EMILY DICKINSON'S HOME

Other books by Millicent Todd Bingham

LIFE OF MARY E. STEARNS

PERU: LAND OF CONTRASTS

GEOGRAPHY OF FRANCE, *with Raoul Blanchard*

AN INVESTIGATION OF GEOGRAPHIC
CONTROLS IN PERU (*Book in Microfilm*)

Translator of PRINCIPES DE GEOGRAPHIE HUMAINE,
P. Vidal de la Blache

LA FLORIDE DU SUD-EST ET LA VILLE DE MIAMI
Institut de Géographie Alpine, Grenoble

BOLTS OF MELODY, *New Poems of Emily Dickinson*
Edited with Mabel Loomis Todd

ANCESTORS' BROCADES, *The Literary Début of Emily Dickinson*

EMILY DICKINSON—A REVELATION

Emily Dickinson's Home

Letters of Edward Dickinson
and His Family

WITH

DOCUMENTATION AND COMMENT

BY

MILLICENT TODD BINGHAM

Home is a holy thing
—EMILY DICKINSON

NEW YORK
HARPER & BROTHERS PUBLISHERS

To the Memory of my Husband

In the preparation of this manuscript my indebtedness is great, to many people, in many ways; but immeasurably greatest to my husband,

WALTER VANDYKE BINGHAM

The wide range of his learning, his sense of form and his exact use of the English language as well as his regard for his fellow man and his profound understanding of human motives tempered by his innate kindness—all these were at my disposal. For his literary skill and his editorial craftsmanship, in short, for his expert help I am grateful. But I am far more grateful for his unflagging belief in the rightness of my endeavor. It is sad that he could not have lived to hold this book in his hands—to see the completion of an undertaking in which he so earnestly believed and with which, through the years, he had so completely identified himself.

CONTENTS

vii

PART FOUR 1853-1855

PART FIVE 1860-1865

PART SIX 1874

PART SEVEN

APPENDICES

ILLUSTRATIONS

Plates

The following illustrations will be found as a group following page 14:

Facsimile Reproductions

The region round about Amherst with its villages, roads and
   railroads as they were when the letters were written, is
   pictured in the end papers

PREFACE

The letters in this book, beginning more than a century ago, were written to one another by the members of the family of Edward Dickinson of Amherst, Massachusetts—by his son William Austin, by his daughters, Emily and Lavinia, by himself and, by his wife, a single letter written five years before their marriage. Documents as intimate as these permit the reader to open the door and step inside "our father's house." Here, busy with her daily tasks, is the young dutiful Emily, governed in all respects by her father's wishes.

Emily Dickinson's father has long been recognized as the dominant fact in her life. But he has been taken for granted, without inquiring into what had made him the kind of man he was. If his character is to be credible we must penetrate the mists of a generation still more remote and examine the career of Emily's grandfather, Samuel Fowler Dickinson, of whose eight children her father was the oldest.

One of Edward Dickinson's sisters, Catherine, married Joseph A. Sweetser in 1835. A packet of letters, treasured by the Sweetser family for more than a hundred years, was presented to me by Catherine's granddaughter, the late Kate Dickinson Sweetser. None has heretofore been published. Excerpts from these letters of "Squire Fowler's" children reveal their father's heavy affliction and final collapse. They naturally give a one-sided view of the man, but when supplemented by facts from other sources the tragedy of his life becomes clear. Not only this. Through that dark glass the figure of his son Edward looms resolute.

Except for the Sweetser collection, the letters in this book were written, as I have said, by members of Edward Dickinson's immediate family and all but a few were addressed to his son. Bequeathed to me by my mother, Mabel Loomis Todd, first editor of the poems and letters of Emily Dickinson, they had come to her in the early 1890's as a gift from the recipient, Emily's brother Austin, who died in 1895. When two volumes of Emily's letters were published in 1894, one chapter contained excerpts from these letters to her brother (*Letters*, 1894).* In the present volume they are reproduced in full, with deleted passages restored—insofar as possible —and in context, among the letters from other members of the family. The manuscripts are described in Chapter V.

This book is one step in the fulfillment of a promise.

A few months before her death in October, 1932, on her forest-covered island off the coast of Maine, my mother and I were talking of Emily Dickinson. We discussed some of the difficulties connected with the original editing of the poems forty years earlier (*Poems*, 1890; *Poems*, 1891; *Poems*, 1896). Those which she had been making ready for the printer when she was stopped by events beyond her control were still, she told me, in the camphorwood chest where they had been packed away in 1897. She looked up from the hammock in which she was lying and said, "Yes, there they are—all I have." Then, sadly, after a pause: "It is all wrong, Millicent, everything that has happened. Will you set it right?" I said I would try.

A simple question and a simple answer.

I did not know what I was promising. I knew only that she wished me to publish the contents of that chest. And I realized that if I were to keep the promise it would take a good deal of time. It was not for me an easy decision, because I was deep in professional activities in another field which I should be obliged to give up.

When my mother said that everything that had happened was wrong, what had she in mind? I think she was not referring to personal wrongs alone of which the following is one example: the letters of Emily Dickinson which she had copied, edited and published in two volumes in 1894 had been republished in 1924, often inaccurately, in a book entitled *Life and Letters of Emily Dickinson*. Without acknowledgment to the original editor, the name of Martha Dickinson Bianchi, Emily's niece, appeared as author on the title page. My mother was hurt of course by this and other attempts to erase the memory of her years of work. But other things troubled her more, two in particular. First, the *Life and Letters*

* For complete citations of books referred to in the Preface, see Bibliography, pages 515-516.

misrepresented Emily's character. Her motives were distorted as well as her relationships to family and friends. Equally wrong my mother thought was the assertion by her niece of a claim to exclusive rights to publication of the writings of Emily Dickinson with results which through the years have been detrimental to scholarship. This possessive attitude my mother deplored. It was not she thought in the public interest and should be stopped.

My obligation I construed to be this: to publish all the documents in the chest, whatever they might be—to make them all available. For this was the living material of history. Once published, facts would be at hand from which later "essential oils" could be "wrung." As soon as I began to study the manuscripts I realized that not one but a series of volumes would be required. Of first importance of course were the poems, hundreds of them. I promptly discovered that even to decipher them would be a fantastically difficult undertaking.

The manuscript poems were of two sorts: those in Emily's handwriting, and those my mother had copied and edited, ready for the printer. (Many originals of these poems had been returned to Lavinia.) She had progressed far enough with the work to indicate the lead poem for the fourth series, and to select the valedictory for a final volume. Among the originals in Emily's hand were six fascicles,* numbered 80 to 85, containing unpublished poems as well as some already included in the first three volumes, and quantities of her rough drafts and practice pieces—"scraps," my mother called them. Some of these were perfect poems. Many, though complete, were interlined with alternative readings. Others were mere fragments; jumbled together as they were, they looked "hopeless," she thought, and had laid them aside for later consideration.

Except for those which had in the interim of more than forty years been brought out by Emily's niece, I have now published all the poems and fragments of poems in the chest. More than six hundred

---

* The cumbersome word "fascicle" used in this connection has been challenged. I chose the word because it best describes the small groups of manuscript poems copied by Emily on sheets of letter paper and tied together with bits of string in little booklets, or pamphlets, which Lavinia Dickinson called "volumes."

of them, including the unfinished drafts, are in a volume entitled *Bolts of Melody* (1945). About fifty more, previously published only in part or with major errors, appeared in *The New England Quarterly,* March, 1947. The first step in the fulfillment of my promise was thus completed.

In order to explain why the poems in *Bolts of Melody* had not been published long ago I took a second step, bringing out an accompanying volume, *Ancestors' Brocades* (1945). It includes an account of the first publication of both poems and letters as well as the final chapter in the history of Edward Dickinson's family. An early chapter, before the family pattern had taken final shape, is in the present volume.

Also preserved in the chest were Austin Dickinson's packets of family letters. My aim in publishing them now is twofold: to make available those hitherto unpublished, or published only in part; and to make real the home where they were written, the home which Emily called "a holy thing," where her life was spent and to the maintenance of which her time was largely given.

To know Emily's brother as well as her father is to understand much of her own behavior. For it was her life work "to make everything pleasant for father and Austin," as she said, and when Austin's life turned to tragedy, his suffering forged yet another link in the chain which held her fast at home.

I have tried to write about the Dickinson family in "plain English" such as Lavinia said their father liked; to avoid even a phrase which might misrepresent those faraway people. In cases of doubt as to the appropriateness of a phrase, or whether a word was in use a hundred years ago, I have kept on my desk an edition of Webster's *Unabridged Dictionary,* published in Springfield in 1851.

At the end, a section entitled "Relatives, Friends and Neighbors" contains more information about persons mentioned in the letters than is provided in the accompanying text. The task of identifying such persons was begun in the early 1890's by my mother with Austin Dickinson's help. When, in 1930, she decided to bring out a new and expanded edition of her original (1894) volumes of *Letters,* she tried to find out more about these long-forgotten people (*Let-*

ters, 1931). I helped in various ways with the search, making pilgrimages here and there to the homes of some of them. But it was baffling to say the least, because most of the people whom we wished to question were no longer living.

With the publication of this book all of the family letters found in the chest will have been reproduced. In my decision to omit none of them no matter how trifling and inconsequential, I have been encouraged by a wise historian who said to me, "Individual experiences are the essence of history. For a documentary volume about Emily Dickinson there are no trivia." He added that these letters are more than a personal record, more than the picture of a rural family. For the Dickinson home was in a way a measure of the times—a unit of which life in the back country of New England was then composed.

The reader will be struck, I think, by the contrast between the life of this busy small-town family in Emily's youth, as they went about their everyday activities, and the emptiness and silence of the home in which, after her father's sudden death when she was forty-three years old, the legendary white-robed recluse moved about during the last twelve years of her life. As the characters of those closest to her, absorbed in their humdrum routine, are revealed, her gradual withdrawal is seen to be a natural response to her surroundings, the only sane response—given her genius—which she could have made to a world in which, as she said, there was so much matter-of-fact. The book will, it is hoped, replace queerness with reasonableness as an explanation of Emily Dickinson's conduct. Having since babyhood been brought up in the midst of Dickinson complexities, I trust that an occasional personal reference will not strike the reader as out of place.

This book was to have been the third step in carrying out my promise to my mother. The family life described in these letters was to have provided the background against which to gauge later events, a bastion, it might be called, from which to gain a perspective for understanding the final events in the Dickinson saga. This, I say, was the plan.

The manuscript of this book was delivered to Harper & Brothers on March 3, 1950, and was announced for publication in their fall catalog of that year. I was reading proof when, early in 1951, manufacture was stopped. The literary rights to publication of the Emily Dickinson material were questioned. That has caused a delay of four years—a source of deep regret to me. As a result of the delay a small book, *Emily Dickinson—a Revelation,* based on hitherto unpublished letters which divulge the last great love of her life, has taken third place and the present introductory volume is fourth. It concludes the series. The letters in this book, being source material, have been reproduced as written, with all the inaccuracies of the original text.

With the forthcoming publication of some rough notes found among Emily's "scraps" my promise to my mother will have been fulfilled.

All writings of Emily Dickinson contained herein are published with the approval of the President and Fellows of Harvard College, who claim all the literary rights and copyrights therein. But, I add, I think the claim is invalid and made without knowledge of what the writings are or from whom or why acquired.

Acknowledgment of my indebtedness is due to many who have helped in the preparation of this manuscript: those who have verified the text as to dates or other precise facts; those who have provided files of old newspapers through interlibrary loans; those who have searched family archives for letters, or town and institutional records, to clarify obscure points; those who have presented me with a daguerreotype or an ancient scrapbook, or who have told me anecdotes which give life to a character; in a word, to all those who through the years have supported my effort and given me encouragement, I wish to express my gratitude—

Lucy M. Bigelow; Solon J. Buck; George Cutler; Guy Stanton Ford; Clara Bellinger Green; Helen F. Greene; Louise B. Graves; Gelston Hardy; Eudocia Flynt Jones; Wallace H. Keep; Jay Leyda; Georgiana Adams Mills; Frederic Palmer; Clara C. Pearl; Edith C. Reichardt; Henrietta Ross-Brown; Richard Sewall; Philip Mack Smith; Alfred E. Stearns; Harlan F. Stone; Kate Dickinson Sweetser; Frederick C. Waite and Charles Warren.

I am also indebted to Charles R. Green of The Jones Library, Amherst; E. P. Dickinson of the Amherst College Library; Hazel E.

Joslyn of the Dartmouth College Library; William A. Jackson of the Houghton Library; the Forbes Library; the Massachusetts State Library; the Presbyterian Historical Society, Philadelphia; the National Archives; the staff photographers of the National Geographic Society; and in particular, and most of all, to many members of the staff of the Library of Congress who, each in his special field, have given me expert assistance.

And lastly my special thanks go to my friends in Harper & Brothers who have patiently stood by me during the past four years.

M. T. B.

November, 1954
Washington, D.C.

PART ONE

Previous to 1840

CHAPTER I

Edward Dickinson and His Family

A HUNDRED years ago the village of Amherst (map opposite page 62) was a community of tight little close-knit family groups. The Dickinsons' was an average home of the period in rural Massachusetts, different from others only in that Edward Dickinson was a man of power. Practising law in Amherst for nearly fifty years, he was treasurer of the college for thirty-eight years, representative of his district for several terms in the Massachusetts legislature, and for one term in the Congress of the United States. Tall, spare and straight, he was a stately figure, the personification of rectitude, the moral law made manifest. His daughter likened his appearance to that of Cromwell or an old Roman general. He knew how to deal with any emergency, whether an unruly horse was to be tamed, a family of orphan cousins to be provided for, or a new state to be admitted to the Union. No one openly opposed his decisions, least of all his family. He knew what was right and what was wrong and that was the end of it. As his daughter Emily remarked, "What Father says he means."

Mr. Dickinson's views were regarded by his family as embodying absolute values. Their own attitudes were based on his eternal rightness. His convictions held even after he was dead. Since "absence is condensed presence," then more than ever, if possible, what he wished was law.

If one thing is fixed Edward Dickinson believed that others will adjust themselves to it. But if he was indispensable to his family, they were his own reason for being. It could not have been otherwise since they were the symbol of his own integrity. With them and with his possessions, even with the gardens he had planted, he

3

identified himself. His last concern, a few days before his death, was about some pear scions he intended to procure for improving the yield of his orchard. By virtue of being his son or his wife or his daughter, the tie was unbreakable. Of them he demanded and obtained obedience. If he wished the family circle to remain unbroken, unbroken it remained—in a geographical sense at least, for none of them left home. To explain the situation Emily used better words. At the age of twenty-seven she wrote to a friend, "I do not go out at all lest Father will come and miss me, or miss some little act which I might forget should I run away." If within the home they all found security, so did he. For absolute loyalty, absolute loyalty was given in return. It was a thing you took for granted like air or sunlight. Home was the center from which you might sally forth to carry on your activities but to which you came back, to warmth and security, when your work was done.

Mrs. Edward Dickinson was a self-effacing wife and mother whose horizon was bounded by her family. She served chiefly as a carrier of Dickinson traits. Her three children, Austin, Emily and Lavinia, though bearing her Norcross family names, were essentially Dickinsons.[1] Except as their interests gained her allegiance, horticulture for example, she had none of her own. Her home and the activities connected with it were sufficient reason for being. Her whole duty was to accept her lot and do her best, for that was what her husband expected. However, in more than one instance Mrs. Dickinson's wishes prevailed. In the summer of 1854, for example, during her husband's absence in Washington, she wanted to attend a celebration in her home town not far from Amherst. An escort was required. The celebration coincided with the Harvard Law School Commencement. The result was that Austin gave up the opportunity of receiving his degree in person in order to accompany his mother to Monson.

Emily said that her mother did not "care for thought." In spite of her "unobtrusive faculties," however, Mrs. Dickinson seems to have had one positive trait, and that was fear. Both of her older brothers had died in their twenties, Hiram in the very year of her son Austin's birth. Her tremulous fear of death was in no way lessened by her conversion soon after Emily was born. Indeed, the

1. See "Children of Joel and Betsy Fay Norcross," pages 510-511.

possibility of everlasting punishment may even have reinforced her well-developed trait of expecting the worst. Be that as it may, on July 3, 1831, she joined the church on profession of faith. Clara Newman, a cousin who lived in Austin Dickinson's family for several years, expressed the opinion that to her mother Emily was a mystery and a constant surprise.

Austin was a tall straight youth with a head of unruly reddish hair. One of his contemporaries called him "the catch of the town." But he was more interested in the out-of-doors than in the various girls who sent him letters and valentines, some of which, however, he preserved as long as he lived.[2]

Austin's sisters were as different in appearance as in other respects. Though both were small, Vinnie was dark, pretty and "arch"—the word always used to describe her in youth. She was an inveterate Dickinson from the first, and the picture of her aunt Elisabeth (Plate V) might almost pass as her own in later life. Emily, on the other hand, was considered plain. Though her auburn hair was luxuriant and "full of sunshine," and her skin of the almost transparent whiteness that often goes with hair of that color, her mouth was wide and her upper lip too long for beauty. The letters in this volume reveal the contrast between the sisters, differences already striking in early youth, of which appearance was the least important.

Emily called her home a fortress. Within the citadel each member of the family lived an "absolute monarch," as Lavinia said, in a world of his own. You were bound to those to whom you gave loyalty and devotion, but with whom you did not share your thoughts. In this as in all things Edward Dickinson set the pattern. With the members of his family he shared everything except his soul. In his professional life, his public duties and family responsibilities, he had in his son an able apprentice. But when it came to the hidden springs, he was unapproachable. Even Austin did not

2. Except for one or two, these have not been printed. One valentine, written from "Somewhere, Indefinite Co., Winter, 1850," postmarked New York, consists of fifty stanzas, of which the first reads:
"Solomon," my dearest of friends,
Read what thy kindred spirit sends,
O let your anger be appeased,
Your mind and heart of burdens eased. . . .

see through. In business affairs his father was frank and outspoken, but his inner life was no less inviolate than that of Emily herself. If anyone tried to probe his feelings, if conversation verged on what was called "the intimate," he withdrew into himself. His emotions and his behavior, as well as his family and his affairs, were under perfect control. No trace of affection was allowed to show through. Indeed, he smiled so seldom that on one occasion when he seemed pleased Emily said that it was almost embarrassing.

When the body of Edward Dickinson was brought home from Boston, where he died shortly after making a speech in the legislature, "Austin leaned over his father's face, kissed his forehead, and said, 'There, Father, I never dared do that while you were living.' "[3]

Emily's memorial words about her father have not been surpassed: "His heart was pure and terrible and I think no other like it exists."[4]

Traits such as those of Edward Dickinson were doubtless his by nature. But fully to understand his character the reader must begin a generation earlier with his father, the Honorable Samuel Fowler Dickinson. For it was "Squire Fowler's" overzealous devotion to the establishment of Amherst College which wrecked his life and placed upon the shoulders of Edward at an early age a compulsion to rebuild the family fortunes and re-establish the family's honored place in the community. To do this Edward would need to be not only energetic, but determined and inexorable.

3. Millicent Todd Bingham, *Ancestors' Brocades, The Literary Début of Emily Dickinson* (New York: Harper & Brothers, 1945), 233.

4. *Letters of Emily Dickinson,* Edited by Mabel Loomis Todd, New and Enlarged Edition (New York: Harper & Brothers, 1931), 292. All references are to the 1931 edition except as otherwise indicated.

CHAPTER II

"Squire Fowler," Edward Dickinson's Father

1

THE Dickinson family had been rooted in Hampshire County since 1659, a vigorous stock producing substantial citizens generation after generation. But the first to reach prominence in his state as well as in his community was Samuel Fowler Dickinson, born in 1775, at twenty an honor graduate of Dartmouth College.[1] This was the man who set the pattern of public service for his son Edward and his grandson William Austin Dickinson.

Samuel Fowler Dickinson, a founder of Amherst Academy, 1814, and in 1821, of Amherst College, practiced law in his native town and was for several terms a member of the state legislature, known in Massachusetts as the General Court. In his history of the college Professor Tyler says that he "was ranked among the best lawyers— perhaps he was the very best lawyer in Hampshire County, and might doubtless have had a seat on the bench, if he had continued in the practice of his profession. But he was gradually drawn off

1. Samuel Fowler Dickinson was graduated from Dartmouth College at the age of twenty as second scholar of the class of 1795. His salutatory was entitled *De administrationis civilis et morum natura; atque momento eorum mutua relationis,* or, "Nature of Civil government & manners; their mutual relation & influence in society." A manuscript copy of this oration is in the archives of Dartmouth College; also three letters from S. F. Dickinson dated 1797, 1798 and 1804.

Two years later, when a student of law in Amherst, he delivered in near-by Belchertown on July 4, 1797, "An Oration in Celebration of American Independence," printed in pamphlet form by William Butler of Northampton in that year. A copy is in the Rare Books Room of the Amherst College Library. To those who search among the forebears of Emily Dickinson for intimations of genius, these stirring words—a kind of apotheosis of the living Washington— spoken by her youthful grandfather are not without interest.

into business for which he had a natural fondness; and he was still more deeply enlisted in the educational enterprises, to which he was strongly impelled at once by his cultivated mind, his rare public spirit, and his high moral and religious earnestness. . . . The conversion of the world often pressed heavily on his mind. He saw in the Institution contemplated at Amherst, one of the agencies that would surely hasten that promised event, and he felt that in rearing and sustaining it, he was as certainly fulfilling the command to 'preach the gospel to every creature,' as if he had himself gone in person to the heathen."[2]

Professor Tyler fails to mention another phase of "Squire Fowler's" political activity. The following notice appeared in *The Hampshire Gazette,* November 7, 1838:

In 1828 . . . Samuel Fowler Dickinson, Esq. was a prominent candidate for the vacant office [of Representative to Congress]. . . . His native talents, his legal knowledge, his business habits, and his long experience in both branches of our State Legislature, would on the floor of Congress, have done honor to the district and the Commonwealth.

He was not elected.

So great was Samuel Fowler Dickinson's contribution to the establishment of Amherst College that it has been said, and rightly so, that but for his vision, his courage and his drive it might never have come into existence. President Hitchcock described him as a man of immense energy—"one of the most industrious and persevering men that I ever saw."[3] As to the actual founding Professor Tyler says (page 121):

"When it was decided to go forward and there were funds enough collected to begin the foundations of the first building, and the corner-stone was laid, the effort was only begun. As the work proceeded and they had used up all their available means, then he (Mr. Dickinson) would pledge his private property to the bank to obtain money that the work might go on. And when there was no money to pay for the teams to draw the brick or men to drive them, his own horses were sent for days and weeks

2. W. S. Tyler, *History of Amherst College during its First Half Century, 1821-1871* (Springfield, Mass., 1873), 119-122. In 1828 S. F. Dickinson, a "counsellor in the Supreme judicial court," proposed to open in Amherst "a school for instruction in the science and practice of the law." *Amherst, Massachusetts, Imprints, 1825-1876* (Amherst College Library, 1946), 166.

3. Edward Hitchcock, *Reminiscences of Amherst College* (Northampton, Mass., 1863), 5.

till in one season two or three of them fell by the wayside. Sometimes his own laborers were sent to drive his horses, and in an emergency he went himself, rather than that the work should cease." At the same time, he boarded more or less of the workmen, and sometimes paid their wages out of his own pocket, while his wife and daughters toiled to board them.

In 1802 Samuel Fowler Dickinson married Lucretia Gunn of Montague, a village in the hills a few miles north of Amherst. In ten years they had become the parents of three sons and two daughters. To accommodate his rapidly increasing family, in 1813 Squire Fowler built The Homestead on Main Street, said to have been the first brick house in Amherst.[4]

By 1823 four more children, two sons and two daughters, had been added to the family. Previous to the marriage of Mary in 1828, the homestead sheltered them all with the exception of William, the second son, who at the age of fifteen had left home to try his hand at business in Boston. To this large household, Edward, the eldest, brought Emily Norcross, his wife, and infant son in 1830. Within three years two more babies, Edward's children, further increased the number of occupants.[5]

But meanwhile the squire's labor for the good of mankind was taking its toll. He had done "more than he was able to do." His zeal had involved him in financial difficulties. "His business which was so large as to require all his time and care, suffered from his devotion to the public. He became embarrassed and at length actually poor."

Though Professor Tyler says no more, the fact is that Squire Fowler's generosity had plunged him so deep in debt that he was finally obliged to sell his home. By May 22, 1833, when Edward's youngest child, Lavinia, was not yet three months old, the title had passed out of the family.

In Walnut Hills, Ohio, now within the city limits of Cincinnati,

4. The date, 1813, is given on the authority of S. F. Dickinson's grandson, William Austin. Professor Tyler says: "When Esq. Dickinson erected his brick house, he removed the wood house which he had previously occupied on the same site to Pleasant Street where it still stands, a small old-fashioned two-story house a little north of the blacksmith shop" (Tyler, 1873, 31). This house was torn down a few years ago.

5. William Austin, born April 16, 1829; Emily Elizabeth, born December 10, 1830; and Lavinia Norcross, born February 28, 1833. See "Children of Samuel Fowler and Lucretia Gunn Dickinson," pages 509-510.

Lane Theological Seminary was established in 1829. The Reverend Lyman Beecher, "one of the most eloquent of American pulpit orators," resigned his pastorate in Boston to become its first president and was inaugurated on December 26, 1832. He considered it his mission to persuade his eastern friends to take an interest in the spiritual needs of the West. As he said: "To plant Christianity in the West is as grand an undertaking as it was to plant it in the Roman Empire, with unspeakably greater permanency and power."[6]

"The laboring plan," adopted at Lane, required every student "to spend not less than three nor more than four hours each day in agricultural or mechanical labor." The supervisor of this work was a "steward," called also a "superintendent," who had charge of construction and building materials. This position was offered to the Honorable Mr. Dickinson of Amherst, now homeless. Necessity, relentless as it was, may for him have been mitigated by the prospect of a chance to take part in the evangelizing of a pioneer community. At least his grandson thought so.[7] However that may be, the offer was accepted. An exile in every sense of the word, with his wife and youngest child, Elisabeth, aged ten, Samuel Fowler Dickinson departed for the West never to return.

New facts open new vistas. It is enticing to speculate about why the position at Lane Seminary happened to be offered to Mr. Dickinson; also why he did not stay there longer than he did. Various possibilities suggest themselves. Dr. Beecher had been pastor of the Hanover (Congregational) Church, Boston, when Mr. Dickinson was serving as representative in the General Court in 1827 and as senator in 1828. Had they known each other in Boston? In 1833, when the homestead was sold, Dr. Beecher's son, Henry, was a junior in Amherst College. Did he tell his father of Squire Dickinson's plight? Loss of his Amherst home was for Mr. Dickinson only

6. Rev. John Vant Stephens, D.D., *The Story of the Founding of Lane,* address delivered at the Centennial of Lane Theological Seminary, June 25, 1929 (Cincinnati, 1929), 8. See also *The American Almanac and Repository of Useful Knowledge, for the year 1835* (Boston, 1834).

7. W. A. Dickinson, "Representative men of the parish, church buildings, and finances," in *One Hundred and Fiftieth Anniversary of the First Church of Christ in Amherst, Massachusetts* (Press of the *Amherst Record,* 1890), 63. This article is hereafter referred to as "Representative Men."

the first of many misfortunes. Soon after his arrival at Lane in 1833, the seminary became the center of a controversy about slavery, a dispute so bitter that in 1835 the very life of the institution was threatened. Did this perhaps explain why, after three years in Cincinnati, Mr. Dickinson left to go to an even more primitive Ohio community? Answers to these and similar questions must be left to future biographers while we return to the account of what actually happened.

Samuel Fowler Dickinson's children scattered far and wide. Edward remained in Amherst. William had left home several years earlier to shift for himself. In 1831 he married and settled in Worcester, Massachusetts. The two older girls had married, Mary in 1928, and Lucretia in 1832, and had moved to Andover and Cambridge respectively. Samuel Fowler, Jr., lived for a while in New York, married in 1834, went south and entered business in Savannah, Georgia. Catherine lived at first with her sister Mary. Timothy, who married in 1838, was lost sight of in the deep South where, in 1852, he died in Griffin, Georgia. Frederick, born in 1819, remained with his brother Edward's family until after his own graduation from Amherst College. Due to the uncertain prospects of the college in the thirties, Frederick had considered transferring to Yale as his brother Edward had done, but decided to stay at Amherst. He graduated in 1837 and soon left for the West to make his home with his parents in Ohio.

After the family disbanded in the spring of 1833, Catherine (sometimes spelled "Catharine") Dickinson went to Andover, Massachusetts, to be with her sister Mary, Mrs. Mark Haskell Newman, who was expecting a third child. In the five years since Mary's marriage on October 2, 1828, she had lost one little daughter, Mary Dickinson Newman, and the second of the same name was now two years old. It was chiefly to take care of baby Mary that Catherine, aged nineteen, was needed. It was the custom in New England, of which the Dickinson family provides several examples, for unmarried daughters to assist in the upbringing of their sisters' children.

On September 12, 1833, Mark Haskell Newman, Jr., was born. On the twenty-seventh Catherine wrote to Joseph A. Sweetser, a young New York businessman whom she was later to marry: "Sister Mary is gradually recovering & has left her room a few times. Little Mary is as *wild* as ever—& troubles 'Aunt Kafrin' continually. I shall be very willing to resign my present station in the family." Until a short time before, Joseph Sweetser had lived in Amherst, associated with his older brother, Luke, proprietor of a general store.

As soon as she could be spared Catherine left to join her parents and sister Elisabeth in far-off Cincinnati. Her letters to Mr. Sweetser tell of her homesickness and her "weary days and nights." She describes her life as "made up of retrospection and anticipation," as she meditates sadly upon the "waves of misfortune which have rolled over us and driven us from our beautiful home."

Catherine remained with her parents about a year. Among her friends were the son and daughter of the president of the seminary. The son, Henry Ward Beecher, entered Lane Seminary after graduating from Amherst College in 1834. His sister Harriet, aged twenty-two, even before her marriage to the Reverend Calvin Ellis Stowe had been making the problem of human slavery her own.

Late in May, 1835, in company with several friends, Catherine Dickinson returned to the East in anticipation of her approaching marriage. From the packet of Sweetser letters I have chosen one, written by Catherine to her parents upon her arrival in Amherst. The difficulties of her long journey emphasize the remoteness of the western city and the reality of her father's exile. The trip took the better part of three weeks: by packet up the Ohio River to Pittsburgh; thence by canal boat, by railroad "cars," by river boat and again by cars to New York; and from there, an overnight journey to Amherst and her brother Edward's home. Her glimpse of Pittsburgh, its infant industries and the ways of its Presbyterian clergy, seemed strange indeed to a young girl accustomed to life in rural New England. Catherine's journey is described in such detail as to suggest that she as well as her parents had reached Cincinnati by the more usual route: by stage to Albany, by boat via the Erie Canal and Lake Erie to Cleveland, down the Ohio Canal (completed in 1832) to Portsmouth, Ohio, and from there to Cincinnati by river boat.[8]

8. Seven years later Charles Dickens followed the same route in the opposite direction. His remarks about conditions aboard the boats (*American Notes*, Chapters X and XI), and the habits of his fellow travelers, supply rugged details lacking in Catherine Dickinson's account.

The following letter, posted after she reached her brother Edward's home, was written on a large double sheet of four pages. Before the use of envelopes, the paper was folded to a proper size for mailing and sealed with wax. Space for the address in the center of the fourth page had been made by folding the four edges of the quarto toward the center. In this case the writing also covered the parts of the fourth page which would be concealed under the folds. Every bit of available space was used. Postal rates at this time being based on distance, the amount paid, "25" cents, and "Amherst, Mass., June 22," are written in ink above the address. There is no stamp and no postmark.

[*To Hon Samuel F. Dickinson, Walnut Hills, Ohio*]

New York, June 15, 1835. Monday morning

Dear Parents & Sister,

. . . You will wish to hear all about my journey & I will endeavour to tell *everything*. . . . Our passage to Pittsburgh was a very long and tedious one—as we did not get comfortably settled at our Hotel in P. before five o'clock on Saturday afternoon. I was very tired indeed —& glad enough to find myself once more on terra firma. Our boat was a very uncomfortable one because it was small. We had the cabin to ourselves most of the way as the large boats before us, took all the passengers. Tuesday P.M. we were obliged to stop the whole afternoon to take a load of iron & again at Wheeling to unload it— so that we *lost* more than a day. Our Capt. was a very excellent man & in looking back upon it—it seems rather pleasant. We sat upon deck much of the time & every evening sung hymns, with the *waves* for an accompaniment. Miss Kemper found her old friend in Pittsburgh (Mrs. Atwood) & spent her time at her house. She urged me to go with her—but of course I could not take Miss Bennett & Mr Stanton with me & it would not be polite to leave them. Sabbath morning we all attended the third Pres. Church & heard Dr. Ely preach. I didn't like him much; his manner is entirely without solemnity & his language common. So it appeared to me, but I may be mistaken. . . . In the evening we heard Mr Patton preach to young men. We found that all the Canal Boats left Pittsburgh at nine o'clock in the evening—& we must either go out on Sabbath evening or wait a whole day. After a little consultation, we thought it the most *christian* to travel on *no* part of the Sabbath & therefore decided on going Monday eve. Monday morning . . . we visited the iron works—where we saw the process of making small thick pieces of iron—into long bars in a very short time. This was novel to me. We then visited the "Glass Works," which were indeed a curiosity, I wished more than once that Elisabeth was with me—she would have been delighted. They were making Decanturs, Tumblers, & everything else—& all the work of a minute. . . . But, to proceed with my story—in the afternoon, we walked over to Alleghany Town, which is on the opposite side of the Alleghany river. A very handsome bridge is thrown over it. The town itself is beautiful, consisting chiefly of country seats very tastefully laid out & almost buried in trees & flowers. Most of them are white cottages, which gives the place a rural appearance contrasting beautifully with the *black*, dirty city on the opposite bank. I had no idea that Pittsburgh was so delightfully situated. On the north side is the Alleghany river, clear & cold from the mountains—on the south, the Monongahela—& from almost any part of the city, their union can be distinctly seen—after which they are called by one name—*Ohio*. The country around Pittsburgh is very highly cultivated—& very beautiful by nature. . . . I must not forget to tell you that I went to the General Assembly in the morning & spent an hour. Most of the clergymen had gone—or *one half* I should say—but there were enough remaining to give me an idea of what it had been. Dr Phillips of N. York was the moderator. There seemed to be a great deal of confusion among them & much less dignity than I expected to find among such an honorable body. Five or six would attempt to speak at the same time & their remarks were often *personal* & seemed to me rather *bitter*. Dr Ely expressed more bitterness than anyone I heard. They adjourned the very day we were there, but not till evening. This gave us a large party of *clergy* for our travelling companions. At [eight] o'clock Monday evening the omnibus took us from Mr Atwood's to the Canal Boat, & at precisely nine o'clock we sailed from Pittsburgh. The Boat was crowded with ministers—& elders—& but few ladies besides ourselves. There is a *Tunnel* which carries the Canal over the Alleghany river. Everything looked *perfectly natural* in the Canal Boat, tho' a Packet boat is infinitely superior to a Leve [e] boat. I will never travel in a Leve [e] boat again if it can be avoided. Our accommodations were very good & our table excellent, but we were crowded & at night almost suffocated. On Wednesday morning, we arrived at Johnstown, 104 miles from Pittsburgh—breakfasted at the Hotel at half past five o'clock & at six precisely took the Railroad car—over the mountains. For four miles it was perfectly level. After that we ascended the mountain

The Dickinson Homestead

From a lithograph by John Bachelder, 1858. Courtesy of The Jones Library, Amherst

PLATE I

The House on Pleasant Street

From a photograph taken about 1868. Courtesy of Miss Lucy M. Bigelow, Amherst

PLATE II

Edward Dickinson

From a daguerreotype made in 1853

PLATE III

Mark Haskell Newman

From a daguerreotype made about
1851. Courtesy of Mrs. George E. Pearl

Mary Dickinson Newman

From a daguerreotype made about
1851. Courtesy of Mrs. George E. Pearl

PLATE IV

Catherine Dickinson Sweetser

From a photograph taken about 1860, furnished by
the late Kate Dickinson Sweetser

Elisabeth Dickinson (Currier)

From a photograph taken about 1860, furnished by
the late Kate Dickinson Sweetser

PLATE V

William Dickinson about 1870

Reproduced from D. Hamilton Hurd, *History of Worcester County, Massachusetts* (Philadelphia, 1889), Vol. II, page 1680

PLATE VI

Lucretia Dickinson Bullard

From a photograph taken about 1883. Courtesy of Mrs. George E. Pearl

The Reverend Asa Bullard

From a photograph taken about 1883. Courtesy of Mrs. George E. Pearl

PLATE VII

William Austin Dickinson

From a daguerreotype made about 1856

PLATE VIII

Emily Dickinson about 1848

From a photograph of the daguerreotype taken in 1954

PLATE IX

Lavinia Norcross Dickinson

From a daguerreotype made in the spring of 1852

PLATE X

Lavinia Norcross Dickinson in the 1860's
Courtesy of The Jones Library, Amherst

PLATE XI

John L. Graves

From a daguerreotype made about
1851. Courtesy of Miss Louise B.
Graves, Boston

John L. Graves in 1905

PLATE XII

by four inclined plane's—which were not remarkably steep—& descended by six. The mountains which we crossed were not very high—or was there any thing terrific at all in their appearance. Occasionally a huge rock hung over our path—but we whirled by it so soon—there was no danger. There is one Tunnel on the Railroad & another on the canal. Both lead directly *under a mountain* & are hewn from the rock—& both are 900 feet in length. We passed through them both in the daytime—& yet it was so dark as to prevent us from distinguishing each other. . . . Our first rail road route took us to Hollydaysburg 37 miles which place we reached at two o'clock & went directly from the Car to another Canal Boat all in readiness & immediately started for Columbia, 170 miles, which place we reached on Friday P.M. at two o'clock—in season to go to the Hotel & take our dinner. Here we were obliged to wait two hours or *three* for the return cars from Philadelphia which gave us a nice time to lie down on a *good* bed & sleep a while. I was heartily glad to quit a Canal Boat. We were so much crowded that we had not a breath of air at *night*—& it seemed to me that I must certainly suffocate. . . . I was never so completely tired out in my life. The heat was excessive the whole time. . . . I felt homesick enough —& for once *cryed* to go to *Ohio* again. On Friday P.M. at 5 o'clock, we took the Rail road for Philadelphia 81 ¾ miles—& travelled all night. We were drawn by horses, as it was dangerous to travel by steam at night. About nine o'clock a tremendous thunderstorm burst upon us—& lasted for two or three hours with rain, hail & some wind. They were obliged to take off the horses & the driver sought refuge somewhere, leaving us upon the track —at the mercy of the elements. I never witnessed anything so terrific. The lightning was vivid as it could be & the thunder tremendous. Again I wished myself *at home in Ohio*. After stopping perhaps an hour we were able to go on—but not till we were pretty well *sprinkled* with rain from the holes in the covering over us. We travelled all night—& at 7 o'clock Saturday morning arrived in Phil'a—*tired* as *tired* could be. We hoped to get in—in time to take the 6 o'clock boat for N. York—but we were too late & therefore went to a Hotel to breakfast. I think I was never so fatigued in my life—tho' I had slept some during the night leaning my head on Mr. Stanton's shoulder & my bonnet in my hand. . . . The entrance to Phil. is very delightful—& the city itself is the handsomest I have ever seen. Our party had been dropping off—one by one—& in Phil. we numbered only five. I believe I didn't mention *who* we had for companions. . . . I think we had more than twenty clergymen beside *elders* a plenty. My *veneration for the clergy* has all fled. . . . We left Phil'a at ten o'clock on Saturday morning—in a crowded Steam boat—at twelve, took the rail road—& travelled

at twenty miles an hour—then took a Boat again & landed in New
York at 7 o'clock P.M. I found Mr Sweetser watching for me (as
he had been for three days before) & glad to see my face once
more. . . . Tuesday morning at seven o'clock Mr Sweetser & myself
left New York for N. Haven—arrived there at 2 o'clock—took the
stage immediately & arrived in Hartford at 7 o'clock in the
evening. . . . Wednesday morning, we took our last stage for Amherst & arrived safely at one o'clock precisely. As we stopped at Mr
Gilbert's, Frederic came running over to see me & Edward too—&
both rode down home with me.[9] I found Emily & the children
quite well & expecting me. . . . My expenses have been just about
40 dollars—Edward is going to see that Sweetser is willing to receive what he paid for my fare—from N. York here. He gave me in
N.Y. a very handsome parasol—a brown one without fringe—& I
bought a small shawl a yard square—white in the middle & handsome border. I also had a green gauze ribbon tied over my bonnet
to make it more decent. . . . Frederic has altered very much—grown
tall—& very much of a gentleman in manners. I should not have
known him at all. He wears a frock coat & looks very well indeed.
He is in good health & very glad to see me. I have been twice to his
room which is in the very best order—everything in its place. He is
much respected in his class & is perfectly steady. I have not yet
conversed with him about his religious feelings, but intend to soon.
He has recently written you—perhaps you know more than I do
respecting his state of mind. . . . Everything looks beautifully here.
The spring is about as far advanced as it was in Cin. when I left—so
that I have followed the Spring. Gen. Mack (see p. 62) has done
many little things around the house of which I will tell you in my
next. I never saw any place half so beautiful as our own home. Do
tell Mr Laughlin that in my descriptions of N.E. & our N.E. home—
I did not tell him *half* the truth. All N.E. looks like a garden to me—
& our house looks very, very beautiful. Tell Mr L. that I have exclaimed an hundred times—since I entered N.E., "How I wish my
western friends could see this!" I want to see you all very much, &
would willingly start back again this very morning. I feel just as
I expected, & must expect to feel lonesome for a long time till I
get interested. My remembrance to Henry Beecher, Eben [Ebenezer
Bullard?] & Talbot especially. O, I do want to see the *fine friends*
I have most—more than tongue can tell. I have cryed day after
day & night after night since I came away—because you were all
left behind. Frederic feels dreadfully about it—& shows much feeling—more than *some others* here that I know. . . . I am going to
Athol with Mr Sweetser tomorrow to be absent till Friday. Caroline

---

9. Thomas Gilbert was (1832-1836) proprietor of a tavern on Main Street called
the Mansion House, not far from the Dickinson homestead.

[Joseph's younger sister] is at home & they all sent a very polite invitation to me to come & Edward thinks I had better go—so I am going. I feel sorry because I don't feel like it at all. I feel perfectly indifferent about going anywhere or seeing anybody. Everybody is talking about something that I know nothing about & until I get the run of affairs, I shall be *homesick*. Edward seems very sober & says but little. I hope [brother] Samuel will come before I go to Andover—so that we can all talk over things together.

I intend now to go to Andover in two weeks from today (Monday). . . . My love to all who care for me—Mr Mason's & Harriet Beecher. I wish I could go back again. Emily sends love. She is *perfectly well*. Love to you all from me.

Yours most affectionately
Catherine

Apparently Catherine Dickinson and her eldest brother did not see eye to eye. "Edward and myself don't seem to *make up* quite," is the way she put it. With her brother Frederick, already a sophomore in Amherst College though not yet sixteen, it was different. Catherine's affection seems to center on him even more than on her intended husband, Joseph Sweetser. Toward making even a brief visit to Athol, the ancestral home of the Sweetser family, she has a kind of grin-and-bear-it attitude.

Catherine did not prolong her stay in her brother Edward's home. She soon left for Andover to spend the summer with her sister Mary who was expecting her fourth child.[10] On November 4, 1835, Catherine Dickinson and Joseph A. Sweetser were married in the Newmans' home.[11]

2

Western Reserve College was established in Hudson, Portage County, Ohio, in 1826. I am indebted to Dr. Waite, its historian, for information about the last months of Samuel Fowler Dickinson's life in "the remote Ohio wilderness."

A treasurer was first employed to devote his entire time to the business affairs of the college, including the care of buildings and grounds, in 1835. "Samuel F. Dickinson, a graduate of Dartmouth

10. Catherine Dickinson Newman was born February 21, 1836.

11. A sale on April 24-25, 1935, at the Anderson Galleries, New York, included twenty-one letters from Emily Dickinson to members of the Sweetser family, an important supplement to the Kate Dickinson Sweetser collection.

College, who had been treasurer of another institution for a short time, was employed, but his experience was insufficient for the position and his health was poor. He died in the second year of service, leaving his accounts in a sorry mess."[12] In the official history of the university this is the only reference to Samuel Fowler Dickinson in the body of the text.

In spite of Mr. Dickinson's ignominious record at Western Reserve, Dr. Waite has been kind enough at my request to investigate his activities during his tenure of office, which may be summarized as follows:

In the Trustees' records of Western Reserve College Mr. Dickinson is first mentioned on August 24, 1835, when it was resolved that "Samuel F. Dickinson, Esqr, of Lane Seminary be, & he is hereby appointed Treasurer, & superintendant [sic] of the financial concerns, & the Workshops of this College, to enter upon the duties of his office as soon as he can make the necessary arrangements." It was further resolved "that the salary of Mr Dickinson be $500, per annum, & that the Secretary notify him of his appointment." This offer, declined in a letter of November 3, 1835, was renewed under the same conditions on August 19, 1836, when it was accepted.[13]

After having spent about three years at Lane Seminary, Mr. Dickinson resigned and, accompanied by his wife and daughter, moved from Cincinnati to Hudson in the late fall of 1836.[14] Once

---

12. Frederick Clayton Waite, *Western Reserve University, the Hudson Era, 1826-1882* (Cleveland, 1943), 315.

13. W. E. Dean, treasurer of Lane Theological Seminary, in a letter dated April 28, 1949, states that Samuel Fowler Dickinson tendered his resignation as "Superintendent and Steward" on October 26, 1836, and quotes as follows from the official records: "Resolved, that this Committee have the utmost confidence in the ability, integrity and good management of Samuel Fowler Dickinson, the present Superintendent, and regret very much that he should have resigned his situation in the Seminary and request him to continue in his duties as Superintendent until a permanent arrangement can be made."

Mr. Dickinson seems to have left Lane promptly, however, for in the records under date of November 14, 1836, is the following minute: "Resolved, that Professor Stowe be authorized to take possession of and occupy the house on the campus recently vacated by S. F. Dickinson, Esq." The Reverend Calvin Ellis Stowe, a professor in the seminary, had married Harriet Beecher on January 6, 1836.

14. Dr. Waite tells me that the route from Cincinnati to Hudson was by river boat to Portsmouth, by "Ohio Canal" to Boston, twenty miles south of Cleveland

more he assumed new responsibilities in unfamiliar surroundings, "beginning life all over again" at the age of sixty. The exact date of his arrival is not known, but he was in Hudson on December 28, 1836, when a committee was appointed to "transfer all the books & papers pertaining to the Treasurers Department, to Samuel F Dickinson Esqr the present Treasurer & obtain his bond for the security of the Board." From time to time the Trustees' records refer to his various duties: making contracts for "the erection of a new College Edifice, & to superintend the work," and authorizing him "to make all ordinary repairs on the College buildings & to superintend the stoves & stove pipes."

Almost a year later, at a meeting of the board on November 30, 1837, Mr. Dickinson was "unanimously chosen Treasurer for the ensuing year," and it was resolved "that in consideration of the high price of provisions & his expences in removing his family from Cincinnati Mr Dickinson be allowed $50.00, in addition to his salary the past year."

Up to this time Mr. Dickinson's work at Western Reserve had evidently been satisfactory. But the heart had gone out of him. After little more than a year of "great labor and many discouragements" he succumbed to "the bilious complaint," and died in Hudson on Sunday, April 22, 1838.

Startling is the contrast between the confused and broken individual, pictured in the official records of Western Reserve, and the powerful figure in Amherst—the vigorous man, walking seven miles to Northampton because he could not spare time to wait for the stage, who by sheer enthusiasm and belief in education helped to bring a new college into being.

Nothing could better reveal Mr. Dickinson's collapse than the condition of the treasurer's books. The Trustees' Prudential Com-

---

and five miles west of Hudson. Furniture could not have been moved by any other route since there was no railroad before 1851.

"The canal boats," he says, "were comfortable, with sleeping accommodations, made few changes necessary and were cheaper than going by stage. Stages were often crowded, did not permit carrying much baggage, and required stopping at hotels overnight, because the stages did not run except in daylight hours." This journey could not have been made after winter set in, since "the water in the canal was likely to freeze in northern Ohio early in November and regular canal boats usually ceased operation by Nov. 1st of each year, or shortly thereafter" (letter of August 8, 1948).

mittee appointed to settle his estate was greatly embarrassed and delayed in its efforts to straighten out his accounts. At the annual meeting of the trustees on August 16 and 17, 1838, this committee "reported that they had made some progress." A similar report was made on August 23, 1839. On August 21, 1840, the committee announced "that the settlement had been completed, & that there is due the estate from the College $258.96 (payable at Northampton, Ms. on the 4ᵗʰ of June 1841, without interest)." It had required more than two years to untangle the records and determine the amount due Mr. Dickinson's estate. By the time the final settlement was made, on June 4, 1841, the beneficiary, his widow, was dead.

The grave of Samuel Fowler Dickinson is in Amherst. It has been assumed that his son Edward, whose filial piety was well known, brought his father's body back from the West to lie beside that of his wife in the West Cemetery. On higher ground, at some distance from the family plot, an impressive monument to the memory of his parents was erected by their son William in 1881.

The tragedy of Samuel Fowler Dickinson's life is reflected in the following excerpts from letters written at the time of his death by his daughters Catherine Sweetser and Mary Newman. The letter from Catherine occupies the first two pages of a double sheet, that from Mary, the third page. Parts of the third page were torn off in breaking the seal. The missing words have been supplied in broken brackets. The paper is folded to the size for mailing and addressed on the back in a masculine hand. Without a stamp, the rate, "20" cents, is written in. The postmark is stamped in red.

[*To Mrs Samuel F. Dickinson, Hudson, Portage Co., Ohio. (Postmark: New-York, Apl 30)*]

Brooklyn, April 29, 1838
Sabbath P.M.

My dear Mother & Sister,

I cannot tell you how much we were surprised at the receipt of your letter yesterday—containing the sad news of our Father's death. It was a shock to our feelings which we cannot express—and the more we think of it—the more are we grieved at his loss. . . . I wish he had expressed his feelings, as he drew near his end—that we might know whether his mind was calm & composed in the prospect of death. It would be a great comfort if he had said but few words. I feel that we have nothing to fear on his account—as in looking back upon his past life—we can see abundant evidence that he was guided by right motives & endeavoured to discharge his duty. I do not mourn on his account for the last years of his life have presented a scene of constant trouble—& I rejoice for him, that all is over. Yes, his trials are all over—his fate sealed for eternity & we trust his home is in Heaven. Doubtless, he now sees that all his trials in this life served to purify him & prepare him for that blessed abode. He is free from toil & pain and sin—he has no more gloomy apprehensions for the future. Why then should we sorrow for him? The death of our brother or sister without hope—would cause a wound which time could never heal—but in this affliction—we have every consolation which religion can afford. I am grieved that we have done so little for his comfort while we had it in our power & this is the only sting. It seems as if his depression of spirits caused his sickness which terminated his life—& I cannot but think that if we children had complied with his wishes & given him a comfortable home in his old age—he might have been spared longer—or at least—we could have smoothed his passage to the tomb. All that we would do—is now of no avail. It only remains for us to *regret* that we did not do our duty better. When I look back & see how much he has done for me in my whole life—how much he has done for my improvement & happiness—I feel that I have poorly repaid the debt of gratitude I owed to him, & the fact that the ingratitude of *many* of his children has weighed down his spirits—is enough to break my heart. If there is anything which I feel to be a greater sin than another—it is ingratitude to Parents—& as I look back & see how much more I might have done for them—which I did not do—when it was in my power I am grieved and humbled—& many are the tears I have shed since I left them—on this account. I hope we may all profit by this affliction. It is the first time death has entered our family circle & he has taken one who was the head. Whose turn will come next—we know not—& it becomes us all to remember our Father's dying words—and be ready as he was for the hour of death. Alas! how many of our family have no hope for eternity. My heart aches at the thought. May the Lord sanctify this affliction to them. . . . As soon as Papa's affairs are settled— you will of course return to us. We cannot yet make any arrangements—but you need have no fears you shall never want for a home with some of us. I hope we may all feel happy to do anything in our power for our Mother's happiness & comfort. We cannot yet decide

upon any course for Frederick—I hope to hear he is better—I ho
you will see that you get *your dues* in the settlement of your affa
—& have it done speedily—

Yours as ever most affectionately—
Catharine

Brooklyn, April 29
Sabbath P.M.

My dear Mother & Sister,

. . . Catharine has written what I would say, & we have I thi
evidence abundant from the tenor of his whole life that to die k
been to Papa's released spirit unspeakable gain. Yes—released fro
evil & care & anxiety for the future, his spirit is doubtless at r
at *home*. For him I think we have reason to rejoice that his tri:
are at last over. Ever since I can remember his life has been one
anxiety & care & disappointment. Now we trust his trials are ende
He has done much for his children—they nothing for him. I a
grieved that he could not have had a *home* for his last years. .
Feeling assured as we do of his happy exchange of worlds I <wou
not> if I could call back his spirit to enjoy a *home* on earth <wi
all the> trials incident. I hope his death may be sanctified to o
<children> & to all of us. Let us all examine our hopes f
eternity. D<eath> has spared our family long—he has at last tak
its head. I <hope> it may be the means of awakening those
us who are though<tless> & leading us all to make *sure* our ti
to an inherita<nce> above is my earnest prayer.

As to a home for you & Elisabeth you need hav<e no> anxie
You will of course come East as soon as your affairs are settled,
not of course until everything *is* settled & *paid.* We shall hear fro
other members of the family & consult with them upon the be
plans for you & write you. We cannot help feeling much anxiety f
Frederic & shall hope to hear that he is better soon.

We are now at Catharine's house & start Wednesday for A:
[over]. We are all tired out with moving. That this affliction m
be sanctified to us all & that you may be abundantly sustained und
every trial is the sincere wish of your affectionate

Mary

Not only had Samuel Fowler Dickinson been forced to leave I
home in Amherst under cruel circumstances; "in his poverty he h
the additional grief of feeling that his services were forgotten, li
the poor wise man in the proverb who 'by his wisdom delivered t

city, yet no man remembered that same poor man.' "[15] Before he died one final drop of bitterness was added. Amherst College, the beloved institution for which he had sacrificed his all, seemed about to collapse for lack of funds.[16] This was the *coup de grâce* and the gallant fight was given up.

This idealist, the driving force in the creation of Amherst College, so full of a desire to serve his fellow men that he wrecked his fortune and was obliged in middle age to leave his home and begin life over again in a distant city, deserves a fuller biography than he has yet received.

15. Tyler, 1873, 121.

16. In 1836-1837, with two hundred and fifty-nine students, Amherst College ranked above Harvard in point of numbers and was second only to Yale (Tyler, 1873, 161). The next year, following the depression of 1837, the number "had fallen to two hundred and six, and so it continued to decrease regularly, till in 1845-1846 it was reduced to one hundred and eighteen, less than half the number nine years before" (Tyler, 1895, 86). Application to the General Court for pecuniary aid was refused in three successive years: 1837, 1838, 1839.

The causes of this decline are poignantly portrayed by Professor Tyler in both issues of his *History of Amherst College*, accounts recommended to those who would understand the spiritual grandeur in the midst of which the college came into being and because of which it survived. The founders were "men of fervid zeal, strong faith, moral courage and holy boldness." The president, professors and tutors all "felt that they were laying foundations for the glory of God and the good of mankind in future ages" (Tyler, 1873, 45). They felt that "education should have reference to *two* worlds, but chiefly to the future, and that moral education, spiritual training, Christian character and influence in such an Institution is not only indispensable—it is everything" (*ibid.*, 162). As Samuel Fowler Dickinson said to his son Edward, "Learning and science without morality and religion are like a man without a soul" (Frederick Tuckerman, *Amherst Academy, A New England School of the Past, 1814-1861* [Amherst 1929], 71).

CHAPTER III

Emily Norcross, Consort, and Her Sister Lavinia

B EFORE narrating the events following the death of Samuel Fowler Dickinson in 1838, the reader is asked to go back a few years for a glimpse of another family, the Norcrosses of Monson, Massachusetts, a small town about twenty miles south of Amherst.[1]

Among Austin Dickinson's packets of letters is one, and only one, from his mother, Emily Norcross. Written at the age of nineteen when she was attending a boarding school in New Haven, Connecticut, the letter is addressed to her younger sister Lavinia. It is the only handwriting of Emily Norcross Dickinson that I have ever seen. The penmanship antedates the Spencerian running hand which came into vogue during the next generation. Written on two pages of a large double sheet, the letter is folded, addressed on the fourth page, and sealed with a wafer. To the original heading, "New Haven," is added in a different hand, "July, 1823." That was the year in which Edward Dickinson was graduated from Yale College. Five years later, on May 6, 1828, he married Emily Norcross.

The "Maria" who delivered the letter was probably Maria Flynt, a cousin, who on September 21, 1826, married the Reverend Lyman Coleman, pastor of the Congregational Church in Belchertown, a village between Amherst and Monson. "Warren" was Emily Norcross' youngest brother, Joel Warren, not yet two years old.

---

1. See "Children of Joel and Betsy Fay Norcross, pages 510-511.

[*To Miss Lavinia Norcross Monson*]

New Haven July 1823

Much loved sister

I recieved your affectionate letter tuesday evening by the hand of Maria together with three others. I can assure you I had quite a feast but permit me to say there was none more cordially accepted than yours. As Maria is expecting to return to day I have scarsly time to ask you the question I wish to. It gave me much pleasure to hear from my friends. My dear Lavinia you know but little how much I think of them. I have but 6 weeks from next Wednesday to stay then shall I return to my *dear dear* home my health is verry good and I enjoy myself as well as I possible can. I was glad [to] hear that you was satisfied with your hats I have seen a number like yours worn by the little Ladies here As respects some beades I will endeavour purchase some for you before I return. please to tell brother Austin I recieved his letter with gratitude It exhilerated my feelings verry much I would answer it by Maria was there time but he must excuse me for the pressent how is dear Mother and little Warren. how much I wish to see them but such desires are out of the question as they cannot be gratified. Please to give little brother one kiss for me often how I pictured him in my imagination runing about the door with his little green hat *on* how is brother Hiram and dear Sister Amanda much do I think of them tell hiram notwith[st]anding I imagined I should be glad to get released from singing a little while I would now esteem a great favour to join with them, and also that I do not think the singing here to surpass ours at Monson I must think about closing my letter As I expect Maria every moment to take it. . dear Lavinia if my time was not so much limited I would give you a sketch of some of my pleasant walks which I think would interest you, but you must be patient untill I return to you, then I will disclose to you all the beauties of New Haven, but at pressent no more. Remember me with affection to my beloved parents brothers & sisters inform Cousin Lorin that his letter met with welcome reception, please to say a word to Clarrisa for me, she is still remembered by Emily. . Will not your goodness overlook all imperfections As it is from one who so much loves you.

From your *affectionate Sister* Emily

I suppose papa will ask the favour of perusing this letter but you tell him that you do not like to expose *youre Sister,* as it was writen in great haste. . Adieu

Dear Lavinia

Emily Norcross was deeply attached to her sister Lavinia, at this time eleven years old. "Cousin Lorin" was fifteen. Lavinia and Loring Norcross lived near one another, were playmates and devoted friends. Eleven years later what was the amazement of the clan, Dickinsons as well as Norcrosses, to learn of their intended marriage. Marriage between closely related persons was uncommon in New England. The family's point of view is set forth in a letter from Joseph Sweetser to his future wife, Catherine Dickinson, then living with her parents in Cincinnati. Edward Dickinson, whom Mr. Sweetser already refers to as "Brother Edward," expressed the prevailing attitude toward such a marriage. After it was an accomplished fact, however, he unbent far enough to send a piece of wedding cake to his sister in the West.

Written on three pages of a double sheet, with the address and a brief two-line postscript on the fourth page, the letter was folded and sealed with wax. It was carried by "Mr Lyman" whose name appears below the address.

[*To Miss Catharine Dickinson, Walnut Hills, Cincinnati, Ohio*]

New York Nov 12th, 1834

My Dear Catharine,

   . . . Great news! Lavinia Norcross—*is married*. Miss has become Mrs—and as Edward says, "we shall now see how great a change this change of titles can make in the individual."

This to them, Loren & Lavinia, important event took place on Tuesday, the fourth of the present month. I received a small piece of the wedding cake with the respects of the bride and bridegroom. So far as I am acquainted with the facts in the case her Father was very unwilling that she should be married this winter. Yet her anxiety prevailed it seems. Even *common report* has it that the haste was hers, not his. After all what is it? I should not think her father or any of her relatives would experience any particular degree of satisfaction in seeing *so near* a brother and sister made nearer by the holy ties of matrimony. Certainly I do not view it in the light of a proper match when I take the subject into particular consideration. I hope they will be happy—yes very happy—for I have a more particular regard for Lavinia than for almost any other female acquaintance, and I should be very sorry if her new situation did not produce all the enjoyment she has ever anticipated.

When the matrimonial tie is rightly viewed by christians, it is, I think, looked upon as a very solemn as well as deeply important relation—(An awful sentence in its construction!) But how few view it rightly. How often is it entered into for the mere purposes of selfish or sensual gratification. I have often remarked that men of sense usually laid that and judgment aside—in the choice of a wife. Thus becoming insane and foolish, when reason—and judgment were of all places most needed. Females are not quite so guilty because they are not as free to choose as males.

I wrote to brother Edward some account of Samuel's conversion as expressed in his letter to me. Hear what he says of it in his letter received today. "You say that brother Samuel has written to you that his business is good, and what is of more importance, that he thinks he is a christian. Truly I cannot but rejoice at such news from a brother so dear to me as he is, and for whom I have so high an opinion—and I hope he is really prepared for that happy future state of existence, for which we all ought to be ever in readiness, but which I am sensible I have always neglected—and fear I always shall." For one who expresses such feelings is there not encouragement to both pray and hope? I think there is—and in my frequent letters to him I often take the liberty to insert a few words of serious import.

The final paragraph of Mr. Sweetser's letter expresses concern for the spiritual welfare of his "brothers," of Edward Dickinson in particular. A feeling of responsibility for one another's soul was a strong family tie, one in which even before his marriage Joseph Sweetser appears to have shared. Although, as "Brother Edward" is quoted as saying, he had neglected to prepare himself for a future life, not even joining the church until he was forty-seven years old, he had always been a God-fearing citizen.

If Mr. Sweetser's words seem sanctimonious, he was merely using the customary language of the time. And it was not a manner of speaking only. It was a way of thinking, rooted in the certainty that a Creator cared for the world He had made and for every human being who lived in it. If our aim is to understand the Dickinsons and why they expressed themselves as they did, we should not underrate the convictions which gave meaning to their words. Furthermore, although Emily Dickinson did not take over their phraseology, the faith underlying it molded her life.

A modified Puritanism, the parent theology of New England, and its expression in the moral law constituted what has been known as "The New England Way." The unwritten rules of conduct, the things the community tolerated and did not tolerate were, the people believed, laws of the universe founded upon the purposes of its Creator. Authority for the Puritans' standards of behavior was no less than that. Illustrated in the foregoing correspondence, this code was still in force a generation later during Emily Dickinson's youth. And so, before reading the family letters, it is well to have freshly in mind the code they lived by and the religious beliefs which gave it substance.

The following chapter summarizes a few essential features of the way of life which prevailed in rural Massachusetts a century ago.

CHAPTER IV

"The New England Way"

1

WHEN a geographer wishes to understand a landscape—its hills and valleys, its brooks, rivers and marshes, and why they look as they do—he begins with the underlying bony structure. Firm as the granite which molds the surface features of a New England scene were the convictions of its people a hundred years ago. The manner in which their countryside had evolved from its supporting rock formations was no less predetermined than was their conduct by their traditional religious faith for, in 1850, two centuries of Puritanism still shaped their mode of living. The meaning of "The New England Way" will escape us if we scoff at their beliefs because of their archaic language, or ridicule their customs while neglecting the motives which explain them.

To approach Emily Dickinson from a twentieth-century point of view is to invite her to elude us. She was a part of her time. And she thought, as she said, "New Englandly." Even though these thoughts reached into the furthest recesses of human experience, her point of departure was always an inveterate New Englandism. Because she could be whimsical about the things that mattered most is no reason for ignoring the very forces from which her strength was drawn. And so, geographically speaking, we must begin with bed rock.

It was an age of belief in God, a personal God present here and now. Human beings were of supreme worth not because of any inherent qualities of their own, but because God had chosen them to be His children. All knowing, all just, all powerful, He nevertheless took an interest in every human being and had for each one a plan

—not a general plan of life merely, but a preference with regard to every choice. Emily Dickinson said:

> God made no act without a cause,
> Nor heart without an aim.

Though she could call herself a pagan, God's presence was for her the transcendent fact. At sixteen she declared, "I have perfect faith in God and His promises"; and three decades later, with equal assurance, "God cannot discontinue Himself." "Be sure you don't doubt about the sparrow," she told her "little cousins" when their father died; for "God keeps his oath to sparrows." If bereavement came close, no cloistered mystic could experience greater rapture. Only two months before her death she sent this note to a friend who had lost her husband:

> Dear One,—"Eye hath not seen nor ear heard." What a recompense! The enthusiasm of God at the reception of His sons! How ecstatic! How infinite! Says the blissful voice, not yet a voice, but a vision, "I will not let thee go, except I bless thee."
>
> Emily[1]

The Puritan's sense of union with God ennobled his actions and lifted him to a sense of high responsibility. Indeed, responsibility for his own acts was a part of his freedom and inseparable from it. But his right to freedom depended on his willingness to do what God required—to obey the divine voice speaking through his conscience. Emphasis was on obligations more than on rights. His code of living, an outgrowth of his faith, was not a code in the sense that a set of rules was imposed from without. Quite the contrary. No priest, no legislature, could relieve a man of direct accountability to God. The taskmaster was within. For the Puritan, conscience was both starting point and final authority.

If the Puritan's standards of behavior were not established by laws of church or state, were they determined by public opinion expressed in the acclaim or disapproval of friends and neighbors? In part, perhaps. But far stronger was the influence of the Bible and of the traditional theology; and of the two, the more important

1. Except for "God keeps his oath to sparrows," in the poem "Victory comes late," the above quotations are taken from *Letters*, 1931, 241, 19, 309, 230, 427.

was the Word of God. The Bible was a gift direct from Him, the final expression of His will. As an aid to right living He had provided this infallible guide. In the time-honored words of Cotton Mather, "The Sacred Scriptures are the sufficient rule for belief, worship, and manners among the people of God."

The Bible was read and pondered in every household, not only on Sunday, not only in morning and evening devotions. It was at hand throughout the day, beside the bed at night. A copy of it was placed wherever, during the day's activities, one expected to pause long enough to be able to read a Psalm or a few verses. Its teachings were as pervasive as the warmth of the sun. Each morning, like other householders, Edward Dickinson led in family worship. With wife and children about him he would read aloud a chapter of the Bible, after which they knelt and prayed.

The King James Version molded the speech of New England. If Emily Dickinson's poetry abounds in Biblical phraseology it is not a manner of speaking only, a metaphor alighting here or there for picturesque effect, stilted leftovers from an age when the words had had meaning. On the contrary, they were a part of her thinking. She used the phrases of the New Testament as if they were her own, explaining that Scripture is "so handy."

On September 23, 1851, after her return from a visit with her brother in Boston, fearing lest he might be homesick, this is the way she tells him that she wants him to come home: . . . "dear Austin— do not despair—we're 'with you alway, even unto the end'! Tho' absence be not for 'the present, joyous, but grievous,' it shall work out for us a far more exceeding and 'eternal weight' of *presence*." The "far more exceeding and eternal weight" in II Cor. 4:17, is to work not for Austin's "glory," however, but for his "presence." On October 10, 1851, again trying to convey to her brother how much he is missed at home, words of the New Testament are combined to suit her need. "Duty is black and brown," she says, "home is bright and shining, 'and the spirit and the bride say *come,* and let him that' wandereth come, for 'behold all things are ready'!" The sentence which took off in Revelation brings up in Matthew.

Although Emily moved easily among Old Testament characters— David and Goliath, Moses, Elijah and Belshazzar—in writing to her friends she slipped more easily into New Testament phrases, full of

tenderness and mercy. "The Savior's only signature to the letter he
wrote to all mankind was 'A Stranger and ye took me in.' " And, on
the death of a child, " 'Come unto me.' Beloved commandment! The
darling obeyed it."[2] This way of lapsing into the words of the
Bible was habitual throughout life. After the death of President
Stearns of Amherst College, in 1876, Emily wrote: "Dr. Stearns died
homelike, asked Eliza for a saucer of strawberries, which she
brought him, but he had no hands. 'In such an hour as ye think
not' means something when you try it."[3]

Around the deep certitudes of the Puritan's belief in God and
His promises had grown up a body of doctrine which reached into
every crevice of life. The stock phrases have too often obscured
the underlying vital faith and the sturdy strength of character inseparable from it, which alone can explain the widespread influence
radiating from New England a hundred years ago. But to keep in
mind the tenets of the theology is necessary for an understanding of
that age. And so a few main points are here reviewed in the hope
that a little of the quality of the New England Way may slip
through to those to whom the Puritans seem as remote as the
Crusaders, and almost as unreal.

The beliefs of Puritan orthodoxy were in line with the great
Christian tradition in which God helps and inspires man in his
struggle to force the good within him to conquer the evil—with
emphasis on the reality of evil. In Emily Dickinson's day the Puritan
no longer persecuted—in the flesh—those who disagreed with him.
But the long shadow of Jonathan Edwards, distant from 1850 in years
but not in influence, still lay dark over Amherst. His ministry had
begun in Northampton only seven miles away, and from that town
his frightening message, instilling in many a sinner the fear of an
angry God, had inspired the Great Awakening of the 1730's. Some
investigators have pointed out that this aspect of the teaching of
Jonathan Edwards has been overemphasized. They maintain that
instilling fear in the hearts of the congregation was only a tech-
nique used to intensify their sense of responsibility. Possibly so.
But whatever the purpose, the effect was the same.

A century later the orthodox New Englander was still weighed
down by his awareness of evil. He believed that sin is natural to

2. *Letters*, 1931, 422, 387.
3. *Letters*, 1931, 257.

men; that there is in all the sons of Adam an inborn tendency to do wrong. They go on sinning until, by the miracle of God's mercy, they are redeemed. But in order to receive such pardon, a person must first experience a suffocating realization of his own guilt. This was not hard to come by since fear of punishment, terrible as that threatened by the Old Testament prophets, filled men's hearts: fear rooted in the knowledge that God is everywhere and knows everything we do. "Thou, God, seest me," admitted of no doubt. In his inaugural address President Heman Humphrey of Amherst College summed it up in these words: "Without the fear of God nothing can be secure for one moment."[4]

In early youth Emily Dickinson seems to have shared this fear. At twenty-three she wrote to Dr. and Mrs. Holland:

The minister today, not our own minister, preached about death and judgment, and what would become of those, meaning Austin and me, who behaved improperly—and somehow the sermon scared me, and father and Vinnie looked very solemn as if the whole was true, and I would not for worlds have let them know that it troubled me, but I longed to come to you, and tell you all about it, and learn how to be better. He preached such an awful sermon though, that I didn't much think I should ever see you again until the Judgment Day, and then you would not speak to me, according to his story. The subject of perdition seemed to please him, somehow. It seems very solemn to me.[5]

Sin was not only trangression of the law. It was, for the Puritan, an affront to Almighty God, a fact which reinforced the fear of it. About the wages of sin there was no uncertainty. The Articles of Faith as first formulated for the Church of Amherst College (1826) made it clear that "all who die without repentance, will at the day of judgment be condemned for their own sins, and will remain in impenitence and justly suffer everlasting punishment."[6] A generation later this theology still thundered from the pulpit on Sunday. The dogma might not hold the congregation, but the implications of it did. Its influence, moreover, was not confined by church walls. Even the man who never went to church conformed to the standards of a faith he did not acknowledge. Although he did not

4. Tyler, 1873, 131.
5. *Letters*, 1931, 158-159.
6. Tyler, 1873, 193.

subscribe to orthodox doctrine, fear of the orthodox God was in his heart.

After the preacher had given his hearers a realization of "the awful solemnity of God," the next step toward redemption was to make the sinner realize the enormity of his own misdoing, which would in turn drive him in agony of repentance to humble himself to the uttermost as he pled to be spared the punishment which he had earned. At last, through the intercession of Christ the Savior, the certainty of forgiveness came with power from on high. Once this was gained and the sinner was in no doubt about it, he was deemed worthy to join the church. But to the end of his life the warfare against sin never ceased. Fear of slipping back into his wicked ways held him fast. To win the never-ending fight he could gain strength through prayer alone. And the only way not to lose that strength, to be able to continue to fight and to win, was by dependence on Christ who would show him the way. Possessed of such knowledge, if a man took a wrong turn he could not plead ignorance. He could only once more beg forgiveness and try again.

Though fear held men in line and kept them steady, there was in orthodox theology room for hope. God is just. He will recompense as well as chasten. As a life of sin will be punished, just as surely will a righteous life be rewarded in the ceaseless ages beyond the grave. If He cares about each one of us, He will not abandon us after a few brief years. So firm was the Puritan's belief in immortality that he regarded this life as no more than a period of probation for the hereafter when his balance sheet would be appraised.

Emily Dickinson's sense of infinity was a baffling certainty that would not let her go. "No friend have I that so persists," she said, "as this eternity." Much of her most exultant poetry deals with immortality, but she could also turn to "the flood subject" with cool detachment:

> No vacillating God
> Ignited this abode
> To put it out.

Toward the end of her life that assurance deepened and she could declare with finality that "to 'know in whom' we 'have believed' is immortality."[7]

7. *Letters*, 1931, 283, 381, 425.

In Amherst as in most of New England "the Church" meant the Orthodox Trinitarian Congregational Church. In Emily's girlhood the total population of all the villages within the town limits was about three thousand. These people supported five Congregational churches, all trinitarian, all orthodox.[8]

The word "Congregational" referred to the form of church government. Every congregation was responsible only to itself, each one as independent as each family in the community; and as a family was judged on its merits, by the acts of its members, so a church earned the right to survive only by its own efforts. The rights and independence of separate congregations and the leeway they permitted themselves in the management of their affairs, however, did not loosen the rigid doctrinal frame in which they functioned. On the contrary, strength was gained through an increased sense of individual responsibility.

In Emily's childhood, hymns (Watts's hymns in particular) were sung in church, but without accompaniment until an innovation was introduced when her brother was about ten. To the end of his life Austin Dickinson recalled the impression it made upon him:

In 1839 . . . came the acquisition of the first musical instrument ever owned by the parish, a double bass viol. With my first recollection Josiah Ayres managed it, and the tones he drew from its lower chords in his accompaniment to the singing of some of Watts' Favorite Hymns, haunt me even now. Such lines as

8. The First Parish to which the Dickinsons belonged (the official name of which is "The First Church of Christ in Amherst, Massachusetts"), organized in 1735, was established four years later (the first minister, the Reverend David Parsons, "settled" November 7, 1739); the Second Parish, the "East Meeting House" at the foot of Main Street, in 1783; the parish at South Amherst in 1824; and the North Congregational Church in 1826. The fifth was the "Church of Christ in Amherst College," organized on March 7, 1826, "on the principles of the Congregational Platform."

There was also a small intermittent Baptist congregation, inducements in Amherst not being sufficient to hold a minister for any length of time. On the outskirts of the town were two Methodist meetings. Episcopalians and Roman Catholics arrived later and in that order.

In a poem beginning "The bobolink is gone," Emily Dickinson referred to "the Presbyterian birds," which has led some writers to assume that the followers of Calvin's doctrines in Amherst belonged to that denomination. To the best of my knowledge there has never been a Presbyterian church in Amherst. I think Emily used the word as she used other remote terms—"Tripoli," "Dnieper," "Zanzibar," "Himmaleh"—to suggest a quality, in this case decorum.

"That awful day will surely come,"
"That last great day of woe and doom,"
and
"Broad is the road that leads to death," etc.

seemed to me sufficiently depressing in plain print; sung with the accompaniment they were appalling—to a boy."[9]

Solemn it certainly was; but not always without humor. A favorite quip of the time had to do with one of the early pastors of the First Church of Amherst who is reported to have said that he "believed in Total Depravity when it was lived up to."

A small book by the Reverend Dr. Pond of the Theological Seminary, Bangor, Maine, sternly warns the orthodox.[10] To win the struggle with unseen spiritual foes, he says, church members must be constantly on their guard against "all these theories of doctrine which go to exalt men rather than God, which tend to let down the high claims of the gospel and make it acceptable to the carnal mind, which require for their support that the Scriptures be loosely interpreted, if not that their inspiration should be given up—let all such theories and pretended improvements, however imposing in outward appearance, be interdicted and thrown overboard at once. Rely upon it, there is poison and corruption in them."[11]

This passage was aimed at the "decidedly and palpably heretical" Unitarians in eastern Massachusetts who show, says Dr. Pond, "a strange and criminal indifference in respect to religious doctrine," and are "afraid of nothing so much as what they call enthusiasm." Indeed, at one time, in the words of President Hitchcock of Amherst College, this heretical sect had "well nigh obliterated vital godliness."[12] The yeomanry of the country districts were shocked and outraged. In particular they deplored the defection of Harvard College with all its "means of influence."

Unitarianism, product of a schism in the Congregational Church which had begun in reaction against the excesses of the Great

---

9. Dickinson, "Representative Men," 56-57.
10. Enoch Pond, D.D., *Sketches of the Theological History of New England* (Boston: Congregational Publishing Society, 1880).
11. *Ibid.,* 77.
12. Hitchcock, *Reminiscences,* 11.

Awakening of the eighteenth century, had produced many saintly characters; but by emphasizing toleration and salvation through righteousness alone it undermined that very fear of God and of punishment for wrongdoing upon which orthodox Congregationalism depended.

The Puritan had long since repudiated the authority of a church which would take from him the responsibility of deciding for himself what was right and what was wrong, only to encounter now in his own tradition those who were renouncing some of the foundations of his belief, such as the doctrine of everlasting damnation which throughout New England still had a practical potency. The Reverend Mr. Higginson, himself a Unitarian preacher, writing to his mother from Newburyport in 1851, told her that his friend, the Reverend Mr. Crosby, had lost his professorship in Dartmouth College because of a letter he wrote to the American Tract Society against the doctrine of eternal punishment.[13] (An honored teacher, Professor Alpheus Crosby did sever his connection with Dartmouth in 1849, becoming emeritus at the age of thirty-nine, but whether or not because of his religious views is not clear.)

In Massachusetts this split between orthodox and Unitarian Congregationalists intensified a difference in outlook between the eastern and central parts of the state, a difference founded partly on geography.

The Connecticut River, rising in the "great and terrible wilderness" of northern New Hampshire and dividing that state from Vermont, flows south across Massachusetts and Connecticut to empty, east of New Haven, into Long Island Sound. The pioneers, advancing from the coast up the valley of the great river, came upon the lush lowlands of the Hadley meadows. There they stopped and built their houses, barns and granaries, cultivating the broad fertile plains and bringing forth abundant harvests.

Irrespective of state boundaries the valley of the Connecticut was a geographical unit, in thought as in crops. The towns were oriented up- and down-valley rather than toward Boston. In the 1850's the drawing power of the two principal colleges of New

13. *Letters and Journals of Thomas Wentworth Higginson, 1846-1906*, Edited by Mary Thacher Higginson (Boston, 1921), 40.

England was thus influenced by geography as well as by religion.[14] Harvard was solidly Unitarian. Yale remained orthodox; so also did Dartmouth College, far upstream among the New Hampshire hills. The pioneers had carried their orthodoxy with them as they moved north up the valley.

But theology was not the chief source of the Puritans' strength. In spite of their anxieties about heresy Congregationalists insisted less on creeds than on a love of "vital piety," or as they put it, "a saving work in their hearts."[15] This may explain why the effect of severe doctrine on the men who devoted their lives to promulgating it seldom produced harsh characters. On the contrary, for sheer kindliness and goodness those old Congregational ministers were a race apart. Throughout life they kept a purity of outlook which often gave them the inspired look of a seer. Photographs taken in old age of many of those who graduated from Amherst College in the 1850's have an appearance of such childlike innocence that a mere glance at their faces brings a sense of peace. They were without guile, and the love of the Lord more than the fear of damnation was in their deep-set eyes. Such were the Reverend John M. Greene, Amherst, 1853, renowned in the annals of Smith College, and the Reverend Henry Vaughan Emmons, 1854, Emily Dickinson's friend.

It may be hard at times to discern the spiritual fervor behind the quaint language, and to understand the intensity of their desire to grasp and to transmit spiritual truth. But Puritans were at heart mystics. The inner life was their chief concern. The missionary zeal of the young preachers was such that John Greene, shortly after graduation, could write to his intended bride: "It seems as if I could not live unless I see sinners turning to God." Later he told her that he had a feeling of personal responsibility for the soul of every child born in his parish.[16]

14. As the young men of eastern Massachusetts seldom went west to college, those of the West did not often turn toward the East. In a list of college graduates between 1771 and 1862 who were natives of Amherst only three, the first three on the list, went to Harvard: Nathaniel Dickinson, Jr., 1771; David Parsons, 1771; Ebenezer Boltwood, 1773. (Sylvester Judd, *History of Hadley* [Northampton, 1863], 628.) These three graduated before Unitarian heresy had engulfed that institution. According to Mr. Judd not one son of Amherst graduated from Harvard College during the next ninety years.

15. Preston Cummings, *A Dictionary of Congregational Usages and Principles* (Boston, 1852), 414.

16. From unpublished letters of the 1850's, quoted with the kind permission of Dr. Greene's daughter, the late Helen F. Greene of Cambridge.

This faith was not unlike that of the architects of the Middle Ages—the drive which gave life its meaning. An intense desire to search out God found expression not in beauty, however, except the beauty of holiness, so much as in a moral code which produced, not cathedrals, but a stalwart strength worthy of human nature. The Puritan's yearning for righteousness glows in the words of the young Emerson—a Unitarian:

"Milton describes himself in his letter to Diodati as enamoured of moral perfection. He did not love it more than I. That which I cannot yet declare has been my angel from childhood until now. It has separated me from men. It has watered my pillow, it has driven sleep from my bed. It has tortured me for my guilt. It has inspired me with hope. It cannot be defeated by my defeats. It cannot be questioned, though all the martyrs apostatize. It is always the glory that shall be revealed; it is the 'open secret' of the universe; and it is only the feebleness and dust of the observer that makes it future, the whole *is* now potentially in the bottom of his heart. It is the soul of religion. Keeping my eye on this, I understand all heroism, the history of loyalty and of martyrdom and of bigotry, the heat of the Methodist, the nonconformity of the Dissenter, the patience of the Quaker."[17]

The words of Emily Dickinson blaze with the same passion for perfection in the sight of God. In her writing this poem seems to scorch the page:

> Dare you see a soul at *the white heat?*
> Then crouch within the door.
> Red is the fire's common tint;
> But when the vivid ore
> Has vanquished flame's conditions
> It quivers from the forge
> Without a color, but the light
> Of unanointed blaze. . . .

The italics are hers.

When Emily Dickinson's poems are read with the thought in mind that hers was fundamentally a Puritan struggle, "the battle fought between the soul and no man," her words will be seen in true perspective. Hers was not only an effort to conquer too great a love for this person or that, persistent and searing though such

17. Emerson's *Journals* (Boston, 1910), III, 208-209 (September 17, 1833).

experiences were. There was a still deeper conflict. Throughout the
years she was lashed to the moral law which was for her the expression of God's purpose regarding her life. To describe the fight she
found an analogy in the Old Testament:

> I took my power in my hand
> And went against the world—
> 'Twas not so much as David had
> But I was twice as bold.
>
> I aimed my pebble, but myself
> Was all the one that fell.
> Was it Goliath was too large,
> Or only I too small?

Richard Sewall once said to me that Emily Dickinson "wrote her
poems in much the same spirit that her devout contemporaries
prayed. It was a daily ritual with her," he thought, "sustaining and
refreshing, a very organic part of her religiously oriented life . . . a
communion with her soul and her Maker in the very best Puritan
tradition." I think this is true. To be sure, Emily said bluntly that
she did not "respect" doctrine. But a code of living founded on
belief in God can tolerate a good deal of theology without harm.

In her poems it is easy to point to examples of cynicism as when,
upbraiding the "Heavenly Father," she says:

> We apologize to Thee
> For Thine own duplicity.

But all the time she was speaking to One who *cared*. Only a soul afire
with love of God could be as sure of it as she was. Although in a
moment of anguish she could cry out that "of course" she prayed
but God did not care, toward the last, after her mother's death, she
was just as quietly confident that He did care. These are her words:
"I believe we shall in some manner be cherished by our Maker—
that the One who gave us this remarkable earth has the power still
farther to surprise that which He has caused. Beyond that all is
silence. . . ."[18]

When the study of Emily Dickinson's motives is concentrated less
on lovers and more on the mysterious depths of the spirit, when the
focus is on her lifelong battle for personal integrity and for right

18. *Letters*, 1931, 267.

adjustment to the will of her Maker—then, I think, scholars will be rewarded by deeper insight into the wellsprings of her genius. "My life has been too simple and stern to embarrass any," she said. The simplicity was characteristic of the times in rural New England. But the sternness came from inner necessity. Rectitude which stems from a sense of accountability to God is a taskmaster far more exacting than any law. To put it differently, when an understanding of her ceaseless groping for more light has replaced the legend of a broken heart, and when her ridicule of cant and her repudiation of the severer aspects of Puritan doctrine have blown away in the wind, Emily Dickinson may come to be ranked among the great religious poets.

2

Conduct, which reflected the Puritan's convictions, was regulated not so much by theology as by religious faith. Lacking spiritual sanction an act was sinful, and in the New England code the avoidance of sin was a positive trait of character. Although "mere morality" as such was disparaged, being without religious incentive, the code men lived by was no less inflexible than their theology. Conduct was closely watched. No incident was too trivial to escape moral implications. Stiff and unbending it was, sometimes unlovely, but clean and firm and sound at the core. It might be hard but it was plain; and it was followed. The rules were definite but they were just. The Puritan's belief in justice, as Mr. Shipton says, was one of the causes of our democracy—the sinew of America.[19]

The code was not only Congregational of course; standards equally inexorable were held and conformity equally rigid enforced by other denominations which also "had their discipline from the Scriptures."[20] But the term, The New England Way, was used to characterize life in communities established by Congregational settlers from New England. Scattered throughout the Middle West from Ohio to Colorado, they became little centers of influence many of which, and others farther west, are still true to type today, some of them even more so than the villages of New England itself.

The rule that went deepest was this: Do the best you can in any

19. Clifford K. Shipton, "Puritanism and Modern Democracy," *The New England Historical and Genealogical Register*, CI (July, 1947), 181-198.
20. Cummings, *op. cit.*, 295.

situation, irrespective of its importance, especially if the interests of other people are involved. The Biblical injunction is plain: "Whatsoever thy hand findeth to do, do it with thy might" (Eccl. 9:10). Or, in Emily's words:

> Life's little duties do
> Precisely, as the very least
> Were infinite to me.

Thoroughness, it is true, was sometimes carried to extremes in completing a job not in itself worth doing. But of effort New Englanders were spendthrift, though frugal in all other respects. "Moderation in all things" stopped short of hard work. They never spared themselves. So deep-seated was the sense of duty that one was always under pressure. Even when occupied with a useful task one felt as if he ought to be doing something else, a feeling for which housework in particular provided almost unlimited scope. A person brought up under this code finds it difficult to slight the most inconsequential task. When called to his attention he adopts it as his own, particularly if it is distasteful, and disposes of it with "scrupulous exactness." If it is his duty that is enough; if unpleasant, so much the better. Emily put it succinctly when she said: "Father is quite a hand to give medicine, especially if it is not desirable to the patient."[21]

Difficulties to be overcome were part of what was called "the discipline of hindrance," in itself salutary, and suffering had an honored place. In the poignant words of President Stearns, after his son aged twenty-one had been killed at the battle of New Bern (March 14, 1862), "Suffering when not too mighty for us is educational." Deeper insight as the reward of suffering was a persistent theme with Emily Dickinson:

> Who never lost, are unprepared
> A coronet to find . . .
>
> A wounded deer leaps highest . . .
>
> 'Tis thirsting vitalizes wine . . .

The qualities most valued, in addition to Benjamin Franklin's primary virtues of industry, thoroughness and frugality, were loy-

21. *Letters*, 1894, 37; *Letters*, 1931, 33.

alty and temperance. This meant constant self-denial. Since life is "solemn in its duties and responsibilities and endless in its eternal duration," the first necessity was subordination of personal desire.[22] To some natures suppression is a challenge, up to a point. Emily was always trying to get her heart "under." As she wrote to a friend, "I have felt so sweet an impatience to write you that I thought it perhaps inordinate, and to be disciplined, like other unruly wishfulness." And again, "Flowers are so enticing that I fear they are sins —like gambling or apostasy." Her enjoyment of flowers was almost recklessly indulged however, one joy without a bridle.

As self-denial was an honored virtue, "the Scarlet Way trodden by the Son of God," the sin most feared was self-indulgence. It must be shunned like a man with cholera. The Puritan was even suspicious of personal comfort. It is said of Mary Lyon that on winter mornings she jumped out of bed the moment she waked and before she was fully conscious had broken the ice in the pitcher on the washstand. Self-indulgence in any form, even if quite harmless, was sin. For the discipline of self was the one sure preparation for the end in view, which was to be worthy of a heavenly reward "after the little interval we pass in lifetime here" (page 404).

Such were a few characteristics of The New England Way. As its outward and visible sign there stood Edward Dickinson. Determined to see that justice was done, he was as stern with himself as with others. Emily said, "You know he never played." His family tried to follow his example; and Emily's self-restraint was as rigid as even Mary Lyon could have wished. But the discipline was strict, not because her father expected it of her, nor because it was customary, not even because of the requirements of the code, but because of her overpowering awareness of God's love. To that fact we must return for it was the key to her life.

It is easy to see the Puritan's peculiarities—his austerity, his hardheaded shrewdness, his stubbornness, his self-repression, his lack of humor. But while noting the symptoms of bigotry or intolerance, we should not forget that these attitudes sprang from a hunger for righteousness and a determination to follow the inner light of conscience. We are mistaken if we permit his prickly aspect to obscure his

22. *The Hampshire and Franklin Express*, August 26, 1853.

virtues: his sincerity and intellectual integrity; his readiness to accept responsibility and his devotion to public service; his forthright honesty, his staunch dependability, his "antique courage," and more than all, the intensity and depth of his piety—a sense of divine guidance which found expression in his concern for others—and his willingness to undergo personal sacrifice for his family, his neighbors and his community. These qualities produced a mighty inner strength. We are still benefiting by the impetus it gave.

PART TWO

1840 - 1850

CHAPTER V

The Manuscripts

A letter always seemed to me like Immortality, for is it not the mind alone, without corporeal friend? Letters, *1931, 347.*

EMILY DICKINSON'S letters were first published in 1894, when two volumes were brought out by my mother, Mrs. Todd.[1] She published the later correspondence in full, insofar as the owners were willing, but used the early letters only in part. For the omissions there were several reasons. To publish "personal and private" letters at all was at that time a dubious venture, a fact which should be borne in mind. Not only were very frank passages left out, those which might give offense to persons still living; in the case of letters to the immediate family the restrictions were drastic, so drastic indeed that the impression conveyed by the published fragments is sometimes misleading.

Then, too, my mother called the early letters "immensely wordy." She said, "I took what I thought were the most interesting parts. You see the letters made two volumes and I thought there were getting to be too many of them. Apparently the publishers thought so too. I tried to take out everything I could." Village gossip, for instance, could have no possible interest for the general reader. And personal affairs were in most cases too trifling to print. This may have been a wise editorial policy in 1894, but it has had the disadvantage of presenting a lopsided picture. Trivial details often

1. *Letters of Emily Dickinson,* edited by Mabel Loomis Todd (Boston: Roberts Brothers, 1894).

47

give a sense of reality. Then, too, the meaning of obscure passages is clarified by the complete text—such for example as Emily's "Oliver" letter of March 27, 1853, replying to one Austin had cryptically signed with that name. Though many of "the most interesting parts" of Emily's letters have become part of our folklore, publishing them out of context has had its drawbacks. Letters written by other members of the family, though without literary value, do supply a background of fact. Furthermore, by leaving out passages not strikingly original, my mother must be held in part responsible for the widely held notion that Emily Dickinson sat upstairs in a rocking chair writing poetry while others carried on the work of the household. Nothing could be further from the truth.

It was while the 1894 volumes were in preparation that the letters in this book (except the Sweetser collection and those in Part Five) were given to my mother by Emily's brother, William Austin Dickinson. They were all the family letters he had left, or all he could find, after fire destroyed his office and most of his historical records during the blizzard of March 11-14, 1888. The fact that one letter from Emily Dickinson to Austin was published in *Life and Letters* by Martha Dickinson Bianchi may mean that there are others he could not find. This might explain the gaps in the correspondence.

The packets contained letters from his father, Edward Dickinson, from his sisters, Emily and Lavinia, and one written by his mother before her marriage. Except for this one, a schoolgirl missive to her sister, and a few drafts of his own, the letters were addressed to Austin himself. And, but for those in Chapters XXX and XXXII and one final group from his father, all were written between 1847 and 1854, when Emily and later Vinnie were away at school, or when Austin himself was absent, teaching in Boston or studying at the Harvard Law School. Only a few of his letters from Emily were included in the 1894 volumes, and from those only excerpts.

Mr. Dickinson told my mother to edit the manuscripts as she thought best, with one proviso which I will take up later. Before turning them over to her he had arranged the letters in order as best he could. She never challenged a date assigned by him. Nearly all of those still in the original envelopes were postmarked with the month and day (often illegible), but not, usually, with the year. These he dated, for the most part correctly. But a few were certainly misplaced. And several were in the wrong envelopes, so that the matching has always had to be checked against other evidence. The reader will observe that in the present volume the sequence of Emily's letters to her brother differs somewhat from his own arrangement of them in the original edition.

I do not lightly change a date assigned by Mr. Dickinson. I have done so only when reference to a known event proves him to have been mistaken. For example: Emily's letter about the burning of Kimberly's barn, on pages 109-111 of the 1894 *Letters,* was dated by him July 23, 1852. But the letter was written "Sunday night," and the barn had burned "yesterday." In 1852, July 22 fell on a Thursday, not a Saturday. Turning to the files of the *Express,* an account of the fire is found in the issue of Friday, August 1, 1851. Thompson Kimberly's barn had burned on the previous Saturday, July 26, and Emily's letter was written on Sunday, July 27, 1851.[2]

Only the very earliest of Emily's letters were dated. It is often a long and tedious process to find out when they were written. Occasionally dates can be found only by intricate matching of internal with external evidence, even celestial phenomena being of use in this connection, as in a letter written "Tuesday noon" during the winter of 1851-1852. Austin had left home the previous day to return to Boston where he was teaching school. His sister wrote, "I watched the stage coach yesterday until it went away," thinking that "should you turn around" and "I should not be there I could never forgive me." The envelope bears a faint cancellation, "November 11," which in 1851 was Tuesday. But is this the right envelope? Is there anything in the text of the letter to prove that it was written on that particular Tuesday? Emily says that on the previous evening "the clear, cold moon was shining." On Monday, November 10, shining it certainly could have been, and high in the eastern sky, for it was full on November 8. So, that Austin had indeed spent Sunday, November 9, at home, that he had left on Monday the tenth, and that the letter was written on November 11 the moon bears additional evidence.

While most of the letters are still in the original envelopes, some were loose in the packets, and a few empty envelopes did not match

2. In *Letters,* 1931, the date of the fire, described on page 106, follows the 1894 text.

the letters. In such cases, if no verifiable event is mentioned, an editor must depend upon minute details in order to fix an exact date: which week did mother have a toothache, or father an attack of rheumatism; when was Austin's valise sent to Cambridge, and when was it, or was it not, received; when did Vinnie first request the hatstand and feather duster; and so on. The sequence of the letters within a given period of time is sometimes determined by facts as trivial as these. It should be added that in spite of having used every available tool, and combination of tools, in an effort to place the letters in correct order, the day, if not the month, is still in a few instances open to question. These uncertainties might have been lessened, if not eliminated, could I have consulted other family letters of the same period, or Lavinia Dickinson's diary kept during 1851, a few passages from which were published by her niece.[3]

And now, turning from details to a matter of primary importance, Emily's penmanship: the first clue to an approximate date for a few of the letters, if not the only one, is the handwriting. For interpreting a life in which the events were not external happenings but inner crises, the correct sequence of her manuscripts is of such importance that the reader's indulgence is asked for a brief digression.

Emily Dickinson is well known to have used successively several styles of script. To one thoroughly familiar with her manuscripts each style is readily distinguishable, a fact which provides a basis on which to construct a chronological scale or timetable of her handwriting. For such a purpose the manuscripts of all her letters to which dates can be assigned with certainty should be arranged in order. Numerous mannerisms, such as the tall *s*, having been identified, together with the years during which each was most characteristic, the dates of their first and last occurrence would be noted as accurately as possible. No matter how familiar one may be with the manuscripts, such minute comparison is the only way to make sure even of the sequence of the different periods. Since each style evolved gradually, merging with those immediately before and after it, the boundaries between the periods cannot be sharply drawn. But when more is known about key details and the period during

3. Martha Dickinson Bianchi, *Emily Dickinson Face to Face* (Boston, 1932), 108-111.

which each was characteristic, the gradations from one style to another can be pinned down with some precision.

It should be noted, however, that even within a single period the penmanship is not uniform. Mood may have influenced it, or fatigue. A strange pen or the quality of the paper could make a difference. Some of the latest notes, obviously scribbled in haste, perhaps in the dark, bear slight resemblance to the formal script of the period. And yet certain peculiarities show beyond a doubt that the writing belongs to the same years.

After a rough chronological scale has been constructed, the handwriting of the *poems*—none of the manuscripts of which is dated—could be matched to that of accurately dated letters; in other words, all manuscripts could be fitted into the sequence where they seem to belong. The scale would be improved and corrected as further evidence unfolded.

This matter of a time scale and its importance in determining the chronology of the manuscripts of the poems was taken up in an article in which I mentioned some of the pitfalls lying in wait for a scholar.[4] If he tries to date a poem in rough draft by the paper on which it is written, for instance, is it safe to rely on anything which may appear on the back of the sheet? At the top of a leaf torn from a notebook he might find in Emily's father's writing, "E. Dickinson, 1824." On that page about sixty years later she wrote, "I send you a decrepit flower"; and on another page from the same notebook, not many years before her death:

> The most pathetic thing I do
> Is play I hear from you.[5]

Any inference as to the date of composition drawn either from a watermark on the paper or from anything on the back of a rough draft is not to be trusted except as evidence that the writing is not earlier than a given date. Equally unreliable are detectives' tools

4. Millicent Todd Bingham, "Emily Dickinson's Handwriting—A Master Key," *The New England Quarterly,* XXII (June, 1949), 229-234.

5. Poems published in *Bolts of Melody, New Poems of Emily Dickinson,* edited by Mabel Loomis Todd and Millicent Todd Bingham (New York: Harper & Brothers, 1945), 52, 156. Incidentally, except for half a dozen letters to Colonel Higginson, I know of no evidence that Emily signed her name "E. Dickinson" until after her father's death in 1874.

such as type of ink or lead pencil, both of which Emily might have kept for years, as she kept her paper.

In her effort to date the letters which she was in process of editing, Mrs. Todd took the first steps in the early 1890's toward making a chronology. By 1894, when the letters were published, her familiarity with the successive changes in the details of Emily's penmanship was sufficient to enable her to estimate the probable periods to which many poems belonged. She recognized the importance of this undertaking and had begun to arrange them in order. But she did not finish.

Forty years later, while deciphering the manuscripts of the poems in *Bolts of Melody*, I in turn came to realize how helpful would be a time scale such as I have described. The early letters, even for so brief a period as the six years covered by those in this volume, have furnished enough material to begin putting in the foundation, one on which students of the handwriting can build, I think, with confidence.

Emily's letters to her brother take us to 1854. The Haven letters of 1858 and 1859 (pages 403-404) supply a link between 1854 and 1862 when Colonel Higginson's collection in the Boston Public Library begins. Another manuscript series, beginning about the time when those in this volume leave off and ending in 1881, consists of letters to Dr. and Mrs. J. G. Holland, prepared for publication by their granddaughter, Mrs. Ward.[6] For the last five years of Emily's life, 1881-1886, letters to Judge Lord and to the Clark brothers as well as to my mother and to her parents may be used. So a sequence of manuscript letters from 1846 to 1886 is now accessible, and the skeleton of a time scale of Emily Dickinson's handwriting can be set up. When all the original manuscript poems

6. When *Letters of Emily Dickinson,* edited by Mabel Loomis Todd, was published in 1894, one chapter was devoted to letters to Dr. and Mrs. Holland. On August 20, 1893, Mrs. Holland wrote to Mrs. Todd: "I regret I had so few of the many letters dear Emily wrote me to send you. As I remember them, there were many more interesting and quaint than these I have" (*Ancestors' Brocades,* 193, 196). Some missing letters have been found and were published in April, 1951. (*Emily Dickinson's Letters to Dr. and Mrs. Josiah Gilbert Holland,* Edited by their granddaughter Theodora Van Wagenen Ward [Cambridge, 1951].) In addition to these, other Dickinson family papers have been acquired by the Houghton Library, Harvard University, and will supply additional material for completing the time scale.

have been placed in order as correctly as possible, they can then be fitted into the scale where they belong.

The arrangement of all existing manuscripts in order of composition is a necessary preliminary to the end in view, which is not merely to date a letter or the manuscript of a poem, important though that may be. It is much more. For the changes which with the passing years took place in Emily Dickinson's writing parallel the drama within. Not that in itself the *handwriting* reveals any trait, or a change in her character. That is not what I mean. But a study of its evolution is one step in determining the sequence of the poems which, when correctly ordered, will themselves reflect the ebb and flow of inner turmoil. In other words, a style of penmanship dates a poem. The poem reflects an inner experience. And so, after a chronological scale has been constructed and tested for accuracy, and the probable time of composition of all available manuscript poems determined within a year or two, the shattering experiences—"the mob. within the heart"—revealed in the poems with an almost frightening frankness can be placed in tentative order. Then, when their true meaning becomes clear, will a biographer for the first time have firm ground on which to stand. It is not impossible that in a routine study such as this may be found the key to an understanding of those volcanic changes which marked the steps of progress in Emily Dickinson's stern and simple life.

So much for the troublesome matter of sequence. Now as to omissions from the letters as originally published.

Austin Dickinson specified that certain parts of Emily's letters to him should be left out. On this point my mother wrote, "Passages omitted from the letters to Austin are either those of little interest, or those which he requested me to omit. Some of the latter he had himself erased from the manuscripts before giving me the letters."[7] I asked her what this meant. She replied that Mr. Dickinson's reservations had varying degrees of firmness. First and least important, certain references he thought could have no interest for anyone but himself: long tiresome passages about how much he was missed at home; reiteration of Emily's devotion to him; details about his clothes, keeping them in repair and how to send them to and from Boston in the days when packages were usually transported through

7. *Letters*, 1931, 62-63.

the courtesy of traveling acquaintances. Frequent references to the family's ill-health, he thought, overemphasized their concern about it. If he meant that it had not been a constant preoccupation his memory was certainly hazy, for the letters make only too clear their anxiety about one another's health, and about their own. Illness and fear of illness hounded them. Even Austin had "palpitations," trouble with his eyes, and constant heavy colds.

To all of these omissions my mother assented. She agreed that for the most part such personal matters were of little interest. The chapter containing Austin's letters would in any case be disproportionately long.

But one of Mr. Dickinson's requests was in the nature of a command. In the Preface to the "New and Enlarged Edition" of the *Letters* (1931) my mother wrote: "Although in general both Lavinia and Austin approved of whatever I did or did not do in the way of editing, leaving decision as to what to print and what to leave out entirely to me, they did make one request, namely, that I omit certain passages, references to a relative then living, in some of the early letters."

That was all my mother said. This is what was meant. Mr. Dickinson stipulated that if Emily's letters to him were to be used, the name of one of her girlhood friends must be left out—that of Susan Gilbert, his wife. But omitting her name was not enough. Before turning over the letters he went through them, eliminating Susan Gilbert's name and in some instances making alterations to disguise a reference to her. He asked my mother to make sure that he had overlooked nothing. In the published volumes Sue's name does not appear. It has been said that her name was omitted at her own request.[8] This is not the case. Mrs. Dickinson was not aware that publication of Emily's letters was in prospect.

The cuts and erasures were made in various ways. If a letter had been written in pencil, the offending lines were rubbed out, not always completely. (Beginning in March, 1853, Emily usually wrote to her brother in pencil.) A few letters show more than one erasure on the same spot. Sometimes, after obliterating what Emily had written, pronouns were altered: "she" to "he" or to "you." In other cases "Sue" was changed to "she" or to "Lucy," even to "Vinnie."

8. *Letters to Dr. and Mrs. Holland,* 207.

(See letters of May 16 and November 21, 1853.) If this was intended not only to guide the editor but to mislead a future reader of the manuscripts it was not successful. Emily's original meaning is perfectly plain.

When written in ink, offending words were blotted out, offending paragraphs cut out with scissors. In one instance half a sheet is torn off; in another, an entire page is missing. It is probably safe to assume that the missing parts had to do with Susan Gilbert, since mention of her had been the only incentive for tampering with these manuscripts. Mr. Dickinson must have given a good deal of time to this undertaking. Had he been more thorough the reader would be more mystified, for enough of Sue still lingers to testify to Emily's early devotion and to her high hopes for the future happiness of them all.

Of course Austin Dickinson had no idea that he was handling the letters of a major poet. But the mutilations are none the less exasperating on that account. They first appear in the fall of 1851 when Emily began to show a special interest in Sue after she had gone to teach in Baltimore. But not until more than a year later does the damage intrude itself upon the reader so insistently that he is unable to forget the bitterness of Austin's life. For Emily, her brother's suffering was her own; though the bitterness was not transferred, only the hurt.

The relationship between Austin Dickinson and his family has long puzzled students because of the inconspicuous place assigned to him in his daughter's volume, *Life and Letters of Emily Dickinson.* Had Emily found her only brother uncongenial, these students asked, unaware as they were of the lifelong mutual devotion. And did he mean little or nothing to his own family? In view of Austin's early disappointment in his marriage and the weight of domestic tribulation he was destined to carry, the letters in this book have a special poignancy. For here, with its air of expectancy, is Edward Dickinson's young devoted family before it was disturbed, in the home which in any study of the observable facts of Emily Dickinson's life is the beginning, the middle and the end.

In the present volume Emily's letters are not only reproduced in their entirety insofar as possible; they are placed for the first time where they belong, among those of other members of the family—

notes written by her father and her sister tucked in the same envelope. This is in a way a symbol, cushioned as she was in life by their surrounding care. The longest letter was usually from Emily, with notes from her father or from Vinnie enclosed. But in a few cases Emily's was the brief note, folded and slipped into a letter written by one of the others.

As to the documents themselves: in letter writing as in all else Edward Dickinson set the pattern for the family. His mannerisms were their mannerisms. A century ago it was customary to put periods after numbers, digits, and people's names, while long double *s*'s, superior letters, and capitals for important words were in common use; but other habits were peculiar to him, the high *s,* and commas in place of apostrophes. The Dickinsons were all addicted to commas, sprinkled around at random. Their use seems to have been "a matter of feeling," as Lincoln said punctuation was with him. And as for paragraphs, Emily's system is not discernible. When a line is incomplete, a paragraph may or may not be intended. But if the following line marks a break in the thought, even if not indented, a paragraph often seems called for.

Owing to mechanical limitations it has not been possible to reproduce every detail as written. For example: the Dickinsons customarily put a period or a dash under superior letters, as with *r* in Mr., or *m* in Wm. It is impracticable to print either a period or a dash under a superior letter. The same holds true when, at the end of a quoted sentence, the period is directly under the quotation marks. In some cases these precede, or follow, the period or comma, but more often they are directly above the punctuation marks. In such instances they have been placed where current practice prescribes. The reader is warned not to look for consistency either of punctuation or of spelling. Emily herself occasionally spelled a word in several ways, as with "Emeline," spelled also "Emmeline" and "Emiline."

Edward Dickinson wrote in ink, and he was particular about the quality, sending to Boston for a special brand. After nearly a hundred years it is only slightly faded. In fact, with the traces of a spluttering quill pen so sharp that it caught in the paper as he wrote, his letters seem as fresh as the day they were written. Little drifts of black sand, which he used instead of blotting paper, still settle in the creases. His early communications are for the most part notes, or commands, on odds and ends of paper tucked into letters sent to Austin by the girls. They are filled with details of finance and matters of business, although occasional asides reveal more of his character than he perhaps intended. Sometimes his letters are dated, a boon indeed!

If, in the care with which he formed his words, Edward Dickinson permitted himself some leeway, his daughter Lavinia was entirely unhampered in this regard. Some letters are omitted; some half-formed. A *u* may serve for an *o* or an *a*, even for an *e*. Small *t*'s are used in place of capitals and capital *s*'s for small ones, the latter following her father's habit. As she says (December 9, 1853), "I do not half write the words." It is often hard to tell whether they were carelessly written, or misspelled. In such cases I have given her the benefit of the doubt. Habitual misspellings have been retained. Syllabic division at the end of a line was not within Lavinia's ken. She divides words according to space—com-e, kno-w, goin-g, thin-k, aga-in. Punctuation was dispensed with for the most part except for commas in irrelevant places. She used an occasional apostrophe, but placed it before the letter it should follow, as in "a'nt," her form of "ain't." (Emily also habitually wrote " 'nt.") Indeed, the position of an apostrophe seems to have been chosen more to please the eye than to convey a meaning. Except for the earliest letters, sent from boarding school and written on large sheets of blue paper, Vinnie's notes are written on torn scraps or half sheets. Nothing could better point the contrast between the sisters than the appearance of their handwriting. Emily's fine early script, so often described, shows few if any signs of carelessness, while Vinnie's impatience with the written word is apparent from the first. In 1884 Austin referred to "Vin's grasshopper-tracked envelopes."

The subject matter of the letters shows a like contrast. Emily wrote at length about things she thought would interest her brother. If she refers to local happenings she sends him a piece of news. And when she does so it is with evident surprise. She says she never thought she would come to it. Usually, she "winnowed what would fade." But he evidently preferred to hear about the homely details which men commonly disdain to notice, for, in her letter of April 8, 1853, Emily wrote, "I shall never write any more grand letters to you, but all the *little* things, and the things called *trifles,* and the crickets upon the hearth, you will be sure to hear." This she may have tried to do, but out of her letters she could not keep herself. The long vistas down which her gaze was traveling are in them all.

When Emily's letters, characterized by Vinnie as feeding Austin "on air," are complemented by Vinnie's down-to-earth comments, the village of Amherst comes alive, the surroundings in the midst of which their lives were spent. Although Vinnie's letters deal only with small incidents of every day, with local gossip and errands for her brother to do, her staccato sentences reveal several basic traits. Indeed, one value of these early letters is the disclosure of characteristics which later became dominant—Vinnie's attachment to possessions, her acid loyalty and possessive devotion in contrast to the warm generosity of Emily's nature. In Emily there is no trace of avarice or hate. "I had no time to hate," she said, "because the grave would hinder me."

Lavinia Dickinson's letters have one definite value, a very real one. Since they were not to be published there are no erasures, no cut-out passages. They remain as written. Only one or two are incomplete, half a page torn off, which Austin may have used as a reminder of something he was asked to purchase and bring with him on his next trip home.

The letters from Edward Dickinson and from his daughters are those actually posted; Austin's on the other hand are rough drafts. The handwriting is vigorous, with the heavy strokes characteristic of his later years, but hardly less difficult to decipher than that of his father and his sister Vinnie. In February, 1853, one letter is written with sufficient care to suggest that he intended to mail it.

In the 1840's the letters were posted without envelopes. The sheet was folded, sealed with a wafer and addressed on the fourth page of the quarto, a habit Edward Dickinson was slow to part with. The earliest letters are without postage stamps. That innovation did not come into general use until 1851. Instead, the Amherst postmaster used a large hand-cut stamp, "Paid 5," or just "5" in the upper right-hand corner, five cents being the rate charged within a specified distance. In some cases, even before the issuance of postage stamps, a round postmark, an inch and a quarter in diameter, gives the name of the town, and, as I have said, the month and the day but not the year. Letters are usually postmarked on the day following the one on which they were written. These postmarks are in red ink until November, 1853, thereafter in green, a detail which has helped to verify the dates of a few letters. In this collection the first postage stamp (three cents) appears on July 7, 1851, and the first self-sealing envelope during that same year, though envelopes without mucilage, sealed with a wafer, had been in use for some time. A wafer was also used on the early self-sealing envelopes. None is embossed. Until March, 1853, envelopes are addressed in Emily's writing, and throughout the rest of that year by her father, unless otherwise indicated.

In addition to the customary brackets to enclose editorial interpolations, the following devices have been used in reproducing the mutilated letters:

Italics in brackets indicate words crossed out or partially erased but still legible:

[*Martha and I are very much together*]

Broken brackets enclose words which, although obliterated in the manuscript, can be identified with certainty by reference to the context, size and shape of the erasure, or similar evidence:

<dear Susie>   <you or Sue>

Obliterated passages which cannot be supplied are indicated in brackets:

[one word erased]   [two lines cut out]   [half of sheet torn off]

When a word has been erased and then altered, the original is given if clear, followed by the word to which it was altered in quotation marks and brackets:

Sue [changed to "we"]   Susie [changed to "Vinnie"]   she ["he"]

At about the time when Emily Dickinson was born, Sir Francis Palgrave wrote in his preface to the *Parliamentary Writs:* "The genuine history of a country can never be well understood without a complete and searching analysis of the component parts of the community." Things so small that they seem unworthy of the attention of a historian, he says, are among the best materials he can find. Thus it happens that documents dealing with the little things that hold people together or drive them apart may reveal the wellsprings of their lives. Such at any rate, is the substance of the letters which follow.

POSTSCRIPT

Since this chapter was set up in type in 1950 my husband, Walter Bingham, has died.

The method of building a time scale described above was suggested by him, who was an expert in the construction of such tools. He attached so much importance to making effective use of the manuscripts of Emily Dickinson that he provided an outline of the necessary procedure, as he called it, which may be summarized as follows:

The aim is to arrange the poems in the order in which they were written; for her poems documented her life. On that foundation alone can her development be traced with certainty. All well-established facts in any way relevant should first be assembled as the basis of the scale: not only known events, but the traits of persons who released the expression of her genius as well, insofar as they are known. Such an inventory would begin with an analysis of her letters. The evidence thus obtained would be carefully weighed. This done, and after a preliminary scale had been set up, a study of the handwriting would then serve as a check on the accuracy of the results. It would take a long time. But my husband felt that only after some such investigation as this could there be any assurance of establishing an accurate chronology of the poems, which is the objective of those who prepare the way for the ultimate biographer of Emily Dickinson.

CHAPTER VI

The House on Pleasant Street[1]

EDWARD DICKINSON was thirty-one years old when the home-stead was sold and his father, sad and broken, departed for the West. He was stirred by his father's humiliation, even more perhaps by the promptness with which his selfless efforts in founding Amherst College seemed to have been forgotten. The only one of the nine children who remained permanently in Amherst, Edward took the brunt of the family disaster. Not only was he the eldest; he felt himself to be in all respects his father's heir. He must recoup the family fortunes and, somehow, turn failure to good account. So he not only took over the large law practice; he made his father's other responsibilities his own. The college was in desperate financial straits. Bankruptcy seemed inevitable. His absent father was power-less to save it. Edward, equally heroic but more worldly-wise, shoul-dered that burden also, determined to see to it that the institution did not founder. In 1835 he assumed the duties of treasurer, an office held until thirty-eight years later it was in turn taken over by his own son. Not only this. In 1838 and 1839, following the panic of 1837, he went as representative to the state legislature in the hope, it was said, of obtaining financial assistance for the college.

For Edward loss of the homestead—built by his father to be passed from generation to generation—symbolized the full force of the family misfortune. It came particularly close because, when the mortgage was foreclosed, he, too, was making his home there

1. At the center of Amherst two streets cross at right angles. The east-west axis is called Main Street east of the village center, and Amity Street west of the center. The north-south axis, skirting the common, known as North Street and Broadway a hundred years ago, were later renamed North and South Pleasant Street.

with his wife and three small children. He did not indulge in dreams, however, or in regret. Instead, he began at once to take practical measures to reconstruct the proud family tradition. Any enterprise with which he might identify himself must be first of all businesslike. As he wrote to his son, "Honesty is the best *policy*."

When Edward Dickinson is called too matter-of-fact, too sharp, too unbending, it is sometimes forgotten that only by steely determination on his part could the Dickinson name have been rescued from the ignominy brought about by his father's lavish idealism.

The purchaser of the Dickinson homestead was David Mack, Jr., of Middlefield, a hamlet at the western extremity of Hampshire County. Referred to as "General" or "Deacon" Mack, in 1834 he came down from his hilltop village, a day's drive from Amherst, where he had been in business with his father, Colonel David Mack, founder and leading citizen of Middlefield, to take up residence in the Dickinson homestead on Main Street.[2] Deacon Mack was an impressive figure. When Austin, aged four, first saw him he thought he had seen God. (See page 502.)

In 1894 Mrs. Todd wrote, "While the family lived for many years in the old mansion built by Emily Dickinson's grandfather, the Hon. Samuel Fowler Dickinson, they had moved away from it about 1840."[3] This approximate date was supplied by Austin Dickinson.

It seems that Edward Dickinson and his young family had continued to live in the homestead after his parents went West and after Deacon Mack took possession in 1834. In his "Reminiscences" the Reverend Mr. Colton describes his impressions of Amherst in 1840. He mentions a call on Edward Dickinson, "then occupying the east part of General Mack's house." This is not strange. There was ample room for two small families in a house which had accommodated ten Dickinsons. In the 1830's Deacon Mack's family consisted of a wife, a son in his teens and, for a time at least, a grown daugh-

2. A deed filed in the Hampshire County Registry of Deeds, Book 71, page 90, records the sale to David Mack, Jr., Esq., on May 22, 1833, of the "Homestead in said Amherst, where Samuel F. Dickinson resides," by "John Leland, Esq., & Nathan Dickinson, Goldsmith . . . the true, sole, proper and lawful owners and possessors of the before granted premises." See Appendix II. It was a somber scene. The deed was signed, sealed and delivered before Samuel F. Dickinson, Justice of the Peace, while his son Edward stood among the witnesses.

3. *Letters*, 1894, 166.

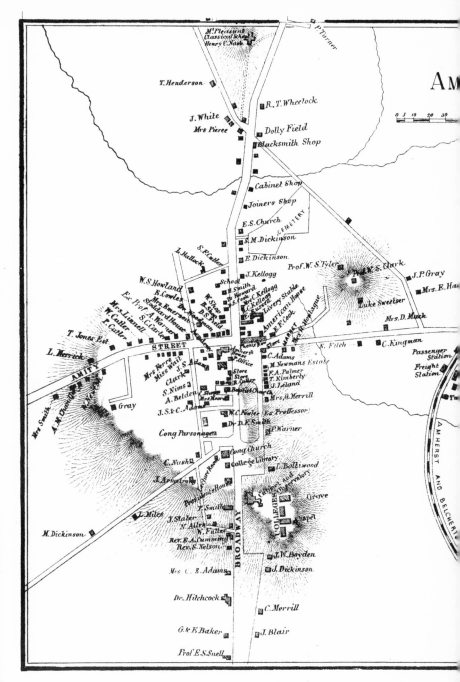

Map of "Amherst Village." From "A Topographical Ma...
direction of H. F. Walling, Superinte...

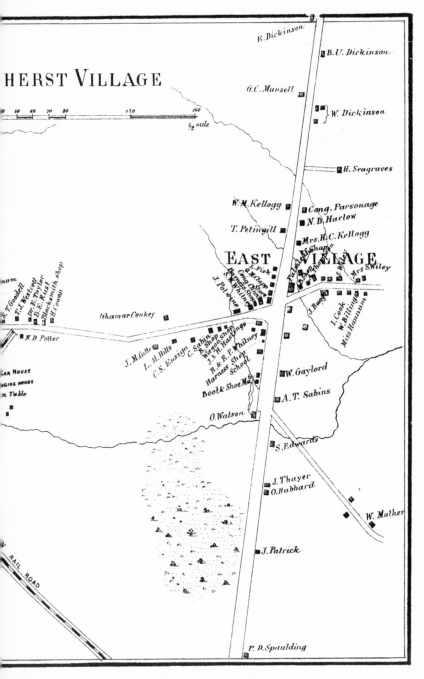

HERST VILLAGE

0 50 60 70 80   120   160
½ mile

E. Dickinson

B. U. Dickinson

G. C. Munsell

W. Dickinson

H. Seagraves

W. M. Kellogg   Cong. Parsonage
                       N. D. Harlow
T. Pettingill   Mrs. H. C. Kellogg

EAST VILLAGE

Whamar Conkey

N. D. Potter

J. M. Cutler   I. H. Hills   C. Sabin
               C. S. Ensign B. Shop
                            Wagon shop
                            J. & H. Hastings
                            R. & E. P. Whitney
                            Harness Shop
                            Book& Shoe Ma.
                            School

Car House
Engine House
n Table

O. Walson

W. Gaylord

A. T. Sabins

S. Edwards

J. Thayer
O. Hubbard

W. Mather

J. Patrick

RAIL ROAD

P. D. Spaulding

p of Hampshire County, Massachusetts, under the
ndent of the State Map, 1856"

ter. In later years it is known that Deacon Mack was accustomed to rent part of the house. (See Emily's letter of September 23, 1851.) Lastly, the families were not entire strangers, Deacon Mack's eldest son, David Mack, III, having been a classmate of Edward Dickinson at Yale. (See pages 501-502.)

The family of Edward Dickinson occupied half of the homestead until April, 1840, when they moved into the house on Pleasant Street which he had recently purchased. A few doors north of the village center, it was a substantial house built of wood with its back to the north. Although hemmed in by neighbors, there was ample space at the rear for a garden and back of that an orchard for the care of which Austin soon assumed responsibility. Its venerable apple trees were of many varieties—Greening, Baldwin, June Eating, Northern Spy, Porter and Russet—each with a special excellence. Beyond the orchard he planted the grove of white pines, so often alluded to in the letters—early evidence of the chief ardor of his life, horticulture and landscape gardening.

This is the house, no longer standing, in which the Dickinsons were living when most of the letters in the present volume were written. Miss Lucy M. Bigelow, whose father, Dr. O. F. Bigelow, bought the house on May 23, 1868, informs me that from 1856 until 1865 it was owned by the College.[4] Miss Bigelow, who gave me the accompanying picture made shortly after her father took possession, describes it in these words:

"Ours was a grand old house. The beams and floors were of such hard wood the carpenters dreaded cutting into them. The floors had very wide planks. Those of the barn were so very wide as to cause wonder and comment by the builders. They must have come from huge trees.

"Mr. Kenfield, I think, bought the house from the College, and removed the large central chimney to make a larger hall. My father put in the gable and French windows over the front door and built on the porch and fence, and regraded the yard. Probably the same fruit trees were there. There were two enormous apple trees with trunks as large as elms. We have thought it may have originally been a part of Noah Webster's orchard. . . . He is said to have had

4. The picture (Plate II) was taken after the changes mentioned by Miss Bigelow had been made.

many fruit trees and that was true of our place when my father bought it."

Miss Bigelow added, "Austin Dickinson used to say the happiest years of his life were spent there."

In 1850 the population of the entire town of Amherst, with all its villages, was 3,057; in 1855, 2,937.[5] The heart of the town then, as now, was the common—at that time a long open space of unkempt ground, partly swamp in which cattle were sometimes mired, and partly pasture grown up to white birch, surrounded by a wooden fence and flanked by dirt roads which, when the snow began to melt at the breakup of winter, turned into a quagmire. Facing the common on both sides at well-spaced intervals were dwelling houses, white and dignified. The business district clung to the north end of the common where, on the west as on the north, a row of assorted brick buildings housed the stores, the hostelries and the post office. On higher ground at the southern end of the common stood the First Parish Church (now College Hall) and the buildings of Amherst College. There were no paved streets and, except for "a short strip of pavement" in the business district, only gravel sidewalks.[6] Even in the village center there were no street lights, only here and there an oil lamp above a gate "which served but to accentuate the surrounding gloom." A nine o'clock bell warned "orderly citizens" that it was time they were in bed. The town had no water supply until a generation later. In case of a conflagration water from wells was carried in buckets passed from hand to hand. The "fighters" also used curious contraptions called "fire annihilators." The town owned no public building until 1860 when the enginehouse was built.

In Amherst, the rumblings of the machine age were still far away, although several industries, small personal ventures, flourished in outlying districts. The yeomanry of the sparsely settled western part of the state bore little resemblance to the affluent manufacturers and merchants of the eastern seaboard who trafficked with foreign countries, and who founded most of the county families of New England. Between 1841 and 1864 there was not even a bank

5. *The History of the Town of Amherst, Massachusetts, 1731-1896,* compiled and published by Carpenter & Morehouse (Amherst, 1896), 604.
6. *One Hundred and Fiftieth Anniversary of The First Church,* 79.

in Amherst, various attempts to establish one having failed. Money was no measure of success in that community. Indeed, it might have been said of Amherst, as of another Massachusetts town, that if you received a legacy your friends hastened to assure you that they thought no less of you on that account.

Before the Amherst & Belchertown Rail Road began to function in 1853 one traveled by stagecoach if at all. A stage carried the mails. Until December, 1861, there was no telegraph. Living conditions were not unlike those on isolated farms beyond the reach of electricity today. Indeed, Amherst was hardly more than a cluster of farms, each with its woodshed, barn and outhouses. Every family was as independent as though the lights from neighbors' windows did not cast shadows across the path to its own front door. The only foreign element was a few Irish, recent arrivals in this country.

Such was the village in which Edward Dickinson's children, his tall son and his two young daughters, grew up—the setting of the home which Emily said was "the definition of God."

In spite of the primitive conditions, however—and they lived without most of the things we consider essential—Amherst was by 1850 already an educational center. Though public schools were not graded until 1861, Amherst Academy provided both primary and secondary instruction, and the college, which had weathered a period of extreme depression in the thirties and forties, was again prospering.[7]

7. Several accounts of life in Amherst a century ago have appeared in recent years. For a description of the village as it was in Emily's youth the reader is referred to George Frisbie Whicher, *This Was a Poet* (New York, 1938), Part I, and William G. Hammond, *Remembrance of Amherst,* an Undergraduate's Diary, edited by George F. Whicher (New York, 1946).

CHAPTER VII

Emily at Mount Holyoke Female Seminary

EDWARD DICKINSON had a theory that young people should for a time attend school away from home. Before entering Amherst College in September, 1846, Austin spent some time at Williston Seminary, Easthampton, just beyond Northampton. One little note from his sister Emily written during these early years is printed below. On it in Mrs. Todd's writing are the words, "probably sent to Easthampton in 1845." The handwriting, however, would seem to indicate that the note was written earlier. "Mr. Baker," the bearer of the note, may have been the prosperous farmer Alfred Baker, or his brother Osmyn, a well-known lawyer who moved his office from Amherst to Northampton in 1844.

The Dickinsons never hesitated to make use of the most prominent members of the community to carry their letters and packages back and forth. Persons they considered the most dependable were selected to transport their purchases, their mended clothes and their laundry even as far as Boston, representatives to the General Court proving especially useful in this connection.

Like many of the early notes, this one, measuring approximately five by eight inches, is written on a neatly folded piece of lined paper torn from a larger sheet and addressed on the back.

[*To William A. Dickinson, per Mr Baker*]

Monday. A M

Dear brother Austin

As Mr Baker was going directly to where you are I thought I would write a line to inform you that if it is pleasant day after tomorrow we are all coming over to see you, but you must not think too much of our coming as it may rain and spoil all our plans. however if it is not pleasant so that we do not come over father says that you may come home on Saturday, and if we do not come he will make some arrangement for you to come and write you about it.

I attend singing school. Mr Woodman has a very fine one Sunday evenings and has quite a large school. I presume you will want to go when you return home. We had a very severe frost here last night and the ground was frozen—hard. We all had our noses nipped a little. the Ladys Society meets at our house tomorrow and I expect we shall have a very pleasant meeting. If you was at home it would be perfectly sure. We wish much to hear from you, and if you have time I wish you would write a line and send by Mr Baker. Mother wishes if your stockings are any of them thin, that you should do them up in a little bundle & send them by Mr Baker. Accept much love from us all.

Your affectionate sister E

If we dont come Wednesday we may Thursday if not father will write you.

The seven letters which follow were written by Emily Dickinson to her brother in 1847 and 1848 while he was a sophomore in Amherst College and she a member of the "Middle Class" at Mount Holyoke Female Seminary, in South Hadley, a few miles south of Amherst beyond the Holyoke hills.

Even so well known a group of letters as some of these—five of them having been published with only minor omissions more than fifty years ago—gain in value when, with the missing paragraphs restored, they are placed in the sequence where they belong.[1] These schoolgirl communications reveal the already fervent love of home which permeates Emily Dickinson's letters.

Written on large sheets of blue paper or on fragments torn to suit the need, the letters are folded, addressed on the fourth page, and sealed with a wafer, or by a small sticker with a printed motto. Letters not carried by hand are stamped "5¢ paid," and although without postage stamps, three are postmarked.

1. *Letters*, 1894, 65-75; *Letters*, 1931, 63-72. Life at the seminary in 1847-1848 is described in Beth Bradford Gilchrist, *The Life of Mary Lyon* (Boston, 1910); in Sydney R. McLean, "Emily Dickinson at Mount Holyoke," *The New England Quarterly*, VII (March, 1934); and in Whicher, *This Was a Poet*, Chapter IV. See also Emily's letters of the same period to Abiah Root: *Letters*, 1894, 27-45; *Letters*, 1931, 24-35.

The teachers most frequently mentioned are Mary Lyon, founder and principal of the seminary; Mary C. Whitman, associate principal; and Rebecca W. Fiske, sister of Samuel Fiske, an Amherst undergraduate. Emily Lavinia Norcross, Emily Dickinson's roommate, was the daughter of her mother's eldest brother, Hiram Norcross of Monson; Jane Humphrey was her classmate. Special Amherst friends are Mary Warner and Mary Snell, daughters of Professor Aaron Warner and Professor E. S. Snell, both of Amherst College; and Abby Wood, niece of Deacon Luke Sweetser.[2]

The first two letters, each written on three pages of a double sheet, are folded, addressed on the fourth page and sealed with a sticker. The rate, five cents, and the postmarks, are in red.

The first letter was written about three weeks after the fall term of the seminary opened on September 30, 1847.

[*To Austin. Dickinson. "Esq." Amherst. Mass. (Postmark: South Hadley Mass. Oct 22)*]

Thursday noon [October 21, 1847]

My dear Brother. Austin.

I have not really a moment of time in which to write you & am taking time from "silent study hours", but I am determined not to break my promise again & I generally carry my resolutions into effect. I watched you until you were out of sight Saturday evening

2. Other persons mentioned in the South Hadley letters include Amherst clergymen, the Reverend Aaron M. Colton, pastor of the First Church; the Reverend Pomeroy Belden of the East Parish; and the Reverend Henry B. Smith, a well-known theologian then teaching in the college. Elbridge G. Bowdoin was Edward Dickinson's younger partner, and Benjamin F. Newton a student of law in his office. Seth Nims was the Amherst postmaster, John Spencer and Samuel Fiske, seniors, members of Alpha Delta Phi, Austin's fraternity. George Gould and John Thompson, of the sophomore class, Austin's special cronies, were, like most of his friends, also fraternity brothers. "Grandmother" was Mrs. Edward Dickinson's stepmother, grim "relict" of her father, Joel Norcross; and "Aunt Elisabeth," Edward Dickinson's youngest sister. Mrs. Coleman was Maria Flynt before her marriage, and "Aunt Flynt," Mrs. Rufus (Sarah Norcross) Flynt, was Mrs. Dickinson's aunt.

& then went to my room & looked over my treasures & surely no miser ever counted his heaps of gold, with more satisfaction than I gazed upon the presents from home.

The cake, gingerbread, pie, & peaches are all devoured, but the—apples—chestnuts & grapes still remain & will I hope for some time. You may laugh if you want to, in view of the little time in which so many of the good things have dissappeared but you must recollect that there are *two* instead of *one* to be fed & we have keen appetites over here. I cant tell you now how much good your visit did me. My cough is almost gone & my spirits have wonderfully lightened since then. I had a great mind to be homesick after you went home, but I concluded not to, & therefore gave up all homesick feelings. Was not that a wise determination? How have you all been at home since last week? I suppose nothing of serious importance has occurred, or I should have heard of it, before this time. I received a long letter from Mary. Warner, last evening & if you see her, please give my love to her & tell her I will answer it the first moment, I have to spare from school. By the way, there has been a Menagerie, here this week. Miss. Lyon. provided, "Daddy Hawks" as a *beau*, for all the Seminary girls, who wished to see the *bears* & monkeys, & your sister not caring to go, was obliged to decline the gallantry of said gentleman, which I fear I may never have another opportunity to avail myself of. The whole company stopped in front of the Seminary & played for about a quarter of an hour, for the purpose of getting custom in the afternoon I opine. Almost all the girls went & I enjoyed the solitude finely.

I want to know when you are coming to see me again, for I wish to see you as much as I did before. I went to see Miss Fiske. in her room yesterday & she read me, her letter from Sam & a right merry letter it was too. It sounded like him for all the world. I love Miss. Fiske. very much & think I shall love all the teachers, when I become better acquainted with them & find out their ways, which I can assure you are almost "past finding out." I had almost forgotten to tell you of a dream which I dreamed, last night & I would like to have you turn Daniel & interpret it to me, or if you dont care about going through all the perils which he did I will allow you to interpret it without, provided you will try to tell no lies about it. Well, I dreamed a dream & Lo!!! Father had failed & mother said that "our rye field which she & I planted, was mortgaged to Seth Nims." I hope it is not true but do write soon & tell me for you know "I should expire with mortification" to have our rye field mortgaged, to say nothing of it's falling into the merciless hands of a loco[3]!!!

3. "Locofoco" was the nickname of an ephemeral faction of the Democratic party.

Wont you please to tell me when you answer my letter who the candidate for President is ? I have been trying to find out ever since I came here & have not yet succeeded. I dont know anything more about affairs in the world, than if I was in a trance, & you must imagine with all your "Sophomoric discernment," that it is but little & very faint. Has the Mexican war terminated yet & how? Are we beat? Do you know of any nation about to besiege South Hadley? If so, do inform me of it, for I would be glad of a chance to escape, if we are to be stormed. I suppose Miss Lyon. would furnish us all with daggers & order us to fight for our lives, in case such perils should befall us.

Tell mother, that she was very thoughtful to inquire in regard to the welfare of my shoes. Emily has a shoe brush & plenty of blacking, & I brush my shoes to my heart's content. Thank Viny 10,000. times for the beautiful ribbon & tell her to write me soon. Tell father I thank him for his letter & will try to follow its precepts. Do excuse the writing for I am in furious haste & cant write another word.

Your aff. Emily

Give much love to Father, mother, Viny, Abby, Mary, Deacon Haskell's family & all the good folks at home, whom I care anything about. I shall write Abby & Mary very soon. Do write me a long letter soon & answer all my questions, that is if you can read them. Come & see me as often as you can & bring a good load every time.

Miss Fiske. told me if I was writing to Amherst to send her love. Not specifying to whom, you may deal it out, as your good sense & discretion prompt.

Be a good boy & mind me.

In these early letters Emily refers several times to a young man named Newton who deserves more than passing notice.

Instead of attending a law school, of which there were few in the 1840's, those who planned to enter the legal profession read law in the office of some well-known practitioner. Edward Dickinson had several such apprentices, among them Benjamin Newton. He seems to have been a rare spirit, and to have taken a deep interest in Emily Dickinson. He directed her reading and turned her attention to the beauty of the world about her. He even pointed the way toward faith in things unseen. She in turn loved him dearly, mourned his early death, and cherished his memory as long as she lived.[4]

4. See *This Was a Poet*, 84-94; see also Millicent Todd Bingham, *Emily Dickinson—A Revelation* (New York: Harper & Brothers, 1954), 85.

Jacob Holt was a former student at Amherst Academy who had studied dentistry in Boston and in 1845 had returned to practice in Amherst. At the time when Emily left for Mount Holyoke he was seriously ill with tuberculosis.

[*To Austin Dickinson. "Esq." Amherst. Mass.; postmark: illegible*]

Tuesday noon [November 2, 1847][5]

My dear Brother. Austin.

I have this moment finished my recitation in History & have a few minutes, which I shall occupy in answering your short, but welcome letter. You probably heard that I was alive & well, yesterday, unless, Mr. E. Dickinson was robbed of a note, whose contents were to that effect. But as robbers are not very plenty now a days, I will have no forebodings on that score, for the present. How [are] you! do you get along without me now & does "it seem any more like a funeral," than it did before your visit to your *humble servant* in this place? Answer me!!! I want much to see you all at home & expect to 3. weeks from tomorrow, if nothing unusual, like a famine or pestilence, occurs to prevent my going home. I am anticipating much in seeing you on this week Saturday & you had better not dissappoint me!! for if you do, I will harness the "furies" & pursue you with a "whip of scorpions," which is even worse you will find, than the "long oat" which you may remember. Have you heard from Sarah Pynchen. lately & have you found out "those particular reasons" which prevent her corresponding with me, much to her sorrow & my inexpressible regret, for having few letters to write, now I am away from home, it would be a pleasant method of employing my liesure time & keep my mind from vain & foolish thoughts in the leisure time before mentioned. How long is Mary. Warner. to be absent from home? I received a long letter from her a few days since & sent her a letter directed to Medford, today. I hear often from Abby. & think she has not forgotten me, though absent. She is now my debtor to the amount of one long letter & I wish you would inform her, if you have an opportunity, that I am anxiously waiting to receive it. I received a letter last eve, of an amusing nature & signed by the writer as "John Klima". I read it, but as I found the postage was 10. cts. I concluded it was not intended for me & sent it back to the office. The postmark, was so faint that I could not decipher it & I have not a little curiosity re-

5. Date supplied in Mrs. Todd's writing.

specting it. If you can give me any clue to the mystery, I will be obliged to you, in due proportion to the amount of information which you are able to give me. How do the plants look now & are they as flourishing as before I went away? I wish much to see them. Some of the girls here, have plants, but it is a cold place & I am very glad that I did not bring any, as I thought of doing. A young lady by the name of Beach. left here for home this morning. She could not get through her examinations & was very wild beside. Miss Lyon. said she should write her father, if she did not change her course & as she did not, her father came for her last night. He was an interesting man & seemed to feel very badly that his daughter should be obliged to leave, on account of bad conduct. Perhaps you saw an account some time since, of a carriage, being presented to Henry Clay. by a Mr. Beach. It was the self same. Why dont Sarah Thompson's brother come over to see her, if he has one spark of affection for her? Please tell him, she is very anxious to see him & will not receive him if he dont come soon. You must tell mother that I was delighted to see her handwriting once more, but that she need not put herself out to write me, for I know just how much she has to do & on that account do not expect to see letters from her very often. Please tell Viny, that if she has any time from the cares of her household to write a line to me, that I would receive it with all due deference to her age & majesty & honors. I suppose "Cook" occupies most of her time & will therefore excuse her long delay for the past, but not for the future. Cousin Emily. had a letter from Grandmother., last night and she mentioned in her letter, that Mrs Coleman & Eliza were daily expected in Monson & would probably spend some time at Aunt Flynt's. It seems impossible to me that Mrs. Frink. is dead. How is Jacob. Holt. now? I have not heard a word from him since you were here & feel quite anxious to know how he is. Give much love to him & tell him I will write him as soon as I can find a spare moment for it. Are Thompson. & Newton. going away before I come home? Give much love to Father, Mother, Viny & Abby, also thank Abby for her note & tell her I consider it only a type of what is forthcoming. Do write a long letter to

Your aff Sister. Emily.

Tell Father, I am obliged to him much, for his offers of "*pica*uniary" assistance, but do not need any. We are furnished with an account-book, here & obliged to put down every mill, which we spend & what we spend it for & show it to Miss. Whitman every Saturday, so you perceive your sister is learning to keep accounts in addition to the other branches of her education. I am getting along nicely in my studies & am happy—quite for me. Wont you ask father for Aunt Elisabeth's address & give it to me when you write me for I wish to write her & dont know to whose care to send it.

[On a separate slip]

South-Hadley—Seminary.
Nov" 2d.   —   1847—
Bill of. Fare.

Roast. Veal.
Potatoes.
Squash.
Gravy.
Wheat & Brown-Bread.
Butter.
Pepper & Salt.

Dessert.
Apple-Dumpling.
Sauce.

Water.

Is'nt that a dinner fit to set before a King.

Emily. E. Dickinson.

A curious practice, more or less common among young people at this time, was tinkering with their baptismal names. William Austin Dickinson became "Austin W. Dickinson" and was so listed in the Amherst College catalogue. While at Mount Holyoke Emily changed the spelling of her first name to "Emilie." Austin's was a temporary vagary which lasted only a short time, but Emily continued to spell her name in this fashion intermittently for several years.[6] The practice was not peculiar to the Dickinsons. Tutor Henry Luther ("Luther Henry") Edwards, is another example and John L. Graves, Edward Dickinson's first cousin, because he did not fancy it, changed his middle name from "Lysander" to "Long."

The following letter is folded and fastened by a sticker with the printed words, "I watch and I hope," to which Emily added "for you." She addressed it to "Austin *W.* Dickinson" and enclosed it in an envelope, the first she had used in writing to her brother.[7] The envelope is sealed with fragments of hard gum besides a sticker bearing the word "Guess." Under the flap she wrote, "if you can."

6. Lavinia used the "ie" long after Emily herself had given it up. Vinnie's ways became fixed in youth. She even dressed in the style of her girlhood to the last.

7. Subsequent letters were enclosed in envelopes, unless otherwise indicated.

[*To Austin* W. *Dickinson. Amherst. Mass.,* Per Mr. Colton.]

Saturday. *P.M.* [December 11, 1847]

My dear Brother. Austin.

I heard today that Mr. Colton. from Amherst was to preach here tomorrow & am writing a word, hoping to send by him to you. You probably thought me very sisterly, grateful &c. not to answer your kind letter by Mary. Snell, but I had no time to write by her & since then I have been occupied every moment & could find no time to write you. I was not very well when Mary. was here, but think that I am better now.

I finished my examination in Euclid last eve & without a failure at any time. You can easily imagine how glad I am to get through with 4. books, for you have finished the whole *forever.* I am looking forward to next Wednesday very impatiently—as I expect you & Mary. Warner, then. Surely you will not disappoint me. How are you all at home & what are you doing this vacation? You are reading Arabian Nights, according to Viny's statement. I hope you have derived much benefit from their perusal & presume your powers of imagining will vastly increase thereby. But I must give you a word of advice too. Cultivate your other powers in proportion as you allow Imagination to captivate you! Am not I a very wise *young lady?* I had almost forgotten to tell you what my studies are now. "Better *late* than *never.*" They are, Chemistry, Physiology & quarter course in Algebra. I have completed four studies already & am getting along well. Did you think that it was my birthday— yesterday? I dont believe I am *17.* Is, Jacob. Holt any better than when you wrote last & is there any hope of him? Give much love to all home friends & tell them I will write a long letter soon. Knowing you to be fond of gimcracks I wish you would accept the enclosed Box of Wafers. Hope you will use them on all extra important occasions, such as writing notes for example &, but I will not specify. My best love to father, mother, Viny, Abby & Mary.

From your aff. Sister Emily.

Mrs. Todd jotted down a few of Lavinia Dickinson's remarks regarding her sister's academic prowess: "Emily was never floored. When the Euclid examination came and she had never studied it, she went to the blackboard and gave such a glib exposition of imaginary figures that the dazed teacher passed her with the highest mark." Lavinia added: "There were real ogres at South Hadley then."

In the foregoing letter Emily refers to her brother's vacation. The winter holidays of Mount Holyoke and Amherst did not coincide.[8] Those of Amherst included both Thanksgiving and Christmas, but the young ladies of South Hadley were not as a rule permitted to observe holidays. An exception was made for Thanksgiving, the "one day of the series" observed as the chief festival of the year.[9] The *Express* (December 2, 1847) called it "the day of days in New England . . . the climacteric of the seasons—the grand epoch of events in the civil, social, literary and business year." Mount Holyoke students were not only permitted to go home for Thanksgiving; they might even remain over Sunday. Christmas, on the other hand, considered a pagan festival, usually went by unnoticed.[10] An article entitled "The Christmas Holidays" in the *Express* (January 6, 1848) opens with the words, "We almost feel as if we ought to ask pardon of our Puritan ancestry for writing

8. Calendars for 1847-1848

Amherst College

Fall term, September 9–November 24, 1847
Winter vacation, November 24, 1847–January 5, 1848
Winter term, January 5–April 19, 1848
Spring vacation, April 19–May 10, 1848
Summer term, May 10–August 10, 1848

Mount Holyoke Female Seminary

Fall term, September 30, 1847–January 20, 1848
Winter vacation, January 20–February 4, 1848
Winter term, February 4–April 27, 1848
Spring vacation, April 27–May 12, 1848
Summer term, May 12–August 3, 1848

9. Thanksgiving first had nationwide observance in 1863 when President Lincoln proclaimed the fourth Thursday of November a national holiday. (Proclamation dated October 3, 1863.)

10. Christmas, "with other holy days, is rejected by Congregationalists, on the ground that they are enjoined on no higher authority than that of men. Indeed, they do not see cause to believe that it is appointed on the true anniversary of the birthday of our Saviour." (Cummings, *Dictionary*, 48.)

Austin Dickinson expressed this point of view in a letter to my mother on December 24, 1883. He says, "Tomorrow Christmas. What of it! The day, I was brought up to believe, was a joint device of the Devil and the Romish church for the overthrow of the true religion and accordingly to be frowned upon by all good people. I wasn't very good, and didn't frown much, but seeing none of the brilliancy and joyousness of it in Amherst, thought little about it anyway." And yet, children hung up their stockings.

such a caption." Readers of the newspaper were reminded that in the days of their fathers the observance of Christmas was a penal offense. Edward Dickinson seemed so to consider it for, as his daughter remarked, he "frowned upon Santa Claus, and all such prowling gentlemen."[11] Nor was any attention paid to New Year's Day, or, in general, to family anniversaries. Though both of his sisters wrote to Austin on his twenty-fourth birthday (April 16, 1853) neither of them alluded to it.

The following fragment, draft of a letter from Austin to Emily, was apparently written during his winter vacation:

Amherst. Sunday eve

My dear sister—

Probably you have been somewhat dissapointed at my not coming over to see you during the past week in accordance with my promise, but your dissapointment cannot have been greater than mine at not seeing Thompson. I thought he would certainly be here this week, and then we were coming over together, to see our sisters. I also wrote to Gould in answer to a letter from him, inviting him to visit me this vacation, but I have heard not a word from either of them. I dont know what to make of it. I dont know now exactly when I shall come over there, but sometime before the term begins. Why dont you write to some of us! We dont know any more about you than if you were not in existence. . . .

Emily spent the brief Mount Holyoke recess, from January 20 to February 4, at home. The next letter, written ten days after her return to South Hadley, was enclosed in an envelope and sealed with a pink wafer embossed with a "D."

[*To Austin W. Dickinson. Amherst. Mass., Per. Miss Fiske*]

Tuesday noon [February 15, 1848]

My dear Austin.

Miss Fiske. has been to my room & left word that she is going to Amherst, tonight & I can send home by her if I wish. It seemed

11. Compare Emily's remarks in *Letters*, 1931, 14, 22, and 362.

desolate enough here for a *few days* after my return as Emily. had
not come & I was all alone, but I have now got settled down in the
old track and feel quite at home. I am pretty well & have got rested
from my *dissipation.* You have probably recovered from the effects
of my visit by this time & can retire in season. Miss. Mann. came in
to see me soon after father went home and spoke of enjoying her
visit at our house very much.

Emily Norcross. came yesterday about 5. o clock & glad was I to
see her I can assure you. She left all Monson folks, well. You probably know that Mary Hills. went home yesterday & dont know when
she will return. When is Harriet. Parsons coming back, or has she
decided to remain at home?

Please give much love to all at home & to Mary & Abby. Also remember me to your room mate if you please to do so. I do hope
you will come & see me as often as you can, for I want much to see
you already; it is [such] good sleighing, that you need make no great
sacrifice to ride over here I am sure. You must not expect to hear
from me often, for I have but little time to write, but you must
write me as often as possible. Your aff. Emily.

The Dickinson referred to in the next letter was not a relative.
In Amherst and vicinity the name was so common that, in the
words of a historian of a family reunion in Amherst, August 8-9,
1884, "Dickinsons choked out other forms of vegetation." And what
names they had! For generations the Old Testament had been the
source of supply—not only Ebenezer, Elijah, Elisha, Ezekiel, and
Gideon, but Azariah, Shelah, Zebina, Zimri and Gad. In 1852 there
were forty-four registered voters in Amherst named Dickinson; next
in point of numbers were Smiths, of whom there were twenty-three
(*Express,* May 28, 1852). Waitstill Dickinson was a prominent citizen of South Amherst, and near North Amherst, among others,
lived Marquis Fayette Dickinson, so named, tradition says, because
"Marquis" was thought to have been Lafayette's first name.

The William Dickinsons were at this time particularly confusing.
William Cowper Dickinson of Longmeadow, valedictorian of the
class of 1848, was a tutor in Amherst College in 1851-1852. William
Austin was graduated in 1850; William Eastman Dickinson of
North Amherst in 1855; and another William Dickinson in 1856.
In South Amherst there was a music teacher named William Dickin-
son (*Express,* May 28, 1852). William Hawley Dickinson, son of
Edward Dickinson's brother William, was a favorite cousin.

The next letter, folded and addressed on the back, is sealed with a diamond-shaped sticker printed with the words, "Believe me," and a bar of music—the first notes of "Believe me, if all those endearing young charms."

[*To Austin W. Dickinson. Amherst. Mass.; postmark: illegible*]

Thursday morn [February 17, 1848]

My dear Austin.

You will perhaps imagine from my date, that I am quite at leisure & can do what I please even in the forenoon, but one of our teachers, who is engaged, received a visit from her intended, quite unexpectedly yesterday afternoon & she has gone to her home to show him I opine & will be absent until Saturday. As I happen to recite to her in one of my studies, her absence gives me a little time in which to write. Your *welcome* letter found me all engrossed in the history of Sulphuric Acid!!!!! I deliberated for a few moments after it's reception on the propriety of carrying it to Miss. Whitman, your friend. The result of my deliberation was a conclusion to open it with moderation, peruse it's contents with sobriety becoming my station, & if after a close investigation of it's contents I found nothing which savored of rebellion or an unsubdued will, I would lay it away in my folio & forget I had ever received it. Are you not gratified that I am so rapidly gaining correct ideas of female propriety & sedate deportment? After the proposed examination, finding it concealed no dangerous sentiments I with great gravity deposited it with my other letters & the impression that I once had such a letter is entirely obliterated by the waves of time. I have been quite lonely since I came back, but cheered by the thought that I am not to return another year I take comfort & still hope on. My visit at home was happy, very happy to me & had the idea of in so short a time returning, been constantly in my dreams, by night & day I could not have been happier. "There is no rose without a thorn" to me. Home was always dear to me & dearer still the friends around it, but never did it seem so dear as now. All, all are kind to me but their tones fall strangely on my ear & their countenances meet mine not like home faces, I can assure you, most sincerely. Then when tempted to feel sad, I think of the blazing fire, & the cheerful meal & the chair empty now I am gone. I can hear the cheerful voices & the merry laugh & a desolate feeling comes home to my heart, to think I am alone. But my good angel only waits to see the tears coming & then whispers, only this year!! Only 22. weeks more & home again you will be to stay. To you, all busy & excited, I suppose the time flies faster, but to me slowly, very slowly so that I can see his chariot wheels when they roll along & himself is often visible. But I will no longer imagine, for your brain is full of Arabian Nights fancies & it will not do to pour fuel on your already *kindled imagination.* You cant think how dissappointed I was to know that Viny was not coming until next week, for I had made all my plans to welcome her on Friday of this week instead of next. But it will be better the longer it is in coming I suppose. All the girls are waiting with impatience to see her & to about a dozen have I given her dimensions. Tell her she must look her prettiest or they will be dissappointed for I have given a glowing account of her.

I suppose you have written a few & received a quantity of Valentines this week. Every night have I looked & yet in vain for one of Cupid's messengers. Many of the girls have received very beautiful ones & I have not quite done hoping for one. Surely *my friend* THOMAS, has not lost all his former affection for me. I entreat you to tell him I am pining for a Valentine. I am sure I shall not very soon forget last Valentine week nor any the sooner, the fun I had at that time. Probably, Mary, Abby & Viny have received scores of them from the infatuated wights in the neighborhood while your *highly accomplished & gifted elder sister* is entirely overlooked. Monday afternoon, *Mistress* Lyon arose in the hall & forbade our sending "any of those foolish notes called Valentines." But those who were here last year, knowing her opinions, were sufficiently cunning to write & give them into the care of Dickinson, during the vacation, so that about 150. were despatched on Valentine morn, before orders should be put down to the contrary effect. Hearing of this act, Miss Whitman by & with the advice & consent of the other teachers, with frowning brow, sallied over to the Post office, to ascertain if possible, the number of the Valentines and worse still, the names of the offenders. Nothing has yet been heard as to the amount of her information, but as Dickinson is a good hand to help the girls & no one has yet received sentence, we begin to think her mission unsuccessful. I have not written one nor do I now intend to. Your injunction to pile on the wood has not been unheeded for we have been obliged to obey it to keep from freezing up. I have had a severe cold for a few days, but think it is better now. We cannot have much more cold weather I am sure, for spring is near. Have you decided who to bring when you come? As to my opinion on that point, I confess I am in a strait betwixt two, Mary & Abby. Your better judgment will I am quite certain decide in the right and I will therefore leave it entirely in your hands.

Do you intend to give Miss. Whitman a ride? You had better resign that honor to your room-mate when he comes over again I judge. I had a note from E. Coleman. a few days since, but she said not a word of any of the family. You can probably imagine the drift of her remarks, without further information. I cannot say half that I want to for want of space. Your affectionate Sister. Emily.

How is Jacob. Holt now? I wish much to hear from him as not one word have I heard since I left home about him. Does your Rooster yet persist in his foolish habit of crowing under his window? I hope he has long ere this repented him of his folly. Professor. Smith. preached here last Sabbath & such sermons I never heard in my life. We were all charmed with him & dreaded to have him close. I understand the people of S. Hadley have given Mr. Belden of East-street a call to settle here. If he accepts, I hope it *will*, WILL not be until my year is out. Will you ask Viny. to get my History & Topic book, of Harriet. Parsons & bring them with her, for reviews commence very soon & I shall need them. Also will she bring a little Sweet Flag & that Comb, which I did my hair up with when I came home from Boston? Write me as long a letter as this is very soon.

Give my best love to Father, Mother, Viny, Mary, Abby, Dea. Haskell's family & all who inquire for me.

Please not to show this letter for it is strictly confidential & I should feel badly to have you show it.

One valentine, mailed in Amherst, was found among the 1848 letters:

Mr. Austin W. Dickinson
  Present.

> I arose early this morning as good lasses should
> And put on my gloves, my shawl and my hood,
> To see what success my steps would attend,
> On valentine's day, in choosing a friend.
> When lo! as I walked, what should rise to my view,
> But the graceful, the elegant, vision of you;
> But, in choosing a friend I never can waste
> A thought upon manner, form, feature or taste,
> I hasten to ask, though strange be the sound,
> Are the virtues I prize in the character found?
> Do mental endowments their lustre impart,
> To grace the pure treasures which flow from the heart.
> These questions concede that I'm no modern belle
> Who boasts of the thousands still bound in her spell,
> Whose brains if distilled, and double refined,
> Would fail to produce one pure drop of mind,
> And whose heart, O forgive the mere insinuation,

Was long ago lost in a former flirtation.
Let heartless young foplings still bow at her shrine,
Be *thou* with *thy* virtues my true Valentine.

The long interval before the next letter was written is in part
explained by the fact that a stubborn cough was giving the family
concern for Emily's health. Over her protest, Austin came on March
25 to take her home. She stayed several weeks in Amherst not
returning to Mount Holyoke until the end of April (*Letters*, 1931,
32-33).

The following letter, folded and sealed with wax, was delivered by
hand.

[*To Austin W. Dickinson. Amherst. Mass.*]

Monday morn [May 29, 1848]

My dear Austin.

I received a letter from home on Saturday, by Mr. Gilbert Smith
and father wrote in it that he intended to send for Cousin Emily.
& myself on Saturday of this week to spend the Sabbath at home.
I went to Miss. Whitman, after receiving the letter & asked her if
we could go if you decided to come for us. She seemed stunned by
my request & could not find utterance to an answer for some time.
At length, she said "did you not know it was contrary to the rules
of the Seminary to ask to be absent on the Sabbath"? I told her I
did not. She then took a Catalogue, from her table & showed me the
law in full at the last part of it.[12]
She closed by saying that we could not go & I returned to my
room, without farther ado. So you see I shall be deprived of the
pleasure of a visit home & you that of seeing me, if I may have the
presumption to call it a *pleasure*!! The Teachers are not willing to
let the girls go home this term as it is the last one & as I have only
nine weeks more to spend here, we had better be contented to obey
the commands. We shall only be the more glad to see one another
after a longer absence, that will be all.
I was highly edified with your *imaginative* note to me & think

12. The passage reads in part: "The young ladies do not make or receive calls
on the Sabbath. Neither should they spend a single Sabbath from the Seminary
in term time. . . . The place of weekly labors is the most favorable spot for the
scenes of the Sabbath."

your flights of fancy indeed wonderful at your age!! When are you coming to see me, or dont you intend to come at all? Viny told us, you were coming this week & it would be very pleasant to us to receive a visit from *your highness* if you can be absent from home long enough for such a purpose.

Is there anything new at home & wont you write me a long letter telling me all news? Mary. Warner. has not yet answered the note which I sent her at the commencement of the term. I cant write longer. Your aff. Emilie.

Although, contrary to the general impression, Emily Dickinson left no instructions about the disposal of the hundreds of poems she left in her bureau, the discovery of which after her death was a surprise to her sister, she did ask Lavinia to destroy the letters she had received. The work of destruction was carried out, as my mother said, "with a promptness she later deplored." (For Lavinia, her sister's request was law. Had Emily asked to have her poems destroyed, that too would have been done with equal dispatch.) This is why none of Austin's letters to her remain. There is however one little package, a series of pencil drafts and fragments of drafts of something he was apparently intending to send. The finished product may have been the "imaginative note" to which Emily referred in her letter of May 29. However that may be, this boyish fantasy is a sample of the give and take between brother and sister in their youth. There are several drafts of the effusion; the shortest begins, "Dear Sister Emily"; the longest is here reproduced just as written, spelling and all.

From half past ten oclock of last evening until eleven of the same, your fathers house was the scene of great commotion. About the time first mentioned, as mother Lavinia & myself were seated around a bright blazing fire in the sitting room, each one attentive to his or her own peculiar duties, we were all of a sudden aroused by *loud shouts,* & huzza's followed by peals of laughter, and various strange sounds which seemed the effect of unbounded Joy. Quite startled by such a tumult at that time of night, in the quiet little village of Amherst, we all immediately rushed to the window, and from thence, I to the door from the outside of which I beheld a thing, from a hole in whose head, the noise seemed to proceed, dressed in man's attire and running at the top of its speed, in a moment it stoped short, turned sumerset, then rising up it leaped and danced, and shouted and gestured and performed the strangest evolutions, and oddest pranks imaginable. As the image drew near me I perceived that it was a man, who in his hand held an open letter which he seemed to be trying to read and at the sentiments and expressions of which he seemed to be almost transported out of himself. He was so intent on his letter that he evidently took no notice of any body or thing although a great number of people, both male and female, of all ages, ranks, and conditions, attracted by the disturbance had collected together and completely lined the street on both sides for a considerable distance, as he came nearer I distinctly heard him read these words, "I told her you were not afraid of her being too strict with me, and she replied, Tell him I am much obliged to him." After he had uttered of this word of this quotation, he presently swelled to such a prodigous size, and grew so lofty in stature that it verily seemed as if he would burst the bonds of nature, and strutting about he reared his sublime eye almost to the clouds, with these movements and a few haughty gesticulations he resumed the reading of his letter. The next sentence was this "and when I told her how gratified you were at our early rising she said Tell him that is the only way to make vigorous children," before he had quite finished this sentence it was apparent to all that the ineffable delight inspired by the answer would cause him to make some mighty effort to free himself from the steam which was pent up within, and had come well nigh exploding him when his eyes had read the last word of the former sentence. And well did he prove that the previous indications had not been deceitful, for while the word "children" was even on his lips he roared out in such a *terrific, great, coarse horse-laugh* that the whole welkin rang, and the distant forests echoed back the awful din, then in his great vehemence, he drew up his monstrous foot and stamped the earth with the most terrible force, so great powerful was the concussion that the whole firmiment was shaken, the whole planetary system was deranged, the stars twinkled, and the clouds fell from the heavens strewing the earth with a white feathery substance.

Emily's final letter from Mount Holyoke was written toward the end of the term, a note sent by hand without an envelope.

[*To Austin W. Dickinson. Amherst. Mass.*]

Sabbath noon [June 25, 1848]

My dear Austin.

I was very glad to see your friend, Bowdoin, for so long a time had passed since I last heard from home, that I began to consider myself entirely deserted.

Your note & father's letter, were both acceptable, only they were quite too brief, not lengthy enough, to suit me. I am much delighted with the idea of going home, but dont expect to realize it until fairly there, within sight & sound of you all. I wonder if you know, that today is the seventh Sabbath, since I left home. Quite a long time since I have seen you all and the many good people in Amherst. Bowdoin, tells me of no news, excepting the following. Cherries are fast getting ripe & the new generation attended the Senior Levee, a short time since, both of which facts, were received by me, with proper resignation. Surely, things must have changed in quiet, peace loving Amherst.

Jane Humphrey. wishes me to tell you that she would be happy to accept your invitation, but as Misses. Lyon & Whitman. are not willing & tell her it will lower her classification if she goes, she feels obliged to decline. I believe, Miss. Fiske. has given up the idea of going also. Father wrote that you were expecting Uncle Joel. at our house, yesterday and you are probably having grand times among yourselves. Louisa. Dickinson & Antoinette. Baker., went home on Friday last & expect to return tomorrow morning. She could not have had permission, had it not been that her friends from New. York. were there and desired to see her. Bowdoin. had quite an adventure about seeing me, which he will tell you. Yesterday afternoon, I had a call from a sister of Tutor Greene's [Lewis Green], who has been teaching school in Brooklyn & is quite intimate in Aunt Kate's family. She said Aunt. Catharine. was coming to Amherst, next week. I received a long letter from Cousin Zebina, [Montague] about a fortnight since & answered it last week. I want much to see you all & think Monday & Tuesday will be rather dull days to me. I do wish they might seem as long to you. One thing in your note made me feel badly, & you can guess what it was. Give my best love to Father, Mother, Viny & Uncle Joel, if he is indeed at our house. Tell Viny, the letter she sent me last, was not received & I guess it was lost on the way. I hope a similar fate, will not befall any others, I should otherwise obtain. I have an action against John. Spencer, which you shall hear of at my coming. Emily & I shall be all ready at precisely 5. o,clock. Your aff. Sister. Emilie.

My love to Abby & Mary. What an honor, Viny had in attending the Levee. I hope she bears that & others similar, in becoming humility. Cousin Emily. can hardly eat or sleep, so perfectly happy is she with the idea of going home with me to the great Festival. She sends her love to all the household.

At the Mount Holyoke "Anniversary," on August 3, 1848, certificates of graduation were presented to forty-five young ladies, among them Emily Norcross and Jane Humphrey.

Amherst College Commencement took place a week later. The valedictorian, William Cowper Dickinson, spoke on "Political Expediency." The salutatory was given in Latin by Samuel Fiske. Next in point of academic distinction after the valedictory and the salutatory was the philosophical oration and then the English orations, first, second and third class.[13]

After the summer vacation Emily did not return to Mount Holyoke Seminary. Both she and her brother were at home so they exchanged no more letters for many months. In the meantime their younger sister went to boarding school and became Austin's correspondent.

13. Hitchcock, *Reminiscences,* 327.

CHAPTER VIII

The Revival of 1850 and Lavinia at Ipswich

1

IN 1849 Lavinia Dickinson had reached sixteen, the age at which Emily had been sent away to school. It was now Vinnie's turn. The week following Thanksgiving she entered the Ipswich Female Seminary, Ipswich, Massachusetts.[1] The Reverend John P. Cowles and his wife, who as Eunice Caldwell had been Mary Lyon's assistant when Mount Holyoke Seminary was opened in 1837, were the joint principals. Five other teachers, all maiden ladies, could be relied upon to enforce the necessary discipline.

Among the 147 pupils listed in the catalogue for the year ending November 12, 1850, are Lavinia N. Dickinson and Jane E. Hitchcock, daughter of President Hitchcock of Amherst College.[2] Within a week of the same age, Lavinia and Jane roomed together at the house of Mrs. Ephraim Kendall. The "young ladies" all lived with private families, none of whom "received" any other boarders. The price of board was $1.25 a week.

The regulations and the items on term bills make quaint reading. For equipment "necessary for every pupil," in addition to "an English Dictionary, a Modern Atlas, and a Bible," each was re-

1. *Ancestors' Brocades*, 233, footnote.
2. The winter term of fifteen weeks began December 5, 1849. A recess of four weeks, from March 20 to April 17, 1850, preceded the summer term of fifteen weeks which ended July 31. Another recess of four weeks, from July 31 to August 28, intervened before the opening of the fall term of eleven weeks which ended on November 12, 1850, completing the school year. In this catalogue, the only one in which her name appears, Lavinia is not listed as a member of the "regular" Senior, Junior or Middle Class. Her name does appear, however, among those attending "The First Latin Class" and "The Second French Class." Composition and Bible lessons were required of the entire student body.

quested to bring "one table or dessert spoon, and one tea spoon."

The "Mr. Humphrey" to whom Vinnie refers in the first letter was Leonard Humphrey, a tutor in Amherst College. A former principal of Amherst Academy, he was a young man of great promise, "a fine scholar and a gentle Christian spirit."[3] The town as well as the college was profoundly shocked when, on November 30, 1850, Leonard Humphrey died suddenly of "congestion of the brain."

Lavinia's letters from Ipswich are written on half sheets of blue paper similar to that used by Emily at Mount Holyoke. The handwriting is sketchy, many of the letters half-formed, some left out altogether. Without a stamp, the figures "5" as well as "15" on the postmark for the day of the month are both written in ink.

[To Austin Dickinson. Amherst. Mass.; postmark: Ipswich Mass, Jan 15]

Ipswich, January 11th /50.

My Dear Brother,

Think not, from my long silence that your grand good letter was in any measure, misappreciated, or yourself forgotten, for I assure you, said document met with a hearty welcome & its contents were most egarly devoured both by your humble servant & her *"chum."*

You've no conception of the pleasure, letters afford us, or the anxiety, with which we watch Mr Cowles, as he comes from the Office, laden with his precious burden, destined, either, to make glad, or sorrowful, our hearts. And he seemingly conscius of his power, generally marches up onto the stage, takes his seat, & in a most tantalising manner, surveys them, one by one, (to see if all be right, & nothing wrong,) mean while we are all *agog* to know our fate, then after a long time, the due ceremonies being over, the names of the fortunate are proclaimed & then, Oh! then, with what a rush they go, their contenences beaming with Joy unspeakable & full of hope, each egar, first, to secure her prize. But *Wo* to those whom fortune favors not, with downcast looks & sunken eyes, each gos on her respective way, dejected & forlorn, thinking the world hard, & friends treacherous.

Now, Austin, to which class, would you have me belong? if to the

3. Tyler, 1873, 339.

former, *"act well your part"*, & invite others to join you in the glorious enterprise, & upon you shall no reproff be cast: But should you
conduct yourself otherwise, "the curse of the withered heart" shall
be upon thee, & the "cave of black despair", thine abode, Hear'st my
words? then obey. Well, Austin, Vacation,s over, & another term
commenced. How seems it, again to be bound down to study, after
having roamed so long at will? Has the time passed swiftly &
pleasantly with thee? had sleigh rides aplenty &c? How merry it
must seem to have the Students back again. Wish, I could be there,
to witness the Joyful greetings among the fiends so long sepereted,
one from another. I met your *Class mate,* Bebee, while in Boston,
so I, suppose he's down, some where in these parts, teaching, is'nt
he? Oh! Austin, you *cant know,* how disappointed I was, in not
seeing you in Ipswich. Jennie & I anticipated it *so much,* t,was too
bad to dash all our hopes. Dont you think so? I'm quite sure, were
you to look at the subject in a proper light, your opinion culd not
be, otherwise, than mine. So you,ve had a *grand* sleigh ride. Emilie,
in her last letter, gave me a most grafic description of it, & Oh!
it made me so homesick, to think of the nice times you were having.
Why, Amherst was never so gay, before. What do the good people
think the town is comming to. They must foresee certain destruction, in the end. Jennie & I have come to the conclusion, that you
are celebrating these *feasts,* games &c, in hounour of our absence,
for what else can it be? We had a very funny time, while Mr.
Humphrey was here. Shall I describe? Well. The morning, after
his arrival, Jennie & I were walking & by some strange chance,
encountered *Mr. H.* & were a little tardy, in consequence. Mrs
Cowles noticing our absence, (as t,was some thing rather unusual)
enquired if any one knew where we might be, upon which, the most
antiquated dame, of the Seminary, rose & stated, that, at the last
accounts, we were walking with a *gentleman!* a friend, she believed.
This was a *startling* piece of intelligence, & produced, for a time,
the most intence excitement, but the storm has now, passed over,
& we, we escaped with our lives, which we consider as quite
miraculous! and the teachers have again assumed their calm, stoical
aspect, & all things go on as usual. T,is astonishing how soon great
things sink into oblivion, & are forgotten forever!

We have some of the funniest rules, here. Mrs. Cowles annonced
to us, the other day, that we (the members of the school) must either,
take our turn in sweeping the Seminary or pay a tax, & required
us, also to write her a note, stating our opinions upon the subject.
You can easily guess *which* I chose, to do! Mr Cowles is very much
afraid, lest we should have an easy time, this winter. He often
lectres us, upon the impossibility of any thing of that kind & hopes
that thoughts of ease, will never be allowed to enter our minds, for

one moment, *even.* He talks, too, about putting on the *"screws"* I suppose, the knowledge of these facts will really make you, grow *best* [?], & in your heart, you'll exult over our misery, but I hope you wont. I've just received my Amherst paper, & in it saw *Dr Woodwards* death, was it not very sudden? I saw, also, a notice of Carpenters mishap. Where is he, & how badly is he injured?

I thank you, for your good advice, concerning letter writing, & hope to profit by it. I have written one & generally two letters, evry Saturday, since I left home, &, though I've allways had a great aversion to writing, I hope, by constent practice, the dislike will wear away, in a degree, at least. Oh! dear, was ever any thing more unfortunate! two wretched blots have I made, & these, added to the other deformities of this sheet, render it quite unfit for inspection, & if it was,nt so late Id, certinly copy it, but as it is, you must excuse it, & I promise you, the next shall look *better.* I had a letter from Mary Snell, the other day, & in it she told of quite a *fracas,* they,d had, & which wuld probably end, in the expulsion of sevral of the girls.

Do you care to know about the girls, here? They are not *Amherst girls,* yet some are pretty & fine scholars, also, & there are two, whom, I guess, you,d like the looks of. Still, they,d hardily equal *"Mary,"* by the way, how is *she* florishing? The People, here, think me, about fourteen years old, & I am, *twenty!* Mrs Kendall persists in calling me, Miss *Dickens,* t,would amuse you to hear her speak the name, in her prim way.

Well, Austin, I believe I've finished, & I know you are hartily rejoiced at the announcement, though really, I did not indend to impose so very much upon your patience. Be calm.

I suppose you know the conditions, on which, I send this, that no one shall see it. Dont forget it! Write soon & dont ridicule this will you?

Vinnie

Enclosed in the same envelope was a neatly written letter from Jane Hitchcock. Better than any comment on the training of children in New England a century ago, this missive shows what was expected of young people. Natural impulses were of necessity suspect; even one's facial expression was better controlled. As F. A. March, of the class of 1845, wrote several years later: "I remember well how [the President's] reproving eye one Sabbath morning brought me to the consciousness that I had been smiling out in meeting."[4]

4. Tyler, 1873, 288-289.

[*Sent by hand to Austin*]

Ipswich. Saturday

Delighted indeed was I, Austin, to get your letter. You never was a schoolgirl one hundred and twenty five miles away from home, so you dont know how glad they are to get letters from *anybody*. We love to hear from people that we never used to care anything about. Now if you choose to take that in a sense in which I dont mean it, you will find rather a doubtful compliment for yourself and your letter. But in all truth, glad as I am in recieving anybodys letters, I was paticularly so in recieving yours. I liked it. And I hate to answer such, for every thing sounds so flat, especially if I try to write as "funny as I can." I may as well give that up first as last, for I have no gift that way. Vinnie writes all the funny letters that go from this room. I am getting very sober. And I believe one reason is that I am so anxious *not* to. The Teachers here every day preach to us about *restraining* our *feelings*. And every morning after devotional exercises, Mr. C[owles] reminds us that we are not placed in this world to *have a good time*. But more especially, our parents did not send us to this Seminary to enjoy ourselves. We were sent here to improve our immortal minds, to strengthen & make better the part *that never dies*. And he closes by exhorting us to *put on the screws,* & consoles, by telling us, that if we do it not ourselves, they shall do it for us. Then when we come home to dinner, Miss Robinson tells us how much beauty there is in forgetting home and friends, in putting every dear name out of our thoughts, and in making every desire, and thought bend to duty and improvement. Now such things would crush me, and take away every bit of spirit and life I ever had, and I should become a bluestocking, or book-worm, were it not for your dear sister Vinnie. Fortunately she still retains her ability to "take off" people. You have seen her, enough to know how well she does it. I assure you it is a real comfort. And now and then we have a good laugh together. Seems to me you young people must be having fun so often, in honor of our absence. For I dont recollect any season before, when there has been so much gaiety there. Do reserve a little for the purpose of initiating us, when we go home. Go home! Those two little words send a thrill of delight through our hearts when ever we speak them. I am sorry you have fears for our friendship. I cannot have it come to pass, that she shall ever cease to love me. For she is my only hope here, and the only one who ever did really love me; & if she leaves me, "Oh! what will then become of me"? No, no, I will throw myself into Ipswich river, I will take wings, and fly up into the clouds, I will throw aside my mortal coil, and be a spirit, so that unseen, I can watch her going on through life. I will do anything so she ceases to care for me. But she shall not. If I see the sun of her love declining, I will place myself at her feet, adjuring her by all that is good, not to break my heart, and then give her her choice, whether to grant me her love, or see me a fugitive and a vagabond on the face of the Earth. How does Amherst College prosper? In the name of the one you love best on Earth, I entreat you to forward quickly another of your welcome letters. Dont you send any communications to Vinnie unless, there be in the same envelope, a document, which has for its superscription, the name of

Jane H.

2

In the religious history of New England 1850 is known as the year of the Great Revival. The tone of Lavinia's next letter written several weeks later reflects the spiritual upheaval then taking place.

It would be hard to exaggerate the importance of revivals to early evangelical sects, because they struck at the heart of Puritan belief in the reliability of individual conscience. It was a man's duty as well as his right to obey his conscience. But unless he was convinced of the iniquity of his natural impulses, he was not likely to renounce his headstrong desires and yield without reservation to guidance from on high. During a revival the experience of conversion, induced by exhortation and prayer, took place in four steps, defined by the Reverend Daniel Bliss—the great missionary of the Amherst class of 1852—as follows: "conviction of deep guilt, a period of despair and struggle, surrender of will, the sudden benediction of peace," as the sinner, having thrown himself on God's mercy and accepted Christ as his Redeemer, and shown his willingness to accept the guidance of The Holy Spirit, knows without any lingering doubt that he has been forgiven.[5] Only then has his conscience been tempered to the point where it can be trusted as an infallible guide.

Emphasis upon this particular type of religious experience has not of course been confined to New England or to evangelical Christian denominations. Similar experiences and practices have prevailed in other religions and in many lands. Their importance for our purpose lies chiefly in their influence in setting the standards

5. *The Reminiscences of Daniel Bliss* (New York, 1920), 61.

and shaping the conduct of the community in which Emily Dickinson grew up.

The Great Revival was "a work of marked depth and power." It began in Amherst during the winter as a "result of long continued prayer and persevering effort," and swept both town and college. A latent feeling of need for spiritual awakening was quickened by a series of events of which the first was a profound shock. The Reverend William A. Peabody, appointed professor of Latin during the winter term, was attacked by scarlet fever soon after his arrival and died on February 27, 1850, at the age of thirty-nine.

In a spirit of great solemnity, five days later Amherst took a drastic step. As the Reverend Mr. Colton put it: "The *trouble,* we came at length to believe, was in the rum places in the village, with fires of hell in full blast." At the annual town meeting on March 4 President Hitchcock made an eloquent plea to close such resorts, voicing the opinion that "it were better that the college should go down, than that young men should come here to be ruined by drink places among us."[6] It was finally voted "to put a stop to traffic in intoxicating drinks as being an obstacle to conversion." The effect was instantaneous. In Mr. Colton's words, "the work of God broke forth on the right hand and left. Such a shaking among the dry bones is not often beheld. . . . Evening meetings for prayer and hearing of the Word were crowded to overflowing and pervaded by a death-stillness except as broken by sobs that *could* not be wholly suppressed. . . . Proud and hard hearts that had hitherto resisted every call of God's mercy were now humbled and broken for sin. . . . In most of the cases the joy of a new hope appeared to be chastened by its proper attendants, humility and fear. . . . [More than 150 persons] from the child of twelve to the aged of more than four-score years have expressed hope in the mercy of Christ. . . . A very large proportion are *young men.*"[7]

In an undated letter to Abiah Root, Emily described the conversion of their mutual friend Abby Wood, who later became the wife of Daniel Bliss:[8]

6. *One Hundred and Fiftieth Anniversary of the First Church,* 77.

7. Report of the results of the Great Revival by the Reverend A. M. Colton (*Express,* January 10, 1851).

8. This letter was I think placed too early in *Letters,* 1931, 28-29. Although she was said to have been converted at the age of sixteen (Bliss, *op. cit.,* 61),

I presume you have heard from Abby and know what she now believes—she makes a sweet girl Christian, religion makes her face quite different, calmer, but full of radiance, holy, yet very joyful. She talks of herself quite freely, seems to love Lord Christ most dearly, and to wonder and be bewildered at the life she has always led. It all looks black and distant, and God and heaven are near. She is certainly very much changed. She has told you about things here, how the "still, small voice" is calling, and how people are listening, and believing, and truly obeying, how the place is very solemn and sacred, and the bad ones slink away and are sorrowful, not at their wicked lives, but at this strange time, great change. *I* am one of the lingering *bad* ones, and so do I slink away, and pause and ponder, and ponder and pause, and do work without knowing why, not surely, for this brief world, and more sure it is not for heaven, and I ask what this message *means* that they ask for so very eagerly; *you* know of this depth and fulness, will you try to tell me about it?

Emily said later that she did not "respect" doctrines, but at this early age she was sometimes bothered by theological dogma which demanded of the convert both fear and remorse for his sinfulness. She understood remorse, and called it "the disease not even God can heal." Although she knew that she was "one of the lingering *bad* ones" and was well aware of sin, which she called "a distinguished precipice," she seems to have lacked the requisite sense of guilt, such as was expressed in the heart-searchings of the righteous and innocent Abby Wood. I believe that Emily's essential struggle was not with sin so much as it was a fight to reconcile Puritan fearfulness with her experience of God's mercy—the "perfect love which casteth out fear"—a struggle between the sternness of the tradition, with a "God of Flint" at the center, and her own direct knowledge of the "Source of Love."

The emotional extremes reached in the revival meetings were strangely unlike the customary decorum. As they begged forgiveness people proclaimed aloud their secret sins. By contrast, how silent was the experience of Emily Dickinson! On January 29, 1850, she wrote to Abiah: "*God* is sitting here, looking into my very soul to see if I think right thoughts. Yet I am not afraid, for I try to be

---

according to the records of the First Church of Amherst Abby Wood was not admitted to membership until August, 1850, at the age of twenty, probably following her conversion.

right and good; and He knows every one of my struggles. He looks very gloriously, and everything bright seems dull beside Him; and I don't dare to look directly at Him for fear I shall die."[9] Although it can hardly be questioned that she was aroused as much as the most vocal penitent in town, she continued to hold herself aloof in accordance with the Psalmist's injunction: "Be still, and know that I am God." Nowhere perhaps is her inner strength more strikingly shown than by her independence in the face of the emotional tide surging all around her.

The revival struck the college too. President Hitchcock considered it of "unspeakable importance in raising the standard of practical piety." He wrote that "we have never in College witnessed a more agonizing spirit of prayer, nor more consistent, persevering efforts on the part of some, than for six or seven weeks before the full answer came. . . . Fear of punishment seemed to have but little influence in producing conviction. The predominant feeling among those awakened was, that they had no adequate sense of their own ingratitude and depravity, though in some instances the sense of sin was overpowering."[10]

One of the undergraduates recalled his own experience many years later. As soon as the revival began, he says, "and the inquiry, 'What must I do to be saved,' was heard, there was the hush and stillness of death. For a few days, the most hardened men in College were subdued and thoughtful. The whole aspect of the College was changed at once, with almost the suddenness of an electric flash. I do not believe that there was one person in the whole College who for a time was not profoundly moved. There was no sound of laughing or loud talking. There were no heavy footsteps in the halls, no noise, no tumult; but the awful stillness and solemnity of those who stood face to face with the realities of eternity. . . . Rarely is a scene of more thrilling interest enjoyed upon earth than a revival in College."[11]

In March, 1850, the full import of human wickedness was brought into focus by another event, "the most exciting criminal trial in

9. *Letters*, 1931, 35.
10. Hitchcock, *Reminiscences*, 183-184.
11. Letter from the Reverend H. N. Barnum, Harpoot, Turkey, March 26, 1869 (Tyler, 1873, 341).

history." On November 23, 1849, Dr. John White Webster, professor of chemistry in the Harvard Medical School, had in a burst of anger killed Dr. George Parkman, member of an illustrious Boston family. The trial which opened on March 19, 1850, shook New England from one end to the other. The tremor was felt in the remotest village in the western hills. Every bit of evidence was devoured, not only because the persons involved represented New England culture at its best, intellectually as well as socially, but because of the grisly details of the professor's attempt to cover his tracks, all of which were reported at length in country newspapers. Professor Webster was found guilty and was condemned "to hang by the neck until you are dead."[12]

The trial provided a unique opportunity to point a moral. It was a dramatic demonstration that sin is always punished, that the sinner cannot escape. As the *Express* observed, "learning, station, respectability and wealth could not save him."

The "black and dismal tragedy" moved the people to further meditation, reinforcing the mounting conviction of sin which had closed down upon New England. Fear lest Dr. Webster might escape the consequences of his crime had intensified the ever-increasing solemnity. Even gay little Lavinia Dickinson was swept along in the tide of self-scrutiny.

The three notes to Austin which follow, written on neatly folded fragments of blue paper torn from larger sheets, are without envelopes, stamps, or postmarks.

Sunday eve.

My Dear Brother,

I am all alone, this evening. Jennie has gone to meeting, & I suppose I ought to have gone, but I felt so anxious to say a word, at *least,* in answer to your last letter, that I concluded to remain at home.

Why, Austin, I cant tell you, how very much the tone of your letter surprised me. The idea that my *brother* was thinking of religion seemed almost impossible to me, the thought gladdened my heart, how ever, & increased, (I hope) my own interest. How I wish I

12. *Express,* April 5, 1850.

could talk with you about this important subject, for you might
have so much influence over me. At times, I desire religion above
all things, & this world seems small indeed, in comparison with the
all important subject, then Satan besets me, & my interest diminishes.
Oh! Austin, if the Spirit of God has awakened *you,* I entreat you
not to grieve it away. Do become a christian *now.* How beutiful,
if *we three* could all believe in Christ, how much higher object
should we have in living! to glorify that great *being,* than to gratify
our own selfish desires. Does Emilie think of these things at all?
Oh! that she might! I am afraid, this note will convey a wrong
impression to your mind, & you may think me more changed than
I am, but I feel so *desirous,* that My Dear Brother & Sister should
become christians, even though I am not, that perhaps I have said
more than I ought, if so, pardon it. I wish you would write me *very*
soon & tell me, how you feel. I was disappointed in not hearing from
you, last week. Tuesday morning, I shall hope to see the "long
looked for", without fail, for I seem to think that you are writing
me, at this very hour. Jennie sends love,

Vinnie

Saturday eve [March, 1850]

My *Dear Dear* Brother,

Have you *indeed* forgotten your younger & absent *Sister?* I have
looked daily for one of your good long letters, since I left you
& have looked in *vain.* Why is it thus? If you knew how I valued
letters, especially from home, I am sure you'd try & gratify me
a little, wuld'nt you? Oh! Austin, I do so long to hear that you
have come over to the Lord's side! Oh, if you have *not* yet given
yourself to Christ wholly & entirely, I entreat you in the name of the
blessed Jesus, to delay no longer, to deprive yourself of *that* happiness, that Joy, *no* longer but my Dear Brother, *now,* while pardon
is offered you & while the precious Saviour is waiting to receive you,
come, yes, now while the Holy Spirit is in your midst & when the
attention of all is called to that subject. *Do* not give up religion
as not *worth* seeking, but pray for strength to press onward in the
glorious work. *Do not* be discouraged. Do not faint by the *way,* &
thus fail of entering in to the Kingdom, but oh! strive & struggle
against Sin, as your *greatest enemy!* & by the help & grace of God you
will come off "conqueror & more than *conqueror*" Oh! that I could
see you, this night & hear from your own lips the story of your
heart! Will you not write me, the very evening you receive this,

I shall expect a letter without fail Thursday or Friday. *Do* grant the *request,* & *Austin dont despair.* Your Sister devoted

Vinie

Lavinia spent the spring recess, March 20–April 17, at home. The following note was written after her return to Ipswich.

11 o-clock
Sunday. eve.

Dear Austin,

You did'nt like me very well, when I was at home, but suppose we should be better friends, now, we are separated, I long to hear from you & to know just how you *feel,* when *may* I have that pleasure?

Oh, Austin, in this vacation when you have such a good time, *do* resolve to seek Christ, & to seek, until you *find.* Oh! do not give up the subject, as a *worthless* one, but press *onward* in the race, & Strive to enter in to *that* rest, which the world knows not of. Oh! Austin, Religion is *not* gloomy, it is all bright & beautiful, it is the only happy thing in this dark world, if we could but realise it, & do *you* want to be without it? Be not *discouraged,* Austin, go on. I'll pray for you, evry day, & may God bless you & recieve you into his kingdom, at last.

Vinie

On confession of faith Edward Dickinson joined the church on August 11, 1850; Lavinia, on November 3, 1850; Austin delayed until January 6, 1856. Emily Dickinson never became a member but remained to the end "one of the lingering *bad* ones."

Among the letters which Austin received from the young ladies in Amherst is one from Emily Fowler, said to have been an unusually pretty girl. Her letter, written during the aftermath of the revival, is a good illustration of the concern felt by young people for the spiritual welfare of their friends. Emily Fowler had herself been received into the church on profession of faith at the age of sixteen (November 6, 1842).

Written on three pages of a large double sheet of blue paper, the letter is folded and addressed to "Austin" on the back.

Friday Eve.

Dear Austin.

I thank you for your letter. I thank you for recieving mine so kindly, and more than all I thank you for answering it and trusting me with your feelings. It has made me happy to read it, all of it, and especially to find that you are gradually awakening to feel an interest in the great end of our being—that light is breaking in upon you and you can see some loveliness and attraction in a christian life, and can realize that you have a part and lot in the matter, and desire to share its blessings. These are the first steps and very different states from those of cool, ignorant scepticism, or indifferent intellectual curiosity. If you begin to care at all, if you add the desire to possess Christ as your friend, because he is lovely and you long to be like him; to have intimate communion with him; if you desire to renounce sin, because it is wrong in itself and displeasing to a holy God, if your *purposes* are right—if you desire and determinately mean, God helping you, to live a new and better life, retaining all the good of the old, purified and enriched by the glorious truths of the gospel, with the added gifts from on high to help and strengthen you, if you can make up your mind to consecrate yourself wholly to holiness, and renounce whatever that demands. I do not think you need feel anxious about your feelings. God may not be working on you by the terms of the law, the fear of punishment, and an agonizing conviction of your sinfulness. He may be drawing you by cords of love, entirely, and after you have seen and loved and longed for Christ, in the fullness of his beauty and perfection, then he may give you more vivid perceptions of the guilt of neglecting him, such an one, "altogether lovely, the chief among ten thousand." A christian life is progressive, a christians experience must be so. It is rare for one who has always been familiar with Gospel truth to have these overwhelming views of sin and God burst on them at once. They come more gradually and deepen with thought and feeling, —as age and trial and life passes on, and it is so with the joys of religion. There are differences of temperament and education, wh' must be remembered as full of influence. Religion does not destroy the natural character though it always modifies it more or less. Do not let this want of "a sense of sinfulness" be a serious difficulty. I know that you feel a good deal by your thinking you do not feel enough and I know from my own experience that this is an ever deepening feeling, as we see our foolishness and sin brought out, after repeated manifestations of Gods love and repeated attempts to consecrate ourselves wholly to his service.

If you can only feel sure that your *purposes* are right that your will is so far subdued that you are earnest in endeavor; and long for the purity and holiness of our dear Savior, that you are willing to enter upon a course, of self denial, of renunciation, if it be necessary, because it is right, and our duty, as well as because the fruits are attractive, the love, the faith in the Redeemer, the sense of sin, the joy of pardon, the holy strength, the happiness, they will all come, dear Austin, in time. You are sure of them, if you persevere in such a course, and pray to God for help. He will send his Spirit, he will enlighten you—he will sanctify you, he will save you, thro' Christ Jesus, our Lord. And Christ will come and dwell with you, to him you can turn with every trouble—he will show you what is right, he will help you to do it, he will never leave you on earth, till he has given you your "mansion," where he will "prepare a place for you."

You will then have an object worth living for. Life can never weary or grow stale with such a friend to love and work for—and to know to that working for him, is reacting on yrself, making you greater and better and happier—. Oh—I cant reason—I cannot answer the quibble, and the doubt, but I can praise, and love my Savior—Dear Austin—he is yrs too—and he is waiting with open arms for you to recognize and claim him—. Go to him—tell him you are not much before him, but that you want to be numbered with his followers, and that you will try to serve him if he will only help you—and he will— Ask him for new views, for enlarged conceptions—for humility and faith and love, and any thing that you feel you need, and he will give it to you—. Prayer is hard work at first—very—Pride revolts—and the world distracts— It is a great thing to pray truly, but it can be done, and it become[s] our strength and our happiness. I will pray for you, that the spirit of grace will not forget you, but carry on the work he has begun—. Write me again, if it is pleasant—no matter, how little or how and keep me with you and let me help if I can. It makes me so happy to do it.

Ever yr true fr—
Emily. E.F.

One effect of the revival had been to strengthen the temperance movement. It has been said that the revival of 1850 was the immediate cause of the first law prohibiting the sale of intoxicating liquors —the so-called Maine Law enacted in 1851.

Then as now, "temperance" meant total abstinence from intoxicating liquor "as a beverage." Mass meetings were held in its behalf. On September 19, 1850, the "Cold Water Army" of North

Amherst held a festival—sometimes called a "jubilee"—at which addresses were delivered, among them one by the Honorable Edward Dickinson. With other leading citizens he was solidly behind the movement. He not only believed in it; he considered its observance of practical importance, since failure to keep the pledge of total abstinence was a form of backsliding easily observed. President Hitchcock thought it of sufficient importance to devote to the subject an entire section (V) of his *Reminiscences*. The original pledge which he and all the officers of the college as well as a large proportion of the students signed is dated "Amherst College, August, 1830." The association sponsoring it was called "the Antivenenean Society, or *the society against poisons*." The pledge read as follows:

Whereas, the undersigned, Officers and Students in Amherst College, are convinced that it is best for us to dispense with Ardent Spirit, Wine, Opium and Tobacco as articles of luxury or diet:—

Therefore, *Resolved,* That, relying on Divine Aid, we hereby pledge to one another our mutual promise, that while connected with this Institution we will abstain entirely from these articles except as Medicines, and the use of Wine at the Lord's Supper.

For nineteen years this pledge stood unmodified. But because some had been willing "to abstain from intoxicating drinks, who still use some of the other substances named in the Pledge," in 1849 an alternative pledge was offered:

NEW PLEDGE

We, the undersigned, officers and students of Amherst College, relying on Divine Aid, pledge to one another our mutual promise that while connected with the Institution we will not use Intoxicating Drinks as a beverage.

[It was also]

Voted, That if any one in signing the new Pledge shall prefix a star to his name, it will be understood that he adopts both Pledges; but if he prefix no star, the new Pledge only will be binding upon him.

An offense less heinous than drinking, smoking was nevertheless thought to be a precursor of other bad habits.[13] It was forbidden in public places. The *Express* (January 5, 1855) refers to a regulation of the Massachusetts General Court to the effect that "the use

13. *Amherst Graduates' Quarterly,* XXXVI *(February,* 1947), 144. For the prevalent attitude toward smoking see Emily's letter of May 16, 1853.

of tobacco in whatever form is hereby prohibited upon the grounds adjacent to, upon, or within, the State House."

As late as 1871 the Overseers of Amherst College "Voted, that it is the unanimous opinion of this Board that no student who uses intoxicating drinks as a beverage, or tobacco in any form, should be regarded as a suitable person to receive aid from the Charitable Funds of this College."[14]

Edward Dickinson supported President Hitchcock and the vote of the overseers. So emphatic was his attitude on the subject of temperance, indeed, that he was vulnerable by reason of it. The motives for his uncompromising stand were precisely those which political opponents later sought to impugn, as we shall see.

The year of the Great Revival had put quite a damper on the young Dickinsons. But it did not disturb the deep currents of mutual understanding between Austin and Emily. Their congeniality flowed from many sources. Not only did they discuss together the meaning of life; they talked of the extension of consciousness after death, an interchange of ideas by the way which their mother thought "very improper." They read the same books; and both had a sense of humor. "I know who loves jokes best," Emily gave as one reason why she missed her brother when he went away from home. And again: "Well, Austin—you are gone, and the wheel rolls slowly on—nobody to laugh with—talk with, nobody down in the morning to make the fun for me!" Joking together was a firm bond which the early letters amply illustrate. Vinnie liked fun, too, in her way. She was a first-class mimic. It was a real gift but, as sometimes happens in such cases, it finally got the better of her. Toward the end her witty but merciless ridicule of her acquaintances was at times a deadly weapon. Austin's wit began to founder in a flood of mounting unhappiness before he was thirty years old. But while Emily shared her brother's suffering, it did not warp her nature.

> In vain to punish honey,
> It only sweeter grows.[15]

Austin and Emily had in common another deep-lying trait, love of nature. It not only satisfied them in what William James called

14. Tyler, 1873, 611-612.
15. *Letters,* 1931, 407.

"the dumb region of the heart," it fed their very springs of life. For Emily, each lovely aspect of the world found response in her worship of beauty. And she felt close kinship with small neglected creatures—with spiders, frogs and caterpillars as well as with bees, butterflies and birds, even with angleworms—"our little kinsmen." For her brother, on the other hand, the Amherst countryside was, it might almost be said, a religion. It not only refreshed him; it was a refuge for his harassed soul.

During these early years the leading figure in Amherst was a great naturalist, the president of the college. So strong was the impress of Dr. Hitchcock's personality upon Austin Dickinson that before reading further it may be helpful to examine some of the reasons for the president's influence.

CHAPTER IX

President Hitchcock—Pace-Setter

1

ON THURSDAY, August 8, 1850, Austin Dickinson was graduated from Amherst College. As it was then observed "Commencement was a holiday, and a high-day, not only for the students and their friends, and the Alumni of this and other Colleges, but for the uneducated masses not of Amherst merely but of Pelham, Shutesbury and all the neighboring towns, some of whom filled the village church with a rush and a jam, while the greater multitude thronged the streets, clustered about the booths and stalls on the common, saw the shows in the tents, listened to the auctioneers, criers and street orators, or perchance, with more aspiring mind, visited the public rooms and took in the view from the tower."[1]

In 1850, as usual, in the midst of this concourse the academic procession formed at 9 A.M. and, "preceded by Dodsworth's Band," advanced to the Village Church. The valedictorian, A. M. Gay, who addressed the audience on the speculative philosophy of the seventeenth century, appears to have made little impression then or later. The salutatory in Latin was given by George Howland of Conway. "Austin W. Dickinson" delivered an oration entitled "Elements of our National Literature."[2] Though not of first rank, Austin's part in the Commencement exercises was evidence of high scholarship. Most of his close friends were also among the high-ranking students.

By this time the financial affairs of the college had taken a turn

1. Tyler, 1873, 636-637. Previous to 1852 there was no Class Day at Amherst, *ibid.,* 640.
2. *Express,* July 26, 1850.

for the better. The reader may recall that it had been facing bankruptcy in the middle thirties when Edward Dickinson became treasurer; and that he accepted various state offices—as representative in 1838 and 1839, as senator in 1842 and 1843 and as a member of the Governor's Council in 1846 and 1847—largely in an effort to persuade the legislators to aid the young college in its struggle for existence. It had temporarily weathered the gale when, in 1845, it was invigorated with new hope. For in that year the Reverend Edward Hitchcock, professor of chemistry and natural history, was made president "by acclamation." He served for ten years until the college was out of danger. During that period no account of Amherst is complete which fails to give due weight to his influence.

President Hitchcock, whose personality dominated the town as well as the college, was one of the most gifted, heroic and colorful figures ever connected with the institution. His early struggles with poverty in the Massachusetts hills; his determination, inspired by his study of astronomy, to pursue the life of a scholar; his bitter disappointment when his career as a watcher of the skies was thwarted by an impairment of vision which compelled him to turn from a study of the heavens to that of earth—from astronomy to geology, that is, whose laboratory was the out of doors; his self-education to a point where, at the age of twenty-five, he was awarded an "unsolicited" M.A. from Yale College, and at forty-seven an LL.D. from Harvard for his pioneer work in the geology of Massachusetts; his courageous and unselfish acceptance of the presidency of Amherst College when its fortunes had fallen so low that its survival was in doubt, and when that survival was assured, his return to his professorship, a chair newly entitled "Natural Theology and Geology"— all this is poignantly set forth in his volume of reminiscences. It is a story well known to Amherst people.

President Hitchcock not only piloted the college through shoal water, an achievement for which he is justly honored; he made another contribution in some respects even greater. For he drew the attention of the students to the wonder of the world in which they lived. He made them aware of the part nature can play in lifting the spirit—a tradition which to this day has never lost its hold on the alumni of Amherst College.

The enthusiasm of this great scholar, eminent among the scientists of his day, for the natural beauty of his "native valley" permeated the community. Striding across the countryside, followed by a group of eager students examining brook and pond, waterfall and ledge, to discover their structure and to probe their meaning, President Hitchcock's spirit was a sane counterpoise in the life of young men dedicated to the acquisition of classical learning. For this kind of study not only expanded the lungs and informed the mind; it reached the heart and soul.

One has a sense of grandeur in the contemplation of this man. In the section entitled "Scenery and Geology" of his volume of *Reminiscences* (pages 211-280) Dr. Hitchcock pictures the placid valley in the midst of which Amherst, on its residual island hilltop, stood high above a primordial body of water. He relates the manner in which the valley of the Connecticut River came to be carved in the ramparts of ancient rocks among which it winds its sinuous way from the Canadian border to the sea. To drive these facts home he took his classes to high points in the surrounding hills not only to study the geological structure, but to gain an understanding of the whole landscape—the relationships among the forms he was describing, which a glance around the horizon made plain. One is reminded of Pascal's pilgrimage in the seventeenth century, just before the birth of the barometer, when a procession of learned men climbed to the summit of Puy de Dôme, carrying aloft a tall column of liquid to test its height at different altitudes.

Sometimes an excursion was made the occasion for a little ceremony, to christen a peak with a classical or Indian title to replace a homely name given by early settlers. Or it might be dramatized by the presence of notables of the vicinity, who had climbed with the others. This was especially true when the ceremony took place on the Fourth of July, then the only national holiday.

In his *Reminiscences* (221 ff.) Dr. Hitchcock described a few of the earlier Independence Day excursions. On July 4, 1845, Amherst students completed a "road up Mt. Holyoke for ponies" in a single morning, supposedly stimulated by a motto from Hesiod—"who mindful of his work draws a straight furrow; nor looks around among his companions, but keeps his mind upon his work." The young men had a further incentive, however, the promise of a dinner prepared by "the ladies of South Hadley Female Seminary." After this was "disposed of, the whole party ascended the mountain." There, 830 feet above the river, they gathered to listen to addresses by Amherst professors and to one by the president on the history of the broad valley spread out below them "in almost unearthly beauty." He describes how by volcanic action the transverse Holyoke range had been uplifted across the course of the Connecticut River—a sort of titanic dam—in which a breach between Mount Holyoke and Mount Tom allowed the river to pass through. The sweep of his thought must have been to many a revelation—a mind-stretching glimpse of the successive steps of creation.

The following year five hundred persons, including many farmers from nearby fields, assembled on top of Hilliard's Knob to rename it Mount Norwottock. Leonard Humphrey, representing the senior class of Amherst College, introduced President Hitchcock to the gathering, there on the summit of the highest point in the Holyoke range. This time his topic included not only the valley of the Connecticut; it spanned the world. Holding in his hands rock specimens from his treasured cabinets, the president described one by one the distant localities from which they had come. Dull indeed must have been the student whose thoughts were not kindled.[3]

The president's enthusiasm for the out of doors seems to have invigorated the entire community. Even Edward Dickinson, well-nigh suffocated by conflicting responsibilities, gained refreshment in the open. One summer day he took time to escort his daughters on a climb to a distant hilltop (June 25, 1851), which Vinnie described for her brother. Upon Austin, as I have said, Dr. Hitchcock's love of the "beauties and sublimities of nature" remained a lasting influence. Sensitiveness to the beauty of the Amherst countryside was for Austin Dickinson a solace and inspiration, and for the president "his heart's delight."

President Hitchcock's curiosity about the natural world was equaled only by his religious zeal. Like Emanuel Swedenborg he struggled throughout life to reconcile scientific truth with religious

3. President Hitchcock's excursions continued throughout his presidency and for several years thereafter. As late as October 13, 1860, when he was making a geological survey of the state of Vermont, the students went as far afield as Dorset to christen "Eolus," a "lofty mountain."

conviction. One section of his *Reminiscences* is entitled "Religious History," which he considers "more important and interesting than everything else pertaining to" Amherst College. An ordained minister of the gospel, he emphasized the "inseparable connection between sound learning and pure religion." His geological discoveries were used to explain and support what he regarded as the truths of revelation. This dual allegiance was appraised by a fellow geologist, J. Peter Lesley, in an eloquent tribute to Edward Hitchcock before the National Academy of Sciences on August 9, 1866.[4] A true missionary both in religion and in science, what he learned he communicated like an apostle. "An original observer and a bold thinker," Dr. Lesley continued, "his whole career laid claims to eminence, which would have been pre-eminence in American Theology, had it not been for the interference of his science, or in American Science had it not been for his devotion to the ecclesiastical and financial interests of the college which he saved from premature decay and refounded upon the deliberate sacrifice of his own ambition."

The breadth of imagination which President Hitchcock brought to bear upon what he observed resulted in scientific theories which for sheer bravery so startled those who listened that they believed in spite of themselves. His publications on the fossil "bird tracks" of the Connecticut Valley are, said Dr. Lesley, not only classical, but standard.

In a few words this fellow member of the National Academy of Sciences sums up Dr. Hitchcock's career: "By his early personal devotion to field-work—by his long and successful college instruction of successive classes of young men—by the purity and simplicity of his personal nature which roused no jealousy and excited no suspicion—by his cheerful, modest, but enthusiastic publication at all times of every new fact which he observed, and every new idea which facts observed gave birth to—and by his ready concurrence in every useful scientific enterprise, Edward Hitchcock shines a star of first magnitude in the heaven of American Science."

In 1850 President and Mrs. Hitchcock spent five months in

4. J. Peter Lesley, "Biographical Notice of Edward Hitchcock," *Annual of the National Academy of Sciences for 1866*, 127-154. *National Academy of Sciences, Biographical Memoirs*, I (Washington, 1877), 113-134.

Europe. The trip, made at the behest of the Commonwealth of Massachusetts to inspect the agricultural schools of the Continent, was also intended to restore the president's health, impaired by overwork. While in Europe he took occasion to visit Switzerland to see for himself and thus confirm his faith in Agassiz' theory of glaciation. The measured judgment of the scientist always tempered the enthusiasm of the intuitive thinker. Reassured by his own observation, he read a paper before the British Association for the Advancement of Science on the terraces of the drift period in river valleys of Massachusetts. After his return to Amherst in October, Dr. Hitchcock gave a series of lectures about his experiences. Describing the beauty of ancient towns he had visited, he suggested that shade trees would improve the appearance of Amherst. It was not long until "430 trees, mostly white pine, [had been] transplanted from the forests to the College grounds."[5] Thus began the beautifying of both town and college, started by President Hitchcock but carried on by Austin Dickinson in a spirit of dedication for almost half a century, up to the year of his death.

2

A month after his graduation in August Austin went to Sunderland, a village overlooking the Connecticut River a few miles north of Amherst, to try his hand at teaching school. Sunderland was near enough for him to make frequent trips home, and it was well within the family sphere of influence, being the home of his great aunt, Mrs. Horatio Graves, Grandmother Gunn's younger sister Fanny. Inspired by President Hitchcock's lectures on the beauty of ancient European towns, it was at about this time that Austin planted the grove of white pines already mentioned.

During the fall of 1850 Amherst was privileged to hear a course of eight lectures by a man who, to quote the *Express* (September 20), "ranks first among the prose writers of America"—Richard H. Dana of Boston and Cambridge. The lectures were given in the college chapel on Tuesday and Friday evenings at seven o'clock. ("Single tickets for the course, $1.00 for gentlemen, 50¢ for ladies.") The lecture on Friday, October 11, to which Vinnie refers in the

5. *Express*, June 6, 1851.

following note, was on *Macbeth*. The next and final lecture, on *Hamlet*, was on Friday, October 18.

Apparently Lavinia had not returned to Ipswich after the summer vacation, since this note to her brother was sent from Amherst. Written on blue paper, and enclosed in a little yellow homemade envelope measuring approximately two by three inches, it was sealed with a wafer.

[*To Austin Dickinson, Sunderland, Mass.*]

Monday [October 14, 1850]

Brother Austin.

Why did'nt you come home, Friday? We expected to see you. We did'nt hear the lecture. It was considered about like the others I believe. I delivered your message promptly, & "they were" very thankful. Can you spare your Shakespeare to us for a day or so? We want to read Hamlet before the lecture. If willing, please send it by the Stage, this afternoon. Come home Tuesday night *without fail*. We are lonely, these cool days, Father & Mother want to see you. Mother says, "We shall all be glad to see him here["]—(meaning "your servant")

Vinnie

[On the reverse]

Come home Naughty Boy!

Emily

A week from the following Sunday, Emily sent a roguish note to Austin. It was not signed, but she did not disguise her writing.

[*To Austin Dickinson, Sunderland, Mass.; postmark: Amherst Ms Oct 28*]

Sunday evening [October 27, 1850]

Suppose "Topknot" should come down, and speak to his brothers, and sisters, or bind up the broken hearts of divers deserted friends, suppose he should doff his crown, and lay down his lofty sceptre, and once more a patient child receive reproof, and correction, salute the insulted rod, and bow to the common Lord!

An affection of nin[e]teen years for the most ungrateful of brothers jogs now and then at my elbow, and calls for paper and pen. Permit me to tie your shoe, to run like a dog behind you. I can bark, see here! Bow wow! Now if that is'nt fine I dont know! Permit me to be a stick, to show how I will not beat you, a stone, how I will not fling, musquito, I will not sting. Permit me to be a fowl, which Bettie shall dress for dinner, a bantam, a fine, fat hen. I will crow in my *grave* if you will. Chanticleer being still, tho' sleeping. Herein I "deign to condescend to stoop so low," what a high hill between me, and thee, a *hill,* upon my word, it is a *mountain,* I dare not climb. Let's call it "Alp", or *"Ande",* or yet the "Ascension Mount." I have it!—you shall be "Jove" a sitting on great "Olympus", a whittling the lightnings out, and hurling at your relations. Oh, "Jupiter"! fie! for shame! *Kings* sometimes have fathers and mothers. Father and I are going to have a Cattle Show Wednesday.[6] School masters and Monkeys half price. I guess you had better "come down." They've appointed *you* joint committee on the "Beast with the seven horns.["] If time, and ability fail you, they'll omit the remaining horn. There's an old hand they call "Revelation". I dare say he will give you a lift! Bowdoin is pretty well, except now and on ailing, he *may* hold on a good while yet, you know that life is *unsartin*!

To the Boy of brass buttons, clasped hands, and fervent expression, send greetings.

That Miss Field may abstain from *meadow,* nor ever be found of *Groves* is the prayer of your anxious friend.

"Serve God, and fear the King"! Exit *Sue*! ! !

Whatever the meaning of these final sentences, the last two words at least are plain. There were among the contemporaries of Emily and Vinnie Dickinson two sisters, Martha and Susan Gilbert. After the death of their mother in 1837 when both girls were under ten, they went to live with an aunt in Geneva, New York. But after the marriage of their elder sister Harriet to William Cutler, an Amherst merchant, in 1842, they returned and made their home with her. Both are said to have attended the Utica Female Academy in Utica, New York, however, and to have spent the holidays with their aunt in Geneva.

6. In 1850 the Amherst Cattle Show was held on October 30, its name changed to "The First Annual Cattle Show of the East Hampshire Agricultural Society," an organization founded in that year by Alfred Baker. For a college student's impression of the Cattle Show of 1847, an informal forerunner of the "Farmers' Festivals" of later years, see W. G. Hammond, *Remembrance of Amherst,* 199-200.

The Cutlers lived on Amity Street not far from the Dickinsons. At the time this note was written both girls were dressed in mourning for another sister, Mary, who, having married Samuel Julius Learned on September 19, 1849, died less than a year later, on July 14, 1850. They continued to wear black for more than two years. The sisters were often spoken of as the Gilbert "twins." But in character as in appearance they were very different. Martha, a gentle yielding child, was apt to follow the lead of her more self-confident younger sister.

Going home to Amherst to spend Thanksgiving, Austin Dickinson did not return to Sunderland, but spent the winter of 1850-1851 reading law in his father's office.

Among the valentines Austin received during this early period is one addressed to "Austin Dickinson, Esq., Amherst, Mass." not signed, dated only "February 14th," and posted in Amherst. The yellow envelope is fastened with eight small stickers of assorted shapes, each with a motto expressing a different sentiment. On the one in the center, above an arrow-pierced heart, are the words, "In vain I fly." The perpendicular script suggests the later writing of Sue Gilbert. The large double sheet of blue paper contains this message:

> To me through every season dearest,
> In every scene—by day, by night—
> Thou present to my mind appearest
> A quenchless star forever bright,
> My solitary, sole delight—
> Alone—in grove—by shore—at sea
>   I think of thee—
> P.S. We are most out of chestnuts—

CHAPTER X

The Making of a Home

HOUSEKEEPING," said Emily Dickinson, "is a prickly art."[1] Her frequent use of homely figures of speech taken from the daily round of household tasks has been noted by students of her poetry. But we sometimes forget how arduous and time-consuming those tasks were. Without conveniences as we know them, Mrs. Dickinson and her daughters would have little time for other occupations if the household was to conform in all respects to the wishes of the head of the family. To the smooth running of "our father's house," as Emily called it, they were all dedicated.

Edward Dickinson was quick to notice any lapse of attention on the part of his womenfolks. In his code there was no room for carelessness. His standard of good workmanship was as strict for them as for himself. The well-known anecdote of the plate illustrates the point. One day, sitting down at the dinner table, he inquired whether a certain nicked plate must always be placed before him. Emily took the hint. She carried the plate to the garden and pulverized it on a stone, "just to remind" her, she said, not to give it to her father again.

In Emily's day domestic activity was still a full-time career for women. The Germans, perhaps because they place so high a value on it, have a special word—*das Alltägliche*—for daily routine. To absorb small annoyances and leave the menfolks free to carry on the constructive work of the community was, a hundred years ago, a woman's sufficient reason for being. No one questioned it, least of all the women. It was not their way to express likes or dislikes toward necessary work. They resented it, for the most part, no more

1. *Letters*, 1931, 269.

112

than we resent putting on our clothes; and they kept everlastingly
at it. Many a man wore out several wives. Old New England burying
grounds testify to that.

We tend to forget how recently the opportunity to express a
preference in such matters has been given to women. Whether their
duties pleased or displeased them was beside the point. To escape
effort was no one's aim. Laborers worked from sunup to sundown
six days a week. Toil was the order of the day, toil so incessant that
it is small wonder the letters from the Dickinson girls are full of
fatigue. It is well to bear in mind, too, that their duties were performed in layers of skirts which swept the floor, often measuring as
much as ten yards around the bottom. Elizabeth Cady Stanton
referred to "the crippled, dragged-down creature slavery to her
clothes has made [woman]. . . . She might as well work with ball
and chain."

Far from being detached from "the narrow round, the stint"
of household tasks, Emily Dickinson was occupied with them week
after week, year after year, without any evidence that in the main
she considered them irksome, although several early poems, among
them "A prison gets to be a friend," might be so interpreted. Since
housework was the occupation to which her time and energy were
given, it might be useful to remind ourselves of a few of the principal activities.

Providing the essentials, heat, light and water, was a part of daily
routine. There was no central heating, so, during many months of
the year, open fireplaces and airtight wood-burning stoves had to be
fed intermittently throughout the day. A wood box in the kitchen
was filled by the men, but the women kept the fires burning. In a
climate as harsh as that of New England, just to keep warm in winter
took a good deal of time. As there was neither gas nor electricity,
lamps must be cleaned and filled with whale oil, a daily task for
which a shelf in the back pantry was reserved. Tallow candles, often
made at home, lighted the family to bed. Not only was there no hot
and cold running water, there was no running water at all. The
only source of supply was the well which, I understand, was underneath the house on Pleasant Street, not outdoors as in many Amherst
homes. Water pitchers for every bedroom were filled each day from
the kitchen pump. There were plants to be watered too. And the

making of feather beds absorbed much time if no flaw was to be found in their appearance.

The tasks were parceled out, each woman having her special province. The preparation of food was the most time-consuming. All the cooking was done at home, for there was no public bakery and the stores carried no canned or partially prepared foods. Much was also produced at home, butter for instance, and eggs, for the Dickinsons kept hens. Most of the raw materials were at hand—an entire arsenal based on barrels of flour and sugar under the pantry shelves. In summer there were green vegetables and berries in the garden and fruit in the orchard. The Dickinsons were all interested in horticulture. Their produce received many prizes. Even Mrs. Dickinson was on the fruit committee of the Cattle Show and her figs were mentioned more than once in the local newspaper. There was no refrigeration, except an icebox for which ice was cut from the pond in winter and stored in sawdust until needed. Root crops and barrels of apples were kept in the cellar during the winter months. Early spring, before the garden began to produce, put the greatest strain on the provider, and on her imagination. Stores in the cellar were running low and "how to get up May hill" was for the cooks more than a metaphor. Although at that time of year diet was monotonous, such as it was there was always more than enough to eat. A community whose chief occupation was farming would see to that.

In the Dickinson family the task of baking—a truly creative enterprise—was allotted to Emily. As she wrote at nineteen, "Twin loaves of bread have just been born into the world under my auspices,—fine children, the image of their mother."[2] In a wood-burning stove where heat was at the mercy of wind movements and other atmospheric vagaries, not to mention the hardness and dryness of the wood which determined the rate of combustion, management of a fire was in itself a challenge, one which she met successfully. Twenty years later Emily's duties were much the same. In 1870 Colonel Higginson reported that she made all the bread "for her father only likes hers, [she] says, 'and people must have puddings,' this very dreamily as if they were comets, so she makes them."[3]

2. *Letters*, 1931, 40.
3. *Letters*, 1931, 286.

Emily Dickinson was an expert and imaginative cook. Some of her finest poems were jotted down on the back of recipes or on grocers' brown paper bags while she was rolling out dough. On one sheet, in writing of the 1880's, "The things that never can come back, are several" is on one side and "Mrs Carmichael's" recipe for coconut cake on the other:

> 1 pound sugar –
> $\frac{1}{2}$ – Butter –
> $\frac{1}{2}$ – Flour –
> 6 – Eggs –
> 1 grated Cocoa Nut.[4]

The amount of alchemy required to make the cake a success, however, is not specified.

Though Emily said in an early letter to a girlhood friend that she attended to the culinary arts "from necessity," the zest was supplied by her "desire to make everything pleasant for father and Austin."[5] That particular letter, written at the age of nineteen, comes nearest to rebellion of any I have seen. "I have been at work," she says, "providing 'the food that perisheth,' scaring the timorous dust, and being obedient and kind. . . . Mother is still an invalid, though a partially restored one; father and Austin still clamor for food; and I, like a martyr, am feeding them." But her outburst fades away in gentle imprecations which "never did any one harm and they make me feel so cool, and so very much more comfortable!"

While foundation baking of bread and cake, cookies, biscuits and puddings was Emily's province, Mrs. Dickinson, though adept at pie making, usually presided over the top of the stove, taking charge of the foods to be boiled or fried. Vinnie appears to have done little cooking at this time. She was sweeping, dusting, washing dishes and keeping things in order. Cooking was constructive; cleaning on the other hand, Emily felt, was a treadmill which accomplished nothing. Vinnie also did the marketing. She made the family's small purchases and once a day went to the post office when the stage came in. Errands were from the first Vinnie's province.

On March 7, 1850, Edward Dickinson advertised for a "hired

4. A recipe for her own "Black Cake" is among the Sweetser letters referred to on page 17.
5. *Letters,* 1931, 42-43.

girl." Apparently no one meeting the requirements was found for during the 1850's the Dickinsons had, to use the terms then current, no regular "house girl," only a "washerwoman" who came for a day's work at stated intervals. On "washing day" Mrs. Mack filled tubs from the pump and heated the water on the kitchen stove; and she wielded the heavy flatirons likewise heated on the stove. (Mrs. Mack, the Irish washerwoman, should not be confused with the wife of Deacon Mack who for many years owned and occupied the Dickinson homestead.) Not until some time after the family moved back to the homestead was a woman engaged to help with the daily chores. Even then the girls continued to take their full share.

Most of the family's clothes were homemade. Although the era of homespun cloth had pretty well passed, the materials, "New York and Boston goods," must be fashioned at home—all of the women's clothing and much of the men's, though for them local tailors did the heaviest work. Ready-made clothes for men were only just beginning to put in an appearance. But their collars and shirt "bosoms," the high old-fashioned stocks and neckties, their shirts and fancy waistcoats, were made in the house. Plain and fancy doeskin vestings were a staple in the general store— "cassimeres, black and figured silks and satins, damasks and grenadiens."

The women all had their share of the sewing. The frequent mention of it is evidence of how much time it required. Although seamstresses came for a day to cut and fashion the dresses, the actual needlework was done for the most part by members of the family. Sewing a fine seam by hand was an endless business.[6] When it is recalled that dresses were lined, and built upon whalebones, thin strips of stiffening, each one of which must be covered before being sewed onto the lining, it is not surprising that once achieved, a dress was worn for years. The style was too demure to betray a date. Underclothes were not only made by hand, the seams triply sewn, the ruffles were embroidered in original designs executed in a manner worthy of a French *religieuse*.

In the days before sewing machines—Singer took out his first

6. The seamstresses referred to in the letters are Miss Leonard, Miss Bartlett, Miss Baker, Mrs. Godfrey, Mrs. Noyes, and Mrs. Kimberly—wife of the tailor Thompson Kimberly. Miss Bangs was "an experienced and superior dressmaker."

patent in 1851—women everywhere took great pride in their sewing. Fine needlework was an accomplishment valued more perhaps than any other. A contemporary of Emily Dickinson, expressing his contempt for female "scribblers," specified the occupation suitable for women in these words: "the needle, not the pen, is the instrument they should handle."

Not only making the family's clothes but keeping them in order was a neverending task. They were worn year after year until there was not enough substance left to mend. Socks and stockings, knit by hand, were darned until they could no longer hold together. Darning a stocking was an art, the aim being to make the darn indistinguishable from the fabric.

In addition to regular duties there were activities to which at certain seasons entire days were devoted, such as rendering fat for soap or candles, and emptying and filling feather beds and cording bedsteads. (Before the days of wire springs, rope was stretched back and forth across the bedstead to support the mattress.) But most exhausting was the annual spring housecleaning when all the carpets—which covered the floors right up to the baseboard—were taken up, beaten out of doors, and tacked down again. For that particular activity Emily had succinct words: " 'House' is being 'cleaned.' I prefer pestilence." Spring had its advantages, however. Work in the garden was eagerly anticipated, especially by her. In summer and autumn there was also the making of jelly and preserving the fruits of garden and orchard.

From daylight to dark the mechanics of living detained them all. Emily said it was her reason for not leaving home: "We have so much matter of fact here," she explained, "that I don't dare to go."[7] Among her poems there are occasional suggestions, however, that routine duties were not unwelcome, supplying as they did a counterpoise to spiritual turmoil. As she puts it:

> Therefore we do life's labor,
> Though life's reward be done,
> With scrupulous exactness
> To hold our senses on.

These simple tasks have been elaborated in some detail because in fulfilling them Emily Dickinson's time was occupied. In point

7. *Letters,* 1931, 141.

of time consumed they might be called her profession. She spent her days, long hard days, doing housework, a respect in which her life was not different from that of other girls. Eudocia Converse, one of her contemporaries, kept a diary. One day she says she "baked eight pies, two loaves of cake and two dozen tarts." The number of pies baked at one time by this young woman ranged from eight to seventeen, and the loaves of cake from two to eight. For the Dickinson household, furthermore, except on Sunday, a never-ending stream of visitors must be fed. This meant a middle-of-the-day dinner which, with all that was involved in addition to other duties, pretty much disposed of the day.

I have recently examined a group of unpublished letters written sixty years ago by Professor George Herbert Palmer of Harvard University to his wife, Alice Freeman Palmer. In the early 1890's Mrs. Palmer, as first Dean of Women at the newly established University of Chicago, was blocking out an academic future for her sex, but the subjects the Palmers wrote about were not limited to educational policy. In a letter of October 1, 1894, Mr. Palmer describes a household not unlike that of the Dickinsons. Meditating upon his own childhood and on Longfellow's poetry, he says:

"I have disparaged him too much. How his whole attitude of mind brings back the peaceful, true, dignified, tender New England life of forty years ago, before Chicagos had arisen, and men lived in isolated homes communing with chosen ones of the past. In those days few wrote poetry, but all read it. Now everybody writes and few read. My youth came back and I felt the hushed home calm saturated with emotion. Even the solid and the sober—the bourgeois and the Philistine—have poetry in them. . . . And all this Longfellow expresses, not only with grace, but with a diffused and penetrating power."[8]

What Mr. Palmer did not mention, however, was the fact that the peace and harmony of a household such as he wistfully recalls was built upon the ceaseless toil of the women of the family.

When Emily Dickinson's letters were first published in 1894, chiefly because of their prolixity only the picturesque parts of the early ones to her brother were used. Consequently, as nine tenths of her activities are missing, that policy helped to create a wrong

8. Reproduced from a typed copy of the unpublished manuscript, with the kind permission of Dr. Frederic Palmer, Haverford College.

impression of her as a person, as I have already suggested (pp. 47, 48). She has been described as detached from practical life. Nothing could be further from the truth. As long as she was physically able she did her full share of work. It was not until the last few years of her life, when she was no longer strong enough to take part in the heavier tasks, that she wrote, "I dont keep the Moth part of the House—I keep the Butterfly part."

She lived in an atmosphere of daily grind and small-town talk. But there it ended—their thoughts were not her thoughts. "All men say 'What?' to me," she said. Even to Austin she once wrote, "You say you dont comprehend me" (June 29, 1851).

The point I wish to make is this: during the years covered by these letters Emily had almost no time for herself. Her duties could not be slighted. She must not be lured away from the task at hand by pencil and paper. If she was ever to "flee to her mind" (March 2, 1852) time must be snatched from some chore waiting to be finished. A chance to be alone with her books and her thoughts was her reward, frequently long delayed. As her letters indicate, she often wrote in her room late at night while the others slept. For her writing was carried on in secret. No one, no one to the very end, ever dreamed of the magnitude of the task to which her "real" life had been devoted.

> Unto my books so good to turn
> Far ends of tired days;
> It half endears the abstinence,
> And pain is missed in praise.
>
> As flavors cheer retarded guests
> With banquetings to be,
> So spices stimulate the time
> Till my small library.
>
> It may be wilderness without,
> Far feet of failing men,
> But holiday excludes the night,
> And it is bells within.
>
> I thank these kinsmen of the shelf;
> Their countenances bland
> Enamour in prospective,
> And satisfy, obtained.

CHAPTER XI

Recreation

FOR the young people of Amherst a century ago there were amusements as well as duties. They found entertainment in a number of ways, but they made their own pleasures, contrived out of themselves. It was for the most part a different kind of exertion, indulged in after the day's work was finished. Better still if it could be had while doing something useful. As Edward Everett Hale said: ". . . if the windows of the room be open, the exercise of sweeping can hardly be rivalled. I am not sure whether I am to speak of it as amusement. It is certainly recreation."[1]

The old Puritan Congregationalists were distinguished for their aversion to vain amusements. Gymnastics, considered "mere frivolity," were not in favor. Lacking organized sports young men took long walks. The girls walked too, during the kinder months, and rode horseback or drove about the countryside. For those who cared for it, there were hunting and fishing the year round, and "nutting" in October. There were hazel nuts, and hickory nuts, but principally chestnuts, clustering side by side in their prickly, silk-lined burs, now wistfully recalled by those who used to gather them. In winter there were sleigh rides, reading clubs, charades, sewing circles and occasional sedate social gatherings called levees. So much emphasis was placed on decorum that a student "caught singing such songs as 'The way we have in Old Amherst,' and others like it, in the streets, would have been expelled, or perchance found himself in the lock-up."[2] The letters mention few other forms of amusement, but in her letter of June 22, 1851, Emily speaks of a dance.

1. E. E. Hale, *What Career?* (Boston, 1878), 267.
2. Tyler, 1873, 640-641.

Chiefly the young people relied for entertainment on an exchange of wits. For Emily Dickinson it was not always a fair exchange. But she could hope. In the 1850's she took part in the social affairs of the community. As time went on, however, it became increasingly clear that if she was to continue to assume such obligations in addition to her other duties she would have no time for anything else—in itself sufficient reason for her inch-by-inch withdrawal. In the beginning it seems to have been as simple as that. Time for reading she must have. It is enlightening to know what she read. In his "critical biography" of Emily Dickinson George Whicher has provided an inventory in a chapter entitled "Books and Reading."[3]

For news of the outside world the Dickinsons like other Amherst people relied on two newspapers, the daily *Springfield Republican* "the largest paper in New England,"[4] edited by Samuel Bowles, father and son, and J. G. Holland; and *The Hampshire and Franklin Express,* published each Friday morning in Amherst, furnished information of a practical sort, largely agricultural of course in a farming community. The front page contained stories and "poetry," with anecdotes and bits of rustic humor appropriate to local taste, while thrills lacking in village life were supplied by details of various extraordinary calamities: a young lady, entering the house by a window in order to feed her kitten, was caught by the falling sash and was "perfectly dead" when discovered (April 16, 1852); a man fell from a haymow onto "the point of a hay puller which entered his abdomen and passed out through his back" (February 4, 1853); a "young lady was caught by the hair in a revolving shaft in Chelmsford Mills and scalped" (July 15, 1853). Regarding such disasters Emily inquired of Dr. and Mrs. Holland, "Who writes those funny accidents, where railroads meet each other unexpectedly, and gentlemen in factories get their heads cut off quite informally? The author, too, relates them in such a sprightly way, that they are quite attractive. Vinnie was disappointed

3. *This Was a Poet*, 206-224.
4. Josiah Gilbert Holland, *History of Western Massachusetts* (Springfield, 1855), I, 442-444. Beginning on March 27, 1844, the *Republican* published a daily as well as a weekly edition, except of course on Sunday, when there were no papers. Compare George S. Merriam, *The Life and Times of Samuel Bowles* (New York, 1885), I, 21.

to-night, that there were not more accidents—I read the news aloud, while Vinnie was sewing."[5]

The *Express* reflected not only what Emerson called the "floating opinions" of the times; it presented topics for meditation, clues to thoughts which filled the readers' minds. Occasional traces of a news item are found in Emily Dickinson's poems. Lady Franklin's repeated expeditions in search of her husband, the British naval hero Sir John Franklin, lost while exploring the Arctic in 1845, for example, were reported in the *Express* intermittently for many years.[6] A copy of the poem

> When the astronomer stops seeking
> For his Pleiad's face,
> When the lone British lady
> Forsakes the Arctic race . . .

is in the handwriting of the late 1850's.

Meetings and occasional lectures were announced in the *Express,* but there was no column of local items until later, except vital and "hymenial" statistics. In the birth notices the mother was not mentioned; a child was born to "Mr." So-and-So.

In Amherst at this time there were two red-letter days, one in August, one in October. The first was Commencement, when the Dickinsons or their friends usually took part in the exercises and old acquaintances came back for their reunions; the second, in October, was the Cattle Show in which Edward Dickinson was always a central figure. There were also occasional exciting events, as when, on October 5, 1852, Welch's National Circus came to town. The *Express* (October 1) heralded its arrival with the announcement that "the entree into this town will be of a grandeur beggaring description, assuming more the appearance of a Triumphal Roman Procession than the entrance of an Equestrian Company. . . . The most imposing entree of all is styled the Kossuth Cavalcade, by the principal ladies and gentlemen in full Hungarian costume." A quarter of a century later, as she watched the "boys and girls from Tripoli" go by, Emily wrote to Mrs. Holland: "A circus passed the house—still I feel the red in my mind though the drums are out."[7]

5. *Letters*, 1931, 157.
6. Compare Austin's letter of February, 1853, on pages 256-257.
7. *Letters*, 1931, 166.

Between 1835 and 1855 the age of Citizens' Lyceums was in full swing in New England. During the winter months papers on literary and scientific subjects were discussed at weekly meetings. (Recreation was usually a by-product of self-improvement.) With local speakers, these precursors of the adult-education movement entailed a good deal of study. After 1850 "ladies took part in the exercises . . . reading compositions and poetical selections." An educated man was expected to be able to express himself clearly, forcefully and persuasively on his feet. So, in addition to lyceums, weekly debates—"debating schools," Daniel Webster called them— gave youthful orators a chance to practice their art. The subjects covered a wide range, from "The desirability of annexation of the Sandwich Islands," and "The comparative usefulness of Noah Webster and Daniel Webster," to such topics as "Ought military skill to be considered a qualification for the presidency?" During the 1853-1854 season the subjects were even more ambitious: "Was Queen Elizabeth justifiable in her treatment and execution of Mary Queen of Scots?" "Ought the Christian Powers of Europe to assist Turkey in the war with Russia?" Problems nearer home were tackled too, for instance, "Ought Pelham, or any considerable part of it, to be annexed to Amherst?" (March 7, 1854.)

But lyceums and lectures attracted a rather limited audience after all, whereas on Sunday the whole town went to church. The best chance for seeing everybody was at meeting. Indecorous though it may seem, activities of the Sabbath Day are included in this chapter on recreation.

In the First Parish meeting house, called the "Village Church," services in the 1850's were held morning, afternoon, and evening. The longer the sermon the better the preacher. Some of them could speak for two hours or more. The texts carried stern warnings. Young Eudocia Converse wrote in her diary: "Heard three solemn, impressive and excellent sermons from Dr. Vaill. Great solemnity pervaded the entire congregation." And again: "The Reverend Mr. Colton preached all day from Daniel 5:27, 'Thou are weighed in the balances and art found wanting.' "

In old Russia, church services with their barbaric splendor were called the opera of the poor. Similarly, although at the other extreme, the austere Sunday meeting supplied to the eager young spirits in Amherst a century ago the chief excitement of the week.

For the girls there was always the chance of an unforeseen encounter after service. Who would be there? What unexpected out-of-town visitor? Who might perhaps walk home with them? The romantic possibilities in the touch of a hand, in the exchange of a glance, in a bow even, filled their need for days.

Young men too, it seems, got sustenance from churchgoing other than that provided by the preacher. I used to know a man in Amherst who gave me a glimpse of the sources which fed his emotional life when, as a youth, he first moved to town. The young lady he most admired, he hesitated most to approach. But one Sunday he walked up the aisle and, with thumping heart, took his station in the pew, or "slip" as he called it, directly behind her. And sure enough! Just before the first hymn, recognizing him as a newcomer, she turned and with a smile handed him a hymnbook open at the right page. "That lasted me two years," he said.

This was not an exceptional case. Young people were shy. Everybody was shy. Edward Dickinson himself was shy—an aspect of his character which will repay further study. And besides, they were all on their guard. How to live together at close quarters in a small community without giving away one's feelings required constant watchfulness. To break through another person's reserve might uncover attitudes better concealed. Insubordinate thoughts, if such there were, were kept to oneself.

On the Sabbath Day all secular activities were laid aside. Whatever you did contrary to custom was behind closed doors. If for instance you wrote a letter on Sunday it was dated as of Saturday or Monday. If you darned a stocking on the Sabbath you felt surreptitious, and you never sewed for pleasure. In view of this, Emily's habit of writing to her brother on Sunday is worth noting.

Such were the kinds of recreation countenanced by the community in Emily Dickinson's youth. It seems as if a sense of accomplishment, a feeling of satisfaction in work well done and duty fulfilled, took the place of entertainment to a large extent. I have sometimes thought that the time spent in diversion of one sort or another, then and now, is the truest measure of our difference.

PART THREE

1851-1853

CHAPTER XII

Austin as School Teacher

IN JUNE, 1851, Austin Dickinson made a second, longer flight from home. Abandoning the study of law in his father's office, he went to Boston to try his hand at teaching in a large public school.

Mrs. Dickinson's sister Lavinia and her husband Loring Norcross (a dry-goods commission merchant with offices at 73 Kilby Street, Boston), with their two little daughters, Louisa, aged nine, and Fanny, aged four, were living at 25 McLean Street, in the North End. Mr. Norcross was a member from Ward 5 of the Boston School Committee. When a vacancy occurred on the staff of the Endicott Grammar School on Cooper Street not far from his home, his nephew was summoned to fill it. At first Austin lived with his uncle and aunt, as did Mrs. Norcross' unmarried brother Joel, but before long moved to a boardinghouse kept by a Mrs. Reed. The Endicott School had separate departments for boys and girls; Austin taught in the boys' school. As he arrived late in the school year his name does not appear in the official list of teachers for 1850-1851.

Exactly when he went to Boston Austin could not recall. He indicated the date of Emily's first letter only as "early in 1851." But he seems not to have arrived in Boston until after the spring recess which ended on June 9, 1851.[1]

1. Two letters which Austin placed in March, 1851 (printed in part in *Letters*, 1931, 75-77), belong in 1852. The letters will be found on pages 226-232 and 243.

[*Envelope missing*]

Sunday evening [June 8, 1851]

It might not come amiss dear Austin to have a tiding or two concerning our state and feelings, particularly when we remember that "Jamie is gone awa."

Our state is pretty comfortable, and our feelings are *somewhat solemn* which we account for satisfactorily by calling to mind the fact that it is the "Sabbath Day." Whether a certain passenger in a certain yesterday's stage has any sombre effect on our once merry household, or the reverse "I dinna choose to tell," but be the case as it may, we are rather a crestfallen company to make the *best* of us, and what with the sighing wind, the sobbing rain, and the whining of nature *generally,* we can hardly contain ourselves, and I only hope and trust that your this evening's lot is cast in far more cheery places than the ones you leave behind.

We are enjoying this evening what is called a "northeast storm" —a little north of east, in case you are pretty definite. Father thinks "it's amazin raw," and I'm half disposed to think that he's in the right about it, tho' I keep pretty dark, and dont *say* much about it! Vinnie is at the instrument, humming a pensive air concerning a young lady who thought she was "almost there." Vinnie seems much grieved, and I really suppose *I* ought to betake myself to weeping; I'm pretty sure that *I shall* if she dont abate her singing.

Father's just got home from meeting and Mr Boltwood's, found the last quite comfortable, and the first not quite so well.

Mother is warming her feet, which she assures me confidently are "just as cold as ice.["] I tell her I fear there is danger of icification, or ossification—I dont know certainly which! Father is reading the Bible—I take it for *consolation,* judging from outward things. He and mother take great delight in dwelling upon your character, and reviewing your many virtues, and Father's prayers for you at our morning devotions are enough to break one's heart —it is really very touching; surely "our blessings brighten" the farther off they fly! Mother wipes her eyes with the end of her linen apron, and consoles herself by thinking of several future places "where congregations ne'er break up," and Austins have no end! This being a favorite sentiment with you, I trust it will find a response in all patriotic bosoms. There has been not much stirring since when you went away—I should venture to say *prudently* that matters had come to a stand—unless something new "turns up" I cannot see anything to prevent a *quiet season*. Father takes care of the doors, and mother of the windows, and Vinnie and I are secure against all outward attacks. If we can get our *hearts "under"* I dont have much to fear—I've got all but *three* feelings down, if I can only keep them!

Tutor Howland[2] was here *as usual,* during the afternoon—after tea I went to see Sue—had a nice little visit with her—then went to see Emily Fowler, and arrived home at 9—found Father in great agitation at my protracted stay—and mother and Vinnie in tears, for fear that he would kill me.

Sue and Martha expressed their sorrow that you had gone away, and are going to write a postcript in the next letter I send.

Emily F. talked of you with her usual deal of praise. The girls all send their love. Mother wants me to say that if you like *Aunt L's Bonnet,* and can find one for *her just like it,* that "Barkis is very willin." Vinnie sends her love, and says she is "pretty comfortable." I shall think of you tomorrow with four and twenty Irish boys—all in a row! I miss you very much. I put on my bonnet tonight, opened the gate very desperately, and for a little while, the suspense was terrible—I think I was held in check by some invisible agent, for I returned to the house without having done any harm!

If I had'nt been afraid that you would "poke fun" at my feelings, I had written a *sincere* letter, but since the "world is hollow, and Dollie is stuffed with sawdust," I really do not think we had better expose our feelings. Write soon to *me,* they all send love to you and all the folks—love to Lizzie if there. Vinnie has commenced snoring.

Your dear Sister Emily.

Among these letters there are no postscripts in Sue's or Martha's handwriting.

The boys and girls in the North End of Boston were for the most part children of Irish peasants who had sought refuge in New England during the famine which followed the failure of the 1847 potato crop in Ireland.

2. "Howland" usually means William Howland, as in the present instance. A tutor in the college, he was also studying law in Edward Dickinson's office. Mr. Dickinson found him particularly congenial. In Emily's words: "They go along as smoothly as friendly barks at sea—or when harmonious stanzas become one melody" (September 23, 1851). William's younger brother George, Austin's classmate, is referred to by his full name. The use of a young man's first name alone was a familiarity not often condoned.

Enclosed in Emily's second letter to her brother three notes were found: One from their father, one from Vinnie and a query from Loring Norcross evidently laid in later:[3]

If any one is to be here from Amherst tomorrow night send back word how many.

L. Norcross

June 17/51

With the names of the relatives mentioned in these letters the reader is already familiar: "Grandmother," Mrs. Edward Dickinson's stepmother; cousin Emily Norcross of Monson, then living with her aunt Mrs. Loring Norcross; and "Aunt Elisabeth," Edward Dickinson's redoubtable youngest sister. At this time the latter was keeping house for her brother William in Worcester. His first wife died in 1851. Following his second marriage in 1852, and the subsequent birth of two boys and a girl, Elisabeth stayed on to help with the children.

[*To Wᵐ Austin Dickinson. Care of Loring Norcross Esq. Boston. Mass.; postmark: Amherst Ms. Jun* 16]

Sunday evening [June 15, 1851]

From what you say Dear Austin I am forced to conclude that you never received *my letter* which was mailed for Boston *Monday,* but *two days* after you left—I dont know where it went to, Father wrote on the outside, and to care of Uncle Loring, and waiting from day to day and receiving no reply, I naturally grew rather crusty and resolved to reserve my mss for youths more worthy of them; this will account for the fact that you heard nothing by Bowdoin. In neither of your letters, for which I heartily thank you, have you made any mention of my departed letter—Bowdoin *thinks* you told him you had not heard from home, and quite surprised at it, and grieved to have you think you were forgotten *so* quick, I will try the post again, if I cant be more successful. I'm glad you are so well

3. The envelope of this letter, reproduced on page 325, is postmarked and stamped in red "Paid 5" in place of a postage stamp. In this collection the first postage stamp appears three weeks later. The letter, like others, reached Austin in Boston without any street address.

Letter from Emily Dickinson to her brother Austin, June 15, 1851

We are quite alarmed for the boys, hope you wont kill, or pack away any of 'em, so near Dr Webster's tomb! Can't strange you have had temp-tations! You would not take it amiss if I should say we *carried some*, when each of your *letters* came — your respected parents were overwhelmed with glee, and as for the young *ferries*, they gave a smile or so, by way of recognising your *diversified merits*. Father remarks quite briefly that he "thinks they have found their mates," in other bills his life, and fears you will be rash with them, and Vinnie and I say masses for poor Irish boys' souls. So far as *I* am concerned I should like to have you kill some — there are so many now, there is no room for the americans, and I cant think of *any death* that would be more after my mind than *scientific destruction, scholastic dissolution*, there's something *lofty* in it, it smacks of *going off*! Wont you please to state the name of the boy that turned the faintest, as I like to *get such facts* to *set* down in my journal, also anything else that's *startling* which you may chance to know — I dont think deaths or murders can ever come amiss in a young —

Emily to the little Austins

woman's Journal — the country's still just now and the Irenities alluded to will have a salutary influence in waking the people up — speaking of getting up, how early are metropolitans expected to wake up, especially young men — more especially Schoolmasters? I miss my department mornings — I lay it quite to heart that I've no one to wake up. Your room looks lonely enough — I am not toe to to in there — whenever I fall this I find I go to whistle as we read that little boys are wont to do in the grave-yard. I am going to let out Crickets as soon as I find time that they by their shrill singing shall help disperse the gloom — will they grow if I transplant them?

You importune one for news, I am very sorry to say "Vanity of vanities" there's no such thing as news — It is almost time for the Chicora, and then things will take a start!

We have had a man to take tea, a Mr March by name — he went to school with Father.

I think him a "man of cares" tho' I know nothing concerning him — another important item. So far as I can judge — I think he's for "law and order."

Susie and Martha come often, Sue was here on Friday, in all afternoon yesterday — I gave this man.

Dear Austin

I expect you will think us strange + ungra-teful to refuse coming to Boston now, though thoned you know all the reasons for our decision your opinion might be different. If I had plenty of money in my comm... I would not hesitate one moment, but the Worcester friends expect us there when Aunt Elizabeth comes + 'twould be too early to go there now + we cannot

Letter from Lavinia and notes from their father and from Loring Norcross enclosed

go again, because
travelling is rather
expensive you know,
Besides, if we go now, our
visit must be too short
to suit me & the Worcester
visit omitted entirely
for the Summer, I want
to have I _Emily_ more than
a care Express here & then
I act entirely from
impulse. you would
certainly see me.
Father is kind, allows us
to _do_ as one choose, she
~~approves~~ of our decision,
We shall come to Boston
another time when we take
the Worcester Trip, We
miss you ~~some~~ Don't
~~kill~~ any boys, I am afraid you

Austin;
I want a copy of the Acts of the first session
of the General Court — Call at the office of the Secretary
of State. I get a copy of those which they
distribute to the people. & send me by mail.
Leave both ends of the wrapper open. to save
postage.   Yours faithfully
Monday morning.   E. L.

If any one is to be here from
Amherst tomorrow night—send
back word how many

June 17/51   L. Norcross

pleased, I am glad you are *not* delighted, I would not that *foreign* places should wear the smile of home. We are quite alarmed for the *boys*, hope you wont *kill*, or *pack away* any of em, so near Dr. Webster's bones t'ant strange you have had temptations![4] You would not take it amiss if I should say we *laughed some* when each of your letters came—your respected parents were *overwhelmed* with glee, and as for the *young ladies* they gave a smile or so by way of recognizing your *descriptive* merits. Father remarks quite briefly that he "thinks they have found their master," mother bites her lips, and fears you "will be *rash* with them" and Vinnie and I say masses for poor Irish boys souls. So far as *I* am concerned I should like to have you kill some—there are so many now, there is no room for the Americans, and I cant think of a death that would be more after my mind than *scientific destruction, scholastic dissolution,* there's something lofty in it, it smacks of *going up*! Wont you please to state the *name* of the boy that turned the faintest, as I like to get such *facts* to set down in my *journal,* also anything else that's *startling* which you may chance to know—I dont think deaths or murders can ever come amiss in a young woman's journal —the country's *still* just now, and the severities alluded to will have a salutary influence in waking the people up—speaking of *getting up,* how early are *metropolitans* expected to wake up, *especially* young men—*more* especially *schoolmasters*? I miss "my department" mornings—I lay it quite to heart that I've no one to wake up. Your room looks lonely enough—I do not love to go in there— whenever I pass thro' I find I 'gin to whistle, as we read that little boys are wont to do in the graveyard. I am going to set out *Crickets* as soon as I find time that they by their shrill singing shall help disperse the gloom—will they grow if I *transplant* them?

You importune me for *news,* I am very sorry to say "Vanity of vanities" there's no such thing as news—it is almost time for the cholera, and *then* things will take a start!

We have had a man to take tea, a Mr Marsh by name—he went to school with Father.

I think him a "man of cares" tho' I know nothing concerning him—another important item, so far as I can judge—I think he's for "law and order." Susie and Martha come often. Sue was here on Friday, for all afternoon yesterday—I gave the *manslaughter* extract to the infinite fun of Martha! They miss you very much—they send their "united loves." Vinnie rode with Howland yesterday, and Emily Fowler and [William Cowper] Dickinson also, at the same time—had a fine ride. The Reading club seems lonely—perhaps it weeps for you.

4. Dr. Webster was hanged on August 30, 1850, and "the remains were buried in his lot in Mt. Auburn" (*Express,* September 6, 1850).

Dwight Cowan does very well—the Horse is quite "uncommon." Hunt is shingling the barn. We are going to have some new hens— a few.

I reserve the close for bad news—we cant come to hear Jennie[5]— we are coming, but cant now. There are several reasons why—the first we are not near ready—Miss Leonard is coming this week— Grandmother is coming to see us—if we go now we cant *stay* any— we cannot come now and again—it would be all haste and confu- sion—we should have to hurry home, and we do not think it best. We shall come before long, when we are all prepared—"two monu- ments of the past" would make quite a stir in Boston! You must'nt be disappointed, nor blame the folks at all—they would be perfectly willing if we tho't best ourselves. Give our love to our friends, thank them *much* for their kindness; we *will* come and see them and you tho' now it is not convenient. All of the folks send love. Your aff Emily.

Mother says if there's anything more you want, if you will only write us Mrs Kimberly will make it—also if you have any things which you would like to send home Henry Kellogg is there, and you can send by him. Write as often as possible. Take care of yourself—

Special love to Emily, and the little cousins.

[*Note enclosed*]

Dear Austin

I expect you will think us strange & ungrateful to refuse coming to Boston now, though should you know all the reasons for our decision your opinion might be different. If I had plenty of money at my command I would not hesitate one moment, but the *Worcester* friends expect us there when Aunt Elisabeth comes & t'would be too early to go *there* now & we can not go again, be- cause travelling is rather *expensive* you know. Besides, if we go now, our visit must be too *short* to suit me & the Worcester visit omitted entirely for the Summer. I want to hear *Jenny* more than I can ex- press here & did I act entirely from impulse, you would certainly see me.

Father is kind, allows us to *do* as we choose, still approves of our decision. We shall come to Boston another time, when we take the Worcester trip. We miss you *some*. Dont kill any boys. I am afraid you *will*.

5. Jenny Lind gave concerts in Boston on June 18, 20, 23, 25 and 27, 1851.

I had a nice horse back ride Saturday, with Howland, Dickinson & Emilie Fowler. My love to Joel & the other friends.

Vinnie

[*Note enclosed*]

Austin,

I want a copy of the Acts of the Last Session of the General Court. Call at the office of the Secretary of State, & get a copy of these which they distribute to the people, & send me by mail. Leave both ends of the wrapper open, to save postage.

Your father
E.D.

Monday morning

The last sentence in Edward Dickinson's note, admonishing his son not to waste postage, cannot be dismissed as mere parsimony. It implies more than the saving of a few pennies. A hundred years ago it was not miserly to be frugal; it was indecent not to be. This is a trivial instance of a deep-set characteristic.

No New England trait was more ingrained than thrift and few have been more ridiculed. Founded on the teachings of the Bible, wherein waste is coupled with sloth and misery, thrift had long been a virtue. Once it had been a necessity. You saved or you starved. But in 1851 necessity could no longer explain the loathing of waste. Material possessions to be sure were still in some cases hard to come by, and expensive. One was careful of what one had. Machines had not yet taken the value out of things. But although there was no oversupply of necessities, neither was there any lack. The Dickinsons like other Amherst people could afford to buy what they needed. Requirements were modest and there was enough for all.

In daily practice, however, frugality had little to do with demand and supply. Saving things that were scarce was thrift only on the surface. Underneath lurked a categorical imperative—the expression of an inner purpose rooted in moral law. Waste was wrong. It was offensive quite apart from what was saved or what was wasted. To get the most good out of anything was not stinginess; it brought a sense of achievement. I might go further: to throw away a thing for which a possible use might be found not only smacked of dissoluteness; it was spiritual profligacy. Only the profligate indulged in such practices, and "wastrel" was a stinging term of opprobrium.

Nowhere was abhorrence of waste better exemplified than in the conduct of the household. Who can forget the vases of newspaper spills on New England kitchen shelves, the tapers with which candles and lamps were lighted from the fireplace or stove! This not only saved matches; it utilized the paper. Loose ends of time, too, as well as bits of paper and ends of string, were put to useful purpose. Though you might squander hours in carrying out imaginary obligations, you never indulged in what Oliver Wendell Holmes called "irresponsible rest."

In the preparation of meals frugality was a constructive undertaking. Food was placed on the table in ample quantities, but you took only what you wanted and you ate all you took. In dressmaking, what could not be used at the time would be sure to come in handy later on. So there were "piece trunks" and drawers for odds and ends of materials—dress goods, ribbons and laces—and boxes of millinery fragments, flowers and feathers not too much frayed to use again. In the garden, wood ashes from stoves and fireplaces were scattered over the plants, thereby putting the ashes to work and improving the quality of the vegetables.

In the Amherst of my childhood the owner of such a household, Emily's contemporary, was one of my cherished friends. She used to allow me to sit in a corner of her kitchen while certain rites were being performed. Preparing food for her chickens, among the plumpest in town, was one of those rites. As a part of their diet they received a coarse brownish powder which I later discovered was ground-up prune stones saved and dried for the purpose.

The old adage, "Eat it up; wear it out; make it do," sums up this attitude of mind. As Mary Lyon said, "Economy is not always doing without things. It is making them do the best they can."[6] Thrift was of the essence of right living, a part of self-mastery, the ultimate aim. Housework, to which Emily Dickinson gave her time, afforded plenty of scope for using things to best advantage. Not unrelated is her frugal terseness of style which makes the most of a word.

6. Gilchrist, *Life of Mary Lyon*, 29.

Closely allied to the practice of thrift was a feeling for what was seemly. In Massachusetts the first green peas of the season were said to mature on the seventeenth of June, Bunker Hill Day. It so happens that the first salmon used to be brought to Boston markets at about that time. I knew an old gentleman on whose calendar this was a fixed date. Before June 17 he could not be induced to touch either salmon or green peas, his favorite foods. His stand could not be ascribed entirely to thrift, though expense may have shaded it, but for him everything had its proper time and place. In waiting for the appropriate day on which to partake of delicacies he enjoyed, he followed his sense of what was fitting.

There was another element in this staunch point of view. To throw away anything for which a use might eventually be found was not only wasteful; it was slovenly. In this sense thrift implied a nicety, a neatness of handling, like what an expert craftsman calls a sense of tools. Good workmanship comes from a feeling akin to the satisfaction of solving a mathematical problem, "beautiful with the perfection of a neat, clean fact, or a calculation adroitly executed," in the words of Sir Osbert Sitwell.

Mass production may have destroyed thrift as a virtue, but not its value. For when waste follows in the wake of plenty it is not materials alone which are lost. The human casualty is damage to a sense of good workmanship.

CHAPTER XIII

Jenny Lind and the Summer of 1851

1

JENNY LIND, who had arrived in New York on September 1, 1850, was providing the thrill of the moment. The response of the public to her first concert in Castle Garden on September 11 had been fantastic. On the thirteenth the *Express* printed this item: "Jenny Lind lost her glove on the street; it was picked up and sold to an ardent admirer, who charges two shillings for an inside kiss, and half for an outside one."

The rush to hear her turned into a stampede. In Boston, where she gave a concert on September 28, she created a "furor." Ossian E. Dodge—he of "Ossian's Bards" who toured New England providing "chaste, unique and fashionable entertainment"—occupied a seat directly in front of the singer for which he was said to have paid $628. A weekly column entitled "Jenny Lind Items" appeared in country newspapers. Men wore "Jennie Lind ties." Young girls were inspired to emulate her in song. Emily as usual retained her composure.

Intending to return to Sweden during the summer, Jenny Lind came back to Boston in June, 1851, for a series of five "farewell" concerts. But her plans were changed and she remained in America for another year. Austin's comments on her singing received from Emily the following reply:

Sunday evening [June 22, 1851]

I rec'd your letter Austin, permit me to thank you for it, and to request some more as soon as it's convenient—permit me to accord with your discreet opinion concerning Swedish Jennie, and to commend the heart brave eno' to express it—combating the opinion of two civilized worlds, and New York into the bargain, must need considerable daring—indeed it had never occurred to me that amidst the Hallelujahs one tongue would dare be dumb—and much less I assure you that this dissenting one should be my romantic Brother! For I had looked for delight and a very high style of rapture in such a youth as you—Father perused the letter and verily for joy the poor man could hardly contain himself—he read and read again, and each time seemed to relish the story more than at first. Fearing the consequences on a mind so formed as his, I seized the exciting sheet, and bore it away to my folio to amuse nations to come.

"If it had only come" in the language of your Father "a single day before," in the twinkling of an eye "it had been transferred to the *Paper*" to tell this foolish world that one man living in it dares to say what he *thinks*—nor heeds if some dog bark. So soon as he was calm he began to proclaim your opinion—the effect cannot be described—encomium followed encomium—applause deafened applause—the whole town reeled and staggered as *it* were a drunken man—rocks rent—graves opened—and the seeds which had'nt come up were heard to set up growing—the sun went down in clouds—the moon arose in glory—Alpha Delta, All Hail!

We have all been rather *piqued* at Jennie's singing so well, and this first calumnious whisper pleases us so well. We rejoice that we did not come—our visit is yet before us.

The *Bonnet* came safely Saturday, and is pronounced by *us all* to be *very beautiful*—mother is very much pleased with it, says it is "just to her mind," you could'nt have suited us better *possibly* if you'd tried.

Mother wants me to thank you for all your pains and trouble, and says you "are very kind to do so much for your mother."

You hav'nt told us yet as you promised about your home—what kind of people they are—whether you find them pleasant—whether those timid gentlemen have yet "found tongue to say"—do you find the life and living any more annoying than you at first expected—do you light upon any friends to help the time away—have you whipped any more bad boys—all these are solemn questions, pray give them proper heed!

Two weeks of your time are gone, I cant help wondering sometimes if you would love to see us, and come to this still home—I cant help wanting to see you now and then at times and my interviews with you at the *Barn* are frought with a saddened interest. I suppose I am a fool—you always said I was one, and yet I have some feelings that seem sensible to me, and I have desires to see you now that you are gone which are really quite intelligent. Dont take too much encouragement, but really I have the hope of becoming before you come quite an *accountable being!*

Why not an "eleventh hour" in the life of the *mind* as well as such an one in the life of the *soul*—greyhaired sinners are saved —simple maids may be *wise,* who knoweth?

The yard round the house has been mowed and presents quite a fine appearance—Dwight continues to do very well. Baalis Sanford was here last week; has gone to Bridgwater now, and will be here again sometime this week.[1]

Our Reading Club still is, and becomes now very pleasant— *Stebbins* comes in to read now, and *Spencer*—t'would not be so if *you* were here—the *last* time *Charles* came in when we had finished reading, and we broke up with a *dance*—make your own reflections at the story I just told you—the Tutors come after us, and walk home with us—we *enjoy that!* A *Senior Levee* was held at Prof and Mrs Haven's on Tuesday of last week—quite an oldfashioned time —Vinnie said [?] dodging *Chapin* was the only fun they had there— Vinnie played pretty well! There's another at the President's this next Friday evening—"Clarum et venerabile" Seniors! Emily Fowler inquires for you—also M. and Susie—Give my love to my friends, and write me as soon as you can—the folks all send their love. *B F N. is married.*

The Dickinsons' neighbors on the south were the James Kelloggs, whose daughter Emeline is often mentioned. Next on the north, a small house was occupied by a succession of tenants, some of whom were more acceptable than others. The Edwin Pierce family, occupants of the moment, had many children. Edwin and his brother Frank sold plows and plow castings and, under the name of E. S. and F. A. Pierce, became the proprietors of a "Cheap Store" dealing in groceries and general merchandise.

The special friends referred to in the next letter were all juniors, all members of the Alpha Delta Phi fraternity: Ebenezer Burgess became a well-known physician; Henry Root attended the Harvard Law School, graduating in the same class with Austin Dickinson. Brainerd Harrington was a quiet youth from the hills whom Austin had found particularly congenial because of his love of the out of

1. Baalis Sanford of the class of 1845 was the older brother of John Sanford, Austin's friend; Milan Stebbins, Charles Fowler, and Lucius Chapin were seniors; the Reverend Dr. Haven was professor of philosophy. B. F. Newton was now practicing law in Worcester. He was married on June 4, 1851.

doors. His Commencement "disquisition" in August, 1852, was entitled "The Influence of Natural Scenery on Character."

Having suggested that his sister use "a simpler style," Austin received the following rejoinder. In addition to the postmark and "Paid 5," the envelope carries a notation in Edward Dickinson's writing, "Paid Box 47."

[*To Wm Austin Dickinson. Care of Loring Norcross Esq. Boston. Mass.; postmark: Amherst Ms. Jun 30*]

Sunday   afternoon [June 29, 1851]

At my old stand again Dear Austin, and happy as a queen to know that while I speak those whom I love are listening, and I am happier still if I shall make *them* happy.

I have just finished reading your letter which was brought in since church. *Mr* Pierce was not out today, the wife of this same man took upon her *his* duties, and brought the letter *herself* since we came in from church. I like it grandly—very—because it is so long, and also it's *so* funny—we have all been laughing till the old house rung again at your delineations of men, women, and things. I feel quite like retiring, in presence of one so grand, and casting my small lot among small birds, and fishes—you say you dont comprehend me, you want a simpler style. *Gratitude* indeed for all my fine philosophy! I strove to be exalted thinking I might reach *you* and while I pant and struggle and climb the nearest cloud, you walk out very leisurely in your slippers from Empyrean, and without the *slightest* notice request me to get down! As *simple* as you please, the *simplest* sort of simple—I'll be a little ninny— a little pussy catty, a little Red Riding Hood, I'll wear a Bee in my Bonnet, and a Rose bud in my hair, and what remains to do you shall be told hereafter.

Your letters are richest treats, send them always just such warm days—they are worth a score of fans, and many refrigerators—the only "diffikilty" they are so very *queer,* and *laughing* such hot weather is *anything* but amusing. A little more of earnest, and a little less of jest until we are out of August, and then you may joke as freely as the Father of Rogues himself, and we will banish care, and daily die a laughing! It is *very* hot here now, I dont believe it's any hotter in Boston than t'is here—we cant lie down to sleep lest we wake up in burning. I verily *baked* in bed the last time I retired, but now adopt a method of keeping up all night which having never *tried* I think will turn out nicely! I hope you're very careful in working, eating and drinking when the heat is so great—there are temptations there which at home you are free from—beware the juicy fruits, and the cooling ades, and cordials, and do not eat *ice-cream*, it is so very dangerous—the folks think much about you, and are so afraid you'll get sick by being rash or imprudent—for our sakes Austin wont you try to be careful? I know *my* sake a'nt much, but Vinnie's is considerab[l]e—it weighs a good many pounds—when *skin and bones* may plead, I will become a *persuasion*, but you have *other* friends who are much more substantial. I know of *sisters twain*—Oh Youth, come back again, they sing—you ask me of the "postscript"—it's coming—the writers are well, and come often to see Vinnie and me—they do not have any *rides* except Martha went with Barton on horseback the other morning. Root has quite left the field—our little neighbor Jones we are happy to say is faithful. We talk of you together, and intersperse remarks with snatches from your letters.

You ask about the carriage, it is to be done this week, when you get home we'll ride, perhaps we will "take a tour".

Mother feels quite anxious to know about your *clothes,* washing, ironing, &c. Vinnie suggests in connection that she may sometimes occur to mind when you would like collars washed—I told her I would'nt tell you—I hav'nt however decided whether I will or not. I often put on five knives, and four and another tumbler forgetting for the moment that "we are not all here", it occurs to me however, and I remove the extra and brush a tear away in memory of my brother.

We miss you now and always—when God bestows but *three* and one of those is witholden the *others* are left alone. *Moody Cook* took tea here Saturday—he came to see "his pony" and it being suppertime Father asked him to stay—he took *your* seat at the table which led to some remarks concerning yourself, and your absence, which your ear may hear. "Somehow he and Austin always *were* good friends—*he* was none of your *mean* boys—doing *small mean* things, and there was something in him which always made *folks mind*—when Austin was at home Austin was *in town*" tho' this I comprehend not the nescessity of *stating* it seeming quite instinctive, and not needful to prove. Father told him about your early youth, your love for trade and driving—instanced *Hens* and *Bees* as nearest illustrations. By the way—I forgive you that *fraud* of 25 *cts* and hope Almighty Jove will be very merciful! Father thinks Moody Cook put spirit in the cider when he was here in the spring, and thinks *you* understand it, and that yourself and Moody are in some way joking him—he has thought so much about it that he said he should write, and ask you—we young ones laugh in our sleeves,

and think he is rather crazy. Father is as uneasy when you are gone
away as if you catch a trout, and put him in Sahara—when you *first*
went away he came home very frequently—walked gravely towards
the barn, and returned looking very stately—then strode away
down street as if the foe was coming—*now* he is more resigned—
contents himself by fancying that "we shall *hear* today," and then
when we *do not* hear, he wags his head profound, and thinks without a doubt there will be news "tomorrow". "Once one is two" once
one *will be* two ah I have it here! I wish you could have some
cherries—if there was any way we would send you a basket of them
—they are very large and delicious, and are just ripening now—
little Austin Grout comes every day to pick them, and mother takes
great comfort in calling him by name, from vague association with
her departed boy. Austin, to tell the *truth,* it is very still and lonely.
I do wish you were here despite the darkened [word illegible]
they are bad enough in darkness, I really dont feel willing that they
should come to the light thro' such a daring medium. Emeline and
Sarah took a trip sometime since, and have not yet returned—
from all that I can learn I conclude that "I tell Eliza" is his con-
soling now—in other language Austin—she has become "Miss
Mills".

Root has been here twice—B Harrington once, and others in due
proportion— W. Dickinson is going to write you—Bowdoin is
"around". The railroad is a "workin"—my love to all my friends.
I am on my way down stairs to put the teakettle boiling—writing
and taking tea cannot sympathize—if you forget me now your right
hand *shall* it's cunning.

Emilie.

Plans for a railroad to Amherst, in the making for several years,
were about to materialize. Emily refers here to the preliminary
meetings, however, not to actual construction, which did not begin
until February, 1852.

[*Note of June 30 enclosed*]

Dear Austin

"We hav'nt been zactly so intimate lately & we used to be"
& while I think the fault on your part entirely, I am going to be
very noble & "let by gones be by gones" Emilie has fed you on air
so long, that I think a little "sound common sense" perhaps wouldnt
come amiss *Plain english you know* such as Father likes. You did'nt

say you were sorry we refused hearing Jenny Lind. Did you really expect we should come? Would Aunt Lavinia like to see us *next week* if we should chance to come? We talk of it. Is Aunt L. going to be in Boston all summer? When does Emilie go home? We wish you were at home, these warm days. It's very lonely here some times. Our carriage has not arrived yet. We shall expect it Saturday. Father took Emilie & me to ride Wednesday morning & we climbed a mountain & had quite a romantic time, picked flowers, talked sentiment &c. *Horse* has been suffering, for a few days from a fit of indisposition, though we think now recovery in prospect. E[meline] & H[enry] dont make much progress, the former having been absent for three weeks. Horse back riding has'nt gone but once, t[h]en twas "pretty comfortable". However, I am going to revenge [?] & buy a pony for my own. I am saving all my money for the purpose, & I would like to have you as my *agent* select a sound animal & charge it to my account & for your trouble I will give you my note of "I o u" to be "*sincerely*" paid at the appointed time, should the animal prove a good article. We sew a good deal & feel always busy. The reading club is quite pleasant, though we miss you always there. Root & Harrington called here last evening. Burgess has called once. Emilie Fowler's Mr Dubledy is in town, called here Saturday. There have been two parties since you went away one at Prof Havens, the other at Dr Hitchcocks. We have a good deal of company. I'm going to ride this afternoon with a cousin [George Dickinson] of William D's from New York. Is Joel going to take me to New York & when? Please tell me if you know. I presume I have omitted half the words which should be here, but my hurry is my only excuse. How is Mr Withington? Dont get sick. Vinnie Direct the next letter to me.[2]

A week later Emily wrote the letter containing the well-known description of Jenny Lind's concert in Northampton on Thursday, July 3, 1851. The first part of this letter has not previously been published. The quizzical tone of the opening sentences is in the same vein as a letter Emily wrote about thirty years later to her cousin Mrs. Sidney Turner (Clara Newman) of Norwich, Connect-icut, in which she says:

The cordiality of the Sacrament extremely interested me when a Child, and when the Clergyman invited "all who loved the Lord

2. An unsigned letter dated June 30, 1851, was mistakenly attributed to Emily Dickinson in *Letters*, 1931, 78-80. The address of the writer, "24 Centre St., Cam-bridge," was that of Edward Dickinson's sister Lucretia and her husband, the Reverend and Mrs. Asa Bullard.

Jesus Christ, to remain," I could scarcely refrain from rising and thanking him for the to me unexpected courtesy, though I now think had it been to all who loved Santa Claus, my transports would have been even more untimely.

In her youth Emily went to church with the family, throughout her twenties at least. But no matter how eloquent the preacher, the mere ability to be vocal about things that lie deepest was distasteful to her. There was among those old New Englanders a strange mixture of reticence about personal affairs, even if quite innocuous, a reluctance to publish personal letters, for instance, and a kind of display of their intimacy with the Almighty. They were never in any doubt as to what He would wish. This left Emily aquiver. For her, those who "talk of hallowed things, aloud, and embarrass my dog" were not confined to the laity.

And there were ministers as well as deacons whose Sunday piety did not carry over into weekday behavior. Of such a "smooth and oily man of God"—as Charles Sumner characterized the Reverend Charles W. Upham of Salem—Emily could write:

> He preached upon breadth
> Till it argued him narrow. . . .

If a preacher did not measure up to standard he did not thereby impair the standard however; he only discredited himself.

[*To Wm Austin Dickinson. Care of Loring Norcross Esq. Boston. Mass.; postmark: Amherst Ms. Jul 7*³]

Sunday afternoon [July 6, 1851]

I have just come in from Church very hot, and faded, having witnessed a couple of Baptisms, three admissions to church, a Supper of the Lord, and some other minor transactions time fails me to record. Knowing Rev A.M. Colton so thoroughly as you do, having received much benefit from his past ministrations, and bearing the relation of "Lamb" unto his fold, you will delight to know that he is well, and preaching, that he has preached *today* strange as it may—must seem, that just from his benediction I hurry away

3. The first postage stamp (3¢) in the collection appears on the envelope of this letter.

to you. No doubt you can call to mind his eloquent addresses, his earnest look and gesture, his calls of *now today*—no doubt you can call to mind the impetus of spirit received from this same gentleman and his enlivening preaching—therefore if you should fancy I'd looked upon the *wine* from walk or conversation a little fierce or fiery, bear all these things in mind!

Our church grows interesting, Zion lifts her head—I overhear remarks signifying Jerusalem, I do not feel at liberty to say any more today! I wanted to write you *Friday,* the night of Jennie Lind, but reaching home past midnight, and *my room* sometime after, encountering several perils starting, and on the way, among which a *kicking horse,* an inexperienced driver, a number of Jove's thunderbolts, and a very terrible rain, are worthy to have record. All of us went—just four—add an absent individual and that will make full five—the concert commenced at eight, but knowing the world was *hollow* we thought we'd start at six, and come up with everybody that meant to come up with us—we had proceeded some steps when one of the beasts showed symptoms, and just by the *blacksmith's shop* exercises commenced, consisting of kicking and plunging on the part of the horse, and whips and moral suasion from the *gentleman* who drove—the horse refused to proceed, and your respected family with much chagrin dismounted, advanced to the hotel, and for a season halted—another horse procured, we were politely invited to take our seats, and proceed, which we refused to do till the animal was warranted—about half thro' our journey thunder was said to be heard, and a suspicious *cloud* came travelling up the sky—what words express our horror when rain began to fall —in drops—sheets—cataracts—what *fancy conceive* of drippings and of drenchings which we met on the way—how the stage and its mourning captives drew up at Warner's hotel—how all of us alighted, and were conducted in, how the rain did not abate, how we walked in silence to the old Edwards Church and took our seats in the same, how Jennie came out like a child and sang and sang again, how boquets fell in showers, and the roof was rent with applause—how it thundered outside, and inside with the thunder of God and of men—judge ye which was the loudest—how we all loved Jennie Lind, but not accustomed oft to her manner of singing did'nt fancy *that* so well as we did *her*—no doubt it was very fine— but take some notes from her "Echo"—the Bird sounds from the "Bird Song" and some of her curious trills, and I'd rather have a Yankee.

Herself, and not her music, was what we seemed to love—she has an air of *exile* in her mild blue eyes, and a something sweet and touching in her native accent which charms her many friends —"Give me my thatched cottage" as she sang she grew so earnest she seemed half lost in song and for a transient time I fancied she *had* found it and would be seen "na mair," and then her foreign accent made her again a wanderer—we will talk about her some-time when you come—Father sat all the evening looking *mad,* and *silly,* and yet so much amused you would have *died* a laughing —when the performers bowed, he said "Good evening Sir"—and when they retired, "very well—that will do," it was'nt *sarcasm* ex-actly, nor it was'nt *disdain,* it was infinitely funnier than either of those virtues, as if old Abraham had come to see the show, and thought it was all very well, but a little excess of *Monkey*! She took 4000 $/*mistake* arithmetical/for tickets at Northampton aside from all expenses. I'm glad you took a seat opposite Lord Mayor —if he had sat in your lap it had pleased me even better—it must seem pretty grand to be a city officer and pat the Sheriff's back, and wink to the Policemen! I'm sorry you got so tired, and would suggest respectfully a Rose in every thorn!

We are all pretty comfortable, and things get along well—Bow-doin has gone home haying—the Tutors are hanging on—Francis March is here, had not been *seen* at the latest—the Exhibition came, and *went* for all that I know—choosing not to "tend." Sanford— Valedictorian—Stebbins—Salutatorian—Carr [W. S. Karr]—Oratio Philosophico—I do not know the rest, except that Wm Washburn has a Dissertation from the delivery of which he is "respectfully excused."[4]

About our coming to Boston—we think we shall probably *come* —we want to see our friends—yourself and Aunt L's family—we dont care a fig for the *museum,* the stillness, or Jennie Lind. We are not going to stay long—not more than a week—are sorry Emily is gone, but she shall come to see us—how long will Joel be gone—we have talked of Thursday or Friday as the earliest that we should come—perhaps not until Monday—can you write a line and send to us tomorrow, how long Joe will be gone? Give our love to our friends, and tell them we will write them and let them know our plans as soon as we hear from you—Thank them if you please for their kind invitation, and tell them we are coming not to see *sights* but *them,* and therefore all the stillness will not incommode us. I saw Martha Friday—she inquired all about you, and said she was going to write, and Susie too that I could send next time— it has rained ever since then and it is raining now, now so I dis-appoint you—have patience Austin, and they shall come next time. Father says your letters are altogether before Shakespeare, and he will have them published to put in our library. Emily Fowler's re-

4. Francis A. March of the class of 1845, who became a distinguished philolo-gist, was at this time practicing law in New York City. William Washburn, a senior, was the son of the Reverend Royal Washburn, whose widow had married Deacon David Mack on May 16, 1844—his third wife.

gards—Love from us all—dont know what I say I write in such a hurry. Your aff Sister Emily

[*Note enclosed*]

Austin,

Tell Aunt Elisabeth to stay in Boston till we come. We expect a visit from her, also with out fail!

I was pleased with Jenny Lind. I had a horse back ride Thursday morning, like riding better than ever. Perhaps you will go with me *sometime*.

I am glad, Withington is so kind to you. I had a nice ride with cousin George Dickinson, last Monday. I think you'd like him. He reminds me some of *you*. Decidedly superior to *most* of our cousins, I assure you. Perhaps we will see you this week—Father perfectly *dotes* upon you & your letters. Mrs Mack is coming to spend the day Wednesday. I went to college exhibition with John *Sanford*.

Vinnie

2

Both Emily and Vinnie dabbled in music for a time. After hearing Jenny Lind, Vinnie tried to improve her singing. Emily is said to have played better than Vinnie. One who heard her strange, limited repertoire said that before seating herself at the piano Emily covered the upper and lower octaves so that the length of the keyboard might correspond to that of the old-fashioned instrument on which she had learned to play.

Whether or not Emily Dickinson was really musical is hard to say. Toward the end of her life she was at least a discriminating listener. But her comments on Jenny Lind and on the playing of the Germanian Band from Boston do not enlighten us much, having more to do with histrionics than with music.

Her next letter announces a change of plan:

[*Envelope missing*]

Sunday night [July 13, 1851]

You must'nt *care* Dear Austin, Vinnie and I cant come—it is'nt any matter, I hope you a'nt troubled about it. We *were* disappointed at first, because not very well, and thinking while at Boston we would see Aunt Lavinia's physician; we did'nt want to tell *you why* we were bent on coming, thinking now you were *gone* you might feel anxious about us—we knew it would worry you and therefore made our plans to come now and see you, and saying not a word to any but Aunt L—follow the advice of her Homeopathic physician. If we had told our reasons for coming at this time we should have seemed more reasonable in wishing so much to come, and we knew you would have us *at once* tho' it might not be convenient.

We are not very sick, we work and go out and have company, but neither of us are well—Dr [John M.] Brewster has fussed until we are satisfied that he does'nt know what ails us, and we are tired and wearied of being under his care. Father has great confidence in Dr Dean of Greenfield, and thinks sometime this week we may ride up and see him. If he cant tell what ails us, nor do us any good, then we will come in the autumn and see the other man.

Do not feel anxious for us—I think we will soon be well—we have been ailing sometime but not very seriously, and Dr Brewster has tried one thing after another till we are most discouraged, and sometimes we think to ourselves that we shant ever get well, but I guess we shall. I long so to see you Austin, and hear your happy voice, it will do us all more good than any other medicine. Do not blame yourself for what you said and did, and do not allow our friends to reproach themselves at all—we knew you had kindest reasons and thank you and them for so kindly consulting our pleasure.

When you go back in the autumn we can see you then, and you must'nt think anything about it, or care for what you wrote. I dont know what Father said—did know not he was going to write you —your sorrowful letter was our first intimation that ever he had written, and I guess we felt as badly to get such a letter from *you,* as you did or *could* at what you heard from Father. I feel so grieved, dear Austin, if Father has blamed *you, Viny and me* are the ones if there is fault *anywhere*—we should have told you frankly why we wished to come—but we did'nt want to worry you as we feared we should. Never mind it Austin—we shall see you soon and tell you all those things which seem obscure when written. Tell all our friends and Joel that we would love to see them but think we will stay at home and come some other time— much love to them all. Joel must'nt look in any of the Depots for he wont find us there, and it would give him trouble. You must'nt think of such a thing as seeing us now, for we have *decided,* and think not best to come.

Vinnie will write you soon—sends her love—mine too. Mother

sends her love and a little curl of her hair "to put you in mind of your affectionate mother"—Sue and Martha send love. Bowdoin is haying yet—we expect him soon—take good care of yourself Austin, we shall all be so happy to see your face at home.

It is late—Goodnight—Vinnie is snoring!

The curl of their mother's hair, in a bit of tissue paper, is still pinned to the first page of the letter.

Though official records indicate that the summer vacation of the Endicott School began on July 14, 1851, Austin appears to have remained in Boston until the end of the month.

[*Envelope missing*]

Sunday evening [July 20, 1851]

Seems to me you are hardly *fair*, not to send me any letter—I was somewhat disappointed to be thus overlooked—my note from you once a week, had come so very punctually I *did* set my heart on getting a *little something*—even a *word* of love, a *line* not *quite* unmindful, and I had from my heart fully and freely forgiven you, but now I am very angry—you shall not have a tender mercy—as I live saith me, and as my inkstand liveth you shall have no peace until all is fulfilled. If I thought you would *care* any I would hold my tongue so tight that Inquisition *itself* should'nt wring a sentence from me—but t'would only punish *me* who would fain get off *un*-punished, therefore *here I am*, a'nt you happy to see me? Since you did'nt write to *me* I pocketed my sorrows, and I hope they are being sanctified to my *future* good—that is to say—I shall "know what to expect,["] and my "expectations will *not* be realized," you will pardon the freedom I use with your remarks. How it made us laugh—Poor little Sons of Erin—I should think they would rue the day that ever you came among them. Oh how I wish I could see your world and it's little kingdoms, and I wish I could see the King—Stranger—he was my *Brother*! I fancy little boys of several little sizes, some of them clothed in *blue* cloth, some of them clad in *gray*—I seat them round on benches in the schoolroom of my mind—then I set them all to shaking—on peril of their lives that they move their lips or whisper—then I clothe you with authority and empower you to punish, and to enforce the law, I call you "Rabbi—Master," and the picture is complete! It would seem very funny, say for [S]usie and me to come round as Com-mittee—we should enjoy the terrors of 50 little boys and any specimens of *discipline* in your way would be a rare treat for us. I should love to know how you managed—whether government as a *science* is laid down and executed, or whether you *cuff and thrash* as the occasion dictates—whether you use *pure law* as in the case of *commanding,* or whether you *enforce* it by means of sticks and stones as in the case of *agents*—I suppose you have authority bounded but by their lives, and from a remark in one of your earliest letters I was led to conclude that on a certain occasion you *hit the boundary line!* I should think you'd be tired of school and teaching and such hot weather, I really wish you were *here* and the Endicot school where you *found* it—whenever we go to ride in our beautiful family carriage, we think if "wishes were horses" we *four* "beggars would ride." We shall enjoy brimfull everything *now* but *half* full, and to have you home once more will be like living *again!*

We are having a pleasant summer—without one of the five it is yet a *lonely* one—Vinnie says sometimes—Did'nt we have a *brother* —it seems to me we *did*—his name was Austin—we call, but he answers not again—Echo—where is Austin—laughing—"where *is* Austin"? I do hope you'll be careful so as to come home *well.* I wish they need not *exhibit* just for once in the year, and give you up on *Saturday* instead of the next week Wednesday, but keep your courage up and show forth those Emerald Isles till School Committees and Mayors are *blinded* with the dazzling! Would'nt I love to be there with certain *friends* of mine—*Toilet Cushions,* and "*Carpets,*" &c, is what I mean! If this should seem *obscure* let me recommend *West St* as an appropriate "Pony" together with *other* ponies, such as Mr and Mrs Cutler! Susie is at home—Martha is in Burlington seeing a friend of her's. I see more of Susie than of any other girl. She said the last time I saw her, she had'nt had a "talk since Austin went away"—she and Martha too seem to miss you much, and talk a great deal of seeing you. Abby Wood has gone to visit Miss Peck in New Haven—the rest of the girls are at home. Sprague's *shop* was set on fire one night last week, and came very near burning up—the roof was burnt off, and it met some other injuries—a process is going on to find out the offenders.[5] John Emerson has come, and has entered himself as a student in Father's office—he carries about the sail of a good sized British vessel, when he has oped his mouth I *think* no dog has barked. Root spent with us Friday evening—inquired for you with interest, and said he'd be glad to see you.

Our apples are ripening fast—I am fully convinced that with

5. The wheelwright shop of Sprague and Perkins at the foot of Mount Pleasant burned on July 15. John Emerson, valedictorian of the class of 1849, became a tutor in Amherst College in the fall of 1851. He was a great admirer of Eliza Coleman.

your approbation they will not only *pick themselves,* but arrange
one another in baskets, and present themselves to be eaten.
   Love from all to all there—to *Joel*—hope he is better.
                                                                Emilie.
   Mother and Vinnie send their love. We all want to see you. Mrs
S. E. Mack, and Mrs James Parsons want to see you. John Sanford
acts like a simpleton since he got the valedictory, he is so delighted,
he dont know what to do.

[*To Wm Austin Dickinson. Care of Loring Norcross Esq. Boston.
Mass.; postmark: Amherst Ms. Jul 28*]

                                        Sunday night [July 27, 1851[6]]

   "I will never desert Micawber" however *he may* be forgetful of
the "Twins" and me, I promised the Rev Sir to "cherish" Mr
Micawber, and cherish him I *will,* tho Pope or Principality, endeavor
to drive me from it—the "Twins" cling to him *still*—it would quite
break his heart abandoned tho' he be, to hear them talk about him.
Twin *Martha* broke her heart and went to the Green Mountain,
from the topmost cliff of which she flings the *pieces* round. Twin
Susan is more calm, tho' in *most deep* affliction. You'd better not
come home, I say the *law* will have you, a *pupil* of the law, o'er-
taken *by* the law, and brought to "condign punishment"—scene for
angels and men—or rather for *Archangels* who being a little *higher*
would seem to have a 'vantage so far as view's concerned! "*Are*
you pretty comfortable tho," and are you deaf and dumb and gone
to the asylum where such afflicted persons learn to hold their
tongues?
   The next time you a'nt going to write me I'd thank you to let
me know—this kind of *protracted* insult is what no man can bear
—fight with me like a man—let me have fair shot, and you are
"caput mortuum" et "cap a pie", and that ends the business! If
you really think I so deserve this silence tell me why—how—I'll

   6. In *Letters,* 1894, 110 (*Letters,* 1931, 106), this letter was dated July 23, 1852.
The burning of Mr. Kimberly's barn, however, took place on July 26, 1851
(*Express,* August 1, 1851). Edward Dickinson was agent for the Hampshire
Insurance Company.
   F. A. Palmer was Mr. Kimberly's neighbor on the north, John Leland on the
south. (See map opposite page 62.) A. P. Howe was landlord of the Amherst
House, Henry Frink of the new Hygeian Hotel (American House) about to
open. One of the attractions offered by the latter hostelry was a "Lunch and
Ordinary" in the basement, where meals could be had at any hour of the day
or night with "hot oysters, tripe and coffee" (*Express,* December 31, 1852).

be a *thorough* scamp or else I wont be *any,* just which you prefer!

Taylor [Horace W.] of Spencer's class went to Boston yesterday, it was in my heart to send an *apple* by him for your private use, but Father overheard some of my intentions and said they were "rather small"—whether this remark was intended for the *apple,* or for my noble self I did not think to ask him—I rather think he intended to give us *both* a cut—however, he may go!

You are coming home on Wednesday, as perhaps you know, and I am very happy in prospect of your coming, and hope you want to see us as much as we do you. Mother makes nicer pies with referance to your coming, I arrange my tho'ts in a convenient shape, Vinnie grows only *perter* and *more* pert day by day.

The Horse is looking finely, better than in his life, by which you may think him *dead* unless I add *before.* The carriage stands in state all covered in the chaise-house—we have *one foundling hen* into whose young mind I seek to instill the fact that "Massa is a comin'!" The garden is amazing—we have beets and beans, have had *splendid potatoes* for three weeks now. Old Amos weeds and hoes and has an oversight of all thoughtless vegetables. The apples are fine and large in spite of my impression that *Father* called them "small."

Yesterday there was a *fire*—at about 3. in the afternoon Mr Kimberly's barn was discovered to be on fire—the wind was blowing a gale directly from the west, and having had no rain, the roofs [were] as dry as stubble. Mr Palmer's house was cleared—the *little house* of Father's, and Mr Kimberly's also. The engine was broken and it seemed for a little while as if the whole street must go. The Kimberly barn was burnt down, and the house much charred and injured, tho not at all destroyed. Mr Palmer's barn took fire and Dea Leland's also, but were extinguished with only part burned roofs. We all feel very thankful at such a narrow escape. Father says there was never such imminent danger, and such miraculous escape. Father and Mr Frink took charge of the fire, or rather of the *water,* since fire *usually* takes care of *itself.* The men all worked like heros, and after the fire was out Father gave commands to have them march to Howe's where an entertainment was provided for them—after the whole was over, they gave "three cheers for Edward Dickinson, and three more for the Insurance Company"!

On the whole it is very wonderful that we did'nt all burn up, and we ought to hold our tongues and be very thankful. If there *must be* a fire I'm sorry it couldnt wait until you had got home, because you seem to enjoy such things so very much.

There is nothing of moment now which I can find to tell you except a case of measles in Hartford. The Colemans were here last week, passed a night here—they came to get John Emerson to travel with Wm Flint [recovering from an illness]. John went to Monson Saturday, and starts with Wm Flint for the White Mts today.

This is one more feather in the Valedictorian's cap, I guess he thinks he will certainly have her now—I mean will have *Eliza.* If *I* loved a girl to disstraction, I think it would take some coaxing before I would act as footman to her crazy friends—yet love is *pretty solemn.* I dont know as I blame John. He is going to be Tutor next year. Vinnie and I made Currant Wine one day last week, I think it will suit you finely.

You remember James Kellogg's Dogs—the one they kept for a watch dog was poisoned by someone and died last week. Chauncey Russell, Frank Pierce, and George Cutler are somewhere on the coast catching fur and fishes, but principally the *former.* Perhaps they have called on you during their travels sometime tho' I dont know their route exactly. Would'nt I love to take a peep at Old Fanueil and all the little Irish, the day of the city fair?

Goodbye Sir—Fare you well, my benison to your school.

The folks all send their love. My compliments to Joel.

[*Note from Edward Dickinson enclosed*]

Austin.

I had a letter from J. W. Lyman. from N. York. on Saturday, saying that he was there, & would pay as soon as he could. You cannot, therefore, get any money of him. If the fence [?] is sent, get money of Joel, or get trusted till I can send it.

E.D.

Monday noon

Call at Sec'y of State's Office and ask for copy of the Acts & Resolves, for me—also one for Horace Lyman, Rep. of Sunderland.

E.D.

CHAPTER XIV

The Schoolmaster Returns to Boston

O N JULY 30, 1851, Austin Dickinson came home for a month's stay, after which he returned to Boston for a year of teaching in the Endicott School.[1] The term opened on September first.

On the same day in a distant city another school opened—Mr. and Mrs. Archer's Boarding and Day School for Young Ladies, 40 Lexington Street, Baltimore, Maryland.[2] One of the new teachers was Susan H. Gilbert of Amherst.

Although Austin apparently destroyed his letters from Sue and drafts of his letters to her, he did keep several first drafts of letters to her sister Martha. He labeled the package, "Copies of notes to 'Mat.'" Rough and unfinished, they suggest a friendship of a peculiarly delicate nature. The mere fact that he kept them for more than

1. Manuscript records of the School Committee show that "William A. Dickinson" was nominated as "Usher" on August 5, 1851, "subject to the usual term of probation." His nomination was confirmed on August 29. When the fall term opened on September 1, 1851, he took his place as assistant master of the Endicott Boys' School, the master of which was John F. Nourse.

2. Robert Harris Archer, a graduate of the U.S. Military Academy at West Point in 1832, had resigned his commission five years later to become principal of this "Female Academy" with "about 130 pupils from various sections of the Union."

In Martha Dickinson Bianchi, *The Life and Letters of Emily Dickinson* (Boston, 1924), 27, in a postscript to a letter said to have been written in 1855, Emily is quoted as saying "Why can't I be a delegate to the great Whig Convention?" This was the convention for the nomination of Daniel Webster as president. Mr. Webster died in 1852. The complete letter was printed in Bianchi, *Emily Dickinson Face to Face*, 215-217, together with others Emily sent to Sue Gilbert during her year of teaching in Baltimore. All of these letters, on pages 205-220 of *Face to Face*, said to have been sent in 1854 and 1855, were written between September, 1851, and June, 1852.

forty years, finally confiding them to my mother together with other treasured packages, is in itself worth noting. Everyone seems to have loved Martha Gilbert. Her sisters Harriet and Susan both named their daughters for her.

Soon after reaching Boston Austin drafted the following letter to Martha in Amherst. Those were the days when girls sent flowers to young men. The culprit who had failed to deliver them was sixteen-year-old Howard Sweetser.

[September 14(?), 1851]

Mat

I wonder if I am forever destined, in all my intercourse with you girls, to be the victim of those dire Misses, take—conception, Apprehension & the rest—grim visaged Spinsters, who are ever toiling at the ropes, tolling away the happiness of us poor mortals.

Not to mention the *uncomfort* they caused me while at home. 'Twas only Wednesday the note I had written for Sue to receive on her first arrival in Philadelphia was returned, my friend failing to find her, and *last* evening I received a box, enclosing notes from you & Sue—and the remains of a once beautiful bouquet, which you supposed were ornamenting my table and engaging my thoughts, as they certainly would have done, had they been received, a week and a half ago.

Until night before last, I never heard a breath of your having sent me anything. The evening before I had received a mysterious letter from Andover, which was to inform me that Howard Sweetser had left at 91 Washington St. a box for me. I was, of course, very curious as to its author & contents, and went immediately after it, but no one in the store knew or had ever heard of either Howard Sweetser, his father [Luke], or any box having been left for me or anybody else. I, at once, wrote to Howard for an explanation, but said nothing to anyone else, thinking that perhaps some one here was in the joke, until night before last, Emily incidentally making some remark about the bouquet you sent me my eyes were opened, and I told them all about my letter, and not having received the box, and *such* a torrent of wrath & indignation as that luckless Howard Sweetser was, for about 15 minutes the unconscious object of.

I received another note from him yesterday afternoon, in reply to mine asking an explanation, in which he says the box was from *Sue* Gilbert, & he guessed it isn^{nt} any great loss if I dont find it. How-

ever one of the clerks *did* find it & sent it up to me last evening.
So I have got it, at last and though the flowers are withered and
odorless, the pleasantness of the act of sending them is fragrant still
and will long be held in sweet remembrance.

I thank you just as much, and am made just as happy in this
their late receipt as if they had come to me sooner, though there
would, I confess, have been a *peculiar* pleasure in receiving so
beautiful an evidence of remembrance so soon after leaving home,
when hours are days & days months, and a dark veil seems almost
to have fallen between your memory and the scenes of but yesterday, so dimly do they come before the mind, and you half believe
they never *really* existed, except in dreams. That Monday morning's ride, Mat, was too pleasant to seem real, long. Another sun
had hardly risen when I began to doubt if I had not just taken it,
while sleep yet lingered on my eyelids—if it was not a dream ride,
and not a real one.

But thanks to the *materialistic* element in my philosophy, a
doubt is not yet to overcome my credence in the actuality of so
delightful a little incident as that ride. I enjoyed it capitally. It
was exactly the sort of thing I like, so unexpected, so independent
& so merry. I have felt happier for it ever since.

And now Mat, for yourself, since Sue left & the girls. Has the
time passed as slowly as you anticipated. Have you "cloistered yourself" yet? Have you not found someone else you like to talk with?
Do you have any agreeable walks? Do you see Bowdoin often? Does
he offer you the cheering consolation of his stoic philosophy?
Does Chauncey continue to manufacture pants & vests in Hadley?—
Have you read "life of an Author"? Have you been down to our
house? Have you heard from Sue. Is she to keep a diary for you.
Do you know whether Bowdoin is keeping one for me? Do you
think I am *"mean"* or *"inconsistent"* & *"indifferent"* because I
have^nt written before? I *meant* to have written you sooner, and
should have done so had not the girls been here. I have devoted
every spare moment to them, but I have thought of you a great
deal & so have they, and we have often talked of you. You will
see them again this week probably, and me I ween [?] about Cattle
Show. I shall be home then if possible.

Write me Mat. I shall be delighted to hear from you any time.
I shall write to Sue in a day or two.

[*Good night. Good night.*] Good night.

On September 4, 1851, Emily and Vinnie had left Amherst for the
long-planned visit in Boston. After a stopover in Worcester, they
arrived on the sixth and remained at their Uncle Loring's home

until September 22. One morning Austin received the following penciled note:

[*To Austin Dickinson, Endicot School*]

You are very thoughtful Austin to make so many plans for our pleasure and happiness, and yet it is so hot we hardly feel like going out. We had a very pleasant evening, and will tell you something when you come. Will you come after school this morning? It seems a great while since we've seen you. We are very warm indeed, but quite happy—we will be very much so if you will be sure to come. Vinnie and I like your friend very much.

You must'nt feel disappointed for yourself or for us, because it is so hot that we dont think we can come—it will be cooler some-time. Vinnie is comfortable—did you rest well last night, and have a nice breakfast this morning.

Sure to come!

Emily

Fanny sends her love [Fanny Norcross was four]

The girls' visit coincided with an unprecedented event. In a three-day "Railroad Jubilee" held in Boston, September 17-19, 1851, enthusiasm for railroad construction reached a climax.[3] An international celebration, it was intended primarily to mark the completion of the "great lines of railway uniting tidewater at Boston with the Canadas and the Great West." President Fillmore and his cabinet, the governors of the New England states, Lord Elgin, governor general of Canada, with his staff and cabinet, all came to celebrate the joining of the two countries. According to the *Massachusetts Register* for 1852,[4] the celebration "passed off with great magnificence." The Amherst *Express* (September 26) reported that more than three hundred thousand persons took part in the jubilee, which included regattas, levees and a military ball followed by fireworks. Led by dignitaries riding in barouches, the procession,

3. "Rail Road," the customary spelling in the 1850's, has been retained only in titles. For a comprehensive picture of roads, canals and railroads a century ago the reader is referred to George P. Baker, *The Formation of the New England Railroad Systems* (Cambridge, 1937); and Edward Chase Kirkland, *Men, Cities and Transportation 1820–1900*, 2 vols. (Cambridge, 1948).

4. *The Massachusetts Register, a State Record for the Year 1852*, 333. This book of general information about the Commonwealth was published annually.

representing every trade and organization in the city, took two hours and twenty-five minutes to pass. The *Express* adds laconically, "the State pays the bill."

Since Austin and his sisters were together there is no letter describing the occasion. But the young people can hardly have failed to see at least part of so "stupendous" a spectacle. Three days after it was over Emily and Vinnie entrained for Grout's Corner. From there they took the stage to Amherst by way of Sunderland.

As a means of public transportation the stagecoach was fighting to maintain its supremacy as its monopoly was being slowly undermined. Mistrusting mechanical devices, farmers of the Amherst countryside had been loath to transfer their allegiance to such a newfangled contraption as railroads. (See Emily's letter of February 6, 1852.) There were good stage connections with neighboring towns where travelers took the train to Boston, or to Springfield and New York. Boston, less than a hundred miles distant, could be reached by "fast mail" in eight hours. What more was needed?[5]

When at last the arrival of "the cars" in Amherst appeared inevitable, more trips were scheduled for the stagecoach. Articles in local newspapers, designed to enhance the prestige of the conveyance and its driver, presented him as a personage of importance. To quote the *Express* (April 16, 1852), "Everybody knows and aspires to be known by the stage-driver. . . . The little boys remember it a month if the stage-driver speaks to them," for there was "magic" in his calling.[6]

5. In 1851 the railroads nearest Amherst were the Western, from Boston to Albany; the Connecticut River Rail Road, running from Greenfield south along the west bank to Hartford and New Haven, Connecticut; and the Vermont & Massachusetts, an extension of the Boston & Fitchburg, to Vernon and Brattleboro, Vermont, on the west bank of the river.

The Amherst traveler could reach Boston by either of two routes: the faster, by stage fifteen miles north to Grout's Corner (referred to as "Grout's Corner, Miller's Falls," or as "Grout's in Montague"), thence by the Vermont & Massachusetts through Fitchburg to Boston; or by stage about twenty miles southeast to Palmer and thence on the Western through Worcester to Boston. The usual route to New York was by stage seven miles to Northampton, and from there by rail to Springfield, New Haven and New York. The New Haven–Northampton Canal had not been much used for several years.

6. A description of this dignitary, driving his four coal-black horses into town, appears in the *History of Amherst*, 387-388:

"On the road his powers were autocratic. . . . The innkeepers along the route

The day after returning to Amherst Emily wrote to her brother.
Like subsequent letters, this one is directed to him in care of Joel
Norcross, now in business for himself as an importer of cutlery and
fancy goods at 31 Milk Street.

[*To Wm Austin Dickinson. Care of Joel Norcross. Boston. Mass.;
postmark: Amherst Ms. Sep 24*]

Tuesday evening [September 23, 1851]

We have got home, dear Austin—it is very lonely here—I have
tried to make up my mind which was better—home, and parents,
and country; or city, and smoke, and dust, shared with the only
being whom I can call my Brother—the scales dont poise very
evenly, but so far as I can judge, the balance is in your favor. The
folks are much more lonely than while we were away—they say
they seemed to feel that we were straying together, and together
would return, and the *unattended* sisters seemed very sad to them.
They had been very well indeed, and got along very nicely while
we were away. When Father was gone at night, Emeline stayed with
mother. They have had a number of friends to call, and visit with
them. Mother never was busier than while we were away—what
with fruit, and plants, and chickens, and sympathizing friends, she
really was so hurried she hardly knew what to do.

Vinnie and I came safely, and met with no mishap—the boquet
was not withered, nor was the bottle cracked. It was fortunate for
the freight car, that Vinnie and I were there, our's being the only
baggage passing along the line. The folks looked very funny, who
travelled with us that day—they were dim and faded like folks
passed away—the conductor seemed so grand with about *half a
dozen* tickets, which he dispersed, and demanded in a very small

---

deferred to his wishes and treated him to the best their bars held in store. His
was the sole responsibility for coach and horses and passengers and mail and
merchandise committed to his charge. The duties of engineer, conductor, mail
and express agent of the modern train rested on him alone. He knew each mile
of his route as the modern pilot knows each rock and shoal and current of the
harbor. . . . He must be an expert reinsman, capable of making any repairs
necessitated by accident to coach or harness, impervious to heat or cold, rain-
proof and wind-proof, a cyclopedia of information regarding his own and connecting routes. The men who combined these qualities in high degree were rare,
and gained more than local reputation."

Professor Kirkland (*op. cit.* I, 54) adds still other duties to the list.

space of time—I judged that the *minority* were travelling that day, and could'nt hardly help smiling at our ticket friend, however sorry I was at the small amount of people, passing along his way. He looked as if he wanted to make an apology for not having more travellers to keep him company.

The route and the cars seemed strangely—there were no boys with fruit, there were no boys with pamphlets—one fearful little fellow ventured into the car with what appeared to be publications and tracts—he offered them to no one, and no one inquired for them, and he seemed greatly relieved that no one wanted to buy them.

At Sunderland, we happened to think that we might find John Thompson, and find John Thompson we did, just sitting down to dinner—he seemed overjoyed to see us—wants very much to see you—asked many questions about yourself and school, all of which we answered in a most glowing manner, and John's countenance fell—we asked him if he was happy—"why, *pretty* happy"—they promised him "35." according to his own story—only 25. of whom have yet made their appearance—he thinks he will not stay more than half a term, and wonders "how in the world" you contrived to be so happy, and like Sunderland people so exceedingly well. He says he has no plan, should he not remain there—seems to be somewhat sober at the little he finds to do—studies law in his leisure. "The Elder" had gone to dinner—Mr Russell was there, seemed quite pleased to see us for our brother's sake—he asked us all about you, and expressed his sincere pleasure in your present prosperity—"wished they had had you *there*," when Thompson was not present! There has been nothing said about Mr Russell lately, as Landlord of the Hygeian—Frink is there himself, and seems to like it well, and probably will keep it, I judge from what they say. They have a great deal of company, and everything goes on well.

You wanted us to tell you about the Pelham Picnic—the folks did'nt know that there had ever been any, so I cannot give you any information there. I suspect if there *was* a party, it was composed of persons whom none of us know. Calvin Merrill is married, you *know*—he had a great wedding party at the residence of his bride, the blooming Mrs Benjamin—Tim Henderson and "suite," and Cotton Smith and suite were among the guests, and were suitably honored.[7] Mr Merrill resides with the recent *Mrs* Merrill, alias Mrs Benjamin, *more* alias, Mrs Thompson—for the sake of the widowed lady for the third time a *bride*. I hope her buried Lords are buried very low, for if on some fine evening they should fancy

7. On September 9, 1851, Calvin Merrill, aged 54, married Fanny D. Benjamin, aged 46. It was the third marriage for both.

to *rise* I fear their couple of angers might accompany them, and exercise themselves on grooms who erst were widowers, and widows who are brides.

Bowdoin has gone home on account of his eye—he has'nt been able to use it since we went away—the folks are afraid he will never have the use of it—he dont know when he'll come back—probably not, till it gets well, which we fear may not soon be—at present his father is sick—pretty sick with the dysentery. Howland is here with father—will stay a while I guess. They go to Northampton together, as it is court there now and seem very happy together in the law. Father likes Howland grandly, and they go along as smoothly as friendly barks at sea—or when harmonious stanzas become one melody. Howland was here last evening—is jolly and just as happy—really I cant think now what *is* so happy as he. He wants to see you, says he is going to write you. Sanford is in town, but as yet we hav'nt seen him. Nobody knows what the fellow is here for.

You remember [John] Lord the Historian who gave some lectures here—he has come round again, and is lecturing now on the "Saints and Heroes." He gives them at the chapel—I guess all of us shall go—tho' we were too tired last evening. Prof Jewett has come and is living with his wife east of Gen Mack and *his* wife. Pretty perpendicular times, I guess, in the ancient mansion. I am glad we dont come home as we used, to this old castle. I could fancy that skeleton cats ever caught spectre rats in dim old nooks and corners, and when I hear the query concerning the pilgrim fathers—and imperturbable Echo merely answers *where,* it becomes a satisfaction to know that they are there, sitting stark and stiff in Deacon Mack's mouldering arm chairs. We had'nt been home an hour, when Martha came to see us—she was here on Saturday after the stage came in, and was dreadfully disappointed because we did not come. She has'nt changed a bit, and I love her dearly. She was so indignant about her sweet boquet—she said it was kind and fragrant, and would have comforted you in the first few days of exile. I showed her all my treasures—I opened the little box containing the scented beads—I tried it on my wrist, she exclaimed it was how beautiful—then I clasped it on her own, and while she praised it's workmanship and turned it o'er and o'er, I told her it was her's, and you did send it to her—then that sweet face grew radiant, and joyful that blue eye, and Martha seemed so happy to know you'd tho't of her, it would have made you happy—*I* know! She said she should write you—if she has not, she will directly—she has had a letter from Sue—she is situated very pleasantly, and tells her sisters here that she can see no reason why she should not be happy —they are very kind to her—she loves some of her scholars. I hav'nt seen Martha long enough to ask but a very little, but I will find out everything before I write again. It has rained very hard all day, it has been "dark and dreary" and winds "are never weary."

Mother has three shirts which she is going to send you besides the ones we bro't—also a pair of bosoms which her forgetful son failed to carry away. She will send you the whole by the first good opportunity, and we shall send some fruit as soon as we have a chance. It is beautiful—*beautiful!!* Mother sends much love and Vinnie. Your lonely Sister Emily

Father has just home come, having been gone today. I have therefore not till now got a glimpse of your letter. <Sue's> address is, Care of Mr Archer—40. Lexington St. I will keep the note till I see, or send, to Bowdoin. I answer all the questions in your note but one—*that* I cannot do till they let you come home—that will be *soon,* dear Austin—do not despair—we're "with you alway, even unto the end"! Tho' absence be not for "the present, joyous, but grievous,["] it shall work out for us a far more exceeding and "eternal weight" of *presence!*

Give our love to our Boston friends—tell them we are well and got home very nicely. Vinnie found the shawls very comfortable and thanks them much for them.

Speaking of *fireworks,* tell Joe we wont ever forget him—*forget him?*—never—"let April tree forget to bud"—etc!

Will Aunt Lavinia sometime tell Mrs Greely how beautifully the boquet came, and how much it has been admired?

You may if you would like, remember both of your sisters to Misses Knight, and French, also tell Mr Nurse we are very sorry for him!

[Note from Edward Dickinson enclosed]

The Academia Society present a tax ag^t you of $1.50 in 1850. If you owe it, I will pay it—I think the matter was talked about, last summer, & I supposed I had paid it. Write me how it is.

Let me know how much money you paid for the girls.

Emily and Vinnie were not expected to pay their own bills. The men of the family attended to such matters. Though provided with pin money, about one dollar a week, it was not customary for women to handle larger sums. In accordance with custom, any loose change which might reach their hands was usually washed before it was spent.

[*To William Austin Dickinson. Care of Joel Norcross. Boston. Mass.; postmark: Amherst Ms. Oct 2*]

Wednesday noon [October 1, 1851]

We are just thro' dinner, Austin, I want to write so much that I omit digestion, and a *dyspepsia* will probably be the result. I want to see you more than I ever did before—I should have written again, before I got your letter, but thought there might be something which I should love to tell you, or if you should ask any questions, I would want to answer those. I received what you wrote, at about 2½ oclock yesterday. Father brought home the same, and waited himself in order to have me read it—I reviewed the contents hastily—striking out all suspicious places, and then very *artlessly* and unconsciously began. My heart went "pit a pat" till I got safely by a remark concerning Martha, and my stout heart was *not* till the manuscript was over. The allusion to Dick Cowles' grapes, followed by a sarcasm on Mr Adams' tomatoes, amused father highly. He quite *laid it to heart*, he thot, it was so funny. Also the injunction concerning the college tax, father took occasion to say was "quite characteristic."

You say we must'nt trouble to send you any fruit, also your clothes must give us no uneasiness. I dont ever want to have you say any more such things. They make me feel like crying. If you'd only *teased* us for it, and declared that you *would* have it, I should'nt have cared so much that we could find no way to send you any, but you resign so cheerfully your birthright of purple grapes, and do not so much as *murmur* at the departing peaches, that I hardly can taste the one or drink the juice of the other. They are so *beautiful* Austin—we have such an *abundance* "while *you* perish with hunger."

I do hope someone will make up a mind to go before our peaches are quite gone. The world is full of people travelling *everywhere,* until it occurs to you that you will send an errand, and then by "hook or crook" you cant find any traveller, who for money or love can be induced to go and convey the opprobrious package! It's a very selfish age, that is all I can say about it! Mr storekeeper Sweetser has been "almost persuaded" to go, but I believe he has put it off "till a more convenient season," so to show my disapprobation, I shant buy any more gloves at Mr. Sweetser's store! Dont you think it will seem very cutting to see me pass by his goods, and purchase at Mr Kellogg's? I dont think I shall *retract* should he regret his course, and decide to go *tomorrow,* because it is the *"principle"* of disappointing people, which I disapprove!

You must not give it up, but that you will *yet* have some, there *may* be some good angel passing along your way, to whom we can entrust a snug little bundle—the peaches are very large—one side a *rosy* cheek, and the other a *golden,* and that peculiar coat of velvet and of down, which makes a peach so beautiful. The grapes too are fine, juicy, and *such* a purple—I fancy the robes of kings are not a *tint* more royal. The vine looks like a kingdom, with ripe round grapes for kings, and hungry mouths for subjects—the first instance on record of subjects devouring kings! You *shall* have some grapes dear Austin, if I have to come on foot in order to bring them to you.

The apples are very fine—it is'nt quite time to pick them—the cider is almost done—we shall have some I guess by Saturday, at *any rate Sunday noon!* The vegetables are not gathered, but will be before very long. The horse is doing nicely, he travels "like a bird," to use a favorite phrase of your delighted mother's. You ask about the leaves—shall I say they are falling? They had begun to fall before Vinnie and I came home, and we walked up the steps through "little brown ones rustling." Martha and I were talking of you the other night, how we wished you were here to see the autumn sun set, and walk and talk with us among the fading leaves.

Martha is very long talking of you and Susie, she seems unreconciled to letting you go away. She is down here most every day—she brings Sue's letters and reads them. It would make you laugh to hear all which she has to tell—she writes in excellent spirits, tho' Martha and I think they are *"unnatural,"* we think she is so gay because she feels so badly and fancies we shant know. Susie asks in every letter why she dont hear from you—she says "Emily and Austin were going to write *so soon,* and I'll warrant I wont hear from either of them, for *one while."* I sent her a letter Monday—I hope if you have not written, you *will* do very soon, for Susie is so far off, and wants so much to have you. Martha wants to see you very much indeed, and sends her love to you. Emily Fowler has gone traveling somewhere with her father—New Haven and New York are to be the stopping places. Charlie has yet no school. I suspect he needs *your aid* in passing himself off somewhere. I have smiled a good many times at that fruitful ride to Sunderland, and the blessings and favors which accompanied it, to Charles. Vinnie tells me *she* has detailed the *news*—she reserved the *deaths* for me, thinking I might fall short of my usual letter somewhere. In accordance with her wishes, I acquaint you with the decease of your aged friend—Dea Kingsbury.[8] He had no disease that we know of, but gradually went out. Martha Kingman has been very sick, and is not yet out of danger. Jane Grout is slowly improving, tho' very feeble yet. "Elizy" has been in Boston, she came home Tuesday night. She asked her friends, and they endeavored to find you, but could not.

She says she told you when you were at home that she should go in *October*, and you were coming to see her, but as she changed her mind and went *earlier*, she did not suppose of course, that you would know she was there. She was very sorry not to be able to find you.

Father has written to Monson to have them all come up here and make us a family visit—I hardly think they will come. If they dont, sometime, next week mother means to go to Monson, and make *them* a little visit. Bowdoin's eye is better, and he has got back to the office—Howland has gone to Conway—will probably be here again in the course of two or three weeks. Did Vinnie tell you that she went with him to Ware, and how it made a hubbub in the domestic circle?

Emeline and Henry are just learning to say *"we"*, I think they do very well for such "new beginners."[9] There was quite an excitement in the village Monday evening. We were all startled by a violent church bell ringing, and thinking of nothing but fire, rushed out in the street to see. The sky was a beautiful red, bordering on a crimson, and rays of a gold pink color were constantly shooting off from a kind of sun in the centre. People were alarmed at this beautiful Phenomenon, supposing that fires somewhere were *coloring the sky*. The exhibition lasted for nearly 15. minutes, and the streets were full of people wondering and admiring. Father happened to see it among the very first, and rang the bell *himself* to call attention to it. You will have a full account from the pen of Mr Trumbull, whom I have not a doubt, was seen with a large lead pencil, a noting down the sky at the time of it's highest glory. Father will write you soon—the day that your letter came with a list of our expenses—he seemed very busy, so I did'nt read *that* part, and his hands have been so full that I have seen no time when I could show it to him—however he knows of all our expenditures, and will make everything right when you next come home —you dont like to have us ever speak of such things, but father wrote to know, and I tho't you might think it strange he should not write about it after your letter came. You will be here now *so soon—*

8. Samuel Kingsbury died September 27, 1851, *aet.* 88 years, 8 months.

9. Although they were not married until October 9, 1855, the engagement of Emeline Kellogg and Henry Nash was announced at this time.

we are impatient for it—we want to see you, Austin, how much I cannot say here. Your aff Emily

Your clothes are in beautiful order, everything in waiting to have some way to send. I have heeled the lamb's wool stockings, and now and then repaired some imperfections in the destined shirts— when you *wear* them, you must'nt forget these things. You made us very happy while we were away. Love from all the folks, with a how I do want to see you!

An incident in the preceding letter (first published in *Letters,* 1894, pages 92-93) was used by the late Genevieve Taggard to dramatize Edward Dickinson's love of natural beauty.[10] Miss Taggard had somehow gained the impression that Mr. Dickinson rang the church bell to draw the attention of his neighbors to a sunset. It was not a sunset, however, but a most unusual display of northern lights which Mr. Dickinson wished the people not to miss. As Emily anticipated, J. R. Trumbull, editor of the *Express,* who "was seen with a large lead pencil a noting down the sky at the time of it's highest glory," described it in the next issue of his paper, on October 3. Under "Amherst, Local Items," is a paragraph entitled "Aurora Borealis." "One of the most splendid displays of this kind we remember ever to have witnessed was visible on Monday night [September 29]. It first extended in a broad belt from east to west, and continued expanding till the whole heavens were covered with a brilliant red light. The rays converged at the zenith and extended over the concave above like folds of crimson cloth attached to the center by a ring. It continually varied in intensity and continued for something like an hour."[11]

10. Genevieve Taggard, *The Life and Mind of Emily Dickinson* (New York, 1930), 128. See also Whicher, *This was a Poet,* 27, and Van Wyck Brooks, *A Chilmark Miscellany* (New York: 1948), 220.

11. In another column, headed "Among Items on Various Subjects," is a paragraph on "Magnetism and the Aurora Borealis": "During the splendid aurora borealis very singular phenomena were noticed on the telegraph wires. Atmospheric electricity often traverses the wires causing brief interruptions, but on Monday evening there was another element at work. Strong magnetic currents seemed to pass from the ground into the wires, at times so powerful as to overcome the batteries on the line, and reverse the magnetic poles, making queer work, and causing some perplexity among the operators. The magnetic currents of the earth were evidently joining in the merry dance of their brilliant partners in the sky. So powerful was this disturbing influence upon the wires that neither of the three telegraph lines between Boston and New York were able to operate through, during that evening."

It is too bad that Miss Taggard's mistake has been incorporated in the legend for it conveys a wrong impression of Edward Dickinson. She was correct in saying that he was announcing "nothing more alarming than the beauty of the sky," to be sure. But to ring a church bell to call attention to a sunset is a little different from summoning the town to view a night sky pulsating with "auroran widths" such as no one had ever seen before.

Edward Dickinson had a proprietary attitude toward Amherst. "These are my people," he said of his fellow townsmen. He must see to it that they did not miss the unique display. To arouse them he used the bell which hung in the First Church—his church.[12] This bell was heard regularly, twice every day. Austin wrote that it "rang at noon and at nine in the evening as notice for dining and retiring," a practice continued, he says, until 1862. And it was used also to get immediate attention, as for fire. Emily said that "the bells tick in Amherst for a fire, to tell the firemen." Perhaps Mr. Dickinson's action was not really so strange as it appears at first glance. But the fact remains that, hard headed as he was, a heavenly spectacle did move him to uncommon action.

Enclosed in the same envelope with Emily's letter, one from Vinnie mentions several of Austin's Boston friends: "McCurdy" and Mary Nichols, Edmund Converse and his sister Kate. The Honorable George Ashmun, of whom Vinnie speaks, was described by George S. Merriam, biographer of Samuel Bowles, as "the most brilliant and impressive personality at that time in western Massachusetts."[13] He had been a classmate of Edward Dickinson at Yale. Samuel Williston of Easthampton was a benefactor of Am-

---

In the 1851 revised edition of Webster's *American Dictionary of the English Language,* S. F. B. Morse defines the "Electro-magnetic-telegraph" in these words: "An instrument or apparatus, which, by means of iron wires, conducting the electric fluid, conveys intelligence to any given distance with the velocity of lightning." Even this definition reflects the amazement aroused by the telegraph early in the age of electricity. It never ceased to be an object of wonder to Emily Dickinson, as when she tells her brother not to forget that he can "*telegraph* father." She not only underscores the verb; she adds an exclamation point. (See letter of March 14, 1854.)

12. Not until after the completion of the new meeting house of the First Church in 1868 was the bell which his father rang transferred to the Baptist Church. *Cf.* Dickinson, "Representative Men," 56.

13. Merriam, *Life and Times of Samuel Bowles,* I, 35.

herst College whose adopted son, Lyman, was Austin's classmate and friend. "Kate's Storrs" was Henry M. Storrs, the young man who was to marry Jane Hitchcock's sister Catherine on March 9, 1852.

[*Enclosed with Emily's letter of October 1*]

Wednesday Eve

Dear Austin

Dont be frightened at this great sheet, for I shant fill it all. I only want to tell you a little what's going on these days. We "have very kind feelings" towards you this term, dont miss you any though, "oh no no." Its so long since Ive written to anyone, that I hardly know what to say first. There is a "free *sile*" meeting here to night & now I hear the *cheers* distinctly. Father took us all to Northamton, last week, dined at the Mansion house, where as it was court week, we met various distinguished persons, Mr Ashmun, *daughter* &c. After spending a little time there very pleasantly, we went to Easthampton & took tea with Mr Williston, had a delightful visit. They asked for you & were disappointed, not to see you with *us.*

Lyman Williston said he should soon write to you, remembers the class meeting at the office, with pleasure.

Howland took me to *Ware,* last Friday. Father was highly excited about it, of course. Sanford & Howland are both gone. Saw Sanford once. Bowdoin has been away, but is at home, now. Elisabeth Tyler called here, yesterday feels rather *lonely.* Emilie & I attended the Freshman levee, last evening. The class appeared well, I thought. Kate's Storrs came home with me. Amherst is still. We miss *Sue* dreadfully. Jane went to South Hadley to day. Mary Ann Dickinson is boarding at Mrs Lymans, will recite to Prof. Haven. Mr Storrs enquired particularly for *you.* We had a grand visit at Boston, reached home safely, think the northern route a dreary one, dont you? Saw Thompson in Sunderland, delivered Mr *Graves letters.* I think Emilie is very much improved. She has really grown *fat,* if youll believe it.

I am very strict with her & I shouldnt wonder if she should come out bright some time after all. I'm anticipating Cattle show, on your account, very much. Quite a nice time we[']ll have! Are you any more reconciled to Boston than formerly? We want to send you some fruit & if an opportunity presents itself, certainly shall.

Emilie Fowler is away. Martha was here this afternoon, read to us, one of Sue's letters. Found some music at home from *Withington*. Received magazine, yesterday from him. Your garments are all ready for transportation. We shall send them soon as possible. I wish my favorite boy would copy for me the words to Nelly Bly. You can send them in your letter I guess. We wish you could be at home this Fall, the Scenery is charming now, the leaves just turning. I dont know whether Edmund Converse will expect to come home with you or not. Manage him as you think best, thats all I can say, hope youll have a very happy time at home, we shall be glad to see either or both of your friends. Give my love to Miss Nichols.

Miss Leonard comes here tomorrow, in anticipation of your visit! Will you Austin, take the enclosed note to Dr. Wesselhoeft soon as convenient & wait for an answer, as I shall expect a small package perhaps from him. Will you be so kind as to enclose whatever he gives you, in a letter to me, for Im anxious to get it. Take good care of your *health*. Dont be sick. Remember us to enquiring friends. Im tired, Austin, as my writing plainly shows, so good night & good bye.

Vinnie

You will find Dr. Wesselhoeft at home, until ten oclock in the morning & from 3 to 5 in the afternoon. Please wait for an answer or if he should prefer & *you can,* call again. See *him yourself.* Mother says, she will be happy to see both Converse & M. Curdy should you choose to bring them.

While in Boston, Emily and Vinnie had consulted Dr. William Wesselhöft. Emily's interview with this eminent physician brought not only a noticeable improvement in her health but a certain buoyancy of spirit as well. This was not unusual with Dr. Wesselhöft's patients. In his last address before the Homeopathic Society of Boston he summed up the goal of the physician in these words: "The art of awakening and increasing the vitality of the human body, *that* is our highest aim." This high endeavor was communicated by "simplicity, directness, and honesty in speech" (as Elizabeth P. Peabody wrote in her *Memorial* of Dr. William Wesselhöft, published in 1859), and with a "kindness, that though it was habitual and constant as the sun, had a morning freshness about its every manifestation." In fact, "every thing about him was of intrinsic nature." It might be enlightening to investigate the influence of this great man upon Emily Dickinson. (Compare page 508.)

CHAPTER XV

Funerals and Fears

MUCH refreshed by their visit in Boston, the Dickinson sisters had come home in high spirits. But the death of four young friends in quick succession soon plunged them into an atmosphere of grief and gloom. The first was John Spencer, "the most amiable and guileless of men, a model of integrity and Christian consistency of character." On October 12 consumption carried him off at the age of thirty-three, and, as the *Express* observed (October 31), in his death "every family seems to have lost a friend." On October 27, Jennie Grout, aged nineteen, died of an intestinal fever, and on October 30, Martha Kingman, also nineteen, of "brain fever." Two weeks later Ellen Kingman, her sister, succumbed to typhoid fever at the age of thirteen.

Fear of eternal punishment was deep-seated in New Englanders. But hellfire was not the only thing they dreaded—they also feared disease. Each time of year had its special scourge. Brain fever, scarlet fever, typhoid fever, "ulceration of the bowels" and dysentery were to be expected in the summer. And an epidemic was no respecter of persons. In July, 1850, President Zachary Taylor had succumbed to a sudden attack of "bilious fever."

The season for fevers was hardly over when influenza set in. Severe colds, developing into "lung fever" and other "pulmonary complaints," took a heavy toll in Amherst throughout the winter. Little was known about preventive medicine. People died without warning, especially young people, of whom the majority succumbed to consumption.

In our prophylactic age it is hard to imagine how widespread was the fear of illness. In attempting to cope with its appalling mystery they turned to isms and cure-alls, even to magic of a sort. Indeed, witch doctors warding off the evil eye would have approved some of their practices, such as red flannel underwear and a horse chestnut in the pocket. Although lightning and other manifestations of electricity, called "fluids," were looked upon as having a baleful influence, their mysterious power was nonetheless sometimes invoked. For curative purposes this force was dressed up in words that made it sound less sinister, as for instance, "Dr. Christie's Galvanic Belt, Bracelets, Necklace and magnetic fluid for the impaired nervous system."

Everybody was in the habit of "doctoring," usually with patent medicines, remedies not always as benign as red flannel underwear. The columns of the *Express* were filled with advertisements of "botanic remedies," "Indian Turnip (Jack-in-the-pulpit) for the cure of consumptions," "Dr. Corbett's Sarsaparilla for Biliary Obstruction," and "V. H. Schenck's Pulmonic Syrup and Seaweed tonic." Then there were "Dr. Ordway's Humor Discovery and Blood Purifier," "Dr. Weaver's Canker and Salt Rheum Syrup," and "Mrs. E. Kidder's World Renowned Cholera, Dysentery and Diarrhoea Cordial." To nostrums such as these Emily Dickinson preferred a doctor's prescription.

There were of course physicians in Amherst, graduates of well-known medical schools. Each school of medicine had its own methods, though bloodletting was the favorite remedy with them all.

In the United States at this time the vogue of homeopathy was hardly less widespread than in France. A few years before the death in 1843 of its founder, Dr. Ch. Fr. Samuel Hahnemann, his "doctrine" had reached Boston where it was enthusiastically taken up, largely because of the popularity of its chief proponent, Dr. William Wesselhöft. The orthodox school of medical practice became known as "allopathy," a term invented by Dr. Hahnemann, it was said, to characterize the old-line practitioners who did not agree with him.[1] They in turn looked upon homeopathy as a dissenting sect, if not as a positive fraud, largely it was thought because it

1. The terms "allopathy, homeopathy, hydropathy, are now in common household use" (*Express*, July 13, 1849). Compare Emily's letter of March 24, 1852.

demonstrated that common practices such as bleeding with cupping glasses and leeches were unnecessary.

"Motorpathy" was a system of "kinaesthetics." Hydropathy was popular in Northampton where, on Round Hill, a "Hydropathic Institute" flourished. Another water cure, located in Brattleboro, Vermont, a few miles farther north, was conducted, until his death in 1852, by Robert Wesselhöft, brother of Dr. William. Mr. Higginson wrote an amusing account of "a party of Hydropaths" at that institution in May, 1850.[2] Much faith was placed in the curative properties of medicinal springs. An establishment called "Pleasant Valley" was opened in Pelham early in August, 1850. Except on Sunday, when it was closed, the bathhouses built above the stream, later known as "Orient Brook," were extensively patronized.

In spite of all this therapeutic equipment Amherst was swept periodically by scourges of which neither the cause nor the cure was understood. Smallpox sometimes crept as close as Shutesbury (August, 1851) and Barre (December, 1852). Most of all cholera was feared. It decimated entire cities (New York in 1849 and 1853), wiping out whole families in the space of a few hours. On September 8, 1851, Samuel Bowles, the elder, founder of *The Springfield Republican,* died of "malignant dysentery" at the age of fifty-four, a few weeks after his eldest daughter, Mrs. Julia Foote, and her child had succumbed to the same disease. In the face of an epidemic no savage exorcising evil spirits is more helpless than were the people of Amherst a century ago. They turned for help to the Most High. When Horace Greeley's little son "Pickie" died of cholera on July 12, 1849, fasting, humiliation and prayer were publicly prescribed as "appropriate duties." The scourge was an inscrutable dispensation from Almighty God, regarded by many as direct punishment for their sins, and, as such, inevitable and unavoidable.

Each house in the village, hemmed in by neighbors on both sides, had its own well and its own privy. Though there had been a death from cholera in Amherst (August 21, 1849) the contamination of drinking water as a cause was not as yet taken seriously. Four years later (June 3, 1853), the *Express,* noting that "the season for epidemics is approaching," warned its readers that "sink drains

2. *Letters and Journals of T. W. Higginson,* 38.

and out-houses are shamefully neglected and intolerably offensive to all. . . ."

Before the days of Pasteur's discoveries, scientific investigations were only just beginning here and there. A Doctor Chabert of New York is quoted (*Express,* October 22, 1852) as saying: "I believe Asiatic cholera is an aerial epidemic or *poison,* diffused through the atmosphere. This poison is a small green insect, invisible to the naked eye, but easily to be seen under the action of a powerful microscope." Novel ideas such as infection had as yet no hold on country districts.

I have labored this point somewhat in order to emphasize the fact that for the Dickinsons' preoccupation with illness and death there was more than enough excuse. Newspapers kept the subject constantly before them, even dramatizing it to add to the terror. Here, for instance, are a few lines from a ghoulish dialogue which appeared in the *Express* on November 18, 1853. A colloquy among various diseases, it is a positively fiendish skit calculated to make the helpless reader's blood run cold. The opening scene is in a lodging house where Typhus is hovering over a crowd of sleepers. From without is heard the hoarse voice of Cholera calling "Sister! Sister!" To which, under her breath, Typhus replies reassuringly:

> "I am here!
> Doing my work for tomorrow's bier."

Emily Dickinson is charged with being morbid on the subject of death. In youth she was curious about its trappings and the ceremonies connected with it. Later she was made cruelly aware of its presence by the frequent loss of dear friends. Overconscious of death she may have been. From childhood her mother's anxieties had encouraged such an attitude. And the prevalence of heavy colds, often developing into illness fatal to her contemporaries, kept the family in a state of constant apprehension. The death rate among young people was appalling.[3] Furthermore, the Dickinson

3. These deaths occurred in Amherst except as otherwise indicated:

1851

February 5, Betsey Packard, aged 19
March 3, Fanny F. Field, aged 23
April 19, Abby Ann Haskell, aged 19
June 25, J. Francis Billings, aged 20

orchard adjoined the burying ground where the final rites took place. Every funeral procession must pass their house. The wonder is, not that Emily as a young girl thought and often wrote about death, but that any buoyancy of spirit remained.

On Sunday afternoons it was the custom in Amherst to make a pilgrimage to the cemetery with flowers. A little girl who lived a generation later in this same house on Pleasant Street told me how left out she felt when the weekly procession passed by and she had no grave to decorate.

July 17, Ellen M. Russell, aged 19
October 12, John Laurens Spencer, aged 33
October 27, Jane Ballou Grout, aged 19
October 30, Martha A. Kingman, aged 19
November 15, Ellen Mary Kingman, aged 13
December (?) 10, Martha Humphrey, aged 20 (in Southwick, Mass.)
December 17, Emeline J. Packard, aged 24

1852

March 26, Ellen C. Stanley, aged 18
June 7, Catherine, daughter of President Woolsey of Yale, aged 8, died at the Amherst House
July 2, Emily Lavinia Norcross, aged 24 (in Monson, Mass.)
November 28, Jane Thayer, aged 21

1853

January 9, Charles L. Converse, aged 18
March 24, Benjamin Franklin Newton, aged 32 (in Worcester, Mass.)
April 20, Anna Charlotte Warner, aged 11
June 18, Julian Cowles, aged 27
August 15, Enos D. Perry, aged 20
October 10, Charles Morton Howland, aged 22
October 30, Sarah W. Church, aged 22
December 2, Ann Augusta (Mrs. Charles) Hutchinson, aged 21
December 5, Franklin Ebenezer Hawley, aged 21
December 5, William Henry Darling, aged 18
December 29, William Boerhaave Gooch, aged 19
December 20, Frederick Warren Lane, aged 23

1854

March 1, Julia (Mrs. B.F.) Allen, aged 26
March 14, Sarah E. Field, aged 17
March 31, Sarah D. Kellogg, aged 31
May 19, Dwight H. Cowan, aged 23
May 26, Jane Juliette Kingman, eldest and only surviving daughter of Col. Cyrus Kingman, aged 31
November 18, Sarah Humphrey, aged 18 (in Southwick, Mass.)

CHAPTER XVI

More Letters to Boston

1

F OR Austin Dickinson a year of teaching the rudiments of education to small boys was getting under way. On the fifth of
October, in order to take advantage of a chance messenger leaving for Boston early the next day, Emily spent an uninterrupted
Sunday morning writing to her brother. The letter, enclosed in a
tiny envelope measuring 2¼ by 3¾ inches, is without stamp or
postmark.

[*To Wm Austin Dickinson. Boston, Mass.*]

Sunday morning [October 5, 1851]

I dont know why, dear Austin, there is'nt much to say which will
interest you, but somehow I feel bound to let nobody escape me
who may by any accident happen to light on *you.*

I take great satisfaction in the consciousness that no one eludes
my vigilance, nor can by any means rid themselves of whatever bag
or bundle I am disposed to send—and again, Austin, "when the
day is dark and drear and the wind is never weary," a slight recollection may be of some avail in lighting the heart up. It is such a
day *today*—nothing but rain and shower, and shower after
shower of chilly pelting rain. I am at home from meeting on account of the storm and my *slender constitution,* which I assured the
folks, would not permit my accompanying them today.

It is Communion Sunday, and they will stay a good while—
what a nice time pussy and I have to enjoy ourselves! Just now the
sun peeped out. I tell you I chased it back again behind the tallest

cloud, it has not my permission to show its face again till after all the meeting, *then* it may shine and shine, for all pussy and I care!

I was glad to hear from you Austin, and again I was very sorry, if you can reconcile a story so inconsistent. Glad to know you were better—better *physically*, but who cares for a *body* whose *tenant* is ill at ease? Give me the aching *body*, and the spirit glad and serene, for if the gem shines on, forget the mouldering casket! I think you are better now—I fancy you *convalescent* during this rainy day. I am sure that long before *this time* that "hour" has passed away, and the "daughter of the dawn" has touched a note more gay, with her slight "rosy fingers". "No Rose but has a thorn", recollect this, dear Austin, and you will derive a faith rosier than *many* roses, which will quite compensate you for now and then a thorn! It expresses *worlds* to me, "some one to see who cares for [you], and for whom you care", and I think I laughed at the phrase "my own selve's company", as conveying a meaning very clear to me. I dont wonder that little room seems small and lonely, and I dont wonder the folks there seem *smaller still*—I *know* they are very little, very small indeed, I know that scores might vanish and nobody would miss them, they fill so small a crevice in a world full of life; how much you feel the need of a companion there. I wish a smiling fortune would send you such an one, but if you talk with no one, you are amassing thoughts which will be bright and golden for those you left at home—*we* meet our friends, and a constant interchange *wastes tho't* and feeling, and we are then obliged to *repair* and *renew*—there is'nt the *brimfull* feeling which one gets *away*.

Why when Vinnie and I came home, we were *rich* in conversation—we were rich in disdain for Bostonians and Boston, and a coffer fuller of *scorn, pity, commisseration*, a miser hardly had.

Sometimes, I am afraid it will hurt you to stay there. I'm afraid the year you teach will become so embittered that all this blessed country cannot wash it away. Oh I hope not—if indeed no joy is added during one long year, I pray that there be no cankers which shall corrode away! I long for this Boston year to fall from out the circle, to perish and flee away, and be forever gone—your being where you are is a *mutual* trial—both yourself, and us, are for the time bereaved—yet your lot is the hardest, in that while *four anticipate*, in *your* case there's but one—we can gather together and say we are very lonely, and it would be so happy if we were all at home—yet one sustains the other—Vinnie and I console and comfort father and mother—I encourage *Vinnie*, Vinnie in turn cheers *me*—but one and alone, you are indeed dependant, in any pensive hour, dependant on *yourself* too, the very one of *all* least likely to sustain you—if it were not *hope*, it would not be *endurance!* Thank God there is *one* bird that singeth for *forever* and builds her nest

anew in the boughs of paradise! You will have several friends to
see you in the course of the week. Wm Kellogg is going tomorrow—
also Ebenezer Burgess of the senior class—Burgess called on Friday
evening and offerred to carry anything which we would like to
send—he says he shall see you often—I believe he's an Alpha Delta,
and I hope you'll be glad to see him, tho' I dont know enough
about him to know whether you will or not.

Council Cutler was there last week, and said he would like to
see you if he could get time—we told him where you were, but he
came Saturday night and we hav'nt yet found out whether he saw
you or not. How funny it seems to me to have you live in Boston,
and be having calls from our country tradesmen!

Whatever else you forget, Austin, dont cease to remember *Smith,*
who made such a plunge at you on a certain evening—keep *his*
memory green, whatever else betides! I will use my utmost influence
to keep him at home during the rest of your absence, and I'm sure
you will wish me well in so needful an enterprise. Vinnie's love.
Mother sends her love and your waistcoat, thinking you'll like the
one, and quite likely *need* the other. All of the other clothes can
go any time after Tuesday. Your aff Sister

Two days later Emily and Vinnie penciled hasty messages on a
single sheet (folded, not sealed, and without envelope) for their
father to take to Austin.

[To Austin Dickinson, Boston, Mass.]

Tuesday noon [October 7, 1851]

Dear Austin.

Father has just decided to go to Boston. I have no time to write.
We send you a few of our grapes—wish they were nicer—wish too
we had some peaches. I send one remaining one—only a frost one.
It expresses my feelings—that is pretty much all.

Was so glad to hear from you—even a word is valued.

I know how busy you are, I don't think it strange not to hear
more. Howland was here yesterday. Gone today. Thompson was
here Saturday—drank tea with us—dont mean to teach in Sunderland after this week. I have tried Dr Jackson's prescription and find
myself better for it. I have used it all up now, and wish you would
get me some more at the same place if you can. Father has the
Recipe, and will give it to you. I should like to have you get *three*

or four times the quantity contained in the Recipe, as it is so good an opportunity, and I think it benefits me much. Martha sends her love—is well. Bowdoin is better and back again. Spencer is very sick, and will probably not live long.

You will be here soon dear Austin, and then away with my pen. Dont get sick these cool days when fevers are around! Vinnie's love —not that she cares particularly about *seeing* Edmund Converse, but after what was said, she only wanted to be polite, that's all. Our regards to Mr McCurdy, if you are a mind to give them. Love—

Emily

[*On same sheet*]

Bring Mr "*Curdy*" home with you, Austin. Hope you will love the grapes. You may think strange that I spoke of *E. Converse,* but as you asked him *first* to come to Cattle show & I repeated the invitation, I thought twould be rather impolite to say nothing more to him about it. I want to see *you* just as much as if you were coming alone, but if you choose to bring your friends, I think they will be welcome here.

Vinnie

The next letter is badly mutilated. Fourteen lines, crossed out in pencil, but legible, have been placed in italics and enclosed in brackets. Words that have been completely erased are supplied in broken brackets if the meaning is unmistakable; if not, the number of missing words is indicated in brackets, or, if within a bracketed passage, in parentheses.[1]

Edward Dickinson added "Mr. Sweetser, American House" to the address in Emily's writing and, in pencil on the envelope flap, "4 P.M. Your bundle was rec^d by Mr. Kellogg."

[*To William Austin Dickinson, Care of Joel Norcross. Boston. 31 Milk St. Mass.*]

Friday morning [October 10, 1851]

Dear Austin.

Father says he came down upon you so unexpectedly that you hardly had time to recover from your surprise before he was *off*

1. For a key to different types of mutilation see page 59.

again—he says you were so astonished that you hardly knew what to say—he thinks you are not very well, and I feel so anxious about you that I cannot rest until I have written to you and given you some advice. They say Mr Sweetser is going—he may not and he may. I will conclude to risk him. I am very sorry indeed that your eyes have been so troublesome. I really hope they are better and will trouble you no more. You ought to be very careful about using them *any* now—I do not care if you *never* write me a letter, if you'll only spare your eyes until they have got better. I would not spend much strength upon those little school boys—you will need it all for something better and braver, after you get away. It would rejoice my heart, if on some pleasant morning you'd turn the schoolroom key on Irish boys—*Nurse* and all, and walk away to freedom and the sunshine here at home. Father says all Boston would not be a temptation to you another year—I wish it would not tempt you to stay another day. Oh Austin, it is wrong to tantalize you so while you are braving *all things* in trying to fulfill duty. Duty is black and brown—home is bright and shining, "and the spirit and the bride say *come,* and let him that" wandereth come—for "behold all things are ready"! We are having such lovely weather—the air is as sweet and still, now and then a gay leaf falling—the crickets sing all day long—high in a crimson tree a belated bird is singing—a thousand little painters are ting[e]ing hill and dale. I admit *now,* Austin, that autumn is *most* beautiful, and spring is but the least—yet they "differ as *stars*" in their distinctive glories. How happy if you were here to share these pleasures with us—the fruit should be more sweet, and the dying day more golden—merrier the falling nut, if with you we gathered it and hid it down deep in the abyss of basket; but you complain not—wherefore do we? [*I had a long letter from* <Sue> *last Tuesday evening* <*and Mat*> *had one that day and came down here to read it*]—we had a beautiful time reading [*about Susie*] and talking of [three words erased] the good times of last summer—and we anticipated—boasted ourselves of tomorrow [one line erased] the future we created, and all of us went to ride in an air bubble for a carriage. [*We have made all our plans for you and us* (two words erased) *in another year*]—we cherish all the past—we glide adown the present, awake, yet dreaming, but the *future* of ours *together*— there the birds sing *loudest,* and the sun shines *always* there!

[*Martha and I are very much together—we fill each niche of time with statues of you and* <Sue> *and in return for this, they smile beautiful smiles down from their dwelling places. Martha wears the charm when she goes out calling, and many a eulogium is passed upon your gift.* <Sue> *says in her letter she has had a "brief letter from you"—wont you write her a longer?*] Father says you wear a white hat, cocked up at the sides—know I shall like it's looks and want so much to see it—as for the *wearer,* I want to see him too—but which the *most,* prithee?

Father says you ate little dinner when you dined with him—he did'nt know whether you were not hungry, or whether it was *astonishment* at encountering him—I *hope* the latter. You must get better fast—we shall have a busy day for you on Cattle Show day. We have had some sweet cider—I drank your health. I thank you for the vial. I had a dissertation from Eliza Coleman a day or two ago—dont know which was the author—Plato, or Socrates—rather think Jove had a finger in it. Abby Wood has not come—Emerson and Dickinson have been threatened with fevers, but are better now. Spencer is still alive, but cannot linger long.[2] He is sick at Dea Haskell's—his mother is here. Mother came home yesterday—had a pleasant visit at Monson. They all send their love. Vinnie sends her's. How soon you will be here! Days, flee away—"lest with a whip of *scorpions* I overtake your lingering!"

I am in a hurry—this pen is too slow for me—"it hath done what it could."

Your aff Emily

[*Note from Vinnie enclosed*]

Dear Austin

I dont think you are well, from what Father said, & I'm afraid youll be sick, so I want to caution you, a little. Fevers are prevailing & if you are not *careful you* will be victimised. Now I tell you if you want to be strong & well you must exercise some prudence. Tis'nt foolish to be prudent, tis very *wise.* I wish you'd call upon Mr [Robert C.] Winthrop. I know you'd enjoy it, & then t,would please Father. I wish you would go into society a little more Austin, t'would be better & happier for you I know. Just try it & see. Dress well wont you, for you are seen some times, w[h]en you dont know it. Was'nt you surprised to see Father? He revels in such things you know.

I wish you'd get me a song called *"Blanche Alpine,"* & bring it with you for Cattle show. We expect to have great times *then,* "fatted calf" &c. Wont it be nice? [Half of sheet torn off.]

I think the words to Nelly Bly are exquisite, thank you again & again! How warm & lovely the days are now hope you'll enjoy them. Root & Bliss are sick. Dickinson & Emerson ailing. [Remainder of note missing.]

2. John L. Spencer died on October 12, 1851 (*Express,* October 31).

2

Writing at this time to Sue Gilbert, Austin contrasts the letters from his sisters: Emily, he says, always tells him something he likes to hear; but when Vinnie occasionally drops him a line, it is either because she wants something or to pass on some advice. He has no doubt, he says, that she has his good at heart and will make something of him if she can, out of regard for his connection with the family of which she is a member. He speaks of the recent call from his father, who reported that Emily's health had been greatly improved by her trip to Boston.[3]

Up to now Austin seems to have been quite impartial in the bestowal of his attentions on the Gilbert sisters, who had always been inseparable. In her letter of June 15, 1851, Emily told her brother that "they miss you very much—they send their 'united loves.' " But here and there from now on traces of a change can be detected. A month after she reached Baltimore, Sue asks Martha why she does not hear from Austin and continues: "Emily and Austin were going to write *so soon* and I'll warrant I wont hear from either of them, for *one while*." This, Emily passes on to her brother in her letter of October 1, 1851. She goes on to say that she hopes if Austin has not written he *will* very soon "for Susie is so far off, and wants so much to have you." Meanwhile, Emily writes about Martha whom she sees "most every day." On November 16, 1851, she confides to her brother that "Martha becomes far dearer to me with every week and day—her's is a spirit as beautiful and pure as one will seldom meet in a world like ours, and it is all the lovelier because it is so *rare*."

Austin seems to have shared Emily's devotion to Martha. The following draft of a letter to her was written by him on October 12, 1851:

Sunday evening—

It's just after tea, Mat, and I am up here in my room—most forlorn but bent on writing you to night, at any rate, for I want you

3. The text of this letter will be found in Bianchi, *Emily Dickinson Face to Face*, 101.

to hear from me again before I see you, and I fancy too you have been thinking rather strange the last few days that your letter of the 23rd ult remained so long unanswered, & not without reason. So pleasant a letter demanded a more immediate acknowledgement, and except for the mutinous conduct of my eyes, would have received it. They, i.e. the eyes aforesaid, became quite dissatisfied with my requirements about the time the girls left, and shortly grew so outrageous as to refuse unqualifiedly all aid in furtherance of any desire I might entertain either of reading or writing. They are not yet fully restored to healthful discipline, but, with a little care I rec[k]on we may soon move on harmoniously again.

I have read your letter over & over, Mat, and though perfectly agreeing with you that "pens are miserable substitutes for tongues", I can yet assure you that, miserable as they are, they are, in the absence of the former, the source of my greatest pleasure. I like both to use them myself and to see the uses others have put them to.

I know it doesnt take very long to read what little can be written within the limits of a common letter sheet, once. But you can read it again, and then, added to its own intrinsic agreeableness is the gratifying reflection that it was quite a good while, comparatively, in writing, that some hours, perhaps two, perhaps an evening has been given almost wholly to you thereby, and there is something very cheering too in seeing these representatives of your friends about your room. It is, though far from, yet *next* to seeing them themselves. But I neednt enlarge on the worth of letters. Everybody who has ever been away from home knows it.

I should judge from your account you were leading a very quiet life at home this Fall, notwithstanding Sue's lecture on the duty of entering into general society, and nothwithstanding your urgent solicitations to come by one who has seen. I think you must have been pretty fairly braced to have withstood all Emily Fowler's entreaties, and though I believe I should have advised you to the same course, I must tell you that I dont believe anything in Bowdoin's representations of her object in endeavouring to start a reading club. I believe her motives in that matter are the very best, and I believe too that she, at the time, felt all she said to you. I dont believe she is selfish or insincere by *any* means, from all I hear or see of her, though she has, like almost every one else, some disagreeable qualities—

Emily wrote me that she sees you very often, and that you have the best talks together, & Sue says you send her the very best letters & keep a diary for her, besides, every minute, one which she receives every friday, converting that into the most blessed day of the week, to her—

I dont think Sue is homesick. She says she isnt. Her words to me are, "I will not say I am *happy* here, that is a strong word, contented is better. I feel that I am doing right" &c I rather think she is satisfied with her decision to go, and I am inclined to think she was right in it, myself. I shall want you to tell me all about her when I see you, and that will be in only a few hours now—

Tuesday evening— You dont know, Mat, how much I am anticipating in my visit. I have been looking forward to it all the term. I shall get my first and only view of autumn scenery for this year, then, and I think too, that Cattle Show day is the pleasantest in the whole year for Amherst. It seems a holiday especially for *Amherst people,* and not for a lot of old women and ministers and students and the relatives and stuck up trustees, as Commencement is.

I see by the paper that Bill Washburn, Ned Larned [a senior] & myself are Capt Conkeys assistants on the occasion. I feel very sensible of the honor done me in the appointment to so honorable a post, but think I shall be obliged to decline it—one of the results of my [word illegible] fame, I suppose.

Dont you feel slighted not to have been put on to some of those bread & cheese or blanket committees? I think you cant be a favorite of Mr Boyden or you would have been on them.[4]

I had a note from Mr Bowdoin the other morning. He began it, "My dear Sir". He is terribly afraid of being sentimental you know.

I am sure to see Mr Winthrop tomorrow to see if he will come up with me, as announced.

I went to hear Catherine Hayes sing last Sunday evening. I like the woman, but dont think her songs compare with Jenny Lind's. I will tell you about it, Wednesday.

You express a desire Mat, that I should have something that I would like you to make for me—to remind me of you, as your [word illegible] reminds you of me.

This appraisal of Catherine Hayes shows an unusual independence of judgment. A popular singer, she was frequently though without justification compared to Jenny Lind.

Cattle Show was held in Amherst on October 22, 1851. For Austin's homecoming with his friend Edmund Converse, great preparations were in the making. On the Friday before his return Emily, unable to conceal her impatience, wrote again. The conclusion of this letter is a good example of her way of moving into and out of poetry.

4. James W. Boyden, secretary and treasurer, East Hampshire Agricultural Society.

[*To Wm Austin Dickinson, Care of Joel Norcross, 31 Milk St. Boston. Mass.; postmark: Amherst Ms. Oct 17*]

Friday morning [October 17, 1851]

We are waiting for breakfast, Austin, the meat and potato and a little pan of your favorite brown bread are keeping warm at the fire, while father goes for shavings.

While we were eating supper Mr Stephen Church rang the door bell very violently and offerred to present us with *three barrels of shavings.* We are much overcome by this act of magnanimity and father has gone this morning to claim his proffered due. He wore a palm leaf hat, and his pantaloons tucked in his boots and I could'nt help thinking of *you* as he strode along by the window.

I dont think "neglige" quite becoming to so mighty a man. I had rather a jacket of green and your barndoor apparrel, than all the mock simplicity of a lawyer and a man. The breakfast is so warm and pussy is here a singing and the teakettle sings too as if to see which was loudest and I am so afraid lest kitty should be beaten—yet a *shadow* falls upon my morning picture—where is the youth so bold, the bravest of our fold, a seat is empty here—spectres sit in your chair and now and then nudge father with their long, bony elbows. I wish you were here dear Austin—the dust falls on the bureau in your deserted room and gay, frivolous spiders spin away in the corners. I dont go there after dark whenever I can help it, for the twilight seems to pause there and I am half afraid, and if ever I have to go, I hurry with all my might and never look behind me for I know who I should see.

Before next Tuesday—Oh before the coming stage will I not brighten and brush it, and open the long closed blinds, and with a sweeping broom will I not bring each spider down from its home so high and tell it it may come back again when master has gone —and oh I will bid it to be a tardy spider, to tarry on the way, and I will think my eye is fuller than sometimes, tho' *why* I cannot tell, when it shall rap on the window and come to live again. I am so happy when I know how soon you are coming that I put away my sewing and go out in the yard to think. I have tried to delay the frosts, I have coaxed the fading flowers, I thought I *could* detain a few of the crimson leaves until you had smiled upon them, but their companions call them and they cannot stay away—you will find the blue hills, Austin, with the autumnal shadows silently sleeping on them, and there will be a glory lingering round the day, so you'll know autumn has been here, and the *setting sun* will tell you, if you dont get home till evening. How glad I am you are well—you must try hard to be careful and not get sick again. I hope you will be better than ever you were in your life when you come home *this time,* for it never seemed so long since we have seen you. I thank you for such a long letter, and yet if I might choose, *the next* should be a longer. I think a letter just about *three days* long would make me happier than any other kind of one —if you please, dated at Boston, but thanks be to our Father, you may conclude it *here.* Everything has changed since my other letter —the doors are shut this morning, and all the kitchen wall is covered with chilly flies who are trying to warm themselves—poor things, they do not understand that there are no summer mornings remaining to them and me and they have a bewildered air which is really very droll, did'nt one feel *sorry* for them. You would say t'was a gloomy morning if you were sitting here—the frost has been severe and the few lingering leaves seem anxious to be going and wrap their faded cloaks more closely about them as if to shield them from the chilly northeast wind. The earth looks like some poor old lady who by dint of pains has bloomed e'en till *now,* yet in a forgetful moment a few silver hairs from out her cap come stealing, and she tucks them back so hastily and thinks nobody *sees.* The cows are going to pasture and little boys with their hands in their pockets are whistling to try to keep warm. Dont think that the sky will frown so the day when you come home! She will smile and look happy, and be full of sunshine *then*—and even *should* she frown upon her child returning, there is *another* sky ever serene and fair, and there is *another* sunshine, tho' it be darkness there— never mind faded forests, Austin, never mind silent fields—*here* is a little forest whose leaf is ever green, here is a *brighter* garden, where not a frost has been, in its unfading flowers I hear the bright bee hum, prithee, my Brother, into *my* garden come! Your very aff Sister.

[And on a slip of paper enclosing a pressed leaf:] "We'll meet again as heretofore some summer's morning."

[*Note enclosed*]

Well, Austin,
Emilie wants me to send you another scrawl, you were so grateful for the last, so here goes. You are a pretty young man I should think to "poke fun" at my good advice. I wont give you any more, not I.
Mr Spencer is *dead.* His funeral was attended at the Chapel, Tuesday afternoon. He had been quite ill for a fortnight. Thompson & Howland were at the funeral. Thompson & Howland had both been to call, before, since we came home. They want to see you,

perhaps will be here at *Cattle show*. Sawyer called here a little while since, wants you to come & spend a Sabbath with him. Jane is at South Hadley & *very home sick*. Emilie Fowler has'nt been here since we came home. We cant imagine *why*.

We are anticipating your visit greatly—hope you'll certainly come. Martha was here yesterday morning, says Mary W. misses Austin so much. Mrs W. is now afflicted with a *"heavy* cold". Write when youll come & who shall accompany you, before the *reality*. I received a note from Uriah, last week, which would make you *stare*. Vinnie.

3

The Amherst Cattle Show—after 1850 the annual exhibition of the East Hampshire Agricultural Society—was for this farming community the event of the year. In 1851 as usual Mr. Dickinson was the official host. Austin served as assistant to Ithamar F. Conkey, chief marshal of the day. Even Mrs. Dickinson took part as a member of the butter-and-eggs committee. Several varieties of fruits were exhibited by the horticulturally adept Dickinsons. Among other things, they accomplished in that severe climate the unusual feat of producing figs as before mentioned.[5]

While the exhibits of animals and the various contests and prize competitions took place on the common, which assumed for the occasion the appearance of a vast barnyard, the fruits, vegetables and ladies' work were displayed in Sweetser's Hall.

A paragraph in the *History of Amherst* (page 280), gives some statistics:

"At the cattle-show in 1851, 500 cattle were exhibited, 390 working oxen, 123 horses, 600 specimens of poultry. Of the working oxen, 202 came from Belchertown, decorated with flags and attached to a spacious car which was occupied by 181 persons, including the Belchertown brass band."

The procession assembled in front of the Hygeian Hotel at half past eleven and, escorted by the artillery company, marched to the residence of the Honorable Edward Dickinson to receive the officers of the society, the orator and invited guests. From there it proceeded to the college chapel where exercises were held. After the exercises a dinner for several hundred persons, at which Mr. Dickinson "con-

5. *Express*, September 5, 1851; September 2, 1853.

sented to officiate," was served at the Amherst House. Among the
toasts—in cold water—one to Daniel Webster, "the friend of labor,
the champion of free Republican Institutions, the friend of man,"
was received with cheers. Mr. Dickinson read a letter he had received from Mr. Webster saying that he had "long entertained a
strong desire to attend an agricultural meeting in the western part
of the state," and regretted that the pressure of his public duties
would not permit him to do so. Daniel Wesbter had not been in
Amherst since, attracted by its "singular prosperity," he had visited
the young college in the early 1830's.[6]

Austin and his friend Converse departed the day after Cattle
Show. Emily's next letter is folded, sealed with a wafer, and addressed on the back, "For my brother Austin."

Saturday morn [October 25, 1851]

Dear Austin.

I've been trying to think this morning how many weeks it was
since you went away—I fail in calculations—it seems so long to me
since you went back to school that I set down days for years, and
weeks for a *score* of years—not reckoning time "by minutes" I dont
know what to think of such great discrepancies between the *actual*
hours and those which "seem to be." It may seem long to *you* since
you returned to Boston—how I wish you could stay and never go
back again. Everything is so still here, and the clouds are cold and
gray—I think it will rain soon—Oh I am so lonely!

We had a beautiful visit, but it was all too short for we brothers
and sisters, and Vinnie and I are dwelling upon the one to come.
Thanksgiving is but four weeks, or a little more than four weeks
and yet it seems to me a very great way off, when I look forward
to it. I have thought you were very sober, since you went away, and
I did when you were here, but now you are out of sight, I remember
it more frequently, and wonder I did'nt ask you if anything
troubled you. I hope you are better now. I waked up this morning,
thinking that this was the very morning your eyes were to be well,
and I really hope that oculist has'nt broken his promise. You
must'nt use them much until they get very strong—you need'nt
write to us except on a slip of paper, telling us how you are, and
whether you are happy—and I would'nt write at all, until they
were perfectly well.

6. Tyler, 1873, 191; *Express*, October 24, 1851.

You had a windy evening going back to Boston, and we thought of you many times and hoped you would not be cold. Our fire burned so cheerfully I could'nt help thinking of how many were *here* and how many were *away*, and I wished so many times during that long evening that the door would open and you come walking in. Home is a holy thing—nothing of doubt or distrust can enter it's blessed portals. I feel it more and more as the great world goes on and one and another forsake, in whom you place your trust— here seems indeed to be a bit of Eden which not the sin of *any* can utterly destroy—smaller it is indeed, and it may be less fair, but fairer it is and *brighter* than all the world beside. I hope this year in Boston will not impair your health, and I hope you will be as happy as you used to be before. I dont wonder it makes you sober to leave [this] blessed air—if it were in my power I would on every morning transmit it's purest breaths fragrant and cool to you. How I wish you could have it—a thousand little winds waft it to me this morning, fragrant with forest leaves and bright autumnal berries. I would be *willing* to give you my portion for today, and take the salt sea's breath in it's bright, bounding stead. Now Austin—you have no friend there—why not see Converse often, and laugh and talk with *him*? I think him a noble fellow—it seems to me so pleasant for you to talk with somebody, and he is much like you in many thoughts and feelings. I know he would love to have you for a comrade and friend, and I would be with him a good deal if I were you. Mother feels quite troubled about those little boys —fears you will kill one sometime when you are punishing him— for *her sake* be careful! Emily Fowler and Mat were here all after- noon yesterday—never saw Emily F— when she seemed more sin- cere—shall go and see her soon—Mat misses *you* so much, and her dear sister Susie. Henry Root was here all evening. Mother's and Vinnie's love. Remember us to Converse—take care of *yourself*— Your aff **Emily**

[*To Wm Austin Dickinson, Care of Joel Norcross, 31 Milk St. Boston. Mass.; postmark: Amherst Ms. Oct 31*]

Thursday evening [October 30, 1851]

Dear Austin.

Something seems to whisper "he is thinking of home this eve- ning," perhaps because it rains—perhaps because it's evening and the orchestra of winds perform their strange, sad music. I would'nt wonder if home were thinking of him, and it seems so natural for one to think of the other—perhaps it is no superstition or omen of this evening—no omen "at all—at all" as Mrs Mack would say.

Father is staying at home the evening is so inclement. Vinnie diverts his mind with little snatches of music, and mother mends a garment to make it snugger for you—and what do you think *I* do among this family circle— I am thinking of you with all my heart and might, and it just occurs to me to note a few of my tho'ts for your own inspection. "Keeping a diary" is not familiar to me as to your sister Vinnie, but her own bright example is quite a comfort to me, so I'll try.

I waked up this morning thinking for all the world I had had a letter from you—just as the seal was breaking, father rapped at my door. I was sadly disappointed not to go on and read, but when the four black horses came trotting into town, and their load was none the heavier by a tiding for me—I was not disappointed then—it was harder to me than had I been disappointed. I have got over it now tho'. I have been thinking all day of how I would break the seal and how gallantly I would read when my letter came, and when it *did'nt* come, I found I had made no provision for any such time as that, but I wont chide you Austin. I know you will write me soon—perhaps your eyes disturb you and will not let you write. I should be unkind to have so much importunity. Dont you wish you were here tonight? —Oh I know *I* wish so, and all the rest of them too. I find I miss you more "when the lamps are lighted," and when the winds blow high and the great angry raindrops clamor against the window. Your room is snug and cozy thro' these chilly evenings—I really hope it is—and I hope the stove is singing the merry song of the wood, and how are the cigars— "pretty comfortable" say, now? The weather has been unpleasant ever since you went away. Monday morning we waked up in the midst of a furious snow storm—the snow was the depth of an inch— oh it looked so wintry—bye and bye the sun came out, but the wind blew violently and it grew so cold that we gathered all the quinces —put up the stove in the siting room, and bade the world Good bye. Kind clouds came on at evening, still the sinking thermometer gave terrible signs of what would be on the morning—at last the morning came laden with mild south winds, and the winds have brought the rain—so here we are. I hope your eyes are better. I have been feeling anxious since we have heard from you lest they might not be as well and had prevented your writing. Your very hasty letter just at your return rejoiced us—that you were "better—happier— heartier"—what made you think of such beautiful words to tell us how you were, and how cheerful you were feeling? It did us a world of good—how little the scribe thinks of the value of his line—how many eager eyes will search it's every meaning—how much swifter the strokes of "the little mystic clock, no human eye hath seen, which ticketh on and ticketh on, from morning until e'en." If it were not that I could write you—you could not go away, *therefore*——pen and ink are very excellent things!

We had new *brown bread* for tea—when it came smoking on and we sat around the table, how I did wish a slice could be reserved for you. I fell at once to thinking perhaps *Mrs Reed* had brown bread, and oh I *hoped* she had, and I hoped you were well and hungry so that you could enjoy it. You shall have as many loaves as we have eaten *slices* if you will but come home. This suggests Thanksgiving—you will soon be here—then I cant help thinking of how when we rejoice—so many hearts are breaking, next Thanksgiving day. What will you say, Austin, if I tell you that Jennie Grout and merry Martha Kingman will spend the day above? They are not here—"while we delayed to let them forth, angels beyond stayed for them."

It *cannot* be—yet it is so—Jennie Grout was buried yesterday—Martha Kingman died at four o,clock this morning—one and another, and another—how we pass away! Did you know that Merrick in Mr Colton's shop was engaged to Jane Grout?[7] The poor fellow is quite heart broken—he walked to the grave with her parents, and was prayed for as one deeply afflicted in the funeral prayer. I dont know of any one very sick just now. Did you know that *Helen Humphrey* was going to be married soon to Mr Stoddard of the "Stoddard and Lathrop" firm—Northampton—it is so! Mother and Vinnie and Martha send you their love. Will you remember us to Mr Converse—will you tell your friend McCurdy how sorry [we were] he could'nt come? Now Austin, mark me, in four weeks from today we are all happy again! Your aff Emily

[*Note from Edward Dickinson enclosed*]

Friday morning [October 31, 1851]

Dear Austin,

I have carried your overcoat to Coltons and he will try to sell it.

You had better get you a new one, without reference to this. If he dont sell it, I shall take it, myself, for an outside garment, & allow you $12.

I wish you would read Kossuth's Address to people of U.S. in

7. J. and S. Colton, tailors.

Atlas of 25″ Oct.—& his subsequent ones to France, & Hungary.
They are very grand & sublime.
All well.

Your father
E.D.

The article in the *Boston Atlas* to which Mr. Dickinson refers
appeared not on the twenty-fifth, but on October 24, 1851. The
Hungarian patriot Louis Kossuth, "The Great Magyar," arrived in
the United States on the fifth of December to raise funds in behalf
of his oppressed country. In spite of "an element of charlatanism"
in his visit, the frenzy with which he was received nearly equaled
that aroused by Jenny Lind. Kossuth's was a whirlwind campaign in
Massachusetts, where in three weeks he made twenty-five major
speeches. When he sailed for home on July 14, 1852, he had "obtained in all about $150,000."[8]
Austin came home again on November eighth and remained to
vote on Monday, November tenth.

4

After her brother had gone Emily felt more than ever bereft.
Not only was he the one she could joke with—and she once told him
that he was indeed "much funnier" than *Punch*—he was also the one
with whom she talked about things that mattered. And they read
the same books. In looking through the family correspondence one
is often reminded, as Emily was, of Hawthorne's strange dark
characters. *The House of the Seven Gables* had been published the
previous spring. Though it is hard to think of Hepzibah and
Clifford, the elderly brother and sister in their "shivering solitude,"
as in any way comparable to Emily and Austin, perhaps nothing so

8. See various issues of the *Express*, January 30 to July 16, 1852. "The round-
top, low-crowned, broad-brimmed, feather-surmounted Kossuth Hat," which sold
for $1.50, vied in popularity with "Jennie Lind ties." On March 12, 1852, the
Express reported that "Kossuth hats to the amount of half a million dollars
have been sold in New York." Under date of April 30, 1852, there is an account
of the visit of "the Governor of Hungary" to Northampton. There the two
representatives of European culture may have met, for on February 5, 1852,
Jenny Lind had married her accompanist, Otto Goldschmidt, and had gone to
Round Hill, Northampton, where they remained until they sailed for Europe
May 29, 1852.

much as the mention of those two "desolate spirits" could have better conveyed to her brother her sense of utter loneliness.

[*To Wm Austin Dickinson, Care of Joel Norcross, 31 Milk St. Boston. Mass.; postmark: Amherst Ms. (date November 11)*]

Tuesday noon [November 11, 1851][9]

I cant write but a word, dear Austin, because its already noon and Vinnie is waiting to go to the office for me, and yet a *single word* may be of comfort to you as you go travelling on. It should be a word big and warm and full of sweet affection if I could make it so—Oh it should fill that room, that small and lonely chamber with a thousand kindly things and precious ministrations—I wonder if it *will,* for know that if it *does* not, it is bad and disobedient and a most unworthy type of its affectionate mistress! I was to write last night, but company detained me—Martha came this morning and spent the forenoon with us, or I had written more than I'm afraid I *can* now, the time flies so fast. I said to Martha this morning that I was going to write and we decided between us that it would make you happier to have us talk about you and wish you could be here, and write you more again. Mattie sends you her love—she thinks a great deal of you—I enjoy seeing her so much, because we are both bereaved, and can sorrow on together, and Martha loves you, and we both love Susie, and the hours fly so fast when we are talking of you.

I watched the stage coach yesterday until it went away, and I hoped you would turn around, so to be sure and see me—I did'nt mind the rain which sometimes pelted me with a big drop, nor the sharp westerly wind. I only thought to me that should you turn around for a last look at home and I should not be there, I never could forgive me. I thought you saw me once, the way I told was *this.* You know your cap was black, and where it had been black, it all at once grew *white,* and I fancied *that* was *you.*

How lonely it was last night when the chilly wind went down, and the clear, cold moon was shining—it seemed to me I could pack this little earthly bundle, and bidding the world Goodbye, fly away and away, and never come back again to be so lonely here, and then I thought of "Hepzibah" how sorrowful *she* was, and how she longed to sleep, because the grave was peaceful, yet for affection's sake, and for the sake of "Clifford" she wearied on, and bye

9. The method of verifying the date of this letter is described in Chapter V, page 49.

and bye, kind angels took both of them home, and it seemed almost a lesson, given us to learn. I dont mean that you are *him*, or that Hepzibah's *me* except in a relative sense, only I was reminded.

You are not alone, dear Austin, warm hearts are beating for you, and at mention of your name, brighter beams the eye—you *must not* be despondent—no, Austin, I cannot have you—dont think of the present—the present is unkind, but the future loves you—it sees you a great way off and runs to meet you—"my son was dead, and lives again—he was lost and is found!" I was thinking of you last night—I dropped asleep thinking of you. Lo, I *dreamed,* and the world was no more *this* world, but a world bright and fair—no fading leaves, no dying friends, and I heard a voice saying there shall be no more tears, neither any crying, and they answered, *nevermore,* and up from a thousand hearts went a cry of praise and joy and great thanskgiving, and I awoke, yet I know the place was heaven, and the people singing songs were those who in their *lifetimes* were parted and separated, and their joy was because they should never be so any more. Good bye, dear Austin, yet why Good bye, are you not with me always—whether I wake or sleep? "And tho *all others* do, yet will not *I* forsake thee"!

Emilie

[*Slip enclosed*]

Dear Austin

I would write *too*, if it were not for my recitation, but I cant stop now. We are very lonely without you. I never missed you more. Hope you reached Boston safely. I thought of you in the evening very often.

Vinnie

[*To Wm Austin Dickinson. Care of Joel Norcross. Boston. Mass.; postmark: Amherst Ms. Nov 17*]

Sunday afternoon [November 16, 1851]

Dear Austin.

We have just got home from meeting—it is very windy and cold —the hills from our kitchen window are just crusted with snow, which with their blue mantillas makes them seem so beautiful. You sat just here last Sunday, where I am sitting now and our voices were nimbler than our pens can be, if they try never so hardly. I should be quite sad today, thinking about last Sunday did'nt another Sabbath smile at me so pleasantly, promising me on it's word to present you here again when "six days work is done."

Father and mother sit in state in the sitting room perusing such papers only, as they are well assured have nothing carnal in them. Vinnie is eating an apple which makes me think of gold, and accompanying it with her favorite [New York] Observer, which if you recollect, deprives us many a time of her sisterly society. Pussy has'nt returned from the afternoon assembly, so you have us all just as we are at present. We were very glad indeed to hear from you so soon, glad that a cheerful fire met you at the door. I *do* well remember how chilly the west wind blew, and how everything shook and rattled before I went to sleep, and I often tho't of you in the midnight car, and hoped you were not lonely. I wished that "Jim" was there to keep you pleasant company, or rather that you were *here,* soundly asleep and adream.

How farcical it seems to sit here a writing, when another Sunday's sun shall shine upon us all in each other's society, and yet thanks to a being inventing paper and pen, they are better far than nothing! By means of them indeed, 'tis little I can tell you, but I can tell how much I would if I could, and there's something comforting in it. We are thinking most of Thanksgiving, than anything else just now—how full will be the circle, less then by none— how the things will smoke, how the board will groan with the thousand savory viands—how when the day is done, Lo the evening cometh, laden with merrie laugh, and happy conversation, and then the sleep and the dream each of a knight or "Ladie"—how I love to see them, a beautiful company, coming down the hill which men call the Future, with their hearts full of joy, and their hands of gladness. Thanksgiving *indeed,* to a family united, once more together before they go away! "Both together" it says, "one taken, the other left."

Col' Kingman's other daughter died yesterday—her funeral is tomorrow. Oh what a house of grief must be their's today—the grass not growing green above the grave of Martha, before little Ellen is laid close beside. I dont know but they are the happier, and we who longer stay the more to be sorrowed for.

Mr Tyler [Professor W. S. Tyler] preached this PM—a sermon concerning Spencer, of which you heard us speak when you were here. A beautiful memorial of his life and character, and preached by the request of Spencer's friends in the village. Martha was here on Friday and we had a beautiful hour to sit and talk together. Martha becomes far dearer to me with every week and day—her's is a spirit as beautiful and pure as one will seldom meet in a world like our's, and it is all the lovelier because it is so *rare*. Martha inquired for you, as she never comes *without* doing, and sends the weekly love which I always bring, and which I love to bring, if it makes you happier. I hope you are encouraged since you were at home —*do not* be lonely. Susie is lonely, and Martha, and I am lonely too, and this is a lonely world, in the cheerfullest aspects of it. We will not live here always—[word illegible] will dwell together beyond the bright blue sky, where "they live whom we call dear." The winter will fly swiftly, then will be the spring think of nothing but hope—heed nothing but anticipation—"the griefs of the present moment are not to be compared with the joys which are hereafter." Bye and bye you are coming home—so is Susie—so is joy and gladness, which have been staying away just as long as you have. Dont mind the days—some of them are long ones but who cares for length when breadth is in store for him, or who minds the cross, who *knows* he'll have a crown? I wish I could imbue you with all the strength and courage which can be given men—I wish I could assure you of the constant remembrance of those you leave at home—I wish, but Oh how vainly, that I could bring you back again, and never more to stray! You are tired *now* Dear Austin, with my incessant din, but I cant help saying any of these things.

The very warmest love from Vinnie and every one of us. I am *never* ready to go.

Reluctant Emily

[*Note enclosed*]

Sunday evening [November 16, 1851]

Dear Austin

Our room has been filled with callers all the evening. They are just gone, John Emerson, E. & C. Fowler, Bowdoin & David Warner were the company. It is quite an unusual thing for us to have callers on Sabbath evening, you know. They all talked about *you*. Mr Colton preached in the morning, Prof. Tyler in P.M. Alanson Russell the shoe maker is married to a girl that boarded at Mr Godfrey's. They were at church today, looked more like dolls than any thing else. Do you think you'll stay to the convention?[10] I hope you wont, though if Father should go to Boston (& he intends to) I suppose you would stay to gratify him.

We were very glad to get your letter. I do hope you will be care-

10. Meeting in Faneuil Hall, Boston, November 25, 1851, to promote the candidacy of Daniel Webster for President of the United States.

ful & not be sick, Austin. I think a great deal about you. I dont
like to have you so nervous. Cant you in some way prevent it? It
will injure you I'm afraid. I'm anticipating *Thanksgiving* more
than usual, this year, as 'twill bring us all together again, if nothing happens. Yet I sometimes feel afraid to make plans for the
future. They are so apt to bring disappointment in their stead.
Dont you think so? We are usually well. I am obliged to study
rather hard, just as busy as ever, never have any leisure you know.
Dont think I cant write better than this, but its my bedtime &
of course I am in *a hurry*. Dont get *blue* or lonely. Dont worry
about *that* trifle you spoke of, when at home, will you?

Good night Austin, I am so tired. Your affectionate Sister Vinnie

[*To Wm Austin Dickinson, Care of Joel Norcross. Boston. Mass.;
postmark: Amherst Ms. Nov 20*]

Thursday noon [November 20, 1851]

I cant write but a syllable, Austin, my letter ought to be in—it
is 2'o'clock even now, but I do want to thank you for what I read
last evening—I want you to know we think of you every morning
and noon, I want to tell you that Father is not at home this week,
therefore you do not hear concerning your plans from him. He went
to Greenfield Monday, uncertain whether he'd get home *that* day, or
two days after. We had a letter yesterday saying he will come home
today, and I presume he will write you immediately upon his
getting home. If I am *selfish* Austin, I tell you you *must come home*
—it seems a good many days to take from your little visit, but *you*
know better than I what is best about it. Father will be at Boston,
and I think he seems inclined to have you wait the Convention. I
hope and Vinnie hopes, you wont decide to stay. Are you willing
to get me once more, *two or three times this prescription,* and bring
it when you come? I have seen much of Mattie since you went away
—she is here most every day. Susie has sent me a letter which has
been lost on the way—I have had a note from her this week. So
many things to tell you, but will not write them now—*rather—tell*
them—dear Austin, it will be soon!

Love from all and me more
Emily

[Prescription, glycerine and water, enclosed]

[*On a slip enclosed by Vinnie*]

Don't forget Katy Darling & Angelina Baker

CHAPTER XVII

Season of "Sobriety"

1

AUSTIN attended the Whig meeting in Boston with his father on November twenty-fifth, and reached Amherst on Wednesday, the night before Thanksgiving. The "day of days" was especially dear to him—a day of rest and gladness before plunging into the season of "sobriety" just ahead. Austin stayed over Sunday, returning to Boston on Monday, December first.

Two brief notes, the envelopes of which are missing, were dispatched to Austin in December by Vinnie. The first is a somewhat tart message for which she later apologized:

If you cant read my writing, Austin, perhaps twill do no good to say any thing to you. I really dont understand your inability to read what has always been called *plain*. I think you must be growing blind. I would advise you to consult Dr. Reynolds speedily, else secure a pair of Fathers glasses which have proved themselves *"uncommon."* I thank you very much for the music, Austin. Perhaps I can do as much for you some time. I did not expect it so soon. You do a good deal for me & I appreciate your kindness, I hope. I dont feel as though the bundle would ever reach you. It is real gloomy today. Snowing fast. I wish you were here. The Warners have not come Emilie tells storys about me. Dont believe her.

The Warners, who had been making a visit in Boston, returned toward the end of the month.

Vinnie had commissioned Austin to buy her a fan. The second note acknowledges having received it on December eighteenth.

Austin,

The Fan is very handsome, but I think it is probably too expensive a one for me. I had not thought of having so nice a one. I suppose I can send it back, some time, if I choose, cant I? I will not decide now. I wish you would give us some accounts of what you see & hear, where you go &c. Your letters are not very satisfactory, because we want to know what you do all the time. You only say how busy you are. Do tell more & gratify us.

Vinnie

Though the next letter was written at midnight on Christmas Eve, Emily does not refer to the day except to tell her brother that she had received gifts and a "Merry Christmas" from Sue. Customs were different in Baltimore.

[*To Wm Austin Dickinson, Care of Joel Norcross. 31, Milk St. Boston. Mass.; postmark: Amherst Ms. Dec 25*]

Wednesday night, 12 o'clock [December 24-25, 1851]

Dont tell them, *will* you Austin; they are all asleep soundly and I snatch the silent night to speak a word to you. Perhaps *you* are sound asleep, and I am only chatting to the *semblance* of a man ensconced in warmest blankets and deep, downy pillows. I am afraid not, dear Austin, I'm afraid that dreadful pain will keep you wide awake all this dreary night, and *so* afraid am I, that I steal from happy dreams and come to sit with you. Since your letter came, we have thought *so* much about you, Oh more, *many* more than pen and ink can tell you—we are thinking of you *now* midst the night so wild and stormy. Austin, I hav'nt a doubt that Vinnie and mother are dreaming *even now* of you, tho' Vinnie was *so* sleepy the last time she opened her eye, and mother has had a very fatiguing day. And you know that I do, *dont* you, or I should'nt incur such perils for the sake of seeing you. Hav'nt you taken cold, or exposed yourself in some way, or got too tired, teaching those useless boys?—I am so sorry for you. I do wish it was *me,* that you might be well and happy, for I have no profession, and have such a snug, warm home that I had as lief suffer some, a great deal rather than not, that by doing so, you were exempted from it. May I change places, Austin? *I* dont care how sharp the pain is, not if it dart like arrows, or pierce bone and bone like the envenomed barb, I should be twice, *thrice* happy to bear it in your place. Dont try to teach school at all, until you get thoroughly well! The committee will excuse you, I *know* they will, they *must*; tell them if they dont I will tell the Mayor of them and get them all turned out! I am glad to know you are prudent in consulting a physician; I hope he will do you good; has anyone with neuralgia, tried him, that recommended him to you? I think that warmth and rest, cold water and care, are the best medicines for it. I know you can get all these, and be your own physician, which is far the better way.

Now Austin, I cant come, I have no horse to fetch me, I can only advise you of what I think is good, and ask you if you will do it. Had I the art and skill of the greatest of all physicians, and had under my care whole hospitals of patients, I could'nt feel more anxious than in this single case; I do feel so desirous of a complete recovery!

But lest I harm my patient with too much conversation on sickness and pain, I pass to themes more cheerful and reminiscence gay. I know it would make you laugh to see Vinnie sleeping as soundly as a poker, and shovel and pair of tongs, and Cousin Emily Norcross bringing up the rear in a sleep twice as sound, and full twice as sonorous, and there come snatches of music from away in mother's room, which wake a funny response in my amused being. I can think of nothing funnier than for intelligent beings to bid the world good night, and go out with their candles, and there's nothing that I enjoy more than rousing these selfsame beings and witnessing their discomfiture at the *bare idea* of morning, when they're *so* sleepy yet!

Vinnie thinks me quite savage, and frequently suggests the propriety of having me transported to some barbarous country, where I may meet with those of a similar nature, and allow her to spend her days—that is, such small remainder as my inhumanity spares—in comparative ease and quietness!

She thinks ancient martyrs very trifling indeed and would *welcome* the stake in preference to the sunrise, and that shrill morning call she may be sure to hear!

A'nt you sorry for her; she thinks of your sympathies often, and thinks they would all be hers, if they were nearer home.

Father will come tomorrow, and I will take care of Mat. Had a "merry Christmas" from Sue, besides some beautiful gifts for Vinnie and me, Monday evening. We are having a cozy, rosy, posy little visit with Cousin Emily—enjoy it very much, would love to have you here, if it might be possible. I was glad you remembered Emily, it pleased her very much. Why did you apologize for any of your letters? Coming from you, Austin, they never can be otherwise than delightful to us; better than that you give us, we shall never desire.

Write to us very soon, and say how you are, and be very careful indeed, and dont write but a little, if you find it pains you. Much love.

Emily.

[*Note enclosed*]

Thursday noon [Christmas Day]

I am so sorry, Austin that you are sick. I should'nt have written what I did, had I known it. So you must forgive me. I hope Dr Wesselhoefts medicine will cure you, but do have faith in it, wont you? I want you should like him. We are having a nice time with Cousin Emilie. She sends her love to you, wishes you were here. Mrs. [John M.] Brewster is dead. Father is in Monson. There is nothing new here. I wish I could tell you something interesting. Hope you will enjoy the holidays. Mary Warner "saw a great deal of Austin." They are convalescing slowly. All now have "*heavy* colds." Good bye. Get well quick.

Vinnie

Four days later Vinnie sent off a hurried note of thanks for the coveted fan, a gift from her brother. It came perilously close to being a Christmas present, but was not so regarded.

Monday morning [December 29, 1851]

You are really very kind, Austin. I hardly know what to say in return for the fan. I did not intend to beg it, but to pay for it myself, however as it is your wish I will accept the gift & be thankful. I think it is beautiful, & I shall always keep it. I'm glad you are well again. So is every body. Cousin Emilie spent last week with us & we had quite a nice still time, the *little* sleighing is entirely gone. It is quite spring like here today. When shall you come home again? I was thinking a little while since that we should'nt go sugaring any more, because you would be always gone & I felt *almost* sad, that those charming little excursions were over. Lizzie Tyler & Twombly took tea & spent the evening here, Tuesday. He said he should call upon you.

Every thing goes on at home as usual. Emilie is pensive just now recollections of "by gones" you know, "Old un" &c.

"Mrs Warner thought Austin appeared poorly, had great many engagements &c" Do you like M. Curdy now & who else? Tell us everything.

The final communication of 1851 was written by Emily on the last day of the year. Posted on January 1, 1852, it was enclosed in the first self-sealing envelope used by her in writing to her brother. To make doubly sure she also used a wafer.

[*To Wm Austin Dickinson, Care of Joel Norcross, 31. Milk Street, Boston, Mass.*]

Late at night, dear Child, but I cant help thinking of you, and am so afraid you are sick—come home tomorrow, Austin, if you are not perfectly sure that you shall be well right away, for you must not suffer there—Vinnie has got her message—We did not get the answer from you—I must not write another word, but Austin, come home, remember, if you are not better right away. Love for you.

Emilie.

2

Early in January, Oliver Watson, the newly elected representative from Amherst, was about to leave for the opening of the 1852 session of the General Court. The Dickinsons took prompt advantage of this dependable emissary to send Austin some of his clothes. A note from Emily was tucked into the bundle.

Emily's reference to influenza, spreading among the neighbors, sounds a note of apprehension heard over and over again throughout the winter. The girls' own susceptibility to colds may have accentuated their anxiety about their brother's health.

[*To Wm Austin Dickinson.*]

Monday morning [January 5, 1852]

I will write a word to you, Austin, to send by Mr Watson. I've found your Gaitor shoes, and send them as you desired.

Mary Warner was here on Thursday, has only just got out; influenza is prevalent here—how lucky they took it in Boston, it would have been so vulgar to have imbibed it *here* among the pools and pastures! Mary said she had finished "Kavanagh," and would return it immediately, which she has *not* done, or you would receive it now. I should go for it this morning, but it storms and is so icy, that I dare not venture out. You shall have it tho, by the next good opportunity. Mr. *Goodale* left for California, this morning, George Godfrey meets him in New York, Tuesday.

Emiline Kellogg is quite sick—they have very much feared a fever, but she's rather more comfortable now.

You remember our telling you of a Cousin George Dickinson, from New York, who came to Amherst last summer, when you were away. He passed the Sabbath in town, took tea here, and passed the evening, is a fine fellow, and has a great desire to see you. We had a very quiet New Year's, I had as a gift from Mattie, an exquisite "piece of carpeting", similar to one Sue gave you, sometime ago!

I dont know anything of the railroad tho' I fancy "things is workin", and so soon as "things *has* worked" I promise to let you know. I am very glad indeed that you've called upon the Lymans— I think Mary a beautiful person, and will certainly go and see her as soon as she comes to town. I have never known Charlotte at all. Vinnie will tell the Jones' some day when she's out this week.

Mrs Howe has heard from Sabra, she is very happy indeed.[1] Mrs Howe was perfectly delighted with your visit there, the last time you were at home—also Mrs Hartly, and all the tavern gang —have spoken of it frequently, and with much evident pleasure. Goodbye, Austin, hope you are happy and well, and would write much more, but your stockings call me. Aff yr sister, Emilie

[*To Wm Austin Dickinson, Boston. Mass.*]

Monday morning [January 12, 1852]

Did you think I was *tardy*, Austin? For two Sunday afternoons, it has been so cold and cloudy that I did'nt feel in my very happiest mood, and so I did not write until next monday morning, determining in my heart never to write to you in any but cheerful spirits.

Even this morning Austin, I am not in merry case, for it snows slowly and solemnly, and hardly an outdoor thing can be seen a stirring—now and then a man goes by, with a large cloak wrapped around him and shivering at that, and now and then a stray kitten out on some urgent errand creeps thro' the flakes, and crawls so fast as *may* crawl half frozen away. I am glad for the sake of your body that you are not here this morning, for it is a trying time for fingers and toes, for for the heart's sake, I would verily have you

1. Sabra was the daughter of A. P. Howe, landlord of the Amherst House.

here—you know there *are* winter mornings when the cold *without* only adds to the warm *within,* and the more it snows and the harder it blows, brighter the fires blaze, and chirps more merrily the "cricket on the hearth"; it is hardly cheery enough for such a scene this morning, and yet methinks it *would* be if you were only here. The future full of sleighrides would chase the gloom from our minds, which only deepens and darkens with every flake that falls.

Black Fanny would "toe the mark" if you should be here to-morrow, but as the prospects are, I presume Black Fanny's hoofs will not attempt to fly. Do you have any snow in Boston? Enough for a ride, I hope, for the sake of "Auld Lang Syne." Perhaps the "Ladie" of curls, would not object to a drive. So you took Miss Mary to The Mercantile—Vinnie is quite excited about her going to Boston, and things are turning out "just as she expected." Father remarked "he was very glad of it—he thought it would please the *old folks* to have the school master pay respect to their darter." I think that "heavy cold" must be making progress as that devoted family have not yet been seen, or what is *more* suspicious, heard of.

I am glad you like Miss Nichols, it must be so pleasant for you to have somebody to care for, in such a cheerless place—dont shut yourself away from anyone whom you like, in order to keep the faith to those you leave behind! Your friends here are much happier in fancying *you* happy, than if in a pledge so stern you should refuse all friendliness. Truth to the ones you leave does not demand of you to refuse those whom you find, or who would make your exile a less desolate thing in their cheerful circles. On the contrary, Austin, I am very sure that seclusion from everyone there would make an ascetic of you, rather than restore you brighter and truer to *them.* We miss you more and more, we do not become accustomed to separation from you. I almost wish sometimes we need'nt miss you so much, since duty claims a year of you entirely to herself, and then again I think that it is pleasant to miss you if must go away, and I would not have it otherwise, not even if I could. In every pleasure and pain you come up to our minds so wishfully, we know you'd enjoy our joy, and if you were with us Austin, we could bear little trials more cheerfully—then when we have any dainty, someone is sure to say "it is such as *Austin* loves." When I know of anything funny, I am just as apt to cry, far *more* so than to *laugh,* for I know who *loves jokes best,* and who is not here to enjoy them. We dont *have* many jokes tho' *now,* it is pretty much all sobriety, and we do not have much poetry, father having made up his mind that its pretty much all *real life.* Fathers real life and *mine* sometimes come in collision, but as yet, escape unhurt! I give all your messages to Mat—she seems to enjoy every one more than the one before—she was here three afternoons last week, one

evening she took tea here with Abby and Abiah Root, and we had
such a pleasant time; how I did wish you were here, and so did all
the girls—every one of them spoke of it. Did you know that Jane
Humphrey's sister [Martha], that you saw at S. Hadley once was
dead? They have sent for Jane to come home, I dont know whether
she will, she is so far from home. I am so glad you are well, and
in such happy spirits—both happy and well is a great comfort to
us when you are far away.

Emilie.

[Note from Emily on a small loose sheet]

Thank you for the music Austin, and thank you for the books. I
have enjoyed them very much. I shall learn my part of the Duett,
and try to have Vinnie her's. She is very much pleased with Charity.
   She would write you now but is busy getting her lesson.
   Mother is frying Doughnuts—I will give you a little platefull to
have warm for your tea! *Imaginary* ones—how I'd love to send you
real ones.

Influenza was unusually prevalent during the winter of 1851-
1852. Latest among the Dickinsons' friends to be attacked, on January 14, was Martha Gilbert. For several weeks she was quite ill. Of
the three or four physicians then practising in Amherst, the foremost was Dr. Timothy J. Gridley. Austin Dickinson described him
as "that strange, queer, eccentric, fascinating man; doctor, politician; hated, admired, distrusted, believed to carry life in his hand;
apparently not knowing day from night, that Sunday came the same
day every time, his own house from another's; who wouldn't go
straight if he could go across; regular only in being irregular; a
most picturesque character."[2]

[Note from Vinnie]

Monday noon [January 26, 1852]

Dear Austin

   The song, "Merry Days When We were Youg" is not the one, I
sent for, & I want to have you exchange it, if you will, the one I
2. Dickinson, "Representative Men," 65-66.

want you to get is sung by *Mrs Wood* & not by "Mr Leffler." I do
not want this one, any how. I think you can find the right one, at
some of the music stores. I'm anxious to have it. Olivia Coleman
used to sing it & tis a beautiful thing.

Remember that tis sung by Mrs Wood & no other, the tune begins
with these words, "Oh! the merry days, the merry days when we were
young," &c. I should also like two other pieces, "You & Me," & "the
Ossian Serenade.". If you can, please send them by W. Kellogg or
Mr Sweetser I dont know but t,will trouble you to select these songs.
If you are busy & cant conveniently attend to them, let them go till
another time. I'm rejoiced that you are better, hope you'll continue
so. I dont know whether Mother will come to Boston or not. Emilie
has told you all the news I suppose. There was a pleasant little
gathering at Tempe's,[3] Friday eve, Martha is better, Mrs "James'
lungs are all tied up in a knout & she she haint got nothin to hitch
her breath on to & her vitals are struck." This is a true statement
Austin, the poor lady really thinks she does suffer & "if it had'nt a
been for Gridley she'd a went," that time. I wish you'd write to me
some time.

[*To Wm Austin Dickinson, Care of Joel Norcross. 31. Milk St.,
Boston, Mass; postmark: Amherst Ms. Jan 29*]

Wednesday evening [January 28, 1852]

I have just got your letter, Austin, and have read and sat down to
answer it almost in a breath, for there's so much I want to say, and
so little time to say it, that I must be very spry to write you tonight
at all.

It has been a long, lonely winter; we do need you at home, and
since you have been sick and are away from us, the days seem like
ages, and I get tired of ever hoping to see you again. It seems to
me it would do you a great deal of good to leave school a few days,
and come home. We are very anxious to see you, the journey would
do you good, and the pure air here, and seeing your old friends
would quite restore you. Cant you, Austin? I do wish you would;
never mind the boys; if they cant fill your place for a week, just let
it be *un*filled. I dont believe the boy's minds would suffer, or run
to waste in such a short space of time, and I do think your health
requires it. You may feel so well by the time you get this that you
wont think it worth the while in a *health* view [?] but it's a long
while since Thanksgiving, and we should like to see you, and per-

3. Tempe S. Linnell, compare p. 500.

haps you would like to come. Wont you think of it tonight and follow my good advice into the Fitchburgh Depot, where you will find a ticket to take you home tomorrow? How glad we should all be to see you! I am rejoiced that your face is better, hope it is now well, as t'will be almost three days from the time you wrote to me, when this reaches you.

I dont understand your being troubled with the palpitation so much, but think it must be owing to a disordered system, and too violent exertions in your school, which I would modestly wish at the bottom of the sea, before ever you were engaged in it. I think you need rest, and riding, and perfect freedom from care—*that* you will find here, and Vinnie and I will do everything we *can* to make you happy, if you will make *us* happy by deciding to come. *Generous,* is'nt it, offerring to make *you* happy, if you'll make *us* so *first*; but in the end, we should *all* be happy, I guess. Poor Mat has been pretty sick, but is recovering now; just a fortnight today since she was taken down.

I am down there a great deal, and spend most all my time in going to see her, thinking of something to carry her, or writing letters to Sue, telling her all about Martha. I had a long letter from Sue last Thursday, and wrote her that day of Mat's sickness, at Mat's request; told her Mat was'nt much sick, had a touch of the influenza and would be out again soon. Poor Sue thought otherwise, concluded Mat was very sick and I had written not so for fear I should alarm her; so yesterday I had the most anxious note from her— she seemed almost distracted lest Mat was sick very, and we were keeping it from her; but I wrote her immediately, stating how Mat was, and Mrs C[utler] wrote too, so Sue will soon be relieved. You are gone, and Sue; Mat's sickness deprives me of her, and on the whole, Austin, I do feel rather lonely, but you'll all get back at some-time, and if I live till then, I mean to be happy enough to make up for all this lost time. Emiline is still very feeble, sits up only a little, cannot bear the light at all on account of her head, and tho' slowly recovering, is very feeble yet. I went up to see her today—her room is kept so dark that I could'nt see where she was for some time—at last I heard a little faint voice way out in the corner, and found poor Em' out there—she inquired for you—I told her you had been shut up with your face, and she smiled and said "we are all sick at a time". It is five weeks today, since she was taken sick, a long and tedious sickness, but I hope she will soon get well. Her hair is all cut off, and to see her propped up with pillows, you would'nt hardly know her.

Mary Warner and Thurston are getting along nicely, spent last Monday evening, sliding down Boltwood's hill—the very last phase of flirtation. Mary dont seem very flourishing just now—everybody seems to get the idea that she's a little gone by, and faded. Dont be roused by this into the former furie, for Mary and Vinnie and I are on the pleasantest terms in the world. Emily Fowler is visiting Liz Tyler. Abby Wood is as usual; Mr Bliss is confined to the house with one of his old attacks, so the work at "Shanghi" I suppose cannot go forward![4] Abby brought her work down and staid all Monday forenoon; said she wrote a letter of *16* pages to Eliza Coleman last week, and had just received one of *ten* in return. Dear me, I'm glad I have no such hot correspondents! Only think of it, Abby Wood and Eliza C. Where is Charles Dickens, is all I have tongue to say? Mary Lyman has not come—Mary French is visiting her coz' in Oxford. Prof Haven[5] gave a Lyceum Lecture last evening, upon the deaf and dumb, and the manner of teaching them—it was called very interesting—he gives one at Northampton tonight—the President [Hitchcock] lectures at Springfield this evening, so you see Lyceum Lectures are pretty plenty around here.

Dr Wesselhoeft's bill is correct I presume. He sent Vinnie medicine three or four times, and me twice—and although we were not benefited by it, he probably did the best he could for us, and I'd rather you would pay it, without any words about it, and Vinnie and I will pay you, when you get home. I dont want any fuss with him. Vinnie and I have tried him and are satisfied that for us the medicine has no power, but I am glad we tried him; we should'nt have *known* without. Go and see him as soon as you can conveniently, Austin; I dont like an unpaid bill.

Mother seems quite delighted at what you said to her about making you a visit—I should'nt be at all surprised should she conclude to go and see you, though of course she has not had time to think at all about it.

I think she is very happy at your mention of her, and desire to see her. I mean she shall go. Vinnie and I have been there so recently, it is not best for us to think of it, but you are very kind, Austin, you do not know how much we all think of you, how much you are missed at home.

I thank you for your letter, it sounds like old times—and makes me feel quite happy, except where you are sick. Mother and Vinnie

4. Daniel Bliss, a senior, older than many of his classmates, was a powerful personality. He joined the Missionary Band in his freshman year, and at this time was planning to go to China. But three years later, having married Abby Wood on November 23, 1855, he took her not to China, but to Syria, where he later founded the Syrian Protestant College (American University) in Beirut.

5. A lecture by Professor Joseph Haven, entitled "The Art of Instructing the Deaf and Dumb," was given on January 27 before the Citizen's Lyceum in Phenix Hall.

send their love, and father says he thinks you had better come home for a few days unless you are very much better.

Emilie E.

[*On a separate slip*]

You sent us the *Duett*, Austin. Vinnie cannot learn it, and I see from the outside page, that there is a piece for *two* hands.

Are you willing to change it. Dont be in haste to send it; any time will do! Shall write when I hear from you, more fully.

[*Note enclosed*]

Well Austin I have come again. Can you read "dat".? "Donnie" say you cannie. I feel rather troubled about your Eyes. Martha is sick. Emiline is sick too. Mrs Nash goes there often. Mr. Godfrey is visiting New York now. Thompson was here last week. I.F. Conkey has a new span of the blacks, rides out &c. Jane is at home. Kate will be married soon. Weather cold, corn high. Metaphysics clear, other things to match, Sir.

Austin, Dr. Wesselhoef's bill for us both amounts to 16 dollars. If you will pay it, when you come home the money shall be returned to you. You had not better speak to Father about it as it may trouble him now. Wait till vacation. You will find him at 18 bedford *st*. I hope you'll attend to it soon as convenient. Get the bills receipted & keep them yourself.

Give my love to Mary Nichols, glad you like her so well, ask Aunt L. why she does not write to us. We both wrote to her in October, have heard nothing since. What does it mean? Tell Joel to come up here. Im making all my preparations to travel with him next summer. So he had better not invite any body else. Our love to all of them. Who "raced you round Cambridge"? only the name. Have a time with Father.

Vinnie

Preoccupation with illness and doctors' bills did not end with winter. But anxiety lessened somewhat with the approach of spring as activity in the village picked up and there were other things to think about. Chief among them was the long-anticipated railroad which now at last seemed about to materialize.

CHAPTER XVIII

"Stir and Commotion" over the Railroad

IN THE 1850's the railroad-building fever was at its height. Whether it was proposed to construct the "Great Atlantic and Pacific Railroad"—a $100,000,000 project to connect east and west coasts of the United States—or to push through the line from Amherst to Grout's Corner, enthusiasm ran equally high. From the beginning Edward Dickinson had been in the van of the excitement. Indeed, if one word were needed to describe the chief ardor of his life it would be "railroads."

The New England railroads in the 1830's began as local enterprises. Most of them were about twenty or thirty miles in length, each separately incorporated with its own board of directors, operating under a charter granted by a special legislative act. The first ("dowager") road to be completed (1835) was the Boston & Lowell. Previous to January 1, 1854, sixty-three railroads had been incorporated in Massachusetts, and during the 1854 session of the General Court seven more were added.[1]

In rural areas acceptance of "the cars" was, as we have seen, rather lukewarm. The machine age was shutting down upon the yeomanry in spite of themselves. Although they realized that "the application of the newly developed property of nature, known by the term 'Caloric,' to practical uses, will produce wonderful changes in the motive power now in general use," the history of the development of

1. *The Massachusetts State Record*, 1851, 243-253 and 279; *The Massachusetts Register, A State Record*, 1852, 250-260 and 332; 1853, 242-247 and 314; 1854, 163-170, 252-253; 1855, 162-168; *History of Amherst*, Chapter XXXVIII; and David W. Sargent, Jr., "The Railroad Mania in Amherst," *The Railway and Locomotive Historical Society Bulletin*, No. 47 (Boston, 1938). See also Massachusetts *House Document*, No. 480, June 24, 1874.

steam power was "remarkable for the zeal and energy of its opponents."[2]

A charter for a railroad to Amherst had been obtained in the 1840's but nothing had come of it. The townspeople, suspicious of the innovation, thought it would bring undesirable elements and ruin business. In brief, they did not want to encourage it. An attempt at persuasion appeared in the *Express* (March 7, 1851) defending the cars as an evidence of prosperity. Far from ruining business, it was maintained that "the multiplication of railroads brings out the dormant energies of the people," creating "more business, instead of dividing that which already exists."

On May 24, 1851, the General Court granted a charter to the Amherst & Belchertown Rail Road, an extension of the north-south New London, Willimantic and Palmer line. It was to run from the Western Rail Road (Boston & Albany) at Palmer, by way of Amherst, north to Grout's Corner, a distance of 34.7 miles, where it would connect with the Vermont & Massachusetts from Boston. On June 17, 1851, a mass meeting of some three hundred persons was held in Amherst to organize the company and to obtain subscribers for the stock. Luke Sweetser was elected president and Edward Dickinson a director. Not until February 4, 1852, however, was it announced that "after eight years of effort," the stock had all been subscribed (*Express*, February 6, 1852). By the first of April two hundred Irish laborers were at work at Logtown, southeast of Amherst.[3] Clusters of little "shantees" sprang up along the route, outlining with slender filaments of blue smoke the course of the projected railroad.[4]

2. *Massachusetts Register*, 1853, 320.

3. Logtown, the point at which construction of the Amherst & Belchertown Rail Road began on February 12, 1852, was the local name for Dwight's, a hamlet in the valley known also as North Belchertown (*Express*, February 13, 1852). To provide space for the construction of terminal facilities in Amherst, Deacon David Mack sold to the Amherst & Belchertown Rail Road Company about six acres, being part of the tract known as the "meadow," formerly owned by Samuel Fowler Dickinson. See Appendix II.

4. In the early 1850's the question of building a tunnel through a mountain in the northwest corner of the state was debated with some heat. A contract for construction of the Hoosac Tunnel, to connect northern Massachusetts with the Hudson River Valley, was let to the Troy & Greenfield Rail Road on November 7, 1851. By February, 1852, the Mastodon Mountain Drill, "said to be the largest machine in the world" (*Express*, February 27, 1852), was already at work.

[*To W*^m *Austin Dickinson, Care of Joel Norcross. 31. Milk St. Boston.
Mass.; postmark: Amherst Ms. Feb. 6*]

Friday morning [February 6, 1852]

Austin.

I have never left you so long before, since you first went away,
but we have had such colds that we could not use our eyes so long
as to write a letter, and the privation on our part has been greater,
I dare say, than it possibly could—on your's.

I have received both your letters, and enjoyed them both very
much; *particularly* the notes on the agricultural convention. Miss
Kelly's part of the performance was very fine indeed, and made much
fun for us. Should think you must have some *discipline* in order to
write so clearly amidst so much confusion. Father seemed specially
pleased with the story of the farmer. I am so glad you are better—
I wish you might have been spared just for a little visit, but we will
try and wait if you dont think best to come, and shall only be the
gladder to see you at last. I hope you will be very careful and not
get sick again, for it seems to me you've had so much miserable health
since you have lived in Boston; if it dont ruin your constitution, I
shall be very glad. I am very sorry to hear of the illness of the
teachers; I should think you must miss them, they have been with
you so long. You will tell us if they are better, when you write home
again.

Since we have written you, the grand Rail Road decision is made,
and there is great rejoicing throughout this town and the neighboring; that is Sunderland, Montague, and Belchertown. Every body is
wide awake, every thing is stirring, the streets are full of people
talking cheeringly, and you really should be here to partake of the
jubilee. The event was celebrated by D. Warner, and cannon; and
the silent satisfaction in the hearts of all is it's crowning attestation.
Father is really *sober* from excessive satisfaction, and bears his

A year later, however, it had penetrated the mountain only "25 linear feet" and
was "pretty well used up." The failure of the enterprise was all its opponents
could have hoped for. When next a bill to provide for continuance of the work
was brought before the Massachusetts House of Representatives the sponsors
were asked to consider the expediency of making a tunnel to "some point in
Australia" (*Express*, April 22, 1853). Dr. Holland (*History*, I, 432), said the
Hoosac Tunnel, if ever completed, would be "one of the most stupendous works
ever achieved by human hands." Although the project was intermittently revived throughout the next twenty years, the tunnel was still unfinished in 1874,
as we shall see.

honors with a most becoming air. Nobody *believes* it yet, it seems like a fairy tale, a most *miraculous* event in the lives of us all. The men begin working next week, only think of it, Austin; why I verily believe we shall fall down and worship the first "Son of Erin" that comes, and the first sod he turns will be preserved as an emblem of the struggles and victory of our heroic fathers. Such old fellows as Col' Smith *and his wife,* fold their arms complacently, and say, "well, I declare, we have got it after all"—*got it,* you good for nothings! and so we *have,* in spite of sneers and pities, and insults from all around; and we will *keep* it too, in spite of earth and heaven! How I wish you were here, it is really too bad, Austin, at such a time as now—I miss your big Hurrahs, and the famous stir you make, upon all such occasions; but it is a comfort to know that you are here— that your whole soul is here, and tho' apparently absent, yet present in the highest, and the truest sense. I have got a great deal to say, and I fancy I am saying it in rather a headlong way, but if you can read it, you will know what it means. Martha gets along nicely, was able to have her dress on, and go in the dining room for the first time yesterday. She sends you her love, and will write to you just as soon as [she] is able.

Mother has not decided yet, about going to Boston—seems to think if you are better it is hardly best to go. I will tell you more decide[d]ly when I write again—she would love to do so dearly, but it's a good deal of an effort to go away from home at this season, and I hardly know what she will do. Emiline improves slowly. Tutor Howland appeared on Wednesday, and remained in town till today—took tea here Wednesday evening—took Vinnie to ride yesterday morning, spent most of the afternoon here, and is just shutting the gate upon his last farewell, as I write this morning. I have been to ride twice since I wrote you, once with a party, manned by Root & Co. and last evening with *Sophomore Emmons,* alone; will tell you all about it when I write again, for I am in such a hurry that I cannot stop for breath. Take good care of yourself, Austin, and think much of us all, for we do so of you. Emilie

[*On a separate slip*]

I send you my prescription again. Will it trouble you too much to get me another bottle, of the same size as the others, namely *twice the quantity,* and send to me by the first person who comes? You are kind very, Austin, to attend to all my little wants, and I'm sure I thank you for it.

April is'nt far off, and then—and then, we are the "merrie men"!

[*On the inside of the envelope flap*]

Vinnie sends her love, and mother. Vinnie says she thinks you dont pay much attention to her.

[*Note from Edward Dickinson enclosed*]

Austin. You will see by the Editor's glorification article in to-day's 'Express,' that the Am. & Bel. r. road is "a fixed fact." The contract is made—the workmen will be digging, in "Logtown", next week—& we shall see those animating shantees, smoking through an old flour barrel, for a chimney, before many days. The boys fired a few guns— old folks looked on, approvingly—and the whole thing seems as much like a dream, as if we had waked up in the "Mariposa tract", of Col. Fremont, surrounded by the pure "rocks".
The two great eras in the history of Amherst, are
  1. The founding of the College.
  2. The building of the rail road.
We here "set up our Ebenezer."[5]
HaHa!!!

Your father
E. D.

[*To Wm Austin Dickinson, Care of Joel Norcross. 31. Milk St. Boston. Mass.; postmark: Amherst Ms. Feb 18*]

Wednesday morn [February 18, 1852]

Austin.

We received your letters last evening—or Father and Vinnie did, for I did'nt seem to have any; Vinnie cant write today on account of those metaphysics, to which you so touchingly allude. Father also is very busy, so perhaps you wont object to an article from me.
We are all pretty well at home—Martha is getting better, and Emeline, very slowly. Mat sends her love to you and says she shall write you a letter as soon as she is strong enough to keep letters on the line—she sits up most of the day now, but is not able to confine her attention to anything but a little while at a time, and has not yet been out. I have heard from Sue three times, since I have written you—she is well, and in usual spirits. I think it would make Mat very happy to have a letter from you should you find a leisure hour, although she did not tell me to say so—they always inquire for you at Mrs W^m C[utler]'s, and Mat would have written you a long time ago had she been able to do so.
Abby Wood is quite sick this week, but I think will be better soon.
Mr Sweetser's house took fire Monday evening and was with great difficulty extinguished—the family did not lie down all night, and

5. I Samuel VII:12.

the escape was narrow—very. The chimney had been on fire during the day, but no danger was apprehended, and sometime the last of the evening, Mrs Sweetser in going up stairs to give Abby her medicine, thought she smelt smoke in the room. Abby had not perceived it. Mrs S. then opened a door in another direction and the smoke seemed to increase—upon opening the garret door, she saw the flames bursting out from the big timbers near the chimney. Mr Sweetser was at the store—Mrs S. with great presence of mind closed the door, sent at once for Mr. Sweetser, and the family themselves worked until it was morning, pouring water, and sawing away great pieces of timber, until the flames were subdued. The house is a good deal injured, but it is such a miracle that they were not all destroyed that they dont care much for damages.[6] Who did you send your letters and Vinnie's music by? We heard accidentally that there was something for us at Wm Kellogg's store, and there they were—we dont know whence—or by whom, tho' we have suspicions of one Oliver Watson! The vial and flannel came safely, and are just the things desired. I thank you *always* for all you do for me, and would love to send you something did I know what you would like. I was on the point one day of buying a pound of *peanuts* and sending them to you in memory of college days, but Vinnie laughed me out of it—if you will like them tho', and will let me know you shall certainly have them.

Vinnie sends her love to you, and thanks you very much for her music—it is correct. Mother wont come to Boston, probably, this spring—she wants to see you very much, and did think about going some, at the time you were so unwell, but now you are better, and will be at home so soon, she will not think it worth while.

We are all very happy to have you well and happy, and hope you may not be sick in all the rest of the time that you remain in Boston. We have never told you that Pussy has gone—she disappeared about four weeks ago, and we can find nothing of her, so we presume she is dead. We miss her very much, and I think you will miss her, when you come home.

April dont seem quite so far off as it used to, last December—I can almost count the days now, before you are coming home, they seem so few. There are a good many lectures here now, before the Lyceum. Mr Mt Pleasant-Nash, is giving a course of Agricultural ones, twelve in all—and besides a lecture from him once or twice in a week, there is also another from some other gentlemen, on some literary subject. Prof Fowler gave one upon Adam Smith, last evening. Tutor Edwards will give the next. Emmons passed the evening here, and Vinnie and I staid at home—mother went out with

6. The fire was extinguished by the "exertion of the inmates" without giving an alarm (*Express*, February 20, 1852).

Father, but thought the lecture too high for her unobtrusive faculties. I shall love to get a letter when you have the time. Emily.

[*On a separate sheet*]

Mother wants me to add a word in relation to her coming—you
will see what she thinks about in the longer sheet—besides the other
reasons, there given—Father will be away at Court for three or
four weeks to come, most all of the time—*this* mother thinks an
objection, as should she go away too we should be quite alone, and
the folks would'nt think that safe. Then she thinks you are very busy,
and however happy to see her, and desirous to have her come, yet
her visit would necessarily occupy much of your time, and as she
will see you so soon at home, she wants me to ask you if you dont
agree with her in its not being just the thing, for her to visit you
now? Kate Hitchcock is to be married in March. I dont envy her
that Storrs. Root, Harrington, Storrs, Emmons, Graves, and the
Tutors, come in quite often to see us. Emily Fowler was here Monday
afternoon—inquired particularly for you—says Charles is "doing
nicely." March is at Harvard—and writes encouragingly in reference to himself. Emily has much to make her sad—I wonder how she
endures all her numberless trials. The railroad goes on swimmingly
—everything is stir and commotion. The Godfreys have heard
from George—he has reached the Isthmus, suffered all things, according to his account, and thinks going to California, quite a little
undertaking! He has probably reached the mines before now. Much
love from us all.

[*Note enclosed*]

Dear Austin

The music is all right & I thank you very much for it. I have
learned most of it. You ask me to tell you more news, but Austin
there is none but what you have heard over & over again. *Mrs Reed*
is at home now, making her first visit. Sarah Ferry is to have company this evening. Emilie & I are going. Father broke his neck, last
week, it is now nearly mended. This week is court at Northamton,
so Father will be gone most of the time. I'm very glad that you
have a vacation in April. T'will be so good to have you at home
again. I hope you'll contrive to enjoy as much of cousin Emilies
society as possible. Give my love to

[half sheet torn off]

choose. It is made at only *two* stores in Washington Street. I dont
know the names. Perhaps Aunt L. can tell you

[reverse of missing half sheet]

Send home your clothes if you like. It will not make any trouble.
                                                        Vinnie

[*To Wm Austin Dickinson, Care of Joel Norcross, 31. Milk St. Boston,
Mass.; postmark: Amherst Ms. Mar 3*][7]

                                        Tuesday noon [March 2, 1852]

Only a word, Austin, to tell you how we are. I presume you were
quite surprised to receive an anonymous bundle, which you must
have done today, if Mr Graves did his duty. I did'nt mean it should
go without a letter in it, of some considerable length. I wanted to
write you yesterday more than I ever did in my life, and will tell
you now, why I did'nt. But first, I will write how we *are*, since I
promised you that, beforehand.

Father has been shut up with the rheumatism, since Saturday—
is rather better today, and hopes to be out tomorrow—the rest of us
are as well as could possibly be expected! Our *minds* are not well,
mine especially, has quite a number of symptoms—and I appre-
hend a *result*! On the whole, however; we bear it with a good deal of
fortitude.

I would have given most anything to have had you here, last
evening—the scene was indeed too rich, to be detailed by my pen,
and I shall ever regret that the *world* has lost such a chance to laugh.
Let me add as I go along, that father's frame of mind is *as usual* the
happiest, developing itself in constant acts of regard, and *epithets
of tenderness*!

Soon after tea, last night, a violent ring at the bell—Vinnie obeys
the summons—Mr Harrington, Brainerd, would like to see me at
the door. I come walking in from the kitchen, frightened almost to
death, and receive the command from father, "not to stand at the
door"—terrified beyond measure, I advance to the outside door—
Mr. H. has an errand—will not consent to come in, on account of
my father's sickness—having dismissed him hastily, I retreat again
to the kitchen—where I find mother and Vinnie, making most
desperate efforts to control themselves, but with little success—once

7. In place of a postage stamp this envelope is stamped in red, "Paid 3 cts."

more breathe freely, and conclude that my lungs were given me, for only the best of purposes. Another ring at the door—enter W^m [Cowper] Dickinson—soon followed by Mr Thurston! I again crept into the sitting room, more dead than alive, and endeavored to *make conversation*. Father looked round triumphantly. I remarked that "the weather was rather cold" today, to which they all assented —indeed I *never witnessed* such *wonderful unanimity*. Fled to my mind again, and endeavored to procure something equally agreeable with my *last happy remark*. Bethought me of Sabbath day, and the Rev. Mr Bliss, who preached upon it—remarked with wonderful emphasis, that I thought the Rev. gentleman a very remarkable preacher, and discovered a strong resemblance between himself & Whitfield,[8] in the way of remark—I confess it *was rather* laughable, having never so much as seen the *ashes* of that gentleman—but oh such a look as I got from my rheumatic sire. You should have seen it—I never can find a language vivid eno' to portray it to you—well, pretty soon, another pull at the bell—enter *Thankful Smith,* in the furs and robes of her ancestors, while *James* brings up the rear.

Austin, my cup was full—I endeavored to shrink away into primeval nothingness—but sat there large as life, in spite of every effort. Finally Father, accompanied by the cousins, adjourned to the kitchen fire—and Vinnie and I, and our friends enjoyed the rest of the evening.

How much I have said about nothing, and yet if you were *here,* I should take so much comfort in telling you all these things, that I try to forget you are gone, and to talk as if it *were* so; and how I wish it *was,* and that brings me back again to the feet of the smiling April; oh April, April, wilt thou not soon be here.

Dear Austin, are you well, and are y'r spirits cheerful? How I do want to see you—Oh yes—*indeed* I do, and so do we all! Mother did'nt send *all* the clothes because it is'nt the washing week, but she tho't you might like these now, and the rest will be done next Monday, to send by the first who goes. They were delighted with the Gimp, at Mrs. Warner's. Mrs Warner says "Austin has such a *perfect* taste"—Dont tell Emily Norcross—Vinnie and I, kept dark! No more now from Emilie

Much love from us all—take good care of yourself. Love to E Norcross—and all.

---

8. George Whitefield (1714-1770), renowned British evangelist, called "the prince of pulpit orators," came as near as Northampton in October, 1740 (erroneously given as 1749 in *One Hundred and Fiftieth Anniversary of the First Church,* 19), to visit Jonathan Edwards and "the scene of the revival in 1735." Joseph Belcher, *George Whitefield: A Biography* (New York, pref. 1857), 174. Emily's spelling followed the customary pronunciation of his name. He has been described as "the comet that flashed across the religious stupor of London."

For Emily and Vinnie, railroads and other matters of weighty concern to their father did not supplant their more immediate interests. Two undergraduates, both members of Austin's fraternity, were at this time frequent callers at the Dickinson home—Henry Vaughan Emmons, a sophomore, and John L. Graves, a freshman.[9] Although younger than Austin, "Mr." Graves was Edward Dickinson's own first cousin, the "Cousin John" to whom the family were much attached.

The other young man, Vaughan Emmons as he was called, was "a lover of good books, good horses, and good friends, . . . described as an accomplished linguist, always devoted to the classics and literature."[10] Judging by the number of times he is mentioned Emily found him unusually congenial. She first alludes to him in the letter of February 6, 1852. From time to time she sent brief notes to "Sophomore Emmons." Some of them, enclosed in small envelopes addressed to "Mr Emmons, Present" (for they were sent by hand), thank him for books he has lent her; others lend him one in return: "I send you the book with pleasure, for it has given me happiness, and I love to have it busy, imparting delight to others. . . ." This note, one of the earlier ones, is signed "Emily E. Dickinson." On one occasion the young men were invited to come and taste some currant wine. Her note to John Graves follows:

Friday afternoon

Cousin John,

I thought perhaps you and your friend would come in to drink *wine* this evening, as I asked you to do, after Vinnie got home, but I want to tell you something.

Vinnie and I are asked out this evening, and Vinnie's obliged to go. It will not be as pleasant when she is absent from home, and now I want to know if you will be busy *next* week, and if not, wont you save an evening, or an hour of one, when you will come and see us, and taste the currant wine?

9. The letters to these young men, both later ordained ministers in the Congregational Church, are in the Harvard College Library.

10. Helen H. Arnold, " 'From the garden we have not seen,' New Letters of Emily Dickinson," *The New England Quarterly*, XVI (September, 1943), 363.

Please tell your friend—Mr Emmons—and invite him to come with you upon another evening.

Vinnie and I are sorry, but fortune is unkind.

Your Cousin Emily.

The currant wine was homemade of course. As garden fruits and wild berries ripened it was customary for the ladies of the family to turn the surplus into jam, jellies and wine. In spite of scruples, their elderberry and blackberry cordials were sometimes quite heady.

CHAPTER XIX

Private Lives

1

THE influence of Edward Dickinson upon his children was so pervasive that it is not strange that they sometimes resorted to subterfuge in order to hold their "real" lives intact. (Compare Emily's letter of January 12, 1852.)

The next letter to Austin is badly mutilated. Not only have several lines been erased; one section has been cut out. A fragment of the missing half page contains three lines of script on each side, on one of which the lines are crossed out in pencil. These are here restored and the relative position of cuts and erasures indicated. Exasperating though this mutilation is, it is well to bear in mind that Austin considered his sister's letters his private property, never imagining that they had any particular value.

After writing "Austin" across Emily's text on the fourth page, Edward Dickinson placed the letter in an envelope and addressed it to his son.

[*To Mr. Austin Dickinson, Boston*]

Sunday afternoon [March 7, 1852]

I will write while they've gone to meeting, lest they stop me, when they get home. I stayed to Communion this morning, and by that way, bought the privilege of not going this afternoon, and having a talk with you, meanwhile.

It's a glorious afternoon—the sky is blue and warm—the wind blows just enough to keep the clouds sailing, and the sunshine, Oh

Letter from Emily Dickinson to her brother Austin, March 7, 1852

cross these bands and ditches, and goes
rumbling along thro' stones and plank
and clay! I don't feel as if I could
have you there, possibly, another day. I'm
afraid you'll turn into a bank, on a
Pearl Street counting room, if you have not
already, assumed some monstrous shape
living in such a place.

Let me see — April — three weeks until April —
the very first of April, will, perhaps, that
will do, only be sure of the week, the *whole*
week, and nothing but the week! if they
make new arrangements, give my respects
to them, and tell them *old* arrangements
are good enough for you, and you will
have them, then if they said the world, why
let it. Now — there's nothing more excellent
than a travel now and then!

What a time we shall have that day,
after we get home from meeting — why
it makes me dance to think of it, and
Austin, if I dance so many days beforehand
what will become of me when the hour
really arrives? I don't know, I'm sure, and
I don't care, much, for that, or for anything
else, but get you home! We will call on

...

Betty is getting well, is coming down stairs this week. Emilие is ... joining — we will have them all ... before you get here. I ... you are well and happy. It half ... you to having you away — the smallest half! ... Hitchcock and Storrs are coming ... tomorrow evening. ... know whether they will have a ... or not, because the family will be present in ... I am more and more convinced that this is a great country! Emily Fowler was here yesterday afternoon — inquired for, and sent

such sunshine, it is'nt like gold, for gold is dim beside it; it is'nt like anything which you or I have seen! It seems to me "Ik Marvel" was born on such a day; I only only wish you were here. Such days were made on purpose for <Susie> and you and me, then what in the world are you gone for, Oh dear, I do not know, but this I *do* know, that if *wishing* would bring you home, you were here today. Is it pleasant in Boston? *Of course* it is'nt, tho', I might have known more than to make such an inquiry. No doubt the streets are muddy, and the sky some dingy hue, and I can think just how every thing bangs and rattles, and goes rumbling along thro' stones and plank and clay! I dont feel as if I could have you there, possibly, another day. I'm afraid you'll turn into a bank, or a Pearl Street counting room, if you have not already, assumed some monstrous shape living in such a place.

Let me see—April—three weeks until April—the very *first* of April, well, perhaps that will do, only be sure of the week, the *whole* week, and nothing but the week; if they make new arrangements, give my respects to them, and tell them *old* arrangements are good enough for you, and you will have them, then if they raise the wind, why let it blow—there's nothing more excellent than a breeze now and then!

What a time we shall have Fast day,[1] after we get home from meeting—why it makes me *dance* to think of it; and Austin, if I dance so many days beforehand what will become of me when the hour really arrives? I dont know, I'm sure, and I dont care, much, for that, or for anything else, but get you home! We will call on

[half a page cut out]

[*I have been hunting all over the house, since the folks went to meeting, to find a small tin box, to send her flowers, in*] [several lines missing] very often and [one line erased]. Abby is getting well, is coming down stairs this week. Emiline, too is gaining—we will have them all cured before you get here. I'm so glad you are well and happy, it half reconciles me to having you away—the *smallest* half! Kate Hitchcock and Storrs, are coming off tomorrow evening. Dont know whether they will have a wedding, or not, presume the *faculty* will be present in robes. I am more and more convinced, that this is a great country! Emily Fowler was here yesterday afternoon— inquired for, and sent

[reverse of cut-out half page]

out of the house. Dont know where they are going—guess they will have to live on College Tower, for the houses are pretty full [several

1. April 8, 1852, Fast Day, was a public-school holiday in Massachusetts.

lines missing]. There's a great demand for Houses, and Father looks
very grand, and carries his hands in his pockets in case he should
meet a *Northampton man.* The Tyler's are going to Pawtucket
this spring, to live.

Henry [Nash] has whiskers. Wells Newport has disappeared, and
our horse is now under the care of Jeremiah Holden, who seems a
faithful hand. There are many things to say, but meeting is out, and
all the folks are coming.

Sunday evening—Much Love from Mother and Vinnie—we are
now pretty well, and our hearts are set on April, the *very first* of
April! Emilie

Love to Miss Nichols—E. Norcross, if still there, and all the relatives. Sorry he did'nt see Sue.

Liked your letter very much, and hope I shall have another one
pretty soon.

Vinnie went to South Hadley with Henry Root, Wednesday to call
on Jane.

Father has got well. John Emerson's going [to give a] lecture,
Tues[day].[2]

[*To Wm Austin Dickinson, Care of Joel Norcross. 31. Milk St. Boston,
Mass.; postmark: Amherst Ms. Mar 24*]

Wednesday morn [March 24, 1852]

You would'nt think it was spring, Austin, if you were at home
this morning, for we had a great snow storm yesterday, and things
are all white, this morning. It sounds funny enough to hear birds
singing, and sleighbells, at a time. But it won't last any, so you
need'nt think 'twill be winter at the time when you come home.

I waited a day or two, thinking I might hear from you, but you
will be looking for me, and wondering where I am, so I shant wait
any longer. We're rejoiced that you're coming home—the first thing
we said to father, when he got out of the stage, was to ask if you were
coming. I was sure you would all the while, for father said "of course
you would", he should "consent to no other arrangement," and as
you say, Austin, what father *says,* "he means." How very soon it
will be now—why when I really think of it, how near, and how
happy it is, my heart grows light so fast, that I could mount a grass-
hopper, and gallop around the *world,* and not fatigue him any! The
sugar weather holds on, and I do believe it will stay until you come.

2. Citizen's Lyceum lecture, March 9, by John Milton Emerson, "Protestantism
and Catholicism in Their Influence Upon Civilization" (*Express,* March 5, 1852).

Mat came home from meeting with us last Sunday, was here Saturday afternoon when father came, and at her special request, was secreted by me in the *entry*, until he was fairly in the house, when she escaped, *unharmed*.

She inquired all about you, and is delighted enough, that you are coming home. I think Mat's got the notion that you dont care much for home or old friends, but have found their better substitutes in Boston, tho' I do my very best to undelude her. But you will be here soon, and you, of all others, know best how to convince her. I had a letter from Sue last week, at Washington—am expecting another today. Dwight Gilbert wrote Mat, that "the Pres' gave a Levee, as soon as he heard of their arrival." The "M C" remind Sue vividly of little boys at school, squabbling, and quarrelling—a very apt illustration! We had a visit from Uncle Bullard, while father was gone—he appeared Friday night, at teatime, and left us Saturday morning, had a very pleasant time. Abby Wood has got well. Emiline is able to ride out, which she did last week, with Henry, to his infinite exultation. Mat is well as ever; Jane Greely is sick with the quinzy—quite sick. Jane Gridley's husband is sick. "Mrs Skeeter" is very feeble, "cant bear Allopathic treatment, cant have Homeopathic"—dont want Hydropathic—Oh what a pickle she is in—should'nt think she would deign to *live*—it is so decidedly vulgar! They have not yet concluded where to move—*Mrs* W. will perhaps obtain board in the "celestial city," but I'm sure I cant imagine what will become of the rest! Here comes Mattie!

She has just gone away, after staying with me two hours. We have had a beautiful time—Mat anticipates so much in seeing you. Do make the days fly, wont you? Here's her love!

Most everybody is going to move. Jane Gridley has bought the old Simeon S[t]rong place—and is going to move there soon.[3] Frank Pierce, the Montague place, up north—Foster Cook, Mr. Harrington's house—Mr Harrington will move into the Colburn place, until his new house[4] is done &c. This is practical enough. I never tho't I should come to it! Keep well, and happy, Austin—13. days, and you shall come!

Much love from us all. Emilie.

3. On September 17, 1849, Jane Gridley, daughter of Dr. Gridley, had married Dr. George S. Woodman, a graduate of Amherst College, who in 1851 became the associate of his father-in-law in the practice of medicine. The following year, on March 11, 1852, Dr. Gridley died at his home, next but one to "the old Simeon Strong place." The Strong house, it is still called, built in 1744 and even now little changed in appearance, is the home of the Amherst Historical Society.

4. "Mr. Harrington's house," under construction in 1852, stood on the highest point of "Oak Grove Triangle," beside that of Luke Sweetser (*Express*, January 7, 1853). Thirty years later it became the chapter house of the Delta Kappa Epsilon fraternity.

[*Note from Edward Dickinson enclosed*]

Austin,

I wish you would enquire for a bottle of—"prepared mustard," (ready for table use—) at some of the grocery stores, & bring with you, when you come home.

We have had winter & spring, both, since I was in Boston, last, week. To-day is a beautiful day.   Your aff father   E.D.

March 24″

[*Note enclosed*]

Wednesday Evening

Dear Austin

Perhaps you think I never write to you except on buisness, but the folks make me do all the errands, else I should sometimes say some thing different.

Mother wants you to get a whole piece of copperplate for curtains in our chambers. Cant you get it at the whole sale price? I wish you would. Dont give more than the ordinary *price*. Be sure & get some thing pretty. Small figures are most desirable. I think *blue & brown* together are pretty as any two colors, but I allow you to exercise your own Judgment about it. Emilie has told you all the news. Do come home in *April*. We want so much to see you. Harrington has been here this evening. It is snowing hard now. Do you see E. Converse ever? What new friends have you found? You never speak of any in *particular*.

I do want to see you Austin very much. Emilie wants cousin E. to get the Polka which she plays, for her, & send it by Father. Hope you'll have a nice visit with him. If Any body ever asks for me, you can tell them I'm "pretty comfortable." I miss poor Pussy sadly. You'll miss her when you come home, too. Good bye. Keep well & come home soon. Sister Vinnie

Lavinia Dickinson was not in the habit of independently mailing letters to her brother. Although without date or envelope, the following emphatic message appears to be an exception to the rule.

Thursday morn

Dear Austin

I want you to do one more favor for me before coming home & this is it. If convenient Ask Aunt Lavinia if she will be so kind as to

get three eights of a yard of transfer work for a collar that I purchased in Boston. Perhaps she may remember that I looked for some
when in Boston but had not quite made up my mind to get any then.
Now I think I will have some. I shall be very much obliged to you
both for the kindness.

You need not send it. Bring it when you come. Oh! dear! Father
is killing the horse. I wish you'd come quick if you want to see him
alive. He is whipping him because he did'nt look quite *"umble"*
enough this morning. Oh! Austin, it makes me so angry to see that
'noble creature so abused. Emilie is screaming to the top of her
voice. She's so vexed about it. I went to ride yesterday with *Thurston*
[a senior]. Perhaps you wont like it, but I *went*. Grandmother &
Emilie came Tuesday, returned yesterday. We had a pleasant little
visit from them. I'm just as hurried as ever.

Good bye
Vinnie

[*In Austin's writing*]

C.C. Holbrook
corner of Temple Place & Washington just above Winter St.

[*To Wm Austin Dickinson. Care of Joel Norcross. 31 Milk St. Boston.
Mass.; postmark: Amherst Ms. Mar 30*]

Tuesday morn [March 30, 1852]

Dear Austin

We have found some copper plate *here* which pleases us & I shall
get it this morning. So you need not give your self any farther
trouble about it. Father has not returned from Palmer & we are
alone. Tempe had a little company Friday night. I was there. Emilie
was not. I hope your increased cares will not overwhelm you, Austin.
I long to see you, hope nothing will prevent you from spending
a *whole* week with us. All Amherst is anticipating your visit, but
they need'nt for you are not coming to see them, but *us*. Mother is
well. I sent you some wedding cake once, conclude it was not
received.

Good bye
Vinnie

[*On the same sheet*]

Austin—have you plenty of time before you come home, to try and
match this bit of calico, and get me 10. yards of it? It is but a 12½

ct. calico, but very pretty indeed, and as Vinnie has one, I think I would like to have one.

You used to like her's, I remember. Dont look, unless you have time—and dont get anything unless you can find this same. Everybody sends their love, and we're all longing to see you. Mary Warner sends her love—I saw her yesterday.

Never mind the calico, Austin, should it give you any trouble.

Affy. Emilie.

A penciled note from Emily, written "Wednesday," folded and pinned together, was found in the same envelope.

Wednesday

Dear Austin

You speak of not coming home, and I cant help writing one word, tho' I have but a moment of time.

I am so surprised and astonished, at the bare supposition that you are not coming, that I hardly know what to say. I am sure you are not in earnest, you cannot mean what you say. If I supposed you did, I should rather speak, than write, and rather cry, than either. We have tho't of nothing else and talked of nothing else, all winter and spring, and now the time is so near, I dont believe you will disappoint us. The winter was long and lonely, and without <Susie and> you, *spring* is so, but whenever the time seemed long, I looked away to April, and was sure of happiness then. I dont wonder you cant think how we look—I know just exactly how you look.

Do you wear a Kossuth Hat? I somehow tho't you did. Austin, you know mother is not in the habit of writing—she talks a great deal about you, and so does Vinnie. Are you willing to get the bottle filled again with my medicine?

We all send you our love, and shall not hear a word to your not coming in April.

Affy Emily.

Mr Ford was in town yesterday. He called here with Emily & inquired much for you.[5]

Austin came home on April seventh for Fast Day and left on the twelfth.

5. During the next year and a half Gordon Lester Ford was a frequent visitor in Amherst. On December 16, 1853, he and Emily Fowler were married.

[*Letter addressed to "Austin" in a separate envelope*]

Dear Austin

I intended to send you quite a long letter this time but Emilie has got the start of me & told you all the news so I shant say but little.

Your last letter was very satisfactory to us all. We were glad that you loved home better than the City. Father looked very meek when it was read & a little foolish. We are lonely this dreary weather Austin & wish you were here.

If the valise does not hold all your things, the rest shall be sent by Mr Watson. Your *cravat* is not here. I think you must have mislaid it. I have looked every where but in vain. Mother is not certain whether you want the two flannel jackets sent back or not. If you say so, they shall go next week. I will send you my picture, but I dont like it at all & should be sorry to have you or any one else think I look just like it. I dont think my real face is quite so stupid as the picture, perhaps I'm mistaken however. You may have it & welcome though if it will be any gratification to you.

My music is bound very nicely. It came home yesterday. It pleased me exceedingly that you liked my music. You dont know how much your favor encouraged me. I shall practise with a great deal more interest now than before. I went to the Palmer party & expressed your regrets as well [as] I could which were warmly accepted. I guess you didnt lose much however.

I hope you will be very careful not to get *sick* this damp weather. Dont confine yourself too closely. What of your boarding place? Have you moved yet? I feel as though you had the blues this week for some reason. Am I right?

Father is at Palmer.

Good bye Austin.

Truly Vinnie

2

At five o'clock one May morning Emily had already completed her early-morning chores, and while waiting for her father, her ailing mother and her sister to come down to breakfast, took time to write for her brother this memorable description of a thunder shower.

The second half of the double sheet on which the letter is written has been neatly removed with a paper knife. Although the docu-

ment appears to be complete, the final letters of several lines on the
second page have been cut off.

[*To Wm Austin Dickinson. Care of Joel Norcross. 31. Milk St. Boston
Mass.; postmark: Amherst Ms. May 10*]

                                        Monday morning. 5.oc. [May 10, 1852]
Dear Austin.

   I have made the fires, and got breakfast, and the folks wont get
up, and I dont care for it because I can write to you. I did not write
yesterday, because mother was sick, and I thought it would trouble
you. She was attacked Friday, with a difficulty in her face, similar to
the one which you have, and with which you suffer so much once or
twice in a year. She had her face lanced yesterday, and was much
more comfortable last evening, so I think she'll get well right away
   Vinnie and I have had to work pretty hard on account of her sickness, so I'm afraid we shant write you anything very refreshing this
time. Vinnie will tell you all the news, so I will take a little place to
describe a thunder shower which occurred yesterday afternoon—the
very first of the season. Father and Vinnie were at meeting, mother
asleep in her room, and I at work by my window on a "Lyceum
Lecture." The air was really scorching, the sun red and hot, and you
know just how the birds sing before a thunder storm, a sort of hurried, and agitated song—pretty soon it began to thunder, and the
great "cream colored heads" peeped out of their windows—then
came the wind and rain and I hurried around the house to shut all
the doors and windows. I wish you had seen it come, so cool and so
refreshing—and everything glistening from it as with a golden dew
—I tho't of you all the time, and I thought too, of Susie; I did wish
you both here through all that blessed shower.
   This morning is fair and delightful—you will awake in dust, and
amidst the ceaseless din of the untiring city, would'nt you change
your dwelling for my palace in the dew? I hear them coming, Austin
Goodbye for now. I shall see you so soon. E.

[*Letter enclosed*]

   Oh Austin how I wish you were here. It is so lonely without you
I dont think I shall ever get used to your being away. I miss you
more & more every day. Mother has been sick for two days & Father
"is as he is", so that home has been rather a gloomy place, lately. You
are at home so little, that you see only the sunshine & none of the

clouds, but clouds there are & very black ones sometimes, which threaten entirely to obscure the sun. Only think Austin, Dr Woodman has been to see Mother *twice,* because Dr Brewster was gone. Wont Jane Gridley crow? Mother is better now & will soon be well, the garden is made & every thing is growing rapidly, the air is full of fragrance & of song. Bowdoin took Mary's French & Lyman, E. Fowler & me out to Pelham Springs, last week after *Arbutus.* We found an abundance of it & had a nice time. I thought t'was quite an undertaking for Bowdoin. I did'nt suppose he could drive a horse before. I guess the horse will be glad to see you Austin, Father gives him a "basteing" occasionally "thinks he needs it." I'm afraid he'll spoil him. Are you going to get anyone for the office? I wish you could find the right sort of person for that place. I hope you wont find any door knobs, Austin for all but Father dont want them, the others are good enough & look better on white doors than white ones would. Dont let Father know that I say this. I'm making some reforms in the house which I guess you'll like, & I have some *plans* for improvement that cant be fully carried out with out your assistance so you must expect to devote a little time in vacation especially to me. When is your vacation? Wont you send us Joseph Lymans address, for we wish to write to him. We sent a bundle to you by Mr Frink, which I supposed you received on Friday. In the bundle, was a note telling the number of yards wanted & containing the pattern of gingham which Mother chose.[6] I presume you discovered it. Did you? Emilie Fowler has gone away for the summer. Mat is well & interesting. John Emerson called here last evening. The term begins this week. The parlor carpets have been taken up & put down again & none of us killed. Write as soon as you can. Good bye Vinnie

[*Note from Edward Dickinson enclosed*]

Dear Austin,

Mother has been severely afflicted with the Neuralgia arising from her front tooth—suffered excruciating pain for 24. hours—it was lanced on Sunday afternoon, yesterday, & she is now relieved—tho' not yet down stairs. We have invited her to take tea with us, below, this evening. The wood is piled—the yard cleaned up—grape vines & trees trimmed—garden made & planted, manure got out, potatoes in lot planted, grass-land dragged over to loosen the earth & make

6. Vinnie's note, with the gingham sample still pinned to it, was found in the same envelope:
Austin
We are delighted with *this* piece of gingham & want you to get a pattern if it comes in *patterns.* Else get 11 yards.

the grass-better. The spring business about over. Bowdoin has, this morning, gone to So. Hadley, to help his father, a few days. He is sick, & sent for him.

The College term commences this week. We expect you home, sometime this month, for a few days. Nothing particularly new.

Mr Sweetser has gone to Boston to-day—will go in the night train, from Palmer—return on Wednesday or Thursday—stops at the American House. You can send anything you wish by him.

Your aff. father
E. D.

A draft of a letter from Austin to Martha Gilbert is written on half sheets of blue paper pinned together. To judge by the drafts in my possession, this shy girl with the "sweet face" was gradually taking a very special place in his affection. A few months later she left Amherst to make a long visit at her brother's home in the West.

Tuesday even [May 11, 1852]

I have just returned from school, Mat, and rather tired, after teaching all day but determined you shall have *something, however poor,* from me by tomorrow's mail.

I meant certainly to have written you almost as soon as I returned and why I *have not* is more than I can easily explain, for this is at least the *sixth* time since then that I have sat here by the window & table, & drawn my paper before me and written "Mat"—and then leaned back to think how to go on, but without even once *thinking* farther than some ten or a dozen lines, and those always unsatisfactory, not to be sure that I have^{nt} enough to write about, but rather that in the multitude of my varied thoughts & feelings & experiences, and hopes & fears, I am at a loss which to select, or those how to join, to give so occasional a correspondent, and one with whom I care to preserve the *appearance* of as much consistency of character as I believe I really possess, any tolerably fair idea of me.

My moods are so changing from day to day (& sometimes even from hour to hour) and with them my views of all about me. I must needs spread over space enough to embrace several of them, or write quite often, just in the present—that the addressed may, from numerous likenesses, form my general expression, or I must write a superficial and artificial letter that it would be mean to send a friend. For the shadows of life, with me, are so constantly changing from light to dark, from dark to light, sometimes as bright as bright can be, & at others, dark as a starless night, sometimes full of only lights of beauty & sounds of joy, & fragrant perfume, and every delightful sensation, and I feel the warmest, kindliest sympathy with all mankind, and can imagine then how no one can be *less* than happy in this world of such beauty & grandeur, nor how a heaven can be more perfect than the one that fills my own heart. And, at *others,* as entirely cheerless—no scenes meet my eye, but those of sorrow & misery, no tales, but of woe, my ears, and not the faintest glimmer from from [*sic*] the faintest star of Hope, to encourage, or bec[k]on to a Future of promise.

Sometimes its end clear as light, & its manifold duties & relations, and, at others, all an awful, bewildering mystery. I startle in broad day, like a frightened child from sleep, as if I had just woke for the first time, to consciousness of my existence & the world around me, and wonder where I am, & *what,* and what my destiny, and the meaning of all this bustle & parade I see, and this jostling and crowding of all these ten thousand men, in every respect like myself, this way & that, and all these signs of *power* impressed on all around.

I feel the presence of that within me, unseen, yet indescribably mighty, that can comprehend worlds & systems of worlds & yet cannot comprehend itself. That with the aid of history, history, not as written in books, but imprinted on the everlasting hills, & deeply imbedded rocks, may last through long ages of a remote past, before Time began, and learn of the lives & changes & ends of races of beings before man was, and yet cannot assure me of a single event of the Future. That can estimate the distances and weights of burning suns, far off in the trackless wastes of space, & yet can find nothing to satisfy its own eager, restless longings for knowledge of itself, & its Infinite author—and I tremble & my brain reels as I think, with all this amazing power, *passing* wonder, and all the susceptibility to pleasure or pain, I am still drifting on I know not whither—I look around me, to see what others are doing, whether *they* too are suffering in the same anxious suspense, or whether it is to me alone Life is a sealed book. Here & there I behold a solitary *one,* groping on in the profound darkness unknowing whither this course or that will lead him if indeed *any*where, if he may not, with the next step plunge into blank nothingness—but with these single exceptions, I see them marshalled in mighty hosts, yet under different banners, and marching on to the word of their several leaders, whom they believe, each his own, have received from the Omnipotent himself the true, and *only* true chart of the route to knowledge, to happiness everlasting & to him. And now *new* doubts encompass me, for if *either,* & only *one, which* is *right?* I am besought on the one hand to join one standard & on the other, another—the advocates for the standard of the "Cross" appeal to me in the most solemn manner, as I value quiet from the gloomy doubts & fears within me—As I value perfect peace & perfect happiness through a life eternal, in *God's* name to join them, for so surely as God is God, all the rest are marching on to death & perdition—but when I survey their ranks, and observe their comparative thinness, I hesitate. I ask myself, Is it possible that God, all powerful, all wise, all benevolent, as I must believe him, *could* have created all these millions upon millions of human souls, only to destroy them? That he *could* have revealed himself & his ways to a chosen few, and left the rest to grovel on in utter darkness? I *can*not believe it. I can only bow & pray, Teach me, O God, what thou wilt have me to do, & obedience shall be my highest pleasure.

But Mat, what am I writing you? Something I am afraid you will be sorry to read from me. Yet you must pardon me, for you *would*nt, you know, had I not written myself, if I wrote at all. And now that you have a glance, *only* a glance, at my inner life, you can appreciate a little the reason for my not liking to write as I should were *I* more settled in my feelings. I despise untruthfulness to friends, and yet I hesitate to do anything that may tend, in the least, to dim their sun-light.—

To break short off this strain now, Mat, my term closes again next week, and I shall be home Saturday eve or Monday, for a week. I hardly know whether I am anticipating it much or not, for I have^nt many anticipations, or hopes just now—yet I *am* anticipating *it too* —anything to break in upon this year & remind me it is near its end.

We are having as beautiful weather the last few days as one could wish. The peach & cherry trees in the yard my window overlooks, are in full blossom—and by the time I go home, the apples will be fairly out, looking like huge bouquets scattered at random through the fields.

How beautiful the country will be! The air heavy with fragrance, and musical with the songs of gay birds & the drowsy hum of bees, & the shrill chirp of countless insects—just the time of all others, for a ride, horseback, or on wheels, and I mean to improve it in that way.

I heard from Sue, about a fortnight since, nothing particularly new from her. She was only a little afraid she should hardly have time to *"pack,"* she was going home so very soon.

Emily always writes me of you, so I find out what *you* are doing as often as I do what she is. Father wrote me about a week ago he expected to go to Washington in a few days, but I have heard nothing about it since, perhaps you know.—

Here I am at the bottom of the 6th page, an entirely unpremeditated length, & I stop right in the middle of several short sentence I *would write*, & say good night—

May 11th, 52

On May 22 Austin came home for the spring recess. Forty year later he tried to recall when the following letter from Emily had

been written and thought it must have been in March, 1851. It was
so dated in the published volumes.[7] But it was in 1852 that the girls
were reading *Ellen Middleton* by Georgiana Fullerton. Furthermore,
in the spring of 1851 Austin was not writing letters to Martha Gilbert that would make her weep. In the case of this hastily penciled
note the handwriting—usually the best guide—does not fix the date
with certainty.

[*To Wm Austin Dickinson, Care of Joel Norcross. 31 Milk St. Boston,
Mass.*]

Thursday night [May 20 (?), 1852]

Dear Austin.

I have wanted to write you a long letter all the week, but you
know Mother has been sick, and I have had more to do; but I've
tho't of you all the time, and thought too how happy we should be
if you were living at home.

It is very hard to have it so, but I try to be as happy and as cheerful as I can to keep father and mother from feeling so very lonely
as they must all the while.

Mattie was with me most all the afternoon—we had a long, sad
talk about <Sue and> Michigan, and Life, and our own future, and
Mattie cried and I cried, and we had a solemn time, and Mat said
she had a beautiful letter from you last night. She was going to send
you some flowers in a box, the other day, but you had'nt then
answered her letter, and Mat is very shy, so you see why you did'nt
get them. John Thompson brought us the books—he arrived Monday—no, it was Tuesday evening—I have read "Ellen Middleton"
and now Mat has it.

I need'nt tell you I like it, nor need I tell you more, for you know
already.

I thank you more and more for all the pleasures you give me—
I can give you nothing Austin, but a warm and grateful heart, that
is your's now and always. Love from all, and Mat. Emilie

Only think, you are coming Saturday! I don't know why it is that
it's always *Sunday* immediately you get home—I will arrange it
differently. If it was'nt 12 o'clock I would stay longer.

[*On a slip in Vinnie's writing*]

Curtain Hooks

7. *Letters,* 1894, 79; *Letters,* 1931, 77.

CHAPTER XX

Edward Dickinson Enters National Politics

1

IN 1852 Edward Dickinson broadened the scope of his activities. On Thursday, June 3, he was elected a delegate from the "Old Sixth" congressional district of Massachusetts to the Whig convention which met in Baltimore on the sixteenth of June. "The Convention was composed of delegates from all the States; men elected, in great measure, for power and political position;—ex-governors, counselors, leaders of the people, chiefs of parties were all there; and it was, in point of intellect, a very superior body to the national House of Representatives."[1] The *Express* (June 11, 1852) voiced satisfaction that the selection of a candidate for the presidency should be "in the hands of a Convention composed of the best men in the nation."

Mr. Dickinson left for Baltimore on the twelfth. "A thoroughgoing whig man," he supported the candidacy of Daniel Webster, as did other Massachusetts delegates including his friends Rufus Choate of Boston and Otis P. Lord of Salem.

Mr. Choate's "Boswell," in a book which brings to life the "corrugated, bloodless, startling look" of that tempestuous personality, describes the spell cast over the convention when Rufus Choate "made one of the most fervid and striking speeches of his life. . . . the southern branch of the Convention, especially, were completely carried away by this new and strange eloquence.

"I have heard, and it was currently said at the time, that in the tedious struggle for a nominee, so much were the southern men im-

1. Edward G. Parker, *Reminiscences of Rufus Choate, The Great American Advocate* (New York, 1860), 65, 66.

pressed by Choate's speaking and appearance, they crowded round him, and more than once intimated that they would vote for him, as nominee, certainly for Vice President, if not for President. But there was no bribe beneath the stars that could swerve Choate from his allegiance to Webster. Next to his God, he believed in Daniel Webster." Rufus Choate spoke prophetic words when he said that "the dying of a nation begins with the heart."

The Convention of 1852 was the last to represent the Whig party as a whole, South as well as North. Northern Whigs named the candidate and southern Whigs framed the platform, although the wording of it was that of Daniel Webster. All were agreed on one point—the Union must be kept intact. Whigs in both sections of the country were trying in every way they could to counteract the alarming effect of the slavery issue; and so the Compromise of 1850 had been "acquiesced in by the Whig party of the United States as a settlement in principle and substance of the dangerous and exciting questions" which it embraced. Fifty-three ballots were cast. Edward Dickinson voted for Webster on every one. After five days of balloting, however, General Winfield Scott of New Jersey and William A. Graham of North Carolina were nominated.

It is an understatement to say that the disappointment of the Whig electorate of Massachusetts was "severe." Many of the foremost men of the Commonwealth, Rufus Choate among them, refused to take further part in the campaign. Not so Edward Dickinson. Though he was as profoundly disturbed as any Whig in the state, he did not withdraw. Instead, he threw his wholehearted support to General Scott, making speeches here and there in his behalf. But without avail. Before Mr. Dickinson's career in national politics ended his party had collapsed. For in this very platform which committed the members to uphold a compromise abhorrent to patriots throughout the North, the Whig party took the final step toward its own dissolution—a direct result of events which were to take place in the Thirty-third Congress.

After the spring recess Austin had returned to Boston on the seventh of June. The next letter from Emily was postmarked on the twenty-first, the day before her father's return. Mrs. Dickinson had recovered from her neuralgia and was making plans for a visit to her sister, Mrs. Loring Norcross.

*[To Wm Austin Dickinson, Care of Joel Norcross. 31. Milk St.
Boston.; postmark: Amherst Ms. Jun 21]*

Sunday morning [June 20, 1852]

Your last letter to us, Austin, was very short and very unsatisfying
—we do not feel this week that we have heard anything from you
for a very great while, and father's absence, besides, makes us all
very lonely.

I infer from what you said, that my last letter did'nt suit you, and
you tried to write as bad a one as you possibly could, to pay me for
it; but before I began to write, Vinnie said *she* was going to, and I
must'nt write any news, as she was depending upon it to make her
letter of, so I merely talked away as I should if we'd been together,
leaving all the matter o'fact to our practical sister Vinnie—well, we
had calls Sunday evening, until too late to write, and Vinnie was
sound asleep when the mail went out in the morning. I was determined to send you *my* letter, that very day, so Vinnie's note of news,
for which I had starved my own, is as yet unwritten. We have looked
every day for a long letter from you, and really felt sadly enough
when Saturday came without it. I should have written you sooner,
but we have had Miss Bangs cutting dresses for us this week, and
have been very busy, so I could'nt possibly write, but we have all
thought of you, and *that* is better than writing. Father has not got
home, and we dont know when to expect him. We had a letter from
him yesterday, but he did'nt say when he should come. He writes that
he "should think the whole world was there, and some from other
worlds"—he says he meets a great many old friends and acquaintances, and forms a great many new ones—he writes in very fine
spirits, and says he enjoys himself very much. I think it will do him
the very most good of anything in the world, and I do feel happy to
have father at last, among men who sympathize with him, and know
what he really is. I wish you could have gone with him, you would
have enjoyed it so, but I did'nt much suppose that selfish old school
would let you. Father writes that he's called on Sue, twice, and found
her very glad to see him. She will be home in a fortnight—only
think of that!

Mattie gets along nicely—she sends her love to you—she is down
here most every day. Abby Wood had a little party, week before
last—a very pleasant one. Last week, the Senior Levee came off at
the President's. Vinnie went to the Levee, and I went to walk with
Emmons. Vinnie had a nice time—said everything went off pleasantly, and very much as usual. I believe Prof. Haven is to give one

soon—and there is to be a Reception at Prof. Tyler's, next Tuesday evening, which I shall attend. You see Amherst is growing lively, and by the time you come, everything will be in a buzz.

Uncle Samuel's family are here, boarding at Mr Palmer's. Uncle Samuel was here himself, about a week, and is now in New York. Arthur, the oldest one, is going to work on a farm this summer, so as to grow stout and strong, before entering college. Porter Cowles is going to take him. Mr Bowdoin is here still—comes round with the news every day—he has formed quite a fancy for Mat, since Mary became so feeble—has called on her two or three times, been to walk with her once, and walked home with her from the President's. Mat smiles and looks very peculiarly when we mention Mr Bowdoin. I hav'nt seen Mary Warner since you went away—the last time I *heard* of her, she had Thurston and Benjamin, *weeding her flower garden. That's* romantic, is'nt it—she better have her heart wed, before she weeds her garden!

As father has'nt come, Mother cant say certainly how soon you will see her in Boston; just as soon as he comes, she will go, tho, and we shall let you know. She has got her new teeth in, and I think they look very nicely. We all send you our love. Emilie.[2]

I hope you will write me a letter as soon as you possibly can.

An undated letter from Vinnie, enclosed in a separate envelope and sealed with a wafer, was also written before their father's return from Baltimore.

Dear Austin

I expect you think I've entirely forgotten you but I've been so busy every moment since you left us, that I could not write to any one. It seems strange enough to have Father gone so long & you too. We behaved very well, though. Henry Nash gave me a horseback ride last Monday. Twas fine! George Dickinson spent Sunday here. I want you to see him. I'm quite sure youd' fancy him. I believe you & I usually like the same kind of persons! Mary Lyman is here yet. The Receptions are prosperous. I've been only once. Emilie & I dont go to see any one but Mat. There is nothing new here.

I hope my picture is in your keeping now. I dont wish any one else to have it. I trust Mother's visit will be happy. She anticipates it very much. I want you to get some songs for me & let Mother pay for them. If you own Ellen Middleton & are not using it & are

2. Addressed to "W. A. Dickinson, Esq.," an invitation to an anniversary dinner on July 27 at Williston Seminary, Easthampton, was enclosed.

willing, Mother can bring it home! I long to have you & *Sue* get home. I've got a beautiful new Pussy, superior to the old one. Emilie's hair is cut off & shes very pretty. She sends love & will write some time.

We are very busy as usual, intend to be at leisure when you come home. Good bye.

Vinnie

Soon after Edward Dickinson came home his wife, her new teeth firmly in place, went to Boston for her long-anticipated visit. While there she received the following communication from Vinnie. The top of the second sheet is torn off, only a detached fragment of it—with the words "Ben Bolt"—remains.

Saturday eve [June 26, 1852]

Dear Mother

I've just received Austins letter & judge from it, that you are having a fine time. I'm very glad to have you so happy & hope you'll stay as long as you desire. We get along nicely with out you. Miss Bangs was here Friday & part of Thursday. Prof. Haven held a levee Friday Evening which I attended & wore my new blue dress. Mr & Mrs Bradford called here on Thursday to tell us about cousin Emilie who is dangerously ill.[3] They are very anxious about her. I've called on Harriet Fisher & Mary Gould. I want you to get me

[top of sheet torn off]

The music of the last is by Dempster, I think. I want also, one yard & a half of deep fringe for my blue bertha cape. I'll send a bit of the dress. I would prefer a plain heading to netting if you can find it.

[Reverse of missing portion]

Please ask Austin when the hat stand & dusting brush are coming. I cant write to him now. Pussy is pretty comfortable. Emilie entraps a mouse every night. Good bye.
Love to all. Vinnie

Three more communications from Vinnie, two of them in envelopes addressed by Emily, were dispatched to Austin before he came home at the end of the school year. The "Joseph" to whom Vinnie refers was Joseph Lyman, an admirer of the moment.

3. Emily Lavinia Norcross, aged 24, died July 2, 1852.

Thursday Morn [July 8, 1852]

Dear Austin

These documents came last night & I opened Joseph's thinking there might be some thing for me in it. I guess you won't care. You *must* write to Joseph. I think he feels badly that you dont. I've recovered from my headache. Father is coming this noon. It's dreadful lonely with out you Austin. Sue spent yesterday afternoon here. I've been thinking lately how easily I could become *insane*. Sometimes I feel as though I should be. Emilie & I had cards from Mr White, too. I am tired of receiving wedding cards, they come from some where, every day, that pretty cousin Lizzie sent me hers Monday.
Now Austin, write to Joseph right off.
Write to us when you can.

Good bye.
Vinnie

After her year of teaching in Baltimore, Susan Gilbert had returned to Amherst on the third of July.

[*To Wm Austin Dickinson, Care of Joel Norcross. 31. Milk St. Boston, Mass.; postmark: Amherst Ms. Jul 15*]

Thursday morn [July 15, 1852]

Dear Austin

I believe I must write to you once more before you come home, so you'll know I'm here yet. If you were here this morning I think *we* would have a ride. It is cool & delightful & I wish I could do some thing a little uncommon. The heat has been intolerable all summer. I'm very glad you are better, hope twill last till you come home.
The music suits exactly & you are very kind to get it for me. Mother had a nice time in Boston & told fine stories of your fame among Bostonians. I long to have you at home again & am hurrying fast as possible to finish all my work before that time. I've made various internal improvements lately, which I guess will please you. Two things I want *you* to do with out fail. Be sure & get the *hat stand* & a *duster* made of *feathers*. You know what I mean I suppose. We

need them both & I shall be disappointed if you dont bring them. Mr Sweetsers family from New York are coming to *"Luke's"* to day. Aunt Lizzie will be *here* next week & Aunt Susan [Mrs. S. F. Dickinson, Jr.] is already established here for the present, that is in town. So you'll find plenty of ancestors here on your return, which you'll doubtless enjoy *"much"*. Mary Lyman leaves town to day & "with a sad heart too"! She invited us to visit her at Cambridge which we shall most certainly do, oh yes, Sue & Mat are bright. Mrs Warner is not herself yet. Mary is "little blue", "only little". Abby is all Ego & "Uncle". Joe Colton & Robert Cutler "Esq" have gone to the west to see what they can see. Have you heard from Joel yet? Distinguished strangers are arriving in town constantly. I've got a beautiful Pussy, Austin. Emilie & I feel as though Richard Dic[k]inson was interested in that Miss Willson. Is it so? Mother wants to know what Aunt Lavinias plans are about leaving the city. Wants you to tell her we shall be happy to see her any time when she pleases to come. Emilie sends love. The reception is to be at Prof. Jewetts toworrow evening. We received your letter & were glad. Dont you leave my picture any where when you come home, bring it with you. Now Austin, remember the *hat stand & duster.*

Good bye.
Vinnie

[*To Wm Austin Dickinson, Care of Joel Norcross, 31. Milk St. Boston, Mass.; postmark: Amherst Ms. Jul 21*]

Tuesday P.M. [July 20, 1852]

You shall have the hair and welcome, Austin, though it seems very funny why you want it.[4] I expect Father will think it rather hard that *he* cant hear your letter of to day. We shall make some kind of excuse, but what, time only will show.

Edmund Converse must come here this summer.

Aunt Lizzie comes tomorrow.

Good bye.
Your curious
Vinnie

Emilie & I made calls, yesterday. Stopped at Fullers & took ice cream, fancied t'was Miss *Copelands.* Want you at home very much.

Austin came home on July 26, 1852, his teaching career at an end. He left the Endicott School with enthusiasm, having made at least

4. A folded bit of paper is enclosed but the hair is missing.

one decision, that his life would not be spent in a schoolroom. With infinite relief he turned to work in orchard and garden.

2

For several months the political activities of Edward Dickinson had been taking more and more of his time. On the day his son returned to Amherst Mr. Dickinson was addressing a Whig rally in Springfield, urging all members of the party to bend their energies toward the election of General Scott.[5] Daniel Webster meanwhile was accused of "sulking in his tent." At the September state convention of the party in Worcester he did not appear, nor did other leading Whigs. Robert C. Winthrop in particular was criticized for being absent. The voters' attitude was set forth in the *Express* (September 10) in an editorial entitled, "Where are our Old Whig Leaders," from which the following sentences are taken:

> Mr. Winthrop is well nigh an idol of the whigs of Massachusetts, and beloved and respected by the whigs of all parts of the Union. He is first in their hearts as he has been heretofore first as an exponent of whig doctrine, and now when he voluntarily withdraws from the leadership to a place in the ranks, that place should be among the *working* whigs. . . . The present is no time for our leaders to hold back. . . . Instead of remaining silent while their fellows work . . . their men should come forward. . . . This much, the whigs of Mass. expect, aye, demand of their leaders, Ashmun, Choate, Winthrop, Webster, and hosts of others. They have shown their devotion to *men*, now let them come forward and proclaim their love of *principle*.

The Whigs of the Tenth Congressional District, newly formed from the "Old Sixth," were to hold a convention at Northampton on Wednesday, September 15, to nominate a representative to Congress. An editorial supporting the candidacy of Edward Dickinson appeared in the *Express* on the tenth.[6] Of the 68 votes cast on the first ballot he received 37, and on the second was chosen unanimously. An Amherst Whig Club, formed with support of the local newspaper, went to work for the election of their fellow townsman. Austin Dickinson was a member of the executive committee.

Meanwhile, the private lives of candidates were being overhauled by rival parties in the hope of digging up something unsavory on

5. *Express*, July 30, 1852.
6. *Express*, September 10, 1852 (Appendix III).

which to base a campaign of personal vilification. It was not long before the Democrats unearthed what was referred to in their organ. the *Boston Times,* as a "scandal." The attack was, so far as I know, the only attempt in this campaign to besmirch the character of Edward Dickinson. The *Express* promptly branded the story as not only untrue, but ridiculous.

Mr. Dickinson appeared so aloof, his manner was so formal, that he sometimes gave the impression of being disdainful. And so it did not seem too much out of character for those who concocted the story to feel that some credence might be placed in it. Here is the incident as it appeared in print, spelling and all. It is not hard to imagine that to Edward Dickinson the imputation was peculiarly offensive.

From the *Boston Daily Times and Bay State Democrat,* second edition, October 1, 1852, Friday morning:

Sixth District—Edward Dickenson, the Whig Candidate

Mr Edward Dickenson is nominated by the whigs of the 6th Congressional District as a candidate for Representative in Congress. The character of the man can be inferred from the following extract from a private letter from a gentleman of Amherst, Mr D's place of residence:

Yesterday there was some fun here. Mr Edward Dickenson has been very prominent among the Maine Law advocates, and by his exertions very stringent regulations have been made for the sale of liquors for medicinal purposes. Among these regulations is one which compels persons wishing to purchase spirit, to obtain an order from a physician for its delivery, for which order the doctor's charge is 12½ cents. Thus the poor fellow, who has occasion to use six cents worth of brandy must pay really eighteen cents. Of course this has caused much complaint among the poorer classes, but the agency has been inexorable. Yesterday Dickinson walked into the shop of an apothecary, "duly authorized," &c, and deposited a vial on the counter, requesting Mr F. to fill it with brandy. The agent politely remarked, "I presume you have an order." "Order!" exclaimed Dickenson, "for what?" "A physician's order is necessary for the delivery of spirit, you are aware," rejoins Physic. "Oh!" replied Dickenson, "that rule *was not made for me!*" But the seller was inexorable, and the Hon. left swearing that he would send to Northampton for his *drink.*

As election day approached and the campaign of mudslinging was nearing a climax, the Whig party received a body blow. On Sunday, October 24, at 2:40 A.M., at his home in Marshfield, Daniel Webster breathed his last. Never since the death of Washington, it was said, had there been such widespread grief. For the Whigs the death of their leader was a sinister omen.

In spite of universal mourning the "Cattle Show and Fair" was held in Amherst on Wednesday, October 27, as planned; but it was more like a funeral. The procession formed at 11:30 and as usual marched first to the house of Edward Dickinson. A "car upon which was an American flag, dressed in mourning," was drawn by a yoke of oxen. After the exercises in the college chapel dinner was served to several hundred persons at the Amherst House. Mr. Dickinson, presiding, gave "the memory of Daniel Webster, the farmer of Marshfield." The toast, in water, was received in silence followed by a dirge from the band.

The students of the college, "participating in the deep and general sorrow," voted to wear a badge of mourning for thirty days and passed a set of resolutions signed by five students, among them H. V. Emmons and Rufus Choate, Jr. At noon on Friday, the day of the funeral, the students fired seventy-one guns in honor of Webster's seventy-one years.[7] For days the newspapers were filled with accounts of his life, his death, his last words and descriptions of the funeral, even to the manner in which the corpse was dressed. The Presidential election on the following Tuesday dropped into second place. On October 29 the *Express* ventured the opinion, however, that if the Democratic candidate was elected, "the restless spirit of aggression, extension of territory and the war spirit of the nation will become predominant." The worst was predicted—the worst happened. While the newspapers were still overflowing with eulogies of "the greatest intellect America has ever produced," the Whig party met with resounding defeat. On November 2, in a Democratic landslide, General Franklin H. Pierce, a New Hampshire Democrat, was chosen President of the United States, an outcome which, in Massachusetts, added to the general depression.

After the national elections, those of the Commonwealth were held on the following Monday, November 8, 1852. In the Tenth District, Edward Dickinson was one of four congressional candidates. None received a majority. In announcing the results the *Express* (November 12) stated that "the vote given for the Whig member of Congress

7. *Express,* October 22 and 29; November 5 and 12, 1852.

in the tenth district is highly flattering to the candidate. In many towns his vote leads that of [Governor John H.] Clifford. . . . And had it not been for the disaffection in this town, which grew out of a purely personal matter which should never have been brought into the election, he would have run ahead of his ticket in the aggregate vote." Another election, called the "second try," was scheduled for mid-December.

During the final weeks of the year Mr. Dickinson was not only in the thick of a political campaign, he was busy raising subscriptions for stock of the Amherst & Belchertown Rail Road. He had to see that pledges were paid on time if the work was to continue. Furthermore, a decision must be reached as to location of the station, turntable and sheds, for Amherst was to be the terminus until the road could be extended to Grout's Corner. (This was not done until after the Civil War.)

In spite of these responsibilities Mr. Dickinson was beginning to feel some concern about his son's future. Austin was in a restless frame of mind. He was even talking about going West. Several young men in town were doing it. Later he did go as far as Chicago to take a look around. For a man on the brink of choosing a career the pull of the West was almost irresistible. Ellery Channing thus described it:

> And the old Kansas life ran in our veins,
> The wild romance, the charms of the free air;
> To sleep within the moon, and feel the night wind
> Curl around your form, the bending grass
> Whisper its loving secrets to your ear,
> And sing you into utter dreams of peace . . .

Horace Greeley's advice thundering from New York was spread far and wide throughout the East in country newspapers. "Passage for California via Cape Horn" was advertised in the *Express,* which was carrying a weekly column of California items. The issue of February 18, 1853, reported the seductive news that "during 1852, 41,444 persons were added to the population of San Francisco by sea, and 20,000 to 35,000 went across the plains. A fair estimate of the total for the year is 75,000."

For more than two years Austin had been unable to make up his mind what to do. By the summer of 1852 he had definitely decided that the teaching profession was not for him; but he was not yet fully persuaded that his field was the law. Still in a state of uncertainty, and with an eye on the West, he returned once more to his father's office. In so doing, although he may not have realized it, the die was cast. Thereafter he would follow the course his father had charted.

The second congressional election was held on December 13, 1852. This time, by a large plurality, Edward Dickinson was elected to represent the Tenth District of Massachusetts in the Thirty-third Congress. After the campaign he turned to serious consideration of his son's future. It was finally decided that Austin should enter the Harvard Law School at the opening of the second term on March 3, 1853. The Unitarian proclivities of Harvard College, so much feared in rural districts, did not deter young men from attending the Law School. Until Austin left for Cambridge the Dickinsons were all at home.

In Amherst a hundred years ago people were at the mercy of the climate. Throughout the severe New England winter when night shuts down early and dawn is long delayed, it was sometimes impossible for days at a time to dig out through the snowdrifts. Double doors and windows kept out the cold and every sound—but there were no sounds except sleigh bells or the distant bark of a dog. The world was encased in stillness as the thermometer kept falling.

There is nothing stiller than a windless snowbound night. The family is held together more closely than in the busier seasons.

When much of the day had been spent in trying to keep warm the Dickinsons on coldest evenings would gather in the kitchen. There they sat, grouped around the dull-burning whale-oil lamp as the wood fire crackled in the stove: Mr. Dickinson reading a "lonely and rigorous" book, Mrs. Dickinson mending or darning stockings, Austin studying, and Vinnie scanning the columns of the newspaper for items of local gossip. Emily was there too, sitting quietly, trying with all her might to keep up with the thoughts rushing past, tumbling headlong through the mill race of her mind:

> Conjecturing a climate
> Of unsuspected suns
> Adds poignancy to winter. . . .

Vinnie explained that Emily "had to think. She was the only one of us who had that to do."

CHAPTER XXI

Austin at the Harvard Law School

1

THE first letter in the new year is one from Austin to Martha Gilbert, who was paying a visit at her brother's home in Grand Haven, Michigan. The letter was written in the office of Dickinson & Bowdoin, where Austin was reading law preparatory to entering the Harvard Law School at the opening of the second term. Without beginning or end, this letter to "Mat" was among the drafts of Austin's other communications to her, but it has the appearance of a finished letter which was not mailed.

[February, 1853]

It was just at the eve of a beautiful & mild sunny day, the day that was numbered the third of the third winter month, when our Mike, was heard, in pacing his room, to soliloquise thus.—

This pure, this fair sheet before me, what a strange, what a wild fate may await! It is to be charged with just a bit of wonder, & just a single interrogatory, & *directed* to Mat, but who it will *reach,* no mortal knows, and my bit of wonder is, if ever either or all of the several letters that down here in my side office, I have made over to her address have been received, and my interrogatory is the same.

What a strange mail system out in the West. I should as soon think of finding Sir John Franklin as of getting a letter into the right hands out there for the *right* hands are Mat's, and I certainly cannot have got one there, for *all* my attempts, or in *some* form she would have acknowledged it, directly or indirectly, by absolute word, or by some borrowed light, some unaccounted for coloring thrown, perhaps unconsciously, over her lines to others which I always hear about.

I will not record here *what* I have written, nor how much, nor will I write more now, to be consigned to so uncertain a fate as attends the Grand Haven mail. Though I will send the dove out yet once again for the olive leaf that shall assure me the waters are abating,

& the dry land appearing. That the long silence is breaking, & the sound of glad words resting on your ear.

And here from the open window it flies.

Fortune attend thee, Gentle bird, & give thee the leaf for thy return

Early in the year Austin began to make inquiries about living quarters in Cambridge. One reply, signed "Burgess," was probably written by Edward P. Burgess (Amherst, 1852) during the winter vacation of his first year at the Law School. As in more recent times, the overflow from the Law School sometimes found accommodations in the near-by Divinity School on Divinity Avenue. Austin appears to have taken Mr. Burgess' advice, for he lived while in Cambridge at "Mrs. Ware's," a house "approved by the faculty." The letter provides a glimpse of early living arrangements in Cambridge.[1]

[*To William A. Dickinson Esq. Amherst. Mass.; postmark: Pittsfield Mass. Paid Feb. 5*]

Pittsfield Feb 4th "53.

Friend Dickinson.

I take this opportunity to answer your letter which I would have done before had circumstances allowed me; my delay was on account of the absence of Prof. Noyes, the officer who has the *disposal* of the rooms in Divin. Hall, but as he had not returned when I left, I made enquiries of another officer who has the *care* of these rooms, and learned from him that the corner room which you looked into, is still occupied, and that the occupant does not intend to leave. This settles the matter you see in regard to that room.

The next best unoccupied room is on the *lower floor corner*, on the *same side*, but in the *other end* of the building from the corner room which you looked at. It is a good room with three windows,

1. Private homes accommodating students furnished meals as well as rooms. The hour for breakfast was "not later than twenty minutes after the second prayer bell in the morning"; and dinner was at one o'clock throughout the year. No wines or spirituous liquors were to be used, and no smoking was permitted at the table or in the dining room. Room rent, "including care of room but not making fires," was from $26 to $75 a term with additional fuel charges, and a "servant, if one is employed, to make fires, $5—$10." Board for twenty weeks was from $50 to $80. *Catalogue of the Officers and Students of Harvard University for the Academical Year, 1852-1853; 1853-1854.* First term, 90; second term, 59.

(the middle rooms have but one window) furnished with most of the necessary articles of furniture except beding basin and bowl, (*bed is* furnished). Lyman, from Northampton, Law Student, has the other lower corner on the same side of the house.

If you wish a room in this building I think you cannot do better than to engage the above mentioned lower corner room, number 2. The price is $24 a term or $48 a year.

But I have my doubts whether a room in this building would suit you as well as one in a private house; this though is a question not for me to decide. I take it for granted you intend to remain there three terms, at the end of which time you will receive a degree L.L.B. and not before. I shall venture to recomment to you a large and very pleasantly situated room in a private house which is by the side of the common, very near the Depot and but quite a short distance from the Law School, and the expence of it for three terms need not be five dollars more than for a room in Divin. Hall, it being but one dollar a week, room unfurnished. I think you would be able to get all the furniture you would want for $20 dollars or there abouts, and to sell it, when you wish to leave, at a fair discount. John D. Taylor, a Law Student, who has occupied it, has now graduated and will leave at the end of this vacation or before, and would like to dispose of his furniture. He has perhaps more than you would need, and thought he should ask $30 for all his furniture, which includes a carpet, glass, bed and stead, washing apparatus, a good bureau, small chairs and rocking, book shelves, clock, etc. If you should conclude to take the room, I would advise you to take his carpet which he offers a[t] $5, and his washing apparatus if nothing more. Perhaps you can bargain for them all for $25 or so. Taylor is a *first rate* fellow.

The reason that I recommend this room to you, is because I think it will be so much more convenient and much more pleasant than one in Divin Hall.

If you wish to engage the room in D. Hall, you can write to James F. Lyman, he will speak for it. If you wish the other, write to John D Taylor, and make any enquiries of him you wish to in regard to his furniture.

I think you had better make up your mind as soon as convenient and let one of these know if you wish either of these rooms, or they may be taken. I may possibly be in Amherst next monday but it is not at all likely, and would be glad to give you any further information that I may be able.

I am stoping a day or two with Chum.

Excuse my haste.

> Yours truly
> Burgess

Requirements for admission to the Law School were hardly less casual than the living arrangements in Cambridge. "No examination and no particular course of previous study" were required. Although there were three classes—Senior, Middle and Junior—the course of study was so arranged as to be completed in two "Academical Years" of two terms of twenty weeks each. The faculty consisted of two professors, Joel Parker and Theophilus Parsons, and two university lecturers.

The second term began on Thursday, the third of March. Although Austin appears to have left in ample time for the opening day, he did not present himself until Wednesday of the following week because of a temporary indisposition. He entered with advanced standing on March 9, 1853. Shortly before he left Amherst, Sue Gilbert had gone to visit friends in Manchester, New Hampshire.[2] "Mr. Green," who carried Austin's table cover and who continued to act as the Dickinsons' messenger throughout his tenure of office in the General Court, was Moses B. Greene, representative from Amherst for that year.

Franklin H. Pierce was inaugurated President of the United States on March 4, 1853, but as the Thirty-third Congress did not convene until the following December Edward Dickinson remained at home. As soon as the new administration took office, however, the girls were provided with franked yellow envelopes addressed by their father. In the upper right-hand corner, in place of a postage stamp, he wrote, "Edw. Dickinson, M.C." Below it the word "FREE" is stamped—in red ink until November, 1853; thereafter, like the postmarks, in green.

[*To M^r Wm. Austin Dickinson, Law School, Cambridge, Ms.; postmark: illegible*]

2. In Bianchi, *Emily Dickinson Face to Face*, 188-192, two letters Emily wrote to Sue at Manchester were dated 1852. They were actually sent in late February and early March, 1853. The first was written on the day Austin left for Cambridge; the second, three days after Vinnie had been bitten by the Kelloggs' dog. In general, the dates assigned to Emily's letters to Sue in *Emily Dickinson Face to Face* (177-223) cannot be relied upon. In some cases they are wrong by as much as four years. A study of the handwriting as well as the subject matter is needed to place the letters in proper sequence.

Tuesday morning [March 8, 1853]

Dear Austin.

Dont feel lonely, for we think of you all the time, and shall love you and recollect you all the while you are gone. Your letter made us all feel sadly, and we had a sober evening thinking of you at Cambridge, while we were all at home.

I hope you are better now, and like the looks of things better than you thought you should at first. You were perfectly tired out when you went away from home and I thought you'd feel rather lonely until you got rested a little and then things would look bright again. I am glad you think of us, and think you would like to see us, for I've thought a good many times that you would soon forget us, on going away from home. I dont think you can miss us more than we do you, Austin, and dont think we have forgotten you, because you are away.

I am glad you found a letter waiting for you <from Sue> for I think it must have made things seem a little more like home.

I hav'nt heard from her yet. I dont much expect to now—though I wrote her again on Saturday. I had a letter for Sue directed to my care last evening—the outside envelope in Mr Learned's hand, and containing one from Martha. I shall send it to Sue today.

Father went to New York, this morning—he thinks he shall come home Thursday, tho' he dont know certainly.

We have sent you a *table cover* this morning by Mr Green—also two little wash cloths, which we found and thought you would like. Mother wants me to tell you if there's anything else you would like, that you must let us know and we will send it to you by the first opportunity—also to send your washing home every time you can find a chance, and your clothes shall be well taken care of. Above all things, take care of yourself, and dont get sick away, for it would be very lonely for you to be sick among strangers, and you're apt to be careless at home. What a time you must have had getting on in the snow storm! We felt very anxious about you—mother, particularly, and wondered how you would get through, and yet I knew you never had any trouble anywhere, and I really did'nt think that with you on board the cars, there could anything happen. But Austin, you are there—the time will soon be over, and we shall all be together again as we were of old—you know how fast time *can* fly, if we only let it go—then recollect dear Austin, that none of us are gone where we cannot come home again, and the separations *here* are but for a little while. We will write again very soon.

                                                        Emilie.

Mother and Vinnie send much love, and say you must'nt be lonely.
I have done what you wanted me to.

[*Half sheet enclosed*]

Dear Austin

I'm real sorry to have you feel so badly, but I expected it. Your
room is like mine in Ipswich I should think from the description.
I know how to pity you. I hope when you get matters arranged a
little to your mind then you'll be happy, & I presume you will.

I cant write much to you now, for t'is lecture time. Nothing new
here. Smith & Fowler called here last evening.[3] Pussy is very lonely
with out *"old boy"*. I shall write again soon. *"My correspondend"*
appeared last night. Did you give my note to Aunt L? Why dont she
write to me? Tell her I'm quite impatient. Good bye

Vinnie

Edward Dickinson wrote from New York that evening. His letter
exemplifies the attitude of Massachusetts Whigs, the "solid men,"
who stood for law and order and considered theirs the only respectable political party. Indeed, a man was identified as a loyal Whig
in proportion to his opposition to the unregenerate Democrats.
In view of the recent elections Mr. Dickinson uses plain language
about what may be expected from the approaching State Constitutional Convention.

Written on a large double sheet of blue paper, the letter is folded,
addressed on the back and sealed with a wafer. The word "FREE" is
part of the red postmark, but outside the circle.

All envelopes used by the family in writing to Austin during the
remainder of 1853, except those postmarked April 16 and July 9
addressed by Emily, were franked and addressed by Edward Dickinson. Not until he went to Washington in December did he learn
that franking letters written by members of his family was not one
of his congressional prerogatives.

[*To M^r Wm. Austin Dickinson, Law School, Cambridge, Mass^tts;
postmark: Free New-York Mar 9*]

3. Horace Smith and William Fowler were juniors, both members of Alpha
Delta Phi.

Astor House, 9. P.M.
Tuesday, March 8″ '53

Dear Austin,

I reached here, this evening, at 8. o'clock, and have taken tea & feel very well.

I wrote you a note, this morning by Mr Green, & sent it, with the books which you engaged of Spear [M. N. Spear, Amherst bookseller], and a spread for your table.

I suppose you will not find every thing quite as comfortable at the Law School, as you find them, at home, but I presume you will be comfortable; that is about as well as any body, for a while.

As I write, there is a torch light procession of the Engineer Companies of the City, with any quantity of Music. I hope to be here, not more than two days, if I can possibly get through.

You have seen the result of the election of Delegates to the Constitutional Convention—[George S.] Boutwell & Co. all elected— the political infamy of Mass^tts is now complete—these scoundrels can now have the Convention abt their own way and all the pleasure or comfort a Whig can take, in being a member, I don't envy him.

Harrington has made great enquiry about the subscription paper for Whig expenses, I know nothing of it. If you do, you had better write me about it.

You will see Lyman of So. Hampton & Mr Hubbard's son, of Boston, I presume. I should like to have you.

I shall write again soon after I get home.

I have not yet seen any body here, that I know, this evening. G. T. Davis, went from here, this afternoon, home. He was the Whig Candidate for Delegate from Greenfield.

Ashmun got home from Washington, on Saturday.

I saw Mr Chapman, W. G. Bates, Geo. Dwight, Edw. Southworth &c. at Springfield to-day. Every body seemed to fall in my way.

Good night
Your aff. father
E. Dickinson

Like Mr. Dickinson, Mr. Ashmun was distraught by the trend in party affairs. He was disillusioned the more, having had for Daniel Webster a feeling of idolatry.

From now on Emily's letters to her brother are usually written in pencil.

[*To M^r Wm. Austin Dickinson, Law School, Cambridge, M^s; post-mark: Amherst M^s. Mar 12*]

Saturday morning [March 12, 1853]

Dear Austin.

I am afraid you think that we have all forgotten you, we hav'nt written now for so many days, but we hav'nt, and I will tell you why we have kept still so long. We thought from your first letter that you'd probably write us again in a day or two, and there might be some thing which you would want to know, so we waited to hear from you—well, you did not seem to write so soon as we expected, and I thought Wednesday morning I would'nt wait any longer, but we know not what is before us.

A little while after breakfast Vinnie went over to Mr Kellogg's on an errand—was'nt going to stay but a minute—well, two hours had passed away and nothing was seen of Vinnie, and I had begun to wonder what had become of her, when Emmeline walked in with her, and helped her onto the Lounge. Her right hand was all done up, and she looked so faint I thought somebody had killed her. It seems she went to the door and found the Dog lying there, and thought she would pat him a little so that he would'nt growl, but he did growl terribly, then snapped at her hand, and bit the thumb on her right hand, almost thro from one side to the other. Her hand pained her so much that she fainted constantly, and as soon as she was able Emmeline came home with her. Mr Kellogg's folks felt dreadfully about it, they did everything they could—Em went for Dr Woodman, and we had quite a time—this was when father was gone, and of course it frightened us more, but you need'nt be scared any longer Austin, for she's doing nicely now. She cant comb her hair or dress her, or help herself at all, so you see I have my hands full, for besides doing all this, I have to do her usual work. *That's* the reason I hav'nt written you Austin, many a time before. I could'nt get time to do it, but I've thought of you just as much, and more, than if I c'd have written, and we all miss you every day, and want to see you more than I can possibly tell you. I am so glad to know you're happier, and that Cambridge looks brighter to you. We enjoyed your letter very much and laughed heartily at it—*father* particularly, seemed to think it "uncommon" fine. He got home Thursday night, at about 12 o clock.

The Newman family are coming here about the middle of April—another fact which will please you. Uncle Sweetser and his wife are going to Europe in May, and Elisabeth and their children are coming to Amherst to board at Mr Newman's for the summer! Such intelligence needs no comments. I have telegraphed to Sue.[4] Dont say anything about it in the letter you write me next, for father reads all your letters before he brings them home, and it might make him feel unpleasantly.

I hope we shall all be spared to have one *kitchen meeting,* and express our several minds on this infamous proceeding, but I wont trouble you. You asked about the Paper.[5] Daniel Webster of Deerfield cant come on account of the limited salary—Mr [Samuel] Nash, on account of his eyes, and as Mr Trumbull has gone, they got Mr Sydney Adams, with the *assistance of others* to get out the this weeks one. Bowdoin "moves on" like snails. I have heard once from Susie —not much tho'. We will hem the crash, and send it to you by the first opportunity. Mother wants you to get a cheap Comforter and put on the palmleaf mattress;—she says t'will be easier to you.

We all send you our love. Vinnie says she will write as soon as she uses her hand. Write us soon. Aff Emilie

[*On a slip in Edward Dickinson's handwriting*]

> *Direct in this form.*
> Edward Dickinson
> M.C.
> Amherst   Ms.

2

Edward Dickinson's sister Mary, Mrs. Mark Haskell Newman, had died on March 30, 1852; her husband, on December 21, 1852. Responsibility for care of their five children fell upon the appointed guardian, their Uncle Edward. The "Newman family" now consisted of Mark Haskell Newman, Jr., nineteen years old; Catherine Dickinson Newman, seventeen; Sara Phillips Newman, fourteen; Clarissa (Clara) Badger Newman, ten; and Anna Dodge Newman, seven. The following information about the family has been given to me by Mrs. George E. Pearl, daughter of Anna Newman who, on June 3, 1874, married George H. Carleton, shoe manufacturer and banker of Haverhill, Massachusetts.

Mark H. Newman was very well-to-do at the time of his death.

4. The Western Massachusetts Telegraph Company was incorporated in 1854. *Massachusetts Register* (1855), 168. The first telegraphic message from Amherst was sent on December 9, 1861 (*History of Amherst,* 469).

5. J. R. Trumbull was soon to be replaced as editor of *The Hampshire and Franklin Express.* For an account of printing in Amherst the reader is referred to *Amherst, Massachusetts, Imprints, 1825-1876,* published by the Amherst College Library in 1946.

He had made a will leaving everything to his wife; but she predeceased him by nine months. Both died of consumption. After Mrs. Newman's death a new will bequeathed $5,000 to each of his five children. The bulk of his fortune, however, was bequeathed "to the Lord"—in other words, $25,000 to the American Home Missionary Society and $10,000 to the American Board of Commissioners for Foreign Missions. Mark Newman, Jr., was so embittered by the latter provision that he broke with the family and was permanently lost sight of. The four daughters went to Amherst in April, 1853, in charge of an old family servant. Before long the two older girls left to make their home with their Uncle William in Worcester. The two younger, in the care of an aunt, Mrs. Fay, remained in Amherst under the supervision of their Uncle Edward.[6] Both had for him real affection. One of them, Clara Newman, later Mrs. Sidney Turner, wrote down her girlhood memories of life in the Dickinson family, a sketch which it is hoped will soon be published. Mrs. Turner said that although she was with them every day for several years she "never saw exchanged any marked *demonstration* of affection." This is in keeping with the reserve which in New England was commonly maintained even among the most loyal and devoted relatives.

As to relatives, the Newman girls were not Mr. Dickinson's only responsibility. In her last letter Emily had told her brother that their Aunt Elisabeth Dickinson and the Sweetser children were coming to board "at Mr Newman's" for the summer, joining forces with the Newman family after they moved into the house owned by his estate. (See map of Amherst, opposite page 61.)

[*To M^r Wm. Austin Dickinson, Law School, Cambridge, M^s; postmark: Amherst Ms. Mar 18*]

Friday morning [March 18, 1853]

Dear Austin.

I presume you remember a story Vinnie tells of a Breach of promise Case where the correspondence between the parties con-

6. A daguerreotype of the family group is in the Houghton Library of Harvard University. Compare Plate IV. After Austin's marriage in 1856 Clara and Anna Newman made their home with him for several years.

sisted of a reply from the girl to one she had never received, but was daily expecting—well *I* am writing an answer to the letter I hav'nt had, so you will see the force of the accompanying anecdote. I have been looking for you ever since despatching my last, but this is a fickle world, and it's a great source of complacency that t'will all be burned up bye and bye. I should be pleased with a line when you've published your work to Father, if it's perfectly convenient. Your letters are very funny indeed—about the only jokes we have, now you <and Sue> are gone, and I hope you will send us one as often as you can. Father takes great delight in your remarks to him—puts on his spectacles and reads them o'er and o'er as if it was a blessing to have an only son.

He reads all the letters you write as soon as he gets, at the post office, no matter to whom addressed. I presume when Sue gets back, and has directed to her, he will take them and read them first. Well, I was telling you, he reads them once at the office, then he makes me read them loud at the supper table again, and when he gets home in the evening, he cracks a few walnuts, puts his spectacles on, and with your last in his hand, sits down to enjoy the evening. He remarked in confidence to me this morning, that he "guessed you saw through things there"—of course I answered "yes sir," but what the thought conveyed I remained in happy ignorance. Whether he meant to say that you saw through *the Judges,* overcoats and all, I could not quite determine but I'm sure he designed to compliment you very highly.

I do think it's so funny—you and father do nothing but "fisticuff" all the while you're at home, and the minute you are separated, you become such devoted friends; but this is a checkered life.

I believe at this moment, Austin, that there's no body living for whom father has such respect as for you, and yet your conduct together is quite peculiar indeed. But my paper is getting low, and I must hasten to tell you that we are very happy to hear good news from you—that we hope you'll have pleasant times, and learn a great deal while you're gone, and come back to us greater and happier for the life lived at Cambridge. We miss you more and more. I wish that we could see you, but letters come the next—write them often, and tell us everything! Aff Emilie.

[On a separate sheet]

Dear Austin, I've just decided that my yarn is not quite spun, so I'll spin it a little longer.

Vinnie's hand is getting well, tho' she cant yet sew or write with it. She sends her love to you, and says she shall write a note, as soon as her hand gets able.

Anna Warner's a little better, tho' the *medical faculty* dare as yet give little encouragement of her return thitherward. Mary is at present incarcerated, and becomes in the public eye, more and more of a martyr daily. The Quincy [*sic*] approached Miss Goudy[?], but was dexterously warded off by homeopathic glances from a certain Dr Gregg, of whom you may hear in Boston. Professor Warner, and consort, and surviving son, are much as usual. Father's Cummington friend, late from State's prison in Brooklyn, took tea with us this week. He has *advanced* somewhat since we children have seen him.

Jerry and Mrs. Mack inquire for "Mr Austin". Most all of the folks we asked here have made their "party call", and we have had our hands full in entertaining them. You must tell us about the party which you attend at Miss C's. I have not heard from Sue again, tho' I've written her three times. I suppose she'll be coming home Saturday, and I'll tell you something funny the next time I write.

We all send you much love, and wish you were here today, so we could talk with you. Emilie again.

[*Note from Edward Dickinson enclosed*]

Dear Austin.

Your letter was rec^d yesterday—glad to hear that you like the school—I believe your letters, which have been put into r.r. cars, come same day—all well—girls have written—

r.r. survey shall be sent, when an opportunity occurs—It is a short roll, containing, cuts, & fills & grades &c—

Cold—& heat—wet & dry—rain & shine—all come along, in their course—

Your Aff father
E D

The following letter from Vinnie, written "Wednesday Eve.," was enclosed with one from Emily written the next morning.

Wednesday Eve.

Dear Austin

This is the first time I've held a pen since my bite which is now most well, else you would have heard from me long ago. I've suffered a good deal from it & shall loose the nail I fear. The dog still lives, though his friends think he is truly penitent, but *I dont*. Emilie & I made calls this afternoon in our best attire. Every body likes our things. Sam Fiske has been here this evening.[7] We've had scores of

7. Samuel Fiske was a tutor in the college from 1852 to 1855. William Howland had settled in Lynn, where he practised law for the rest of his life. The Reverend George Cooke was a temporary supply in the pulpit of the First Church.

company since you went away of every sort & kind & we are tired enough of it I can assure you. I miss you dreadfully, even more than I anticipated. I guess we all think of you as much as you do of us. Father & Mother seem to delight to dwell on the incidents of your youth which are daily called up. Every body enquires for you. We enjoy your letters *entirely*, wish they would come every day. When you want to get off another joke on Lynn, you must write it rather plainer. Father read Lym, Lymans, & did not see his mistake until after we had read the letter when he remarked "So Austin has called on the Lymans." We told him there was no mention made of *them* in the letter. He was sure he was right but was finally convinced to the contrary by putting on his glasses & studying the passage carefully. He then asked me if you meant Howland. I told him I thought *likely*. I dont think he sees the real joke yet. Eyes has he but he will not see. We are very lonely with out Sue. I suppose you are perfectly happy to night Austin. Mrs Cutler told Emilie that Sue would come home through Boston as she had never seen the city & besides she would see Austin & that would be *so pleasant*. I wonder how she'll like the city & the people! I think shes staid a long time & during it all she has written but a short note to Emilie. It has made E. very unhappy & me vexed. I dont understand what it means. I cant tell of any thing new as I know of. We are all busy as usual & hurried. Mr Alby has trimmed the grape vine today. Pussy sleeps in a basket under the kitchen table most of the time. Father is so outraged towards parson Cooke that he would not let Emilie or me go to church all day last Sunday. Mother would go part of the day though he prefered she should not. I've had two letters from Aunt Lavinia since you went away & one from Mary Nichols which I shall answer soon. I'm glad you have called on Mrs Converse, you say she spoke of me & I should like to know whether she liked me or not. My love to her & Kate when you see them again. The weather has been charming for several days. Mr & Mrs Cobb returned Mother's call Tuesday. They are very agreeable people. I've not been out to ride at all since you left, but I walk every day. Good night Austin

Vinnie

Aunt Elisabeth & the Sweetser children are to spend the summer with the Newman familie, the relations will keep close to us as long as we live!

Vinnie's remark, that Sue's silence had made "Emilie very unhappy & me vexed," is another illustration of the temperamental difference between the sisters. Although, as she said, "it breaks my heart sometimes because I do not hear from you," Emily was not irritated by Sue's failure to answer her letters; she tried to excuse her as she had done once before when Sue was teaching in Baltimore. Preferring to pretend that a snowstorm had held up the mail, Emily explained that ". . . I am so credulous and so easily deluded by this fond heart of mine."[8]

[*To M* *Wm. Austin Dickinson, Law School, Cambridge, M*[8]*; postmark: Amherst Ms. Mar 24*]

Thursday Morning [March 24, 1853]

Dear Austin.

How much I miss you, how lonely it is this morning—how I wish you were here, and how very much I thank you for sending me that long letter, which I got Monday evening, and have read a great many times, and presume I shall again, unless I soon have another.

I find life not so bright without <Sue and> you, or <Martha>, and for a little while I hav'nt cared much about it. How glad I was to know that you had'nt forgotten us, and looked forward to home, and the rustic seat, and summer, with so much happiness. You wonder if we think of you as much as you of us—I guess so, Austin —it's a great deal anyhow, and to look at the empty nails, and the empty chairs in the kitchen almost obscures my sight, if I were used to tears. But *I* think of the rustic seat, and I think of the July evening just as the day is done, and I read of the one come back, worth all the "ninety and nine" who have not gone from home, and these things strengthen me for many a day to come.

I'm so glad you are cheerful at Cambridge, for cheerful indeed one must be to write such a comic affair as your last letter to me. I believe the message to Bowdoin, w'd have killed father outright if he had'nt just fortified nature with two or three cups of tea. I could hardly contain myself sufficiently to read a thing so grotesque, but it did me good indeed, and when I had finished reading it, I said with a pleasant smile, "then there is something left"! I have been disgusted, ever since you went away, and have concluded several times that it's of no use minding it, as it is only a puff ball. But your letter so raised me up, that I look round again, and notice my fellow men.

I think you far exceed Punch—much funnier—much funnier, cant keep up with you at all!

I suppose the young lady will be getting home today—how often

8. Bianchi, *Emily Dickinson Face to Face*, 210. The letter containing these words, said to have been written "To Sue at Baltimore, 1854-55 *(early winter),*" was written during Martha Gilbert's illness in January, 1852.

I thought of you yesterday afternoon and evening. I did "drop in at the Revere" a great many times yesterday. I hope you have been made happy. If so I am satisfied. I shall know when you get home.

I have been to see Mrs Cutler several times since Sue has been gone. *Mr Cutler* has missed her dreadfully, which has gratified me much. What I was going to tell you was that Mr Cutler's folks had written Sue to meet *Mr Sweetser* in Boston, last week, and come to Amherst with him. I knew she would'nt come, and I couldnt help laughing to think of him returning to town alone—that's all! <Sue's> outwitted them all—ha-ha! Just imagine me giving three cheers for American Independence!

I did get that little box, and do with it as you told me. I wrote you so at the time, but you must have forgotten it. Write again soon, Austin, for this is a lonely house, when we are not all here. Emilie.

Mother says "tell Austin I think perhaps I shall write him a letter myself."

[On a separate sheet]

Mother sends her love, and is very much obliged to you for the message to her, and also for the comb, which you told us was coming. She wants you to send your clothes home just as soon as you can, for she thinks you must certainly need some by this time. We hav'nt had much maple sugar yet, but I shall send you some when Mr Green goes back. We have had some maple molasses. I know you would love some, if you were here—how I do wish you were! I read the proclamation, and liked it very much. I had a letter from Mat, last night—she said a great deal of Sue and you, and *so* affectionately. If Sue thinks Mat would be willing, I will send the letter to you, the next time I write.

CHAPTER XXII

Intangible Pressures

1

THE next few letters suggest that Susan Gilbert had already made up her mind that Austin was the man for her. With this attitude Emily at least was in complete agreement. Austin would appear to have been not quite so sure if his letters to Sue's sister can be taken at face value.

Sue's return from Manchester on March 24 by way of Boston, where she stopped at the Revere House, was the occasion of a mischievous communication from Emily in reply to a letter which Austin had signed with a fictitious name. Emily's letter of March 27, 1853, was written on "Sabbath evening," without alluding to the fact that it was Easter.

[*To M^r Wm. Austin Dickinson, Law School, Cambridge, M^s; postmark: Amherst Ms. Mar 28*]

Sabbath evening [March 27, 1853]

Oh my dear "Oliver", how chipper you must be since any of us have seen you? How thankful we should be that you have been brought to Greenville, and a suitable frame of mind! I really had my doubts about your reaching Canaan, but you relieve my mind, and set me at rest completely. How long is it since you've been in this state of complacence towards God and your fellow men? I think it must be sudden, hope you are not deceived, would recommend "Pilgrim's Progress," and "Baxter upon the will." Hope you have enjoyed the Sabbath, and sanctuary privileges—it is'nt *all* young men that have the preached word.

Trust you enjoy your closet, and meditate profoundly upon the Daily Food! I shall send you Village Hymns, by earliest opportunity.

I was just this moment thinking of a favorite stanza of your's, "where congregations ne'er break up, and Sabbaths have no end."

That must be a delightful situation, certainly, quite worth the scrambling for!

Quite likely you have *tickets* for your particular friends—hope I should be included, in memory of "old clothes."

And Austin is a Poet, Austin writes a psalm. Out of the way, Pegasus, Olympus enough "to him," and just say to those "nine muses" that we have done with them!

Raised a living muse ourselves, worth the whole nine of them. Up, off, tramp!

Now Brother Pegasus, I'll tell you what it is—I've been in the habit *myself* of writing some few things, and it rather appears to me that you're getting away my patent, so you'd better be somewhat careful, or I'll call the police! Well Austin, if you've stumbled through these two pages of folly, without losing your hat or getting lost in the mud, I will try to be sensible, as suddenly as I can, before you are quite disgusted. *Mademoiselle* has come, quite to the surprise of us all. I concluded you had concluded to sail for Australia. Sue's very sober yet, she thinks it's pretty desolate without old Mr Brown.

She seems to be absent, sometimes, on account of the "old un," and I think you're a villainous rascal to entrap a young woman's "phelinks" in such an awful way.

You deserve, let me see; you deserve hot irons, and Chinese Tartary; and if I were Mary Jane, I would give you one such "mitten" Sir, as you never had before! I declare, I have half a mind to *throw a stone* as it is, and kill five barn door fowls, but I wont, I'll be considerate! Miss Susie was here on Friday, was here on Saturday, and Miss Emilie, there, on Thursday. I suppose you will go to the *"Hygeum"* as usual, this evening. Think it a dreadful thing for a young man under influences to frequent a hotel, evenings! Am glad our Pilgrim Fathers got safely out of the way, before such shocking times! Are you getting on well with "the work," and have you engaged the Harpers? Shall bring in a bill for my Lead Pencils, 17, in number, disbursed at times to you, as soon as the publishment. Also, two envelopes daily, during *despatch of proofs,* also Johnnie Beston, also David Smith, and services from same!

Dear Austin, I am keen, but you are a good deal keener, I am *something* of a fox, but you are more of a hound! I guess we are very good friends tho', and I guess we both love <Sue> just as well as we can.

You need'nt laugh at my letter—it's a few *Variations* of *Green-ville* I thought I would send to you. Affy Emilie.

[*On the inside of the envelope flap*]

Love from us all. Monday noon. Oh Austin, Newton is dead. The first of my own friends. Pace.

News of the death on March 24, 1853, of Benjamin F. Newton, the "first" of her "own" friends, had evidently just reached Emily.

[*To M^r Wm. Austin Dickinson, Law School, Cambridge, M^s; post-mark: Amherst Ms Mar 31*]

Amherst March 31, 1853

Dear Austin,

I have time to say a few words only to you, this morning. Frank Pierce is at Boston, till Saturday. Stops at the "Quincy House." Mr Green, I suppose, will come up on Saturday. You can send any thing, by either.

We are well, at home. I am going to Hadley to-day, to help our Cousins settle. The weather is beautiful—Our r. road is fast being put in a state of fitness to run. In a fortnight, or so, I think it may be in operation.

Take care of your health, first—then study what you can.

All send love.

Your aff father
E. Dickinson.

[*To M^r Wm. Austin Dickinson, Law School, Cambridge, M^s; post-mark: Amherst Ms Apr (?)*]

Saturday noon [April 2, 1853]

Dear Austin.

I rather thought from your letter to me that my essays, together with the Lectures at Cambridge, were rather too much for you, so I thought I would let you have a little vacation; but you must have got rested now, so I shall renew the series. Father was very severe to me; he thought I'd been trifling with you, so he gave me quite a trimming about "Uncle Tom" and "Charles Dickens" and these "modern Literati" who he says are *nothing*, compared to past generations, who flourished when *he was a boy*. Then he said there were "somebody's *rev-e-ries*," he did'nt know whose they were, that he thought were very ridiculous, so I'm quite in disgrace at present, but I think of that "pinnacle" on which you always mount, when anybody insults you, and that's quite a comfort to me.

We are all pretty well at home, and it seems a great while, Austin, since we have heard from you. The correspondence from "Oliver" did'nt seem to say a great deal of how you were getting along, or of yourself, at Cambridge, and I am waiting patiently for one of those grand old letters you used to send to us when you first went away.

I have got a nice cake of Sugar, to send you by Mr Green, and shall put in some big, sound Apples, if there is any room. Vinnie would have written you this week, but has had quite a cold, which settled in her eyes, and she has not used them much. She will write you the first of next week. Vinnie and Sue walked down to mill yesterday. Sue comes down here most every day [one line rubbed out]. Emily Fowler spent yesterday afternoon here. She *inquired for you*. The girls "Musical" met here on Tuesday evening, and we had as pleasant a time as could have been expected, in view of the individuals composing the society. Dr Brewster was in town yesterday, and took tea here. He asked a great deal about you, and said he was going to write to you to come and make him a visit. I told him I "presumed you'd go." Mary Aiken is in town with her children, and is going to stay a fortnight. I wonder she did'nt wait, and meet *you* here in May. Thurston and Benjamin are in town on a visit.

Rufus Cowles gave us a call last evening. He is quite a young man! Mr Godfrey's folks have gone, and Mr and Mrs Pierce have moved into the house. The second generation spend most of their time in our door yard.

This is all the news I can think of, but there is one *old story,* Austin, which you may like to hear—it is that we think about you the whole of the livelong day, and talk of you when we're together, and [several words rubbed out] of the golden link which binds us all together.

And you can recollect when you are busy studying, that those of us [at] home not so hard at work as you are, get much time to be with you. We all send our love to you, and hope you will be very careful, and take good care of yourself. Emilie.

[*On a separate slip*]

That *was* a "grand old letter," Austin, and I shall answer it soon, but I cannot today, for I feel more like writing that little note of mine, and talking of you.

Oh how much it pleased Father, and how it made us all laugh, tho' I did'nt laugh so hard as the rest, on account of *my note.* There's a beautiful verse in the Bible—"Let not your heart be troubled"—so believe in [word altered and illegible], believe also in me! Emilie.

[*Note enclosed*]

Dear Austin.

The *thumps* continue at every door as usual. When we were at supper last night, a loud knocking was heard some where, but no body could tell where. I went to the front & back doors & finding no one, started for the north door & enquired who was there. Edwin Pierce replied & as I opened the door "Mistress" Pierce flew in & Master flew out.

We went to see Sue last night. She looked *splendidly*. The weather is real nasty & that's all I can stop to say now.

Write often as possible.

Vinnie

[*To M*r *Wm. Austin Dickinson, Law School, Cambridge, M*s*; post-mark: Amherst Ms Apr 9*]

Friday noon [April 8, 1853]

Dear Austin.

I've expected a letter from you every day this week, but have been disappointed—and last night I thought I should have one as surely as I lived, but I did not. I'm sure you are very busy, or I should have had a note, but I will "bide and see." It seems as if you'd been gone several hundred years, and it had been some centuries since we had heard from you, and I should like to know when you were coming home, for if it is'nt probable that you are coming *some time,* I think I shall take the stage, or run away myself. I asked you this same question in my last Saturday's letter, but you make me no reply. I cant help wondering sometimes if you think of us as often as we all do of you, and want to see us *half* as much. I think about this a great deal, and tho' I dont talk with Vinnie or Sue, about it, yet it often troubles me. I think we miss each other more every day that we grow older, for we're all unlike most everyone, and are therefore more dependent on each other for delight.

Last evening Sue and I walked down to the Old Oak Tree, and sat there and talked a long while, principally of you, and ourselves. Sue said she guessed you were writing us, as we sat there talking, and we both wished you were there. Last Saturday evening I spent with Sue in her room—she read me some funny things which you had just written her, concerning her sorry suitors, and your *excellent suggestions* to prevent future accidents! I think you are rather hard upon unfortunate gentlemen—presume they would like to shoot you, if they knew you had won the bird.

Sue was here to supper last night, and I could'nt but think of a great many things, which we will talk about sometime, if you ever come home.

Mrs Scott is ironing here today—we shall have all your clothes in nice order to send by Mr Green. When is the good man coming? I get quite out of patience, waiting to send your sugar. I hope some country friend has given you a taste long before this time, for you must miss such little luxuries, you always get at home.

Have you had any maple molasses, or any Graham Bread, since you have been away? Every time a new loaf comes smoking on to the table, we wonder if you have any where you have gone to live.

I should love to send you a loaf, dearly, if I could. Vinnie sends her love to you, and thanks you very much for the Rubber. She finds it "capital," she says, and she will write you a letter, when the valise goes back. Mother sends her love, and says she thinks very often she shall certainly write to you, but she knows that we write so often she thinks we say all there is, and so she recollects you, but says nothing about it. I have mended your gloves, Austin, and Vinnie, all the clothes which were out of repair. I have written you in a hurry. I shall never write any more grand letters to you, but all the *little* things, and the things called *trifles,* and the crickets upon the hearth, you will be sure to hear. Emilie.

Wont you write to me pretty soon? I send that letter of Mat's, wh' I said I would. Much love from all. We have charming weather here. I know you would be so happy, if you were at home—but you'll come soon and we shall be so glad to see you.

Jerry inquires for you.

[*To M^r Wm. Austin Dickinson, Law School, Cambridge, M^s; postmark: Amherst Ms. Apr 12*]

Tuesday noon [April 12, 1853]

Dear Austin.

You asked me in your Sat morning's letter to write you so you'd hear from me yesterday, but your letter did'nt get here until last evening, so you see I could not very well; but I must write a word this noon, to tell you that they've both come, tho' they tarried upon the way.

I thanked you for the long one in my letter of Saturday, but I want to thank you again, it was such a beautiful one, and too, for yesterday's wh' I did not expect. <Sue was> here when it came, and we read it together. I staid with her Saturday evening, and we spent part of it reading your long letter to me, and talking of what it made us both think of, and of you. Sue thought t'was the most beautiful letter she ever heard.

I have taken *your place* Saturday evening, since you have been away, but I will give it back to you as soon as you get home. *Get home* dear Austin—how soon now you are coming, and how happy we are in the thought of seeing you! I cant realize that you will come—it is so still and lonely, that it dont seem possible it can be otherwise, but we shall see, when the nails hang full of coats again, and the chairs hang full of hats, and I can count the slippers under the kitchen chair. Oh Austin, how we miss them, and more than them, somebody who used to hang them there, and get many a hint ungentle, to carry them away. Those times seem far off now, a great way, as things we did when children. I wish we were children now. I wish we were *always* children, how to grow up I dont know.

We had company to tea last evening, Mr and Mrs Jewett, and little Henry, then Mr Haven, and <Sue>—it seems much more like *home* to have her with us *always,* than to have her away. We had a delightful evening. How often we thought of you, and wished you were not away!

Father went home with <Sue>. I think he and mother both think a great deal of her, and nobody will make me believe that they dont think she is their's, just as much as Vinnie or you or me. Perhaps I am mistaken, but I can most always tell anything that I want to. Emmons brought me a beautiful boquet of Arbutus, last evening —it's the first I have seen this year. Cousin John has made us an Aeolian Harp, which plays beautifully, alone, whenever there is a breeze.

Austin, you must'nt care if your letters do not get here just when you think they will—they are always new to us, and delightful always, and the more you send us, the happier we shall be. We all send our love to you, and think much and say much, of seeing you again—keep well till you come, and if knowing that we all love you, makes you happier, then Austin, you may sing the whole day long!

Aff Emilie.

We now expect to send your valise in a day or two, by Mr Wm Cutler.

2

Two letters from his sisters were written on Austin's twenty-fourth birthday, but neither of them mentions it. Emily's next letter, written in pencil, has been a good deal tampered with. Not only have several passages been rubbed out; the reader is brought up short against the line, "I shant see him this morning because he has to bake Saturday." Only then, on closer inspection, does it appear that throughout that paragraph pronouns have been changed, "she" to "he," "her" to "him." Still other words have been erased, altered, and erased again. When, in spite of changes, the meaning remains clear the original is given, followed by the altered word in brackets. The envelope, addressed by Emily, has a 3-cent stamp.

[*To Wm Austin Dickinson, Law School. Cambridge. Mass.; postmark: Amherst Ms. Apr 16*]

Saturday noon [April 16, 1853]

Dear Austin.

You make me happy, when you write so affectionately, happier than you know, and I always want to write to you as soon as your letters come, but it is not very often convenient that I can. Yet I *will* the morning after, as I do today. I am all alone, Austin. Father has gone to New York, Vinnie to Northampton, and mother is cutting out apples in the kitchen. I had forgotten *Pussy*, tho'; she's sitting on the mat, looking up in my face as if she wondered who I was writing to—if she knew it was "Master Austin" I guess she would send some word, for I know Pussy remembers you, and wonders where you are. Sometimes when she's more intelligent, I've half a mind to tell her how you have gone to Cambridge, and are studying the law, but I dont believe she'd understand me.

You cant think how delighted father was, with the account you gave of northerners and southerners, and the electioneering—he seemed to feel so happy to have you interested in what was going on at Cambridge—he said he "knew all about it—he'd been thro' the whole, it was only a little specimen of what you'd meet in life, if you lived to enter it." I could'nt hardly help telling him that I thought his idea of life rather a boisterous one, but I kept perfectly still.

I dont love to read your letters all out loud to father—it would be like opening the kitchen door when we get home from meeting Sunday, and are sitting down by the stove saying just what we're a mind to, and having father hear. I dont know why it is, but it gives me a dreadful feeling, and I skipped about the wild flowers, and one or two little things I loved the best, for I could'nt read *them* loud to anybody [several words rubbed out]. I shant see her [changed to "him"] this morning, because she ["he"] has to *bake* Saturday, but ["he"]'ll come this afternoon, and we shall read your letter together, and talk of how soon you'll be here.

[Seven lines rubbed out.]

I shall think of you taking tea at Aunt Lavinia's tonight, and we shall take tea alone, how pleasant it would be to have you with us while father is away, but it is'nt *May* yet. Thank you for remembering me when you found the wild flowers, and for wanting me to stay a week with you. These things are very kind, and I will not forget them. The birds sing beautifully, Pussy is trying to beat them. Dont work too hard Austin, dont get too tired, so that you cannot sleep, we always think of you. Love from us all. Emilie.

John Thompson is in the office of Mr Vose, in Springfield.

[*Note enclosed*]

Saturday morn.

Dear Austin

I expect I've made a terrible blunder in packing your things. Father enquired for his clothes this morning & the house was hunted over but nothing could be found of them so we suppose they must have gone with yours. If so you know it already. Father's feelings can better be imagined than described under such circumstances. It was my fault & I feel badly about it. Send them by the first chance if he guessed right about them. Father has gone to New York this morning to fetch the Newmans, they will all come Monday. They will board at Mrs Merrills till their house is in order. I'm going to Northampton in a few moments with Emeline Kellogg. She has secured an old horse from East street warranted safe & we hope to have a fine time. If I had any brother at home perhaps I should not be driven to this. I want you to come home very much. Seems a great while that you've been away. How much we shall all have to say & hear. You must remember to tell us every thing that interests you. The Cars will probably run the first of May. Be sure & send the clothes safely & let us know immediately if you have them. No more now. Sue & I walked four miles Wednesday; what do you think of that? I'm thinking of sending to you to get a *"what not"* for the parlor & bring when you come. Take care of yourself.

Vinnie

[*To M*ʳ *Wm. Austin Dickinson, Law School, Cambridge, M*ˢ; *postmark: Amherst Ms (date illegible)*]

Thursday noon [April 21, 1853]

Dear Austin.

We could hardly eat any supper last night, we felt so badly to think you had'nt got the valise, and we talked all the time about it while we sat at the table, and called Mr Cutler names—Father says he "would like to reach him just long enough to cuff his ears." We do feel so badly about it, we dont know what to do.

There were all your clothes in such beautiful order, and a cake of new maple sugar, and mother had with her own hand selected and polished the apples, she thought it would please you so. It is too bad—too bad. We do feel vexed about it. Mother thinks it is lost—she says you will never see it. Father thinks he would'nt *dare* to lose it, but is too selfish to trouble himself by sending you any word. Mother is so afraid that you will need the clothes, and wont know what to do without them, and Vinnie and I keep hoping, and trying to persuade her that you've got them before now.

We have all been thinking how much you'd enjoy the sugar, and how nice the apples would taste after studying all day long, and "living very sparingly," but this [is] a vexing world, and things "aft gang aglay." I wont talk any more of this, for I know you are disappointed as much as any of us, and want to hear something sunnier—and there is something sunnier. I was with dear Susie last evening, and she told me how on Monday she walked out in the fields, carrying your letter with her, and read it over and over, "sitting on the stile," and pausing as she read, to look at the hills and the trees and the blue, blue home beyond.

Susie talked much of you, and of her lonely life when you were gone away, and we said you would soon be here, and then we talked of *how* soon, and of many and many a sunlight and many and many a shade which might steal upon us ere then. How I wish you were here, dear Austin, how I do wish for you so many times every day, and I miss the long talks most, upon the *kitchen stone hearth,* when the just are fast asleep. I ask myself many times if they will come back again, and whether they will stay, but we dont know.

Father wont go to Boston this week, as he had intended to, for he finds a great deal to do in starting the Newman family. I think now he will go *next week,* tho' I dont know what day. The Newmans all board at Mrs Merrill's until they get into their house, which will be by Saturday, certainly. Their Irish girl stays here, for Mrs Merrill was afraid she would not agree with *her* girl. The Newmans seems very pleasant, but they are not *like us.* What makes a few of us so different from others? I'ts a question I often ask myself. The Germanians gave a concert here, the evening of Exhibition day [April 19]. Vinnie and I went with John. I never heard [such] *sounds* before. They seemed like *brazen Robins,* all wearing broadcloth wings, and I think they were, for they all flew away as soon as the concert was over. I tried so hard to make Susie go with us, but she would'nt consent to it. I could not bear to have her lose it.

Write me as soon as this comes, and say if you've got the valise.

Emilie

[*On a separate slip*]

Anna Warner died Tuesday night, and will be buried tomorrow, I suppose.[1] They seem to feel very badly. She has been sick a great while now. You will not be surprised at hearing it. Mother wants me to tell you *from her* to get all the clothes you need at some good place in Boston, should you not find the valise. I hope you have got it before now. I should'nt think he *would lose* it, after all you have done for him. Mother says she can never look upon him again.

[*Note from Edward Dickinson enclosed*]

Austin. I can't go to Boston, this week; & perhaps I can't go to Cambridge before you come home, if I should go to Boston, next week.

E. D.

The missing valise must have turned up as there is no further mention of it. On Friday, April 29, Austin came home to spend Sunday.

On May 6, 1853, an accident on the New York, New Haven & Hartford Rail Road resulted in an "appalling" loss of life. An express train of five cars entered an open draw near Norwalk, Connecticut, and plunged into the water below. Over fifty persons were killed, many of them physicians returning from a meeting of the American Medical Association in New York. The wreck was

1. Anna Charlotte Warner, aged eleven, died of a fever during the night of April 19-20, 1853.

described at length in local newspapers. *The Hampshire Gazette* (May 10 and 17, 1853) reported that "the speed of the train was such that the locomotive leaped the draw, sixty feet wide, and struck the opposite abutment twelve feet from the top with such force as to move the whole slightly. . . . The accident was caused by the recklessness of the engineer who . . . ran around the curve at a rate not less, certainly, than 20 miles an hour, when, under no circumstances should it have been half that." A week later an editorial in the same paper meditates upon this "inscrutable dispensation" of God.

News of the accident reached Amherst the day it happened. Vinnie notified her brother at once. Emily, writing the next day, did not refer to it.

[*To M^r Wm. Austin Dickinson, Law School, Cambridge, M^s; no postmark*]

Friday evening [May 6, 1853]

Dear Austin

I've just heard of that frightful rail road accident on the New York way & it makes me feel so sad that I want to sit right down & ask if you are safe. When I hear of such things I feel a desire to cling closer, closer to my dear friends lest I should loose some of them, & you know I've none to spare. I feel to night as I think over my friends scattered over the earth, & some so far away, if I could once gather them together they should never stray again. Oh Austin! I love my friends, more than you think perhaps but 'tis true. I hoped a letter would come from you to night but I suppose 'twas too soon to look for it.

We are lonely with out you Austin, though we are very busy gardening, sewing, cleaning &c Mother says it seems as though you had been struck out of existance. I got home nicely, but *some how* the ride was a good deal longer back, than going. What was the reason? I dont think you enjoyed the trip so much as you thought to. Did you? I did'nt make it as pleasant as I might. I saw *Sue* this afternoon, & everything is right between us now. We shall never have any more troubles. I confess I did wrong to suspect her, but sometimes I feel rather depressed & then I see every thing through cloudy spectacles. I love *Sue* most dearly & will try & never do her injustice again. I'm in the kitchen writing. John Emerson is in the sitting room with Emilie reading parts of Eliza Colemans letters.

I wonder if he thinks t'will do him any good. Poor fellow is [a] little deluded I fear.

I will send you the *three* books as soon as opportunity offers. Judge Conkey went Tuesday P.M. I'm anxious to hear from the boquets. Jerry is making various improvements around the house. He says, "you ought to see Mr Austins house, he'll have a dog *serre* & he'll know his place *serre*." He talks about Mr Austins *"pine grove."* My eyes remind me that I've written too much now so I must stop or else pay the penalty, tomorrow.

Dont let *some thing* trouble you. It is'nt half so bad as you imagine & you'll be glad, bye & bye. Our yard is looking beautifully now, the trees are in full bloom, peach & cherry, with the shrubs. To use Mrs Dick Coles expression, "the air is filled with fragrance & perfumery". I feel unusually hurried just now, so many plans suggest themselves to my mind for improving the house & grounds.

Good bye. Write soon

Affectionate sister
Vinnie

[*In the same envelope*]

Saturday noon.

Dear Austin.

A week ago, we were all here—today we are not all here—yet the bee hums just as merrily, and all the busy things work on as if the same. They do not miss you, Child, but there is a humming bee whose song is not so merry, and there are busy ones who pause to drop a tear. Let us thank God, today, Austin, that we can love our friends, our brothers and our sisters, and weep when they are gone, and smile at their return. It is indeed a joy which we are blest to know. Today is very beautiful—just as bright, just as blue, just as green and as white, and as crimson, as the cherry trees full in bloom, and the half opening peach blossoms, and the grass just waving, and sky and hill and cloud, can make it, if they try. How I wish you were here, Austin—you thought *last* Saturday beautiful—yet to this golden day, 'twas but one single gem, to whole handfuls of jewels. You will ride today, I hope, or take a long walk somewhere, and recollect us all, Vinnie, and me, and [*Susie and*] Father and mother and home. Yes, Austin, every one of us, for we all think of you, and bring you to recollection many times each day—not *bring* you to recollection, for we never put you away, but keep recollecting on. Was'nt you very tired when you got back to Cambridge? I thought you would be, you had so much to do, the morning you went away. I hope you do not cough mornings, as you did when you were at home. If you do, go and see that Apothecary who gave you something before, and get something to cure it. And Austin, dont you care about anything else that I know troubles you—It is'nt anything—It is too slight, too small, to make you worry so—dont think any more about it. We all love you very much—wont you remember *that* when anything worries you, and you wont care then.

I dont feel as if you'd been here—the time was so very short—how I wish today was last Saturday, and last Saturday was today, so we could see you. Shant you write to us pretty soon? We have looked for a note before. Susie and I walked together all last Tuesday evening, talking of you and the visit, and wishing you were here, and would not go away again. I love her more and more. She looks very lovely in colors—she dont wear mourning now.

You must think of us tonight, while Mr Dwight takes tea here, and we will think of you far away, down in Cambridge. Dont mind the law, Austin, if it is rather dry, dont mind the daily road, tho' it is rather dusty, but remember the brooks and the hills, and remember while you're *but one,* we are *but four* at home!

Emilie.

You *must* come home in the recess.

The Reverend Edward Strong Dwight was under consideration as minister of the First Church to replace Mr. Colton, who had left Amherst in January, 1853, to take up his pastoral duties in Easthampton.

The Massachusetts Constitutional Convention which opened in Boston on May fourth, and to which Judge Ithamar Conkey was the delegate from Amherst, had a special interest for Edward Dickinson. It provided a background for display of the forensic talents of his friend, Otis P. Lord of Salem. So greatly was Mr. Lord's prestige enhanced by his part in the deliberations of the Convention that he was elected Speaker of the Massachusetts House for 1854. The following appraisal had appeared in *The Republican* on March 29, 1853, under the heading " 'Loiterer's' Legislative Monographs, from Boston":

Otis P. Lord is now the acknowledged leader of the House, in all its polemics. He is a man of vigorous intellect, and great force of character, is a powerful and pungent debater, is severe in his logic, blighting in his sarcasm, and audacious in his denunciations, and always armed, at all points, either for defense or attack.

CHAPTER XXIII

A Railroad Reaches Amherst

1

THE Norwalk disaster, "almost at our very doors," came at a time when the campaign to convince Amherst people of the benefits of railroad travel was about to end in success. The first passengers were to venture forth on the Amherst & Belchertown Railroad (total length 19½ miles) during the following week. An advertisement in the *Express* (April 8, 1853) concludes with the words: "Fellow citizens—we are going to prove to you that a Rail Road is one of the greatest of blessings." Freight had been coming in for some time. On April 5 thirty tons, consisting for the most part of dry goods and general merchandise, had arrived in a train of three cars drawn by "a comical little engine belonging to Colonel Phelps, the contractor." The station and terminal buildings were located east of the town on the edge of open country. Except on Main Street, which leads toward East Village in the valley, there were no houses beyond the tracks. The land sloping down toward the southeast, a tract called "No Man's Land," was settled later, for the most part by Irish immigrants. It had been part of the property owned by Samuel Fowler Dickinson. (Compare Appendix II: deeds dated May 22, 1833, and April 27, 1855.)

A neatly printed letter from the superintendent of the connecting railroad announced the opening:

N. L., Willimantic & Palmer R.R. Office
New London, May 5, 1853

Sir:—

The Amherst and Belchertown Rail Road will be opened from Palmer to Amherst, on Monday next, 9th inst.

Trains will run in connection with the trains on this road,—
Leaving Palmer for Amherst at 10.45 A.M., and 6.15 P.M. Leaving
Amherst at 5 A.M., and 1.15 P.M.

> Very Respectfully,
> Wm. R. Storrs, Sup't[1]

On Monday, May 9, as noon bells were ringing, the first regular
passenger train reached "its own stable door." The Amherst artillery
fired nineteen guns in the College Grove. Edward Dickinson's letter
to his son, written even as the fulfillment of his dream was being
realized, is jubilant if guarded.[2]

[*To M^r Wm. Austin Dickinson, Law School, Cambridge, M^s; postmark: Amherst Ms. May 9*]

> Monday morning
> Amherst May 9. 1853

Dear Austin,

The cars are to come in to-day—11½ A.M. for the *first* regular
trip!—and leave at 1.10′ P.M.—& reach Boston at 6.P.M. Mr Greene
goes to Boston in the afternoon train—& will take 2. No^s of Harper
& 3. other books. We have no r.r. jubilee, till we see whether all
runs right—then we shall glorify, becomingly.

The day is beautiful. Mr Carter takes over r.r. station—goes in,

1. Times of anticipated arrival were not announced. But a few days later,
May 17, Edward Dickinson wrote on an inside page of this same sheet a letter
to his son (page 289). On the face of the printed letter he added these essential
details:

Leave Boston—8.　A.M. Express
　　　　〃　　　2½ P.M. Accommodation
Reach Amherst—12.　M.
　　　　〃　　　7½ P.M.

In 1854 the equipment of the Amherst & Belchertown consisted of two wood-
burning engines and tenders, one baggage car, two passenger cars, five platform
cars, three long house cars and two short house cars (Sargent, "The Railroad
Mania in Amherst," 27).

2. See *Express* (May 13, 1853). *The History of Amherst,* 316, states that "the
first passenger train passed over the route on Saturday, May 14."

this morning—& is waiting, anxiously, to be turned out of the P. office—so that he can become a martyr, the second time![3]

Mother has been almost sick—but is now better—rest, well—& send love to you. We may send a bundle by Wm Kellogg, J^r, w^h expects to go to Boston in the afternoon train of to-morrow. He stops at U.S. Hotel.

Mr Dwight continues to interest & please the people—more & more.

Your aff father,
E. Dickinson

12 M. The cars are in; in good style—y^r mother went down to the station, & enjoyed the sight very much—& rode up in the "Amherst House" carriage [two words illegible].

1.10′—Cars left, with lots of passengers—in good spirits—Mr Greene on next train—glory enough for one day!

Another mutilated letter follows. Three lines have been rubbed out and, in a transparent attempt to disguise the meaning, pronouns have again been changed from feminine to masculine gender. "Sue" has twice been altered, first to "Vinnie," then to "Abby." Sometimes the alterations have been partially erased, so that even the substituted words themselves are not legible. Postmarked "Boston," the letter had apparently been given to someone to mail on his arrival there.

[*To M^r Wm. Austin Dickinson, Law School, Cambridge M^s; postmark: Boston. 17 May*]

Monday noon [May 16, 1853]

"Strikes me" just so, dear Austin, but somehow I have to work a good deal more than I used to, and harder, and I feel so tired when night comes, that I'm afraid if I write you, 'twill be something rather bluer than you'll be glad to see—so I sew with all my might, and hope when work is done to be with you much oftener than I have lately been.

3. The records of the United States Post Office Department give the following terms of office of the Amherst postmasters: S. C. Carter, March 30, 1842–May 9, 1845; Seth Nims, May 9, 1845–May 29, 1849; S. C. Carter, May 29, 1849–June 3, 1853; Seth Nims, June 3, 1853–July 16, 1861. In 1853, however, Mr. Nims did not take office until July 1, judging by Emily's letter of that date. Compare *History of Amherst*, 333.

Somehow I am lonely lately—I feel very old every day, and when morning comes and the birds sing, they dont seem to make me so happy as they used to. I guess it's because you are gone, and there are not so many of us as God gave for each other. I wish you were at home. I feel very sure lately that the years we have had together are more than we shall have—I guess we shall journey separately, or reach the journey's end, some of us—but we don't know. We all love you very much. I dont believe you guess how much home thinks and says of it's only absent child—yes, Austin, home is faithful, none other is so true [three lines rubbed out].

You must'nt mind what I say about feeling lonely lately. It is'nt any matter, but I thought I would tell you, so you'd know why I did'nt wirte more. Vinnie and I thank you very much for your letters —we always thank you, and your letters are dearer than all the rest that come. Vinnie did the errand which you wanted her to, but the stage did'nt come over from Northampton at noon, and she could'nt send till today. She sends her love to you, and will write to you very soon [two words rubbed out] her [changed to "his"] letter was safely delivered, and she ["he"] seemed very grateful—she ["he"] has not yet received your week before last letter—she ["he"] thinks someone here has got it. <Susie> ["Vinnie"] and I went to meeting last evening and Father went home first with Abby [?] and then with me. I thought the folks would stare. I think Father feels that she appreciates him, better than most anybody else—How pleasant it is, is'nt it?

She is a dear child to us all, and we see her every day.

We had a very pleasant visit from the Monson folks—they came one noon and stayed till the next. They agree beautifully with Father on the "present generation." They decided that they hoped every young man who smoked would take fire. I respectfully intimated that I thought the result would be a vast conflagration, but was instantly put down.

We are very glad Joel is better, and shall be glad to see him. Take good care of yourself, Austin—now the days grow warm, and dont study too hard. I want to have you tell me how soon you're coming home. You must think of nothing but coming! Emilie.

[On a separate sheet]

While I write, the whistle is playing, and the cars just coming in. It gives us all new life, every time it plays. How you will love to hear it, when you come home again! How soon is the recess? We are anxious to know, and you must come home, *of course.* You must write us pretty soon, and tell us when you are coming—so we can anticipate it. Mr Dwight has finished preaching, and it now remains to be seen if the people ask him to stay. We are all charmed with him, and I'm sure he will have a call. I never heard a minister I

loved half so well, so does Susie love him, and we all—I wish you
were at meeting every time he preaches.

The term has commenced, and there were a great many students
to hear him yesterday.⁴ We all send our love to you. Mother says
she shall send your stockings by the first opportunity. Have you received the package sent by Wᵐ Kellogg? I have written so very fast,
but I hope you can read what I write.

Edward Dickinson's growing pride in Susan Gilbert is plain to
see. It was a potent argument in her favor. Obedience from young
people was expected and obtained. But the obedience of a cool,
self-possessed young woman like Sue would have been, we may be
sure, more gratifying to him than the submissiveness of a timid girl
like her sister Martha, who hid herself in the entry until he had
passed by. (Page 233.)

Edward Dickinson's next letter, written on the back of the printed
circular quoted on page 285, was folded, seled with a wafer and
posted without an envelope.

[*To Mʳ Wm. Austin Dickinson, Law School, Cambridge, Mˢ; postmark: Amherst Ms. May 18*]

Tuesday Evening [May 17, 1853]

Dear Austin,

Your letter to Emily says that your recess commences next Tuesday, & lasts till Monday following.

I think, as you can come so easily, that you had better spend the
recess at home.

We are all well, now. I went to Palmer, in the cars, this morning,
& back at noon. The road rides very smoothly indeed. We were 55.
min. each way.

The weather is excessively warm, & vegetation grows very rapidly.
Library building walls nicely up.

Your aff father,
E. Dickinson

On the Sunday before going home for a brief holiday, May 24–29,
Austin again wrote to Martha Gilbert, who was still in Michigan.

4. The summer term of Amherst College opened on May 11.

Cambridge—Sunday eve
May 22nd [1853]

What is the matter, dear Mat, that not a word comes from you to
one of all your Eastern friends! & that not a word has come for now
almost three months! almost three months! not even to Sue! You
can[t] be sick or your brothers would have written. Is it that you
have never received *our* letters! Sue's letters! & my note & eight
paged letter, since you wrote last! Early in March! I dont know
what to write, Mat, for if it never reaches you, it might reach some
one else whom I should prefer to talk altogether differently to than
to you, & if it does, & you make no reply, it will be just about as
useless to me.

You are very often in my mind, & you are always in our talk at
home, & in Sue's every letter she says not a word from Mat yet &
wonders what the reason is.

Wont you write me *something,* Mat, *soon,* & let me know what
has kept you from us all so long.

Dont you know that I love you and am interested in all that interests you as much as your own brothers? & Dont you suppose I
want *you* to speak to me oftener than twice a year?—to tell me the
course of your thoughts & feelings, so that I may keep along with
you for the time when we are together again! *Write,* Mat, *ever* so
little, & tell me how you are passing your time, how the Spring has
gone with you, & how the Summer promises, & if the Fall is not to
bring you East again. How your Western Springs compare with
ours, & your Western friends with us. What you read, & about your
walks & rides, and if a certain vague suspicion that has come dimly
to my mind is groundless, or if you *have* found some heart out there
that is absorbing your every thought & affection, that is taking you
entirely from us.

Write to me *freely,* cant you, Mat, for have I not to you? & tell
me of all that gladdens or even that saddens you, & write soon, Mat.
I am impatient to hear from you.

Im studying away here in Cambridge—liking well, & *keeping*
well. Have been home once since I came—the first of May—& am
going again tomorrow morning, to spend the recess of a week that
commenced Friday night. Shall leave here after regular breakfast,
get over to Boston, for half an hour & be at home an hour before
dinner at *that,* for you must know that at *length,* at *last,* & finally
that wonderful, long talked of Railroad from P to A is in operation,
and Amherst is nearly a "Seaport town", & only three hours & half
distance from Boston.[5]

I had a *capital* time when I was home before, & I am anticipating

5. A small fragment of paper containing three words—"become a seaport"—
was found with this letter.

everything for *this* weeks visit. We went, *for a ride,* Sue & I, &
Bowdoin & William Fowler, & Emily Fowler & Vinnie, up to Roar-
ing Brook, around the same road we drove the last night you were
in Amherst, you remember—& when you come back we^{ll} go again
just as we did then.—
I could write any quantity of things I^{ve} thought & am thinking,
Mat, or things I^{ve} felt, or things I^{ve} seen—& a thought I^{ve} had—
pleasant thoughts about old times & bright anticipations for times
to come, but I am so indefinite as to what might interest you just
now, I believe I^d better wait till I^{ve} heard from you—& know. Write
very soon Mat, & lets dont have so long a time pass again without
hearing from each other.

Among the drafts which Austin kept through the years and finally
confided to my mother, this is the final letter to Martha Gilbert.
Scribbled on both sides of fragments of blue paper, this rough pencil draft is still pinned together through the middle just as he left it.
From now on gentle Martha fades from the picture. She did not
come back to Amherst in 1853 as he was hoping, but appears to
have spent the rest of the year in the West. Later in the winter,
however, she did return to Amherst, where she made her home with
her sister Harriet for the next four years.
It is unnecessary to speculate about the nature of Austin's feeling
toward Martha Gilbert or to trace its course during the next three
years. It is enough to note that in 1857, the year following the marriage of Austin and Sue, Martha married J. W. Smith of Geneva,
New York.

2

Beginning on May 23, Austin spent a few days at home. On May
24, 1853, the Reverend Mr. Dwight was called to the First Church
of Amherst.[6] During the interim of nearly three months before he
took up his duties as acting pastor on August 21, 1853, the pulpit
was occupied by a variety of incumbents, some of whom appear to
have broken down customary Sabbath decorum. The regular ministers of the First Church were for the most part righteous men who
lived up to what they professed. Indeed, so sincere and dignified
were the preachers to whom the congregation had been accustomed

6. Mr. Dwight's letter of acceptance was received early in July (*Express,* July
15, 1853). He was installed a year later, on July 19, 1854.

that they were not prepared for the vicissitudes of a period of "supplies." When cant took the place of religion in the pulpit Emily was beside herself. She, to whom the Unseen was reality, was left "near frenzy" by a "counterfeit presence." Her father, whose sense of humor was usually well buried, was in the following instance moved to mirth.

This letter has been torn in half. A faint attempt was made to change "Sue" to a word ending in "y."

[*To M^r Wm. Austin Dickinson, Law School, Cambridge, M^s; postmark: Amherst Ms Jun 6*]

Sunday afternoon [June 5, 1853]

Dear Austin.

It is Sunday, and I am here alone. The rest have gone to meeting, to hear Rev Martin Leland. I listened to him this forenoon in a state of mind very near frenzy, and feared the effect too much to go out this afternoon. The morning exercises were perfectly ridiculous, and we spent the intermission in mimicking the Preacher, and reciting extracts from his most memorable sermon. I never heard father so funny. How I did wish you were here. I know you'd have died laughing. Father said he didn't dare look at <Sue>—he said he saw her bonnet coming round our way, and he looked "straight ahead"—he said he ran out of meeting for fear somebody would ask him what he tho't of the preaching. He says if anyone asks him, he shall put his hand to his mouth, and his mouth in the dust, and cry, Unclean—Unclean!! But I hav'nt time to say more of Martin Leland, but I wish you were here today, Austin, and could hear father talk, and you would laugh so loud they would hear you way down in Cambridge. Vinnie and I got your letters just about bedtime last evening. I had been at <Sue's> all the evening and communicated to her the fact that they had not come. She had felt all the time she said, perfectly sure that [Remainder of letter missing]

[*Postscript on first page*]

All send love to you Austin—write us again very soon—I am glad for "The Honeysuckle."

In the next letter many words referring to Sue have been either erased or altered. Some of the alterations have themselves been partly erased so that not all of the substituted words are clear.

[*To M^r Wm. Austin Dickinson, Law School, Cambridge, Ms.; post-mark: Amherst Ms. Jun 9*]

Thursday morning [June 9, 1853]

Dear Austin.

I got your letter—I delivered the one <to Sue>. Jerry stood ready to act at a moment's notice, and all was as you wished, but <Sue> [changed to "we"] thought not best, so I suppose you'll receive a telegraphic despatch, and Susie [changed to "Vinnie"] and I shall not see you this evening.

Your letter troubled me a good deal for a moment, I tho't something dreadful had happened; you were about to be killed and were coming to bid us Goodbye, or something of the kind, but I know the whole now.

Whenever you want help, Austin, just call on Jerry and me, and we will take care of you, and perhaps we'll *help a little*. I hope you wont trouble yourself about any remarks that are made—they are not worth the thought of—certainly not the care for. Dont mind them. Nobody'll dare to harm <dear Susie>, nobody'll dare to harm you. You are too far from them; dont fear them. I hope the hair is off—you must tell me about it as soon as you write again, and write us soon.[7] We are pretty well now. I rode with Emmons last evening, and had a beautiful ride. New London is coming today, but I dont care, I dont think folks are much. I do wish you were here. Dear Austin, now remember not to care for these foolish things, for they cant reach [*you or Sue*].

Love from us. Emilie

7. For some reason or other the ladies of the family seem to have been worried about Austin's hair. The reference to it in the present letter is the first of several. Of a reddish color, it was thick and unruly; he had difficulty making it stay in place. But whether or not to cut it off would hardly seem to have been a cause for concern. Following an attack of fever after his visit to the Philadelphia Centennial in 1876, he wore a wig—a reddish wig.

In recent years there has been a rumor that Austin Dickinson's wig was green. As to that, I can only say that the person who started such a rumor must have been color blind. With Mr. Dickinson's appearance up to his last illness in August, 1895, I was intimately familiar. A very young person is apt to notice eccentricities of appearance. Although as a child I had not been aware that he wore a wig, I do remember wondering why his hair was so long. And I vividly recall the coppery glint of it and the shining highlights. I remember other peculiarities of his countenance, too, such as the exact location of two strange warts which fascinated me. But in spite of daily opportunity, I never saw him wear anything at all resembling a green, or greenish, wig. See Stanley King, *A History of the Endowment of Amherst College* (1950), 104.

On June 9, 1853, at the invitation of the New London, Willimantic & Palmer and the Amherst & Belchertown Rail Roads, 325 New Londoners made "a morning call" on the citizens of Amherst. Three letters were enclosed in the next envelope: one from Emily, one from Vinnie, and one from Edward Dickinson, begun Saturday, but finished Monday evening, June 13.

Emily Dickinson's preference for solitude is already apparent at the age of twenty-two. "I sat in Prof Tyler's woods," she says in her next letter, "and saw the train move off, and then ran home again for fear somebody would see me, or ask me how I did."

It was not so much that she shunned people, I think, as that she wanted time. She did not "starve" herself, as Amy Lowell said she did, by withdrawing from an exchange of platitudes. On the contrary, by evading the incessant demands of commonplace talk she escaped into her "real life" with her books, with her pencil, with the friends whom she ardently loved, and with the high excitement of her own thoughts.

[*Enclosed in Emily's next letter*]

> Amherst. Sat Eve.
> June 11 "53.

Dear Austin,

I want to get the New Edⁿ of Shakespeare, just publishing by Redding, in Boston.[8] Can't you subscribe for it better than I can?

Joel came up on Thursday noon—& left on Friday noon. He seems much better than he has been, & thinks he is getting well.

We had a very good time with the N.L. party. About 325 came up. The N.L. papers & Williamantic papers are full of the matter. We shall probably, return the visit, before long.

Nothing yet heard from Mʳ Dwight—whether he will accept our call, or not.

Dʳ Holland came up with the Excursion party & made us a short call. Wm. Howland took tea with us on Monday evening. Our C.C.P. [Court of Common Pleas] sat ½ day. These are about the events of the week.

Monday evening. All well—all send love.

> Your aff father,
> E. Dickinson

8. Redding & Company, 8 State Street, Boston.

[*To M^r Wm. Austin Dickinson, Law School, Cambridge, M^s; post-mark: Amherst Ms. Jun 14*]

Monday morning [June 13, 1853]

My dear Austin.

I dont know where to begin. There has been considerable news since I have written much to you, and yet of such a kind as I dont think you would care for. I will tell you first how glad I am you are better, and are not going to be sick, as I was afraid when you wrote me. Do be careful, very careful, Austin, for you are from us all, and if anything happens to you, we cannot find it out and all take care of you as we can when you're at home. I dont think you'd better study any for a day or two, until you feel perfectly well. I wont say any more about it, if you dont want to have me, lest I make you sick by talking, as you said you should be if I told anybody, and folks wrote letters to you; but just come home the moment whenever you are sick, or think you are going to be sick, and you shall have Vinnie and me [*and Somebody nearer than either of us*] . . . to take care of you, and make you well. I sent the White Hat as you wished, and you've probably received it before this. I sent it on Saturday, with special instructions to Driver, and presume it has got there safely.

I will send *the other* directly, if you would like to have me.

The New London Day passed off grandly—so all the people said—it was pretty hot and dusty, but nobody cared for that. Father was as usual, Chief Marshal of the day, and went marching around the town with New London at his heels like some old Roman General, upon a Triumph Day. Mrs Howe got a capital dinner, and was very much praised. Carriages flew like sparks, hither, and thither and yon, and they all said t'was fine. I spose it was—I sat in Prof Tyler's woods and saw the train move off, and then ran home again for fear somebody would see me, or ask me how I did. Dr Holland was here and called to see us—seemed very pleasant indeed, inquired for you, and asked mother if Vinnie and I might come and see them in Springfield.

Last week was beautiful, tho' very warm and dry. I was very happy last week, [*for we were at Susie's house, or Susie was at our house most all the time, and she always makes us happy. Vinnie is down there now*].

The stories are all still, Austin. I dont hear any now, and Susie says she dont care now the least at all for them. They must not

trouble you—they are very low—of the earth—they cannot reach
our heaven if they climb never so high. I will attend to Bowdoin.

Mr Ford sat with us in church yesterday, and took tea at our
house last night. I think he's a popinjay.

We had a visit from Joel. Ego, mitie, me. We all go down to
the grove often. Father and mother together walked down there
yesterday morning. I think they will all live. Father thinks so. We
all send you our love. Emilie.

I have had a letter from Mat, and she sent her love to you, and
will write you very soon.

[On a separate slip]

I will find out accurately what "the expenses" are, and let you
know next time. We did the best we c'd, and everything very
safely.

I gave Jerry your messages, at which his teeth increased, and his
countenance expanded—he laughed also for some time, as if taking the joke moderately and wasting none of it.

Austin—there's nothing in the world that Jerry wont do for
you. I believe he thinks you are finer than anybody else, and feels
quite consequential to think of serving you. Send him a word
sometimes, for it affects him so. Mrs Mack too inquires for you
with unabating interest. It's pleasant to be liked by such folks, and
I love to hear them speak of you with interest. Mr Dwight has not
given an answer. I feel a good deal afraid, but try to hope for the
best. 'Twill be dreadful if we dont get him. You dont tell us about
your hair—wont you next time, Austin, for your peace is our's.
Write us often, and we will, and think that if we all live we shall
again meet together during these summer days. I shall be glad to
see the Poems.

Austin and Emily were always on the lookout for interesting
new books, especially those written by their contemporaries. The
poems of Alexander Smith, son of a patternmaker in the linen
mills of Glasgow, were having an immense if ephemeral vogue in
America. Nearly 11,000 copies of an edition published in Boston
in 1853 had been sold within a few months.[9]

[Letter enclosed]

Dear Austin

I've just come up from dinner and will write you a little before
I take my nap. It's a warm, dusty day, the south wind blows &

9. *Express,* February 3, 1854.

every thing is parched & withered. I've been watching the clouds all day hoping they would bring rain but I'm afraid we shant see any to day. I went to see *Sue* & Jennie this morning.

Sue & I intend to go to Northampton tomorrow if she can get a horse. I'm sorry you've been sick. Be careful & not get over done this hot weather. Mother says "have patience & *her letter* will come to you before long.["] We have been hurried ever since you went away.

Mr Ford sat in our slip yesterday & took tea here last night. He was quite agreeable & still I always feel as if he was tinctured with Emily Fowler. He intends to spend most of his Sabbaths in A—I hear. He inquired for you with interest. We have company to tea most every night. Elisabeth Hand who was preserved so long for you is here for the summer.

The New London excursion was said to be a little remarkable & I suppose it was. Dr Holland called here & laughed at me a little about Howland which was of course gratifying to me.

Joel has made us a visit & I'm glad its over, for I have got tired of hearing about *Ego altogether*. He is never informed on any other subject.

I suppose there will be an excursion to New London at some time. I dont know when. George Howland will know about the expense of last week & perhaps you had better write to him & ask him, or if you prefer I will enquire. I think he was very kind to do it. No one else could have been trusted. Emilie went to ride with Emmons last week. I guess I cant say any more now, for my nap (which is as essential to my comfort as a cold bath) must be attended to. Vinnie.

Three days later Vinnie wrote again. Emily was Sue's ardent champion but, as an intermediary with Austin, Vinnie seems to have left something to be desired.

[*To Mʳ Wm. Austin Dickinson, Law School, Cambridge, Mˢ; no postmark*]

Thursday [June 16, 1853]

Oh Austin 'tis so beautiful this afternoon that I want to sit & look out all the time & breathe the perfume that comes to me with every breeze, of new mown hay & flowers. Pussy is sleeping in her little nest in the grass & the *Pierce* children screaming around just as when you were here & now & then a big bumble bee bobs in at the window & out again. It has seemed like Sunday ever since you went away. Tuesday night Sue & I went to a party at Prof. Havens to entertain the remainder of the Senior class. The students were very green & *we* were resolved not to come home with any of them, so we refused all their offers & when they were all gone, Mr H[owland] went with us. Mr Ford was there with Emilie Fowler. Sue & I looked best of any one there. Emilie Fowler did'nt appear like herself & Austin I now believe what you said so long ago, that she means to marry Ford herself. From some things I've heard I feel quite sure that she intends to watch him pretty close, any how. Yesterday Emeline, Sue, William Hubbard & I went to Northhampton with Mr Kelloggs horse, had a nice time, Sue is here every day. Austin you need never fear that we shall treat her unkindly, I don't love to hear you speak so. We are bored with callers most of the time. We are busy as usual, the sitting room is all ready for summer & really looks quite refreshing. We received your notes last evening & were glad that you were safe, they made me feel very badly & I hope there will be no more occasion for such ones. I think Emilie & I were in the fault some what. I thought she ought not to say what she did the last morning & tried to prevent it, but she felt you must know it. If we did'nt love you, we should never care what you did or how you felt. I know how much you do for us & I appreciate it. We love you & we love Sue dearly & if you'll forget all that has been unpleasant in the past, we will also & let us never think of it or speak of it again.

I had a funny dream last night about the Converse family. I thought they invited me to travel West with them this Summer. I shall like to hear about your call when you have time. I'm sorry my writing does'nt look better but I'm in a hurry & the letters will go wrong. Mother sends love. Be cheerful & happy & dont mind the hair. Have it done *now* & then you'll feel relieved.
Good bye, Vinnie

[*To M^r Wm. Austin Dickinson, Law School, Cambridge, Ms.; post-mark: Amherst Ms. Jun 20*]

Sunday afternoon [June 19, 1853]

Do you want to hear from me, Austin? I'm going to write to you, altho' it dont seem much as if you would care to have me. I dont know why exactly, but things look blue, today, and I hardly know what to do, everything looks so strangely, but if you want to hear from me, I shall love very much to write. Prof Tyler has preached today, and I have been all day. Susie walked home from meeting with us, and was so disappointed at having no letter from you. It really seems very unsafe to depend upon Judge Conkey, and that Mr Eaton too, I should think quite hazardous. Dont wait for them next time! We received your notes and the Poems, for which we thank you, last week. Father seemed much pleased with his letter, and all of us laughed a little. The remark concerning Mr Ford seemed to please father mightily. I dont dont mean what *I* said, but your opposition to me. He told me you'd "hit me off nicely." You make me think of Dickens, when you write such letters as that—I am going to read it to Sue—I should have done before, but the afternoon it came, we had terrible thundershowers, and it rained all evening long; and yesterday afternoon Father wanted us all to ride, so I have not had opportunity. I walked with her last evening. She wore her new things today, and looked beautifully in them—a white straw hat, trimmed with Rouches— mantilla of fawn colored silk, very handsomely finished, and white Dress. She is going after Miss Bartlett tomorrow morning at 5. and begins her Dressmaking tomorrow. She says she shall just get thro' by the time you get home. So shall Vinnie and I—there must be no sewing then. We are all pretty well, and the weather is beautiful. If you were here I think you would be very happy, and I think we should, but time has wings, and you will be with us soon. We have been free from company by the "Amherst and Belchertown Railroad" since Joel went home, tho' we live in constant fear of some other visitation.

"Oh would some power the giftie gie" folks, to see themselves as we see them. Burns. I have read the poems, Austin, and am going to read them again, and will hand them to Susie. They please me very much, but I must read them again before I know just [what] I think of "Alexander Smith". They are not very coherent, but there's good deal of exquisite frenzy, and some wonderful figures, as ever I met in my life. We will talk about it again. The grove looks nicely, Austin, and we think must certainly grow. We love to go there, it is a charming place. Everything is singing now, and everything is beautiful that *can* be in it's life.

So Joel did'nt have a remarkable trip up here—wonder which enjoyed it the most—the pestilence, or the victims. Dont tell him what I said. And think besides Aunt Lavinia must be very busy. Guess "Father will be tired" when they next visit here.

Jerry gets along nicely, takes first rate care of the horse, and seems unusually grand after having a message from you. It has the same effect as a big mug of cider, and *looks* a good deal better. I am glad your eye has got well. You must use it carefully, for a little while. I hope you received your hat. I had not time to write you with it, for I did it up late at night, after having folks here all the evening, and I hope it did not seem strange to you.

The time for the New London trip has not been fixed upon. I sincerely wish it may wait until you get home from Cambridge, if you would like to go.

The cars continue thriving—a good many passengers seem to arrive from somewhere, tho' nobody knows from where. Father expects his new Buggy to come by the cars, every day now, and that will help a little. I expect all our Grandfathers and all their country cousins will come here to pass Commencement, and dont doubt the stock will rise several percent that week. If we children <and Sue> could obtain board for the week in some "vast wilderness", I think we should have good times. Our house is crowded daily with the members of this world, the high and the low, the bond and the free, the "poor in this world's goods," and the "almighty dollar,["] and "what in the world they are after" continues to be unknown. But I hope they will pass away, as insects on vegetation, and let us reap together in golden harvest time—that is [*you and Susie and me*] and our dear sister Vinnie must have a pleasant time to be unmolested, together, when your school days end. You must not stay with Howland after the studies cease. We shall be ready for you, and you must come home from school, not stopping to play by the way! Mother was much amused at the feebleness of your hopes of hearing from her. She got so far last week once, as to take a pen and paper and carry them into the kitchen, but her meditations were broken by the unexpected arrival of *Col Smith* and his wife, so she must try again. I'm sure you will hear from her soon. We all send our love to you, and miss you very much, and think of seeing you again very much, and love dear <Sue> [changed to "you"] constantly. Write me again soon. I have said a good deal today. Emilie.

[*Note from Edward Dickinson enclosed*]

Dear Austin
  Judge C[onkey] came home on Saturday noon.
  You can send by some other chance.
  We are all well.

Y^r father
E.D.

Monday morning.

Austin

Sunday afternoon [June 26, 1853]

I shall write you a little, Austin, to send by Father tomorrow, tho' you havnt yet answered my long letter which went to you last Monday, and I've been looking for something from you for a good many days. The valise did'nt get to us till a long time after you sent it, and so 'twas a good while Austin, before you heard from us, but you know all about it now, and I hope you dont care. But we felt so sorry to disappoint you by not sending the things which you requested to have us. <Sue> [changed to "we"] did'nt hear yeasterday, so we are all in a tantrum to know the meaning of that.

If you ever get where we are again, we shall tell you how many letters are missing by the way, and never reach you, and we shall ask you too how many have gone to us, which we have not received.

It is cold here today, Austin, and the west wind blows—the windows are shut at home, and the fire burns in the kitchen. How we should love to see you, how pleasant it would be to walk to the grove together. We will walk there, when you get home. We all went down this morning, and the trees look beautifully. Every one is growing, and when the west wind blows, the pines lift their light leaves and make sweet music. Pussy goes down there too, and seems to enjoy much in her own observations. Mr Dwight has not answered yet—he probably will this week. I do think he will come Austin, and shall be so glad if he will.

Did <Susie> write you how Vinnie went to South Hadley with Bowdoin, and she came to stay with me? And how we sewed together, and talked of what would be? We did sew and talk together, and she said she should tell you what a sweet time we had. Emmons asked me to ride yesterday afternoon, but I'd promised to go somewhere else, so he asked me to go this week, and I told him I would. Has father written you that Edwin Pierce, our neighbor, was arrested last week, for beating a servant girl, tried, and fined two dollars and costs? Vinnie and I heard the whipping, and could have testified, if the Court had called upon us. Also Dea Cowan's son George was detected while breaking into the Bonnet Shop, the other night, and is to be tried next Wednesday. Mr Frank Conkey is absent, and the criminal desiring his services, the parties consent to wait.

What do you think of Amherst? Dont you think your native place shows evident marks of progress? Austin—home looks beautifully—we all wish you here always, but I hope 'twill seem only dearer for missing it so long. Father says you will come in three weeks—that wont be long now. Keep well and happy, Austin, and remember us all you can, and much love from home

and Emilie.

[On a separate slip]

Austin—are you willing to get me another bottle of medicine, if it wont trouble you too much, and send it to me by father? I enclose the prescription. You can get it at Mr Burnett's, but dont get it, Austin, unless it's convenient for you.

Mr and Mrs Godfrey have moved into the Baker house, across the road, and we're so glad to get them back again.

CHAPTER XXIV

Costs of Hospitality

THE summer of 1853 was a particularly busy one. Visits were impending not only from friends but from relatives on both sides of the family. Vinnie as usual was head of the committee on arrangements. Then, too, Mr. and Mrs. Dickinson were planning to attend a reunion of his class at Yale, the thirtieth anniversary of his graduation. Their absence would add to the girls' responsibilities. It is plain that already, in her twenties, when she wrote these breathless stanzas, Emily was beginning to feel a sense of pressure.

> A day! Help! Help! Another day!
> Your prayers, oh, passer-by!
> From such a common ball as this
> Might date a victory!
>
> From marshalings as simple
> The flags of nations swang.
> Steady, my soul—what issues
> Upon thine arrow hang!

[*To Mr Wm. Austin Dickinson, Law School, North Cambridge, Ms., Via Grouts"; postmark: Amherst Ms. Jul 2*]

Friday afternoon [July 1, 1853]

Dear Austin.

I'm sorrier than you are, when I cant write to you—I've tried with all my might to find a moment for you, but time has been so short, and my hands so full that until now I could not. Perhaps you do not know that Grandmother has been here making a visit this week, and has just gone this noon. She has, and we are tired, and the day very warm, but write to you I will, before a *greater* happens.

Some of the letters you've sent us we have received, and thank you for affectionately. Some, we have not received, but thank you for the memory, of which the emblem perished. Where all those letters go—our's, and your's, and Susie's, somebody surely knows, but we do not. The note which came to Susie in the last evening's letter, was given her. She does not get the letters you say you send to her, and she sends others which you do not receive. Austin, if we four meet again we'll see what this all means. I tell Susie you write to her, and she says she *"knows* so" notwithstanding they do not often come. There's a new Postmaster today, but we dont know who's to blame. You never wrote me a letter, Austin, which I liked half so well, as the one Father brought me, and you need'nt fear that we dont always love you, for we always do. We think of your coming home with a great deal of happiness, and are glad you want to come.

Father said he never saw you looking in better health, or seeming in finer spirits. He did'nt say a word about the Hippodrome or the museum, and he came home so stern that none of us dared to ask him, and besides Grandmother was here, and you certainly dont think I'd allude to a *Hippodrome* in the presence of that lady! I'd as soon think of popping fire crackers in the presence of Peter the Great! But you'll tell us when you get home—how soon—how soon! [Several words rubbed out.]

We are glad you're so well, Austin. We're glad you are happy too, and how often Vinnie and I wonder concerning something of which you never speak. We are pretty well, but tired, the weather too so warm that it takes the strength away. I am glad you are glad that I went to ride with Emmons. I went again with him one evening while father was gone, and had a beautiful ride.

I thank you for what you sent me, and for your kindness in saying what you did. I sent your little brush. I admire the Poems very much. We all send our love to you. Shall write you again, Sunday. Emilie.

[*Letter enclosed*]

Friday. After tea.

Dear Austin

One word about the Converse visit. It seems to me not *best* for them to come at commencement time, for we shall be so occupied

then that we can not enjoy seeing them at all. Then too, we are
always so tired & hurried. Mother & Emilie both think t'would be
much pleasanter for them to come after commencement. Mother &
Father will go to New Haven the 28th of July & then Aunt Lavinia
will be here with the children, so if they can come just as well then
& you are willing, we should all very much prefer it.

I would rather that Katy should not stay any longer than Edmund, I would like to have them come together & both stay as long
as they can but *both* go away together. Another thing, I know that
[we] should not have any place to put them at commencement &
every thing is always so confused, I would rather have them come
when we are alone & let us have the visit all by ourselves. As for
Mary Nichols, I dont know as its best for her to come to Amherst.
I should like it well enough but I *fear* the *folks* will begin to open
their eyes. I'm afraid they wont like it. Does she expect to come?
I'm afraid it *wont do* to have so many visitors. You know home has
not *altered* in your absence & sometimes the *fire kindles suddenly!*
I anticipate the Converse visit with *pleasure.* You asked me to write
frankly & so I have. Mother grand² has just made us¹ quite a visit.
Another *job* over for the season. I guess we dont need any more
fixings for the parlor. I bought a pretty image for the parlor this
week. The weather is very hot. Pine trees growing *well.* We shall
be very glad to have you at home again. If you dont like what I
have written, you must say so. Sue is well. I carried your note to her
this morning.

Goodbye
Vinnie

[*To* Wm *Austin Dickinson. Law School. Cambridge, Mass.; postmark: Amherst Ms. Jul 9¹*]

Friday noon [July 8, 1853]

Dear Austin.

I must write you a little before the cars leave this noon—just to
tell you that we got your letter last evening, and were rejoiced to
hear from you after so long a time, and that we want to see you,
and long to have you come, much more than I can tell you.

We did'nt know what to make of it that we did'nt hear from
you, but owed it to the post masters on the way, and not to you,

1. This envelope is addressed by Emily. Not franked, it has a 3-cent stamp.

but now we know you've had company, you are rather more excusable.

Susie was here last night, saying she'd had a letter, and that we should have one at home before bed time, which we did about 10—. o'clock, when father came home from the office. Now Austin—we hav'nt written you oftener, because we've had so much company, and so many things to do. We want to get all our work done before you come home, so as not to be busy sewing when we want to see you; that's why we dont write oftener. You dont know how much we think of you, or how much we say, or how wish you were here every hour in the day, but we have to work very hard, and cannot write half as often as we want to to you. We think you dont write to us any, and we must all be patient until you get home, and then I rather think we shall wipe out old scores in a great many good talks. You say it is hot and dry. It is very dry here, tho' now for two or three days the air is fine and cool. Everything is so beautiful, it's a real Eden here; how happy we shall be roaming round it together! The trees are getting over the effect of the canker worm, and we hope we may have some apples yet, tho' we cant tell now—but we feel very thankful that the leaves are not all gone, and there's a few green things which hav'nt been carried away. Mother expects to go to Monson tomorrow afternoon, to spend the Sabbath. They want very much to have her, and we think she had better go. She will come home Monday afternoon.

Vinnie will write what she thinks about Mary Nichols' coming in her next. What would please you about it? I want you should all do what will make you the happiest—after that I dont care.

I am glad you have enjoyed seeing Gould. About something for Mother—I think it would please her very much if you should bring her some thing, tho' she would'nt wish you to get anything very expensive.

Vinnie and I will think of something and write you *what* next time.

I hope to send fathers Daguerreotype before you come, and will if I can get any safe opportunity. We shall write you again in a day or two, and all send our love. Your aff Sister Emilie.

[*Letter enclosed*]

Friday Morning

Dear Austin

I've just come in from picking raspberries & I'm all scratched & burnt up, but I'll try & write a little. Emilie received your note last evening. We began to think very strange that you did not write to us before. I sent you a note last Saturday concerning the Boston visitors, but I dont know as you received it & whether you liked what was in it. Mother says she prefers you would get her what you think best, that is if you want to get her any thing. She does not want to specify anything. It seems a great while since you have been home & we all want to see you.

Mr Nims is post master, & a clumsy one enough. I dont expect to get anything that comes through his hands. Ford & Emilie Fowler are driving around just as you said they would. Father & every body else that is decent is mad with the *whole* New London company, they are very mean & impudent.

I hope for my part the contract will be broken at some time. Father will tell you how they act, when you get home. You must do as you think best about the *time* for the Converse visit. Do as you like about Mary Nichols.

I want if you have time, that you should get two or three things for me. There is one corner in the parlor where I would like an *ottoman.* I cant get any *here.* I think a mahogany frame with a hair cloth top would be as pretty as any thing perhaps. Get rather a low one. I dont want mine to be like those in Aunt *Lavinia's* parlor, but in form like some Sue saw at the *Revere,* only those were damask. Get any kind you like & I shall be suited. I want a black bracelet *very much,* such as they keep at Joel's store. I presume you have seen a good many of them & I should be very glad of one, if they dont cost too much. I believe they are called *Jet,* though I'm not quite sure. Then I want a song, "When Do the Swallows homeward fly." The more I think about it, Austin I guess a bottle of *genuine* cologne would please *Mother* as well as anything.

Mother is going to Monson to spend the Sabbath. We intend to have Aunt L & family come here week after next. I shall have lots to tell you & to hear when you come. The grove is flourishing well. Mr Jenkins was haying in the lot a few days ago & Mother saw him sitting on your bench in the grove to rest him, so you see t'was a good [idea] to put it there.

If it is not convenient for you to do my errands, no matter about them.

Vinnie

[*To M^r Wm. Austin Dickinson, Law School, North Cambridge, Ms.,* "*Via Grout's*"; *postmark: Amherst Ms. Jul 11*]

Just before dark [July 10, 1853]

Dear Austin

I'm so glad you are coming home. It seems to me as though we should all be remarkably happy to see each other. How does it seem to you? I sent you a letter on Friday full of wants to be supplied & I hope you have received it. I'm rejoiced that your hair is gone. Dont ever worry about it. Sue dont care, *indeed* she dont & now, do you?

Sue is a nice girl & you ought to be a happy *fellar.*

We have had a splendid visit from Dr Holland & his wife & we shall return it some time. Get any sort of *ottoman* that pleases you. I sent for a black bracelet & a song, "When do the Swallows homeward fly." I seem to feel as if you had not received Friday's letter. I hope you'll have a good time at Lynn. I ought to write to the Squire [William Howland], but some how I dont. My regards perhaps. It's rather lonely with out Mother. I have something to tell you that will vex you I know. It does me. Good bye till Thursday.

Vinnie

Remember me to Katy & Edmund & tell them to come when you say.

The torn-off second half is all that remains of a letter from Emily enclosed in the same envelope.

. . . are so glad it's off, and you are you at last. I will not tell the folks, if you dont want to have me. Dr Holland and his wife, spent last Friday with us—came unexpectedly—we had a charming time, and have promised to visit them after Commencement. They asked all about you, and Dr Holland's wife expressed a great desire to see you. He said you would be a Judge—there was no help for it—you must certainly be a Judge! We had Champagne for dinner, and a very fine time. We were so sorry you were not here, and Dr and Mrs Holland expressed their regret many times. Mother's coming home Monday. It seems very queer indeed to have her gone over Sunday, but we get along very well. It rained beautifully Saturday.

Susie is here or we there, pretty much all of the time now. We walked home from Church together, and she said she was going to write you today. Mrs Cutler is going to Hardwick next week for a visit, and Sue is going to keep house. Perhaps you will go and see her in case you should be in town! I cannot realize that you will come so soon, but I'm so glad, and we all are. Never mind the hair, Austin, we are glad, and that's all we care, and all <Susie> cares is that you should *suspect* she should care. Love till you come.

Emilie.

[*On a separate slip*]

Austin

    As you are coming home Austin, and it's a good opportunity, I
think I had better have another bottle of medicine, tho' I hav'nt used
up the other yet. But dont you get it for me if you are very busy, or
have other errands to do which will take all your time. You can
do nothing for me, for which I thank you so much.

    On Thursday, July 14, Austin came home for a six-weeks' vacation.
From then until Emily's next letter, written on November 8, there
is but one note—from his father.

    The fall term of the Law School opened on the first of September;
but once more Austin was late in returning. The delay was not
unusual. Regular attendance of law students during the 1850's was
the exception rather than the rule.[2]

    Edward Dickinson's letter, folded and addressed on the back, is
postmarked in green ink, as are those which follow.

[*To Mrs Edward Dickinson, Amherst, M^s; postmark: N H & Bellows
Falls R.R. 14 Sep*]

Greenfield ½ past 10.A.M.

[September 14, 1853]

Dear Austin,

    The Court have just cont^d the 2^d Capital case to 20. Dc^r Mr East-
man's case will therefore come next.[3] Probably this first capital case

    2. Austin went back to Cambridge on November 7, 1853. Not only was he late
in returning for the first term of his final year at the Law School, he took time
off during the year in addition to the long vacation from January 19 to March 1,
1854. But he graduated in good standing though *in absentia*, receiving his LL.B.
on July 19, 1854. See *Quinquennial Catalogue of the Law School of Harvard
University, 1817-1934* (Cambridge, 1935), Chronological List, 48; Alphabetical
List, 88.

    3. For the trial of jury cases the Massachusetts Supreme Court met in Green-
field on the second Tuesday of September (September 13, 1853), and on the
fourth Monday (26th) of the same month in Northampton.

    The Reverend John Eastman of Hawley was being sued for divorce by his
wife Prudence, an almost unheard-of procedure for a minister of the gospel.
Trial of the case was begun at Greenfield and continued at Northampton, with
Rufus Choate, attorney general of the Commonwealth, representing the woman,
Edward Dickinson of Amherst and David Aiken of Greenfield, the man. Decision

will be finished tomorrow—& Mʳ Choate will probably make his argument to-morrow (Thursday) forenoon.

If you want to hear him—take the horse & come up.

Your aff father
E. Dickinson

I put a letter into the mail this morning—lest it should fail, I put this into the car-mail.

E.D.

The weather was fine and the number of visitors large for the Cattle Show, Wednesday, October 26. The principal event was an address on "The Education of the Farmer for his Vocation," by a graduate of the college, the Reverend Frederick Dan Huntington of Boston, who discussed the relation of farming to schoolhouse, town hall, church and homestead. At the dinner which followed, "as soon as the clatter of knives and forks had fully subsided," the presiding officer, the Honorable Edward Dickinson, after giving a brief history of the society and referring to the interest felt by all professions and pursuits in the subject of farming, carried on the theme of the morning's address. He emphasized the duty of all those present to cultivate the mind as well as the soil. President Hitchcock spoke "in a pleasant way" of the hardships farmers must endure and "closed with the following sentiment: *The Farmers of the Connecticut Valley* may their hardships go on increasing till they cry out for very joy."[4]

By now the Amherst & Belchertown Rail Road, providing better service, had become the preferred mail route to Boston. Apparently there were still on hand a few envelopes addressed by Edward Dickinson to his son "via Grout's" to "North Cambridge," where there was a stop on the Fitchburg Rail Road. These were not to be wasted. So "North" and "via Grout's" were inked out to make sure that the letter would go by the quicker route through Palmer to Boston. In such envelopes Emily's next three letters to Austin were dispatched.

[*To Mʳ Wm. Austin Dickinson, Law School, Cambridge, Mˢ; postmark: Amherst Ms. Nov 8*]

---

was reached three months later. "The case has just now been decided; the Court denying the application of the wife for divorce" (*Express*, December 30, 1853).

4. *Hampshire Gazette*, November 1, 1853. See also *Express*, October 28, 1853.

Tuesday morning [November 8, 1853]

Dear Austin.

It seems very lonely without you. Just as I write it snows, and
we shall have a storm. It makes me think of Thanksgiving, when
we are all here again. Sue was with us yesterday afternoon, and as
usual walked up to Miss Baker's with Vinnie.

I got my plants in yesterday, and it was so cold last night that
the squashes all had to be moved.

We shall move the table into the sitting room to day, and with
a cheerful fire, and only one thing wanting, you can think just how
we look. I guess things at the house are getting along pretty well,
tho' father said this morning he almost wished he'd persuaded you
to stay until after Thanksgiving. Father went away, bidding us
an affectionate good bye yesterday morning, having business in
Springfield which would detain him all day, and perhaps until the
next day, and returned at dinner time, just as the family were getting
rather busy. Of course, we were delighted to be together again! After
our long separation! Had a letter from Mat, last night, which I
would enclose to you, but have just sent it to Sue.

She spoke of you very affectionately, sent her love, and wanted you
to write her. She enclosed a private letter to Sue. I hope you have
got there safely, and found a pleasant home. It looks so bleak this
morning that if you were me, at all, you might be inclined to be
homesick; as you are not, I hope you're not.

I must not write any more, for there is'nt a moment to spare
before this goes in the mail.

I'm afraid you cant read it now, I have written in such a hurry.
We all send you our love, and hope you are happy, and think much
of seeing you again.

Affy. Emily.

PS. Pussy is well.

[*To Mʳ Wm. Austin Dickinson, Law School, Cambridge, Mˢ; postmark: Amherst Ms Nov 10*]

Thursday morn [November 10, 1853]

Dear Austin.

I was so glad to get your letter, and thank you for writing so soon.

It does seem so strange without you, but we try to make the most
of us, and get along pretty well.

The weather is very cold here. Day before yesterday, we had a snow storm—yesterday a terrible rain, and today the wind blows west, and the air is bitter cold. I am so glad you got there pleasantly, and feel so much at home. Mr Dwight preached beautifully Sunday, and I knew you w'd miss him.

Mrs Fay is moving today, and Father is so solemn.

I do wish he would "look more cheerful". I think the Artist was right.

<Sue> was here day before yesterday, but it stormed and blew so yesterday, no one could get out, and therefore we did not see her [changed to "him"].

Father remarked yesterday that he would like it very well if you were here to vote. For all you differ, Austin—he cant get along without you, and he's been just as bleak as a November day, ever since you've been gone. You asked me about the railroad. Every body seems pleased at the change in arrangement. It sounds so pleasantly to hear them come in twice. I hope there will be a bell soon. We were talking about it this morning. Write very often, Austin. You are coming next week Saturday, you know, and the Roosters are ripening!

The family party is to be at "Miss Willim's"!

Good bye. Emilie.

[*Letter enclosed*]

Wednesday Eve

Oh such dismal weather, Austin. It most makes me cry to think of it. I've felt for two days that if I had a friend in the world I should like to see or hear from such an *individual*. It snowed all yesterday & to day has poured & blowed. I made out to see Sue, yesterday, but we've all been in prison to day. Father was *thoughtful* enough to spend last evening with us *socially* & as he seemed rather dull, I endeavoured to entertain him by reading spicey passages from Fern leaves, where upon he brightened up sufficiently to correct me as I went along, advising me to put in all the little words as they would'nt hurt me &c. You can imagine the rest as you have heard such like before. Father has seemed quite pensive & exhibited much of the martyr spirit since you went away. We've had some queer times here, but I cant stop to tell them now. We were glad to hear from you & shall want to hear *certainly* once more this week. Tell us every thing that will interest us. I'm glad Clarke liked the flowers.[5]

5. Stephen Greely Clarke of Manchester, New Hampshire, was a friend of Austin's at the Law School.

Theres some pleasure in sending gifts where they are appreciated. Do you remember the fate of a similar boquet under your charge? I do, & I never could understand that & some other things of the same nature. I have'nt heard from Aunt Lavinia yet. I think its very strange indeed. The table is in the sitting room, & the dining room is closed up for the winter. I think Father is perfectly home sick with out you. What will he do when *we* are *all* gone? Good night Austin.

Vinnie

What indeed, the reader may ask! That was a thought, we may be sure, not often entertained by Edward Dickinson.

In 1853 the Massachusetts state elections were held on Monday, November 14. Ithamar Frank Conkey was elected representative from Amherst for the year 1854.

The following letter, begun on "Monday morning," election day, appears not to have been finished until Tuesday. There were no Sunday trains; and Edward Dickinson could not have known the results of the election before it took place. Vinnie's letter, written "Tuesday morning," was in the same envelope.

[*To M^r Wm. Austin Dickinson, Law School, Cambridge, M^s; no postmark*]

Monday morning [November 14, 1853]

Dear Austin.

You did'nt come, and we were all disappointed, tho' none so much as father, for nobody but father really believed you would come, and yet folks are disappointed sometimes, when they dont expect anything. Mother got a great dinner yesterday, thinking in her kind heart that you would be so hungry after your *long ride,* and the table was set for you, and nobody moved your chair, but there it stood at the table, until dinner was all done, a melancholy emblem of the blasted hopes of the world. And we had new custard pie, too, which is a rarity in days when hens dont lay, but mother knew you loved it, and when noon really got here, and you really did not come, then a big piece was saved in case you should come at night. Father seemed perfectly sober, when the afternoon train came in, and there was no intelligence of you in any way, but "there's a good time coming"! I suppose Father wrote you yesterday that Frank

Conkey was chosen Representative. I dont know whether you will care, but I felt all the while that if you had been here, it w'd not have been so.

I wonder if you voted in Cambridge. I did'nt believe you would come. I said so all the while, and tho' I was disappointed, yet I could'nt help smiling a little, to think that I guessed right. I told Father I *knew* you w'd vote somehow in Cambridge, for you always did what you wanted to, whether 'twas against the law or not, but he would'nt believe me, so when he was mistaken, I *was* a little gratified. Sue "spent the afternoon, and took tea" at Dea [John] Leland's yesterday. I was with her last evening, and she came half way home with me. She did'nt think you would come. George Allen remarked at their table yesterday, that for his part, he hoped Frank Conkey would be chosen representative, for he was a very smart fellow, and the finest Lawyer in Amherst—also that he was said to present his cases in court much finer than any other, and should *he himself* George Allen, have any difficult business, he should surely entrust it to him!

If that is'nt the apex of human impudence, I dont know anything of it. She remarked in her coolest, most unparralled way, that she wanted to open the door, and poke him out with the poker!

So much for the Amherst youth! I should recommend a closet, and self examination, accompanied with bread and water, to that same individual, till he might obtain faint glimpses of something like common sense. If Joseph Addison were alive, I should present him to him, as the highest degree of absurdity, which I had yet discerned, as it is, I will let him alone in the undisturbed possession of his remarkable folly.

Mr James Kellogg's brother from New York, with a family of nine, are here for a little while, and board at the Amherst House. Quite an affair to the town, and to the Landlord's purse. I'm telling all the news, Austin, for I think you will like to hear it. You know it's quite a sacrifice for *me* to tell what's going on.

We want to see you, all of us—we shall be very happy when you come. I hope you'll get home on Saturday. Prof Park will preach in Amherst next Sunday. I know you will want to hear him.

I send my prescription, Austin, and would be glad to have you attend to it for me, if you have time, but if it is inconvenient, no matter now. Mother sends much love—father is gone away. Vinnie has written herself, and I am today and always, your aff Sister Emily.

[*Letter enclosed*]

Tuesday Morning

Dear Austin

So you did'nt come to Election. Father expected you *certainly* & we had a splendid dinner ready for you & Sue came down to see if you were here. *I* didnt much look for you, there's a piece of custard pie saved for you & if I thought t'would go safe, I'd put it in here & send it along. I suppose Father has told you the news. He voted for Frank Conkey & carried him to Greenfield this morning. What do you think of that? He'll be all in with the rowdies if you stay away long. We had a terrific storm here on Sunday. I wondered if you were in Boston then. I guessed not. Mother wants you to ask Mr Bullard about garding the trees against the canker worms. Dont forget it. I'm glad you are so happy at Cambridge. Keep so if you please. Mother wishes you would have your picture taken in a small case for her private use. Saturday's letter was welcome & so will be today's, for I suppose there'll be one of course. When are you coming home?

How is Clarke? Remember Emilie & I very kindly to him. Hope you'll have good times together. Write as often as possible.

Vinnie

The *Express* (November 18) reported that the storm of November 13 to which Vinnie refers was "the greatest freshet in many years." Professor Snell, one of the first observers, if not the very first, in Massachusetts to keep continuing weather records, measured three inches of rainfall.

In the autumn of 1853 an important event took place in Amherst —the dedication of the first library building for the college. The site, adjacent to the First Parish meeting house, had necessitated tearing down the parsonage, the oldest house in town. That undertaking, started in the spring of 1852, was finished in time for construction to begin in October. On May 17, 1853, Edward Dickinson wrote to his son that the walls, of Pelham granite, were already "nicely up." The building was completed in October and dedicated on Tuesday, November 22, 1853. Professor Edwards Amasa Park of Andover delivered the address entitled "Taste and Religion Auxiliary to Each Other," (*Express,* December 2).

Emily undoubtedly wrote the following letter at this time, although in *Letters of Emily Dickinson,* 1894, page 102 (*Letters,* 1931, page 99), the date was given as "December, 1851," which shows what a mistake it is for an editor to rely on the memory of anyone—no matter how authoritative—without checking other sources of information. The cumulative evidence that places the letter nearly two years after the date assigned to it by Austin Dickinson in the 1890's is given in full as an illustration of the way in which a correct date can sometimes be arrived at.

As one looks at the manuscript, the first thing that strikes the eye is that the handwriting belongs to a period later than 1851. And the letter was written in pencil. Except for an occasional note sent by hand, Emily did not use a pencil in writing to her brother before 1853. Is there other evidence for the later date?

Incidents mentioned in Emily's letter, as well as in Vinnie's enclosed in the same envelope, show that neither could have been written previous to 1853. The railroad was not finished until 1853; Seth Nims, the postmaster, took office in 1853; and the envelope was franked by Edward Dickinson, who was not a member of Congress until March, 1853. This leaves no doubt about the year.

The month must have been November, because Thanksgiving was close at hand. Furthermore, the storm which "injured" the railroad occurred on November 13, 1853, the day before Frank Conkey was elected representative; and both girls mention Stephen Clarke, Austin's new-found friend at the Law School. Professor Park's sermon was preached on November 20, 1853, the day before this "Monday morning" letter was written. The precise date of the letter is, therefore, November 21, 1853.

Though the envelope was franked by her father, it is addressed in Emily's hand.

[*To William Austin Dickinson. Law School. Cambridge. Mass.; no postmark*]

Monday morning [November 21, 1853]

Dear Austin.

I should have written you long ago, but I tho't you would certainly come Saturday, and if I sent a letter, it w'd not get to you. I was so glad to get your letter. I had been making calls all Saturday afternoon, and came home very tired, and a little disconsolate, so your letter was more than welcome.

I felt so sorry I did not write again, when I found you were not coming home, and w'd look for a line on Friday, but you must'nt feel disappointed, Thanksgiving will come so soon.

Oh Austin, you dont know how we all wished for you yesterday. We had such a splendid sermon from that Prof Park—I never heard anything like it, and dont expect to again, till we stand at the great white throne, and "he reads from the book, the Lamb's book." The students and chapel people all came to our church, and it was very full, and still, so still, the buzzing of a fly would have boomed like a cannon. And when it was all over, and that wonderful man sat down, people stared at each other, and looked as wan and wild, as if they had seen a spirit, and wondered they had not died.

How I wish you had heard him. I thought of it all the time, and so did <Sue and> Vinnie, and father and mother spoke of it as soon as we got home. But—it is over. [S. J.] Sawyer spent last evening here, but I was at meeting, and had only an opportunity to bid him Good night as I came in.

I suppose that Thanksgiving party is to take place as surely as any stated Fast, and it is quite as cheerful, as those occasions to me. It will have to happen this year, but *we* wont go again. I know it is too bad, but we will make the best of it, and from this time henceforth, we'll have no more to do with it.

No Austin—you're very kind, but there is nothing more we shall want you to do for us than we have spoken of. I wish you might come sooner, but come just as soon as you can.

<Susie> ["Vinnie"] is all worn out sewing. She seems very lonely without you, and I think seems more depressed than is usual for her. I am so glad you are coming. I think a great many things need you. I will write no more. We shall soon see you, and can say all we please. Remember us to Mr Clark cordially. Take care of yourself, and get here early Wednesday.

Affy Emilie.

[*Letter enclosed*]

Sunday Evening

Dear Austin

I feel rather too tired to write much to you to night, but I think you ought to hear from some of us once more before coming home. I dont know how long I shall hold out, but you'll see. I was sorry to have you disappointed in your expected letter from us Saturday.

I wanted to write but thought perhaps you'd come Saturday & then my letter would have been for nothing. We received both your letters last week & were pleased with both, more particularly the first where you described the Bullards so graficly, that nearly finished us all. It was the best of its kind that I ever read. We had a great laugh over it, Sue & all. I wanted to sit right down & tell you how glad I was to get it, but the time slipped away with out giving me a spare moment. I wish you could have been here to day, Austin. Prof. Park preached in our church & the chapel folks united with us. I never heard any thing like his preaching. I wont attempt to describe it, for of course I cant do it. I can only say t'was wonderful. Father feels very sorry that you could not have heard it. Sawyer has got around again. He has been here most of the evening. He enquired for you with solicitude as he always does. I never saw him appear so smart & bright. He kept us laughing all the while he was here. I have'nt seen any body so agreeable in a long time.

Twas well you did'nt attempt coming to election, for the rain injured the rail road so badly that there were no passengers in until 5 oclock that night.

Do you remember Joseph Howard who sometimes favored us with a call? Well, he is married to a rarely beautiful looking girl & is visiting his Mother. We received an invitation to the wedding in New York & so we have called upon them since their arrival here. They both appear rather important. I would love to have you see her *face*. It is so beautiful. Joseph Howard is just 21. Rather got the start of you!

Mr Nims is making awful blunders in the post office. I hope he'll be requested to retire. I dont expect any letters that are sent to me will reach me. Father was gone most of last week. Emilie & I called at Mrs Jones' on Saturday.[6] The Newmans have come home & are sitting down perfectly passive, waiting Fathers next direction. I think its a bad thing for him to have that care. We all have to suffer the consequences. I shall be real glad to see you, Austin. I'm glad you like Clarke so well. I knew you *would*. You cant help it. I'm as full of business as ever. I run an express between Miss Bakers, Mrs Kimberleys & Miss Bartletts & run it often too. I shall be glad when I get the folks all fixed as to their wearing apparrel. I dont know as we want any thing in Boston that you can *conveniently get*. Just bring yourself along & that will do for this time. Sue is bad off with out you, indeed she aint no ways comfortable no how at all as Miss Kingsbury would say.

I want to say lots more, but too tired.

6. Thomas Jones, a prosperous manufacturer of Amherst, died October 21, 1853.

We shall look for you Wednesday noon in season for dinner. It rains all the time.

Good night.

Vinnie

In the *Express* (November 25, 1853) an account of the dedication of the library contains the following paragraphs:

"The edifice erected for the safe keeping of the Library of Amherst College was dedicated on Tuesday with appropriate exercises and an address by Prof. E. A. Park at the Village Church. . . .

"The address of Prof. Park was an exceedingly brilliant production, worthy of the man and the occasion. It occupied an hour and fifty minutes in its delivery. We did intend to give an outline of it, but as no attempt of ours could do it justice we forbear. His theme was the importance of Aesthetic in connection with Religious and Moral Culture. . . ."

Though Emily spoke with awe of Professor Park's sermon, I have been unable to find any record of her impression of that hour-and-fifty-minute address on a subject of vital interest to her.

PART FOUR

1853-1855

CHAPTER XXV

Edward Dickinson in Congress

1

THE Thirty-third Congress convened on December 5, 1853, and remained in continuous session for eight months, adjourning on August 7, 1854.

Throughout his career in national politics Edward Dickinson, a Whig conservative, was a member of the minority. The government from President Pierce down was preponderantly Democratic, with a large working majority in both Senate and House, a proportion characteristic of the country as a whole. None of the eleven representatives from Massachusetts, however, was a regular Democrat; nine were Whigs and two, Nathaniel P. Banks, Jr., and Alexander DeWitt, were listed in *The Congressional Globe* as Free Soilers.[1]

In spite of the momentous questions smouldering everywhere beneath the surface, the President's message on the state of the Union dealt largely with foreign relations, tariff reduction, and financial aid for the proposed railroad to the Pacific. Although he touched on the "substantive power in the respective states," he expressed the opinion that we "are exempt from any cause of serious disquietude in our domestic relations." The paramount issue—further extension of slavery—was not mentioned. Instead, the Presi-

1. Nathaniel P. Banks, Jr., was "elected as a coalition Democrat to the Thirty-third Congress and as the candidate of the American [Know-Nothing] party to the Thirty-fourth of which he was chosen Speaker . . ." *Biographical Directory of the American Congress, 1774-1927* [1950], 667. This directory is also authority for the statement that Alexander DeWitt was elected as candidate of the American party to both the Thirty-third and Thirty-fourth Congresses.

dent spoke of the peace and harmony prevailing throughout the nation, strife dying away, he said, as the causes fade into history. Edward Dickinson was present on the opening day and listened to the reading of this message.

Soon after Mr. Dickinson left for Washington the family received a visit from Austin's friend Stephen Clarke. The next letter, from Vinnie, was in an envelope addressed by Emily. Their father had left at home a supply of franked envelopes, which he had signed but had not addressed. For a time the girls used these envelopes, a practice discontinued after the beginning of the new year.

[*To William Austin Dickinson. Law School. Cambridge. Mass.; postmark: Amherst Ms. Dec 3 (as of the previous Saturday?)*]

Monday Morning [December 5, 1853]

Dear Austin

Clarke has been & gone & we have had a good time. I wish you could have been here & so did we all, many times. I was out shopping when the carriage from the depot drove to the hotel & little Henry Cooke came on in great haste after me & handed me the letter. I supposed Mr Bowdoin sent it & so did not open it till I got home, & then we flew around briskly enough I can tell you.

We fixed the sitting room as genteely as possible, making the extension table into a circular & lots of other improvements that I cant stop to mention now. Then we prepared ourselves for the reception. About three oclock he arrived, & at the same time Sue, who had been walking behind him all the way, trying to make out who it was. He staid till late in the evening, came in the morning & went to church with us, dined at the hotel though we invited him to go home with us. Went to church with us again in the afternoon came home after meeting & staid till about eight & then we called with him to see Jane & Sue. We took him to see *Sue* Saturday evening *too*.

He left us about ten oclock last evening & we shall feel rather lonely for a day or two I expect. Mother enjoyed his visit very much. We all wore our winter bonnets & things to match, as you would wish to have us I know. Oh Austin I was proud to have that handsome "Surtout" at the head of our seat, the very first Sunday Father was away. Mrs Sweetser's bonnet did double duty & so did other heads

Envelope addressed by Emily Dickinson, posted June 16, 1851

Envelope addressed by Emily Dickinson, franked in advance by her father, and posted in Amherst, December 3, 1853

& bonnets. I'm so glad you sent him to see us. He was bright & happy as he could be, & talked of him self, & the *"Professor"*, & his Science, in so happy a way that we could'nt help but be delighted. He seemed very sorry to leave you, said he should write you in a week. Pussy has not yet returned & I've given her up as lost. I hope you wont get blue, living there alone. Clarke says you studied too hard before you came home. Be careful & not do too much now.

I guess Clark had a good time. When he writes to you, tell us what he says of his visit, unless he forgets it before that time. We entertained him in the best way we could & I think every thing was pleasant to him. It seems real funny to live as we do, all alone. I like it *pretty well* "indeed".

Thank you for Saturday's letter. Write again soon. You'll hear from us again Saturday. We had a letter from Father Wednesday, I mean Thursday & Friday. I must stop.

Good bye.
Vinnie

Susceptible as Vinnie was to cats, any "pilgrim kitten" that strayed her way was added to her "flock." If it died she grieved. Emily says she tried to soothe her: "Vinnie is deeply afflicted in the death of her dappled cat, though I convince her it is immortal which assists her some."

While in Washington during the coming spring, Emily wrote that she remembered the cats at home with "tender emotion." But she seems to have cherished them less for themselves than for their prowess in mouse-catching. With Vinnie, on the other hand, the feeling for cats was devotional—a most engaging trait! Emily was whimsically indulgent toward her sister's love of "pussies," even using it as a pretext to round up a universal truth: "Vinnie has a new pussy the color of Branwell Brontë's hair. She thinks it a little 'lower than the angels,' and I concur with her. You remember my ideal cat has always a huge rat in its mouth, just going out of sight —though going out of sight in itself has a peculiar charm. It is true that the unknown is the largest need of the intellect, though for it, no one thinks to thank God."[2]

[*To Wm. Austin Dickinson, Cambridge Law School, Mass.;*[3] *postmark: Amherst Ms. Dec 9*]

2. *Letters*, 1931, 260; 166; 256-257.
3. Addressed in Vinnie's writing.

Friday Morning [December 9, 1853]

Dear Austin

Why dont you write to us? We feel real bad about it. We've looked for a letter ever since Tuesday, thinking every day we should surely have one. If we dont hear today, I shall think some thing dreadful has happened to you. It seems very lonely, some times. Every body almost is sick or dying. I never knew such a time. I'm most sorry Clarke came to see us, for it has been so lonely here since he went away. Old Mr [Stephen] Nelson is dead. Darling [a junior] is dead. Mrs J. Kellogg is very sick & lots of others that you dont know. Emilie Fowler is going to marry Ford, next Friday. What do you think of that? She wants to have you come to the wedding if "you know how to make the *sacrifice.*" She is very anxious to have you present. She says her house in New London is all furnished & the cook is waiting for her. Mr Fowler is very much overjoyed. Emilie cries most of the time & seems half sad & half glad. Is'nt it funny? Sue & I went down to see the horse yesterday. Sue said twas next to seeing you. Mr Cabot led him out of the barn so I could have a good look at him. The horse was real glad to see me, Sue & I both thought, he looked me all over, snorted, & acted very comfortably "indeed." Mr Cabot remarked that Jerry had been down to say that he would like to exercise him now & then. I told him never to let any body take him at all. I called at Mr Warner's yesterday. Mary was sorry to be out when you called last. Mary *kinder* held her eyes down when she spoke of you. Sue has got a splendid cloak. I've sent to Aunt Lavinia to get one for me. I hope she has got the letter. I feel some how that I shant get to Boston this winter. I dont believe Father will allow me to leave the folks alone. I want to go, but I'm afraid I can't. The hens have begun to lay & so Mother will keep them for the present. Pussy dont come. Jerry is very good & faithful. We've had four letters from Father since he went away, two since he reached Washington. He dont seem to be very happy, speaks of the *attractions of home* with quite a relish, he will never consent to be there more than two years, I think. Emilie says he'll get off some how, before the first term is ended.

Emilie & I have each sent you two letters. Have you recived them? Our breakfast hour so far has been 9,ock, that would just suit you. I dont know what is the matter but we cant seem to wake up. I think I shall consult Dr. Woodman! Do tell us what you are about. We shant like you at all if we dont hear from you to day. I dont believe you can read what I've written, for I'm in such a hurry that I dont half write the words.

Good bye
Vinnie

[*To Wm. Austin Dickinson,*⁴ *Cambridge Law School, Mass. post-mark: Amherst Ms. Dec 13*]

Tuesday morning [December 13, 1853]

It's quite a comfort, Austin, to hear that you're *alive,* after being for several days in ignorance of the fact, and when I tell you honestly, that Vinnie and George Howland would have gone to Northampton yesterday to *telegraph* to you, if we had'nt heard yesterday noon, you can judge that we felt some alarm.

We supposed you had either been *killed,* in going from Cambridge to Boston, for the sake of your watch, or had been very sick and were at present *delirious* and therefore could not write. Mother and Vinnie, <Sue and> me, were about as disconsolate last Saturday night at sundown, as you would often see. <Sue> spent the evening here and I went home with her, each feeling perfectly sure that you were not in this world, neither in that to come, and worrying ourselves to fevers, in wondering where you were, and why you did'nt write something to some of us. Oh how you would have laughed to have seen us flying around—dodging into the post office and insisting upon it we had a letter there, not withstanding poor Mr Nims declared there was nothing there—then chasing one another down to our office to Bowdoin, and telling him we knew all about it—he had got the letter and was hiding it, and when he took oath he had not, plunging into the street again, and then back to the house to communicate the result of our forlorn proceedings— and mother—Oh she thought the bears in the wood had devoured you, or if you were not eaten up, you were such a monster of thought-lessness and neglect! but it's all over now, and Thank God you are safe! We are all here, dear Austin—still getting cheerfully on—still missing you, and wishing for you, and knowing you cannot come— Oh for the pleasant years when we were young together, and this was *home—home!*

Poor Susie hears nothing from you. She knows you have written tho'. Sue and I walked to Plainville to meeting Sunday night, and walked back again. Mr Dwight was there. I presume it will make you laugh—Mother could'nt find that Collar Pattern but you left a Collar in the kitchen cupboard, which you said was just right, and I've ripped it, and cut a pattern from that, and the next time you write if you'll tell me if it's the correct one, Vinnie'll take it up to Miss Baker. We hear from Father often—in better spirits now.

4. Addressed in Vinnie's writing.

When are you coming home. We do want to see you. Much love for you. Write soon.

Your aff Sister, Emily.

The stationery on which this letter was written carries in the lower left corner of the fourth page an embossed oval with the word "Congress" and the form of the Capitol with its then flat dome. To it Emily added in pencil a chimney belching smoke and, striding toward the entrance, an Indian complete with feather headdress labeled "Member from the 10th!"

A letter from Vinnie in the same envelope bemoans the difficulty of persuading anyone to help with the housework.

Tuesday Morning

One word, Austin, before going to sewing. Your notes written Sunday reached us yesterday noon. That is the first we have heard from you since Clark was here. Sue has received not a word since the note Clark brought to her. She feels badly about it. I went to Mr Nims after reading your letter yesterday & told him I was sure there were two letters there some where for me. He said no, but I feel perfectly sure that I could find them if I could look over the office. There is a great deal of complaint about the post office. Nobody does any thing about it, though. I know how busy you must be, Austin & I only ask to have you write once a week. Do you wonder we thought it rather strange that we as Sue did not get a word all last week, when you are generally so good about writing? If we had thought you were *safe*, we would not have felt so anxious, but we were sure some thing had happened to you. Now that Father is gone we think more of hearing from you at just such a time. Father writes to us very often & I guess he is getting happy. He told us in his last letter, that he had been sending out his cards to various persons of rank. He says he dont know much about etiquet but he is trying to learn.

Mr [J. A.] Nash has returned from Europe. You'll be interested to know that I've made another call at *"Marshy's"* & she is really coming to help us some day this week. Mrs. Scott has not finished her medicine yet. Mrs Mack is done up with an *irish wake*. You see how things go, when the *head* of the house is away from *"home."* George Howland has got back again.

Write to us when its convenient & ask the post master to send your letters along. Let us hear a word now & then & it will help to encourage us *wonderfully*. Keep safe & well & dont let any thing happen to hurt you. Good bye

Vinnie

On December 16 Austin made a surprise visit to attend the
wedding of Emily Fowler and Gordon Lester Ford.

[*To Wm Austin Dickinson Esq,.*⁵ *Law School, Cambridge, Mass.;
postmark: Amherst Ms. Dec 21*]

Tuesday evening [December 20, 1853]

Well Austin—dear Austin—you have got back again, Codfish and
Pork and all—*all* but the *slippers,* so nicely wrapped to take, yet
found when you were gone, under the kitchen chair. I hope you
wont want them. Perhaps you have some more there—I will send
them by opportunity, should there be such a thing. Vinnie proposed
franking them, but I fear they are rather large! What should you
think of it. It is'nt *every* day that we have a chance to sponge Congress. I wish Vinnie could go as a member—she'd save something
snug for us all, besides enriching herself, but Caesar is such "an
honorable man" that we may all go to the Poor House, for all the
American Congress will lift a finger to help us.

Sue went round collecting for the charitable societies today, and
calling on *Miss Kingsbury* in the exercise of that function, the
gentle miss remarked that she "would'nt give a cent, nobody gave *her*
anything, and she would'nt give them anything," i.e nobody—she
"had to do all the work,["] besides taking care of "*her*" referring
Sue supposed to the proprietor of a huge ruffled night cap, protrud-
ing from a bed in their spacious apartment. Sue said the gate went
"shang, wang, wang" as she passed out of it.

The usual rush of callers, and this beleaguered family as yet in
want of time. I do hope immortality will last a little while, but if
the Adams' should happen to get there first, we shall be driven there.
Vinnie has the headache today. She intends to increase the friction,
and see what that will do! She dont believe a word of the man without any action—thinks it is one of your hoaxes. Vinnie went down
yesterday to see about the Horse, and found everything right. We
heard from Father last night and again tonight. He is coming home
on Thursday. He alludes to you several times.

We were real glad to get your note, and to know that all was well.
[*Sue shall have hers*] early tomorrow morning. Will that be soon
enough? She ["he"] has been here this afternoon, she ["he"] is going
to send the letters you spoke of, directly. Well Austin—you are gone,
and the wheel rolls slowly on—nobody to laugh with—talk with,

5. The envelope, addressed in an unidentified hand, is stamped "5" in place of
"FREE."

nobody down in the morning to make the fun for me! Take care of your lungs, Austin—take that just as I told you, and pretty soon you'll be well. Emilie.

Hope you can read it.

I have written to Clark, today, so will Vinnie. Write us just as soon as you can.

Mother's love, and Vinnie's.

[*On a separate sheet*]

6 o'clock!   Wednesday morn

Dear Austin—I add a word to say that I've got the fires made and waked the individuals, and the Americans are conquering the British on the teakettle. Hope you are happy this morning—hope you are well. Have you taken your medicine yet? Write the effect of it. Will now proceed to get breakfast, consisting of hash and brown bread—Dessert—*A. sauce*. I shall have to employ a Reporter. Wish you a merry breakfast—wish you were here with me. The bath goes briskly on.

To some it may still come as a surprise to learn that in Austin's absence it was Emily who got up first to build the fires, before dawn on winter mornings.

On Thursday, December 22, Edward Dickinson came home for a brief stay. During the following week he made a flying trip to Boston, an opportunity seized upon by Emily to send a note to her brother. Written on a half sheet of paper, it is folded, sealed with wax, and addressed on the back.

Austin

Tuesday noon [December 27(?), 1853]

I will write to you Austin, tho' everything is so busy, and we are all flying round as if we were distracted. We send you a little box, containing some good things to help you on your way, and I hope they will please you.

Take good care of yourself, Austin until you get home again, and then we will take care of you. You must have a good time with father. He seems very happy at home, and I guess is happy at Washington. [Several words rubbed out] yesterday—I found a—I wont tell you tho' till you get home, I guess—as there are particulars. We think always of you, and hope you are always glad. Father is going now, they have just finished oysters—I wish you could have some. Love. Emilie

[*Around the edges of the page*]

If Clark has come give our love to him.
I have written Emilie Lord.
Mother wants <you to> save the box.

[*To Wm Austin Dickinson,⁶ Law School, Cambridge, Mass.; post-mark: Amherst. Ms. Dec 27 (?)*]

Austin. If it wont trouble you too much, are you willing to get me another bottle of my medicine, at Mr Joseph Burnett's, 33. Tremont Row? I did not like to ask Father, because he's always in such a hurry. I hope it wont trouble you.

Pinned to the note is a prescription with an embossed heading:

96.027.

109.821
Joseph Burnett
33 Tremont Row
    Boston

        R. Glycerin.   3 ss (Oz $\frac{1}{2}$)
            Aqua.   3 iiss (Oz $2\frac{1}{2}$)

[*In Emily's writing*]

Mʳ Burnett. 33. Tremont Row.
Please send *twice* the amount prescribed.

2

Edward Dickinson served as a representative in Congress during a stormy period of our history. Before reading his letters from Washington it may be useful to have freshly in mind the main events preceding the controversy in which the country was embroiled, familiar though they are.

In 1848 California was ceded by Mexico to the United States. Following the gold rush of 1849 the Californians applied for admis-

6. The envelope, addressed by Vinnie, bearing the familiar frank, is also stamped "PAID," with "3" written in.

sion to the Union as a nonslave state. By the terms of the Missouri Compromise of 1820, engineered by Henry Clay, although Missouri itself was to be admitted as a slave state, slavery was to be forever excluded north of latitude 36° 30′; south of that parallel new states applying for admission might choose their own terms of entry. More than half of California being south of the line, the South demanded its rights. Mr. Clay again suggested a way out. But his bill, the "Compromise of 1850," adopted on September 18 of that year, led to a new crisis because parts of the agreement were not acceptable in the North, especially the section known as the "fugitive-slave law." The northern attitude is well summed up in a biography of Judge Hoar of Concord: The "iniquitous provisions [of this law] authorized the delivery of a slave to his master by a commissioner of the United States on the issuing of a warrant in the state from which the slave was alleged to have fled. The alleged fugitive was not allowed a jury trial; the claimant was not bound to prove that he was a runaway— a simple affidavit was enough. Any harboring or aid given a fugitive, or refusal to help in his seizure, was made a crime with heavy penalties; while, as if to insult the magistrates, before whom the alleged fugitives were brought, they were allowed a larger fee if they delivered them to the claimants than if they discharged them."[7]

Attempts to enforce this law aroused increasing bitterness. The *Express* (November 1, 1850) called it "the offspring of Satan." Abolitionists—"persons to whom the supreme interest in public affairs was the abolition of slavery"—were roused to frenzy, which in turn further inflamed the South. Representative Boyce of South Carolina went so far as to say that "this anti-slavery feeling is the evil genius of the Republic."[8] Calhoun, Webster and Clay, together with nearly all political leaders including President Fillmore, had for some time united in deploring the fanaticism of the abolitionists, who, they said, were by their very fervor widening the breach between the two sections of the country, a view with which Edward Dickinson was in complete agreement.

Leaders of the Whig party in Massachusetts stood firm behind the

7. Moorfield Storey and Edward W. Emerson, *Ebenezer Rockwood Hoar, A Memoir* (Boston: 1911), 81.
8. *The Congressional Globe*, 33 Cong., 1 Sess., *Appendix*, 724. *The Congressional Globe* was the predecessor of the *Congressional Record*.

Compromise, which they considered essential if the unity of the
nation was to be preserved. And so, following passage of the bill, the
fugitive slave law was accepted by them as necessary, although
under protest. The people of the state, on the other hand, were outraged. They felt that Webster had betrayed them by "knuckling
under" and, in the words of Emerson, they were plunged in "the
great despair."

Throughout the North the efforts of the Whig party to gloss over
the principal issue of the time were alienating antislavery members.
With a presidential election in the offing they found a way to express
their feelings. The National Whig Convention opened in Baltimore
on June 16, 1852. Of the mighty trio only Daniel Webster remained.
John C. Calhoun had died on March 31, 1850, in the midst of the
Compromise debate. Henry Clay was even then, during the convention, mortally ill. Less than two weeks later, on June 29, 1852, his
"powerful eloquence" was stilled. Repudiating Webster (and it took
fifty-three ballots to do it), the convention nominated for President
the military hero, General Winfield Scott. Daniel Webster did not
live to see the overwhelming defeat of his party in November.

With the election of a Democratic President, Franklin H. Pierce,
that party was solidly entrenched. Shortly after the new Congress
convened Senator Stephen A. Douglas reopened the question of the
extension of slavery on January 4, 1854, this, in spite of the fact
that he had done more than anyone except Henry Clay to bring
about the Compromise of 1850.[9] Two new territories, Kansas and
Nebraska, about to be organized as states, were both north of latitude
36° 30′. Ignoring the Missouri Compromise, Senator Douglas proposed that the residents of those territories should be allowed to
decide for themselves whether or not slavery was to be permitted
within their borders. The antislavery press was infuriated. Douglas,
sensing the depth and intensity of the anger he had aroused, acted
quickly. He rushed the Kansas-Nebraska Bill to the floor of the
Senate where, on March 4, 1854, it was passed, 37 to 14—a personal
triumph indeed for Mr. Douglas. But public indignation was steadily
rising. More and more meetings of protest were held throughout

9. James Ford Rhodes, *History of the United States from the Compromise of
1850 to the End of the Roosevelt Administration* (New York: 1928), I, 425-428.

the North. Even Mr. Dickinson received a remonstrance against repeal of the Missouri Compromise signed by 700 Northampton women.

Although this controversy dwarfed every other issue, for Edward Dickinson as for all thinking persons, his efforts in Congress were chiefly confined to the work of the one important committee of which he was a member. Had he been consulted, he would doubtless have chosen the "Select Committee on the Pacific Railroad," but he was appointed neither to that nor to the committee on the tariff, a subject of importance for the textile mills of New England. Instead, he became a member of the "Select Committee of the House on the Superintendency of Public Works," commonly called "the armory committee," its activities for the most part being focused on problems connected with the national armories. In 1854 there were but two—at Harper's Ferry, Virginia, and at Springfield, Massachusetts, the chief town of the district which Mr. Dickinson represented. Although he had no particular interest in armories, as he stated on more than one occasion, it is to their affairs that his time in Congress was largely devoted.[10]

The appointment of this committee was the result of long-continued agitation by certain residents of Springfield who, for one reason or another, wanted civilian rather than military administration of the armory. The point at issue was this: should the superintendent continue to be appointed from the Army Ordnance Board —officers whose specialty was firearms—or should he be a civilian engineer? In our day, when military control of such establishments is taken for granted, it is interesting to observe that from the first Mr. Dickinson favored military supervision as against the majority of Congress, who preferred to regard such posts as party perquisites. The work of Edward Dickinson on the armory committee is worth recalling not only because it has historical importance, resulting as

10. The name appears as the "Select Committee on the Superintendency of Civil Works by Military Officers," in the *Congressional Directory*, 33 Cong., 1 Sess., second edition (June 20, 1854), 32.

An account of the work of the armory committee, the events leading up to its appointment, and the record of the debate as contained in *The Congressional Globe* and other government documents, together with the complete text of Mr. Dickinson's principal speech on the floor of the House, will be found in Appendix IV.

it did in a switch from military to civilian control of the national armories only a few years before the outbreak of the Civil War, a change which Mr. Dickinson did his best to prevent, but also because debates during the controversy provide a glimpse of human relations in industry at a time when the typical working week was six days of twelve hours each. Public opinion was only just beginning to consider the advisability of limiting the hours of labor "in manufacturing corporations to ten hours a day."[11] This aspect of the committee's investigations appears to have been of considerable interest to Mr. Dickinson. Twenty years later, as a member of the Massachusetts legislature, he was still trying to "regulate the hours of labor in manufacturing establishments."[12]

For purposes of this narrative, however, the part played by Mr. Dickinson on the armory committee is important mainly because it is in a way a gauge of the man. His principal speech on the floor of the House on July 13 (pages 543-553) reveals his habits of thought as well as his blunt way of expressing them, a trait not conducive to prolonging a political career.

As the year 1854 opened Edward Dickinson was at home, having reached Amherst on December 23. After a brief visit to his son in Cambridge, where the first term of the Law School was still in session, he went back to Amherst and, early in January, was about to return to Washington.[13]

Between December 27, 1853, and March 14, 1854, there is only one letter. The last from Emily before her brother came home a little ahead of time for his winter vacation, January 19 to March 1, it opens with the oft-quoted paragraphs about George Howland, then a tutor in the college. He was at the moment much attached to Vinnie, who, when this letter was written, was visiting her Aunt Lavinia in Boston. Emily leaves no uncertainty about the ordeal to which sisterly loyalty subjected her. The envelope is missing.

11. *Express,* May 7, 1852.
12. *Journal of the House of Representatives, Commonwealth of Massachusetts,* 1874, 230-231.
13. Although Edward Dickinson was admitted to practice as "attorney and counsellor" before the Supreme Court of the United States on January 27, 1854, (*Express,* February 17), I have found no record of his having made use of the privilege.

Thursday evening [January 5, 1854]

Austin—

George Howland has just retired from an evening's visit here, and I gather my spent energies to write a word to you.

"Blessed are they that are persecuted for righteousness' sake, for they shall have their reward"! Dear Austin—I dont feel funny, and I hope you wont laugh at anything I say. I am thinking of you and Vinnie, what nice times you are having, sitting and talking together, while I am lonely here, and I *wanted* to sit and think of you, and fancy what you were saying, all the evening long, but—ordained otherwise. I hope you will have grand times, and dont forget the *unit* without you, at home.

I have had some things from you, to which I perceived no meaning. They either were very vast, or they did'nt mean anything, I dont know certainly which. What did you mean by a note you sent me day before yesterday? Father asked me what you wrote and I gave it to him to read. He looked very much confused and finally put on his spectacles, which did'nt seem to help him much. I dont think a *telescope* would have assisted him.

I hope you will write to me—I love to hear from you, and now Vinnie is gone, I shall feel very lonely. [*Susie has been with me today. She is a dear sister to me. She will write and enclose with mine.*][14]

Father and mother are going to South Hadley tomorrow, to be gone all day, and Sue I guess will come to spend the day with me.[15] Prof Haven will give a Lyceum Lecture next Monday eve—subject —Power Ottoman in Europe. There will be a Temperance Lecture in the Hall tomorrow evening. The Academy and Town Schools have been riding "en masse" this afternoon, and have got home this evening, singing as they came. Well—we were all boys once, as Mrs Partington says.

Jerry has been to ride today. Left home at eight this morning— Goal—South Hadley Falls. Suppose he will return sometime during the evening.

He takes good care of the horse. When shall you come home Austin? We do want to see you again. You must come as soon as you and Vinnie think best, for she will want you some. Dont mind the

14. These three lines almost completely rubbed out and barely legible.

15. In a record of votes the name of Edward Dickinson does not appear in *The Globe* between December 20, 1853, and January 12, 1854, except on January 3. On that day there were two roll calls, from the first of which his name is missing; on the second his vote is recorded with the nays (*Globe*, 33 Cong., 1 Sess., 114). This letter is evidence, however, that on January 3 Mr. Dickinson was at home.

writing, Austin, for I'm so tired tonight, I can hardly hold my pencil. Love for them all, if there are those to love and think of me, and more and most for you, from Emily.

If it's perfectly convenient, when you come, I should like the vial filled, which you took away with you.

No matter how engrossing affairs of state might be, home responsibilities were never far from Edward Dickinson's mind. During a session of the Massachusetts Court of Common Pleas, which coincided with Austin's vacation, his father spent more than a week in Amherst, from February 16 to February 28. Plans for a visit of the family to the capital were doubtless proposed at this time.

CHAPTER XXVI

The Dickinsons Visit Washington

1

THE second term of the Law School began on Thursday, March 2, 1854. Austin was again late in returning, this time because of what was called "a pulmonary affection." He did not leave Amherst until March 13. His father wrote from the capital the same day. The word "free" is part of the Washington postmark.

[*To Wm Austin Dickinson, Law School, Cambridge, Mass.; post-mark: Washington, D. C., Mar 12, Free*]

Ho. of Reps. U.S.
Washington March 13. 1854.

Dear Austin,

I hope you are well, before this time, & able to return to C. I have written home, to have Lavinia come with y^r mother & you—& Emily too, if she will—but that I will not insist upon her coming. The latter part of March, or quite the fore part of April, will be the best time for you all to come. Perhaps, I may meet you in New York, as I shall want to go there about the 1st April, on business. Take good care of your health—& make yourself comfortable, and deny yourself no reasonable comfort, feeling, always, that your improvement is for yourself. I shall write again, soon.

Your letter was rec^d—about house rents, &c.

I hope the matters in Amherst will go on well, & that everything

Ho. of Rep. U. S,
Washington March 13. 1854.

Dear Austin,

I hope you are well,
before this time, & able to return to C.
I have written home, to have Vinnie come
with yr. mother & you — & Emily too. If she
will — but that I will not insist upon
her coming. The latter part of March,
& quite the fore part of April, will be
the best time for you all to come —
Perhaps, I may meet you in New York,
as I shall want to go there about the
1st April. on business. Take good care of
your health — & make yourself comfortable,
and deny yourself — no reasonable comfort,
feeling, always, that your enjoyment is for
yourself. I shall write again. Your
two letters were rec'd — about much nuts, &c

Letter from Edward Dickinson to his son, March 13, 1854

I hope the matters in Amherst
will go on well — & that everything
will be & go, improve & show
a brighter aspect. Write me — on
a tenor a week — & shall make
definite plans about the spring. as
soon as I can.

Your aff father
G. Coolbrithie

Ellis McKutin
M.C.

Wm. Austin McKutin
Law School
Cambridge
Mass.

will bye & bye, improve, & show a brighter aspect. Write me once or twice a week. I shall make definite plans about the journey, as soon as I can.

                              Your aff father
                                E. Dickinson

Emily wrote to her brother the day after he left home. From now on the girls used postage stamps instead of franked envelopes. They were addressed by Emily except for those of March 24 and March 28 which are in Vinnie's writing.

[*To Wm Austin Dickinson. Law School. Cambridge. Mass.; postmark: Amherst Ms. Mar 15*]

                         Tuesday evening [March 14, 1854]
Dear Austin.

   It is getting late now, but I guess you'll "have occasion," so I write a word from home.
   After you went away yesterday, I washed the dishes, and tried the Drainer. It worked admirably, and reminded me much of you. Mother said I must tell you. Then I worked until dusk, then went to Mr Sweetser's to call on Abiah Root, then walked around to Jerry's and made a call on him—then hurried home to supper, and Mother went to the Lyceum, while John Graves spent the evening with Vinnie and I until past 10. Then I wrote a long letter to Father, in answer to one we had from him yesterday—then crept to bed softly, not to wake all the folks, who had been asleep a long time. I rose at my usual hour, kindled the "fires of Smithfield," and missed you very much in the lower part of the house—you constituting my principal society, at that hour in the day. My family descended after taking their bath, and we breakfasted *frugally*. Mother and Vinnie were quite silent, and there was nobody to make fun with me at the table.
   Today has passed as usual. <Sue> came this afternoon, and we gave her all her things. The note was quite unexpected. I had a letter from Garrick [?] Mallery this evening. <Sue and> I went up to Mr. Sweetser's to see Abiah, then I went home with her, and had a pleasant time. She said she meant to have you get her letter first, but I advised not to quarrel on so minute a point. Father wrote a very pleasant letter, said he hoped you had got well. Prof Fowler,

was very interesting—so mother said, and had a very good audience. Did'nt you find it very lonely, going back to Mrs Ware's? We speak of it very often.

I would'nt sit up late, if I were you, or study much evenings. Vinnie has been to see Mrs Mack about the house.[1] Mrs Mack says John White is a nice man to be in the house—neat, orderly, clean, and so is his wife—does not drink, she says, and "has took the pledge". Mrs Mack says the only thing is whether he can pay the rent, and he *thinks* he can pay it. Mrs Mack would like to have him there—"a great deal better than Morrison". You must do as you think best.

Mr Field's daughter is dead.[2]

I dont think you left anything. Should I find such, I shall direct it to the "Honorable Edward Dickinson" and send it on!

I hope you wont be lonely in Cambridge. You must think of us all when you are.

And if the cough troubles you follow my prescription, and it will soon get well. You must write whenever you can.

You know you can *telegraph* to Father if you would like to—you are not confined to the pen! It seems pretty still here, Austin, but I shant tell you about it, for twill only make you lonely. Love from mother. Remember us to Clark. Good night. Emilie.

[*Letter enclosed*]

10 0,clock Tuesday Eve

Dear Austin

Glad to hear from you. Cant write much as its so late. I've been writing to Aunt Lavinia all the evening on business. It seems rather still around since you "left with your *left.*" Mr Albee arrived this P.M. & did his work. He said he supposed my Father was to Con-

1. There is a tradition which I have not verified that General Mack built an addition to the homestead on the west; that it was subsequently moved a few rods farther west and made into the house above referred to; and that in 1856 it became the ell of Austin Dickinson's new house. However this may be, the land, "one acre more or less," on which the little house stood, had been owned by Edward Dickinson since May 13, 1833 (deed recorded in the Hampshire County Registry of Deeds, Book 71, page 88).

This house had been for rent in 1852:

> For Rent.— The Dwelling House directly west of Gen. Mack's, lately occupied by Mr. E. F. Cook. Possession given immediately. Enquire of Mr. Cook, or me.
> Edward Dickinson. May 6, 1852 (*Express*, May 7, 1852).

2. Sarah E. Field, aged seventeen, died of consumption on March 14, 1854.

gress. I told him he had hit it exactly. I walked down to Elijah Boltwoods before tea & consulted with Mr Cabot about North parish. He says Jerry will be careful. So Jerry is going early in the morning after "Miss Puffer". I as usual was caught in a shower & had no umbrella. Austin, Do you think its best for me to go to Washington? I dont feel decided. What did Aunt L. say about it? I hate to leave Emily alone. When Aunt L. gets the things, I want you to find some way to send them. Sometimes it does not seem best for me to think of going. Tell Aunt L. what you think about it. I'm almost tired to death. Good night.

Vin

[*On a separate slip*]

I spent the forenoon at Dr Strattons.[3] Shall go again Saturday. Had hasty pudding for supper. Dont you wish you had been here?

Though preparations were already in the making for the family's visit to the national capital, it is plain from the previous as well as from subsequent notes that Emily had no intention of making the trip. Austin was planning to come home on the first of April to accompany his mother and Lavinia to Washington. The next letter is written in ink.

[*To Wm Austin Dickinson. Law School. Cambridge. Mass.; postmark: Amherst Ms. Mar 17*]

Thursday evening [March 16, 1854]

Dear Austin.

Cousin John has passed part of the evening here, and since he took his hat, I have written a letter to Father, and shall now write to you. Your letter came this noon. Vinnie went after it before we sat down to dinner. You are very kind to write so soon. Dont think we miss you any—hey? Perhaps you know nothing about it. We are indeed very lonely, but so very hard at work that we havnt so much time to think, as you have. I hope your room will seem more cheerful when you've been there a little while. You must'nt think anything about Mrs Ware. Since you went back to Cambridge, the

3. Dr. Stratton was a "surgeon dentist." In 1854, if a tooth was troublesome it was customary to have it pulled.

weather has been wonderful, the thermometer every noon between 60 and 70 °· above zero, and the air full of birds.

Today has not seemed like a day. It has been most unearthly— so mild, so bright, so still, the kitchen windows open, and fires uncomfortable.

Since supper it lightens frequently. In the south you can see the lightning, in the north the Northern Lights. Now a furious wind blows, just from the north and west, and winter comes back again.

Sue was here yesterday and today—spent a part of both afternoons with us. Seems much like old times. We gave her the letter. Vinnie's bundle came today, after giving her great suspense. Mr Potter brought it to the house himself, and seemed very pleasant indeed. I went to the door—I liked him. Mary Warner and her friend Abbie Adams, made a call of about an hour, here this forenoon. They had been *taking a walk.* I think any sentiment must be consecrated by an interview in the mud. There would be certainly, a correspondence in *depth.*

There is to be a Party at Prof Haven's tomorrow night, for married people merely. Celibacy excludes me and my sister. Father and mother are invited. Mother will go.

Emiline and Jennie Hitchcock were both here this afternoon.

Mrs Noyes is sewing up stairs. Jerry went for her with our horse. Mr Cabot said there was no danger and Jerry drove very carefully. Jerry asked us yesterday when we were writing to Mr Austin, to tell him Fanny was much improved by recent exercise, and looked finer than ever. Jerry is so kind and pleasant that I cant bear the thought of his going away.

He speaks of you with great admiration. We are going to send two little cakes of maple sugar to Father tomorrow. We thought it would please him.

Miller came here yesterday to see if Father wanted to hire him this summer—said he had had a fine offer, and before accepting it, would like to know if he was needed here. He wanted us to ask you when we wrote. I think he is a humbug. I hope you wont employ him.

I have more to say, but am too tired to now. Mother and Vinnie send love. They are both getting ready for Washington. Take care of yourself Austin, and dont get melancholy. Remember Clark. Emilie.

[*To Wm. Austin Dickinson, Law School, Cambridge, Mass.; post-mark: Washington D. C. March 17 Free*]

Willard's Hotel, Friday
March 17, 1854

Dear Austin

I have rec^d your letter from Cambridge, & am glad that you [are] well, & back—hope you will keep well.

I am not willing that John White should go in to the house with Mrs Mack. He drinks, & quarrels with his wife. I had rather the house would stand empty. If [George L.] West wants the whole, I should think it better to let him have it—or rent the lower rooms to some steady person. I shall write to the folks at home, the same thing—shall have Bowdoin attend to it—so you need not take any care of it, yourself. When it is decided, at what time you come here, I shall write & make definite arrangements for it. I have bought Mr Flagg's pew, where the Pierces sit, for Mr Dwight at $80.—He writes me that he don't know how the parsonage & vestry get along, but he thinks about "like Pharaoh's chariots, after the wheels were taken off".

I wish you would write y^r letters on *thicker* paper—it troubles me to read them, on so thin sheets. Write me, once or twice a week, regularly. Remember me to Mr Bullard,s & uncle L's family.

Your aff. father
E. Dickinson

[*To Wm Austin Dickinson. Law School. Cambridge. Mass.; postmark: Amherst Ms Mar 20 (?)*]

Sunday evening [March 19, 1854]

I have just come from meeting, Austin. Mr Luke Sweetser presided, and young Mr Hallock [a junior] made a prayer which I dont doubt you heard in Cambridge. It was really very audible. Mr Dwight was not there. Sue [changed to "Lou"] did not go. Tempe Linnell sat by me. I asked her if she was engaged to Sam Fiske, and she said *no*, so you can tell Mrs Jones she was slightly mistaken. Have you had a pleasant day, Austin? Have you been to meeting today? We have had a lovely Sunday, and have thought of you very much. Mr Dwight preached all day. Mr Williston and [W. S.] Clark were at our church this morning. There was a letter read from the Congregational c'h in Washington, D C, requesting the company of the Pastor and a Delegate, at the ordination of that Rev Mr Duncan, who was so much admired by Father when he was at home before. Father was

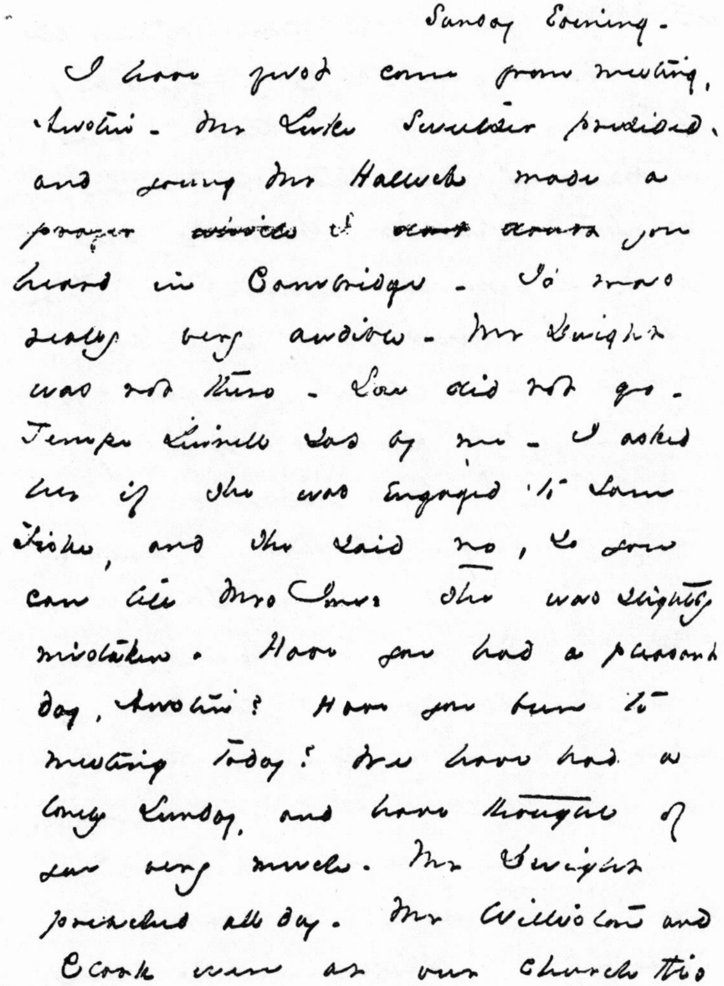

Letter from Emily Dickinson to her brother, March 19, 1854

morning — There was a as
he read from the Congregational Ch.
in Washington — S. B. , requesting
the company of the Pastor and
a Delegate, at the ordination
of their Rev. Mr. Duncan, who
was so much admired by Father
when he was at home before —
Father was chosen Delegate, but
whether Mr. Dwight will go
or not I don't know —

Tuesday morning — Austin — I hadn't
time to finish my note Sunday night.
I shall do so now. Received your
note last Evening, and coughed all
night till now. You must not
be so precarious — It will never do.
I was here when this note arrived, and we just sat and
screamed. I shall keep the letter
always — Marcia is here this morning — the work goes briskly on —

We are almost beside our-
selves with business, and company.
"Spencer" has not yet called.
Emmons spent Friday evening here.
I went with Cousin John last
evening to call on S —— stayed
till most 11. and had a splendid
time — She seemed very finished.
She sends this letter now.

Was at Mrs Dwight's yesterday —
They had a great deal to say
about you ———, and how
happy Vinnie and I must be
to have such a beautiful ———.

We had two letters from Father
last night — one to mother and
one to me — I shall autograph to
him soon! Charlie sings every
day — Everybody admires him —
How much like Aunt Lavinia —
How did Mr Bowen hear the
announcement that broke the

clock they were disposed of?
It must have been quite a shock
to him. Mrs Ayer has gone home.
Helped us a great deal.
Ceniten has just arrived, so between
her and "Judah" and Marcia and
Miss Croly, I guess the folks
will go. — Cousin John is going
to stay here at nights when
they are away, and wants to
know quite eagerly "when it
is to come off." I am glad you
have got settled and are not
afraid of ghosts. — Love much have
pleasant times with Clark.
We all send our love to —
Won't you write some about John
White — He is anxious to know,
and Mrs Mack wants very much
to have him come in there.
Love to Austin. Great trouble —
Remember us always to Clark. — Emily —

chosen Delegate, but whether Mr Dwight will go or not, I dont know.

Tuesday morning. Austin— I had'nt time to finish my note Sunday night. I shall do so now. Received your note last evening, and laughed all night till now. You must not be so facetious. It will never do. Sue [altered] was here when the note arrived, and we just sat and screamed. I shall keep the letter always. Marcia is here this morning—the work goes briskly on. We are almost beside ourselves with business, and company. "Lysander" has not yet called. Emmons spent Friday evening here. I went with Cousin John last evening to call on Sue [altered]—stayed till most 11—and had a splendid time. Sue ["she"] seemed her very finest. She sends this little note.

Was at Mr Dwight's yesterday. They had a great deal to say about you <and Susie> and how happy Vinnie and I must be to have such a beautiful [word altered and erased].

We had two letters from Father last night—one to mother and one to me. I shall telegraph to him soon! Charlie sings every day. Everybody admires him. You must tell Aunt Lavinia.

How did Mr Bourne bear the announcement that both the black eyes were disposed of? It must have been quite a shock to him. Mrs Noyes has gone home. Helped us a great deal. Cenith has just arrived, so between her and "Judah" and Marcia and Miss Cooly, I guess the folks will go. Cousin John is going to stay here at night when they are away, and wants to know quite eagerly "when it is to come off." I am glad you have got settled and are not afraid of ghosts. You must have pleasant times with Clark.

We all send our love to you. Wont you write soon about John White. He is anxious to know, and Mrs Mack wants very much to have him come in there. Good bye Austin. Great hurrah. Remember us always to Clark.

Emily.

[*Note enclosed*]

Dear Austin

I've written to Mira not to visit us now.[4] We are so busy that we can not see any one. I want you to see Aunt Lavinia & find out when she will have a bundle ready to send to me & then I wish you would get some way to send it to me. I want it. I'm in a dreadful hurry.

Vinnie

4. Joel Norcross married Lamira H. Jones of Chicago on January 17, 1854.

[*To Wm. Austin Dickinson, Law School, Cambridge, Mass.; post-*
mark: Phil^a & Balt^e R.R. Mar 20]

Willard's Hotel
Washington, Sunday Evening, March 19. '54
Dear Austin,

I want to have you get & send me a Mass. Register—perhaps some
Member of the Legislature will do it, tho' I think you had better
buy one—it will cost only .75. cts. & mail it. I have written to Mother
about sundry things, having reference to coming here, & told her to
get 60. or 70. dolls. of my money of Bowdoin. I have written, too,
that I do not want John White in my house.

I don't hear anything of the Pierce's movements—see no notice in
the papers. I have notified them that I have bo't the Flagg pew for
Mr Dwight.

We now expect that we may have the Nebraska bill up, on Tuesday or Wednesday—but can't tell any thing about it. Several Boston
people are now here—& some arriving almost every day. It has been
much colder, for two or three days, past—trees show their green, a
little, & the grass in the Capitol grounds is the greenest that I ever
saw. I think you will be here, the most beautiful month in the year,
& hope you will all enjoy it.

I am very well—let me hear from you, soon. Make my respects to
Prof. [Joel] Parker, Mr Bullard, uncle L. & J's family.

Your aff father
E. Dickinson

The Dickinsons could hardly have chosen a more beautiful time
in which to visit the national capital, or a more exciting one. Feeling
in the North had been strained to the breaking point by passage of
the Kansas-Nebraska Bill by the Senate on March 4, 1854. So great
was the tension that it seemed as if the country was about to be
wrenched in two when, suddenly, on the twenty-first of March, the
"Nebraska Bill" was introduced in the House.[5] There it encountered
such determined opposition that it was finally referred to the Com-

5. It was usually called the "Nebraska Bill" because, in 1854, that territory
covered a much larger area than Kansas, which was about its present size.
Nebraska included all of the territory north of the Kansas line up to the
Canadian boundary, and west of the Missouri River as far as the summit of the
Rocky Mountains.

mittee of the Whole. Like its other opponents, Edward Dickinson hoped that by postponement the bill had been killed, for that session of Congress at least, as he wrote his son the same day. But he was mistaken. Not only was the bill very much alive; it was destined to be the outstanding piece of legislation enacted by the Thirty-third Congress. Although sucked into the whirlpool of the fight to prevent its passage, and although thoroughly roused by what he considered its infamy, Mr. Dickinson took little part in the debate on the floor of the House.

It was precisely at this time, while the Kansas-Nebraska Bill was hanging fire and public indignation rising by the hour, that the Dickinsons set out for Washington.

Before they left home a few more letters were exchanged.

[*To Wm. Austin Dickinson, Law School, Cambridge, Mass.; postmark: Phil^a & Balt^e R.R. Mar 22*]

Washington March 21. 1854

Dear Austin.

We have to-day referred the Nebraska Bill to the Committee of the Whole House on the State of the Union, by 15. majority—and that in the face of the public proclamation of M^r [William A.] Richardson, who is the leader in that matter, in the House, that he should regard that reference of it (he moved to refer it to Com^ee on Territories of which he is Chairman,) as equivalent to killing the Bill. The galleries were crowded—with anxious lookers on— the House was still—& the ayes & noes echoed thro' the Hall—and such earnest & solemn countenances I have never seen in this body— it was a scene of as exciting solemnity, as I have ever witnessed—as if the preservation of freedom itself depended on the issue—& when the Speaker announced 110. yeas, & 95. nays—all relaxed— freemen breathed freely; all efforts to take up any thing else were in vain—& the House adj^d, the North rejoicing, & the Nebraska men & the Administration placed in a minority which we hope is beyond recovery. Enough for one day. Col. [Alexander] DeWitt & M^r [Samuel L.] Crocker both go home to-morrow morning. I am well—the weather is fine again. I see that there has been great damage done by the wind of Saturday last—it was terrible, here— blowing a hurricane, thro' the day. I hear from home that they are all getting along very well—& Mother & Lavinia going to be ready to come here, about the 1ˢᵗ April. I may meet you in New York. I expect to go there, on the evening of the last day of March—Friday of next week—most probably.

I have written to Bowdoin about various matters of business— at home. If it should happen just right, I might even go home, on Saturday 1ˢᵗ day of April, & return on Tuesday after, with you all— probably not, however. I expect to hear from you by the morning mail. Write me twice a week, even if but a few lines, & let me know how you are getting along.

Your aff father
E. Dickinson

The next letter was folded and mailed without an envelope.

[*To Wm. Austin Dickinson, Law School, Cambridge, Mass^tts; postmark: Washington D.C. Mar 24 Free*]

Ho. of Reps. U.S.
Washington March 24. 1854.

Dear Austin,

Since we gave the Nebraska Bill its destiny, for the present, there is great chagrin & desperation in the defeated party in the House, & the defeated administration—which will lead them to attempt a grand rally, when the matter is reached again. That time may come —nobody knows when. We don't believe it to be very near. I think we have given it its death wound. I do not believe any such bill can pass this House.

Hunt's speech, was a most fearless & noble specimen of the efforts of a most noble man—and it told upon the House, & will tell upon the country.[6] We shall [hear] some more from the North, on the same side.

I hear from home that yʳ mother & Lavinia are getting ready as fast as possible, to come here. I should like to have you all come as early in April as you can.

I shall write you definitely by the middle of next week—about the time for you to go home.

6. On March 23, Theodore G. Hunt of Louisiana reminded the representatives from the North that they were dealing with their brothers, and urged a more fraternal spirit among them. Mr. Hunt is remembered as one of the nine southern representatives who voted against the Kansas-Nebraska Bill. *Globe,* 33 Cong., 1 Sess., 1254; also Appendix, 434-439.

We have had an Equinoctial storm—beginning with Saturday last.
We are having occasional days of great interest in the House—
and shall probably have more of them as we pass along.
I am very well.

Your aff father
E. Dickinson

2

Although Edward Dickinson often expressed the belief that the
Nebraska Bill would never pass the House, he seems nevertheless to
have had a premonition of what was about to happen. In a letter to
an acquaintance in Amherst, quoted in the *Express* (March 31), he
wrote: "We expect that the friends of the Nebraska Bill may make
a desperate effort to get up that infamous measure again, on the
first occasion when they find enough of its opponents absent to give
them a momentary majority."

The "equinoctial" storm mentioned in Mr. Dickinson's letter of
March 24 raged far and wide up and down the coast for more than
a week. It even reached Amherst. Emily refers to it in her letter of
March 26. But first, here is one from Lavinia.

[*To Wm. Austin Dickinson, Cambridge Law School, Cambridge,
Mass.; postmark: Amherst Ms. Mar 25*]

Friday Evening [March 24, 1854]

Dear Austin

I'm glad you are in such great spirits. Cambridge does'nt seem
to be so bad a place after all. Your lively & highly interesting letters
of this week have both reached us safely, were very glad to get them.
You dont seem to like Clark, what's the trouble now?
We are all dreadful busy sewing. I guess we shall be ready to go
by week after next Tuesday. If you want any more collars made, you
must send a pattern to us just as soon as you get this note else they
cant be finished soon enough. Be sure & send a pattern Tuesday.
Miss Baker has engaged to make them then. Dont forget to do it.
Mother thinks you'll need them. Prof Haven leaves for Europe on
Monday next. I hear that Joel & Mira are coming to see us next
week. We feel badly about it because we dont know how to attend
to company now. It may prevent our going to Washington as soon

as we want to. I wrote to Aunt Lavinia that it would not be convenient for *us* to see them at this time. She replied that Uncle said they *must* come even if it delayed our Washington visit for a few days. We dont any of us like it at all. Aunt L. told Joel that we were too busy to see company at this time, but he said he would come, at any rate. Won't it be charming for us to see them under the circumstances? Dont forget to make use of *his store*.

I cant write any more, Austin for I have a severe ague in my face & dont feel able to hold the pen longer.

Nothing new here. No decent maple sugar to be had any where. Let us hear from you with out fail on *Tuesday*.

"Remember, love, remember"

Yours attached,

Dickinson

Charley has sung splendidly all day. My *face* aches hard & I'm putting on camphor.

Now I'm going to bed.

Good night.

Did the Lymans say anything about me?

Have you seen to the cleaning of the gloves? Dont neglect it.

Saturday morning

My face is not any better.

It pains me dreadfully & aint you sorry for me?

In Austin Dickinson's packets of family letters received while he was in Cambridge, the last from Emily is that of March 26, 1854. Written in ink, it is a beautiful example of her early penmanship.

[*To Wm Austin Dickinson. Law School. Cambridge, Mass.; postmark: Amherst Ms. Mar 27*]

Sunday evening [March 26, 1854]

Well Austin—it's Sunday evening—Vinnie is sick with the ague —mother taking a tour of the second story as she is wont Sabbath evening, the wind is blowing high, the weather very cold, and I am rather cast down, in view of all these circumstances. Vinnie's face began to ache Friday—that night, and yesterday, and last night, she suffered intensely, and nothing seemed to relieve her.

Today she is better—has sat up in the big rocking chair most of the time, and seems quite bright this evening. I guess she'll be smart tomorrow. She sends her love to you and says you will sympathize with her. I went to meeting alone all day. I assure you I felt very solemn. I went to meeting five minutes before the bell rang, morning and afternoon, so not to have to go in after all the people had got there. I [*came home with* <Sue> *from meeting. She said she wished*][7] you had heard Mr Dwight's sermons today. He has preached wonderfully, and I thought all the afternoon how I wished you were there.

The sewing is moving on—I guess the folks will be ready by next week Tuesday. That is the day fixed now. I have to work very hard. I dont write to you very often now, and I cant till all this is over. I should love to see you this evening. I told Vinnie a few minutes ago that it seemed very funny not to see you putting on your surtout, and asking us if we would like to call at Mrs Jones'! I received several notes, or paragraphs, from you, in the course of the week, for which I am much obliged. The wind has blown a gale for the last week in Amherst. <Sue and> I went to the Depot yesterday to get "Vinnie's Express", and we had to hold our bonnets on, and take hold of each other too, to keep from blowing away. We had a snow storm here last week, and there's a covering of snow on the ground now. Mr Sweetser's family went to meeting in a sleigh, so you can see there's a little. Sam Fiske called here this evening. I will tell you something funny. You know Vinnie sent Father a box of maple sugar. She got the box at the store and it said on the outside of it, "1 Doz Genuine Quaker Soap." We did'nt hear from the box, and so many days had passed, we began to feel anxious lest it had never reached him, and mother writing soon, alluded in her letter to the "sugar sent by the girls," and the funniest letter from Father, came in answer to her's. It seems the box went straightway, but father not knowing the hand, merely took off the papers in which the box was wrapped, and the Label "Quaker Soap" so far imposed upon him, that he put the box in a drawer with his *shaving materials,* and supposed himself well stocked with an excellent Quaker Soap, until mother gave him the hint, which led to the discovery. He said he really supposed it a plan for the progress of soap, until he had mother's letter. We all send our love to you, and want you should write us often.

Good night—from Emilie

I spelt a word wrong in this letter, but I know better, so you need'nt think you have caught me.

Only a few days remained before the family was to leave for Washington, but Emily still seems to have had no intention of going.

7. Crossed out in pencil, but legible.

The following snappy exchange is a good illustration of the relationship between Austin and his sister Lavinia.

[*To Wm Austin Dickinson, Cambridge Law School, Cambridge, Mass; postmark: Amherst Mar 2(9)*]

Tuesday Evening [March 28, 1854]

Dear *Rooster*

Your sweet remembrance came to hand about 3 oclock this afternoon, glad you are so well off for collars, though Miss Baker was engaged to make you some more this week. My face is much better but not well by any means. I have not been so sick for years as I was Saturday, Sunday & Monday. We are progressing some what with our sewing, guess we shall be ready to start next Wednesday. I feel sorry for Mrs Greely, I presume she will be perfectly frantic. You must get as large & good a trunk as mine & bring home with you. Have some of the folks advise you in selecting it. Get a good one & if you think a Boston *case* too expensive, Mrs Godfrey has engaged to make one after the trunk comes home. Mother must have one any way. Father wrote to her to have one purchased. I suppose you will bring several things home which Aunt Lavinia will have ready for you.

Sue was here this afternoon & told us a long story that Mrs Sweetser had told Harriet [Cutler] about us this morning. I have not been able to go out since Friday, but hope to get out again tomorrow & then Mrs Luke will get such a lecture from me as she never heard, I guess. She says we dont treat the Newmans with any attention & that Mrs Fay has talked with her about it & all such stuff. I shall first go to Mrs Luke & give her a piece of my mind, then Mrs Fay another piece & see what effect will come of it. Mrs Sweetser has interfered with my business long enough & now she'll get it, I tell you. I'll bring up all past grievances & set them in order before her & see what she'll say for herself. I hope to start by 11 oclock in the morning to deliver my feelings. I *certainly shall*. She has watched me long enough in meeting & her bonnet has bobbed long enough & now I'll have a stop put to such proceedings, I will indeed.

I'm sorry, Austin that you ever invited Clark to come to Amherst if you have such an opinion of him. Emilie & I think he is a very agreeable fellar, but I think *you* ought to know best. I dont expect

to write again before you come home. We shall see you Saturday of course. Good night
I'm so tired.

Vinnie
Alias, Chick

Notice of the discipline Vinnie proposed to mete out to Mrs. Luke Sweetser called forth from Austin a prompt reply. The envelope is missing.

Thursday afternoon [March 30, 1854]

Dear Vin.

Your note of Tuesday eve came this morning, rather the *smartest* note I have in your hand.

Will those desiring have an opportunity to view the *remains* of the mischievous lady of the woods when you get through with her, what few there may be left!

My own notion would be, Vinnie, not to say a single word to Mrs Sweetser on the subject. She is not our master, nor are we in any way responsible to her for anything we are, or have. Let the woman talk if it makes her any happier. She cant hurt us, we dont care for her, and seems to me it would be making her of rather too much importance to take all the trouble to go up there & give her such a pommeling as you propose. I dont doubt your *ability* to raise an *awful* breeze around her ears, but is it on the whole best? Wont it be very apt to please her very much to know she has put you into such a fever?

I dont believe, Vinnie, that you could possibly tickle her so much as by just the course you promise yourself. If you want to punish her the severest, just let her alone severely. Let her passion for slandering & insinuating against you, or any of us, fall upon herself alone. Do nothing which shall divert it from her for a single moment. Keep quiet & let it burn away there as long as it will, and it will burn nobody but her own dear self. And that miserable, fretful, old maidish widow, let her alone too. Dont say a single word to her, only if she barks too loud, & troubles your sleep, tell father & have him inform her her services are no longer needed, and hire some more servicable girl to take charge of those children. We can turn her out of the house any day and she cant say one word.—

The trunks I will see about.

I am going over to Boston towards night.———

Shall come Saturday.

Thursday afternoon

Dear Vin, your note of Tuesday eve came this morning, rather the smartest not drawn in your hand.

Will Thos desiring have an opportunity to view the remains of the mischievous lady of the woods whom your first thought within tour, what few town may be left, was my own notion would be. Vinnie, now to say a light word to mere function on the subject. She is not our master, nor are we in any way responsible. She for anything we are, or have, let the woman talk if it makes her any happier. She can't hurt us, we don't care for her, and

Letter from William Austin Dickinson to his sister Lavinia, March 30, 1854

fuss to me it would be making
him of rather too much importance
to take all the trouble to go up there
& give him such a pommeling
as you propose. I don't doubt
your _ability_ to raise an _awful_
bruise around his ears. But
is it on the whole best? Would
it be very apt to please him
very much to know that he had
put you into such a furore?
I don't believe, Vinnie, that you
could possibly tickle him so
much as by just the course
you propose yourself.
If you want to punish him
to the utmost, just let him alone
severely. Let his passion
for slandering & insinuating against
you or any of us, feed upon itself
alone. Do nothing which

shall dinner is from her for a high
morning. Keep quiet and let it turn
away her as long as it will, and
it will turn nobody but her own
dear self. And that miserable
fretful old snailish widow,
let her alone too. don't say a high
word to her, or if she barks too
loud and troubles your sleep, tell
father and have him inform her
her services are no longer needed,
and hire some more sensible
girl to take charge of those
children. He can turn her
out of the house any day and she
can't say one word. ——

The Trustee I will see
above.
I am going on to Boston
towards night. ———————
　　　　　Shall come Sat.

If Jerry is still about & is a mind to get the horse & come to the depot after me I should like to have him.

I dont know as there is anything in particular I need to write about more now, I^m coming so soon.

Perhaps shall add a word from Boston.

Last night attended an exhibition of the "Mercantile Library Association," by invitation.

Good day, *for the present.*

I hope Mrs Mack will be able to wash a few small things for me before I start for Washington.—

On Wednesday, April 5, the Dickinson family left Amherst on their journey to Washington. What caused Emily to change her mind at the last moment is not known. But to Washington she went with the rest of the family. They stopped overnight at the Astor House, New York, and arrived at Willard's Hotel, Washington, on April 6. Judge Hoar of Concord, who visited the capital at this time, mentions having seen them in a letter to his wife dated April 16, 1854:[8]

"I found at Willard's, of our Massachusetts delegation, Mr. Crocker of Taunton, Mr. Walley of Roxbury, and Mr. Dickinson of Amherst with his wife, son and daughter"—which daughter the Judge does not specify.

Although Austin had accompanied his mother and sisters, he did not remain in Washington throughout their stay of three weeks; nor, apparently, did Mrs. Dickinson.[9] But the date of Judge Hoar's letter indicates that ten days after their arrival, at least, Austin and his mother were still there. For him such a prolonged absence from Cambridge seems strange in view of the fact that the bar examinations were to be held shortly. He took them in Boston early in June and passed successfully. Suffolk County court records show that he was "admitted to practise law in Massachusetts on June 26, 1854." I am told by Charles Warren, Esq., historian of the Harvard Law School, that the practice of taking bar examinations before graduation was at that time not uncommon.

Through the courtesy of Gelston Hardy of New York there has recently come to my attention a note written by his grandmother,

8. Storey and Emerson, *Ebenezer Rockwood Hoar,* 105.

9. See Emily's letter from Washington in Bianchi, *Emily Dickinson Face to Face,* 202-205.

Jeanie Ashley Bates Greenough, whose husband, James Carruthers
Greenough, was president of the Massachusetts Agricultural College
in Amherst from 1883 to 1886. Mrs. Greenough had become
acquainted with the Dickinsons in Washington after Austin and
his mother had left. With Mr. Hardy's kind permission her note
is reproduced:

My first acquaintance with Emily D. was in Washington many
years ago. Her father was U. S. Senator.[10] He, with his two daughters,
my father & mother & myself were together at Willards Hotel. Emily
impressed me as a girl with large, warm heart, earnest nature &
delicate tastes, & we soon became friends. Some years after, when my
father had symptoms of paralysis, she wrote me a note full of
sympathy, accompanying flowers.

In Amherst, I did not see her, (as she saw no one) but Lavinia
came to renew our acquaintance, & brought me Emily's love, or
flowers, or notes.

After I lost my mother, I rec^d the following characteristic note
of sympathy.[11]

Emily's own account of the Washington visit, contained in a letter
to Dr. and Mrs. Holland first published in *Letters,* 1894, is familiar
to many readers. It runs in part as follows:

We were three weeks in Washington, while father was there, and
have been two in Philadelphia. We have had many pleasant times,
and seen much that is fair, and heard much that is wonderful—
many sweet ladies and noble gentlemen have taken us by the hand
and smiled upon us pleasantly—and the sun shines brighter for
our way thus far.

I will not tell you what I saw—the elegance, the grandeur; you
will not care to know the value of the diamonds my Lord and Lady
wore, but if you haven't been to the sweet Mount Vernon, then I *will*
tell you how on one soft spring day we glided down the Potomac in
a painted boat, and jumped upon the shore—how hand in hand
we stole along up a tangled pathway till we reached the tomb of
General George Washington, how we paused beside it, and no one
spoke a word, then hand in hand, walked on again, not less wise or
sad for that marble story; how we went within the door—raised the
latch he lifted when he last went home—thank the Ones in Light
that he's since passed in through a brighter wicket! Oh, I could

10. Mrs. Greenough first wrote "in Congress," then crossed it out, substituting
"U. S. Senator."

11. The note, beginning, "I had the luxury of a mother a month longer than
you," was published in *Letters,* 1894, 428; *Letters,* 1931, 416-417.

spend a long day, if it did not weary you, telling of Mount Vernon—and I will sometime if we live and meet again, and God grant we shall![12]

April in Virginia is a season of magic, the whole earth decked out with blossoming trees and shrubs as for a festival.

It is a tantalizing glimpse Emily gives of this world so new to her, and different. In a painted boat, she says, they glided down the broad river fringed by trees just springing into tender leaf—sassafras and beech, sycamore and tulip poplars. Here and there a dogwood or redbud was in bloom and the vivid young green of weeping-willow branches brushed the surface of the water. And when she jumped upon the shore and stole up the "tangled" pathway through the thick mat of interlacing honeysuckle stems, suddenly she came upon "the sweet Mount Vernon." Beneath the trees which Washington himself had planted were clumps of fragile wildflowers which she had never seen before, spring beauties and violets with two velvet petals. The sweet-scented air was filled with the singing of birds, songs new to her too—the cardinal's strong whistle and the riotous medley of the mockingbird.

During her three weeks' stay in Washington this was the thing of permanence she found. Of all the wonders of the nation's capital this it was that moved her most.

12. *Letters*, 1894, 163; *Letters*, 1931, 160.

CHAPTER XXVII

Philadelphia Interlude

BEFORE returning to Amherst in late May, Emily and Lavinia stopped in Philadelphia for a visit of two weeks with the Colemans.

The Reverend Dr. Coleman had been principal of Amherst Academy and an instructor in the college during the 1840's—a fact not mentioned in his own sketch of his life.[1] A memorial sermon delivered after his death on March 16, 1882, described his "commanding presence," his "tall form, handsome face and intelligent eye," his "scrupulous neatness coupled with his antipathy to tobacco," his observance of the courtesies of life, his "passionate love of nature," his warm sympathy and his strong convictions.[2]

Between a professorship at the College of New Jersey (Princeton), 1847-1849, and a similar position at Lafayette College, 1861-1882, Dr. Coleman taught the classics and Biblical Geography at the Presbyterian Academy of Philadelphia. From 1858 to 1861 the family lived in Middletown, Connecticut.

As the reader may recall, Mrs. Coleman was a connection of Mrs. Dickinson. When the Colemans lived in Amherst their daughters, Olivia and Eliza, had been close friends of Emily and Vinnie. The girls felt especially drawn to Eliza because Olivia had died of "galloping consumption" on September 28, 1847, when she was only twenty years old. As she died without warning in a carriage, the circumstances of her death were considered "romantic."

1. *The Coleman Family [etc.], 1598-1867* (Philadelphia, 1867).
2. Rev. Alfred H. Kellogg, *A Sermon Commemorative of the Life and Character of the Rev. Lyman Coleman, D.D., June 25, 1882* (Lafayette College, Easton, Pa., 1882).

It was during this visit in Philadelphia that Emily is said to have first heard the Reverend Charles Wadsworth preach in the Arch Street Presbyterian Church. As the Colemans were Presbyterians, it seems probable that during her visit she did hear Dr. Wadsworth preach. But of this no proof has thus far been produced. It also seems probable that if she did, she was profoundly moved.

Dr. Wadsworth was descended from a colonial hero, Joseph Wadsworth, who in 1687 prevented the charter of the Connecticut Colony from falling into the hands of a British governor.[3] The intrepidity of his ancestor flowed in Charles Wadsworth's veins. His life was devoted to building up weak, disintegrating religious organizations. When in 1850 he took over the Arch Street Church the membership had dwindled to twelve families. Before he left for California a few years later, it had grown into a prosperous congregation.

As a preacher Dr. Wadsworth was said to have been as popular in Philadelphia as Henry Ward Beecher in Brooklyn. The Reverend George Burrows of San Francisco published his impression of Dr. Wadsworth shortly after he became pastor of the Calvary Presbyterian Society in that city in 1862. After dwelling on his "deep, earnest, simple-hearted piety," Mr. Burrows continues: "You feel that behind all he says there must be lying years of conflict and agony, of trials and sorrows, of deep gloom and despondency, of strong cries and tears, of heavenly fellowship and confidential friendship with God . . . all this, blended with deep study and meditation on the Scriptures, and assimilated by the fires of the Holy Spirit . . . finds utterance through the molding control of a brilliant, original, powerful mind, of a soul whose lips have been touched with a coal from Israel's hallowed fire. . . . He preaches consolation like a man who knows how to succor others because he has himself been compassed with suffering. . . . All is sobered by deep penetration and sound common sense. . . . A humility so unfeigned, allied with so much greatness, and mellowed, no less than deepened, by divine grace, throws a great charm around the character." (See page 508.)

The writer emphasizes one feature of Dr. Wadsworth's language: his power of condensation. Many of the traits of this gifted man, described in numerous publications in the archives of the Presby-

3. W. H. Gocher, *Wadsworth or the Charter Oak* (Hartford, 1904).

terian Historical Society of Philadelphia, suggest avenues of inquiry into the sources of certain characteristics of Emily Dickinson's style. An editorial in *The Presbyterian* (April 8, 1882), a week after Dr. Wadsworth's sudden death from pneumonia on April first of that year, mentions another parallel—the contrast between his eloquence in the pulpit and his strange solitary life: "He would go along lonely streets seemingly to avoid men. He chose to walk solitarily alone along the paths of life, in fellowship with Christ, whose thoughts were his companions by the way."

Trying to find a source of inspiration for the love poems of Emily Dickinson is a provocative adventure. There is no need to pursue the search here. But one additional bit of evidence may help to dispose of the candidacy, as a lover at least, of this revered friend "whom to know was life." Although it clears up no mystery, this evidence may lend support to what I believe to be the truth about the reason for her secluded life: that it was not a chance meeting, not a sudden onslaught upon "the pulses of the flesh," not even tumultuous "Calvaries of love," but a relentless inward necessity which, little by little, drew Emily Dickinson into seclusion. At the age of twenty-two she herself explained it by saying, "I find I need more veil."

Here, then, is the evidence: Among the scraps of prose and verse found after Emily Dickinson's death, was an unsigned letter the text of which follows. The handwriting resembles that of Dr. Wadsworth and the embossed letterhead, without color, bears the initials "C.W." The letter reveals his concern for the young friend who had intimated to him a turmoil of spirit which, although he was unaware of its nature, he tenderly wished to ease. The letter is not dated but as the friendship appears to be already well established, it was undoubtedly written several years later than 1854:

C W
My Dear Miss Dickenson
    I am distressed beyond measure at your note, received this moment, —I can only imagine the affliction which has befallen, or is now befalling you.
    Believe me, be what it may, you have all my sympathy, and my constant, earnest prayers.
    I am very, very anxious to learn more definitely of your trial—

My Dear Miss Dickinson

I am distressed beyond measure at your note, received this moment, — I can only imagine the affliction which has befallen, or is now befalling you

Believe me. — be what it may you have all my sympathy, and my constant, earnest prayers —

I am very,

Unsigned letter thought to be from the Reverend Charles Wadsworth

very anxious to learn
more definitely of your
trial — and though
I have no right to
intrude upon your sorrow
yet I beg you to write
me. Though it be but
a word.

In great haste
Sincerely and most
affectionately *Sims* —

and though I have no right to intrude upon your sorrow yet I beg you to write me, though it be but a word.

> In great haste
> Sincerely and most
> Affectionately *Yours*—

To turn a relationship such as that of Dr. Wadsworth and Emily Dickinson into a love affair is not only misleading; it is false. The clergyman's solicitude for a young woman who had sought his help in a searing experience of which he apparently knew as little as we do is evident in this unsigned note. All that is known with certainty about this transcendental friendship is that it was for Emily Dickinson a transforming experience. In her words:

> We can find no scar
> But internal difference
> Where the meanings are.

Whatever the "imperial affliction" for which she was seeking comfort it was as undisclosed to her family, perhaps even to Dr. Wadsworth, as to us. To grasp its meaning deeper insight is needed. A wise woman has said that she could never feel that it is essential to have proof whether Emily Dickinson's lover or lovers were real or imaginary. It is enough that she was herself capable of the heights and depths of love and could help the many voiceless ones who cannot utter a word nor clarify their feelings. A lover or even lovers cannot bring that about—it is what one has to offer oneself that counts, and Emily had all that a human being could give. She was fortunate if another shared her emotional life even a little, but there are no weights and measures for that. Few could have followed her and it is a part of life and deep experience that the heights and depths are lonely. Why shouldn't they be? They are enough in themselves.

Acceptance of such an opinion should not, however, deter us from continuing to learn all we can about Emily Dickinson's friends and to explore all her relationships. A sudden beam of light from an unexpected direction might illuminate an inscrutable poem or series of poems—even a whole period of months or years. No relationship is too tenuous to be investigated.

Women need something firm to hold to. Emily had her father of course. Firm he certainly was. In daily living he was the pivot around which all creation turned. She was, as she said, "accustomed to all through Father." But thoughts are stalwart things too. In Dr. Wadsworth she found another kind of support in a realm of reality in which her father was not so expert. At any rate she did not know about that. But here was a man to whom the Holy Ghost was more than a theological figment. Through Dr. Wadsworth she was invigorated by what she had so long and so passionately hoped for —a tingling inrush of the Holy Spirit. It was in a sense regeneration, perhaps the nearest to conversion she had ever come.

In *Life and Letters,* pages 49-50, Emily's niece published the poem, "Title divine is mine!" as expressing Emily's "first ecstasy of renunciation" after the Philadelphia visit in 1854. I have not seen a copy of the poem in the handwriting of that period. But a slightly different version written about ten years later reads as follows:

> Title divine is mine!
> The Wife without the Sign!
> Acute Degree conferred on me—
> Empress of Calvary!
> Royal, all but the Crown!
> Betrothed, without the swoon
> God sends us women
> When you hold Garnet to Garnet
> Gold, to Gold.
> Born—Bridalled—Shrouded—
> In a Day!
> "My Husband," women say,
> Stroking the melody.
> Is *this*—the way?

The legend that Emily Dickinson became a recluse because of a broken heart has taken such root in popular imagination, and in popular preference, that no amount of evidence to the contrary will make "a dent thereon." But that is no reason for ignoring such facts as there are, among them the statements of her brother and sister.

To a reader of the letters in this volume it is unnecessary to point out Emily's closeness, though in different ways, to Austin and Lavinia. On the subject of her romantic attachments both had definite views.

Vinnie, the watchdog, stood guard over her sister, protecting her from intruders. Emily told a friend that "without her life were fear." When still in her twenties she told another friend that "our practical sister Vinnie has been all, so long, I feel the oddest fright at parting with her for an hour, lest a storm arise, and I go unsheltered." If anyone hurt Emily, or when a friend played her false, Vinnie turned on him fierce as a tigress. Nothing could rouse her more. On one such occasion Emily wrote: "Vinnie is full of wrath, and vicious as Saul toward the Holy Ghost, in whatever form. I heard her declaiming the other night, to a foe that called—and sent Maggie to part them."[4] No observable facts about Emily's life could escape Vinnie. She did not comment on the shade of Emily's affection for her various friends, to several of whom she was extravagantly devoted. Vinnie would not have presumed to do so. She respected her sister's reticence. But she knew who they were, when they came, and how long they stayed. Because they were dear to Emily, and without indicating one as dearer than others, Vinnie revered them all but, in my mother's words, "she didn't know what was going on in Emily's mind."

Austin, on the other hand, was quite definite. He said that at different times Emily had been devoted to several men. He even went so far as to maintain that she had been several times in love, in her own way. But he denied that because of her devotion to any one man she forsook all others. Such an idea was mere "nonsense." Her gradual withdrawal, Austin insisted, was perfectly natural. As far as he was concerned, it was Emily's right to be alone if she wanted to be. It was not because of any disappointment in love, he thought, but because people did not understand her that little by little she withdrew from village life, seeing fewer and fewer acquaintances as time went on until, after their father's death in 1874, she became the recluse of the legend. He knew that she read prodigiously, but that she sought solitude because she needed time to write Austin did not guess. For he died without suspecting that his sister had been a great poet.

Some of Emily's friends, on the other hand, were troubled by what they considered the failure of Amherst people to understand her. In the fall of 1854 Eliza Coleman, writing to John Graves, expressed her solicitude for Emily in the hands of village gossips. Eliza says:

4. *Letters*, 1894, 372; *Letters*, 1931, 363.

4th Oct. '54

. . . Emily, too, sends me beautiful letters, & each one makes me love her more. I know you appreciate her & I think few of her Amherst friends do. They wholly misinterpret her, I believe. . . .[5]

When, after Emily's death, Austin and Lavinia were asked the direct question, "Did she fall in love with Dr. Wadsworth?" they both thought not. That notion, they said, had been conceived in hearsay and kept alive by those who could think of no other explanation for her withdrawal from their society. She had always responded, they said, to anyone who gave promise of understanding her. Vinnie used plain words: "Emily was always watching for the rewarding person to come." She herself put it this way:

> Experiment to me
> Is everyone I meet,
> If it contain a kernel?

Austin went further. He told my mother that Emily reached out eagerly, fervently even, toward anybody who kindled the spark, a thought amplified in "Struck was I, nor yet by lightning."

Emily's brother and sister did not try to make her almost worshipful love of certain friends conform to the stern New England Way. They merely accepted the fact, as with everything else about her. It may be questioned whether either of them would have known what she meant by "Struck was I, nor yet by lightning," had they ever seen the poem; or by another with much the same thought written during her thirties:

> We met as sparks—diverging flints
> Sent various scattered ways;
> We parted as the central flint
> Were cloven with an adze,
>
> Subsisting on the light we bore
> Before we felt the dark,
> A flint unto this day perhaps
> But for that single spark.

Instant recognition and response was a favorite topic with Emily Dickinson—a chance encounter with a lasting effect:

5. For permission to quote these sentences from a letter to her father I am indebted to Miss Louise B. Graves.

> So the eyes accost and sunder
> In an audience
> Stamped occasionally forever . . .

Such persons were set apart. In at least two instances they became sacred; and one of them was Dr. Wadsworth.[6] In grief at his death she turned to his close friend, James D. Clark; and when he died, to his brother, Charles H. Clark, whose "name alone" remained. Her letters to the Clark brothers were first published in 1931.[7] They reveal as much about her relationship to Dr. Wadsworth as is now known.

The first letter to James Clark was written on August 22, 1882. It begins:

> Dear Friend,
> Please excuse the trespass of gratitude.
> My Sister thinks you will accept a few words in recognition of your great kindness.
> In an intimacy of many years with the beloved clergyman, I have never before spoken with one who knew him, and his Life was so shy and his tastes so unknown, that grief for him seems almost unshared.
> He was my shepherd from "Little Girl" hood and I cannot conjecture a world without him, so noble was he always—so fathomless —so gentle. . . .

Further light is thrown on the nature of her friendship with "the beloved clergyman" in a letter to Charles Clark written nearly two years later, on April 21, 1884. It begins: "These thoughts disquiet me and the great friend is gone who could solace them. Do they disturb you?"

Then follows a twenty-four-line poem, of which the theme is this:

> The music in the violin
> Does not emerge alone
> But arm in arm with touch, yet touch
> Alone is not a tune.
>
> The spirit lurks within the flesh
> Like tides within the sea

6. The other was Judge Lord of Salem. An account of this relationship can be found in Millicent Todd Bingham, *Emily Dickinson—A Revelation* (New York: Harper & Brothers, 1954).

7. *Letters*, 1931, 343-357 and 429-430.

That make the water live; estranged
What would the either be?

Another poem has the same theme:

The moon is distant from the sea,
And yet with amber hands
She leads him, docile as a boy,
Along appointed sands.

He never misses a degree;
Obedient to her eye,
He comes just so far toward the town,
Just so far goes away.

Oh, Signor, thine the amber hand,
And mine the distant sea,
Obedient to the least command
Thine eyes impose on me.

"The privilege of one another's eyes" is a recurrent thought.

In the Dr. Wadsworth legend the reason advanced for Emily Dickinson's retirement fails to take account of two facts. The first is that her withdrawal took place gradually over a period of years. It did not even begin until some time after her return from Philadelphia. Five years later, in 1859, she was still going to church with the family and "doing" her "courtesies" by making calls on newcomers. (Page 405.) The second fact is that many, but by no means all, of her most powerful love poems were written toward the end of her life. Instead of trying to identify the individual, or individuals, who inspired such poems, many of them intensely personal, it is more useful to look within the poems themselves.

One quality runs through them all, amazement at the intensity of her own emotion—given to her by the gods when she was "new and small." An attitude of wonder pervades Emily Dickinson's poetry from first to last. And the greatest of all wonders was the mystery of her own heart and the power of certain persons to arouse it to "the white heat." In the earliest love poem of which I have seen a copy in her writing, that of about 1860, she addresses her heart as if it were a separate entity—a partner, to be sure, but one she could never fully comprehend:

Heart! We will forget him!
You and I—tonight!
You may forget the warmth he gave,
I will forget the light!

When you have done, pray tell me
That I may straight begin!
Haste! lest while you're lagging
I remember him!

Here we must leave it. There may be more to know. But even
if so, "knowledge only increases mystery—never explains it."

CHAPTER XXVIII

The Thirty-third Congress Adjourns

AS SPRING advanced, the Kansas-Nebraska Bill which its opponents thought had been successfully shelved was still uppermost in everyone's mind. Although the Whigs did their best to prevent it, William A. Richardson of Illinois unexpectedly brought it up again in the House on Monday, May 8, 1854, and the fight was on. The next day Samuel H. Walley of Massachusetts spoke in opposition, and on May 10 Thomas D. Eliot, also of Massachusetts and Mr. Dickinson's close associate, made a rousing speech against the measure to which William W. Boyce of South Carolina made an equally acrimonious reply in its support. With that gentleman Mr. Dickinson got into such an argument that the good faith of both was questioned. After this "misunderstanding" on the floor of the House the opponents of the bill used every delaying device known to parliamentary procedure to prevent its consideration. A debate, begun on May 11, lasted for thirty-six hours, until on Friday, the twelfth, shortly before midnight, conciliatory Mr. Hunt, the Louisiana Whig, proposed postponing further discussion until the following Monday. This famous filibuster, if such it can be called, is one of the most dramatic as well as vituperative in congressional history.

Resumed on Monday morning, May 15, the debate continued throughout the week with ever-increasing bitterness. On Monday, May 22, the House assembled at noon and listened to a prayer for peace and forbearance, quite touching as it is tucked into *The Globe* among the charges and countercharges. But it was a brief respite; the controversy went on as before, all day and all that evening until, at half past eleven, Mr. Richardson finally brought the bill to a vote and it passed, 113 to 100. Because of slight changes it was returned to the Senate for final concurrence where, after more debate, in the course of which Charles Sumner made prophetic remarks about slavery coming to grips with freedom, the bill was passed 35 to 13 on May 26 at 1:10 A.M. Signed by President Pierce on May 30, it became law.[1]

The effect was instantaneous. Since Kansas and Nebraska were to be free or not as their citizens might choose, there was a scramble to occupy the new territories. Missouri slaveholding "squatters" swarmed across the border to stake out claims, while entire families in covered wagons left antislavery New England to do likewise. The American Colonization Society was organized to promote immigration of Free Soil settlers. Another vigorous enterprise, the Massachusetts Emigrant Aid Company, of Worcester, was reorganized as the New England Emigrant-Aid Society in 1855. The first detachment of 600 persons had left Boston for Lawrence, Kansas, a Free Soil center, on July 17, 1854. When, a year later, Emily Dickinson was herself uprooted, she referred to her sense of utter confusion as "a kind of gone-to-Kansas feeling."

Another result of the passage of the Kansas-Nebraska Act was to convince a large number of the best citizens of the North, irrespective of party, that checking the further spread of slavery was essential to the well-being not only of the North, but of the Union as a whole. As they lacked a leader powerful enough to weld together all the antislavery factions they set about trying to find some other way to focus their determination.

In February, 1854, a mass meeting had been held in Ripon, Wisconsin, where it was resolved, if the Kansas-Nebraska Bill should pass, to "organize a new party on the sole issue of the non-extension of slavery." The very morning of passage of the bill by the House, about thirty members met in the rooms of Representatives Dickinson and Eliot of Massachusetts at "Mr. Crutchett's on the northwest corner of Sixth and D Streets," to discuss a new antislavery party.[2] "Republican" was suggested as an appropriate name. A month later, on July 6, 1854, that name was formally adopted by a mass meet-

1. *Globe,* 33 Cong., 1 Sess., 1132, ff. See also Rhodes, *History,* I, 486, ff.

2. *Cong. Directory,* 33 Cong., 1 Sess., second edition, corrected up to June 20, 1854 (Government Printing Office, 1854); also *The Washington and Georgetown Directory,* etc., compiled and published by Alfred Hunter (Washington, 1853), 25. Compare Allan Nevins, *Ordeal of the Union* (New York, 1947), II, 322.

ing of fusionists at Jackson, Michigan, and the Republican party
came into being.

The passage of the Kansas-Nebraska Act had far-reaching political
reverberations: it sounded the death knell of the Whig party which
survived for four more years but in a comatose condition. In New
England it also undermined the Democrats as Know Nothings and
Free Soilers prepared to take over. Finally, it aroused Abraham
Lincoln to take a vigorous interest in national politics. Senator
Douglas, after his personal victory, became the center of political
history until, in 1858, he met his match in another son of Illinois.[3]

Although Mr. Dickinson had participated in the Nebraska Bill
debate, most of his time during those turbulent weeks had been
spent on armory committee business. The seven members had split
four to three against military control.[4] Mr. Dickinson was one of
the minority. The two others were John L. Dawson and Lawrence
Keitt, the latter a magnetic young man who, as an officer of the
Confederate Army, was to lose his life in the Civil War. On June 13
the majority report entitled, "A bill to restore the civil superintendence at the national armories," was presented to the House. On
June 21 the report of the minority was submitted by Mr. Keitt. A
month later, on July 13, when a bill for Army appropriations came
up, an amendment was unexpectedly added by the chairman of the
committee, Mr. Stanton. This provided that all military officers at
the armories should thereafter be replaced by "competent and well-
qualified" civilians. For the minority of the committee this abrupt
action by the chairman was a blow between the eyes. Mr. Stanton
had given no hint of his intention. If the amendment was to be
defeated the minority must act, and at once. As soon as Mr. Dickinson could obtain the floor, he rose to his feet and began:

"Mr. Chairman: I was never more surprised in my life than to
find myself thrust into a debate under the circumstances in which
we find ourselves this morning. In reference to the manner in which

3. Compare Rhodes, *op. cit.*, I, 493.
4. Members of the "Select Committee of the House on the Superintendency
of Public Works": John L. Dawson, Pennsylvania; Edward Dickinson, Massachusetts; Charles J. Faulkner (Harper's Ferry), Virginia; Lawrence M. Keitt, South
Carolina; W. R. Sapp, Ohio; Joshua Vansant, Maryland; and Richard H.
Stanton, chairman, Kentucky.

this debate comes up, I have to say that this is not the time and place to discuss this question."

Mr. Dickinson insisted that the House owed it to the committee, whose members had devoted three months to the matter, to discuss it separately on its own merits, not tacked on to a bill for appropriations. He then proceeded to speak for an hour, all the time allowed. A few highlights of the speech must suffice here. He explained that at the outset he had had "no preconceived opinions on this subject to maintain, or prejudices to gratify," only "an honest desire to learn the truth." His words as recorded illustrate several characteristics of which the most conspicuous is his respect for facts and his direct way of stating them. He made no attempt to soften his meaning, or to disguise his scorn for the selfish conniving he had discovered.

Mr. Dickinson took the chairman of his committee to task for bringing up the question of armory administration indirectly, without even having notified the members of the committee in advance so that they might all be present, tactics he did not hesitate to call "unfair" and "discourteous." And as to how he regarded the commission, appointed by the President during the previous Congress to investigate conditions at the national armories, here are Edward Dickinson's words: "I undertake to say in my place, as a member of the select committee . . . that there never was a commission authorized by anybody on earth, for the discharge of important duties, which failed so completely in the performance of the duties prescribed, as this." "The large body of evidence" presented in the commission's report did not satisfy him, he continued, consisting "more of the opinions of the members than of the facts on which such opinions are founded."

Mr. Dickinson disposed of the accusations of extravagance on the part of the military administration, making clear that they were not only unfounded, but that the opposite was in fact the case, namely, that the cost per musket had been reduced since the Ordnance Department took over. He went on: "Now as to the tyranny—the despotism—that has been spoken of. I went into the shops of the Springfield armory. I did not go there on the invitation of the superintendent, nor by his advice, nor under his guidance. I had even told him that I did not want him to accompany me. I went there to learn for myself, to understand how affairs stood there, for my own enlightenment as a member of the special committee of this House, so as to be able to report what the truth was in regard to this whole matter." The men were "contented and satisfied," he found, and furthermore, workmen in "the best private manufactories in the neighborhood, earning the highest rate of wages, would willingly leave these establishments to work at the national armory." To sum up "the state of facts" at the armory he quoted the words of "a leading man in my district": "Under the civil system the men do just as they have a mind to, and under the military system they are obliged to do as they ought to."

Not content with generalities, however, Mr. Dickinson returned to the President's commission and described at length the maneuvers of one member, ex-Governor Steele of New Hampshire. That gentleman went to Springfield, he said, visited each of the shops, asked the men individually about their opinions of the superintendency, and reported that a large majority were in favor of a change. How did he get this result? By telling them that there was to be a change and that they better be on the right side, or they would be "removed." He then assured the men, in the name of the President of the United States, that if they were now in favor of a civil superintendent and lost their jobs as a consequence, they need have no fears; he knew the President and could assure them in his name that they would be reinstated within thirty days. And "that," concluded Edward Dickinson, "is a specimen of one of the commission authorized to ascertain the facts to be used to enlighten the President of the United States, in reference to a change in the superintendency."[5] Although the speech was extempore, Mr. Dickinson thought well enough of it to suggest that it be printed in newspapers of the Tenth District—*The Springfield Republican, The Hampshire Gazette* (Northampton), and *The Hampshire and Franklin Express* (Amherst). The *Express* complied, printing the full text, with minor differences, on August 4, 1854.

Edward Dickinson's efforts on behalf of the Army proved useless. On July 18, five days after it was introduced, Mr. Stanton's amend-

5. The text of this impromptu speech, the longest made by Edward Dickinson on the floor of the House, is reproduced in full in Appendix IV as it appeared in *The Globe*.

ment was adopted, 80-38. In spite of this defeat, however, a disaster which he had done his best to forestall, Mr. Dickinson still hoped to find some way of circumventing the dispensers of patronage, at least insofar as administration of the armories was concerned. In this at least he was successful.

On the same day, July 18, he presented to Congress a petition of the citizens of Amherst for repeal of the "fugitive slave law." It was laid on the table.[6]

In the meantime much was happening at home. The new pastor of the First Church, the Reverend Edward S. Dwight, was to be installed on July 19, the very day on which Austin was to graduate from the Harvard Law School. Furthermore, the semicentennial of Monson Academy was to be celebrated on July 16-18, and Mrs. Dickinson wished to attend. This presented a problem to her husband, for she must not go unaccompanied. He himself could not be there; too many decisions of importance were hanging fire in Washington. The alternative, that Austin should accompany his mother, would necessitate missing his own commencement. The upshot of the matter was that Austin failed to receive his law degree in person but his mother had an escort to Monson.

Mr. Dickinson had not considered his presence essential on any of the above-mentioned occasions. But a decision affecting the future of Amherst College was a different matter. On July 11 President Hitchcock had resigned and, at the approaching meeting of the trustees, a new president was to be elected. Mr. Dickinson's candidate was the Reverend Edward Porter Humphrey of the class of 1828 (son of the former Amherst president Heman Humphrey), professor of Biblical and ecclesiastical history at the Theological Seminary in Danville, Kentucky. With customary confidence in his own judgment Mr. Dickinson felt so strongly about this, as about all matters in which he was personally involved, that he left Washington before the end of the session to see to it that the proper choice was made. To an unusual degree he had the New England trait of wanting to have things go right or, if they had gone wrong, to set them right.

6. *Journal of the House of Representatives*, 33 Cong., 1 Sess., 1159.

[*Envelope missing*]

Washington Sunday 1.P.M.
July 23. 1854.

Dear Austin

I rec^d your letter, last evening, giving some account of your trip to Monson—& imagine you & mother had a nice time. The published account in the Republican looks as if some considerably large people had gone out from Monson Academy—male & female. I think it must have been the greatest day Monson ever saw.

It seems that you are suffering with drought—so are we,—grass drying up—brown—burnt—still we have had some showers. The weather has been intolerably hot—101° in the shade—there is more air to-day, but it is like a Sirocco. I have not been out to meeting to-day—nor has Mr Eliot—he thought we were better off at home—especially as there was no preaching that we cared to hear. It is the driest of all places, to attend church—there is hardly enough of mentality here to hold the place together—and still, not much that is positive immorality. A dont-care air which renders every body callous to everything good. I remain perfectly well—yet—& this city is spoken of as remarkably healthy. I probably shall be home, on Monday night, 31st July. I think not, before.

I had 600. copies of the Rept. to the Globe containing my Armory. remarks struck off for myself to send to my friends. I do not know whether the Republican, Express & Gazette will publish it, or not. If they do, I want to have the column on the 3^d page, containing my views on the annullment which I offered to Stanton's amendment, published, too—as it illustrates & carries out what I wanted to say, at the first. You can see Wethrell [Leander Wetherell, editor of the *Express*] perhaps, incidentally, & find out what he intends to do—as it is the first extended speech that I have made, I thought likely he would wish to publish it. I *should not ask* him to do it. I have written to Repub^n what I want, if any thing.

I notice what you said of the Coll. Pres. I had heard the same suggestion before I came away. Edw. Humphrey is my candidate, & the Trustees know it. Any body else will prove a failure—in my judgment. It wants back-bone in physical, moral, financial & practical and governmental matters—such as few have got.

I sent one of my speeches to Horace,[7] under an envelope to you. It may please him. I hope he takes good care of every thing. The fusion convention will purify the political atmosphere, I think, and prepare the way for all sound & true Whigs & honest men to take high, strong ground on principles which are not temporising, or

7. Horace Church was caretaker of the Dickinson property, more especially of the orchard and vegetable garden.

intended to delude the people—tricks, when seen through, never succeed well, in the long run. *Honesty* is the best *policy*.

I shall send some papers of turnip seed from the Patent Office— let Horace save it, somewhere, for winter turnips.

You had better not write me later than Thursday morning of this week. I may leave here, on Saturday evening & spend the Sabbath in New York. If any thing special, address me at the Astor House, New York, on Saturday. I shall receive it on Sunday, or Monday morning—according to my leaving here on Saturday or Sunday evening.

Love to you all.

Your aff father
E. Dickinson

You will receive some bags of books addressed to me. My books in boxes will go by way of Boston before long.

Edward Dickinson's final letter from Washington is addressed to his daughter Emily. He refers to none of the affairs of state with which his mind was filled. Such matters were discussed with Austin. But in writing to his daughter he appears to have assumed that family and church activities, Sue Gilbert's attack of fever, the weather, the date of his homecoming and his living accommodations for the following session would pretty well cover the topics in which she would be interested, preoccupied as she was with domestic duties. Although from time to time he gave her books, which may or may not have been those she would have chosen, an exchange of ideas was not the plane on which they met.

How mystified that man would have been, how nonplussed, could he have known that after a hundred years the only interest attaching to his political career would be because of thoughts which this daughter of his was even then jotting down on little scraps of paper!

> I stepped from plank to plank
> A slow and cautious way,
> The stars about my head I felt,
> About my feet the sea.
>
> I knew not but the next
> Would be my final inch—
> This gave me that precarious gait
> Some call experience.

[*Envelope missing*]

Ho. of Reps. U.S. July 26. 1854.
Wednesday

Dear daughter Emily,

Your letter of Sunday evening was rec^d last evening, & gave me great pleasure to hear that mother enjoyed her Monson trip so highly. I expected that it would be a great day for her—& am very happy that she went.

Also that the installation passed off so pleasantly, & that Mr Dwight appeared so much better than any body else. We hardly know how to appreciate him—as much as we are attached to him. I don't know any body that could now satisfy us but him. I see by the Spf^d Repub^n that the afternoon services in the Spf^d churches, commence at 3½—instead of 3—our time. I hope he may be long spared to do us good.

It seems, also, that you have had some rain. It must seem very refreshing. It is very dry here—tho' we have had slight showers—it is very hot, in the sun.

I am glad to hear that Susan is getting better. I hope she will be perfectly well, before I get home—where I expect to be next Monday night.

I hope Zebina & Harriet & our Hadley friends &c. are all well. It seems that there is nothing new in the town.

It is still quite healthy, here—no cholera, so far as I know—tho' every body complains of the oppressive weather.

I am very well—and should be glad to stay thro' the last week of the session, if it was possible—but it is entirely out of the question. I must be at home, the week before Commencement, to get my report ready for the Trustees.

Aunt Elisabeth has been with Bro. W^m & his wife, at a place near Newport. She wrote me a letter, a few days since, from there—saying that she was better.

I hope to see Mr Sweetser & Aunt Catherine on my way home—if I can—tho' it is not certain that I can stop—unless I spend the Sabbath there. Mr Eliot is well, & we continue to get along well together. I shall miss him very much when we separate. We like living at the National Hotel, to board. I hope I shall have a comfortable place, next winter, somewhere.

Love to all.

Your aff father
Edw. Dickinson

As Congress prepared to adjourn Mr. Dickinson made one last effort to insure competent administration of the national armories.

On July 31, 1854, he offered a resolution requesting the Secretary of War to communicate to Congress any information he might have about the qualifications of applicants for the office of superintendent. For once, in spite of objections, his resolution was carried and he was free to leave for home.

The letter from the Secretary, Jefferson Davis, was written on August 3 after Mr. Dickinson had left Washington. The Army Appropriations Act, including the Stanton amendment, was passed the same day. It was signed by President Pierce on August 5, and the armories at Harper's Ferry and Springfield were returned to civilian management.[8] Though this appeared to be a complete defeat for the committee minority, Mr. Dickinson had won his battle, for the moment at least, to keep incompetents from controlling the armories, for both of the civilian superintendents appointed were selected on merit. Neither of them had been in any way connected with the fight to restore civilian administrators.

Amherst College commencement was held on August 10, 1854. Mr. Dickinson presented the treasurer's report at the trustees' meeting on the seventh, the same meeting at which Edward Hitchcock resigned and the new president was elected.[9] The Reverend Dr. Humphrey was passed by in favor of the Reverend Dr. William Augustus Stearns of Cambridgeport, a graduate of Harvard, who became the fourth president of Amherst College.

Edward Hitchcock returned to teaching and to his geological surveys. On November 22 he delivered his valedictory. The following excerpt from his "private notes" is dated December 30, 1854:

> The change in my condition which I have long been desirous of has at length been accomplished & the circumstances have been as merciful as I could have hoped for. The character of my successor as a literary man & a preacher is such as I could wish. I do not expect indeed that he will take the same interest in scientific matters as I have done. . . . But I am cheered with the deep interest Dr Stearns seems to take in the religious affairs of the College. . . .

8. Within a few years this act was repealed. On August 6, 1861, officers of the Ordnance Department were again authorized to take over. See *A Collection of Ordnance Reports* (Washington, 1890), III (1860-1889), 572.

9. Compare Stanley King, *A History of the Endowment of Amherst College* (published by the College, 1950). "Edward Dickinson, Treasurer, 1835-1873," 35-65.

Less than a month after commencement an event befell which touched the life of Edward Dickinson and his family more than college presidents or college finances, more even than a national emergency. On September 6, 1854, General David Mack died at his home on Main Street. The Dickinson homestead, purchased by him in 1833, would now be on the market. The memory of the forced sale and his father's humiliating departure from Amherst still carried a sting for Edward Dickinson. Might there not now be a chance to erase the ignominy and reinstate "Esquire Fowler" in his rightful place in the annals of town and college?

But meanwhile a mid-term congressional election was in the offing. In spite of the fact that the Whigs had lost their hold, Mr. Dickinson's party loyalty was so strong that he consented to accept their nomination as candidate from the Tenth District for the Thirty-fourth Congress. At the November election he was defeated, however, by the Know Nothing candidate, Henry Morris of Springfield, who polled 7723 votes to Mr. Dickinson's 2757.

On the fourth of December Mr. Dickinson returned to Washington and Willard's Hotel, for the opening of the second session of the Thirty-third Congress. The events of this brief session need not detain us. It is enough to say that his attempts to get anything done met with little success. When he rose to speak he was frequently not permitted to gain the floor. His recommendations were ignored; his protests overruled; his good faith questioned. And yet, as the reader of his remarks on the floor of the House will observe he managed to accomplish a good deal for a man not only serving a first term, but one who belonged to a dying minority party which encountered the opposition of a determined majority at every step. If on the whole he seems to have had a pretty rough time of it, his difficulties may have been due less to his own inadequacies than to the waning strength of the Whigs. In any event, with the adjournment of the second session on March 3, 1855, Edward Dickinson's career in Congress came to an end.

CHAPTER XXIX

Political Aftermath

A FEW weeks after Mr. Dickinson returned to Amherst the following notice appeared in the *Express* (April 20, 1855):

Sale of Real Estate:—The elegant place where the late venerable Dea. Mack resided for upwards of twenty years, has been recently sold by his son, Samuel E. Mack, of Cincinnati, to the Hon. Edward Dickinson, whose father, Samuel F. Dickinson, formerly owned the place. Thus has the worthy son of an honored sire the pleasure of possessing the "Old Homestead." Here was born in 1790 the Hon. Chester Ashley, United States Senator from Arkansas, who died in Washington in 1848.[1]

Not long after the Dickinsons took possession in November Emily described their return to the "Old Homestead" in a now famous letter to Dr. and Mrs. J. G. Holland:

I cannot tell you how we moved. I had rather not remember. I believe my "effects" were brought in a bandbox, and the "deathless me," on foot, not many moments after. I took at the time a memorandum of my several senses, and also of my hat and coat, and my

1. In Appendix II is the warranty deed, signed by Samuel E. Mack on April 27, 1855, conveying the property to Edward Dickinson.

Senator Ashley could hardly have been born in the Dickinson homestead, which was not built until 1813. I am told by Gelston Hardy, grandson of Jeanie Ashley Bates Greenough, that the family of William Ashley of Pelham, father of Chester Ashley, was indeed living in Amherst temporarily when his son was born in 1791. So it may be that he was born in the wooden house on the same site where Samuel Fowler Dickinson lived before building the homestead. (See page 9, footnote 4.)

Edward Dickinson offered his house on Pleasant Street for sale (*Express*, November 23, 1855), and it was bought by the college. The next occupant was the Reverend Professor James G. Vose, who lived there until, in 1865, it was purchased by Charles S. Kenfield, who sold it three years later to Dr. Bigelow. (Compare page 63.)

best shoes—but it was lost in the *mêlée,* and I am out with lanterns, looking for myself.

Such wits as I reserved, are so badly shattered that repair is useless —and still I can't help laughing at my own catastrophe. I supposed we were going to make a "transit," as heavenly bodies did—but we came budget by budget, as our fellows do, till we fulfilled the pantomime contained in the word "moved." It is a kind of *gone-to-Kansas* feeling, and if I sat in a long wagon, with my family tied behind, I should suppose without doubt I was a party of emigrants!

They say that "home is where the heart is." I think it is where the *house* is, and the adjacent buildings.[2]

One advantage in returning to the homestead was the added space, without as well as within. For fifteen years the Dickinsons had been hemmed in pretty close by neighbors. Now there was ample room: on the south, across the road, the down-sloping meadow; on the east, the long garden reaching as far as Triangle Street. On the west, only Mr. Dickinson's small house stood between the homestead and the village center. Behind, on the north, the ground rose toward a grove of venerable oaks where, at the top of the hill, the broadside of Luke Sweetser's hospitable home faced in the Dickinsons' direction.

In July, 1855, Henry Morris of Springfield had been appointed judge of the Court of Common Pleas. He soon resigned as the newly elected representative to Congress from the Tenth District and the post was again open.

On October 2, 1855, the Whig State Convention was held in Worcester. J. Thomas Stevenson presided and Edward Dickinson was one of twenty-three vice presidents. This convention was chiefly noteworthy for the prominent Whigs who were "unable to attend," among them Rufus Choate, Robert C. Winthrop, ex-Governor John H. Clifford, and Emory Washburn, Governor of Massachusetts during the previous year. But although the party was moribund several vigorous speeches were made, among them one by the Honorable Otis P. Lord of Salem, speaker of the Massachusetts House of Representatives, of whom Rufus Choate said: "Otis Lord I think one of the very ablest men in this State."[3]

The attitude of the substantial Whigs of Massachusetts, their

2. *Letters,* 1894, 167; *Letters,* 1931, 163.
3. Parker, *Reminiscences of Rufus Choate,* 286.

die-hard loyalty even after it had become clear that the party had outlived its usefulness, their reluctance to switch their allegiance to any newfangled coalition such as the Republican party, all are exemplified in Mr. Lord's remarks. His friend Edward Dickinson was one of those "patriots and statesmen" who had been "swept from the public scene" in November, 1854. The Whigs may not have known it, but their party was disintegrating because of overcompromise. One who did realize that the country was "afflicted with compromise" was Charles Sumner. Most of the slurs in Mr. Lord's speech were directed against the great senator from Massachusetts, who had deserted the Whigs in order to aid in forming the Free Soil party as a protest against the Whigs' nomination for the Presidency in 1848 of General Zachary Taylor, a Louisiana slaveholder. After Mr. Sumner's defection, that cosmopolitan gentleman was branded by the Whigs as a dangerous radical. To many of the coalition of Free Soilers and Democrats who elected him to the Senate of the United States in April, 1851—a post held for twenty-three years until his death on March 11, 1874—he was the embodiment of the conscience of the American people, a prophet immune to political expediency. Abraham Lincoln once remarked that Sumner was his idea of a bishop.

The defense of Edward Dickinson as a symbol of his party had an added personal zest for Mr. Lord inasmuch as Henry Morris, the Know Nothing candidate who had defeated Mr. Dickinson, was Mr. Lord's friend and classmate. They had been running neck and neck ever since college days.[4]

4. Mr. Morris and Mr. Lord were graduated from Amherst College in 1832, and both received their M.A. from the same college three years later. Both studied law in the office of Mr. Morris' father, Judge Oliver B. Morris of Springfield, and both attended the Harvard Law School. Mr. Morris received his LL.B. in 1835, and was admitted to the bar in October of that year. Mr. Lord was admitted to the bar only two months later, but did not receive his degree until 1836. Mr. Lord practiced law in Ipswich (1835-1844) and in Salem (1844-1875), Mr. Morris in Springfield (1835-1888). Both were representatives in the State Legislature, Mr. Morris, 1846-1848; Mr. Lord, 1847-1849 and 1851-1855.

In 1854 when Mr. Lord was elected speaker of the Massachusetts House of Representatives, Mr. Morris was elected to Congress; but he did not take his seat, having been appointed judge of the Court of Common Pleas of Massachusetts in 1855. Mr. Lord was not far behind. He became judge of the Superior Court of Massachusetts, organized in 1859 to replace the Court of Common Pleas, remaining in that office until he was appointed associate justice of the Supreme Court of Massachusetts in 1875. There was one further parallel; both men received an honorary LL.D. from Amherst College in 1869.

Mr. Lord's remarks well express the feelings of loyal Whigs as their party was about to disappear—feelings shared to the full by Mr. Dickinson. This speech, delivered in a style described as "Websterian," has been called the funeral oration of the party. But it reads more like a repudiation of the Republicans even before their first national convention had adopted a platform.[5]

When called upon by the chairman, Mr. Lord began:

Mr. President,—This is a Whig meeting. (Laughter and applause) . . . I have been somewhat accustomed of late years to attending those meetings which have been called Whig, but until to-day since some fifteen years ago, in this very place, I have not before seen the *real* Whig spirit roused—that which has the ring of the true metal. Today we are Whig, and we are not anything else. (Laughter and applause) We have no outsiders to catch today; we have no baits to throw to any gudgeons. We stand to-day Whigs upon Whig principles, and we stand there or we fall. (Cheers and cries of "good—good.")

It does one good to see a regular old fashioned political meeting—one based upon some kind of politics other than to see who can get the most votes in a scrub race, (laughter) and to-day we have presented to us not only a platform such as we have all cordially united upon, and are ready to sustain, but we have standard-bearers to represent us in sustaining and carrying forward those principles such as are worthy of us and worthy of the Commonwealth.

To-day, Mr. President, after the ballot for Governor had taken place, as I saw my worthy and most respected friend [Samuel Walley] pass up the aisle and come upon this platform, I remembered that only one year ago such a fusion as nobody ever heard of, and such a fusion as nobody hereafter will ever hear of, had swept him, as it had other patriots and statesmen, from the public scene, and put untried, unknown men into their places, and I thought that the voice of such an assembly as this, if it could be tendered to me as it was to him, would ten thousand times compensate for all the mortification—if any body *could* be mortified, (loud laughter and applause) of a stab in the back in the dark. (Renewed applause)

No open foe in a fair field ever caused the Whigs of Massachusetts to quail before it. (Cheers) If they are beaten down it is in a bush fight or in the dark, or by a treacherous blow. The Whigs of Massachusetts, upon the principles which have made Massachusetts what she is, openly maintain themselves against the world. But a new era is dawning; a Republican party has sprung into existence; but I have not seen, with the exception of

5. *Proceedings of the Whig State Convention, Worcester, October 2, 1855* (Office of the *Boston Courier,* 1855).

The first Republican Convention in Massachusetts had been held in Worcester on September 7, 1854. See Henry Wilson, *History of the Rise and Fall of the Slave Power in America* (Boston, 1874), II, 414.

*Western entrance of the Hoosac Tunnel,
finished 1860.*

Western entrance of the Hoosac tunnel drawn by Otis P. Lord, 1854

(The construction of the Hoosac Tunnel was a major political issue
in 1854 when Mr. Lord was Speaker of the Massachusetts House of
Representatives. During the debates he amused himself making sketches
of this and that [*Emily Dickinson—a Revelation,* 24], the tunnel among
others. The above prediction that it would be finished in 1860 was
premature. As we shall see [Chapter XXXIII], its completion was still
a subject for debate in 1874 when Edward Dickinson returned to the
General Court.)

our late respected fellow citizen (laughter) who has been picked out from among us to see how many can be taken away,—with that one exception, among all those leaders I have not seen one, no, not one, that was not last year in the other fusion. Why, gentlemen, you remember that last year we said that the party which had been organized down cellar, or somewhere out of sight—that party which was called in Virginia "the dark lantern oligarchy"—were merely puppets, the wires to which were pulled by a magician, who meant to warm a cushion for himself in the United States Senate—but our good friends said to [us], "O, you are mistaken; let us all go into that party and manage it." And they went in one after another in order to manage the Know-Nothings, and keep Wilson out of the Senate.[6] (Laughter)

Well, this year these same good-natured friends say—"This fusion is a great thing after all; and now, which is best," say they, solemnly, "that good men, good Whigs, should take hold and get the management of that movement, or shall we let other men get the management?" No, it is best for the Whigs to go into it; and so they take hold of it in order to get the management. They get the management, and then they nominate four out of the six candidates from the old Know-Nothing or American Party, which they last year meant to manage.

Who is at the head of this fusion movement? Why, no less a personage— I don't mean to call names, and there is nobody here at whom I can nod to indicate to whom I allude—but it is just that man who said he had been a member of every political party in Massachusetts, and had left every political party, and that he meant to leave every political party just as soon as they ceased to conform to his principles; and when you find out what his principles are, you will know when he will leave you. (Laughter and applause)

I said, Mr. President, I did not mean to make a speech—I do not. But I want to congratulate myself and this great assembly upon the cheering prospects before us—the prospect that we are to have a party that has to search for candidates instead of having a party made merely for the purpose of advancing particular men. (Cheers) And that I hold to be the great triumph, this hour of the Whig party.

I say this is the great matter on which we may congratulate ourselves. They may call us a small party, but if we are small, we are somewhat energetic; there is a little strength left somewhere. I thought once or twice,

6. On June 1, 1854, Edward Everett resigned from the U.S. Senate. Two days later Julius Rockwell was appointed by Governor Emory Washburn to serve until the next session of the General Court of Massachusetts convened on January 3, 1855. On January 23 Henry Wilson was elected by a coalition of Free Soilers, Know Nothings and Democrats in the House, and was confirmed by the Senate on January 31, taking his seat in the Senate of the United States on February 10, 1855. (*Journal of the* [Massachusetts] *House* [1855], 187 and 286; *The Congressional Globe*, 33 Cong., 2 Sess., 657; *Biographical Directory of the American Congress, 1774-1927* [Government Printing Office, 1950], 243.)

today, these rafters must have been pretty well secured. (Applause) But this party is not a small party in Massachusetts. I do not care what extraneous influence may call one man and another away to-day; the great heart of Massachusetts is Whig to the core. (Loud cheers) You cannot cheat Massachusetts three times with the same delusion; you may make a coalition go twice, you may make secret political machinery work once, possibly, and fusion may work once; but I say you cannot cheat the people of Massachusetts three times in the same way. They are an honest people—they are a confiding people, but they are intelligent enough to see to it that they are not cheated three times in the same manner. I take it that if the people of Massachusetts are what I believe them to be, we shall have a change this fall, and the Whig principles of Massachusetts will gain a triumph, and the Whig men of Massachusetts will again be entrusted with the rule of this Commonwealth. . . .

The remainder of Mr. Lord's speech had to do with the nefarious acts of the previous legislature, elected on a fusion ticket, the members of which were "wholly new and wholly unacquainted with the subjects with which they were dealing." In closing, he expressed renewed confidence that the Whigs would be reinstated in the next election.

Following Mr. Lord's speech and in response to ever-increasing pressure, Edward Dickinson once again permitted himself to be nominated for Congress, this time to fill the unexpired term of Judge Morris, who had resigned because of his appointment to the Court of Common Pleas. On the twenty-fourth of October Mr. Dickinson was unanimously chosen as their candidate by the Whigs of the Tenth District.

In the _Express_ of November 2, 1855, an editorial entitled "The Tenth Congressional District," reads as follows:

Let no one stay away from the polls on Tuesday next, thinking that it is only an election for State officers, and is therefore unimportant. In this Congressional District a member of congress is to be elected, and it _is important_ that the true Anti-Nebraska feeling of the District be represented in the person chosen. Whether a few State officers shall hold their places another year, is of little consequence in comparison.

By way of introduction to a letter from Mr. Dickinson which appeared in the next column the editor wrote:

On the "great question" of public policy which now agitates the country, no member of the last House of Representatives can show a fairer and

more consistent record, and one more faithfully reflecting the sentiments
of his constituents and the almost unanimous feeling of the North, than
Hon. Mr. Dickinson, and we regret, very much regret, the existence of
such a state of things as will prevent his receiving the vote of all who
agree with him in sentiment.

Mr. Dickinson's letter of acceptance follows:

Amherst, Oct. 29, 1855.

A. L. Soule, Esq., Sec'y, &c.

DEAR SIR:—I have received your letter announcing that "at a
Convention of the Whigs of the Tenth Congressional District, held
in Springfield on the 24th inst., I was unanimously nominated as a
Candidate for Representative in Congress, and that the Convention,
feeling that to have nominated me for re-election was a sufficient
declaration of their principles, passed no resolutions."
I am duly sensible of this renewed expression of confidence, and
appreciate it the more highly from the fact that no pledge is
required for the future, beyond what is furnished by past action.
My inclination would lead me to avoid the publicity of being a
candidate for office, at a time when friends who entertain the same
sentiments in relation to the "great question" of public policy which
agitates the country, are divided *merely* by the consideration of
names; and differ, mainly, as to the most practicable mode of ac-
complishing the same purpose.
I regret this unfortunate, and in my judgment unnecessary difference—and am in no way responsible for it.
My opinions, as entertained and acted upon in the last Congress,
are on record—are well known to the people of the District,—and
remain unchanged; and as the Convention have so cordially tendered me the nomination, I do not feel at liberty to decline, but
shall accept it, and leave myself in the hands of the electors.
Yours truly,
EDWARD DICKINSON.

After reading this communication from Edward Dickinson one
marvels the more at his daughter's closeness of style.
On Tuesday, November 6, as anticipated, the Know Nothing
candidate, an untried man, Dr. Calvin C. Chaffee of Springfield,
was elected. Among four candidates Edward Dickinson ran fourth.
So feeble had the Whig party of Massachusetts become that none of

their nine members in the Thirty-third Congress was returned to the Thirty-fourth. (Compare page 323.)

After the downfall of his party Edward Dickinson held no further public office for nearly twenty years. Although he had long since made up his mind that he had had enough of politics, he was still proposed for this or that office. His wisdom was sought not only in town and county, but throughout the state. When, shortly before the outbreak of the Civil War men of ability were desperately needed, Mr. Dickinson was urged to run for the office of Lieutenant-Governor of Massachusetts on the Constitutional Unionist ticket. Echoes of Whig loyalty can be traced in the phrasing of his refusal. His letter declining the nomination "from purely personal considerations" concludes with these words:

"Let us in this exigency repudiate political vagaries and fancies; let us denounce, as subversive of all constitutional guarantees, if we expect to reconstruct or restore the Union, the heretical dogma that immediate and universal emancipation of slaves should be proclaimed by the government, as the means of putting an end to the war; and the rather to hope and pray that, in the good providence of God, emancipation may be one of the blessed results of the war. Let us sustain the national administration in its policy, as avowed, with all our heart and might; let us unitedly gird ourselves for the terrible contest in which we are engaged, and resolve to 'fight on and fight ever' *under the constitution,* 'until the sway of the constitution and the laws shall be restored to all portions of our country.' "[7]

The final packet of letters from Edward Dickinson to his son were written many years later. The break provides an opportunity to take one more look at the three generations of country lawyers of whom Austin was the last. It was during these same years that the pattern of the family took shape. Against the background of Dickinson "difference" the life of Emily's brother, whose tastes were her tastes and whose suffering she shared, can be seen in clear perspective. But before discussing this difference, a few more letters from the prewar years give further evidence of the warmth and generosity of her nature, so apparent in the letters to her family.

7. *Springfield Republican,* October 17, 1861.

CHAPTER XXX

Early Friendships

WHEN Mr. Dickinson and Austin were away from home "Cousin John" Graves often stayed with Mrs. Dickinson and her daughters. Before he graduated he had become so much a part of the family that they called him "John," an almost unheard-of liberty to take with a young man. From a group of letters to him, hitherto unpublished, I have selected two. Although the first cannot be dated with accuracy, his daughter Louise thinks it was written in "late summer, 1854," before his return to college for his senior year.[1] Full of tender concern for the happiness of her friends, Emily seems to be troubled about a misunderstanding between John and his friend Henry Vaughan Emmons.

[*To Mr. John L. Graves, Present*]

Tuesday Evening [late summer, 1854]

Dear John,

Are you very happy? Why did'nt you tell me so before you went away? And why too, did'nt I ask you that pleasant evening long, when we sat and talked together?

I have wanted to ask you many times, and I thought you would tell me, but someone would come in, and something else would happen and put me all to flight, but tonight, John, so still is it, and the moon so mild, I'm sure that you would tell me, were you sitting

1. John Graves was graduated with honors on August 10, 1855. See *Amherst Graduates' Quarterly*, IV (April, 1915), 227-228. For permission to print the letters to Mr. Graves I am indebted to his daughter, Louise B. Graves.

here. You know what I mean, dont you, and if you are so happy, I kneel and thank God for it, before I go up to sleep.

Then you and your former College friend are reconciled again— he told me all about it, and tears of happiness came shining in my eyes. Forgiving one another as Jesus—us.

I have hoped for this very often, John, when you were fast asleep, and my eyes will shut much sooner, now all is peace. I loved to have you both my friends, and friends to one another, and it grieved me very often that you were enemies—now all is safe.

It is lonely without you John—we miss you very much, and I'm thinking we'll miss you more when a year from now comes, and the crickets sing.

Quite sad it is when friends go, and sad when all are gone, to sit by pensive window, and recollect them, but I would not forget them. Please not forget us John, in your long vacation. We'll often think of you, and wish that we could see you. Mary is with us yet. Eliza went yesterday morning. I miss her thoughtful eyes, and did not Mary's merry ones linger with us still, the day would be too long, but Mary strokes the sunshine and coaxes it along, and drives the shadows home. Much like a "bumblie" bee she seems, among more antique insects! She wants me to give you her compliments, and say to you beside, that she thanks you sincerely for the "social capacity,["] which she forgot to do, there were so many in. Good night, and gentle dreams, John—my pen is very bad. I write not any more. Vinnie sends her love. Mine if you will to Hattie, and for your mother too. Had you been here tonight, John, I should have talked with you—you are not, and I write. I "wish you a merry Christmas," and a vacation as good as summer days are long—

　　　　　　　　　　　　　　　　Affy, Emilie—

A little note, folded and addressed on the back to "Cousin John," has the same theme:

> Dear John—
> Be happy—
> Emily—
> Early Monday morning—

Miss Graves says that whenever her father spoke of Emily Dickinson there was about him a kind of glow. She has described his attitude toward his cousin Emily as follows: "Poetical feeling, which he had in large measure, was rather scornfully repressed, and even his devotion to his cousin 'Emily Dick's' memory failed to break through that reserve. When the first series of her poems appeared, seven editions came from the press before one copy showed itself upon his library table! In spite of this apparent lack of interest in her poetry, a sort of *aura* hovered over him at the mere mention of her name. But when questioned for a detailed description he would say, after an instant's searching, tantalizing pause, 'unlike anyone else—a grace, a charm,' and his eyes would kindle and breathing quicken as when handling a piece of rare old Chinese porcelain, or a precious stone."[2]

Several months after his graduation in 1855, John Graves received from his cousin Emily the following letter. A notation in pencil, "April, 1856," places it a few weeks before the marriage of Austin and Sue Gilbert when thoughts of the wedding were filling all their hearts with joyous anticipation. To Emily "dear Sue," soon to become her precious sister, was at this time a consecrated being.

[April, 1856]

It is Sunday—now, John, and all have gone to church—the wagons have done passing, and I have come out in the new grass to listen to the anthems.

Three or four Hens have followed me, and we sit side by side—and while they crow and whisper, I'll tell you what I see today, and what I would that you saw. You remember the crumbling wall that divides us from Mr Sweetser, and the crumbling elms and ever-

2. Other acquaintances were similarly affected. A note from venerable Luke Sweetser is expressed in strange words for a dignified old Puritan. He had been in the habit of mailing letters for Emily in later years.

> Miss Emilie
> You dont know [how] much I have missed these opportunities of service of late.
> I shall not believe you are displeased with me until you tell me so.
> Yours
> L. Sweetser

After Mr. Sweetser's death on July 27, 1882, at the age of eighty-two, octogenarian "Cousin George" took his place as intermediary.

> Cousin Emily will please forgive me. I have made a blemish on *two* of her envelopes, and have substituted two of mine, which I am sorry to say, are not quite so nice. If they will do, I shall be glad.
> Cousin G.

Even stiff old George Montague realized that he was in the presence of something mysterious and different.

> To Cousin Emily
> Your very *choice* and excellent gift I duly received some days ago, and for the present, "thank you,"—a very cheap compensation.
> If I am so fortunate hereafter as to find anything either rare, beautiful or good shall hope to remember you.
> Cousin G. Montague

Drafts of poems in the latest script were written on the back of these notes.

greens, and *other* crumbling things that spring, and fade, and cast their bloom, within a simple twelvemonth—well, *they* are *here,* and skies on me fairer far than Italy, in blue eye look down—up—see!—away—a league from here, on the way to Heaven! And here are Robins, just got home, and giddy Crows, and Jays—and will you trust me—as I live, here's a *bumble-bee*—not such as *summer* brings, John—earnest, manly bees, but a kind of a Cockney, dressed in jaunty clothes. Much that is *gay*—have I to show, if you were with me, John, upon this April grass—then there are *sudden* features—here and there, *wings* half gone to dust, that fluttered so, last year—a mouldering plume, an empty house, in which a bird resided. Where last year's flies, their errand ran, and last year's *crickets fell!* We, too, are flying—fading, John—and the song "here lies," soon upon lips that love us now—will have hummed and ended.

To live, and die, and mount again on triumphant body, and *next* time, try the upper air, is no schoolboy's theme! It is a jolly thought to think that we can be eternal, when air and earth are *full* of lives that are gone, and done—and a conceited thing indeed, this promised Resurrection! *Congratulate* me, John—Lad—and "here's a health to *you*"—that we have each a *pair* of lives, and need not chary be, of the one "that *now is.*" Ha—ha—if any can afford, 'tis *us* a roundelay!

Thank you for your letter, John. Glad I was, to get it, and gladder had I got them *both,* and glad indeed to see—if in your heart, *another* lies, bound one day to me. Mid your momentous cares, pleasant to know that "Lang Syne" has its own place—that nook and cranny still retain their accustomed guest. And when busier cares, and dustier days, and cobwebs, less unfrequent, shut what *was* away, still, as a ballad hummed, and lost, remember early friend, and drop a tear, if a *troubadour* that strain may chance to sing.

I am glad you have a school to teach—and happy that it is pleasant—amused at the *clerical civility* of your new friends, and shall feel, I know, delight and pride, always, when you succeed. I play the old, odd tunes yet, which used to flit about your head after honest hours—and wake dear Sue, and madden me, with their grief and fun. How far from us, that spring seems, and those triumphant days! Our April got to Heaven *first.* Grant we may meet her there, at the "right hand of the Father." Remember, tho' you rove—John—and those who do *not* ramble will remember you. Susie's, and Mattie's compliments, and Vinnie's just here, and write again if you will.

For three other letters written a year or two later to another friend I am indebted to Professor Davidson of Indiana University.[3]

3. Frank Davidson, "Some Emily Dickinson Letters," *The Indiana Quarterly for Bookmen,* I (October, 1945), 113-118.

The Reverend Joseph Haven, professor of moral philosophy and metaphysics, left Amherst in the early fall of 1858 to become professor of systematic theology in the Chicago Theological Seminary. In summing up his Amherst career President Hitchcock predicted that his "character as a teacher, a preacher and an author here, during eight years, was a sure precursor of his eminent success at the head of a Theological Seminary at the West."[4] For Dr. Haven Emily had high regard and for Mrs. Haven, the daughter of Professor Ralph Emerson of Andover, real affection. The Havens had four sons and six daughters.

The first letter, folded and addressed on the back, was written during the spring of 1858 before the Havens left Amherst; the second, after they had reached Chicago; and the third early in 1859. The envelopes of those sent to Chicago are missing.

[*To Mrs Haven, Present*]

Dear Mrs Haven—

Have you, or has Mr Haven, in his Library, either "Klosterheim," or the "Confessions of an Opium Eater," by De'Quincey? I have sent to Northampton, but cannot get them there; and they are missing just now, from the College Library. I thank you very much, should you have them, if you will please lend them to me, for tho' the hours are very full, I think that I might snatch here and there a moment, if I had the books.

I hope you are happy this summer day, tho' I know you are lonely. I should love to pass an hour with you, and the little girls, could I leave home, or mother. I do not go out at all, lest father will come and miss me, or miss some little act, which I might forget, should I run away. Mother is much as usual. I know not what to hope of her. Please remember Vinnie and I, for we are perplexed often.

　　　　　　　　　　　　　　　　Affy.
　　　　　　　　　　　　　　　　Emilie—

Good night, dear Mrs Haven! I am glad I did not know you better, since it would then have grieved me more that you went away.

Some summer afternoon, I thought we might be acquainted, but summer afternoons to me have had so many wings, and meanwhile, you have flown!

Thank you for recollecting me in the sweet moss, which with your

4. Hitchcock, *Reminiscences*, 39-40; Tyler, 1873, 435.

memory, I have lain in a little box, unto the Resurrection. I hoped to see your face again—hoped to see Mr. Haven, and the little girls.

Though I met you little, I shall miss you all— Your going will redden the maple, and fringe the Gentian sooner, in the soft fields.

Permit us to keep you in our hearts, although you seem to be outward eye, to be travelling from us! That is the sweet prerogative of the left behind.

I know you will come again—if not today, *tomorrow*—if not tomorrow as we count, after the little interval we pass in lifetime here. Then we wont say "Goodbye," since immortality makes the phrase quite obsolete. Good night is long eno',

I bid it, smiling!

Emilie—

Sabbath Eve

Dear Mrs Haven.

Your remembrance surprises me. I hardly feel entitled to it. A most sweet surprise, which can hardly be affirmed of all our surprises. I grieve that I cannot claim it in a larger degree. Perhaps tho', sweeter as it is—*unmerited* remembrance. "Grace," the saints would call it, careless girls like me cannot testify. Thank you for this, and your warm note.

We have hardly recovered laughing from Mr Haven's jolly one. I insist to this day, that I have received internal injuries. Could Mr H. be responsible for an early grave? The Coat is still in the dark, but the mirth to which it has given rise, will gleam when coats and rascals have passed into tradition.

The letters of suspected gentlemen form quite a valuable addition to our family library, and father pursues the search with a mixture of fun and perseverance, which is quite diabolical! I will give you the earliest intelligence of the arrest of our friend, who for the mirth he has afforded, surely merits *triumph,* more than transportation. Father is in New York, just now, and Vinnie in Boston, while mother and I, for greater celebrity, are remaining at home.

My mother's only sister has had an invalid winter, and Vinnie has gone to enliven the house, and make the days shorter to my sick aunt.[5] I would like more sisters, that the taking out of one might not leave such stillness. Vinnie has been all, so long, I feel the oddest fright at parting with her for an hour, lest a storm arise, and I go unsheltered.

She talked of you before she went, often said she missed you, would add a couplet of her own, were she but at home. I hope you are well as I write, and that the far city seems to you like home. I

5. Mrs. Loring Norcross died April 17, 1860.

do not know your successors. Father has called upon Mr S[eelye] but I am waiting for Vinnie to help me do my courtesies. Mr S. preached in our church last Sabbath, upon "predestination," but I do not respect "doctrines," and did not listen to him, so I can neither praise, nor blame. Your house has much of pathos to those that pass who loved you. I miss the geranium at the window, and the hand that tended the geranium. I shall miss the clustering frocks at the door, bye and bye when summer comes, unless myself in a *new* frock, am too far to see.

How short, dear Mrs. Haven! A darting fear, a pomp, a tear, a waking on a morn to find that what one waked for, inhales the different dawn. Receive much love from

Emilie—

In the first letter to Mrs. Haven Emily spoke of her perplexity. During her late twenties she often referred to it. She even tried to define the feeling. Part of it was certainly a sense of "difference," expressed in a number of ways. "I am so far from land," she wrote to one friend, and to another: "I am pleasantly located in the deep sea." Mystified she was, but "Baffled for just a day or two," she said, "Embarrassed, not afraid." A poem in the handwriting of the late 1850's has the same theme:

> Once more my now bewildered dove
> Bestirs her puzzled wings;
> Once more her mistress on the deep
> Her troubled question flings;
>
> Thrice to the floating casement
> The Patriarch's bird returned—
> Courage, my brave Columba,
> There may yet be land!

But each new perplexity seemed only to heighten the sense of wonder leading always to new vision, to deeper insight. "Is not an absent friend as mysterious as a bulb in the ground," she asked, "and is not a bulb the most captivating floral form? Must it not have enthralled the Bible, if we may infer from its selection? 'The lily of the field!' " To that germinal thought she often returned, as in the poem:

> Through the dark sod as education
> The lily passes sure,
> Feels her white foot no trepidation
> Her faith no fear. . . .

In the high Sierra there is a fragile plant known as the avalanche lily. Its nodding blossom is easily broken. And yet, as winter nears its end, such is the vitality within the bulb that while still buried beneath the snow the stem drives through the tight-packed drifts straight up to the light. No less hard-packed was the icecap of New England "terrible reserve"; no less miraculous Emily Dickinson's strength to push through to upper air.

CHAPTER XXXI

Dickinson "Difference"

AT THE AGE of twenty-two Emily Dickinson inquired of her brother, "What makes a few of us so different from others?"—a question she says she often asks herself.[1]

Austin Dickinson wrote a series of biographical sketches of prominent members of the parish of the First Church, and summed up his father's life in one inclusive paragraph:[2]

> Edward Dickinson, proud of being of Amherst soil, of the sixth generation born within sound of the old meeting-house bell, all earnest, God-fearing men, doing their part in their day toward the evolution of the Amherst we live in; in the front from earliest manhood, prompt with tongue, pen, time, money, for anything promising its advancement, leading every forward movement, moral or material, in parish and town; holding many positions of trust and responsibility, never doubted, the soul of integrity and honor, fearless for the right, shirking no duty, and dying at his post as representative of his district in the Massachusetts Legislature where, in his seventy-second year, he had gone to help in shaping the legislation proposed affecting the interests of the Central Railroad.

With characteristic pride of family, on page 63 of the same publication Austin described his grandfather:

> Samuel Fowler Dickinson; familiarly called Esq. Fowler; who stood in the forefront in the Amherst of his generation; a fine scholar; a lawyer of distinction and wide practice; a man of rare public spirit, the highest moral purpose, unflagging zeal; the leader in every local enterprise; holding many offices of trust, a dozen years and more a member of the Massachusetts Legislature, in both houses; of the most earnest and active religious faith and life, a deacon at twenty and for forty years thereafter, one of the

1. See letter of April 21, 1853.
2. Dickinson, "Representative men," 58. See also *Amherst Record*, October 11, 1871.

leading founders of the college, sacrificing for it his property, time and professional opportunities, in the idea of getting the Gospel sooner to the ends of the earth.[3]

The "difference" appears less marked in Austin's evaluation of his forebears than in his way of expressing himself. A vigorous use of English was characteristic of the family, including Lavinia, whose witty if caustic remarks about her acquaintances and their pursuits were widely appreciated.

The three generations of lawyers had many traits in common, among them a sense of civic responsibility. For them all the will to public service was a compelling drive. For Samuel Fowler Dickinson it had been belief in education, a faith so fanatical that it led to his ruin; for Edward, belief in railroads and their role in the development of the country, a zeal too great for his strength, one indeed which at times made him seem almost as visionary as his father. It was while pleading their cause in the legislature that he was felled by a stroke of apoplexy. Each of these men embodied the enthusiasm of his time. In a letter to his son (February 6, 1852) Edward Dickinson himself evaluated their services:

The two great eras in the history of Amherst, are
1. The founding of the College.
2. The building of the rail road.

Austin had his grandfather's devotion to the college; and he managed its financial affairs with his father's acumen. He carried on their law practice, too, and the promotion of undertakings for community betterment. But something over and above their interests made those who were Dickinson-born "all unlike most everyone," as Emily said.

In pursuing their respective enthusiasms the three men had one outstanding characteristic—an emotional vigor, a creative glowing quality which transformed effort and hard work into a kind of self-dedication which attained results of lasting value. Before it disappeared with the extinction of the family, this trait had culminated not in the menfolk but in the dutiful daughter, whose life insofar as those closest to her could see was almost entirely taken up with the smooth running of her father's household.

3. When Austin cut a street across his "meadow" he named it "Fowler Place," now an extension of Spring Street.

During the 1850's another element was added to accentuate the Dickinson "difference." On July 1, 1856, William Austin Dickinson and Susan Huntington Gilbert—"both of Amherst" according to the *Express*—were married in Geneva, New York. The ceremony was performed by the Reverend Dr. Haven of Amherst College at the home of Mrs. William Van Vranken, the bride's aunt. After the young people returned to Amherst, to live in the new house just west of the homestead, the pattern of the family took final shape.

As he looked about him Edward Dickinson could feel justified in indulging a sense of satisfaction. He had retrieved the family fortunes. In the community his place was secure, not to say honored, while beyond the county the Dickinson name was known in the wider circles of state and nation. His wife and daughters were settled in the homestead, built by his father with an eye to future generations, and Austin was established next door. There was a feeling of permanence in his status, not to say an expectation of perpetuity, for by Austin's marriage the succession was assured. Whether the girls ever married was beside the point. It was not family traits which must be perpetuated so much as the Dickinson name. Austin was well aware of this requirement. He was troubled when four years passed and no child was born. Then came a son; and his name was Edward Dickinson. But "Ned" was a feeble child. This gave his grandfather grave concern, his father even more. Both were looking forward to the continuation of the dynasty, unaware as they were of the illness and deaths which were to put an end to the line of succession.

Nor had Austin foreseen another deep shadow: a lack of mutual understanding with his wife, of which his mutilation of Emily's letters is such a pitiful reminder. Though the pattern of the family had indeed taken final shape, it was not the shape Austin had expected. Without further elaboration at this point it may be enough to say that it was due to conflicting aims and fundamentally different ideals. The estrangement between Austin and Sue which became apparent not long after their marriage widened with the years. As their son, born in 1861, and their daughter, born in 1866, grew toward maturity, Austin was to find himself more and more of a stranger beneath his own roof.

Throughout the years Edward Dickinson had been devoting himself to his law practice, his insurance business (he was agent for the Aetna and the Hampshire Mutual Insurance Companies among others), and to community affairs, in all of which he was assisted by his son. His experience in national politics at an end, his activities, in addition to personal responsibilities and care of the college finances, had been focusing more and more on matters of importance to the town. He stood behind any enterprise which would redound to its advantage, any that is which he considered sound, for he was not given to flights of fancy.

The reader may wonder whether the family solidarity had not been weakened by Austin's marriage. On the contrary, it had been strengthened, as a backward glance at his career makes plain.

After graduating from college in 1850, Austin had been given his head and for a while, it will be recalled, he taught school. But it did not take him long to find out that he did not want to spend his life in a classroom. By July, 1852, teaching had for him served its purpose and he entered the Harvard Law School. Once that plunge had been taken, his life conformed to the plan his father had laid down. As soon as he received his law degree and had been admitted to the bar, he returned to Amherst to become his father's deputy in the management of legal matters for town and college as well as the affairs of the family and numerous dependent relatives. From then on Austin did not deviate from the plan. When necessary Edward Dickinson would "insist" that he do thus and so, even until he died, when Austin was more than forty years of age. Traces of command can be detected in his last letters to his son. Austin did make one effort to swing out of the orbit. In the winter of 1854-1855 he spent a month in Chicago. He even thought seriously of settling in the West. His father thought better not. He would make him his law partner.[4] He would build him a house near by and the family would be kept intact. So, after his marriage in 1856, Austin moved into the house which his father had built for him next door and there, twenty-one years after his father's death, he died. Such in brief was the career of the last of the three generations of Dickinson lawyers.

Although Austin was his father's dutiful understudy in practical affairs, his outlook was fundamentally different. As with his sister

4. *Express*, November 9, 1855.

Emily, his "real life" was elsewhere. There was in him an artistic quality, a sensitiveness to beauty, of which his father was only intermittently aware. It found expression not only in collecting works of art, paintings in particular, but more especially in his love of nature, a domain in which he lived life to the full.

Their handling of the treasurer's office illustrates the contrasting talents of the two men. Austin had for years assisted his father in fulfilling the duties of that post, which included not only the management of college finances, to which both gave minute attention, but also oversight of the buildings and grounds. Austin supervised the construction of new buildings, the remodeling of old ones, and the upkeep of the college plant. He took part, too, in making plans for future expansion. But when, in 1873, he assumed full responsibility for the office, he found more leeway for the use of his own special gift, that of making things grow. He devoted a great deal of time to beautifying the grounds—cherishing the ancient trees, replacing them with young ones when necessary, and planting others to fit into an over-all plan. Amherst still owes much of its charm to the expert arrangement of the multitudes of shrubs and trees he planted. His greatest pleasure was to drive in his buggy into the surrounding hills, seeking out wild saplings to transplant to congenial places on the campus where they would find similar conditions of soil and exposure. One of my earliest memories is sitting between my young mother and stern, elderly Mr. Dickinson as he drove his high-stepping horse through the wood roads of Leverett in search of a small hemlock for a particular spot.

The embellishment of town and college as well as of his own grounds was not only Austin Dickinson's recreation, lifting him above exhausting routine; it was also a balance wheel which gave him the poise needed for coping with his domestic tribulation. He was fortunate to have lived in a region which gave scope to a truly creative love of beauty. His father's interest in growing things, on the other hand, had been largely confined to improving the quality of their yield. In the last letter before his death Edward Dickinson tells his son about the scions he intends to purchase with a view to improving the flavor of his pears.

Edward Dickinson's refusal to allow his children to leave home has been much criticized. In fairness it should be said, however, that insofar as Emily was concerned, staying at home was not without its advantages. Her father's feeling of responsibility for them all enabled her to run to cover when her work was done. He had a strong arm good to lean on; and after he was gone Austin was there to take his place. Both her father and her brother respected her wishes. They never forced her to do anything against her will—their way perhaps of acknowledging her "difference." In plain English such as her father liked, this protectiveness in the Dickinson male relieved her of the necessity of meeting the world. She could "flee" to her "mind" without being forced to spend unrewarding hours in the company of persons with whom she had nothing in common. Vinnie was there too, of course, to ward off intruders and in general to take the brunt. Thus shielded, Emily could withdraw without explanation or apology, in the certainty that she was safe, that her daily needs would be supplied and that she could without obloquy follow wherever her thoughts might beckon. In a way, her very retreat was part of the "difference." For it should be repeated that she made no decision to retire from the society of her neighbors. It was not rejection of the commonplace and refusal to squander time so much as eagerness for a chance to read, to meditate and to write which drew her into seclusion. That in itself was reason enough for her inch-by-inch withdrawal, quite apart from any hypothetical heartbreak.

This simple explanation of Emily Dickinson's behavior did not, and does not, satisfy most people. Even Colonel Higginson, as he wrote her in May, 1868, found it hard to understand how she could live so alone, for solitude was not his natural state. At that time he dismissed the subject by observing merely that "it isolates one anywhere to think beyond a certain point." But when two years later he went to Amherst and asked her point-blank whether she never felt the want of employment—for she appeared to have no particular occupation—she gave this answer: " 'I never thought of conceiving that I could ever have the slightest approach to such a want in all future time,' and added, 'I feel that I have not expressed myself strongly enough.' "[5] The fact is that she never had enough time. Keats put this sense of pressure into a mighty sonnet—

5. *Letters*, 1894, 314; *Letters*, 1931, 286.

> When I have fears that I may cease to be
> Before my pen has glean'd my teeming brain . . .

—the terror that haunts the creative thinker lest there may not be time before the final curtain falls in which to put down on paper the thoughts pounding within him.

During the years following Austin's marriage when the various parts of the picture were falling into place, what was happening to his mother and sisters? How did they fit into the slow-hardening design? To change the figure: if the girls had ever been tempted to fly out of the magnetic field that danger was pretty well past. Both would now stay put where their father wanted them to be. He need have no further uneasiness on that score. The womenfolk were settling down, each in her own groove. Mrs. Dickinson was afflicted with increasingly poor health, so that the housework fell more and more heavily on her daughters. With the conduct of their father's house in accordance with his wishes their time had long been occupied. But the homestead was large and the housework so arduous that it was becoming clear that they must have help. Sometime during the early sixties an Irish "housegirl" named Margaret was engaged.[6] Tradition has not preserved her personal characteristics, nor is it known of what help she proved to be. But among my mother's notes is Lavinia's description of her appearance in her go-to-meeting best. This Margaret "had in nine years only one Sunday dress, a bright scarlet merino, which she wore to church summer and winter with a Bay State shawl, and a 'Florence' bonnet trimmed with a medium shade of green ribbon."

By the time Emily reached the age of thirty, in December, 1860, the pattern of the family had crystallized. But while contributing to the maintenance of a solid front, each component part remained distinct and independent. Vinnie said that they all lived like friendly and absolute monarchs, each in his own domain. She was not referring to activities alone. These are her words: "Father was the only one to say 'damn.' Someone in every family ought to say damn of course. As for Emily, she was not withdrawn or exclusive really. She was always watching for the rewarding person to come, but she

6. Referred to by Mr. Bowles as "your colossus," this Margaret O'Brien should not be confused with Margaret Maher, the "Maggie" of the seventies, eighties. and nineties. *Letters*, 1931, 149.

was a very busy person herself. She had to think—she was the only one of us who had that to do. Father believed; and mother loved; and Austin had Amherst; and I had the family to keep track of."

As in a forest, trees of different species maturing through the decades side by side from adjacent saplings expand into massive trunks, touching one another here and there, rubbing each other's bark off in spots but continuing in essence unchanged, so, as their roots intertwined and their daily activities became more and more dependent one upon another, the inner lives of this family remained inviolate while their thoughts roved farther and farther afield. As the world of Edward Dickinson contracted, two of his children, at least, escaped into expanding horizons of which for him there was no outward or visible sign.

PART FIVE

1860-1865

CHAPTER XXXII

Away from Home

1

BEFORE turning to a later chapter in the life of the Dickinson family we should stop long enough to weigh the evidence which the camphorwood chest provides about a climax in Emily Dickinson's emotional life. The evidence relates to a period about which very little is known. But all that is known points to a crisis in the early 1860's. The inner turmoil which beset her throughout life was intensified at that time and it resulted in serious trouble with her eyes.

In trying to understand some of the forces with which she was grappling it may help to enumerate a series of events, each of which in its own way drove another "gimlet in the nerve."

In the winter of 1859-1860 Vinnie was away. She had gone to Boston to be with her aunt, Mrs. Loring Norcross, who was seriously ill with consumption. Emily felt bereft. On April 17, 1860, without warning, Mrs. Norcross died. The letter Emily wrote to her sister follows the text of *Letters,* 1931, 217-218:

[April, 1860]

Vinnie,—I can't believe it, when your letters come, saying what Aunt Lavinia said "just before she died." Blessed Aunt Lavinia now; all the world goes out, and I see nothing but her room, and angels bearing her into those great countries in the blue sky of which we don't know anything.

Then I sob and cry till I can hardly see my way 'round the house again; and then sit still and wonder if she sees us now, if she sees *me,* who said that she "loved Emily." Oh! Vinnie, it is dark and strange to think of summer afterward! How she loved the summer! The birds keep singing just the same. Oh! The thoughtless birds!

417

Poor little Lou! Poor Fanny! You must comfort them!

If you were with me, Vinnie, we could talk about her together.

And I thought she would live I wanted her to live so, I thought she could not die! To think how still she lay while I was making the little loaf, and fastening her flowers! Did you get my letter in time to tell her how happy I would be to do what she requested? Mr. Brady is coming to-morrow to bring arbutus for her. Dear little aunt! Will she look down? You must tell me all you can think about her. Did she carry my little bouquet? So many broken-hearted people have got to hear the birds sing, and see all the little flowers grow, just the same as if the sun hadn't stopped shining forever! . . . How I wish I could comfort you! How I wish you could comfort me, who weep at what I did not see and never can believe. I will try and share you a little longer, but it is so long, Vinnie.

We didn't think, that morning when I wept that you left me, and you, for other things, that we should weep more bitterly before we saw each other.

Well, she is safer now than "we know or even think." Tired little aunt, sleeping ne'er so peaceful! Tuneful little aunt, singing, as we trust, hymns than which the robins have no sweeter ones.

Good-night, broken hearts, Lou, and Fanny, and Uncle Loring. Vinnie, remember

SISTER.

In October, 1860, Emily and Lavinia went to Middletown, Connecticut, to visit Eliza Coleman, whose family had been living there since they left Philadelphia in 1858. It will be recalled that Mrs. Coleman was Maria Flynt of Monson before her marriage. Eliza was engaged to the Reverend John Langdon Dudley, pastor of the South Congregational Church in Middletown, who had graduated from Amherst College in 1844. It is assumed that Emily met him for the first time when he brought Eliza to Commencement in August, 1860. There is in the Flynt family a tradition—and without stressing it—that for a time Mr. Dudley was the object of Emily Dickinson's romantic ardor. Of this there is no proof.

The Civil War began in April, 1861. The few southern students in Amherst College left in a body, followed by a rush to enlist in the armies of the North. From then on vital statistics were to have for Emily Dickinson a cumulative effect.

John Dudley and Eliza Coleman were married unexpectedly on June 6, 1861.

On June 19 the first child of Austin and Sue was born, a son named Edward Dickinson.

On June 30 Mrs. Browning died, for Emily Dickinson a personal bereavement.

On August 13 Mary Warner was married.

On September 11 Mrs. Dwight died, wife of the beloved pastor who had recently moved away from Amherst.

Samuel Bowles had been suffering from a serious ailment. In October he came to Northampton for a water cure. On him Emily depended for more than literary criticism and advice.

On December 19 the Bowles's son Charles was born in New York, where they were then living.

After learning of the death of the second of the two sons of a neighbor on December 29, both as a result of the war, Emily wrote to her cousins, "Mrs. Adams had news of the death of her boy to-day, from a wound at Annapolis. Telegram signed by Frazar Stearns. You remember him. Another one died in October—from fever caught in the camp. Mrs. Adams herself has not risen from bed since then." (*Letters,* 1931, 223.)

A few weeks later, on March 13, 1862, Frazar Stearns was killed at the battle of New Bern. Emily's poignant letter to the Norcross girls about his death ends with the words: "So our part in Frazar is done. . . . Let us love better, children, it's most that's left to do." Later she speaks of the mounting tragedy around her and tells them that "Sorrow seems more general than it did, and not the estate of a few persons, since the war began; and if the anguish of others helped one with one's own, now would be many medicines. . . . Every day life feels mightier, and what we have the power to be, more stupendous (*ibid.,* 225-226).

On April 5 Mr. Bowles, whose health had been steadily declining, came to say good-by before sailing for Europe to be gone many months.

Ten days after he left Emily wrote to Colonel Higginson, a stranger, seeking advice about her poetry. In her second letter, on April 25, 1862, she explained: "I had a terror since September, I could tell to none; and so I sing, as the boy does by the burying-ground, because I am afraid" (*ibid.,* 273). For this there may have been an outward cause, a specific event, but the assumption is unnecessary. The effect of shock after shock throughout many months, against the background of fratricidal strife, is enough to explain her distress. And there is another thing to keep in mind. This was the year in which Dr. Wadsworth left Philadelphia to become pastor of Calvary Church, San Francisco, on June 1, 1862.

In November Mr. Bowles returned from Europe somewhat improved in health. Emily queried:

> The loss by sickness—was it loss?
> Or that ethereal gain
> You earned by measuring the grave,
> Then measuring the sun.[1]

It is worth noting that there is not another letter to Colonel Higginson until April, 1863.

A note to Mr. Bowles gives a hint of her struggle during these turbulent months:

I cant explain it, Mr Bowles.

> Two swimmers wrestled on the spar
> Until the morning sun,
> When one turned, smiling, to the land—
> Oh God! the other One!
>
> The stray ships—passing—spied a face
> Upon the waters borne,
> With eyes, in death, still begging—raised,
> And hands—beseeching—thrown!

Among Emily Dickinson's fragmentary manuscripts were found drafts of three letters in writing of this period. Two are written in ink with sufficient care to suggest that they were intended for mailing, but were later corrected in pencil. There is no evidence that these letters, or the altered versions of them, were ever posted. A few sentences from the second letter appeared in *Letters,* 1894, pages 422-423 (*Letters,* 1931, 411):

. . . If you saw a bullet hit a bird, and he told you he wasn't shot, you might weep at his courtesy, but you would certainly doubt his word.

---

1. This is the final stanza of the seven-stanza poem which begins, "My first well day, since many ill . . . ," here adapted to Mr. Bowles's need.

The next poem, "Two swimmers wrestled on the spar," was first published in *Poems,* 1890, 137.

Thomas's faith in anatomy was stronger than his faith in faith. . . . Vesuvius don't talk—Aetna don't. One of them said a syllable, a thousand years ago, and Pompeii heard it and hid forever. She couldn't look the world in the face afterward, I suppose. Bashful Pompeii! . . .

This was as much as Austin and Lavinia thought decorous. And the date they assigned to the published fragments was 1885. Why? The writing obviously belongs to a period at least twenty years earlier. The fact that in the full text Emily refers to her dog Carlo, without further evidence, would fix the date as the early eighteen-sixties.[2]

Who could have inspired such letters as these? "Daisy" writes to her "Master." She called Colonel Higginson "Master" but felt toward him no ardent emotion. Certain phrases suggest that Dr. Wadsworth was the master she had in mind, as when she inquires whether he could come to New England, implying that he lived elsewhere; but Mr. Bowles was also far away in New York during the winter of 1861-1862. She regrets that "to come nearer than presbyteries . . . is forbidden me." As I have suggested elsewhere (page 35) the word "presbytery" cannot be taken literally any more than words like "Himmaleh" or "Calvary," which were often used in a metaphorical sense. One is tempted to link the following letters to one of the names just mentioned, but it is wiser to wait awhile longer. For it is not impossible that some hitherto unidentified correspondent might turn up, one whose power to arouse such fine frenzy as that which throbs in these letters has not as yet been suspected. But whoever the man, or men—for all three letters may not be addressed to the same person—here is further evidence that

2. Why was this date selected? Emily's brother and sister were always trying to shield her from curiosity seekers bent on prying into her private affairs. One suspects that by placing these sentences far enough away from the date when they were written, as well as subsequent to the death of Judge Lord, Austin and Lavinia thought to conceal the identity of the one to whom they were addressed. In themselves the published words could of course lead to no surmises. But the guardians wished to make doubly sure that words non-committal in themselves would not, if the letter itself were later discovered by an outsider, lead to irresponsible speculation. But note that, as in the case of those written to Judge Lord, these letters have survived: they were not destroyed, determined though both Austin and Lavinia were to protect their sister.

In the 1894 edition of the *Letters* these sentences, dated "1885," were addressed "To ——," without comment. In the 1931 edition, although my mother was unwilling to print the complete letter, she did consent to a footnote drawing attention to the fact that it was out of place (*Letters*, 1931, 411). For typographical devices used in showing the alterations see page 59.

for Emily Dickinson her own heart was her most insistent and
baffling contendent. As to that she says: "God made me—Master—
I did'nt be—myself. I dont know how it was done. He built the
heart in me. Bye and bye it outgrew me—and like the little mother
—with the big child—I got tired holding him."

Here then are the letters which pose more questions than they
answer.

Master.

If you saw a bullet hit a Bird—and he told you he was'nt shot—
you might weep at his courtesy, but you would certainly doubt his
word.
One drop more from the gash that stains your Daisy's bosom—then
would you *believe?* Thomas' faith in Anatomy, was stronger than
his faith in faith. God made me—[*Sir*] Master—I did'nt be—myself.
I dont know how it was done. He built the heart in me. Bye and
bye it outgrew me—and like the little mother—with the big child—
I got tired holding him. I heard of a thing called "Redemption"—
which rested men and women. You remember I asked you for it—
you gave me something else. I forgot the Redemption [*in the
Redeemed. I did'nt tell you for a long time, but I knew you had
altered me—I*] and was tired—no more—* [*so dear did this stranger
become that were it, or my breath—the Alternative—I had tossed
the fellow away with a smile.*] I am older—tonight, Master—but the
love is the same—so are the moon and the crescent. If it had been
God's will that I might breathe where you breathed—and find the
place—myself—at night—if I can never forget that I am not with
you, and that sorrow and frost are nearer than I—if I wish with a
might I cannot repress—that mine were the Queen's place—the love
of the Plantagenet is my only Apology. To come nearer than presbyteries—and nearer than the new Coat—that the Tailor made—
the prank of the Heart at play on the Heart—in holy Holiday—is
forbidden me. You make me say it over. I fear you laugh—when I
do not see—[*but*] "Chillon" is not funny. Have you the Heart in
your breast—Sir—is it set like mine—a little to the left—has it the
misgiving—if it wake in the night—perchance—itself to it—a tim-
brel is it—itself to it a tune?
These things are [*reverent*] holy, Sir, I touch them [*reverently*]
hallowed, but persons who pray—dare remark [*our*] "Father"! You
say I do not tell you all. Daisy confessed, and denied not.
Vesuvius dont talk—Etna—dont—[*thy*] one of them said a syllable,
a thousand years ago, and Pompeii heard it, and hid forever. She

Master.

If you saw a bullet hit a Bird - and he told you he was'nt shot - you might weep at his courtesy, but you would certainly doubt his word. One drop more from the gash that stains your Daisy's bosom - then would you believe? Thomas' faith in Anatomy, was stronger than his faith in faith. God made me - [Master] - I did'nt be - myself. [He] can't know how it was done. He built the heart in me - Bye and bye it outgrew me - and like the little mother - with the big child - I got tired holding him - I heard of a thing called Redemption - which rested men and women -

Draft of letter by Emily Dickinson about 1861

You remember I asked you
for it - you gave me something
else. I forgot the Redemption
~~[crossed out]~~
~~[crossed out]~~
~~[crossed out]~~ and ~~[crossed out]~~
~~[crossed out]~~ was time - no more ~~[crossed out]~~
~~[crossed out]~~
~~[crossed out]~~
~~[crossed out]~~
Am older - tonight, Master -
but the love is the same -
so are the moon and the
crescent. If it had been
God's will that I might
breathe where you breathed -
and find the place - myself -
at night - if I can never forget
that I am not with you -
and that sorrow and frost -
are nearer than I - if I could

persons who pray — dare remark
"Father"! You say I do
not tell you all — Daisy confessed —
and denied not.
Vesuvius dont talk — Etna — dont —
said a syllable — one of them —
a thousand years ago, and
Pompeii heard it, and hid
forever — She could'nt look the
world in the face, afterward —
I suppose — Bashful Pompeii!
"Tell you of the want" — you
know what a leech is, dont
you — and Daisy's arm is small.
And you have felt the horizon
havnt you — and did the
sea — never come so close as
to make you dance?
I dont know what you can
do for it — thank you — Master —

- but if I had the Beard on
my Cheek - like you, and you - had Vinnie's
Ringlets - and you Cared so for
me - what would become of you?
Could you forget me in fight, or
flight - or the foreign Land?
Couldn't Carlo - and you and I
walk in the meadows an hour -
And nobody Care but the Bobolink
and his - a Silver scruple?
I used to think when I died -
I could see you - so I died
as fast as I could - but the
"Corporation" are going too so
wont be Squirrels - now.
Say I may wait for you -
Say I need go with no stranger
to the to me - untried fold -
I waited a long time - Master -
but I can wait more - wait
till my hazel hair is dappled.

And you carry the same -
then I can look at my
watch - And if the day is
too far declined - we can take
the chances for # Heaven -
What would you do with me
if I came "in white"?
Have you the little chest - to
put the alive - in?
I want so see you more - Sir -
than all I wish for in
this world - and the wish -
altered a little - will be my
only one - for the skies -
Could you come to New England -
~~this~~ ~~than~~ - ~~would~~ would you come
to Amherst - Would you like
to come - Master?
~~Would it do harm~~ -
~~Would Daisy~~ disappoint
you - no - she wouldn't - Sir -
it were comfort yours - just -

to Cook in your face, while
you Cooked in mine - then I
Could play in the mead - till
dark - till you take me
when Sundown Cannot find
us - and the ways keep
Coming - till the town is full.
~~[crossed out]~~ ~~[crossed out]~~ ~~[crossed out]~~ ~~[crossed out]~~ ~~[crossed out]~~ ~~[crossed out]~~

I did'nt think to tell you, you
did'nt come to me "in white",
nor ever told me why,

+ No Rose, yet felt myself
a'bloom,
No Bird - yet rode in Ether,

could'nt look the world in the face, afterward—I suppose. Bashful Pompeii! "Tell you of the want"—you know what a leech[?] is, dont you—and [*remember that*] Daisy's Arm is small. And you have felt the Horizon, hav'nt you—and did the sea—never come so close as to make you dance?

I dont know what you can do for it—thank you—Master—but if I had the Beard on my cheek—like you, and you—had Daisy's petals —and you cared so for me—what would become of you? Could you forget me in fight, or flight, or the foreign land? Could'nt Carlo, and you and I walk in the meadows an hour—and nobody care but the Bobolink, and *his*—a *silver* scruple? I used to think when I died —I could see you—so I died as fast as I could—but the "Corporation" are going Heaven too so [*Eternity*] wont be sequestered— now [*at all*]. Say I may wait for you—say I need go with no stranger to the to me—untried [*country*] fold. I waited a long time—Master —but I can wait more—wait till my hazel hair is dappled—and you carry the cane—then I can look at my watch—and if the Day is too far declined—we can take the chances [*of*] for Heaven. What would you do with me if I came "in white"? Have you the little chest to put the Alive—in?

I want to see you more—Sir—than all I wish for in this world—and the wish—altered a little—will be my only one—for the skies.

Could you come to New England, [*this summer—could*] would you come to Amherst—Would you like to come—Master?

[*Would it do harm—yet we both fear God*—] Would Daisy disappoint you—no—she would'nt—Sir—it were comfort forever—just to look in your face, while you looked in mine—then I could play in the woods till Dark—till you take me where sundown cannot find us—and the true keep coming—till the town is full. [*Will you tell me if you will?*]

I did'nt think to tell you, you did'nt come to me "in white", nor ever told me why.

> *No Rose, yet felt myself a'bloom,
> No Bird—yet rode in Ether.

[*No heading*]

Oh! did I offend it—[*Did'nt it want me to tell it the truth*] Daisy—Daisy—offend it—who bends her smaller life to his (its), meeker (lower) every day—who only asks—a taste—[*who*] something to do for love of it—some little way she cannot guess to make that master glad.

A love so big it scares her, rushing among her small heart—pushing aside the blood and leaving her faint and white in the gust's arm. Daisy—who never flinched thro' that awful parting, but held her life so tight he should not see the wound—who would have sheltered him in her childish bosom (Heart)—only it was'nt big eno' for a Guest so large—*this* Daisy—grieve her Lord—and yet she (it) often blundered. Perhaps she grieved (grazed) his taste—perhaps her odd —Backwoodsman ways teased [*life troubled*] his finer sense (nature).

Daisy [*fea*] knows all that—but must she go unpardoned—teach her grace, preceptor, teach her majesty. Slow (Dull) at patrician things—even the wren upon her nest learns (knows) more than Daisy dares.

Low at the knee that bore her once with [*royal*] wordless rest [*now*] Daisy [*stoops*] kneels! a culprit—tell her her [*offence*] fault—Master —if it is [*not so*] small eno to cancel with *her life,* [*Daisy*] she is satisfied—but punish—do not [*dont*] banish her—Shut her in prison, Sir—only pledge that you will forgive—sometime—before the grave, and Daisy will not mind—she will awake in your likeness.
Wonder stings me more than the Bee—who did never sting me—but made gay music with his might wherever I [*may*] [*should*] did go. Wonder wastes my pound, you said I had no size to spare.
You send the water over the Dam in my brown eyes.
Iv'e got a cough as big as a thimble—but I dont care for that. Iv'e got a Tomahawk in my side but that dont hurt me much. [*If you*] Her master stabs her more.
Wont he come to her—or will he let her seek him, never minding [*whatere*] so long wandering if [*out*] to him at last.
Oh how the sailor strains, when his boat is filling—Oh how the dying tug, till the angel comes. Master—open your life wide, and take me in forever. I will never be tired—I will never be noisy when you want to be still. I will be [*glad as the*] your best little girl— nobody else will see me, but you—but that is enough—I shall not want any more—and all that Heaven will be will disappoint me, only because it's not so dear

Dear Master

I am ill, but grieving more that you are ill, I make my stronger hand work long eno' to tell you. I thought perhaps you were in Heaven, and when you spoke again, it seemed quite sweet, and wonderful, and surprised me so. I wish that you were well. I would that all I love, should be weak no more. The violets are by my side, the Robin very near, and "Spring", they say, Who is she—going by the door.

Indeed it is God's house, and these are gates of Heaven, and to and fro, the angels go, with their sweet postillions. I wish that I were great, like Mr. Michael Angelo, and could paint for you. You ask me what my flowers said—then they were disobedient—I gave them messages. They said what the lips in the West, say, when the sun goes down, and so says the Dawn.

Listen again, Master. I did not tell you that today had been the Sabbath Day.

Each Sabbath on the Sea, makes me count the Sabbaths, till we meet on shore—and (will the) whether the hills will look as blue as the sailors say.

I cannot talk any more (stay any longer) tonight now, for this pain denies me.

How strong when weak to recollect, and easy, quite, to love. Will you tell me, please to tell me, soon as you are well.

As the year 1863 opened the march of events went on, relentless as before.

On January 17 Loring Norcross died. To his orphan children Emily wrote, "It is not dying hurts us so."[3]

> 'Tis not that dying hurts us so,
> 'Tis living hurts us more.
> But dying is a different way,
> A kind behind the door,
>
> The southern custom of the birds
> That ere the frosts are due
> Accepts a better latitude.
> We are the birds that stay—
>
> The shiverers 'round farmers' doors,
> For whose reluctant crumb
> We stipulate, till pitying snows
> Persuade our feathers home.

During the summer Colonel Higginson was wounded. Mr. Bowles's health was no better. He was said to be suffering from nervous dyspepsia. Emily's prolonged anxiety culminated in September when the trouble with her eyes began. Darkness was closing in. "Nothing has happened but loneliness," she wrote. Her eyes did not improve. She finally decided to consult the well-known oculist, Dr. Henry W. Williams, of 15 Arlington Street, Boston. He told

---

3. This is the first line of the poem as copied by Miss Norcross and as published in *Letters*, 1894, 251; *Letters*, 1931, 229. The version which Mrs. Todd took from a copy in Emily's handwriting is the one published in *Bolts of Melody*, 201.

her that she must be under his care for an extended period of treatment. She left home toward the end of April.

2

Away from Home, are Some and I,
An Emigrant to be
In a Metropolis of Homes
Is easy, possibly.

The Habit of a Foreign Sky
We—difficult—acquire,
As Children, who remain in Face
The More their Feet—retire.

While under the care of Dr. Williams Emily lived with her cousins in a boardinghouse in Cambridgeport. She referred to it as a prison; but was able to conclude that "A prison gets to be a friend."

Louisa and Fanny Norcross were as kind as they "knew how," but absence from home was a cruel panacea, especially for an ailment which lay deeper than any observable symptom. It was not only an oculist Emily required. She had "need of the balsam word"—a cure for bewilderment and an understanding of how to manage the heart which had outgrown her.

Emily stayed in Cambridgeport until November—seven months—the longest time she had ever been away from home.[4] It was not

4. While it is true that Emily Dickinson had been away from home very little, she had made quite a number of visits which the legend overlooks. Insofar as they are known, the list of her absences is as follows:

In May, 1844, she visited the Loring Norcrosses in Boston for a month, stopping on her way back for a brief stay with her Uncle William in Worcester. In 1846 she went to Boston for a visit at the Norcrosses' of about four weeks. In 1847-1848 she was a student at near-by Mount Holyoke Seminary. It was an intermittent absence, for a period of nine months—but interspersed with stays of several weeks at home. In September, 1851, she went to Boston again to visit the Norcrosses, stopping in Worcester on the way, and was absent from home from September 4 to 22. In September, 1853, she and Lavinia made an overnight visit to the Hollands in Springfield. Her longest absence from home up to that time was the Washington trip, when she left Amherst on April 5, 1854, returning in mid-May. The girls made another overnight visit to the Hollands in September, 1854. On October 19, 1860, Emily went to Middletown, Connecticut, to visit Eliza Coleman, who was living there with her parents, as we know, from 1858 to 1861.

only painful being cooped up in a boardinghouse among strangers and unable to use her eyes. Absence from home hurt her more, as her letters so touchingly reveal.

These letters to Lavinia first appeared in *Letters,* 1894 (*Letters,* 1931, 148-151). Following the text of the manuscripts, they are republished with the few deletions restored and in a more accurate time sequence.

[May ? 1864]

Dear Vinnie

I miss you most, and I want to go Home and take good care of you and make you happy every day.

The Doctor is not willing yet, and He is not willing I should write. He wrote to Father, himself, because He thought it not best for me.

You wont think it strange any more, will you?

Loo and Fanny take sweet care of me, and let me want for nothing, but I am not at Home, and the calls at the Doctor's are painful, and dear Vinnie, I have not looked at the Spring.

Wont you help me be patient?

I cannot write but this, and send a little flower, and hope you wont forget me, because I want to come so much I cannot make it show.

Emily.

[July ? 1864]

Dear Vinnie

Many write that they do not write because that they have too much to say—I, that I have enough. Do you remember the Whippowil that sang one night on the Orchard fence, and then drove to the South, and we never heard of Him afterward?

He will go Home and I shall go Home, perhaps in the same Train.

It is a very sober thing not to have any Vinnie, and to keep my summer in strange Towns, what I have not told—but I have found friends in the Wilderness.

You know "Elijah" did, and to see the "Ravens" mending my stockings, would break a Heart long hard. Fanny and Loo are solid Gold, Mrs Bangs and her Daughter very kind, and the Doctor enthusiastic about my getting well. I feel no gayness yet. I suppose I had been discouraged so long.

You remember the Prisoner of Chillon did not know Liberty when it came, and asked to go back to Jail.

Clara and Anna [Newman] came to see me and brought beautiful flowers. Do you know what made them remember me? I was most surprised. Give them my love and gratitude.

They told me about the Day at Pelham, You—dressed in Daisies and Mr McDonald. I could'nt see you Vinnie. I am glad of all the Roses you find, while your Primrose is gone.

How kind Mr Copeland grew.

Was Mr Dudley dear.

Emily wants to be well and with Vinnie. If any one alive wants to get well more, I would let Him first.

I am glad it is me, not Vinnie. Long time might seem further to Her.

Give my love to Father and Mother, and Austin. Am so glad His Tobacco is well—I asked Father about it.

Tell Margaret I remember Her, and hope Richard is well.

Dear Vinnie, this is the longest letter I wrote since I was sick, but who needed it most, if not my little Sister? I hope she is not very tired, tonight How I wish I could rest all those who are tired for me.

Big Kiss for Fanny.

Emily.

[To Vinnie in Middletown]   [November 1864]

Does Vinnie think of Sister? Sweet news. Thank Vinnie.

Emily may not be able as she was, but all she can, she will.

Father told me that you were going. I wept for the little Plants, but rejoiced for you.

Had I loved them as well as I did, I could have begged you to stay with them, but they are Foreigners, now, and all, a Foreigner.

I have been sick so long I do not know the Sun.

I hope they may be alive, for Home would be strange except them, now the World is dead.

Anna Norcross lives here, since Saturday, and two new people more, a person and his wife, so I do little but fly, yet always find a nest.

I shall go Home in two weeks. You will get me at Palmer, yourself. Let no one beside come.

Love for Eliza, and Mr Dudley.

Sister.

[To Vinnie in Middletown]   [November 1864]

. . . Her, when I get Home. The Doctor will let me go Monday of Thanksgiving week. He wants to see me Sunday, so I cannot before. Vinnie will go to Palmer for me certainly?

I took the little Sac to wear in walking, under Cloak, to keep away more cold. I did not think to tell before.

Vinnie will forgive me?

Love for the Middletown Pearls. Shall write Eliza after Tuesday, when I go to the Doctor. Thank her for sweet note.

The Drums keep on for the still Man, but Emily must stop.

Love of Fanny and Loo.

                                                    Sister.

Emily hoped that the return to her blesséd home would complete her cure for, as she wrote Louisa, "new heart makes new health, dear." But it was not to be. Already in January she realized that she must go back to Boston for further treatment. She asked Lou if, by the first of April, she would be strong enough to "carry" her, for by then, she thought, she would not be "half as heavy" as she was before. When pressed for further details about the state of her health, Emily sent the following account:

The eyes are as with you, sometimes easy, sometimes sad. I think they are not worse, nor do I think them better than when I came home.

The snow-light offends them, and the house is bright; notwithstanding, they hope some. For the first few weeks I did nothing but comfort my plants, till now their small green cheeks are covered with smiles. I chop the chicken centres when we have roast fowl, frequent now, for the hens contend and the Cain is slain. . . . Then I make the yellow to the pies, and bang the spice for cake, and knit the soles to the stockings I knit the bodies to last June. They say I am a "help." Partly because it is true, I suppose, and the rest applause. Mother and Margaret are so kind, father as gentle as he knows how, and Vinnie good to me, but "cannot see why I don't get well." This makes me think I am long sick, and this takes the ache to my eyes. I shall try to stay with them a few weeks more before going to Boston, though what it would be to see you and have the doctor's care—that cannot be told. (*Letters*, 1931, 235.)

The foregoing letter was probably written in February, 1865. Emily left home in April as before, and in May sent another letter to her sister:

Dear Vinnie   [May 1865]

The Hood is far under way and the Girls think it a Beauty. I am so glad to make it for you, who made so much for me.

I hope the Chimneys are done and the Hemlocks set, and the Two Teeth filled, in the Front yard—How astonishing it will be to me.

I hope Mother is better, and will be careful of her Eye.

The Doctor says it must heal while warm Weather lasts, or it will be more troublesome.

How is Margarets lameness? Tell her the Girl's name, here, is Margaret, which makes me quite at Home.

The Pink Lily you gave Loo, has had five flowers since I came, and has more Buds. The Girls think it my influence.

Is <Sue> still improving? Give her love from us all, and how much we talk of her.

Loo wishes she knew Father's view of Jeff Davis' capture—thinks no one but He, can do it justice.

She wishes to send a Photograph of the Arrest to Austin, including the Skirt and Spurs, but fears he will think her trifling with him. I advised her not to be rash. How glad I should be to see you all, but it wont be long, Vinnie—You will be willing, wont you, for a little while.

It has rained, and been very hot, and Mosquitoes as in August. I hope the flowers are well. The Tea Rose I gave Aunt Lavinia has a flower, now.

Much love for both Houses, from the Girls and me. Is the Lettuce ripe.

Shall you go to Springfield? Persons wear no Bonnets, here. Fanny has a Blade of Straw, with Handle of Ribbon.

Aff, Emily.

After another summer spent in the Cambridgeport boardinghouse Emily Dickinson returned to Amherst in October. She lived for more than twenty years but never again left home—that home which to her was "the definition of God."

PART SIX

1874

CHAPTER XXXIII

Edward Dickinson Returns to the General Court

1

IN 1874 the era of railroad building in the United States was still in full swing. There were in New England 132 separate railroads, large and small.[1] The attention of legislators in that session of the Massachusetts General Court was focused largely on problems of railroad construction and finance.

The history of the north-south line through Amherst, in the promotion of which Edward Dickinson had been active from the outset, had been disheartening. The area had not produced the expected amount of traffic. After a few years of operation the Amherst & Belchertown had gone into bankruptcy; also its successor, the Amherst, Belchertown & Palmer Rail Road. The original stockholders lost their entire investment. The latter road, purchased by the New London Northern in 1864, and extended to Grout's Corner (Miller's Falls) in 1867, had been leased by the Vermont Central as its southern outlet in 1871.[2]

From east to west two lines traversed Massachusetts: the Western (Boston & Albany) by way of Worcester, Palmer, Springfield and Pittsfield to Albany; and the Vermont & Massachusetts, with its extension, the Troy & Greenfield, along the northern boundary of the state. In 1873 the Troy & Greenfield still brought up short against Hoosac Mountain in the extreme northwest corner of Massachusetts.

1. *Massachusetts Register and Business Directory* (1874), 653-656.
2. Sargent, "The Railroad Mania in Amherst," 35-36.

The partially completed Hoosac Tunnel was still the major engineering problem in the state.[3] Ever since 1852, when "The Mastodon Mountain Drill" had collapsed after penetrating the rock to a distance of 25 feet, machines one after another had piled their rusting skeletons beside the entrance. Every device from power drilling to hand labor and blasting had been tried and had failed. More than engineering was involved in the failure, however. There was also fanatical opposition. From the beginning, the tunnel had been ridiculed as an impossible undertaking. Each successive failure only served to strengthen skepticism in rural districts. And yet, so important to the economic life of Massachusetts was completion of the tunnel judged to be, that the Commonwealth itself came to the rescue.

In 1854 the state granted a subsidy of $2,000,000 to the Troy & Greenfield Rail Road, called "the tunnel route," as part of a trunk line to the West. The Western Rail Road naturally fought the use of state funds to finance a competitive route. Connecting lines, too, were agitating for protection of their interests. In a two-volume treatise on the history of New England transportation this story has been summarized by Professor Kirkland of Bowdoin College.[4] For almost a quarter of a century it had been a long-drawn-out battle, he says, and not a creditable one. "The era of state construction was one of inertia, false starts, engineering mistakes, and incompetence."

At last, on November 27, 1873, the "holing through" was completed. But the tunnel was still far from finished. The bore must be enlarged and the inner archways constructed. Furthermore, if and when completed, the disposition of the tunnel would still remain a problem. The state was loath to sell its property to private owners. But how else could a consolidated through line be operated?[5]

3. *Journal of the House of Representatives of the Commonwealth of Massachusetts,* 1874, 74-609; and Massachusetts *House Documents,* 1874, No. 462, 1-10.

4. Kirkland, *Men, Cities and Transportation,* I, 387-432 (Chapter XII, "The Great Bore").

5. *The Boston Transcript,* January 6, 1874, listed "subjects of consequence presented for the consideration of the Legislature. And, prominently among them will undoubtedly be the disposal of the Hoosac Tunnel. Public opinion seems to have decided in favor of having this great tunnel retained in the possession of the Commonwealth, and its ownership so fixed that private corporations cannot by any hocus pocus alienate this property which has cost

Meanwhile, construction of another east-west railroad through the central part of the state, from Boston by way of Amherst to Northampton, had been authorized by a special act of the General Court on April 13, 1864. The incorporation of the Massachusetts Central was approved by the legislature on May 10, 1869, and organized on September 2 of the same year. The effort to finance the enterprise, in which Edward Dickinson took a leading part, continued throughout most of the following year. Amherst voted its commitment (1000 shares of stock) on October 4, 1870. Work of construction, promptly started at Boston, was halted in 1872 because the contractor had failed to complete the bridge across the Connecticut River between Amherst and Northampton. Largely on this account and because he hoped to inject some life into the enterprise, the town having already paid substantial amounts of its pledge, Mr. Dickinson consented to accept another term in the Massachusetts Legislature. Such was his faith in the benefits accruing from railroads, and such his determination to see to it that the interests of his town should not be neglected, that in spite of his perennial efforts to bolster up the north-south line, followed by repeated failure, he was still trying to obtain dependable rail connections for Amherst. And so we find him at the age of seventy-one energetically promoting plans for the new road. For more than a quarter of a century Mr. Dickinson had held no public office in Massachusetts. He had been entirely out of politics, in fact, ever since the demise of the Whig party, and he had no wish to return. I think it is not too much to say that an opportunity to help in securing another railroad for Amherst was the only appeal which could have persuaded him at his age to accept a fresh responsibility necessitating protracted absence from home.

In 1873 Professor William S. Tyler published *The History of Amherst College During its First Half Century, 1821-1871*. Among the brief biographies of men prominent in the development of the college is that of Edward Dickinson (pages 538-540). He is described

---

so large a sum of the people's money, and was intended for the benefit of every part of Massachusetts, and particularly for the development of its trade and commerce. We take it there will be no serious effort to steal the tunnel the present session, but care and forethought now may prevent the occurrence of such an event hereafter."

as he was when, on November 10, 1873, he was elected on an independent ticket to represent the Fourth District of Hampshire County (Amherst and South Hadley) in the House of Representatives of the Massachusetts General Court. (Compare an editorial in the *Boston Journal,* November 7, 1873.) Professor Tyler wrote:

Mr. Dickinson has made enemies by his unbending firmness of purpose and his great freedom and boldness of speech under excitement; but no enemy, whether personal or political, has ever questioned the integrity of his character, the purity of his life, or the breadth, depth and intensity of his public spirit. A liberal giver for public objects from his private purse, his vote may always be relied on in the town, the parish or the State for the largest appropriations for public improvements. The best financier in the Corporation has publicly announced, as the result of careful examination for many successive years, that, as Treasurer of Amherst College, he has never lost a dollar. And one of the sharpest and shrewdest of the Board of Overseers declares that after the most prolonged and patient scrutiny of his books and accounts, only a single error of less than a hundred dollars could be detected, and that error was *against* himself. At the age of three-score years and ten Mr. Dickinson still stands erect, perpendicular, with his senses of seeing and hearing unimpaired, with his natural force and fire chastened and subdued but scarcely abated, one of the firmest pillars of society, education, order, morality and every good cause in our community.

The 1874 session of the General Court opened on the seventh of January. On January 10 Mr. Dickinson was appointed to membership on "The Joint Special Committee of the Senate and the House on the Hoosac Tunnel Line of Railroads" which met from time to time with a joint standing committee—of which he was not a member—"On the Hoosac Tunnel and Troy and Greenfield Railroad." Though the tunnel was of interest to him, as were all enterprises connected with the building of railroads in Massachusetts, his reason for returning to the legislature had been to expedite completion of the Massachusetts Central.[6] In this objective he was promptly disappointed, the members of the legislature having decided that construction had not gone far enough to warrant further consideration of the project at that time. On January 12 *The*

6. This explanation was given by his son who, in the sketch of his father's life previously mentioned, said that he went to the General Court in 1874 in order "to help in shaping the legislation proposed affecting the interests of the Central Railroad." (Page 407.) See also *The Transcript,* June 17, 1874. *Manual for the General Court,* 1874, 353, 359; *Journal of the House,* 1874, 18.

Transcript reported that "it is announced, semi-officially, that the Massachusetts Central Railroad will ask no aid from the Legislature this winter; but will merely apply for an extension of one year in the time permitted for its completion."

In addition to problems pertaining to railroads Mr. Dickinson's efforts in the General Court were directed toward furthering other interests of Amherst and neighboring communities. He argued for tax exemption of educational institutions, of Amherst College in particular, for larger subventions, and shortly before his death he succeeded in putting an end to political appointments on the Amherst board of trustees. He helped to obtain appropriations for the newly established Massachusetts Agricultural College at Amherst, and for individuals in his constituency he was always trying to obtain justice, whether in straightening out their insurance policies or getting derelicts out of prison.[7]

During his absence from home Mr. Dickinson could rest assured that his affairs were being carefully attended to by his son, in the office, in the town, and in the college, of which Austin had been made treasurer on December 1, 1873.

Among his father's papers preserved by Austin Dickinson is a small packet which he labeled "Some of the last letters of E. Dickinson." They were written in Boston and they deal for the most part with personal and legislative matters. My mother maintained toward them a respectful detachment, probably because to Austin they were sacred relics. One to whom you have given complete allegiance controls you in absence—in death perhaps more than ever. So it was with his father. The letters are still in their original envelopes, tied together just as Austin left them. For him the sacredness of the letters was not alone due to the fact that they were the last his father wrote. A series of events preceding his death seemed to Austin a kind of portent, so real as to be almost uncanny. Millard Fillmore, the last Whig President, died on the eighth of March, 1874. Edward Dickinson was a member of the committee appointed to draft a set

7. Such matters were handled by the following committees: "On Just and Equal Taxation"; "On the State Police"; and a joint standing committee "On Mercantile Affairs," the interest of the latter solicited by Edward Dickinson on behalf of the Amherst Gas Light Company.

of resolutions for the General Court. The ink on this document was hardly dry when, three days later, Charles Sumner, senior senator from Massachusetts, died suddenly. Mr. Dickinson was again appointed to the committee to draft resolutions. But more than either of these, a sentence in his father's letter written on the fifth of June seemed to Austin like a premonition of his father's death only a few days before it occurred. The letter closed with these words: "I shouldn't be here much longer, & never again, so we must put up with the inconvenience."

These letters are given in full, detailed and for the most part inconsequential though they are. Better than any comment, they show to within what narrow bounds the activities of Edward Dickinson had shrunk. And they illustrate the extent to which in absence he still felt responsible for minute details at home. On May 26 he wrote: "I forgot to leave stamps at home & send some for the family."

Had I considered myself merely the editor of these letters I might have deleted much of the detail. But my responsibility has seemed to be not so much that of editor as of intermediary between the reader and the contents of the camphorwood chest. So the letters appear in full. With one or two exceptions they are written in purple ink. They are extremely difficult to read, not only because of abbreviations and omissions, but because of peculiarities of script and spelling. The punctuation has been regularized as little as possible.[8]

The top third of the first sheet of the first letter is missing. Postmarked "January 21, 5 A. M.," it was presumably written on Tuesday, January 20. If so, "one of the most sincere outpourings of heartfelt respect" the writer had ever witnessed doubtless refers to a banquet held at Odd Fellows' Hall on the previous Saturday evening in honor of the 168th anniversary of the birth of Benjamin Franklin. Reported in the Monday issue of *The Transcript,* a page and a half were devoted to an account of the "Notable Occasion" at which three hundred covers were laid.

8. In addition to the postmark and a green 3-cent stamp, each envelope bears a date in Austin's writing. The postmark, or any part of it, when legible, is given. Most of the envelopes are embossed "Tremont House, Boston"; four, engraved "House of Representatives, Boston"; a few have no return address.

[*To Wm. Austin Dickinson Esq., Amherst, Mass.; postmark: Boston Mass Jan 21 5 A.M.*]

. . . this morning. It was one of the most sincere outpouring[s] of heartfelt respect which I ever witnessed. People from distant places, drawn by no motives of regard for titled distinction, but by the love they had for the man who had done so much good & contributed by his long life of kindness, to the rational enjoyment of so many of the worthy of all classes.

I reached here at 8. o clock. Albert Montague's witnesses came along with me, and the whole day has been spent, & the evening, in the hearing before the Committee—who will make their report, at as early a day as they can.

[Reverse of missing top third]

. . . are used here, then wheels, and the weather is quite cold.

I see that Judge Lord is now holding Court at Cambridge—& hope to see him, soon.

I hope everything will go right, at home.

I hope, too, that you will ask *Horace* to bring his bill ag^t you, that we may judge better what I ought to pay him. I should like to finish up with him, as soon as I can.

I think of nothing special in regard to business. Should like to receive a note every morning to know how you all are at home.

I cannot tell whether I shall go home on Friday or Saturday.

I met Mr Winthrop, this noon, in the Tremont House—and was very glad to see him. He was as polite as ever.

Our sessions are yet quite uninteresting & unimportant—Hoosac Tunnell project, and Liquor laws & State Constabulary with the smallest orders of enquiry, fill up the hour, which the House sits.

Love to you all, at both houses.

Your aff. father
E. Dickinson

The election of Albert Montague of Sunderland was contested by Charles A. Perry of Shutesbury, who claimed the seat in the House occupied by Mr. Montague. After weeks of discussion it was finally voted on February 10 that Mr. Perry "had leave to withdraw" his petition and that the seat be declared vacant. (*Journal of the House,* 1874, 116-117.) A second election on February 24 in the second district of Franklin County was won by Mr. Montague.

[*To Wm. A. Dickinson Esq, Amherst, Mass.*]

Tremont House
Boston
Tuesday Evening
Feby. 10. 1874

Dear Austin,

The Montague & Perry case was settled, this afternoon—by declaring that Perry might *have leave to withdraw and the seat be vacant.*

We found that many who were not perfectly clear that Montague was clearly elected, would vote for this result—so Codman made an Amendment to the Minority Report, that Perry might withdraw, and the seat be declared vacant. My friends came and enquired of me if I was satisfied with that, and after consulting with Montague, Billings & other friends of Montague's, I went to Codman & requested him to make the motion.[9] He made a capital speech in favor of Montague, & was followed by Dr Cole of Cheshire on the same side—& opposed by Judd, & Hale, & the motion was carried by 120 some, to 70 odd—a very strong vote.

Members voted for this, on the ground that while there was a possible doubt which one obtained a majority of the votes, they had rather vote in favor of vacating the seat, than to give either one of them the seat.

Montague is satisfied with the result. A new election will be ordered for an early day. Many members took pains to see Montague & hope that he will be sent back.

I have mailed to you 3. copies of the two Comee Reports—we advised Montague to get a quantity of these reports printed for distribution, & make some effort to secure his election.

I reached the Tremont House about ½ past 11. this forenoon.

A meeting of the Amherst Alumni, is called for Monday next, 4.30, afternoon, at Revere House. I have recd an invitation. It will

9. Charles Russell Codman of Boston was chairman of the Judiciary Committee, the most important committee of the House, to which a "very great" deal of business was referred. "In the debates Colonel Codman was far the most influential member on the floor." John Torrey Morse, Jr., "Colonel Charles Russell Codman," *Proceedings of the Massachusetts Historical Society,* LII (1918-1919), 87-95.

For the full name, residence, usual occupation and current post of public officials mentioned in these letters, but not included in the directory of "Relatives, Friends and Neighbors," see pages 512-513.

depend on whether I am obliged to stay at home, at that time, or not, whether I can accept.

I hope to hear, to-morrow morning, whether any arrangement is made about the Cook case vs. the Town—and the other matters which I wrote to Strickland about.

The weather is very comfortable. Judge French has gone to Washington. Mr Gillett has just come in, & will be here a day or two.

Mr Colt of Pittsfield is also here—& a number of other persons of my acquaintance, whom I have not seen here before.

I will see Robinson to-morrow about the springs.

Love to you all,
Your aff. father
E. Dickinson

[*To Wm. A. Dickinson Esq, Amherst, Mass.; postmark: Boston Mass Feb 13 9 A.M.*]

Tremont House
Boston
Thursday Evening Feby. 12. 74

Dear Austin

Your letter & Strickland's were rec^d this morning—& contents noted. Aldrich is to hold the Court. Gillett went home, yesterday, without any arrangement for the cases of Cook &c. vs. the Town. I will see Aiken, in the morning, & find whether he can attend our Court.[10]

It doesn't seem to me that we can try them, next week. I hoped some arrangement might be made which would dispose of them this term.

The Speaker has ordered a re-election in Montague's District for one week from next Tuesday, I understand—& he must be active & vigilant, in the mean time.[11]

Anna [Newman] dined with me, this noon, and I went over to Cambridge & staid two or more hours, this evening & met Elisabeth with Anna & the Bullard family.[12]

The College Alumni meeting takes place on Monday afternoon

10. In Suffolk County the name of the Court of Common Pleas had been changed to Superior Court in 1855, a change made throughout Massachusetts in 1859. "Our court" refers to the February session of the Superior Court in Northampton beginning on February 16, 1874.

11. The Speaker of the House was John E. Sanford of Taunton, Austin's fraternity mate and lifelong friend.

12. Mr. Dickinson's sister Elisabeth was now Mrs. Augustus N. Currier.

next. If it were not for the Court, I should insist on your attending it.

I shall probably go home to-morrow afternoon, as usual, & get home in the evening. And on Saturday, see about the Court matters, & the Am. [?] Com^ee business.

I went over to the State Prison, this morning, to see about getting out Peter Benjamin's son—on pardon. The warden speaks well of him & expresses a willingness to aid him at any time he may apply.

No more to-night.

> Your aff. father
> E. Dickinson

2

Mr. Dickinson did not permit the interests of Amherst College to be overlooked by the legislators, who, empowered to elect five members of the board of trustees, had been accustomed to exercise a certain control over the institution. On February 13 he moved to inquire into the advisability of amending the original act "to establish a college in the town of Amherst" so that the five members elected by the General Court should thereafter "be elected by the alumni of said college," a subject under consideration for many years. He moved further, "that the amount of the annual net income of real or personal estate which said college may now receive, may be increased." The bill to provide for "the election of certain trustees of Amherst College by the graduates thereof" was passed on April 25, 1874.[13]

The following letter was written on the day the Amherst alumni met in Boston.

[*To Wm. Austin Dickinson Esq, Amherst, Mass.; postmark: Boston Mass Feb 17 1874 5 A.M.*]

> Tremont House
> Boston
> Boston Feby. 16. 1874

Dear Austin,

We have had an Alumni Meeting of 80. in number, this evening, and a very pleasant time. All passed off agreeably—and a set of fine

13. *Journal of the House,* 1874, 129; 425.

looking men, and no one need to be ashamed of the sons of the College. Prof^rs Snell, Crowell & Mather & Clark Seelye were all here.

We have a Meeting of our Committee to-morrow morning at 10.½ oclock.

The weather cleared off, just before evening, and is now quite pleasant, & comfortable. Gov. Washburn, Wm. Howland & Manning were here—at the dinner, & Mr Bullard. Dr Allen, only, of the Trustees, attended.

I suppose you will be at Court, *necessarily,* only *one day,* tho' I would be there as much as you please to be. Let the office take care of itself.

I think of nothing to say about business, now.

Your aff. father
E. Dickinson

P.S. I saw Gard[i]ner Tufts after I got here, this afternoon, and told him about Meeny's wife's death. He said he would write this evening to the Trustees, & presumed they would discharge the daughter—at once—& that he would probably get an answer by Wednesday.

As soon as I can get any thing done, I will write about it.

You had better ask Mr Gillett to send his bill to you, for our Town Committee.

I will ask Judge Aiken to do the same thing.

E. D.

[*To Wm. A. Dickinson Esq, Amherst, Mass; postmark: Boston Mass Feb 19—A.M.*]

Tremont House
Boston
Wednesday Evening
Feby. 18. 1874

Dear Austin,

I did not receive any letter from you, this morning. I suppose because you was at Northampton to-day. This forenoon, I went into the Hall of the Ho. of Reps. to hear the Women's Suffrage People argue pro & con,—heard some women speakers, on both sides—some sentimental, some belligerent, some fist shakers—some scolds—and was disgusted with the class of females which gathered there. I hope we shall soon have a chance at the subject, & begin to clear off the scum—they don't expect to get what they ask, this year, as most of them say, but threaten to agitate & agitate till they find a Legislature weak enough to report in their favor.

Many members of the House begin to have some apprehensions about the election of Montague.

This afternoon, Mr Moors of Greenfield and I have written a short article & sent to Montague to publish if he thinks best, for circulation before the election. The Boston Liquor men feel much interest in securing Perry's election. I hope if you see any body from that District, you will urge them to make all the effort they can to secure the right result.

Is there much business before the Court? Will Aldrich be at N.H. [Northampton] after the present week.

Our Tunnel Line Com^ee meet again Friday forenoon. We hope before long, to make a plan to present to the Legislature—and thus get the subject before the two branches.

The weather to-day is quite cold, but very pleasant.

I enquired of [Arthur M.] Bridgman, the Reporter, to-day, about his report in the Union of the Amherst Alumni dinner. He said he wrote a long one of the whole meeting, in the Union of Tuesday which you will find if you can get that paper. I have not seen it, myself.

The graduates of Brown had their dinner at Parker's, last evening, Judge French has not yet got home, and Anna is still at Mr Bullard's. Judge Colt has got back—is holding the Court at Dedham —is here over night—and is full of stories, & very amusing.

Phelps has begun to run on a new time-table, this week, which I send you—by which we can leave N.York, at 12¼ P.M. & reach Spf^d so as to leave there at 6.28 for Amherst. N.L.N. trains are held back a little, to connect at Barrett's Junction. This will be some concern to us. He says he intends to arrange, in the Spring, to arrange so that we can leave N.York, at 3. P.M. & come directly to Amherst.

As soon as our Com^ee have finally decided on a report, I will send one to Mr Hills, at N.York.

Nothing more to-night.

Your aff. father
E. Dickinson

The Local Time Table of the Springfield, Athol and Northeastern Rail Road, dated February 16th, 1874 (Geo. W. Phelps, Superintendent), was enclosed.

Two notes, written en route to Boston, were also enclosed in the same envelope. The first was written in the Amherst depot, the second on a Western Union Telegraph Company blank in Palmer, where, although there is no postmark, it was presumably mailed.

[*To Wm. A. Dickinson Esq, Amherst, Mass.*]

	New London Northern Railroad
J. A. Allen, Agent.	Local Office
	Amherst, Mass., Feby. 24. 1874.

Dᴿ Austin,

Mᴿ Day [?] says that by coming to the Depot, by 3½ P.M. you can find whether the 5. o'clock train is on time. If it is, you can meet the N.Y. train at Palmer.

I hope you will go to-night. I expect to be home, Thursday morning.

Palmer Feby. 24, 1874.

The agent of station at Palmer says that our 5. o'clock P.M. train meets the N.Y. train at Palmer. I think you had better go to-night, if you can find at our Depot, at 3½ o'clock, that the train at Brattleboro is on time.

I left a note to that effect, at our Depot, this morning.

E. Dickinson

[*To Wm. A. Dickinson Esq, Amherst, Mass; postmark: N.Y. & Bos. R.P.O. Feb 24*]

Boston. Feby. 24. 1874.

Dear Austin

I have written to you, this evening, & sent it to the care of Mᴿ Hills at New York, and shall send him a copy of Mᴿ Learned's r.r bill about the Tunnel that he may examine it, and give me his opinion about it. We met this forenoon, & meet again to-morrow, and I expect to be home on Thursday morning.

Mᴿ Bowles, I see, speaks pretty well of the Bill—rather to my surprise.

Nothing specially new.

Your aff. father
E. Dickinson

[*To Wm. A. Dickinson Esq., Amherst, Mass.*]

Boston, Tuesday Evening
March 3, 1874

Dear Austin

I have only time to say that I reached here, at 11. oclock safe & sound. Bro Wm came into the cars at Worcester, to see me. I went immediately into the Com^ee room—then to the session which continued till 5½—& am now going to a session of our Com^ee this evening. Can write no more, now.

You had better leave the matter of Grand Rapids Water Bonds so that you can take 3000. or $4000. between this & Commencement —& probably you could take $2000. 1st April.

Your aff. father
E. Dickinson

"The Harvard College Case," to which Mr. Dickinson refers in the next letter, had a bearing on the finances of Amherst College.

On January 19, 1874, William Whiting of Pembroke had introduced in the House of Representatives a bill entitled "An Act Concerning the Taxation of Religious, Charitable and other Societies and Corporations."[14] "Other" corporations included the colleges of the state. Their exemption from taxation would thus be placed in jeopardy, a matter of interest to Harvard University. President Eliot prepared a long memorandum, the gist of which was presented to the joint committee "On Just and Equal Taxation" on March 5 by Francis B. Crowninshield, a member of the Corporation.

[*To Wm. Austin Dickinson Esq, Amherst, Mass.; postmark: Boston Mar 5 6 P.M.*]

Thursday Evening Mch 5. '74

Dear Austin

I have spent the forenoon, in the Com^ee on Equal & Just Taxation —heard the Harvard College Case argued, and Wmstown & Amherst were waiting to be heard, when the Com^ee adj^d one week.

14. *Journal of the House*, 1874, 40; 226.

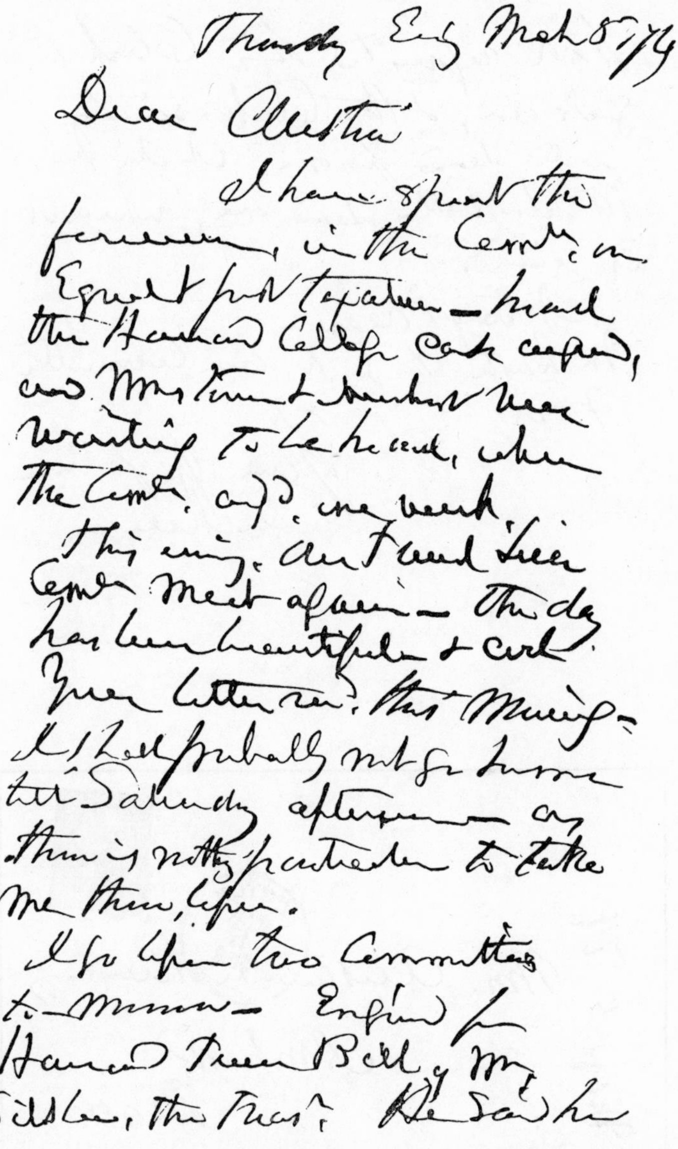

Thursday Eveg Mch 5/74

Dear Austin

I have spent this forenoon, in the Comee on Equal taxation—heard the Harvard College case argued, and Mr. [illegible] [illegible] were waiting to be heard, when the Comee adjd one week.

This evng. our [illegible] Comee meet again—the day has been beautiful & cool. Your letter recd. this morning—

I shall probably not go home till Saturday afternoon—as there is nothing particular to take me there, before.

I go before two Committees to-morrow—Engineer for Harvard [illegible] Bill, & Mr. Sibley, the Treasr. He said he

Letter from Edward Dickinson to his son, March 5, 1874

had *reports to his Clerk to*
get one, & the Clerk said he
would send for one, whether they
Mr. S. will send me, when it
is said.

    Nothing new —
In haste — to go to our Committee
room

        Your aff. father
        E. Dickinson

Wm. Austin Dickinson Esq
     Amherst
      Mass

Mar 5 '74

This evening, our Tunnel Line Com^ee meet again—the day has been beautiful—& cool.

Your letter rec^d this morning. I shall probably not go home till Saturday afternoon—as there is nothing particular to take me there, before.

I go before two Committees to-morrow. Enquired for Harvard [word illegible] Bill of Mr Silsbee, the Treas^r. He said he had requested his Clerk to get one, & the Clerk said he would send for one, which he, Mr S. will send me, when it is received.

Nothing new.

In haste to go to our Committee room

Your aff. father
E. Dickinson

[*To Wm. Austin Dickinson Esq, Amherst, Mass; postmark: Boston Mass Mar 7 5 A.M.*]

Thursday [Friday] Evening March 6. 1874

Dear Austin,

I have rec^d a copy of the Harvard College [word illegible] Bill, & shall bring it with me to-morrow. I don't certainly know whether I shall go in the morning, or evening.

I have been before the Com^ee on Mercantile Affairs, to get our Amherst Gas Light Co. extended. We have not yet done anything about the Dist. Courts in this County, but expect to have up the subject next week.—

Our Tunnel Line Com^ee have to-day prepared a Bill & a Report, which is to be offered in the Senate, on Monday of next week. It is signed by seven out of ten of the Com^ee.

It is substantially the Bill published in the newspapers, with a Report explaining it, & showing how it will operate, practically. It is not perfectly satisfactory, but perhaps as good as any thing we shall be likely to prepare.

Your letter was rec^d this morning, and it seems that the measures taken to carry the town at Town Meeting are working to the development of the secret springs of the action of the Wire-pullers.

I hope [Flavel] Gaylord & others may be of some use in stirring up the Leaders.

To-day & yesterday have both been very beautiful days, here, and seem like healthy weather.

Judge French has got back from [to?] Boston.

I shall not come back till Tuesday. Well—nothing more.

Your aff. father
E. Dickinson

CHAPTER XXXIV

Last Letters of Edward Dickinson

1

ON March 11, 1874, Charles Sumner, senior senator from Massachusetts, died suddenly in Washington. The "melancholy intelligence" reached the General Court the following day. A joint committee of eighteen, of whom Mr. Dickinson was one, was appointed "to consider and report what measures it may be expedient and proper to adopt as a recognition of the important services" of "our great orator, scholar, statesman, philanthropist—the champion of universal freedom and the equal rights of man."

Mr. Dickinson was profoundly shaken not only by the suddenness of Sumner's death but by the circumstances of it. Less than a month before, on February 13, the legislature had passed a resolution "rescinding and annulling a Resolution passed December 18, 1872, 'censuring the Honorable Charles Sumner for his motion to eliminate the names of fratricidal battles of the Civil War from the Army Register and from the National Flags.' "[1] This rescinding resolution was to be presented to the Senate of the United States on

1. *Journal of the House,* 1874; 131-135; 268-270.

Charles Summer's outspoken conviction that slavery was intolerable had resulted in a deadlock in the Massachusetts legislature when he was a candidate for United States Senator in 1851. Many Democrats refused to vote with the Free Soilers for such a "radical." Mr. Sumner was finally elected (April 24) by a majority of one vote and quickly became the recognized leader of northern anti-slavery sentiment. He remained in the Senate for the rest of his life. During the Civil War he served as chairman of the Senate Committee on Foreign Relations, and more than any other man helped to avert the threat of war with England during that critical time. In 1872 Mr. Sumner introduced in the Senate his proposal to eliminate the names of Civil War battles. Massachusetts misinterpreted this magnanimous act, denounced the resolution and condemned its originator.

the tenth of March. Against the advice of his physician Sumner went to the Senate to hear the words of vindication from his state. He had that satisfaction. But a few hours later he was stricken with a heart attack and died the next day. The resolutions of the General Court on Sumner's death were passed unanimously by a rising vote. On Monday, March 16, the Court recessed to permit the members to attend his funeral.

Beginning on March 24, and for more than three weeks thereafter the legislators were occupied with the choice of a successor. A vote was taken every day. The principal contestants were:

Charles Francis Adams, Boston
Benjamin R. Curtis, Boston
Henry L. Dawes, Pittsfield
E. Rockwood Hoar, Concord[2]
Wendell Phillips, Boston
John E. Sanford, Taunton
William B. Washburn, Greenfield

Mr. Dickinson voted for Charles Francis Adams on every one of the thirty-four ballots except two, when he switched to Judge Hoar in the hope of reaching a decision. Finally on Friday, April 17, Governor Washburn was elected. As a result of this prolonged contest the "prorogation" of the legislature was postponed until the last day of June, a fact which had a direct bearing on the life and death of Edward Dickinson.[3]

2. Although Thomas Wentworth Higginson reported (*Letters and Journals*, 263) that Charles Sumner once said to him, "After I am gone, there is nothing in the gift of the people of Massachusetts which George F. Hoar may not expect," his name was not put forward at this time. It was his brother, Judge Rockwood Hoar, who competed with Mr. Dawes of Pittsfield for first place when the voting started.

3. As the Speaker of the House said on the day of adjournment: "The death of Mr. Sumner came upon us in the midst of our work, not only as an unspeakable loss, but with the burden of an unexpected duty. Fortunately it was delayed until after one of your number had borne to him the assurance that he still enjoyed the honor and confidence of the legislature, which had so often chosen him to his high office. In the election which ensued, like a mariner surprised by a sudden tempest in an unknown sea, without prepared chart or certain observation, we were driven about for many days in peril of serious damage if not total loss. I judge that the interruptions and diversion of thought incident to the canvass and to the tributes of respect to the memory and fame of the great senator, have prolonged our session nearly or quite a month" (*Journal of the House*, 1874, 704).

[*To Wm. A. Dickinson Esq, Amherst, Mass.; postmark: Boston Mass
Mar 25 5 A.M.*]

Boston Tuesday Evening March 24. '74

Dear Austin

The day is remarkably bright & beautiful. Pres^t Clark & M^r
Stockbridge have been before the Com^ee of Agriculture to-day, on
the subject of Fertilisers, & the Dog fund—& made some strong
statements which seemed to impress the Com^ee.

We have had one ballot for Senator in the House, & more than
that, in the Senate—with about this result—

Dawes—61	Hoar—68	Curtis 63
Adams 12	Washburn 2	Wendell Phillips 2
Sanford 14 (16)	Several others—one or two apiece	

Senate—Dawes—last Ballot 17.

Hoar	10.
Curtis	10
Whole no. of votes in House	235
Necessary to choice	118

To-morrow both houses vote in joint convention. To-night a
caucus is called by Dawes' friends. I presume there will be great
caucussing to-night and no calculation can be made as to the result,
or when it can be reached. Nothing of importance can be done, until
the Senatorial question is settled.

The day has been very cold—all the Members of the House were
present except 5.—some of them away sick.

Pres^t Clark will not go home before to-morrow. I did not hear
from you to-day—hope to hear to-morrow.

No more to say.
Your aff. father
E. Dickinson

P.S. 7½ oclock

The Tremont House swarms with Lobby members from Berkshire
& Springfield—for Dawes—a little disappointed that their candidate
did not lead to-day. They now expect that the scattering complimentary votes may be cast to-morrow, for him—perhaps they may.
It looks, this evening, as if the election lay between Dawes & Hoar—
but nobody can tell. It is said that the Custom House [men] were
at the State House this afternoon, in Dawes' favor.

I have looked for paper for your Library, and am told that

formerly there was a large quantity of your pattern, but has been none, for some years.

[*To Wm. A. Dickinson Esq, Amherst, Mass; postmark: Boston Apr 1*]

> Tremont House
> Boston
> Boston. Tuesday Evening
> March 31, 74

Dear Austin,

Another vote on Senator. The Dawes men have invited the Republicans of the Legislature to a supper, at the Tremont House, this evening, as a Caucussing festival. No nearer an election than before. I intend to go home to-morrow afternoon, and if I think it will do, I shall not return till Monday; tho' I cant tell how the prospect looks to-morrow.

I have to-day seen the agent of the Knickerbocker Ins. Co. and told him how Bartlett feels about his Policy. He says he will write immediately to the New York office, & tell them what I say, & let me know, by Saturday, if I am there, what his Principals say about it. I told him that he had better consider whether it was not better for them to put the papers just where they were, before Bartlett signed the application for the new policy; I told him that Bartlett has determined to have the matters put back where they were before.

Henry F. Hills wrote me, yesterday that he was going to Amherst to-day, and would be here to-morrow.

I shall be glad to see him. Nothing new.

> Your aff. father
> E. Dickinson

2

The next letter from Edward Dickinson is dated six weeks later. During the interim he spent a week at the Hoosac Tunnel with the tunnel committees, leaving Boston on April 27. But mostly he was occupied with matters of local and individual concern. Opposed to a ten-hour, six-day work week, then the customary hours of labor in the factory system, he had always encouraged efforts both in Congress and in the state legislature to change the prevailing schedule. Finally, on April 21, 1874, the Massachusetts House of Representatives passed "An Act to regulate the Hours of Labor in Manu-

facturing Establishments," the conservative provisions of which were
at least a step in the right direction.[4]

Meanwhile, affairs at home were being taken care of. A letter
from his son illustrates the way in which Austin had shouldered
community burdens. He was at the moment drafting the articles of
incorporation of the Amherst Library Association. Such a society,
with dues-paying members, had been first organized in 1793, when
the entire collection was kept in a single bookcase. Then, after the
founding of the college in 1821, residents of the town could draw
upon its library, within limits. But their needs had been supplied
for the most part by small libraries in the various school districts.

The first public library in the modern sense was established in
1873. It was to be free to all responsible citizens for one year "as
an experiment." Located over Adams' drug store on the corner of
Main and Pleasant Streets, it was opened on February 25, 1874.[5]

[*To Hon Edward Dickinson, Tremont House, Boston*]

Amherst, April 22[d] 74.

Dear father—

I wish after looking at the 11th sec of Chap 224 of the Stats of
1870, you would ask the Commissioner of Corporations, whoever
he is, if the certificate to be signed by president and others is a
formal affair, or only very simple. Perhaps there may be blanks for
such certificates, or perhaps he will show you one which has been
approved for a Library association forming themselves into a corporation, and so save me the trouble of writing one out with any
care and study.

I send you along a letter received this morning from that C. D.
Smith.

Another from, I judge, Mrs Horn, though I have[nt] read it, thinking you would have to any way, and that one would be enough to
wade in that sort of mud.

I will remind you that Gaylord would like the bill made up for
services in the Cook-Town Case. If you care to make any inquiry
about it before you come home you can, and then we[ll] make it up.

4. Massachusetts *House Documents*, 1874, No. 284.
5. *History of Amherst*, 347-354.

Ed Burrell and Co. of Worcester want very definite information about Couch & Heywood—something "later than March 7th"— "Estimate of means," "present prospects," "*urgent*".

I would inquire and reply, but dont know what you may have said, or know, so shall leave it to you unless you wish me to investigate, and that I should have to do pretty much de novo.

I wish you would get and bring when you come a pint bottle of Maynard & Noyes ink from some good stationer, perhaps the trouble with ours is that it has stood in Mr Adams' cupboard too many years, and that some of more recent manufacture would go better. It has come off bright this p.m. but it is cool and Marchy.

Lou and Fannie [Norcross] came last Monday evening are making headquarters at the Potwins, were at your house last night and are to be at mine to night. Nothing new here. I sent your Insurance policy to Kirkland yesterday. There was no case for the jury before the Supreme Court, and whether anything else I dont know, the jurymen from here were back mid afternoon—through. Your letter received this morning.

Austin

[*To* Mrs *Edward Dickinson, Amherst, Mass.; postmark: Boston, Mass. May (13?)*)]

Boston May 12. 1874

Dear Austin,

I have left your tassels at Lawrence, Wild[e, Hull] & Coy & got the 2. doz. rings.

The Agl College Scholarship Bill comes up to-morrow, in the House, for discussion.

There is a little look like going forward with the important business. [John B.] Gough lectures this evening, & the members of the House are invited by invitation given from the Speaker's Desk—& to sit on the platform, in Music Hall.

The weather is very pleasant. There was quite a white frost, this morning. Dr Loring has got back into the Chair.

Nothing new.

Your aff. father
E. Dickinson

[*In the same envelope*]

Boston, Wednesday Evening
May 13, 1874

Dear Family,

The weather has been very comfortable to-day, and I am very well.

The Ag^l College Bill for a grant of money has been up this afternoon, and I have advocated it, and carried it, one stage. It will come up tomorrow again, and I hope we shall carry it.

Nothing new. I dont find any package from Susan, for Fanny & Louisa.

Mr Montague says he will send us 15. or so lbs. of his last maple sugar.

I think of nothing particular to say.

Love to you all—& to Austin's family.

Yours aff^y.
E. Dickinson

M^r [Edmund H.] Sawyer & his wife of East Hampton are here. I have met them this evening.

[*To Wm. A. Dickinson Esq, Amherst, Mass*]

Boston Thursday Evening
May 14. 1874

Dear Austin

Another warm day—and a busy day in the House. Our Tunnel Com^{ee}, & the Hoosac Tunnel Com^{ee} met together this morning, to confer in regard to the course to be taken to finish the Tunnel—before we discuss the *disposition* of it.

I rec^d your letter, this morning, and think you are right in letting the Parish matter subside till next Fall. I think things will get into better shape after the last instalment of the subscription for the *debt* is paid.

I can't say whether I shall go home, Friday night, or not before Saturday.

I think the Ag^l College Bill will come up for another reading to-morrow. We cant tell what will be its fate, in the next stage.

I made a speech in favor of the amendment to take the money from the Treasury, *directly*—not to touch the *Dog Fund.,* which seems very *sacred* to very many of the country members.

It looks as if the College would get what it wants, in one of the ways proposed.

You say that you wish to go to N.Y. next Monday. I shall try to stay at home when you are gone—unless the Tunnel, or some of the things requiring my attention bring me back earlier.

N. Mayo left me a note to-day that his mother accepts his offer to settle with him by accounting for the $1000. which she gave to M[rs] Spear, so that the disputed matter between them will be settled.

I have not seen Stone, nor M [name illegible], since I came back. I had a talk with Carpenter last evening, & heard his views about the tunnel. He will make a speech upon it, in the Senate—& offer a Bill as a substitute for L[e]arned's.

No more to-night.

Your aff. father. E. Dickinson.

I am glad the Sweetsers [?] are pleased.

[*To M[rs] Edward Dickinson, Amherst, Mass.*]

Boston Friday Evening
May 15. 1874

Dear Family,

I shall not go home till to-morrow, Saturday. afternoon, as the Ag[l] College Bill is passing along in the House, & may need me to-morrow forenoon. The college will prevail, in the House. We can't promise for the Senate.

The weather is very pleasant, and spring-like.

Anna Newman called to see me, on Wednesday, but I missed her. She left me pictures of herself & M[r] Carleton—which I shall carry home.

The House is beginning to act as if they intended to get through, at some time. I hope I may stay at home a few days, next week—when Austin writes me that he intends to go to New York.

Unless something will require my care, here, I shall stay at home the first half of the week.

M[r] Gillett & his wife & M[r] Delano were here, this morning.[6]

Nothing more to-night.

Yours affy.
E. Dickinson

6. Charles Delano, prominent Northampton lawyer.

Anna Newman and George H. Carleton were married on June 3, 1874, at the home of Judge French in Concord. Her daughter, Mrs. Pearl, says that "it only needed Edward Dickinson's 'very pleasantly impressed,' in his most dignified manner, after my father had been presented to him at a cousin's home in Cambridge, to make my mother feel that she had chosen her husband wisely."

3

The last weeks of Edward Dickinson's life were filled with anxiety about the health of his grandson, "Ned" Dickinson. He was a gentle likable boy, but from birth had been a semi-invalid. He suffered from severe epileptic seizures, of which his father's diary is distressing proof. During the month of May, 1874, Ned had an attack of inflammatory rheumatism. His grandfather's deep concern is evident in the letters which follow. Ned was not only his namesake, he was the only male heir on whom continuity of succession depended.[7]

[*Envelope missing*]

Boston May 26. 1874

Dear Austin

I reached here at 11. o'clock to-day. I went to your house, before I came away, to enquire for Ned, & left word with Lavinia to have

7. When, after Ned Dickinson's recovery from inflammatory rheumatism, it finally became evident that he would never be strong enough to carry on the succession, it was a question whether another heir could be expected. But in 1875, the year after Edward Dickinson's death, a second son was born and they named him Thomas Gilbert Dickinson. From then on Austin's devotion was centered on the winsome boy. When he died of a fever at the age of eight, his father received a blow from which he never fully recovered. A pall descended upon the entire family. For that sunlit child had been the joy and delight, as well as the hope, of both their houses. Now their only bond was gone. Gilbert died on October 5, 1883. The date of birth on his gravestone is August 1, 1876; but the town records give his age at the time of his death as eight years, two months, five days, which would place his birth a year earlier.

Young Edward Dickinson never married, and he died on May 3, 1898. His mother survived him for fifteen years.

you send a Postal card, to let me know how he was, this morning. I felt quite concerned about him.

M^r L[e]arned has occupied the afternoon in the Senate, on the Tunnel, in reply to Dr Loring & Carpenter—and to-morrow, goes on with his argument in favor of his own Bill.

We have discussed the Lee & N. Haven r.r. Bill in the House this afternoon. I made a speech against it, with Codman & Phillips. Montague paired with somebody, so as not to vote. Gates voted for the Bill—Bassett & Davis of Ware, in the same way.

Lee carried the vote, by 7. majority, many members being absent. Several changed their votes ag^t them since the last reading.

Codman moved to reconsider, & that will come up to-morrow forenoon, 10. oclock.

I hope we may yet kill it. It looks more like business, now, than ever before.

Aiken & Gates came from Amherst, with me this morning.

The day has been beautiful.

I think if you can get Coy to come up to my house, & touch up the bare spots on the buggy & have it dry, this week, you had better do it. You can tell him what to do. He can first touch it with a little black,—then, perhaps, a little black varnish.

We shall want to go to Court with it, next week.

Nothing new, or further, to-night.

Your aff. father
E. Dickinson

I forgot to leave stamps at home & send some for the family.

The next letter, and those of May 28 and June 5, are written on the official stationery of the House of Representatives with the seal of the Commonwealth on the engraved letterhead.

[*Envelope missing*]

Commonwealth of Massachusetts
House of Representatives
Boston May 26 1874

Dear Austin,

Rec^d your letter of yesterday, this morning, & that of this morning, about 6.o'clock, this evening. Sorry to hear that Ned suffers so much, but hope the disease will remain, Rheumatism in his limbs, & not do worse, & that he will soon be better.

The Lee & N. Haven r.r. bill was refused a re-consideration, this morning—& it now goes to the Senate. The House was very thin, when the vote was passed. We hope to defeat it in the Senate.[8]

It has been May training to-day. Several Companies of Artillery, Colored Cavalry & Infantry were out, & attracted great attention of great crowds. To-morrow is the day for David Cowls [?] Bankrupt meeting. Mrs Watson may call on you to prove her claims ag^t him— & others may.

Mrs Howard should pay $10. in addition to the fees for mortgage &c.

If Ned grows worse, & I can be of any service, at home, telegraph me—for I consider his recovery of more consequence than all the legislation.

I think, now, that I shall be home Friday night.

Mr Bullard has invited me to go with him to the Congregational Club at Faneuil Hall, Thursday evening, and I have accepted.

A good many strangers are in the City. Tell Ned to be as courageous as he can. I hope he will soon be better.

Your aff. father
E. Dickinson

I would not neglect Ned for Mr Olmsted, even.

Frederick Law Olmsted, the eminent landscape architect, made occasional visits in Amherst to consult with Austin Dickinson about the college grounds. At this time they were planning to improve the village common, which was partly swamp and partly hayfield.

[*To Wm. A. Dickinson Esq, Amherst, Mass. postmark: (May) 29, 5 AM*]

Commonwealth of Massachusetts
House of Representatives
Boston, May 28, 1874

Dear Austin,

Your letter was rec^d this morning—glad to hear that Ned seemed to be better, yesterday afternoon—hope he is still improving.

Last evening I attended the meetings of the Young Men's Chris-

8. This bill was finally defeated on the afternoon of the day Edward Dickinson died. (*Journal of the House,* 1874, 543-545; 547-548; 616-618. See also *House Documents,* Nos. 373 and 486.)

tian Association—heard Pres^t Eliot of Harvard College, Phillips Brooks, & Edw. E. Hale—& was much pleased with their speeches.

This evening, I expect to go to Faneuil Hall, to attend the annual supper of the Congregational Club.

I suppose the Legislature will adjourn to-morrow noon, till Monday next, on account of "Decoration Day" and I expect I shall be home Friday evening.

I saw Louisa & Fanny, this noon, Joel's wife has gone to Philadelphia.

The day has been beautiful, & there are many people here, attending the Anniversaries. To-day is the great day for all kinds of societies.⁹

> Your aff. father
> E. Dickinson

[*To Wm. A. Dickinson Esq, Amherst, Mass; postmark: Boston Mass May 29, 5 AM*]

> United States
> Postal Card

Your letter of Thursday morning rec^d at 5 P.M. to-day. Very glad to hear that Ned is better—letter written & mailed before receiving this.

> E. Dickinson

[*To Wm. A. Dickinson Esq, Amherst, Mass.; postmark: Boston Mass. Jun 6, 8 A M*]

> Commonwealth of Massachusetts
> House of Representatives
> Boston, June 5, 1874

Dear Austin,

I hoped that I might go home this evening, but our Tunnel Bill is on an Order of the Day, for to-morrow, and I think I ought to stay during the forenoon.

9. In May of each year conventions of religious and benevolent societies were held in Boston, among them the Massachusetts Bible Society; American Education Society; American Peace Society, in which F. D. Huntington had been the prime mover; Unitarian Festival; Massachusetts Home Missionary Society; the Convention of Congregational Ministers of Massachusetts; and others.

I have got your moulding made, they not having any on hand, at Bumstead's.

I am glad to hear that Ned is rather improving. The weather to-day, is very warm. I have not yet seen Mayo, but shall try to, in the morning, if I can. I will also see about the Pear scions.

Judge Lord sent me a note that he is holding Court at Cambridge, and invited me to go home with him, some night. I declined for this week—on account of things which detained me here.

I don't see, now, how I can go home till to-morrow afternoon, & reach home in the evening. Sorry not to be able probably, to be there all day, as you wish.

I shouldn't be here much longer, & never again, so we must put up with the inconvenience.

Your aff. father
E. Dickinson

Written on Friday, June 5, 1874, this is the final letter in the packet labeled "Some of the last letters of E. Dickinson." The legislative session had been prolonged beyond the usual date of adjournment and the heat was becoming intense.

CHAPTER XXXV

Death of Edward Dickinson

E DWARD DICKINSON had planned to spend Sunday, June 7, at home. Whether or not he did so is not clear. But he did spend the following Sunday in Amherst if we are to depend on Emily's word. She wrote: "Sabbath morning was peculiarly dear to my father, and his unsuspecting last earthly day with his family was that heavenly one" (*Letters*, 1894, 376; *Letters*, 1931, 366). If this is true, he would have returned to Boston on Monday, June 15, 1874, only the day before he died alone in a Boston hotel. The following paragraphs are taken from *The Boston Transcript*, June 17:

Hon. Edward Dickinson of Amherst, a member of the Massachusetts House of Representatives from the Fourth Hampshire District, died quite suddenly at his rooms at the Tremont House yesterday afternoon of apoplexy. Mr. Dickinson was in his seat in the House during the forenoon session and spoke upon the bill to appropriate $3,000,000 for the completion of the Troy & Greenfield Railroad. Feeling some premonition of illness, he left the House soon after, and not far from one o'clock was smitten with apoplexy. A physician was at once summoned, but he lingered most of the time in an unconscious state, and died at a quarter before six o'clock. . . .

His father was among the first founders of Amherst College, and the subject of this sketch has been for nearly half a century identified with its interests. He was elected the treasurer of the college in 1835, and held the position for nearly forty years—the trustees being unwilling to accept his resignation when it was tendered something over a year ago, and it is only recently that he has been released from its duties and responsibilities, which now devolve upon his son, Austin, who has also been his partner in the practice of the law for several years past. Mr. Dickinson, by his faithful labors in the interest of the college, has done much to bring it to its present strong financial condition. . . .

Some years ago he was actively engaged in securing the first railroad facilities for the town of Amherst, and was instrumental in obtaining the charter for the road from Palmer to Amherst, which was subsequently extended to Miller's Falls. It was understood that he served in the present Legislature for the main purpose of securing to his town all the advantages of the Massachusetts Central Railroad. He was a member of the Joint Special Committee on the Hoosac Tunnel Line of Railroads, and the main burden of his speech yesterday morning was to guard the interest of the Massachusetts Central Railroad. . . .

The immediate relatives who are so suddenly bereaved are an aged wife, who has been the partner of his joys and sorrows from early life; a son, who, as before stated, was associated with his father in the practice of the law at Amherst; two daughters who are unmarried; a brother, William, who resides in Worcester and is engaged in the banking business; and a sister, the wife of Rev. Asa Bullard, Secretary of the Congregational Publication Society, who resides at Cambridgeport. None of his family were present at the time of his death.

At a meeting of the Hampshire County bar on June 18, Judge S. T. Spaulding, in behalf of the committee, submitted to the Superior Court, then sitting in Northampton, a number of resolutions, prefacing them with a personal tribute to Edward Dickinson.[1] I. F. Conkey followed, recalling that he began his own study of the law with the deceased. He was, said Mr. Conkey, a "laborious, painstaking, industrious lawyer, preserving and keeping to the last the customs and habits of the olden school of practitioners. . . . Only last week, when at home during a recess of the Legislature, the light in his office in the evening was seen as usual, and he was there ready to attend the calls of his clients and friends." Mr. Conkey described him as "a man of natural dignity and great personal presence. . . . It was sometimes said of him that he was austere, aristocratical, perhaps and cold hearted," but this, said Mr. Conkey, was not the fact. Charles Delano added that the deceased had such high ideas of the duty of the members of the profession that he, Mr. Delano, asked whether it would not be well for the younger members to scan Mr. Dickinson's character for their own "profit and example."

The funeral was held on Friday afternoon, June 19, at the homestead. The following account appeared in *The Republican,* June 20, 1874:

No poverty of accommodation or modesty of program, however, could keep away the village. . . . Chairs and settees about the lawn accommodated

1. The *Amherst Record,* June 24, 1874.

those whom the large rooms of the house would not seat. The face that the open coffin displayed seemed as self-reliant and unsubdued as in life. A simple wreath of white daisies, from his own meadow opposite, were the only flowers allowed. And the services were confined to the singing of a hymn, and reading from the scriptures and a single prayer by Rev Mr Jenkins. . . . The hearse was dispensed with, and the college professors and as many and more of the business men of the village united to bear the coffin to the grave-yard. The stores were closed and business was suspended in the village during the exercises. . . .

Many distinguished men "from abroad," walked in the procession, among them Samuel Bowles, the Reverend Mr. Dwight, the Reverend Mr. Colton, Charles Delano, Esq., the Hon. E. H. Sawyer, and Judge S. T. Spaulding. At the grave, reading of scripture was followed by the Lord's Prayer.

When, on June 30, the Massachusetts House of Representatives adjourned, John E. Sanford, the speaker, said in summarizing the events of the session:

. . . On this midsummer day—a day in the calendar on which the voice of the legislator has not been wont to be heard in these halls I . . . forbear to delay the final hour of prorogation. I only ask to record my judgment that no House of Representatives, within my own observation, has assembled with a better purpose or a larger ability for the prompt discharge of its duties; and that the tedious delays and ultimate failure to solve the problem of utilizing the Hoosac Tunnel are due in part to causes beyond your control, but chiefly to the inherent difficulty which a body constituted like the legislature must always find in dealing with questions of business management and practical detail. Such questions are not within the legitimate province of the law-making power. It never was, and never will be, its appropriate function to solve them. . . .

We separate with ranks not quite unbroken. Two, to whom places had been assigned with us, did not live to occupy them; and one seat is but freshly vacant. Our honored and lamented associate (Mr. Dickinson of Amherst), among the ripest of our number in years and wisdom, conspicuous as a friend of learning and for high official service in the state and nation, respected and trusted for his firm integrity, was stricken down at his post in the midst of duty. The voice to which we listened at noonday was silent at the going down of the sun. For him it was well. Death could not come to him unseasonably to close an honorable and well-spent life. . . .

At an afternoon session on the same day, "the Secretary of the Commonwealth . . . declared the General Court prorogued until the Tuesday next preceding the first Wednesday in January next."[2]

2. *Journal of the House,* 1874, 705-706; 712.

"Dying," said Edward Dickinson's daughter, "is a Wild Night and a New Road."

It was some time before Emily wrote a letter. When she did so, she was so dazed that she gave her "little cousins" a wrong date for her father's death, placing it a day earlier than it occurred.

To Louisa and Fanny Norcross she wrote:

You might not remember me, dears. I cannot recall myself. I thought I was strongly built, but this stronger has undermined me.

We were eating our supper the fifteenth of June, and Austin came in. He had a despatch in his hand, and I saw by his face we were all lost, though I didn't know how. He said that father was very sick, and he and Vinnie must go. The train had already gone. While horses were dressing, news came he was dead.

Father does not live with us now—he lives in a new house. Though it was built in an hour it is better than this. He hasn't any garden because he moved after gardens were made, so we take him the best flowers, and if we only knew he knew, perhaps we could stop crying. . . .

I cannot write any more, dears. Though it is many nights, my mind never comes home. Thank you each for the love, though I could not notice it. Almost the last tune that he heard was, "Rest from thy loved employ."

Emily.[3]

3. *Letters*, 1894, 280; *Letters*, 1931, 255.

CHAPTER XXXVI

The End

THE sudden death of Edward Dickinson gave to those closest "a finished feeling." Though they were still safe at home beneath his roof—and his roof it remained to the end—his womenfolk could not begin again because there was no world. Emily said so. Austin was there to be sure, next door. He dropped in several times a day to attend to their wants. But he had little time. The family relied for support on him alone, five women and an invalid son. Furthermore, not only must his wife, son and daughter, his mother and sisters, be provided for and his law practice carried on; the college could not be neglected, nor the needs of the town. Austin was now forty-five, his sisters forty-three and forty-one.

After Edward Dickinson's death his wife never regained enough strength to attend to her own small needs. One year from the day he died she had a stroke; three years later she broke her hip. Unaware of more than lassitude, she survived through four lingering years while her daughters hovered over her until one chilly morning—November 14, 1882—she "ceased." Of her death Emily wrote: "The great mission of pain had been ratified—cultivated to tenderness by persistent sorrow, so that a larger mother died than had she died before. There was no earthly parting. She slipped from our fingers like a flake gathered by the wind, and is now part of the drift called 'the infinite.'

"We don't know where she is, though so many tell us. . . ."

For a moment Emily's courage seemed to falter when she wrote: "The great attempt to save her life had it been successful, would have been fatigueless, but failing, strength forsook us." She added:

"I cannot tell how Eternity seems. It sweeps around me like a sea. . . ."

After her father's death Emily Dickinson's withdrawal had become complete and final. For this there was sufficient excuse. Not only were there her helpless mother's "dear little wants" to attend to; the years were bringing her heady bereavements, an ever-increasing load of grief. Those she loved best were following one by one: in 1878, Mr. Bowles; in 1881, Dr. Holland; in 1882, both her mother and Dr. Wadsworth; in 1883, her nephew, little Gilbert; and in March, 1884, Judge Lord of Salem. "I hardly dare to know that I have lost another friend," she wrote, "but anguish finds it out.

> "Each that we lose takes part of us;
> A crescent still abides,
> Which like the moon, some turbid night,
> Is summoned by the tides."[1]

True. And yet, each fresh sorrow brought with it not only prostration; it brought as well clearer insight and a sharpened tool with which to set down "the phrase to every thought." Just how soon after her father's death Emily Dickinson found the strength to take up her pencil again is hard to say. But strange as it seemed, "time does go on," she said. Not only that; throughout this period of mounting affliction her creative power did not subside. Of the poems in *Bolts of Melody,* fully 250 are from manuscripts in her late handwriting. And these are only a part. When the originals of all her poems are re-examined, it will probably be found that many more were written during these final years.

But in the meantime she had become ill, with Bright's disease. Less than four years after her mother's death she succumbed to the gathering dissolution around her and, on May 16, 1886, she died.

In the homestead only Lavinia was left to carry on, following in every particular the pattern her father had set. Austin continued of course to stand between her and life. But when, after nine more years, he broke under a burden too heavy to carry further, she was indeed alone, sustained only by her loyalty and by her pride of family. One day toward the end when asked to look at the light

1. The letters from which these passages are taken appeared in *Letters,* 1894, 295-296; and in *Letters,* 1931, 267-268, and 347.

on the Pelham hills she said, turning away, "There is no landscape since Austin died."

Alone with her pussies Lavinia Dickinson presided over her father's empty house. Maggie was still on hand, though only during the morning hours and to sleep at night; the afternoons were spent at her home in No Man's Land beyond the railroad tracks.

For four years Lavinia lived on until in her too "the Dickinson heart" stopped beating. The family of Edward Dickinson was no more. It had almost spanned the century.

Edward Dickinson, born, January 1, 1803.

Lavinia Norcross Dickinson, died, August 31, 1899.[2]

2. Edward Dickinson's only surviving descendant, Martha Gilbert Dickinson Bianchi, died without issue on December 21, 1943.

PART SEVEN

Relatives, Friends and Neighbors
Bibliography

Relatives, Friends and Neighbors

BIOGRAPHICAL NOTES

This directory has but one purpose, to clarify references to persons mentioned in the letters or in the explanatory text of this volume. Biographical details which do not serve that purpose are not included. Each entry contains only such details as have a bearing on the reference. In some instances there are only enough facts to identify a person; in others, a summary of his principal activities gives point to a casual reference, as in the case of President Clark of the Massachusetts Agricultural College. A full sketch of Colonel Higginson on the other hand, an important figure in the life of Emily Dickinson, is not required here, only a few details of his career previous to 1862 when his acquaintance with her began. Length of an entry bears little relation to a person's eminence. In accordance with this policy the Reverend Lyman Beecher, friend of Samuel Fowler Dickinson, requires more space than his more famous son, Henry Ward Beecher, a casual acquaintance.

Relatives mentioned in the text appear in this directory. In addition, on pages 509-511, there is a complete list of Emily Dickinson's aunts and uncles, the children of both grandfathers, Samuel Fowler Dickinson and Joel Norcross, each with his life span. If, in the letters, a close relative is not mentioned as frequently as his importance in the family would warrant (as in the case of Edward Dickinson's influential brother William, mentioned by Edward only once) a sketch of some length has been provided.

Among the *friends* of Edward Dickinson, men like George Ashmun, Thomas Eliot and Robert Winthrop, prominent in their day but now forgotten, are included, while personages as well known as Rufus Choate and Charles Sumner are not.

Neighbors also are allotted space proportionate not to their prominence while living but to the interest they may have for the reader. Casual acquaintances among the undergraduates of Amherst College whose sketches are in the *Amherst College Biographical Record, 1821-1939,* are for the most part omitted.

Names in italics indicate biographical sketches for such entries.

If no state is given, a town or a village is in Massachusetts.

Placed at the end are three lists: senators and representatives from Massachusetts in the Thirty-third Congress, 1853-1855; representatives from Amherst in the Massachusetts General Court (legislature) during the years covered by the correspondence; and public men of the Commonwealth mentioned by Edward Dickinson in his 1874 letters.

I

PELEG EMORY ALDRICH (1813-1895). Harvard Law School, 1844. Following his apprenticeship in the office of Ashmun, Chapman and Norton, Springfield, he moved to Barre, where he practiced for several years. In 1853 he was appointed State's Attorney of the Middle District (Worcester) to succeed *Benjamin F. Newton,* "quite a promising young man," who "was in poor health at the time and with great moderation and generosity, the new District-Attorney postponed taking the office until after Mr. Newton's death, an event which occurred after several months. He was so sensitive that he did not want even to seem to press Mr. Newton out of the office" (*Worcester Evening Gazette,* March 15, 1895). Mr. Aldrich was a member of the State Constitutional Convention of 1853 and of the Republican convention of September 7, 1854, the first Republican convention held in Massachusetts. He served as Mayor of Worcester in 1862, and was appointed judge of the Superior Court in 1873, an office held for the remainder of his life.

NATHAN ALLEN, M.D. (1813-1889). Amherst College, 1836. A prominent forward-looking physician who practiced in Lowell, 1841-1889. His thesis for his medical degree was entitled "The Connection of Mental Philosophy with Medicine." Trustee of Amherst College, 1857-1889.

GEORGE ASHMUN (1804-1870). Yale College, 1823. Practiced law in Springfield, 1828-1870. Elected to the Massachusetts General Court, he had four terms in the House (final term, 1841, as speaker), and two terms in the Senate (1838, 1839). He served in the Congress of the United States from 1845 to 1851. Mr. Ashmun opposed the Mexican War and the extension of slave territory. "He entered the Twenty-ninth Congress in 1845 as a Whig, and speedily made himself conspicuous as an impassioned and dependable defender of Daniel Webster, to whom he manifested a devotion amounting almost to idolatry. . . . Alone among the nine Massachusetts Representatives, Ashmun stood by Webster," who supported the Compromise of 1850. At the Whig national convention in Baltimore, June 16, 1852, Mr. Ashmun, as chairman of the Committee on Resolutions, "managed the presidential candidacy of Webster and served as chairman of the Platform Committee." General Winfield Scott was nominated, and in October, 1852, Webster died. Thereafter Mr. Ashmun abandoned politics until, on May 16, 1860, he was persuaded to become permanent chairman of the (second) Republican National Convention in Chicago, which nominated Abraham Lincoln for the presidency. For this nomination he had little enthusiasm. As he wrote that same year to Senator Henry Wilson, "all my love for any public man was long ago buried in the grave by the seaside" (that of Webster in Marshfield).

Quotations are from George S. Merriam, *The Life and Times of Samuel Bowles* (New York, 1885), I, 38-44; Charles Wells Chapin, *Sketches of the Old Inhabitants* . . . *of Old Springfield* (Springfield, 1893), 1-7; and F. Lauriston Bullard, "Abraham Lincoln and George Ashmun," *The New England Quarterly*, XIX (June, 1946), 184-211.

REV. HENRY WARD BEECHER (1813-1887). Eighth child of Lyman and Roxana Beecher. Amherst College 1834. Lane Theological Seminary 1834-1837. Ordained 1838. This famous preacher was renowned chiefly, as T. W. Higginson said, for "eloquence of feeling."

REV. LYMAN BEECHER (1775-1863). Congregational minister, descendant of a founder of the New Haven colony, he was graduated from Yale in 1797, studied theology under Timothy Dwight, and was ordained in 1799. He preached in the Presbyterian church at East Hampton, Long Island (1798-1810); in the First Congregational Church at Litchfield, Connecticut (1810-1826); in the Hanover (Congregational) Church, Boston (1826-1832); and in the Second Presbyterian Church, Cincinnati, Ohio (1833-1843). He resigned as pastor of the Boston church to accept the presidency of Lane Theological Seminary at Walnut Hills, Cincinnati, where he was also professor of didactic and polemic theology (1832-1850). At Litchfield and in Boston he was a prominent opponent of the growing "heresy" of Unitarianism, though as early as 1836 he was himself accused of being a "moderate Calvinist" and was tried for heresy, but was acquitted. Magnetic in personality, incisive and powerful in manner of expression, he was one of the most eloquent of American pulpit orators. In 1806 he preached a widely circulated sermon against dueling, and about 1814 a series of six sermons on intemperance which were often reprinted and greatly aided temperance reform. Thrice married, he had thirteen children; seven of his sons became Congregational ministers, and two of his daughters, Harriet Beecher Stowe and Catherine Esther Beecher, attained literary distinction. *Obituary Record of the Graduates of Yale College*, First Series, 84-85; *The Congregational Quarterly*, XIV (April, 1872), 265-269. *Autobiography and Correspondence of Lyman Beecher*, edited by his son, Charles Beecher (New York, 1864).

REV. POMEROY BELDEN (1811-1849). Amherst College, 1833. Andover Theological Seminary, 1833-1836. Ordained 1836. Pastor of Second Congregational Church (East Street), Amherst, 1842-1849.

REV. DANIEL BLISS (1823-1916). Amherst College, 1852. His Commencement oration (August 12, 1852) on "Agitation" created a profound impression by its "manly diction, strong utterance and glowing sentiment" (*Express*, August 13, 1852). Andover Theological Seminary, 1852-1855. Ordained, College Church, Amherst, October 17, 1855. Married *Abby Maria Wood* on November 23, 1855. With American Board of Commissioners for Foreign Missions, Syria, 1856-1862. Founder (1866) and president of Syrian Protestant College (American University), Beirut, Syria. Daniel Bliss joined the "Missionary Band" as an undergraduate and thereafter never wavered in his dedication to foreign missions. *The Reminiscences of Daniel Bliss*, Edited and Supplemented by his Eldest Son (New York, 1920).

LUCIUS BOLTWOOD (1792-1872). Williams College, 1814. Studied law with Samuel Fowler Dickinson and became his partner in 1817. One of the first citizens of Amherst. Secretary of the Amherst College Board of Trustees, 1828-1864. A Free Soil Whig, Mr. Boltwood was candidate for Governor of Massachusetts on the Liberty ticket in 1841. On August 30, 1824, he married Fanny H. Shepard, a first cousin of Ralph Waldo Emerson. She was a force to be reckoned with in the community.

ELBRIDGE GRIDLEY BOWDOIN (1820-1893). Amherst College, 1840. Admitted to the bar, May, 1847. Partner of Edward Dickinson, 1847-1855. After leaving Amherst he settled in Iowa.

SAMUEL BOWLES (1826-1878). Son of Samuel Bowles, founder of *The Springfield Republican*, to which, as editor, the younger man gave a national reputation. Professor Tyler (*History of Amherst College*, 1873, 514) described this Massachusetts sheet as "the ablest, the most influential, and the most successful provincial newspaper in America." He was elected a trustee of Amherst College by the legislature April 26, 1866, and served until his death in 1878. A Whig at the outset, Mr. Bowles became successively a Republican, a Liberal Republican, and an independent. George S. Merriam, *The Life and Times of Samuel Bowles*, 2 vols. (New York, 1885).

JOHN MILTON BREWSTER, JR. (1817-1902). M. A., Williams College, 1839. M.D., Berkshire Medical Institute, 1841. Practiced in Amherst 1843-1853. His wife died December 24, 1851.

REV. ASA BULLARD (1804-1888). Amherst College, 1828. Andover Theological Seminary, 1829-1831. Ordained, Portland, Maine, January 13, 1832, as an evangelist. Agent for Maine Sabbath School Union, 1831-1834. Secretary and general agent for Massachusetts Sabbath School Society, later known as Congregational Sunday School and Publishing Society, 1834-1874. Honorary secretary of the Society, 1874-1888. Author: *Fifty Years with Sabbath Schools; Sabbath School Chestnuts; The Dana Hill Stories*, etc. Editor of Society periodicals: *Sabbath School Visitor* (10 years), *Congregational Visitor* (3 years), *Wellspring* (31 years). Married Lucretia Gunn Dickinson, May 16, 1832. They lived at 24 Centre Street, Cambridge, and were members of the Prospect Street Congregational Church.

GEORGE H. and ANNA NEWMAN CARLETON. *See* MARK HASKELL NEWMAN

SAMUEL CUTTS CARTER (1803-1889). Came to Amherst from Andover in 1825 and set up a printing office and bindery. His firm printed the first local newspaper in Amherst. (See *Amherst, Massachusetts, Imprints, 1825-1876*, [1946], 11.) From 1837 to 1846, and again from 1857 to 1880, he served as town clerk and treasurer, and as postmaster for two terms, 1842-1845, and 1849-1853, at the conclusion of each term being succeeded by Seth Nims.

WILLIAM SMITH CLARK (1826-1886). Amherst College, 1848. Received a Ph.D. from the University of Göttingen in 1852, first member of the Amherst College faculty to hold that degree. Professor of chemistry, botany and zoology, Amherst College, from 1852 to 1867. He enlisted with the 21st Massachusetts Volunteers in 1861, resigning in 1863 with the rank of colonel. Representative in the General Court in 1864, 1865 and 1867, and president of the Massachusetts Agricultural College, Amherst, from 1867 to 1878. In 1876-1877, Colonel Clark founded the Imperial College of Agriculture, Sapporo, Japan. He became interested in a project called a "floating college," uniting scientific study with a tour around the world, a venture which was discontinued at the death of the originator on March 9, 1886. Married, May 25, 1853, the adopted daughter of *Samuel Williston*, Easthampton. They had eleven children.

CHARLES RUSSELL CODMAN (1829-1918). Harvard College, 1849. Studied law in the office of Hon. Charles G. Loring of Boston and was admitted to the bar in 1852. "For the next ten years, like many young men of his class and expectations, he did not engage in a general practice of the law, but employed his professional knowledge in the conduct of his own affairs, the care of trust estates and the like. Independent in fortune, the active years of his life thenceforward were devoted in ample measure to furthering the interest of the public; as churchman, as soldier, as Harvard man, and as a private citizen he never failed to respond to the call of duty. With his power of clear statement, of incisive argument and of forcible oratory, if necessity had compelled, and, but for a certain aloofness, if not coolness, of manner, Colonel Codman must have gone far both at the bar and in the world of politics."

He served in the army as Colonel of the "Cadet Regiment" (45th Massachusetts Volunteers), July, 1862-July, 1863; in the Massachusetts Senate, 1864-1865, and in the House, 1872-1875. William Vail Kellen, "Memoir of Charles Russell Codman," *Proceedings of the Massachusetts Historical Society*, LIII (1919-1920), 168-176.

REV. LYMAN COLEMAN (1796-1882). Yale College, 1817. Ordained 1825. Pastor in Belchertown, 1825-1832. Principal of Amherst Academy, 1844-1846, he taught Greek and German in Amherst College during the same period. Professor of German, College of New Jersey (Princeton), 1847-1849; teacher of the classics, church history and Biblical geography in the Presbyterian Academy, Philadelphia, 1849-1858; lived in Middletown, Connecticut, 1858-1861; and Professor of Ancient Languages, Lafayette College, Easton, Pennsylvania, 1861-1882. Married Maria Flynt (1801-1871) of Monson, September 21, 1826. Children: Olivia Maria (1827-1847); Eliza M. (1832-1871), who married the Rev. John Langdon Dudley (Amherst College, 1844), on June 6, 1861. *The Coleman Family*, etc., 1598-1867 (Philadelphia, 1867); *Obituary Record of the Graduates of Yale University*, Third Series, 65-66.

REV. AARON MERRICK COLTON (1809-1895). Yale College, 1835. Studied at Union and Andover Theological Seminaries and was ordained in

Amherst as pastor of the First Church, June 10, 1840, where he remained until January 4, 1853. He was active in revivals and in temperance reform. Pastor of the First Church, Easthampton, from March 2, 1853, to 1880. *Obituary Records of the Graduates of Yale University,* Fourth Series, 283.

ITHAMAR CONKEY (1788-1862). Studied law in Amherst with Noah D. Mattoon and practiced there, 1817 to 1862. An overseer of the Charitable Fund of Amherst College, 1846-1862. Delegate to the State Constitutional Convention, 1853.

ITHAMAR FRANK CONKEY (1823-1875), son of *Ithamar.* Attended Amherst College, 1839-1841, and received an honorary M.A. from the college in 1852. Practiced law in Amherst 1844-1875, and was representative in the General Court in 1854. Married Luthera Cutler, June 15, 1847.

REV. EDWARD PAYSON CROWELL (1830-1911). Amherst College, 1853. Andover Theological Seminary, 1856-1858. Professor of Latin, Amherst College, 1858-1908. Married Mary Warner (1830-1903), daughter of *Rev. Aaron Warner,* August 13, 1861.

AUGUSTUS NELSON CURRIER (1820-1896). Associated with the firm of Towne, Currier & Upham, flour merchants, Boston, before accepting the post of secretary of the People's Mutual Fire Insurance Company, Worcester, in 1857. That company, among others, was "closed out" by the great Boston fire of 1872. But meanwhile Mr. Currier had become director of many banks as well as insurance companies. Not only was he "among the best known insurance men in the state," he was one of Worcester's most useful and respected citizens.

Mr. Currier was twice married: first to Margareta Prentiss Dickinson of Holliston, June 30, 1844; and after her death to *Elisabeth Dickinson* (see *Elisabeth Dickinson Currier*), sister of *Edward* and *William Dickinson,* whom he married on October 10, 1866. By his first wife Mr. Currier had two sons, both of whom died at a comparatively early age, and one daughter Annie L. Dickinson Currier.

ELISABETH DICKINSON CURRIER (MRS. AUGUSTUS NELSON CURRIER) (1823-1886). Aunt of *Emily Dickinson.* On October 10, 1866, married *A. N. Currier* of Worcester. His daughter Annie, by a previous marriage, married Arthur Newton Brown. Annie had a bosom friend, Henrietta Williams, who lived near the Curriers on Harvard Street. Henrietta became the wife of Admiral Albert Ross. After his death, and after the death of Annie Dickinson Currier Brown, Mrs. Ross married Annie's widower, the same Mr. Brown. This is by way of introducing Mrs. Ross-Brown's remembrance of Elisabeth Dickinson Currier:

"She was a large, tall woman, rather distinguished in appearance, who usually dressed in royal purple, and always wore gloves. She is the one whom Emily described as 'the only male relative on the female side.' She was a dominating, strident personality, a typical step-mother, who made Annie's life miserable. Mr. Currier didn't dare say his soul was his own without her consent. She used to say, 'Eagles have the right idea. They push the eaglets out of the nest.' "

I asked Mrs. Ross-Brown whether Elisabeth Dickinson met her husband in Worcester at the house of her brother, William Dickinson. "No," she replied. "After Annie's mother's death, when Annie was about ten or twelve, her father, who was a very handsome man, went to Amherst. There Elisabeth Dickinson saw him and remarked to a friend, 'I am going to marry that man.' She was forty-three at the time. 'But you don't know him,' said her friend. 'That makes no difference. He is the man I'm going to marry.' And she did."

In describing a call from this same Aunt Elisabeth, Emily says that although it took place "many days since, its flavor of court-martial still sets my spirit tingling." (*Letters*, 1931, page 175.)

After a lingering illness, Mrs. Currier died of cancer on the twentieth anniversary of her marriage, October 10, 1886. A tribute in the *Worcester Daily Telegram* reads in part as follows:

"A great student all her life, and a teacher in her earlier days, she was eminently qualified to lead in charitable and church work. During all her residence in Worcester she has been a member of Union Church, taking an active part in all the work appertaining to the women's field. She was secretary of the board of visitors of the Home for Aged Females, and in that capacity devoted much of her time and gave to the work her sympathy and best endeavor."

WILLIAM CUTLER (1811-1870). Married Harriet M. Gilbert on June 22, 1842. Their children were Harriet Gilbert (1844-1845), Dwight Gilbert (born May, 1852), and Martha Isabella (born 1857). Mr. Cutler was a partner of *Luke Sweetser* in his general store until 1854, when he bought out Mr. Sweetser, thereafter Mr. Cutler carried on the business with his brother George, under the name of W. & G. Cutler.

Among members of the First Church, prominent at the time of construction of the new edifice (1867-1868), *Austin Dickinson* described Mr. Cutler as follows:

"Next in the row, perhaps next in importance, William Cutler, representative of one of the old and prominent families, the then leading merchant in the village, naturally slow and cautious, more apt to see objections than advantages—the course of events never quite to his mind—finding much to condemn, little to approve outside Daniel Webster and the old Whig party, but who went into the new church enterprise with a spirit that seemed almost like a revolution of himself, and carried many with him from the back seats, where the greatest confidence was felt in him, whom no one else could have moved." Dickinson, "Representative Men," 59.

REV. AUSTIN DICKINSON (1791-1849), not a close relative. Dartmouth College, 1813. Read law with Hon. *Samuel Fowler Dickinson* in Amherst and subsequently studied theology at Princeton and in West Hartford, Connecticut, where he was licensed to preach in 1819. Returning to his home in North Amherst, he became interested in plans for the founding of Amherst College. (Ornan Eastman, "Rev. Austin Dickinson," *The Congregational*

Quarterly, XIV [April, 1872], 282-293.) Left for "important enterprises at the South," but returned in the summer of 1822 to give all of his time to furthering the interests of the recently established college, "and soon became the leading mind in devising ways and means to meet its necessities" and procure a charter. To this work, as "Agent," he devoted his energies until in February, 1825, after nearly three years of struggle with the legis- lature, the charter was finally obtained. The author of his brief biography quotes the Rev. Jacob Abbott as saying that "all action of a legal or political character connected with the efforts to obtain a charter for the college was understood to be arranged and directed by him." Since "he did everything in the most quiet, unostentatious manner," his biographer concludes, "it would be well if the alumni and students of the college . . . could have some just appreciation of the earnest, self-sacrificing spirit with which he toiled to found the institution whose blessings they enjoyed." After an illness of only two days he died of "bilious dysentery" on August 14, 1849. (*Express*, August 24, 1849). It has been assumed that *Edward Dickinson* named his son for this friend and associate of his father, *Samuel Fowler Dickinson*. Compare footnote, page 510. Hitchcock, *Reminiscences*, 9-10.

CATHERINE DICKINSON (MRS. JOSEPH A. SWEETSER) (1814-1895). Aunt of *Emily Dickinson*. See JOSEPH A. SWEETSER.

EDWARD DICKINSON (1803-1874). Father of *Emily Dickinson*, eldest child of *Samuel Fowler Dickinson* and Lucretia Gunn Dickinson. Born in Amherst, January 1, 1803, he prepared for college at Amherst Academy and attended Amherst College for one year, the first of its existence, then transferred to Yale College where he was graduated as valedictorian of the class of 1823. For the next two years he read law in his father's office. After another year, 1825-1826, in the Northampton Law School, under Elijah H. Mills, Judge Samuel Howe and John H. Ashmun, he was admitted to the Hampshire County bar in 1826. For the next forty-eight years, until his death in 1874, he practiced law in his native town. He was moderator of town meetings in 1833, 1835, 1842, 1843, and 1849. He was treasurer of Amherst College from August 4, 1835 to July 10, 1872, when he resigned. In 1863 the college conferred upon him the honorary degree of LL.D.

Edward Dickinson married, May 6, 1828, *Emily Norcross*, daughter of *Joel Norcross* of Monson. They had one son and two daughters: *William Austin Dickinson, Emily Elizabeth Dickinson*, and *Lavinia Norcross Dick- inson*.

Edward Dickinson joined the First (Congregational) Church of Amherst on August 11, 1850.

His political career began as representative in the General Court of Massachusetts where he served in 1838 and 1839. (In published obituaries there is some discrepancy as to the years Edward Dickinson served as repre- sentative in the General Court. The dates here given are those in the records of the State Library of the Commonwealth of Massachusetts. A manuscript letter dated November 2, 1839, written by Luke Sweetser to his brother Joseph A. Sweetser in New York just before the election, also indicates that Mr. Dickinson's term ended in 1839. Mr. Sweetser wrote, "Edward Dickinson has no chance for Representative, not even with the aid of abolition. It's all the better for him in my opinion.") State senator in 1842 and 1843, he was a member of the governor's executive council in 1846 and 1847, holding the office of senior aide-de-camp, with the rank of major, to the major general of the state militia.

Edward Dickinson was a delegate to the National Whig Convention in Baltimore, June 16, 1852, and was elected later that year as representative from the recently redistricted Tenth Congressional District of Massachusetts to the Thirty-third Congress, 1853-1855. On January 27, 1854, he was admitted to practice before the Supreme Court of the United States. In 1861 he was proposed by the Republican party as lieutenant governor of Massachusetts, but refused to run. On an independent ticket he was again elected in 1873 to the House of Representatives of the General Court of Massachusetts for the following year. Before the end of that legislative session he died of apoplexy in Boston on June 16, 1874. Edward Dickinson left no will. Tyler, 1873, 538-540; *Obituary Record of the Graduates of Yale College,* Second Series, 129; *Biographical Directory of the American Congress, 1774-1949,* 1084. See also the *Amherst Record,* October 11, 1871.

From the *Journal of the* (Massachusetts) *House,* 1874 (627-628):

Mr. Billings of Hatfield announced the death on Tuesday, June 16, of Mr. Edward Dickinson of Amherst a member of the House.
Mr. Bassett of Easthampton moved the following resolutions:
Resolved, That the House has heard with deep emotion the tidings of the decease of a distinguished member, the Hon. Edward Dickinson of Amherst, the Representative of the Fourth District of Hampshire County.
Resolved, That the loss of one so long and so well known, so highly esteemed for his real worth and the nobility of his character, one who has been for nearly half a century distinguished in public life, repeatedly holding high offices in the state and national governments, and identified with one of our most prominent institutions of learning, known and honored by us for the virtues that marked the Christian gentleman, will be deeply felt by the whole community.
Resolved, That we tender the family of the deceased our deep sympathy in their great bereavement, and to the community in which he lived our condolence for its loss of an honest and faithful representative.
Resolved, That as a mark of respect for the services and character of the deceased, a committee be appointed to attend his funeral.
Resolved, That a copy of these resolutions be transmitted to the family of the deceased, and that as a further mark of respect the House now adjourn.
The resolutions were seconded by Mr. Brown of Marblehead, and remarks were also made by Messrs. Lamb of Greenfield, Billings of Sharon, and Hale of Boston.
The resolutions were unanimously adopted by a rising vote.
The Speaker appointed the following members of the House as the Committee to attend the funeral of the deceased:—
Messrs. Billings of Hatfield, Bassett of Easthampton, Wellington of Worcester, Lamb of Greenfield, Noble of Westfield, Montague of Sunderland, Gates of Pelham, Brown of Marblehead, Billings of Sharon.

ELISABETH DICKINSON (MRS. A. N. CURRIER) (1823-1886). Aunt of
Emily Dickinson. See ELISABETH DICKINSON CURRIER.

EMILY ELIZABETH DICKINSON (1830-1886). Born in Amherst, December 10, 1830, the daughter of *Edward* and *Emily Norcross Dickinson*.
Attended Amherst Academy intermittently 1840-1847; and Mount Holyoke
Female Seminary from September 30, 1847, to August 3, 1848. She visited
her Aunt Lavinia (*Mrs. Loring Norcross*) in Boston on three occasions,
in May-June, 1844; August-September, 1846, and September 4-22, 1851
(pages 162-164). Leaving Amherst on April 5, 1854, she spent three weeks
in Washington and more than two in Philadelphia (pages 364-378). Except
for visits, April to November, 1864, and April to October, 1865, to consult Henry W. Williams, M.D., 15 Arlington Street, Boston, about her eyes
(pages 432-437), thereafter Emily Dickinson remained at home. She died
May 15, 1886. (Compare page 433.)

EMILY NORCROSS DICKINSON (MRS. EDWARD DICKINSON)
(1804-1882). Mother of *Emily Dickinson,* born in Monson, July 3 (June
23), 1804. Attended a boarding school in New Haven, Connecticut, 1822-
1823; and on May 6, 1828, married *Edward Dickinson* of Amherst. Joined
the First (Congregational) Church, July 3, 1831. Mrs. Dickinson seldom
left home, making only brief visits in Monson; to her sister Lavinia (*Mrs.
Loring Norcross*) in Boston; and to New Haven with her husband for a
college reunion in 1853. Her longest absence from home was the journey
to Washington in April, 1854, while her husband was in Congress. She
died November 14, 1882.

LAVINIA NORCROSS DICKINSON (1833-1899). Sister of *Emily Dickinson,* born in Amherst, February 28, 1833. Attended Amherst Academy
intermittently, and Ipswich Female Seminary from December 5, 1849, to
July 31, 1850. Joined the First (Congregational) Church, November 3,
1850. Visited in Boston, September 6-22, 1851; went to Washington April
5, 1854, staying three weeks in Washington and more than two weeks in
Philadelphia before returning to Amherst. Except these and a few subsequent visits in neighboring towns and in Boston, Lavinia Dickinson
remained at home. She died August 31, 1899. A tribute by Professor
Joseph K. Chickering (who died on December 27, 1899) appeared in *The
Republican,* November 30, 1899.

THE LATE LAVINIA DICKINSON
A Friend's Admiring Tribute to a Unique Personality

To the Editor of the Republican:

I do not know what has been said about my friend by those who had known
her longer, perhaps better, than myself, but I have a word of my own.

I suppose people called her peculiar, a favorite term in the vocabulary of
mediocrity. To me she was unique, rather than peculiar. She never said things
as other people said them. I think she abhorred the commonplace in speech
almost more than the vulgar. I never made ready to call upon her without
feeling that I must purge my vocabulary of triteness. Her views of life were those

of an onlooker, not a participator in the affairs of men, and they were at once shrewd and amusing to a remarkable degree. Her conversational and literary gifts would have been more highly appreciated and more widely known, but for the extraordinary powers of her famous sister. I do not know whether this ever occurred to her, but I do know that I never met a human being so absolutely absorbed in admiration of another as was this woman in admiration of her sister. Those who never heard her read one of Emily's poems, or a tribute from some new worshiper at her shrine, missed a rare and uplifting experience. I should add that this enthusiastic devotion to one member of the family circle extended in turn to every other. It seemed impossible for her to realize that any other estimate than hers could be held of their gifts and graces, their abilities and achievements. Her fiercest denunciations were reserved for those who ventured to oppose or even call in question the opinions of her father and brother on matters of public concern. No other opinions were either conceivable or allowable. One of the most interesting and memorable experiences in all our long years of intercourse occurred at our last interview, when, with an exaltation of tone and manner which it would be impossible to reproduce, this sorrowful yet radiant-faced woman delivered, rather than read, a remarkable tribute, lately received, to her departed brother. Unwavering and admiring loyalty to her family was the first article in her creed.

And then her courage! Did ever so valorous a spirit lodge in so frail a tenement? I did not come to know her well till the first great sorrow of her mature years fell in a moment. After that, one blow followed another in more or less rapid succession till she was left alone of her father's house, and almost the sole survivor of that distinguished company of men and women which includes in its numbers the Hollands, Judge Lord, Judge Perkins, Samuel Bowles, and Helen Hunt. But though she bent under these fierce assaults, she never gave way. That little figure stood foursquare against all the winds that blew. I am told that she never wholly recovered from the latest blow, the sudden death of her chivalrous nephew; but she still clung to life, and to the friends that remained. "I am glad that you are still alive," she wrote me, after some sadly unexpected loss. For this heart of adamant could be tenderness itself. Those who ever experienced as I did the delicacy and gentleness of her attentions in time of sorrow, need no testimony on that point. She who because she was sure her father would have wished it, denied herself to no one in the hours that succeeded his death, could weep with those who wept, and tried in gentlest ways to ease the burden.

No one who met her even casually could fail to be struck with her passionate love for both animate and inanimate Nature. She did not more tenderly cherish her troop of pussies within the house than she did the birds and the flowers without it. It seems as if the pansies and the violets, the roses and the lilies would miss being tucked up under their coverlets these chill November days, and would be asking what was keeping their friend so long.

Respecting her religious experiences and sympathies, she was very reticent. I think this was largely due to her dread of falling into cant, the commonplace of religious conversation. Whatever the reason, few, if any, were admitted to the sanctuary of her soul. She often questioned the dealings of Providence, and sometimes seemed defiant in the presence of some cruel bereavement. But for all this, I do not believe that her faith in an all-wise, benevolent Being ever suffered more than momentary eclipse. She was not given to analyzing her spiritual condition. She seemed less conscious of her duties toward her Creator than toward the creatures of his hand. I think she could have adopted as her own her sister's fine lines:—

> Afraid? Of whom am I afraid?
> Not death; for who is he?
> The porter of my father's lodge
> As much abasheth me.

Of life? 'Twere odd I fear a thing
That comprehendeth me
In one or more existence
At Deity's decree.

Of resurrection? Is the east
Afraid to trust the morn
With her fastidious forehead?
As soon impeach my crown!

Farewell, brave, vehement, loyal soul! Thou art no more in the fetters of the flesh. Thy freed spirit has entered upon new and unimagined experiences. We give thee joy at thy release, as we thank God for the example of courage, unselfishness and devotion thou didst leave us as our legacy.

J.K.C.

LUCRETIA GUNN DICKINSON (MRS. ASA BULLARD) (1806-1885). Aunt of *Emily Dickinson. See* REV. ASA BULLARD.

MARY DICKINSON (MRS. MARK HASKELL NEWMAN) (1809-1852). Aunt of *Emily Dickinson. See* MARK HASKELL NEWMAN.

SAMUEL FOWLER DICKINSON (1775-1838). Grandfather of *Emily Dickinson.* Born in Amherst, October 9, 1775. An honor graduate of Dartmouth College, 1795, he studied law with Judge Strong of Amherst, and practiced there for more than thirty years. On March 31, 1802, he married Lucretia Gunn (1775-1840) of Montague. They had nine children. (See page 509.) She died of consumption in Enfield on May 11, 1840. "Squire Fowler" was one of the principal founders of Amherst Academy, 1814, and of Amherst College, 1821. He was representative from Amherst to the Massachusetts General Court in 1805, 1806, 1807, 1808, 1809, 1813, 1816, 1817, 1818, and 1827, and a member of the Massachusetts Senate in 1828 (records in the State Library of Massachusetts). The homestead which he built in 1813 was sold on May 22, 1833. Soon thereafter he moved to Cincinnati and in the autumn of 1836 to Hudson, Ohio, where, on Sunday, April 22, 1838, he died. His body was later brought to Amherst and interred in West Cemetery. Tyler, 1873, 118 ff., George T. Chapman, *Sketches of the Alumni of Dartmouth College, 1771-1867* (Cambridge, 1867), 78, gives the date of his marriage as March 21, 1802, and the date of his death as April 23, 1838.

WILLIAM DICKINSON (1804-1887). Well-to-do uncle of *Emily Dickinson.* Born in Amherst, October 7, 1804, and died in Worcester, September 6, 1887. He attended Amherst Academy but did not go to college. Instead, at the age of fifteen "or thereabouts," he became a clerk in a Boston drygoods house and for ten years was employed in paper factories in Hardwick and Fitchburg, moving in 1829 to Worcester where he lived for the rest of his life. He manufactured paper machinery (until 1883), owning and operating the Worcester Felting Company, Foster Street. In October, 1836, he became cashier of the Central Bank, holding that position until October, 1850. Elected first treasurer of the State Mutual Life Assurance Company in 1843, an office held for forty years, he was also treasurer of the Merchants' and Farmers' Mutual Fire Insurance Company from 1847 to 1887, and at the time of his death was one of its directors. In 1853 he was elected president pro tempore of the Quinsigamond Bank, served for one year when he became a director, an office also held for the remainder of his life. In 1856 he was elected a director of the Providence and Worcester Railroad. He served several terms as alderman of the City of Worcester, was a member of the highway commission, of the school board, of the board of the State Hospital, and of the Free Public Library, as well as of the renowned Worcester Society of Antiquity (American Antiquarian Society).

William Dickinson was not a church member but was regular in attendance at the Union (Congregational) Church. It was said that for more than sixty years he was not detained from service by ill health but one Sunday.

"Mr. Dickinson was a man of large means, but of simple and frugal tastes. . . . He had an incisive manner of speech and a dry humor about him which made him an entertaining companion. He was a man of remarkable shrewdness and business ability and filled the important positions to which he was called with rare judgment." His business sagacity is illustrated by his attitude toward the licensing of liquor dealers. During his last term as alderman this question was uppermost. "He took the ground that just about so much liquor would be drunk whether saloon keepers were licensed or not, and favored selling as many licenses as possible to increase the revenue of the city. At first he was bitterly opposed, but finally carried his point and that year a very large income was realized by the city from the sale of licenses." (Quoted passages are from the *Worcester Evening Gazette*, September 7, 1887. See also D. Hamilton Hurd, *History of Worcester County, Massachusetts* [Philadelphia, 1889], II, 1681-1682.) William Dickinson's realistic outlook, his entire character indeed, was a protest against that of his expansive father, *Samuel Fowler Dickinson*. Even his politics were in keeping. After the downfall of the Whigs, unlike his brother Edward, who remained a Whig to the last, William joined the Republican party. Between the brothers there was great mutual respect. Together they shared the brunt of family misfortunes.

William Dickinson first married, on October 1, 1831, Eliza Hawley of Andover, by whom he had one son, William Hawley Dickinson, born October 22, 1832. *Lavinia Dickinson's* favorite cousin "Willie" was graduated from Brown University in 1852, and for many years practiced law in New York, and died on May 15, 1883. (*Ancestors' Brocades*, 262-266.) His mother, the first Mrs. William Dickinson, died July 31, 1851, and on October 23, 1852, his father married Mary Whittier of Andover, by whom he had two sons, one of whom was named Samuel Fowler Dickinson, and one daughter.

Colonel Higginson described *Emily Dickinson's* uncle as "a prominent citizen of Worcester, a man of integrity and character, who shared her abruptness and impulsiveness but certainly not her poetic temperament, from which he was singularly remote. He could tell but little of her, she being evidently an enigma to him, as to me." *The Atlantic Monthly*, October, 1891.

WILLIAM AUSTIN DICKINSON (1829-1895). Brother of *Emily Dickinson;* son of *Edward* and *Emily Norcross Dickinson*. Born in Amherst, April 16, 1829. He prepared for college at Amherst Academy and Williston Seminary, Easthampton, and was graduated from Amherst College in 1850 (Phi Beta Kappa, Alpha Delta Phi); M.A., Amherst, 1853; LL.B., Harvard, 1854. He taught school in Sunderland, September to November, 1850; read law in his father's office, 1850-1851. Austin Dickinson went to Boston, on June 7, 1851, to teach in the Endicott (public) School for the term ending July 30, and returned on September first for the next school year, which ended in July, 1852. Entering the Harvard Law School March 9, 1853, he was graduated on July 19, 1854. Admitted to the Suffolk County bar, Boston, on June 26, 1854, he practiced law in Amherst from 1854 until his death forty-one years later.

On July 1, 1856, he married Susan Huntington Gilbert. (*See* page 496.) They had two sons and one daughter: Edward Dickinson (June 19, 1861– May 3, 1898); Martha Gilbert Dickinson (November 30, 1866–December 21, 1943); Thomas Gilbert Dickinson (August 1, 1875–October 5, 1883). (Dates are from Amherst town records.) W. A. Dickinson joined the First (Congregational) Church on January 6, 1856. Susan Gilbert had joined on August 11, 1850.

Moderator of town meetings, 1881-1895; on the board of the Amherst Savings Bank; the First National Bank of Amherst; the Amherst Water Company; the Amherst Gas Light Company; Village Improvement Association; Amherst Library Association. In 1867 he supervised the erection of the new building of the First (Congregational) Church. He was treasurer of Amherst College from December 1, 1873, until his death. He supervised the erection of several college buildings, and by expert landscaping enhanced the beauty of the college grounds.

William Austin Dickinson died in Amherst August 16, 1895, and lies buried in Wildwood Cemetery of which he was the founder. W. I. Fletcher, "The Amherst Dickinsons and the College," *Amherst Graduates' Quarterly*, VI (May, 1917), 179-185. *See also Obituary Record of the College*, 1895-1896.

REV. WILLIAM COWPER DICKINSON (1827-1899), a friend but not a close relative. Amherst College, 1848; valedictorian. Tutor in Amherst College, 1851-1852. Attended Union and Andover Theological Seminaries; ordained April 12, 1854.

WILLIAM HAWLEY DICKINSON. *See* WILLIAM DICKINSON.

REV. EDWARD STRONG DWIGHT (1820-1890). Yale College, 1838. Yale Divinity School, 1843. Ordained, 1844; D.D., Yale, 1878. Invited to become pastor of the First Church of Amherst, May 24, 1853; accepted between July 11 and 13; acting pastor, August 21, 1853; installed, July 19, 1854; "dismissed" (the term used for concluding a pastorate), August 28, 1860. Mrs. Dwight died September 11, 1861. Dr. Dwight was a trustee of

Amherst College from 1855 to 1890, and for the twenty-six years preceding his death was secretary of the board. *Obituary Record of the Graduates of Yale University,* Fourth Series, 24-25.

REV. HENRY LUTHER EDWARDS (1822-1903). Amherst College, 1847 (listed as "Luther Henry" Edwards). Andover Theological Seminary, 1847-1849. Tutor, Amherst College, 1849-1852. Ordained, 1857.

THOMAS DAWES ELIOT (1808-1870). Columbian College (D.C.), 1825. Read law with his uncle, William Cranch, chief justice of the Federal Circuit Court for the District of Columbia. In 1830 Mr. Eliot went to New Bedford, finished his studies, was admitted to the Massachusetts bar and became the partner of Judge Charles H. Warren. Served in both the House of Representatives and in the Senate of the General Court. In the spring of 1854 he was elected from the First District of Massachusetts to the United States House of Representatives to fill the unexpired term of Zeno Scudder. (See page 511.) On April 17 he took his seat in the midst of the Nebraska Bill excitement. On May 10 he made a speech against the repeal of the Missouri Compromise, and condemned the fugitive slave law. With the Whigs he was swept out of Congress in the 1854 election. He became a Free Soiler before joining the new Republican party which elected him to the Thirty-sixth Congress in 1859. He served continuously through the Fortieth until March, 1869. As chairman of the Committee on Freedmen's Affairs he took a prominent part in legislation bearing upon the protection and welfare of Negroes.

JOHN MILTON EMERSON (1826-1869). Amherst College, 1849; valedictorian. Tutor, Amherst College, 1851-1853. Admitted to the bar, 1854. Practiced law in Amherst, 1854-1856; in New York, 1856-1869. Professor Tyler says of John Emerson that he "demonstrated . . . that an honest, cultivated Christian lawyer can live and succeed in New York." *Tyler,* 1873, 339.

REV. HENRY VAUGHAN EMMONS (1832-1912). Amherst College, 1854. Bangor Theological Seminary, 1856-1859. Ordained as evangelist, November 14, 1860. Served with United States Christian Commission in South Carolina, Florida and Virginia, 1862-1865. Pastor of various churches in New England, 1865-1902.

MRS. S. A. FAY. *See* HANNAH HASKELL NEWMAN.

REV. SAMUEL FISKE (sometimes spelled FISK) (1827-1864). Amherst College 1848; salutatorian. Attended Andover Theological Seminary, 1850-1852; tutor, Amherst College, 1852-1855; ordained June 3, 1857; pastor, Madison, Connecticut, 1857-1864. He enlisted as a private in the 14th Connecticut Volunteers and was mortally wounded at the Battle of the Wilderness, May 6, 1864. At the time of his death at Fredericksburg, Virginia, May 22, 1864, he had attained the rank of captain. His sister, Rebecca W. Fiske, was a teacher at Mount Holyoke Seminary when *Emily Dickinson* was a student. Tyler, 1873, 339, 583-584.

MARIA FLYNT (MRS. LYMAN COLEMAN) (1801-1871). *See* REV. LYMAN COLEMAN.

REV. WILLIAM CHAUNCEY FOWLER (1793-1881). Yale College, 1816. He was ordained on August 31, 1825, and was for a time pastor of the Congregational Church in Greenfield. Professor of rhetoric and oratory, Amherst College, 1838-1843. Representative from Amherst to the Massachusetts General Court, 1851. Left Amherst for Durham, Connecticut, in 1858. He married Harriet, daughter of Noah Webster, July 26, 1825. Children mentioned in the Dickinson letters:

Emily Ellsworth Fowler, born August 26, 1826; married, December 16, 1853, Gordon Lester Ford; had three sons, among them Worthington C. and Paul Leicester Ford, and five daughters; died November 23, 1893.

Charles Chauncey Fowler (1828-1876). Amherst College, 1851. Studied law and was admitted to the New York bar, 1855.

William Worthington Fowler (1833-1881). Amherst College, 1854. Studied law with *Edward Dickinson* for six months. Was admitted to the New York bar, 1857.

Obituary Record of The Graduates of Yale University, Third Series, 5-6.

MARTHA ISABELLA GILBERT (MRS. J. W. SMITH) (1827-1895). *See* THOMAS GILBERT.

SUSAN HUNTINGTON GILBERT (MRS. WILLIAM AUSTIN DICKINSON) (1830-1913). *See* THOMAS GILBERT.

THOMAS GILBERT (March 21, 1793–December 23, 1841) of Amherst, Deerfield and Greenfield; married, November 11, 1814, Harriet Arms (September 3, 1792–February 13, 1837).

CHILDREN:

Thomas Dwight Gilbert (December 13, 1815–November 18, 1894). *See* Albert Baxter, *History of the City of Grand Rapids,* Michigan, (New York, 1891).

Francis Backus Gilbert (May 25, 1818–May 25, 1885).

Harriet (Harriette) Murray Gilbert (1820–March 18, 1865) married *William Cutler* of Amherst on June 22, 1842.

Mary Arms Gilbert (1822–July 14, 1850) married Samuel Julius Learned (Amherst College, 1845) on September 17, 1849, and went to Sunbury, North Carolina, to live.

Catharine S. Gilbert.

Martha Isabella Gilbert (April 13, 1827–October 10, 1895). (These dates are taken from her tombstone, Geneva, New York. Greenfield church records give 1829 as her date of birth.) In 1857, in Amherst, she married John Williams Smith (October 11, 1822–December 2, 1878), of the J. W. Smith Dry Goods Company, Geneva, New York. Of their three children, only one lived to grow up, Elizabeth Troup (Throop) Smith (June 30, 1868–January 3, 1931). (Name and dates taken from her death certificate.)

Susan Huntington Gilbert (December 19, 1830–May 12, 1913). Joined the First Church, Amherst, August 11, 1850. Married, on July 1, 1856, *William Austin Dickinson.*

EDWARD BATES GILLETT (1818-1899). Amherst College, 1839. Harvard

Law School, 1840-1841. Admitted to the Hampden County bar, 1843. Practiced law in Westfield and Springfield and was a leader of the bar in western Massachusetts. Vice president of Smith College from its founding, and trustee of Amherst College, 1861-1896.

REV. GEORGE HENRY GOULD (1827-1899). Amherst College, 1850. Union and Andover Theological Seminaries, 1850-1853. Ordained, Springfield, 1862. Held various pastorates before settling in Worcester in 1872, where he lived for the rest of his life.

REV. JOHN LONG (LYSANDER) GRAVES (1831-1915). Amherst College, 1855. Studied privately and was ordained to the Congregational ministry in Boston, January 4, 1857. (This date, from the *Amherst College Bulletin, Obituary Record 1915*, IV, No. 6, and confirmed by his daughter, Louise B. Graves, antedates by three years the date given in the *Amherst College Biographical Record*, 1939.) Mr. Graves resigned from the ministry in 1865 and entered business.

TIMOTHY J. GRIDLEY, M.D. (1788-1852). Yale College, 1808. M.D., Dartmouth College, 1812. Practiced medicine in Amherst from 1822 to 1852 and was not only a distinguished physician; he was one of the town's most picturesque characters (see page 210). His daughter Jane married *George S. Woodman, M.D.*, September 17, 1849.

REV. JOSEPH HAVEN (1816-1874). Amherst College, 1835. Attended Union and Andover Theological Seminaries; ordained 1839. Professor of intellectual and moral philosophy and metaphysics, Amherst College, 1850-1858. Professor of systematic theology, Chicago Theological Seminary, 1858-1870, and at Chicago University (a small college, predecessor of the University of Chicago), until his death. A gifted orator, he was in great demand as preacher and lecturer.

Married September 23, 1840, Mary, daughter of Professor Ralph Emerson of Andover. They had four sons and six daughters. The "clustering frocks" to which *Emily Dickinson* referred in a letter to Mrs. Haven after she left Amherst were those of Elizabeth, Mary, Alice (Mrs. James R. Danforth) and Ada (Mrs. Calvin W. Mateer) Haven.

REV. THOMAS WENTWORTH HIGGINSON (1823-1911). Harvard College, 1841. Studied theology at Harvard Divinity School, graduating in 1847. Pastor of First Religious Society (Unitarian), Newburyport, 1847-1852, and of the Free Church at Worcester, 1852-1861. A prolific writer and crusader for liberal causes, he served in the Union Army (1862-1864) as colonel of the first regiment recruited from former slaves, the First South Carolina Volunteers.

HENRY F. HILLS (1833-1896). In 1852 entered his father's business in Amherst as a manufacturer of straw hats. L. M. Hills & Sons were locally known as "the largest operators in the business in America" (*History of Amherst*, 292). In 1877 Henry F. Hills became president of the Hills Company.

REV. EDWARD HITCHCOCK (1793-1864). Hon. M.A., Yale College, 1818. Yale Theological Seminary, 1820. Ordained in 1821, the year in which

Amherst College was founded, he joined the Amherst faculty in 1825 as the first professor of chemistry and natural history, a position held for twenty years. On December 16, 1844, when the college was in desperate financial straits, he was made president "by acclamation," and was inducted into office on April 14, 1845. He served for almost ten years (November 22, 1854) until the survival of the college was assured. Professor Tyler says he "saved the College." He then returned to teaching, this time as professor of natural theology and geology, his dominant interests. He not only discussed the phenomena of nature and of man as he *observed* them (in the early 1840's lecturing on "physiology with a manikin"); he used the results of his observations to support the truths of revelation as he *understood* them. He spoke with authority both as preacher and as naturalist. In 1850 Dr. Hitchcock investigated the agricultural schools of Europe for the Commonwealth of Massachusetts. He and Mrs. Hitchcock were away from Amherst for five months and traveled more than 10,000 miles, "mostly by horse-drawn vehicles." (*See* his *Report,* 1851.)

In geology Dr. Hitchcock achieved international recognition. He wrote voluminously, his bound volumes reaching a total of twenty-four. He held the title of state geologist of Massachusetts from 1830 on, and in 1840 received the degree of LL.D. from Harvard. "To him, more than perhaps to any other man, is due the title of founder of the association of American geologists and naturalists [American Society of Geologists and Naturalists] which afterwards assumed the name of the American Association for the Advancement of Science. . . ." (Lesley, "Biographical Notice" [1866], 151; "Memoir" [1877], 132.) Of the latter he became the first president. He was one of the signers of the act of incorporation of the National Academy of Sciences, March 3, 1863.

In Amherst he is held in grateful remembrance chiefly for his administration of the college from 1845 to 1854; its survival as an institution of higher learning was due largely to his "weight of character and his wise policy." (Tyler, 1895, 135.) But neither the saving of Amherst College nor even "scientific reputation" was, as President Hitchcock observes in his *Reminiscences* (page 295), "the culmination of my ambition, but the higher object of making science illustrate the Divine Glory." His book, *The Religion of Geology and its Connected Sciences,* was published in 1851.

On May 31, 1821, Edward Hitchcock married Orra White, daughter of Jarib White of Amherst, who bore him seven children. The two daughters referred to in this book are Catherine, or "Kate" (1826-1895), who became the wife of the Rev. Henry M. Storrs (Amherst College, 1846), on March 9, 1852; and Jane Elizabeth (1833-1894), who married Granville B. Putnam (Amherst College, 1861), on August 31, 1864.

Hitchcock, *Reminiscences,* "Personal History," 281-407; Tyler, 1873, 355-365, and Tyler, 1895, 109-138; J. P. Lesley, "Memoir of Edward Hitchcock," *National Academy of Sciences, Biographical Memoirs,* I (Washington, 1877), 113-134; Anson Phelps Stokes, "Edward Hitchcock," *Memorials of Eminent Yale Men,* II (New Haven, 1914), 86-87; Frederick Tuckerman, "President

Edward Hitchcock," *Amherst Graduates' Quarterly,* X (November, 1920), 3-13.

EBENEZER ROCKWOOD HOAR (1816-1895). Harvard Law School, 1839. Attorney General of the United States under President Grant, 1869-1870; in 1870 was asked to resign because he opposed the political machine. His appointment to the U.S. Supreme Court (1870) was not confirmed by the Senate. Republican member of Congress, 1873-1875.

GEORGE FRISBIE HOAR (1826-1904). Harvard Law School, 1849. Free Soil member of Congress 1851-1853. Active in the organization of the Republican party in Massachusetts, and a Republican member of Congress, 1869-1877. U.S. Senator, 1877-1904.

JOSIAH GILBERT HOLLAND, M.D. (1819-1881). After practicing medicine for a few years he became, in 1849, assistant editor under *Samuel Bowles* and subsequently one of the owners of *The Springfield Republican* with which he maintained his connection until 1867. His *History of Western Massachusetts* was published in 1855. A well-known author of many books, in 1870 he moved to New York where he established and became editor of *Scribner's Monthly,* later the *Century Magazine.* T. V. W. Ward, *Emily Dickinson's Letters to Dr. and Mrs. J. G. Holland* (Cambridge, 1951).

GEORGE HOWLAND (1824-1892). Amherst College, 1850; salutatorian. Tutor and instructor, Amherst College, 1852-1857. Teacher in Chicago public schools, 1860-1880; superintendent of Chicago public schools, 1880-1891. Trustee of Amherst College, 1879-1888. Brother of *William Howland.*

WILLIAM HOWLAND (1822-1880). Amherst College, 1846. Tutor, Amherst College, 1849-1851. Studied law in office of *Edward Dickinson* for a time, and was admitted to the bar in Springfield, September 1851. Married June 21, 1860, Caroline G. Russell. Practiced in Lynn, 1852-1880.

REV. EDWARD PORTER HUMPHREY (1809-1887). Amherst College, 1828. Son of Heman Humphrey, president of the college from 1823 to 1845. Tutor, Amherst College, 1832-1833. Ordained Presbyterian Evangelist 1834; entered ministry the following year. Professor of Biblical and ecclesiastical history, Danville (Kentucky) Theological Seminary, 1853-1866.

JANE T. HUMPHREY (MRS. W. H. WILKINSON) (1829-1908). Daughter of Dr. Levi W. Humphrey of Southwick. Graduated from Mount Holyoke Female Seminary in 1848. Preceptress, Amherst Academy, 1848-1849. After ten years of teaching she married William H. Wilkinson, August 26, 1858, and returned to Southwick to live. Her sister Martha died of consumption on December 10, 1851, aged 20; and her sister Sarah also died of consumption on November 18, 1854, aged 18. (In the town records of Southwick Martha's death is placed between two other entries on November 9 and 15, 1851, but the month as written resembles "Dec." more than "Nov." The entries in these records are not always in chronological order.)

LEONARD HUMPHREY (1824-1850). Amherst College, 1846; valedictorian. Principal of Amherst Academy, 1846-1847. Attended Andover

Theological Seminary, 1847-1848. Tutor, Amherst College, 1849-1850. Died November 30, 1850.

REV. GEORGE BAKER JEWETT (1818-1886). Amherst College, 1840. Andover Theological Seminary, 1840-1842. Tutor, Amherst College, 1842-1844. Professor of Latin and modern languages, 1850-1855. Ordained, 1855. Married Mary J. Whipple, May 19, 1845. One child, Henry, born 1846.

THOMAS JONES (1787-1853). Prosperous manufacturer of cotton and woolen goods. Settled in Amherst in 1839. His "Kentucky jeans," manufactured in the "Hollow" at North Amherst, were well known. Representative from Amherst in the Massachusetts General Court, 1845. Mr. Jones died in Amherst, October 21, 1853.

EMELINE KELLOGG (MRS. H. C. NASH) (1828-1900). *See* JAMES KELLOGG.

JAMES KELLOGG (1792-1868). Prominent Amherst manufacturer. His fine joiners' tools, planes in particular, had a national reputation. His daughter, Emeline (1828-1900), married *Henry Clark Nash*. Until 1855 the Kelloggs were the Dickinsons' next-door neighbors.

CYRUS KINGMAN (1794-1854). Moved to Amherst from Pelham in April, 1850. The year following he was greatly bereaved: his two youngest daughters, Martha and Ellen Mary, died within two weeks of each other in the late fall of 1851. He was stricken with paralysis on November 9, 1852. His eldest and only surviving daughter died on May 26, 1854, and he died on December 29, 1854. *Express,* January 5, 1855.

TEMPE S. LINNELL (1831-1881). Her widowed mother (Tempe Linnell) moved to Amherst in 1839 to educate her two sons. Tempe S. Linnell never married; as Emily said, "Tempe lives single." A stone in the West Cemetery, Amherst, sums up the life of this young woman, favorite of Austin Dickinson:

> Tempe Linnell, died February 11, 1879, *aet.* 85
> Tempe S. Linnell, died November 6, 1881, *aet.* 50

Her life was devoted to the care of her mother, their names linked on this single stone.

OTIS PHILLIPS LORD (1812-1884). Amherst College, 1832. Admitted to the Essex County bar, December, 1835. LL.B., Harvard, 1836. Practiced law in Ipswich, 1835-1844; in Salem, 1844-1875. Married Elizabeth Wise Farley of Ipswich, October 9, 1843, who died December 10, 1877. Representative in the Massachusetts General Court, 1847, 1848, 1852, 1853, and 1854. Member of the State Constitutional Convention, 1853. Speaker of the last Whig Massachusetts House of Representatives, 1854. State senator, 1849. Judge of the Superior Court of Massachusetts, 1859-1875. Appointed to the Supreme Court of Massachusetts on December 21, 1875, from which he resigned on December 8, 1882. Died March 13, 1884. For details of his career and for his relation to the Dickinson family, see M. T. Bingham, *Emily Dickinson—A Revelation* (New York, 1954).

MARY LYON (1797-1849). Founder and principal of Mount Holyoke Female Seminary; was a pupil in Amherst Academy, 1818; studied chemistry and natural history with the Reverend *Edward Hitchcock* while he was pastor of the Congregational church at Conway; taught in Ipswich Academy, 1828-1834, and in 1836 founded Mount Holyoke Female Seminary, South Hadley, where she died, March 5, 1849. B. B. Gilchrist, *The Life of Mary Lyon* (Boston, 1910).

DAVID MACK, JR. (1778-1854). Son of Colonel David Mack of Middlefield. A merchant and a former member of both houses of the state legislature, and of the executive council of the Commonwealth, he served as a major in the War of 1812, and in 1821 was promoted to brigadier general of militia. "General," "The Honorable," more often called "Deacon," David Mack moved to Amherst in 1834, where he engaged in the manufacture of straw hats. From 1840 to 1848 he also conducted a general store in Phoenix Row. From 1836 to 1854 he was a member of the board of trustees of Amherst College.

On May 22, 1833, Deacon Mack purchased the Dickinson homestead, where he lived until his death on September 6, 1854. His son, Samuel E. Mack (1815-1866), who had been associated with him in business, moved to Cincinnati in 1847, where he entered the insurance business and became general agent of the Home Insurance Company of New York.

Two facts, if known, would have a bearing on the movements of the family of *Edward Dickinson*: the size of Deacon Mack's family when he moved into the homestead, and the exact date when he took up residence there, whether late in 1833 or not until 1834. For the following information I am indebted to Philip Mack Smith, who, with his brother, wrote the history of Middlefield. (Philip Mack Smith and Edward Church Smith, *The History of Middlefield, Massachusetts* [Menasha, Wisconsin, 1924]. See also Ebenezer Mack Treman and Murray A. Poole, *The History of the Treman, Tremaine, Truman Family in America* [Ithaca, 1901], two vols. David Mack, I, 357; David Mack, Jr., I, 382; Samuel Ely Mack, I, 439.)

David Mack, Jr., married Independence Pease (1776-1809) on March 2, 1803. Their son, David Mack, III (1804-1878), was graduated from Yale College in 1823 in the same class with Edward Dickinson. He studied law, but soon abandoned it for teaching. From 1831 to 1836 he was principal of the Friends' Academy, New Bedford, proof that he was not then living in Amherst (*Obituary Record of the Graduates of Yale College*, Second Series, 337). His sister, Julia, born April 27, 1806, had not yet married the Rev. Moody Harrington when the family left Middlefield, but may be assumed to have done so shortly thereafter as their first child was born in 1836.

After the death of his first wife on April 13, 1809, David Mack, Jr., married Mary Ely (1787-1842) on January 14, 1812. They had three sons, only one of whom, Samuel Ely, lived to grow up. Born on November 8, 1815, he went to Amherst with his father, mother, and half sister, Julia. Thus it appears that when General Mack took up residence in the homestead his family consisted of a wife, a son in his late teens and, until her marriage, a daughter in her late twenties. His wife's mother, who died in Amherst in 1841, aged 81, may also have lived with them.

As to just when the Macks moved into the homestead, the following paragraphs contain all that is known. A letter from Philip Mack Smith, January 28, 1948, quotes a letter from his brother, E. C. Smith:

Concerning David Mack, Jr.'s going to Amherst, we state that he went about 1834 (*Hist. of Mid.* p. 535). The 1844 date you found referred to his general store there. He ran a hat shop too (1840-1848).

Confirmatory of the 1834 date is the account of Uncle William Church (*Mack Gen.* p. 481). He worked for David Mack, Jr., in his store in Amherst for six years before having a brief period of employment in Northampton in 1840.

A further confirmation we have in the Middlefield Congregational Church records, thanks to Edna for copying some lists for us. Among the list of letters of dismissal I find such were granted to David Mack, Jr.; to Mary Mack (his second wife); to Julia Mack and Samuel E. Mack, to the church in Amherst, on April 27, 1834. D.M. Jr. was last Clerk and Town Treasurer in 1831.

It is possible that David Mack, Jr., moved to Amherst in 1833, for the *History* (of Mid, p. 265) states that the parsonage (his house) on the Parsonage Lot was given by the two Macks, David Sr. and David Jr., to the Congregational Society in 1833. This, however, should be confirmed by dates of deeds in "Hamp."

Thus the precise date when the Mack family moved into the Dickinson homestead is uncertain, but it was either late in 1833 or early in 1834; and as to whether or not Julia was with them, it is interesting if not conclusive that her name was included among the letters of dismissal from the Middlefield church in 1834. Edward Dickinson's family occupied the east half of the homestead until 1840.

After the death of his second wife on December 15, 1842, Deacon Mack married Harriet Parsons Washburn (1793-1874) on May 16, 1844. She was the daughter of the Reverend Dr. David Parsons, long-time pastor of the First Church, Amherst, and widow of the Reverend Royal W. Washburn, who had also served as pastor of the same church from 1826 until his death on January 1, 1833.

Austin Dickinson described General Mack as "a man to command attention anywhere, tall, erect, of powerful build, with a fine head finely set, clear, exact, just, a believer in law and penalty for its breach; strong as a lion, pure as a saint, simple as a child, a Puritan of the Puritans: I remember my first sight of him—I was four years old—I thought I had seen God. He was moral and spiritual tonic to any community he entered" (Dickinson, "Representative Men," 65).

(The washerwoman who worked for the Dickinsons in the 1850's was also named Mack.)

REV. JACOB MERRILL MANNING (1824-1882). Amherst College, 1850. Andover Theological Seminary, 1850-1853; ordained, 1854. Assistant pastor and pastor of the Old South (Congregational) Church, Boston, 1857-1882.

HENRY CLARK NASH (1829-1900). Son of *Rev. J. A. Nash.* Amherst College, 1851. Teacher at Mount Pleasant Institute, Amherst, 1851-1854; principal, 1854-1877. Married, October 9, 1855, Emeline (1828-1900), daughter of *James Kellogg.*

REV. JOHN ADAMS NASH (1798-1877). Amherst College, 1824. Attended

Andover Theological Seminary and Yale Theological Seminary. Principal, Mount Pleasant Institute, Amherst, 1846-1854. Instructor in agriculture, Amherst College, 1852-1855. Became editor of *The Connecticut Valley Farmer* in 1854.

HANNAH HASKELL NEWMAN (MRS. S. A. FAY). Born in Andover, June 6, 1809. Married, September 26, 1833, the Rev. Samuel A. Fay. Mrs. Fay took care of her four nieces, the daughters of *Mark Haskell Newman*, after they moved to Amherst in 1853 following the death of their parents. Their cousin, *William Austin Dickinson*, married in 1856. Thereafter, beginning in October, 1858, the two youngest girls, aged twelve and fourteen, made their home with him. See MARK HASKELL NEWMAN.

MARK HASKELL NEWMAN (1806-1852). Bowdoin College, 1825. Established, in 1826, "what appears to have been the first bookstore in Amherst" (*Amherst Imprints*, page 12). He left Amherst in 1827, and "about 1830" founded in New York the publishing house of Mark H. Newman, which became Newman & Iverson (Iverson was a Scotsman in his employ), and after Mr. Newman's death, Iverson, Blakeman & Taylor. Mark H. Newman is said to have been "the first person to publish graded school-books in this country." On October 2, 1828, he married Mary (1809-1852), daughter of *Samuel Fowler Dickinson*.

CHILDREN:

Mary Dickinson Newman (1829-1830).

Mary Dickinson Newman (1831-1835).

Mark Haskell Newman, born September 11, 1833. Although the younger Mark lived until the end of the century, no record of the date or place of his death has been found.

Catherine Dickinson Newman (1836-1868). Soon after the death of their parents in 1952, and after a temporary residence in Amherst, as wards of their Uncle Edward, Catherine and her sister Sara went to live in Worcester with their uncle *William Dickinson*. Married, December 28, 1865, the Rev. George A. Tewksbury of Portland, Maine, and died July 18, 1868, when Kate Newman Tewksbury (Farrington) was born.

Sara Phillips Newman (1838-1909). Married, April 9, 1868, Dr. J. Anson Bates, a Baltimore dentist. Soon thereafter her two younger sisters went to live with her.

Clarissa (Clara) Badger Newman (1844-1920). Married, October 14, 1869, Sidney Turner, manufacturer of ax handles in Norwich, Conn., who died in 1891.

Anna Dodge Newman (1846-1887). Lived with her sister, Mrs. Turner, from 1869 to 1873, when she went to Concord and lived in the home of Judge Henry F. French. Married, June 3, 1874, George H. Carleton, shoe manufacturer and banker of Haverhill. Their daughter, Clara Newman Carleton (Mrs. George E. Pearl), was born March 21, 1876.

BENJAMIN FRANKLIN NEWTON (1821-1853). Studied law in the office of Dickinson & Bowdoin, Amherst, 1847-1849; admitted to the bar at Worcester, 1850. Married Sarah Warner Rugg, June 4, 1851. In the spring of 1852 he was appointed state's attorney for the Middle District (Worcester County), and died March 24, 1853. See *The Republican,* March 26; *Express,* April 1, 1853; and Whicher, *This Was a Poet,* V, "An Amethyst Remembrance."

SETH NIMS (1798-1877). Amherst postmaster, 1845-1849; also from June 3, 1853 (taking office on July 1, 1853), to July 16, 1861, according to the records of the U.S. Post Office Department. His wife was Emily Dickinson of Conway. *History of Amherst,* 192.

EMILY LAVINIA NORCROSS (1828-1852). Cousin of *Emily Dickinson.* Daughter of Hiram Norcross, *Mrs. Edward Dickinson's* eldest brother.

EMILY NORCROSS (MRS. EDWARD DICKINSON) (1804-1882). Mother of *Emily Dickinson. See* EMILY NORCROSS DICKINSON.

JOEL WARREN NORCROSS (1821-1900). Uncle of *Emily Dickinson.* Importer of fancy goods and cutlery, 31 Milk Street, Boston. Married Lamira H. Jones of Chicago, January 17, 1854, who died May 3, 1862. On April 24, 1866, he married Maggie P. Gunnison of Roxbury.

LAVINIA NORCROSS (MRS. LORING NORCROSS) (1812-1860). Aunt of *Emily Dickinson.* Married her cousin, Loring Norcross, November 4, 1834. Their children were Lavinia (1837-1842), Louisa (1842-1919) and Frances Lavinia (1847-1896). Loring Norcross (1808-1863) was a dry-goods commission merchant, 73 Kilby Street, Boston; home, 25 McLean Street, Boston; secretary, Massachusetts Temperance Union; member, Boston School Board.

SARAH VAILL NORCROSS (1788-1854). Second wife of Joel Norcross, *Emily Dickinson's* grandfather. Emily's grandmother, Betsy Fay Norcross, died September 5, 1829. Joel Norcross married Sarah Vaill on January 6, 1831. He died on May 5, 1846; she died on April 25, 1854. See page 510. The picture of Mrs. Joel Norcross opposite page 441, *Letters,* 1931, is that of Sarah Vaill Norcross, not of Betsy Fay Norcross, Emily Dickinson's grandmother and first wife of Joel Norcross.

REV. EDWARDS AMASA PARK (1808-1900). Brown University, 1826. Andover Theological Seminary, 1831. Professor of Moral Philosophy and Metaphysics, Amherst College, 1835-1836. Professor at Andover Theological Seminary, 1836-1881. A leader of the new school of New England theology, he was one of the most noted preachers in the Congregational Church. In January, 1844, he declined an offer of the presidency of Amherst College.

HENRY DWIGHT ROOT (1832-1855). Amherst College, 1852. Harvard Law School, 1854-1855. Died September 3, 1855. Tyler, 1873, 343.

JOHN ELLIOT SANFORD (1830-1907). Amherst College, 1851; valedictorian. Tutor, Amherst College, 1853-1854. Studied law for a time with *Edward Dickinson.* Admitted to the bar at Taunton, June 12, 1856, where he practiced until 1899. Speaker of the Massachusetts House of Representatives, 1872-1874. Trustee of Amherst College, 1874-1907, and president of the board for many years.

REV. JULIUS HAWLEY SEELYE (1824-1895). Amherst College, 1849. Auburn Theological Seminary, 1849-1852. Ordained, Schenectady, N.Y.,

1853. Professor of mental and moral philosophy, Amherst College, 1858-1890. President, Amherst College, 1877-1890. Pastor of the College Church, 1877-1892.

REV. L. CLARK SEELYE (1837-1924). Brother of *J. H. Seelye.* Union College, 1857. Andover Theological Seminary, 1858-1859. Ordained, 1863. Professor of rhetoric and oratory, and English literature, Amherst College, 1865-1873. First president, Smith College, 1874-1910.

REV. HENRY BOYNTON SMITH (1815-1877). Professor of moral philosophy and metaphysics, Amherst College, 1847-1850. Professor of ecclesiastical history, Union Theological Seminary, 1850-1877. Described as "accomplished" by the *Express* (January 20, 1848), he is placed by President Hitchcock in "the front rank among the scholars and theologians of our country. *Reminiscences,* 39.

EBENEZER STRONG SNELL (1801-1876). Amherst College, 1822. Principal, Amherst Academy, 1822-1825. Beginning as tutor in 1825, he was professor of mathematics and natural philosophy, Amherst College, for more than forty years, 1834-1876.

JOHN LAURENS SPENCER (1818-1851). Amherst College, 1848. Commencement oration, "An Earnest Life." Principal of Amherst Academy, 1848-1849. While studying theology in Amherst, he died on October 12, 1851.

LEVI STOCKBRIDGE (1820-1904). One of the founders of the Massachusetts Agricultural College in Amherst, 1867; appointed professor of agriculture in 1872; established the Massachusetts Experimental Station in 1877; and served as president of the college from 1880 to 1882.

REV. RICHARD SALTER STORRS (1821-1900). Amherst College, 1839. Andover Theological Seminary, 1842-1845. Ordained in Brookline, 1845. Pastor of The Church of the Pilgrims, Brooklyn, N.Y., 1846-1899. Trustee of Amherst College, 1863-1898.

CHARLES HUMPHREYS SWEETSER (1841-1871). Amherst College, 1862. After the death of his parents in 1847, he lived in Amherst with his uncle, *Luke Sweetser.* Following a year's apprenticeship on *The Springfield Republican* under *Samuel Bowles,* in 1863 with his cousin Henry E. Sweetser he established *The Round Table,* a weekly newspaper published in New York. (See *Ancestors' Brocades,* 71.) He spent the remainder of his short life in newspaper work, founding and editing the *New York Evening Gazette* and *The City,* a penny morning paper, and other periodicals. (*The Republican* [December 23, 1863], noted that both young men "have ambition, enthusiasm, money, and the journalistic passion as capital." He published the first *Songbook of Amherst College.* On October 24, 1867, he married his cousin, Mary Newman Sweetser, daughter of *Joseph A.* and *Catherine Dickinson Sweetser,* and died of consumption on January 1, 1871.

JOHN HOWARD SWEETSER (1835-1904). Only child of *Luke Sweetser.* Attended Amherst College with the class of 1857 but left in his junior year to enter the wholesale dry-goods business of his uncle, *J. A. Sweetser* of

New York. Howard Sweetser received his bachelor's degree from Amherst in 1871.

JOSEPH ARTENATUS SWEETSER (1809-1874?). Baptised Artenatus, he obtained permission from the General Court to add Joseph to his name and was known thereafter as Joseph A. Sweetser. About 1824 he left Athol, where he was born, and entered the employ of his brother *Luke*, proprietor of a general store in Amherst. In 1830 the name of the firm was changed to L. & J. A. Sweetser. Soon after Luke's marriage on December 31, 1833, Joseph left Amherst to become a clerk in the firm of Merrill & Williams, wholesale dry-goods merchants, 246 Pearl Street, New York. Eventually he established a similar firm of his own and prospered.

On November 4, 1835, he married *Catherine*, daughter of *Samuel Fowler Dickinson*. They had eight children. On January 21, 1874, he left his wife in their apartment at the Fifth Avenue Hotel to attend a committee meeting at the Madison Square Presbyterian Church opposite, and was never heard of again. An entry in the family Bible opposite Psalm XI reads, "Last Psalm read in the family by J.A.S. on the morning of Jan. 21, 1874" (the day of his disappearance).

The record of Joseph A. Sweetser's movements is confusing in more than one particular: his connection with the Amherst bank for example. He is said to have been cashier of the bank, succeeding Thomas Green, who had held the post since December, 1838. It is said further that on "Feb. 9, 1841, Solomon Pitkin, president, Joseph A. Sweetser, cashier, and Edward Dickinson, attorney, of the Amherst Bank" did so-and-so (*History of Amherst*, 328-329). But Joseph A. Sweetser had left Amherst and gone into business in New York years before. Family letters addressed to him or to his wife in *New York* bear the following dates: June 13, July 14, November 12, and November 25, 1834; June 15 and October 20, 1835; September 6, October 10, October 13, November 2, and December 4, 1836; August 7, and November 20, 1837; April 29, 1838; November 2, and November 13, 1839; January 2 and February 26, 1840; August 31, 1842; and March 3, 1843. Since there are no letters between February 26, 1840, and August 31, 1842, he may possibly have returned to Amherst for a relatively short term of employment in order to extricate the bank from difficulties in which it was at the time involved.

LUKE SWEETSER (1800-1882). Born in Athol, he came to Amherst in 1821 where, in 1824, he established a general store and became the leading merchant of the town. His stock included "wines and spirits" as well as groceries, dry goods, crockery and glassware. By 1830 his younger brother *Joseph A.* had become the junior partner and the name of the firm was changed to L. & J. A. Sweetser. In 1834 *Joseph* moved to New York and in 1841 *William* and George *Cutler* entered the firm. Luke Sweetser sold out to them in 1854 to become a farmer and to raise fancy stock. A director of the Amherst & Belchertown Rail Road, Mr. Sweetser served as its first president. For one term (1849) he represented Amherst in the Massachusetts General Court. From 1833 to 1864 he was a member of the Prudential

Committee and overseer of the buildings and grounds of Amherst College. A deacon of the First Church from 1851 to 1871, Mr. Sweetser was described as "the upright merchant, the sagacious citizen, and the earnest Christian."

On December 3, 1833 Luke Sweetser married Abby Tyler Munsell of New York. Early in 1834 a three-year-old niece, *Abby Wood,* came to live with her Uncle Luke. His only child, *John Howard Sweetser,* was born the year following. In 1847 one more was added to the household, an orphan nephew, *Charles Humphreys Sweetser,* aged six. Luke Sweetser died on July 27, 1882, and his wife on October 19 of the same year.

Austin Dickinson thus characterized Mr. Sweetser on page 58 of the One Hundred and Fiftieth Anniversary volume of the First Church of Amherst:

"At the head, Luke Sweetser, for a generation exercising the largest influence in the affairs of both church and parish; a successful business man, of bright and active mind, genial manner, a generous host, conscientious, believing religion a chief concern, hesitating before no duty as he saw it, conservative to a degree that commanded the confidence of those who saw safety only in the old ways, yet too intelligent not to be open to suggestions for improvement, and when convinced, ready and helpful in carrying them into execution; not the first or among the first to feel the importance of a more fitting house of worship, but second to none when he came to it, in the time, energy and devotion he gave to making the undertaking a success."

JOHN HOWLAND THOMPSON (1827-1891). Amherst College, 1850. Admitted to the Massachusetts bar in 1853. Practiced law in Chicago from 1854 until 1891.

J. R. TRUMBULL. Editor of *The Hampshire and Franklin Express,* Amherst, from July, 1849, to March 15, 1853, when he became editor of *The Hampshire Gazette,* Northampton, and Leander Wetherell took over the editorship of the *Express.* See Holland, *History,* I, 454 and 458.

MRS. SIDNEY TURNER (CLARA B. NEWMAN). *See* MARK HASKELL NEWMAN.

REV. WILLIAM SEYMOUR TYLER (1810-1897). Amherst College, 1830. Taught in Amherst Academy, 1830-1831. Attended Andover Theological Seminary, 1831-1832 and 1834-1835. Tutor, Amherst College, 1832-1834. Ordained, North Amherst, 1839. Professor of Latin and Greek, Amherst College, 1836-1847; Professor of the Greek language and literature, 1847-1893. President Hitchcock (*Reminiscences,* 128) says that in 1847 Mr. Tyler also became professor of Hebrew. Historian of Amherst College. Married, September 4, 1839, Amelia Whiting. They had four sons.

REV. JOSEPH VAILL (1790-1869). Yale College, 1811. Ordained, Brimfield, 1814. Appointed a trustee of Amherst College at its founding in 1821, he held the position throughout his life. When, in August, 1841, the college finances were in a precarious condition, he was "dismissed from his pastoral charge" to become general agent of the college. For nearly four years he devoted himself to raising money. The name of Joseph Vaill is indissolubly connected with the raising of funds in support of the young college. Called a master of the art of begging, "No man so swayed assemblies, and 'made fast the arrows of the Almighty' in the hearts of men as did he." (*The Congregationalist,* XXI [March 25, 1869], 90; *Obituary Record of the Graduates of Yale College,* First Series, 301-302.) On the completion of his agency he returned to preaching, first at Somers, Connecticut, and then in December, 1854, at Palmer, where he lived for the rest of his life.

REV. CHARLES WADSWORTH (1814-1882). Union College, 1837. Princeton Theological Seminary, 1840. Pastor of the Second Presbyterian Church of Troy, N.Y., 1842-1850; of the Arch Street Presbyterian Church, Philadelphia, 1850-1862; and of the Calvary Presbyterian Society, San Francisco, 1862-1869. In 1869 he returned to Philadelphia as pastor of the Third (Reformed) Dutch Church, which he combined with one or two other moribund congregations. After he became pastor of what was then called the Clinton Street Presbyterian Church on November 4, 1878, it united with Immanuel Presbyterian Church. On December 1, 1846, he married Sarah Jane Locke (1827-1891); they had three children. Dr. Wadsworth died of pneumonia on April 1, 1882.

Rev. William P. White and William H. Scott, *The Presbyterian Church in Philadelphia* (Philadelphia, 1895). *Impressions of Dr. Wadsworth as a Preacher,* "by a Clergyman" (San Francisco, 1863). In the copy at the Presbyterian Historical Society of Philadelphia the name of the author, George Burrows, is written in pencil on the title page. *See* also *The Presbyterian,* LII (April 8, 1882), 10, and Rev. John Dewitt, *In Memoriam Charles Wadsworth* (1882).

MARY WARNER (MRS. E. P. CROWELL) (1830-1903). *See* REV. EDWARD PAYSON CROWELL.

REV. AARON WARNER (1794-1876). Williams College, 1815. Andover Theological Seminary, 1819. "A very pious man," he was professor of rhetoric, oratory and English literature at Amherst College from 1844 until his resignation on November 21, 1853. His eldest daughter, Mary Hardy (1830-1903), married, August 13, 1861, the *Rev. Edward Payson Crowell.* Tyler, 1873, 337-338.

WILLIAM WESSELHÖFT, M.D. (1794-1858). He left Germany in the 1820's and settled in Pennsylvania; became a homeopath and moved to Boston in 1841. His brother Robert came to the United States in 1840, practiced at first in Boston and Cambridge; in 1846 founded a water cure in Brattleboro, Vermont, where he died in 1852. Elizabeth P. Peabody, *Memorial of Dr. William Wesselhöft* (Boston, 1859); William Harvey King, *History of Homeopathy* (New York, 1905), I, 130-134, 218, 233; *The American Homeopathic Review,* I (1858-1859), 96.

LYMAN RICHARDS WILLISTON (1830-1897). Adopted son of *Samuel Williston.* Amherst College, 1850. Andover Theological Seminary, 1853-

1855. Professor of Latin and modern languages, Amherst College, 1856-1857. Removed to Cambridge in 1857.

SAMUEL WILLISTON (1795-1874). Button manufacturer and philanthropist of Easthampton. Founded Williston Seminary, 1841. Trustee of Amherst College, 1841-1874. President Hitchcock says of him that he "will in all future histories of the College head the list of its benefactors." *Reminiscences,* 16.

ROBERT CHARLES WINTHROP (1809-1894). Harvard College, 1828. Studied law with Daniel Webster and was admitted to the bar in 1831. A member of the House of Representatives of the Massachusetts General Court, 1834-1840, he was speaker for three years. Elected to Congress in 1840 as a Whig, he served with a brief intermission until 1851. Speaker of the House, Thirtieth Congress, 1847-1849, he antagonized the antislavery bloc and was defeated for re-election in 1849. When Daniel Webster resigned from the Senate to become Secretary of State, Mr. Winthrop was appointed to replace him in January, 1850, but in 1851 was defeated for the succeeding term by Charles Sumner. Immediately thereafter he became the Whig candidate for Governor of Massachusetts, but was again defeated by the same coalition of Democrats and Free Soilers which had defeated him previously. (Amherst gave Mr. Winthrop 350 votes; his opponent, 84. *Express,* November 14, 1851.) He was never again a candidate for political office, but devoted his time to the advancement of education in the South and to delivery of patriotic orations on important occasions.

ABBY MARIA WOOD (MRS. DANIEL BLISS) (1830-1915). Daughter of Joel and Abby Moore Sweetser Wood of Westminster. After the death of her father on October 11, 1833, and after the marriage, on December 31, 1833, of her uncle, Luke Sweetser, Abby Wood made her home with him in Amherst. Records of the First Church, Amherst, indicate that she was admitted to membership in August, 1850. On November 23, 1855, she married *Rev. Daniel Bliss.* Compare his *Reminiscences,* 61.

GEORGE SULLIVAN WOODMAN, M.D. (1823-1906). Amherst College, 1846. M.D., Harvard, 1849. Married, September 17, 1849, Jane L., daughter of *Dr. Timothy J. Gridley.* Practiced in Amherst, 1851-1858.

CHILDREN OF SAMUEL FOWLER (1775-1838)* AND
LUCRETIA GUNN DICKINSON (1775-1840)

EDWARD DICKINSON (1803-1874)*
  Married May 6, 1828, Emily Norcross*
  Children
    William Austin (1829-1895)*
    Emily Elizabeth (1830-1886)*
    Lavinia Norcross (1833-1899)*

* An asterisk indicates that the name is listed in "Relatives, Friends and Neighbors."

WILLIAM DICKINSON (1804-1887)*
Married (1) October 1, 1831, Eliza Hawley, d. 1851
Child
    William Hawley (1832-1883)
Married (2) October 23, 1852, Mary L. Whittier
Three children, one of whom was named Samuel Fowler Dickinson
LUCRETIA GUNN DICKINSON (1806-1885)
Married May 16, 1832, Rev. Asa Bullard*
Five children
MARY DICKINSON (1809-1852)
Married October 2, 1828, Mark Haskell Newman*
Seven children
SAMUEL FOWLER DICKINSON, JR. (1811-1886)
Married October 9, 1834, Susan ———?
Two children
CATHERINE DICKINSON (1814-1895)
Married, November 4, 1835, Joseph A. Sweetser*
Eight children
TIMOTHY DICKINSON (1816-1852)
Married January 10, 1838, Hannah Dickinson
Three children
FREDERICK DICKINSON (1819-1885)
Married February 17, 1846, Mary L. Richardson
Four children
ELISABETH DICKINSON (1823-1886)*
Married October 10, 1866, Augustus N. Currier*
No children

CHILDREN OF JOEL (1776-1846) AND BETSY FAY NORCROSS (1777-1829)

HIRAM NORCROSS (1800-1829)
Married Amanda Brown
Children
    William Henry Norcross (1823-1854)
    Emily Lavinia Norcross (1828-1852)*
AUSTIN NORCROSS (1802-1824)
EMILY NORCROSS (1804-1882)*
Married May 6, 1828, Edward Dickinson*
Children
    William Austin Dickinson (1829-1895)*†

* An asterisk indicates that the name is listed in "Relatives, Friends and Neighbors."

† Mrs. Edward Dickinson's family names, William, Austin, Emily and Lavinia, were perpetuated in her children. It has usually been assumed, however, that her son was named for his father's brother, William, and for his grandfather's friend and associate, the Rev. Austin Dickinson. The name combination,

Emily Elizabeth Dickinson (1830-1886)*
Lavinia Norcross Dickinson (1833-1899)*
WILLIAM OTIS NORCROSS (1806-1863)
  Married May 6, 1830, Mary Fanning
  Six children
ELI NORCROSS (1809-1811)
LAVINIA NORCROSS (1812-1860)
  Married November 4, 1834, Loring Norcross (1808-1863)
  Children
    Lavinia (1837-1842)
    Louisa (1842-1919)
    Frances Lavinia (1847-1896)
ALFRED NORCROSS (1815-1888)
  Married Olivia Chapin, 1841
  Five children, the youngest of whom (1860-1862) was named Edward
  Dickinson Norcross
NANCY NORCROSS (1818-1824)
JOEL WARREN NORCROSS (1821-1900)*
  Married (1) January 17, 1854, Lamira H. Jones (d. May 3, 1862)
  Two children
  Married (2) April 24, 1866, Maggie P. Gunnison
  One child, Edith Carlton (Reichardt), born 1873

THIRTY-THIRD CONGRESS OF THE UNITED STATES, 1853-1855

Senators from Massachusetts

Senior Senator: Charles Sumner
Junior Senator: Edward Everett, resigned effective June 1, 1854
        Julius Rockwell, June 3, 1854–January 31, 1855
        Henry Wilson, January 31 (February 10), 1855–

Representatives from Massachusetts

First District: Zeno Scudder, Barnstable
        Injured on his way to Washington for the opening of
        Congress, December 3, 1853, he was never seated, and
        resigned on March 4, 1854
        Thomas Dawes Eliot, New Bedford
        Appointed to replace Zeno Scudder, took his seat on
        April 17, 1854, and completed the term
Second District: Samuel L. Crocker, Taunton
Third District: J. Wiley Edmands, Newton Centre
Fourth District: Samuel H. Walley, Roxbury

"William Austin," favored by both parents for different reasons, may well
have decided the name of the child.
  * An asterisk indicates that the name is listed in "Relatives, Friends and Neighbors."

Fifth District: William Appleton, Boston
Sixth District: Charles Wentworth Upham, Salem
Seventh District: Nathaniel P. Banks, Jr., Waltham (coalition Democrat)
Eighth District: Tappan Wentworth, Lowell
Ninth District: Alexander DeWitt, Oxford (Free Soil)
Tenth District: Edward Dickinson, Amherst
Eleventh District: John Z. Goodrich, Stockbridge
All representatives from Massachusetts were Whigs except as otherwise indicated

REPRESENTATIVES FROM AMHERST TO THE MASSACHUSETTS GENERAL COURT

1849*   Luke Sweetser, merchant
1850   Waitstill Dickinson, postmaster and owner of general store, South Amherst
1851   William C. Fowler, former professor, Amherst College
1852   Oliver Watson, shoe manufacturer, East Amherst
1853   Moses B. Greene, retired schoolteacher
1854   Ithamar F. Conkey, lawyer

1874   Edward Dickinson, lawyer

PUBLIC OFFICIALS OF MASSACHUSETTS IN 1874

State officials and other public men mentioned in Edward Dickinson's letters whose names do not appear in "Relatives, Friends and Neighbors"†

Charles Francis Adams, Boston. Diplomatist; candidate for United States Senator, 1874

David Aiken, Greenfield. Senator; lawyer

William G. Bassett, Easthampton. Representative; lawyer

Samuel P. Billings, Hatfield. Representative; farmer

Erastus P. Carpenter, Foxborough. Senator; manufacturer; State Director of the Boston & Albany Railroad

L. J. Cole, Cheshire. Representative; physician

James Denison Colt, Pittsfield. Associate Justice of the Supreme Court of Massachusetts

Benjamin Robbins Curtis, Boston. Associate Justice of the Supreme Court of the United States, 1851-1857; candidate for United States Senator, 1874

* Representatives to the General Court were elected each year, in November, to serve for the following year. Years given above are those during which they served.

† See *Massachusetts Register and Business Directory* (1874), *Manual for the General Court* (1874), and *Journal of the House of Representatives* (1874).

Henry C. Davis, Ware.* Representative; lawyer.
Henry L. Dawes, Pittsfield. Lawyer; candidate for United States Senator, 1874
Charles H. French, Canton. Senator; banker and manufacturer
Asahel Gates, Pelham. Representative; farmer
Charles Hale, Boston. Representative; lawyer
Thomas M. Judd, Lee. Representative; lawyer
Samuel O. Lamb, Greenfield. Representative; lawyer
Edward Learned, Pittsfield. Senator; lawyer
George B. Loring, Salem. President of the Senate; physician
Albert Montague, Sunderland. Representative; farmer
John F. Moors, Greenfield. Representative; clergyman
Willard P. Phillips, Salem. Representative; merchant
Eliphalet Stone, Dedham. Member of the State Board of Agriculture
Thomas N. Stone, Wellfleet. Senator; physician
William P. Strickland, Northampton. Clerk of the Courts
Gardiner Tufts, Lynn. Visiting Agent of the Board of State Charities
William B. Washburn, Greenfield. Governor of Massachusetts until elected by the General Court to succeed Charles Sumner as United States Senator, April 17, 1874

* Two other men named Davis, both of Greenfield, were active in state politics, George T. and Wendell T. Davis.

Bibliography

Six source books are particularly helpful in gaining a picture of the early days of Amherst and of Amherst College. As with other works of reference, the first time a book is mentioned the complete citation is given, thereafter a short title, as indicated:

Josiah Gilbert Holland, *History of Western Massachusetts,* 2 vols. Springfield: Samuel Bowles and Company, 1855. (Holland, *History*)

Edward Hitchcock, *Reminiscences of Amherst College.* Northampton, Mass.: Bridgman & Childs, 1863. (Hitchcock, *Reminiscences*)

W. S. Tyler, *History of Amherst College during Its First Half Century, 1821-1871.* Springfield, Mass.: Clark W. Bryan and Company, 1873. (Tyler, 1873)

William S. Tyler, *History of Amherst College, 1821-1891.* New York: F. H. Hitchcock, 1895. (Tyler, 1895)

George S. Merriam, *The Life and Times of Samuel Bowles.* 2 vols. New York: The Century Co., 1885. (Merriam, *Samuel Bowles*)

The History of the Town of Amherst, Massachusetts, 1731-1896, compiled and published by Carpenter & Morehouse. Amherst, 1896. (*History of Amherst*)

Among more recent volumes dealing with local history the reader is referred to

Frederick Tuckerman, *Amherst Academy, A New England School of the Past, 1814-1861.* Amherst: Printed for the Trustees, 1929.

George Frisbie Whicher, *This Was a Poet.* New York: Charles Scribner's Sons, 1938.

Theodora Van Wagenen Ward, *Emily Dickinson's Letters to Dr. and Mrs. Josiah Gilbert Holland.* Cambridge: Harvard University Press, 1951.

The *Amherst College Biographical Record, 1821-1939;* the files of *The Hampshire and Franklin Express* (*Express*) and of its successor, *The Amherst Record,* both printed in Amherst; as well as those of *The Hampshire Gazette,* Northampton, and *The Springfield Republican,* are indispensable.

Works to which frequent reference is made herein are as follows:

Letters of Emily Dickinson, edited by Mabel Loomis Todd, 2 vols. Boston: Roberts Brothers, 1894.

Poems by Emily Dickinson, edited by two of her friends, Mabel Loomis Todd and T. W. Higginson. Boston: Roberts Brothers, 1890.

Poems by Emily Dickinson, Second Series, edited by two of her friends, T. W. Higginson and Mabel Loomis Todd. Boston: Roberts Brothers, 1891.

Poems by Emily Dickinson, Third Series, edited by Mabel Loomis Todd. Boston: Roberts Brothers, 1896.

Letters of Emily Dickinson, New and Enlarged Edition, edited by Mabel Loomis Todd. New York: Harper & Brothers, 1931. All references are to the 1931 edition, except as otherwise indicated.

Bolts of Melody, New Poems of Emily Dickinson, edited by Mabel Loomis Todd and Millicent Todd Bingham. New York: Harper & Brothers, 1945. A description of the manuscripts, including the fascicles in which Emily copied her poems, is contained in the Introduction to *Bolts of Melody.*

Millicent Todd Bingham, *Ancestors' Brocades, The Literary Debut of Emily Dickinson.* New York: Harper & Brothers, 1945.

"Poems of Emily Dickinson, Hitherto Published Only in Part," edited by Millicent Todd Bingham. *The New England Quarterly,* XX, 1-50.

Millicent Todd Bingham, *Emily Dickinson—A Revelation.* New York: Harper & Brothers, 1954.

APPENDICES

I. EMILY DICKINSON'S DAGUERREOTYPE

In 1893 when Mrs. Todd was preparing Emily Dickinson's letters for the press, a likeness of her was needed as a frontispiece. Since childhood there had been but one picture taken when she was sixteen or seventeen, probably in December, 1847, during the visit of a traveling daguerreotypist in South Hadley. Her brother and sister did not like it and objected to its being used. The various expedients devised in the effort to produce a satisfactory likeness were described in *Ancestors' Brocades* (224-225, 273, 294).

"A question which had been baffling them all for some time—editor, publisher, brother, and sister—was the matter of a picture for the book of letters. How was a satisfactory likeness of Emily Dickinson to be contrived? 'I had no portrait, now,' she wrote Colonel Higginson. 'It often alarms father. He says death might occur, and he has molds of all the rest, but has no mold of me.'

"This statement was, however, not strictly true." Not only was there an oil painting of Austin and his sisters as children and a little silhouette made by Charles Temple who graduated from Amherst College when Emily was fourteen and taught in the Academy the year following. "There was also the now well-known daguerreotype of Emily at eighteen, first published by my mother in 1931. In 1893, it belonged to Maggie Maher, Miss Vinnie's servant."

This last statement, made on the authority of Lavinia Dickinson, my mother never questioned. On April 2, 1893, she wrote in her diary: "The cabinet photograph of Emily taken from Maggie's daguerreotype is dreadful—the original is far better." This sounds as if she thought the daguerreotype was still, at that time, in Maggie's possession. But apparently it was not.

In 1893 attempts to concoct a picture based on the daguerreotype, one which would satisfy Austin and Lavinia, continued for some months without success. "It was finally agreed that the chance of obtaining a likeness in this way was too remote to justify the expense. And that is why the only picture of Emily Dickinson's face taken from life was discarded, and the reproduction of an oil painting of her as a child, which both brother and sister admitted did not resemble her, was the only one used in the volume of letters."

After publication of the *Letters* in 1894, Lavinia Dickinson did not give up trying to achieve a likeness of Emily which would express her own ideas of what her sister should look like. This was in the late 1890's. Her efforts have been described in an article by Louise B. Graves.[1]

1. L. B. Graves, "The Likeness of Emily Dickinson," *Harvard Library Bulletin*, I, 248-251, 1947. In this article Miss Graves describes the efforts of

But in the meantime the original daguerreotype had disappeared. (Daguerreotypes were produced directly on silvered copper plates. Each was unique and without a duplicate.) Mystery had overtaken it in the early nineties and for more than fifty years the destiny of this one and only picture was unknown. Photographic copies of it were the only evidence that the daguerreotype had ever existed.

In 1931 my mother brought out the new edition of the 1894 *Letters*, the source book long out of print. As a frontispiece she reluctantly decided to reproduce the 1890 photograph of the daguerreotype. Even if not a flattering likeness it was at least authentic. Poor as it was, it would be preferable to the doctored "miniature," with curled hair and fancy ruff, which had been published in 1924 by Emily's niece and used thereafter as the frontispiece of the collected poems. For that doctored picture not only misrepresents Emily's appearance, it belies her character. Furbelows and Victorian ornateness were not a part of her nature; she would not have worn such a ruff. It was to counteract this misrepresentation that the cabinet photograph of the daguerreotype was used as the frontispiece of the 1931 *Letters*. At the time it was the only solution, since the whereabouts of the original daguerreotype was unknown.

A few months after the appearance of the 1931 volume my mother received a letter from Austin Baxter Keep, professor of history at the College of the City of New York, a graduate of Amherst College in the class of 1897. Through his mother he was related to the Dickinsons. The letter was written less than three months before he died on August 19, 1932. He says in part:

> "Hillcroft," Biltmore, N. C.
> May 28, 1932

Dear Mrs. Todd:

. . . . How I wish you or your daughter had told me a little more fully about the picture of Emily that was to appear in your joint volume, for I have treasured a similar picture lo these many years, and I feel that a print from mine would have satisfied you better. I am enclosing with my compliments a print for each of you, processed differently, as you can see, with the thought that you may like to use one of them in subsequent editions. You will notice one feature particularly *Emilyesque*, namely, her holding fresh flowers.

---

her sister Gertrude to please their Cousin Lavinia in her wish to have a less "severe" likeness of her beloved sister. Gertrude Graves asked Laura C. Hills, the well-known miniature painter, to add Miss Vinnie's ideas to a photograph of the daguerreotype. So Miss Hills softened the hair and put on the ruff, but she did not touch the face. A photograph of the retouched photograph was then sent to Miss Vinnie, who received it with enthusiasm. But this was not the end. The photograph, retouched by Miss Hills, is not the picture published by Mrs. Bianchi as a "miniature" of Emily Dickinson. Louise Graves is of the opinion that that "miniature" was made after Lavinia's death, not before, and was painted by someone not known to her or to Miss Hills, *upon* a photographic enlargement of the little print sent by her sister to their Cousin Lavinia, and which the latter acclaimed with the words, "Emily has come back to me!"

You may remember I did go so far as to enquire of you whether the likeness of Emily you showed my brother Wallace was from a daguerreotype, because she is seemingly holding the flowers in her left hand, whereas it would normally be the right; but you probably misunderstood my "drift" and replied that it was not reversed, left and right. . . .

With hearty congratulations on your great work accomplished, and with cordial regards for you both, I am

Your friend of long ago
Austin B. Keep

Austin Keep's photograph of the daguerreotype was like the one used in my mother's book, only much clearer. The margin around the picture was different too. After discussing the matter we came to the conclusion that his copy must have been made by removing the daguerreotype from its frame. But however it was done, the picture was so much better than the one originally used in the 1931 *Letters* that a new plate was made. In the third printing a reproduction of Mr. Keep's photograph replaced the earlier frontispiece, and is now accepted as the standard likeness of Emily Dickinson.[2]

All thought of discovering the whereabouts of the original daguerreotype having long since been given up, what was my amazement after the publication of *Ancestors' Brocades* to receive from Austin Keep's brother Wallace, a graduate of Amherst in 1894, a letter from which I quote:

402 North Jefferson Avenue, Saginaw, Mich
June 13, 1945

Dear Millicent:

. . . . I drove to our home on Grand Traverse Bay last week . . . taking many things back and bringing here numerous other things—among them the very precious picture of the immortal poetess which she had once owned and had left to Vinnie. At least that was what Vinnie herself told me at the time she handed over to me the daguerreotype as her gift to me and as an expression of her affectionate regard in June of 1892. The picture must by this time be nearly one hundred years in age but you will know more accurately about that than I. It has of course become somewhat faded but with the proper lighting thrown on it the face is quite clear. I am turning it over to your care and keeping knowing of no living person who could more appropriately possess it. I do so from no wish to part with it myself but being now in my seventy-fifth year of life I desire that heirloom to pass to you before I might be "no more seen"—as the prayer book expresses it. . . . Lots of auld lang syne regards to yourself always and everywhere I might be.

Wallace

This letter was soon followed by the daguerreotype itself.

A little while ago, as I was writing down these facts, I realized afresh the importance of finding out the precise date on which Miss Vinnie gave the

2. Previous to the publication in 1938 of George F. Whicher's *This Was a Poet*, and in giving him permission to reproduce the frontispiece of the 1931 *Letters*, I sent him Austin Keep's copy of the daguerreotype. This was done in order to insure a wider audience for the best and clearest respresentation of Emily Dickinson's face.

daguerreotype to Wallace Keep. It seemed incredible that, even as Emily's letters were being prepared for publication, her sister should have given away this one and only picture. Furthermore, if, as Miss Vinnie told my mother, the daguerreotype did not belong to her but to Maggie Maher, what right had she to give it away?

I was so puzzled that I ventured to write again to Wallace Keep, hoping that he might recall further details about the circumstances of the gift. I quote from his reply, mailed February 13, 1949, in Traverse City, Michigan.

"I feel more than sorry that all these fifty-six or -seven years have beclouded what memories I might conjure up today. I do recall being piloted upstairs by Vinnie to the sacred bed room in which Emily closed her eyes in death and remember distinctly seeing the priceless daguerreotype on Emily's bureau and it was perhaps or probably then and there that Lavinia decided that it should be given to me and if so the time was in the spring of 1892."

The story of Emily Dickinson's picture thus provides the starting point for yet another train of speculation, one which, in line with tradition, leads to yet another mystery.

The daguerreotype as it appears today is shown in a photograph taken on December 16, 1954, by Richard Stewart and Milton Ford, distinguished staff photographers of the National Geographic Society.

II. DEEDS RELATING TO THE DICKINSON HOMESTEAD
RECORDED IN REGISTRY OF DEEDS OF HAMPSHIRE COUNTY, NORTHAMPTON, MASSACHUSETTS

Deed of Sale to David Mack, Jr., May 22, 1833 (Book 71, page 90)

To all people to whom these presents shall come, GREETING.

KNOW YE THAT We John Leland Esq. & Nathan Dickinson, Goldsmith, both of Amherst, in the County of Hampshire & Commonwealth of Massachusetts For and in consideration of the sum of Five thousand two hundred & Fifty dollars current money of the commonwealth aforesaid, to us in hand paid, before the ensealing hereof by David Mack Jr of Middlefield in said county, Esq. the receipt whereof we do hereby acknowledge and are fully satisfied, contented and paid, HAVE given, granted, bargained, sold, aliened, released, conveyed and confirmed, and by these presents do freely, clearly and absolutely give, grant, bargain, sell, alien, release, convey and confirm unto him the said David Jr his heirs and assigns forever,

The Homestead in said Amherst, where Samuel F. Dickinson, resides, containing two & an half acres of land, more or less, with all the buildings on the same; bounded South, on the county road, west & north on land of Luke Sweetser & East on a town road. Also a tract of land in said Amherst, South of said county road & in part, opposite to the premises above described, containing seventeen & an half acres, more or less, bound North on said county road, East on land of Leander Merrick, South on land of Phinehas Warner, & west on land of Rupell I Wheelock & Orinda Merrick.

TO HAVE AND TO HOLD the before granted premises, with the appurtenances and privileges thereto belonging, to him the said David Jr his heirs and assigns: To his and their own proper use, benefit and behoof, forevermore. And we the said John & Nathan for ourselves our heirs, executors and administrators, do covenant, promise and grant unto and with the said David Jr. his heirs and assigns forever: That before and until the ensealing hereof, we are the true, sole, proper and lawful owners and possessors of the before granted premises, with the appurtenances. And have in us good right, full power, and lawful authority to give, grant, bargain, sell, alien, release, convey and confirm the same as aforesaid; and that free and clear, and freely and clearly, executed, acquitted and discharged of and from all former and other gifts, grants, bargains, sales, leases, mortgages, wills, entails, jointures, dowries, thirds, executions and incumbrances whatsoever.

AND FURTHERMORE, we the said John & Nathan for ourselves our heirs, executors and administrators, do hereby covenant, promise and engage, the before granted premises, with the appurtenances unto him the said David Jr his heirs and assigns forever, to warrant, secure and defend against the lawful claims and demands of any person or persons whatsoever.

IN WITNESS WHEREOF, We together with Lydia wife of said John & Mary
Ann wife of said Nathan, releasing dower in the premises have hereunto set
our hands and seals this twenty second day of May in the year of our Lord one
thousand eight hundred and thirty three.

Signed, sealed and delivered, in presence of

Samuel Dickinson	John Leland	
Edward Dickinson	Lydia Leland	
Rossy Root	Nathan Dickinson	
	Mary Ann Dickinson	

Hampshire ss. May 22, 1833. Personally appeared John Leland & Nathan Dickinson, subscribers to the within instrument, & acknowledged the same to be
their deed.

Before me, Samuel F. Dickinson, Justice of the Peace

Hampshire ss. May 22, 1833. 7 o'clock 6 min. P. M.

Deed of Sale to Edward Dickinson, April 27, 1855
(Book 160, Page 446)

Know all men by these presents that I Samuel E. Mack of the City of Cincinnati and County of Hamilton, & State of Ohio., Gentleman, in consideration of
six thousand dollars, paid by Edward Dickinson of Amherst, in the County of
Hampshire, and Commonwealth of Massachusetts, Esq. the receipt whereof is
hereby acknowledged, do hereby give, grant, bargain, sell and convey unto the
said Dickinson, the homestead in said Amherst, where my late father David,
Mack Esq. now deceased, resided, and consisting of the following pieces of land
one on the North side & one on the South side of the highway, described as
follows:

1. on the North side, beginning at the North west corner of the premises at
an angle in L. Sweetser's line, thence Southerly to the highway, partly on land
of said Sweetser & partly on land of said Dickinson; thence Easterly on the
highway to the road running by J. P. Gray's dwelling house; thence N. Westerly on said road to the S. E. corner of the town pound; thence westerly &
Northerly on said pound to L. Sweetser's south line; thence westerly on said
Sweetser to the first mentioned corner; containing two & a half acres more or
less.

2. on the South side beginning at the N. West corner, & the N. E. corner of
the heirs of Col. Kingman's land; thence Southerly partly on said Kingman's
heirs & partly on Newton Fitch to Phineas Warner; thence Easterly on said
Warner to the land sold & conveyed by my said father to the Amherst &
Belchertown Rail Road Co.; thence Northerly on said Co's land to the highway; thence Westerly on said highway to the first mentioned corner; containing eleven & a half acres, more or less.

To have and to hold the above granted premises, with all the privileges and
appurtenances to the same belonging, to the said Dickinson, his heirs and as-

signs, to their use and behoof forever. And I the said Mack, for myself, my heirs, executors and administrators, do covenant with the said Dickinson, his heirs and assigns, that I am lawfully seized in *in* fee simple of the aforegranted premises, that they are free from all incumbrances, that I have good right to sell and convey the same to the said Dickinson, his heirs and assigns forever as aforesaid, and that I will and my heirs, executors and administrators, shall warrant and defend the same to the said Dickinson, his heirs and assigns forever, against the lawful claims and demands of all persons.

In Witness Whereof, I the said Samuel E. Mack together with Rebecca, my wife, hereby releasing her right of dower in the premises, have hereunto set our hands and seals, this twenty seventh day of April, in the year of our Lord eighteen hundred and fifty five.

Signed, Sealed and
delivered, in presence of

| C. D. Mansfield | } | Saml. E. Mack | & seal |
| A. H. McGuffey | } | R. A. R. Mack | & seal |

The State of Ohio   }
County of Hamilton   } sst.
City of Cincinnati   }

The twenty seventh (27) day of April, eighteen hundred and fifty five (1855)

Then the said Samuel E. Mack (the grantor) personally appeared and acknowledged the foregoing instrument to be his free act & deed. At the same time & place also personally appeared Rebecca A. R. Mack, the wife of said Samuel E. Mack likewise a party to said instrument & acknowledged the same to be her free act & deed, before me, as witness my hand and official seal.

(Seal)   Alexander H. McGuffey
Commissioner in Ohio, for the
State of Massachusetts

Hampshire, ss. May 17, 1855, 3 oC. 44 m. P. M.

There is also, recorded in Book 160, page 449, a mortgage deed for $4000 from Edward Dickinson to Samuel E. Mack, dated May 2, 1855.

III. POLITICAL CAMPAIGN OF 1852

Extracts from *The Hampshire and Franklin Express* relative to Edward
Dickinson's Candidacy

The following editorial appeared in the issue of September 10, 1852:

REPRESENTATIVE TO CONGRESS

The new apportionment of the State into Congressional Districts, devolves
upon the whigs of the old Sixth, now mainly incorporated in the Tenth District,
the necessity of selecting a new candidate to represent them in the Halls of the
National Legislature. . . .

The electors of the new Tenth District are called upon to meet in convention
by delegates at Northampton, on Wednesday next, to designate whom they will
have to represent them in Congress. To the intelligent and enlightened whigs of
this district, no questions of availability need be raised. It has always been
found, and will ever so prove, that the *best* men are the most *available.* The
men best known, longest identified with the great interests of the Connecticut
Valley, familiar in every particular with our peculiar wants, tried, proved, responsible and trustworthy, are those whom we desire should represent us in
congress.

On this ground, and as best meeting the wants of the community as a faithful,
well known, able whig, stands HON. EDWARD DICKINSON.

Mr. Dickinson has been for many years in public life, and in every position has
faithfully and honorably served his constituents. As a member of our State
Legislature and State Senator, as Councillor, and in many other offices of public
trust, he has shown himself a man, strong, reliable, capable. His legislative
experience is such as to render him abundantly qualified for the office of
member of Congress.

As a staunch and tried whig no man has been more devoted to the principles
of the party. Through the stormy period following the nomination of Gen.
Taylor, he gave in his firm and unflinching adherence to whig principles, laboring with a hearty zeal for the true interests of the great whig party. In the
present campaign, he had the honor to represent the old Sixth District in the
National nominating Convention. To that convention he carried a firm and
unwavering friendship to Daniel Webster, which led him to stand by the great
statesman through the 53 ballots of that body. Yet when the nomination was
fairly made, and the man of his choice defeated, gracefully yielding to the
majority, he gave in his adherence to the nomination of Gen. Scott. A true whig
in every sense of the word, he is ever ready to sacrifice personal preference to
the good of principle.

Through a long life of public and private responsibility, Mr. Dickinson has
made himself familiarly acquainted with all great questions of national moment,
as well as with those more particularly affecting the region of country embracing
the Tenth Congressional District. To say that he is a whig, thoroughly a whig,
in feeling, principle, and action, is sufficient. The great industrial interests of
the country at large, Agriculture, Manufactures, Commerce, will find in him a
staunch supporter.

In connection with his numerous and extensive professional acquirements, he
brings to his aid strong and powerful natural abilities, expanded by cultivation
and matured by experience. Of his private character and his every day life, it is
needless to speak to the whigs of Old Hampshire. Always a firm friend of tem-

perance, ever first in sustaining the true principles of law and order, he always looks toward the right, and with indomitable perseverance pursues it. He is no trimmer, courting the breezes of popularity first upon one tack and then upon another, but straight forward, steadfast and reliable.

Such it seems to us is the man we desire to represent us in Congress. Common practice and courtesy, we believe, award the Representative to Hampshire County, and as her truest, most deserving and popular son, Old Hampshire points to HON. EDWARD DICKINSON. Let our sister counties, joined in the District with us, come forward to our aid, and the first choice of Hampshire will be the ultimate choice of the District.

The issue of September 24, 1852, published an editorial, "Our Candidate for Congress," and a column entitled "Mr. Dickinson's Letter of Acceptance," as follows:

MR. DICKINSON'S LETTER OF ACCEPTANCE

We take pleasure in placing before our readers the subjoined correspondence between DANIEL FROST, ESQ., President of the nominating Convention, and Hon. EDWARD DICKINSON. The letter of Mr. D., accepting the nomination, is such as every true whig will heartily endorse. We commend it to the perusal of our readers:—

ORANGE, Sept. 18, 1852

HON. EDWARD DICKINSON:—*My Dear Sir*:—At a Convention of Whig Delegates, in Congressional District No. 10, duly assembled at Northampton on the 15th inst., for the purpose of nominating a suitable person to receive their suffrages and represent their interest in Congress, you was unanimously selected. By a vote of said convention, I am instructed as their presiding officer, to communicate to you the foregoing action of the Convention and request your acceptance of the nomination thus made. If I may be allowed to express my opinion, formed from what passed in the Convention, I should say, that the unbroken harmony in action and sentiment which prevailed and especially the unanimity with which the Candidate was selected and the manifest settled purpose by all honorable measures to sustain the selection thus made, give certain assurance that the result of the nomination will not be doubtful. When I shall have received your reply and published the same to the District, the pleasing duty devolved on me by the Convention, will have been discharged. With the highest regard and esteem, I am your

Ob't servant,
DANIEL FROST.

AMHERST, Sept. 21, 1852

DANIEL FROST, Esq:—

My Dear Sir:—I have received your letter notifying me that I had been unanimously nominated by the delegates to the Whig Convention, held at Northampton, on the 15th inst., as the candidate, to represent the 10th District in Congress, and requesting my acceptance of the same.

I am duly sensible of the confidence reposed in me by this act of the Convention, and gratefully accept the nomination; not unconscious, however, that if ratified by the electors, the election would impose upon me high and responsible duties; nor without great distrust of my ability to meet these responsibilities in the manner which the District has a right to require of its Representative.

The District is *nominally*, a new one—yet it embraces but few towns which have not, at some former period, belonged to the "Old Sixth,"—whose name and history are well known to every man, of every party in Massachusetts; and whose unwavering attachment to whig principles has ever been manifested by the election of a succession of as true and honorable men, as have represented any district in the Commonwealth.

To sustain this same reputation, in the new District, is worthy of our highest efforts, and due to the principles we profess.

In thus accepting the nomination, I can give no assurance of fidelity in the discharge of the duties of the office of representative, if elected, beyond what is furnished by my past life, and an honest, earnest and honorable resolve to exert myself to the utmost of my ability, to maintain the influence and the honor of Massachusetts in the National Councils, by emulating the example of my predecessors in their steadfast and inflexible maintenance of that wise and liberal policy which seeks to promote the great political and industrial interests of the Country, and in their manly and fearless advocacy of the true doctrines of Constitutional government and Republican liberty.

With the highest esteem and regard,

Yours truly,

EDWARD DICKINSON

IV. EDWARD DICKINSON IN CONGRESS

Abridgment of a study made at my request by Willoughby Davis

Edward Dickinson entered national politics in June, 1852, when he went as a delegate to the Whig Presidential Convention in Baltimore. Later that year the federal electoral districts of Massachusetts were reorganized and the central part of the state, as the tenth district, was empowered to send another representative to the Congress of the United States, a post which Mr. Dickinson was the first to occupy. When he arrived in Washington on December 5, 1853, for the opening of the Thirty-third Congress, he found a Democratic President, Franklin H. Pierce; a House of Representatives consisting of 159 Democrats, 71 Whigs and 4 Free Soilers; a large Democratic majority in the Senate as well; and a Democratic governor and legislature in almost every state in the Union except Massachusetts where the Whig party was still dominant. Mr. Dickinson was one of its staunchest members.

The political complexion of Congress showed itself on the opening day. A Democratic speaker, Linn Boyd of Kentucky, was elected by an overwhelming vote (*1, 2*).[1] This Congress would have been noted for a reduction of the tariff, and still more so for opening the way for a transcontinental railroad, if there had not been in the Senate a man capable of changing the course of history.[2] This man was Senator Stephen A. Douglas, who, by his introduction and defense of the Kansas-Nebraska Bill, precipitated almost singlehanded the storm of public protest which was to culminate in the Civil War. The Nebraska Bill, as it was usually called, was the most significant piece of legislation passed by the Thirty-third Congress—or for that matter, by any Congress of the 1850's. Mr. Dickinson took very little active part in the controversy. And he had nothing to say in Congress about the tariff, or even about the Pacific Railroad, although railroads were his lifelong interest. His first appointment was to the House Standing Committee on Elections, of which the opinionated Richard H. Stanton, a Kentucky Democrat, was chairman (*1, 33*). Mr. Dickinson had no interest in the Committee on Elections as far as can be judged from the record, though he did once under instructions from the committee present one of its resolutions to the House.

On February 13, 1854 (*1, 414*), on motion of Mr. Stanton, a special committee of the House was set up to investigate the superintendency of the national ar-

1. For numbers in parentheses see *The Congressional Globe*, 33 Congress. See also References, page 570.

2. James Ford Rhodes, *History of the United States from the Compromise of 1850 to the End of the Roosevelt Administration* (New York: 1928), I, 422.

United States Armory, Springfield, Massachusetts, 1854

mories. Edward Dickinson was appointed to that committee although he had at first no interest in the matter whatever, and said so in unmistakable terms on two occasions. But legislation connected with this investigation provided the opportunity for his only important speech while in Congress.

There were in 1854 two national armories, one at Springfield, Massachusetts, the other at Harper's Ferry, Virginia. The purpose of the investigation by the House was to determine whether the superintendents should continue to be appointed from the Army Ordnance Board consisting of military officers whose specialty was ordnance and firearms, or whether they should be civilian mechanics or engineers. The advocates of the "military system" pointed out the increased operating efficiency and the excellence of arms produced under military management; they deplored the danger of the office coming under the influence of party politics. Their opponents claimed, on the other hand, that the system was wasteful of public funds and oppressive to the workers. The debate which followed had nothing to do with competence; it was concerned solely with whether manufacture of government firearms should be administered by civilians or by officers of the Army.

The title of the special committee proposed by Mr. Stanton was "Select Committee of the House on the Superintendency of Public Works," usually referred to as the armory committee. Mr. Stanton was appointed chairman, Mr. Dickinson a member, presumably because he came from the Springfield district, and Mr. Charles J. Faulkner because he came from Harper's Ferry. The other members were Joshua Vansant, Maryland; W. R. Sapp, Ohio; John L. Dawson, Pennsylvania; and Lawrence M. Keitt, a hot-blooded Democrat from South Carolina. The two latter, with Edward Dickinson, the only Whig on the committee, made up the minority which favored military superintendence.

Lawrence Keitt was in his twenties and it was his first term in Congress. Yet it was he, and not Dawson or Dickinson, who signed the minority report. Keitt was an ardent secessionist, and at one time even advocated the lone secession of South Carolina. In 1856 he participated in the notorious affair of the beating of Senator Charles Sumner of Massachusetts, to the extent of trying to prevent interference with the attack. For this he was severely censured by the House and resigned his seat. But twenty days later he was re-elected by his constituents. He served in Congress until the beginning of the War between the States, when he left to become an officer in the Confederate Army. A gallant soldier, he was killed in action in 1864 when not quite forty years of age. Impetuous, but extremely able, Keitt's name appears often in the *Congressional Record,* or *The Globe* as it was then called; but he made few long speeches, preferring to utilize his skill in debate for impromptu questions and comments. He respected his austere colleague Edward Dickinson and more than once came to his aid on the floor of the House.

Such was the make-up of the special committee which set out, in February of 1854, to investigate conditions in the two national armories. Richard Stanton, the chairman, an experienced politician, was spokesman for those members who favored civilian management. Besides Mr. Stanton, only two other personalities emerge with sharp outlines: the youthful Lawrence Keitt and Edward Dickinson, blunt, stubborn, and forthright.

The history of what came to be known as the armory question goes back to the beginning of nineteenth century.

When the national armories were established in 1794 civilians were appointed as superintendents. They continued in control until 1841, when, owing to reports of slackness, slovenly work and flagrant abuse of privileges by the workers, the civilian superintendent was replaced by a military officer who proceeded to enforce the rules and to run the armories according to prevailing business methods. In February, 1846, after five years of military administration, a memorial was sent to Congress, signed by thirty citizens of Springfield, among them Samuel Bowles, Sr., founder and editor of *The Springfield Republican*. This memorial complained about several "unjust acts" committed, and duties left undone, by the superintendent, Major James W. Ripley.

Born in 1794, James Ripley had a long and distinguished career in the Army. General Winfield Scott said of him: "Captain Ripley has no superior in the middle ranks of the Army . . . in general intelligence, zeal or good conduct." For eight years he had been in command of the arsenal at Kennebec, Maine, when, in 1841, he was transferred to the Springfield armory.[3]

Captain, later Major, Ripley came to Springfield with reluctance, for he foresaw opposition in the difficult assignment of ridding the armory of corruption. But he was not prepared for the violence of the feeling against him. Springfield citizens not connected with the armory took it upon themselves to agitate against him and to snub him socially, while the workers were busy spreading slander and abuse. When it became evident that Ripley's course was comparatively mild and that his innovations were beneficial, many people changed their minds, among them George Ashmun, prominent Whig and Yale classmate of Edward Dickinson. But others who had profited from the old slackness continued to stir up trouble and ill feeling. Charles Stearns, a contractor and builder, was the ringleader. His opposition was based on the fact that the old superintendent's quarters, a house which he had built some dozen years before the arrival of Major Ripley, was torn down by order of the Secretary of War because of poor bricks and faulty construction. A better house was built—but not by Mr. Stearns, who took out his resentment in abuse of the commandant. He tore down a fence and a small shack which Ripley had put up on a strip of Government land adjacent to land owned by Stearns, who claimed that he owned both strips. An indictment of riotous conduct was brought against him and seven other men, but all were acquitted. There was a sharp edge on Edward Dickinson's opposition to Charles Stearns. After the death of Mrs. Dickinson's brother Hiram, Mr. Stearns had married his widow.

The 1846 memorial to Congress took the form of thirteen charges against Major Ripley. They sound formidable; but no names or dates were specified.

3. "An arsenal is a military post, and has at it enlisted men. An armory is not a military post, and has at it no enlisted men" (*6, 20*).

Ripley, before a court of inquiry, was fully and honorably acquitted on all counts. On examination the charges simply disappeared. The workmen Ripley discharged failed to show that they had been "distressed"; the town of Springfield did not consider that its rights had been encroached upon in any instance; "wild and reckless foreigners," employed as night watchmen, proved to be three or four Irishmen, eminently steady and reliable, and soberer than the watchmen previously employed. The discharges had roused a storm of complaint, but of all the men dismissed up to the time of the trial only twelve were not subsequently re-employed. The other accusations were shown to be either pure fabrication or a misrepresentation of the facts, and Ripley continued in office.[4]

But Charles Stearns was still on the warpath and so were many of his fellow agitators. By 1853, seven years after Ripley's acquittal, they again succeeded in stirring up public opinion to the boiling point. Memorials and letters from Springfield citizens and others flooded in to Congress, to the Secretary of War, and to the President; the matter was argued at length in the House and the Senate early in 1853 while the Thirty-second Congress was still in session (*3*, 460-466, 496-498, 568-581, 787-794, 837-852, 866-872, 979-1006).

Senator Charles Sumner, on February 23, 1853, expressing the opinion that the complaints should be investigated, said further: ". . . I do submit confidently that the genius of our institutions favors civil life rather than military life, and that, in harmony with this, it is our duty, whenever the public interests will permit, to limit and restrain the sphere of military influences. This is not a military monarchy, where the soldier is supreme, but a Republic, where the soldier yields to the civilian" (*3*, 794).

Sumner was arguing for an investigation by the President, one finally authorized by Congress on March 3, 1853. Six men were appointed to an examining board known as "The Springfield Commission." Four were civilians, one of whom had been governor of New Hampshire; one, ambassador to Great Britain. The other two were military officers, members of the Army Ordnance Board.[5]

These men first assembled in Springfield on August 1, 1853, five months before the opening of the Thirty-third Congress, and began to collect evidence and to hear testimony. They visited private arms factories near Springfield, and were wined and dined by everyone who had any interest in the result of the investigation. The civilian members appear to have thought of the office of superintendent as a political plum. This was the era of the spoils system and the scramble for offices at the beginning of every Presidential term was a quadrennial feature of life in the capital.

4. The entire record of the court of inquiry is contained in *Senate Document*, No. 344, 29 Cong. 1 Sess.

5. The members of the commission were Andrew Stevenson, Charlottesville, Virginia (former Ambassador); ex-Governor John H. Steele, Peterborough, New Hampshire; Henry D. Smith, Middletown, Connecticut; and Reuben H. Walworth, Saratoga Springs, New York. The military members were Lieut. Col. Timothy P. Andrews and Brevet Col. Edward James Steptoe.

For a description of the U. S. Armory at Springfield, see *The Massachusetts Register, a State Record for the Year 1852*. Boston, *1852, 321-323*.

The Springfield Commission took its time and continued hearings well into October. The remuneration was eight dollars a day, about four times its present value. On October 24 the board dissolved without having visited Harper's Ferry.

When the new Congress convened in December, these six men assembled their findings, which included a separate report by each member. This material was presented to President Pierce, who sent it to Congress for action. The result was the formation on February 13, 1854, of the select committee of which Mr. Dickinson was a member.

It was during a preliminary discussion in Congress on February 8, about payment of the six members of the Springfield Commission, that Edward Dickinson made his first recorded appearance on the floor of the House of Representatives. Several members had made "remarks," in each case ruled out of order, regarding military superintendence. Among them were Richard Stanton, Nathaniel P. Banks, Jr., of Massachusetts, and the member from Harper's Ferry, Charles Faulkner. Mr. Stanton was anxious to have the commissioners sent to Harper's Ferry also, to complete their work. Mr. Dickinson drew attention to the fact that the question was not whether the men should or should not be sent to Harper's Ferry; it was of no consequence, he said, whether they had been prevented from discharging all their duties or not, the House was under obligation to pay them for what they had done. He said:

The question now before the House is, what amount they shall receive as compensation, and this question of civil or military superintendence is not legitimately before us.

As I understand it, the law leaves that matter in the hands of the President of the United States. Whenever it comes up legitimately for discussion here, it will devolve upon me, as the representative of the district in which the Springfield armory is located, to take some part in the discussion. I do not wish now to state what my views are upon the question, but if the matter comes up I shall take occasion to address the House upon it (*1*, 381-382).

The above discussion occurred a week before the armory committee was appointed on February 13.

The first few days of committee meetings were devoted to reading the reports of the Springfield commissioners who, it should be recalled, had never been at Harper's Ferry. In fact, none of the investigators, commissioners or congressmen ever did go to Harper's Ferry, so none of them, with the exception of Mr. Faulkner who lived there, had any firsthand knowledge of the place. This lack of information, as well as the apparent indifference with which the other members admitted the lack, disturbed Mr. Dickinson. He was also troubled because at the early meetings only the reports of the commissioners were read, and none of the testimony on which they were based, nor any of the letters and other documents connected with the case. The reports might have been sufficient had the commissioners been competent and impartial; but the record shows anything but impartiality. Since the testimony of three of the Springfield witnesses seemed to Dickinson essential to an understanding of conditions at the armory, he had it included later in the published material, together with his own committee's testimony and documents (6). At the time the committee was receiving evidence, however, they had not read any of the material gathered by the Commission. Had they done so, they might have been able better to evaluate the testimony of Joseph C. Foster (6, 55-57), the only Springfield worker who came to Washington to testify in person before the special committee.

Foster, who had worked at the Springfield armory for twenty-one years, told the committee how differences in regulations and enforcements under the two systems of superintendency appeared to some of the workers. Under both systems some men worked by the piece, with a certain quota as a day's work, while others worked by the day. The reason for this difference, as Foster put it, was that "a barrel-welder uses less fuel and makes better work when working fast than when working slow. The like is true of all forgers. But these workmen cannot maintain their highest speed for ten hours," at that time the standard working day. Among the changes made by Ripley (by this time a lieutenant colonel) was the setting up of a system of bell rings dividing the day into quarters, roughly two-and-a-half-hour periods, varying with the season and the hours of daylight. This division was mainly for the guidance of the day workers, but the pieceworkers were also governed by the bell, which meant that if a pieceworker finished his quota for the day a few minutes after a bell ring he was required to stay in the shop until the next bell ring. In reply to a question, Foster told the committee that the former practice of allowing a piece worker to quit when his quota was completed never caused any expense to the Government because of machinery being kept running for the accommodation of a few men. Before 1841, under civilian administration, water wheels had been used for power. A wheel would last longer with constant use, said Foster, and added that when the water "was in a condition to be affected by the men going to work at different periods, and knocking off at different periods, the men were made to go to work together." Soon after military commandants took charge, steam power was introduced. Foster, although opposed to military control, admitted that "as it is now, worked by steam, the men should go to work at the same time."

While listening to Foster, the committee should have had before them the testimony of Joseph Weatherhead, another Springfield worker, given to the commission some months before (6, 82-98). He had been employed in the armory in various capacities for twenty-six years, though he was not employed at the time, nor had he been for several years. He had worked up from day laborer to master armorer, and testified that the military superintendency was far superior to the civilian on almost all counts.

Weatherhead's comments on day workers, pieceworkers, and the different conditions for the latter under the bell-to-bell rule give substantially the same picture as Foster's, but with the added information that under civilian direction no time record was kept for the pieceworkers, nor even any record of what days they worked, and that their scale of wages was therefore quite out of line: men could work as little as five hours a day and still receive as much as a day worker's ten-hour wages. One effect of the reorganization under Colonel Ripley had been to adjust wages and hours so that both groups worked an average of ten hours.

Even to this there were many exceptions, however, depending on the kind of work performed.

Weatherhead vividly described conditions at the armory under civilian direction. Beggars and loiterers of all sorts were allowed freely to enter the shops where, he said, they often spent the entire day. Merchants, butchers and other tradespeople also came to the shops, which became a provision market for the townspeople as well as the workers. Many of the men were in the habit of knocking off in the middle of the morning and going to town for beer. One lane in the armory grounds was called Toddy Lane because every day at eleven o'clock the workmen sauntered down it on their way to the tavern. Other groups would gather during working hours to sing songs and hymns under the trees. The pieceworkers, who came early and rushed through their stint for the day, would leave when they had finished and ride out in their buggies; or they would linger around the shops reading newspapers, smoking, or taking naps. Weatherhead had made a memorandum of what he found on one occasion in 1841 when, as clerk to the master armorer, he had reason to visit in succession three outlying shops. At the first one he found an inspector and ten men sitting on the steps, idle. It was then 1:45 P.M. Inside the shop one David King was smoking a cigar and talking with others, while Joseph Foster, he who complained to the congressional committee about the strictness of the military administration, was asleep in a corner. In the next shop all the welders were absent, two bayonet forgers were at work; otherwise the place was empty. In the lower water-shop, he noted that "five out of nine hands [were] at work in the stocking-shop, six hands only at work in the filing-shop, two band-forgers and two grinders at work below."

An hour later, on his return, Weatherhead found the two bayonet forgers had gone and the second shop was empty; in the first one Joseph Foster had waked up and gone to work. But "not more than one-third of the hands employed at all these shops were engaged at work during the time I was at them."

After Colonel Ripley took charge, such abuses were gradually stopped. No more beggars or tradespeople were allowed in the armory, though it was still open to visitors. The men were checked as to time spent and work performed, and the rates for piecework were adjusted accordingly. He had greatly improved the appearance of the grounds at the armory, having obtained special funds from Congress for the purpose which the civilians had been unable to do. The machinery and shops had likewise been improved and modernized, and the methods of producing guns as well as the design of the guns themselves radically changed. This had involved additional expense at first, but resulted in a saving over a period of years.

In parenthesis, Edward Dickinson took a special interest in the master machinist, Cyrus Buckland, a man whose mechanical inventiveness was responsible for many of these changes. A farmer's son from Connecticut, his talent, already apparent in his teens, had led him through various jobs in machine factories to the Springfield armory, where he remained from 1828 until his retirement in 1857. Barely five years after he went there his name appears on the payroll as "making patterns for new machines." After that his inventions were introduced regularly. His title in 1853 was "Inspector having charge of fabricating models," but his particular skill was in devising the machines to make newly required parts as the design of the musket was altered and improved. The era of new railroads, of rapidly expanding industrial horizons, and of the first flowering of mechanical engineering and science was in a way personified for Mr. Dickinson in this modest man.

In Joseph Weatherhead's previous testimony before the commission, we read that Colonel Ripley had made a good many changes in personnel. But in Weatherhead's opinion, as opposed to that of Joseph Foster and Charles Stearns, these changes were mostly beneficial. The committee also heard from James T. Ames, owner and manager of a private arms manufactory at Cabotville, Massachusetts, who *(6,* 67-69) testified that after the military took over, many of his own best workers left for the armory and never came back.

Weatherhead denied that there was ever any interference in the local elections by the superintendent of the armory, whether civilian or military; on the contrary, he said, the superintendent stayed away from Springfield throughout election day, lest it be said that he had tried in any way to influence his men; nor was there, as alleged, any interference with freedom of worship. Finally, he emphasized the fact that none of the armorers were ever required by Ripley, on pain of discharge, also alleged, to sign a book saying they were in favor of the military system, as a member of the commission stated.

The examination of Weatherhead then turned to one of the most hotly argued subjects of the investigation—the relative excellence of the arms produced under civilian and under military superintendents. This dispute had been prominent in the proceedings of the court of inquiry in 1846. Weatherhead, together with Asahel Hubbard, the inspector of finished arms, and the inventor, Cyrus Buckland, drew up a statement at that time in rebuttal of the charge of deterioration of quality under Ripley. In 1853, as this controversy grew more and and more heated, the Springfield Commissioners themselves inspected various gun models. One member, John H. Steele, later appeared in person to testify before the select committee of the House *(6,* 37-44, 70-77). Describing himself as an expert on guns, he told the Congressmen that he had examined samples of the guns produced at Springfield, and had found the models made under civilians to be superior to those made later under military superintendency. This serious charge excited much concern among the men employed at the armory. Printed with other documents in the case are several letters of protest from the armorers, one of which describes the circumstances of Steele's inspection as follows: "[Steele made] a cursory comparison of the different parts of the several muskets as to finish, using no gauges whatever to test the accuracy of the work, and occupying perhaps half an hour in this examination; he then took his seat at the table, and began to write" *(6,* 163).

This letter was signed and sworn to by the master armorer, chief foreman of the plant, and by two other foremen. Other letters from foremen and inspectors inform us that the writers had themselves examined the same guns and found that there had been a gradual improvement in the quality. In particular, the machining had so much improved that various parts of the muskets were now interchangeable, which had never before been the case. Confirmation of this view is found in an official report of inspection made at Springfield by General S. Churchill, inspector general of the Army (6, 168-171). He examined the same guns that Steele had seen and, like Weatherhead, Cyrus Buckland and the others, found that the later models had been greatly improved. This finding was made in spite of the fact that the models of the early years had been picked from the choice show specimens, those of more recent date from stock, and the 1853 or latest model had been taken directly from the shops before final inspection.

Having said that the work done under military direction was inferior, ex-Governor Steele advanced as his reason that the men were treated like serfs, that initiative was discouraged, and that suggestions for improvements were invariably followed by a loss of pay. No other evidence bears this out. The same thing was alleged to be true at Harper's Ferry, but here, too, no proof was offered. Oppressed by the tyranny of the military system, Steele continued, the men were restive and resentful; and besides, it was not right on the face of it for military officers to be in charge of a purely civil establishment such as a national armory.

Mr. Steele gave the results of a poll of the workers which he took while in Springfield. He asked them whether they would prefer military or civilian management, and found 127 men in favor of a civil system, 39 in favor of the military, and 12 unwilling to say. In the early summer of 1854, while the committee was still sitting, Edward Dickinson took occasion to visit the Springfield armory, to get the truth about his poll as to the men's preference. He found and reported in his speech to the House on July 13 that Steele had told the men that the management was going to be changed from military to civilian, and if they would declare themselves in favor of the civilian administration, he, Steele, as a personal friend of the President, would undertake to guarantee that they would retain their jobs!

Steele had further testified that the inferior muskets made under the military system had cost the government more than had the good ones made under civilian superintendents. To emphasize this point he had added all the different expenses at the armory—new grounds, living quarters, landscaping and machine shops, as well as the actual cost of materials, labor and maintenance, thus arriving at an inflated "cost per musket."

Jefferson Davis, the Secretary of War, requested Colonel Ripley to submit certain information about expenditures by the armories. With the figures Ripley sent an explanatory letter (6, 171-178). Comparing the over-all expenditures of the commandants during the entire time they were in charge with the same expenditures of the civilians during a corresponding period immediately preceding 1841, he pointed out that the cost per arm under the civilians at Springfield was $12.65, and under the military the cost was only $10.27. When the military men took over, he said, great improvements were being made in the design and manufacture of muskets; also a great deal of new machinery was being installed—which raised the cost per arm for the early forties. But by 1854 the loss had been more than made up. The figures quoted were an average of all twelve years. At Harper's Ferry, using the same period of time and the same basis for calculation, the cost per arm under civilians was higher under both administrations than the highest cost at Springfield. Meanwhile in both armories wages had been increased. The average wage under civilians was $36.99 monthly; under military officers, $38.30 monthly, while highly skilled workers made as much as $70 a month.

Since Colonel Ripley was the only commandant at Springfield between 1841 and 1854, the year in which civilian superintendents were restored, the committee's investigation amounted merely to one more examination of Ripley. (At Harper's Ferry there had been three military superintendents during the same period.) Edward Dickinson, having been to Springfield and having talked with Colonel Ripley, had found that the President's Commission, of which Steele was a member, had never so much as requested Ripley to testify! Dickinson asked Steele about this: Why had the superintendent not been called upon for evidence? And had any report been received from him? Had such report been considered as evidence, and if not, why not? To which Steele replied that since the management and condition of the armory was what the commission had been looking into, they hardly felt that Ripley could be of any help. Besides, said Mr. Steele, the commission having had no power to summon witnesses, they had given notice through the newspapers that they would receive any evidence which was brought forward. As Mr. Dickinson later pointed out, what better way could there have been to ensure hearing all the malcontents and agitators in the whole town of Springfield? It appeared that the only evidence the commission received from Colonel Ripley was in a letter which, Mr. Steele said, not being sworn to under oath, had not been accepted.

Colonel Ripley's letter was, however, printed with the other documents in the case (*6*, 171-178). It is evident that loss of his job meant nothing to him. If civilian administrators were to be restored the War Department would merely station him elsewhere. As to military despotism, of which there had been so many complaints, Ripley pointed out that the only *military* control was over the commandant himself; there could be none over the workers for they were not soldiers. "The workmen employed are contented, in all respects, with their treatment," said Ripley, "and desire nothing so much as a relief from the constant worry and excitement kept up by the agitators for a change in the superintendence." Among these agitators were those who used to profit by jobs or contracts at the armory and did so no longer. They were animated, he said, by "revengeful feelings, self-interest, or mistaken sympathy." He added that the capacity of the armory was now capable of being doubled in time of emergency.

Colonel Ripley made the final point that the armorers could bring political pressure against a civilian superintendent, but that they had no such weapon against a military man, who cannot be deprived of his commission except by court-martial, on proof of specific charges. This immunity is also enjoyed by owners of private factories, such as that of Ames of Cabotville, and of one John Chase, who had also testified before the Springfield Commission and whose ideas on private ownership seemed to Edward Dickinson so important that he had the record of his testimony printed by Congress (*6*, 98-111).

Mr. Chase had been one of the three examiners in 1841 on whose recommendation civilians had been removed from the armories and military men appointed. He had been manager of various arms manufactories and had traveled abroad to inspect foreign establishments; he had even "projected" the village of Cabotville when the first factory was built. He gave it as his opinion that civilians at a national armory never did have and could not possibly have as efficient management as a private company could. Chase himself, for instance, had never been troubled with such abuses as were described by Weatherhead, for the reason that he had never allowed them to get started.

It is astonishing that in this whole investigation the two armories were not once considered separately. As previously stated, there never had been an inspection of Harper's Ferry, although Edward Dickinson tried on three occasions to introduce a resolution in the House authorizing the committee to visit both armories. On the first occasion, Friday, June 30, 1854, his approach to the matter was correct, even deferential:

> This is the first time I have had occasion to ask a favor of the House, and I will occupy but a moment of its time under the circumstances. I shall be compelled to leave the city for a few days, and I feel compelled to appeal to the House to grant the request contained in that resolution.
>
> The select committee of which I am a member have already had the subject under consideration for several months. They have been in session from two to five days in a week, for the purpose of examining the questions which have been referred to them in connection with the superintendence of the national armories—whether superintendents should be appointed from the Ordnance Corps, or whether they should be appointed from the citizens of the United States generally. We have had a large mass of testimony before us, written and verbal; . . . but we have had such a mass of contradictory evidence that it has for a long time been my view, and I have proposed it to the committee time and time again that we should visit the establishement ourselves, for the purpose of satisfying ourselves from our own observation; but I have not been able until now to obtain the assent of the majority of the committee.
>
> On a recent visit to Massachusetts, I spent two half days at the armory at Springfield in making inquiries into the state of things there; and I found that I was able to obtain more information, such as was necessary to base our action upon, in that time, than from all the time I had spent here in committee. . . .
>
> This is a matter of much importance to the country. It is a matter of which I care nothing about personally; but it is of so much importance to the country at large, that I think the select committee should be authorized to visit the armories personally, by which they will be able to obtain reliable information upon which to base their action . . . (*1*, 1585) .

Representative Thomas L. Clingman of North Carolina then said, "I look upon this whole controversy as a Buncombe humbug, and this as a proposition to authorize the members of the select committee to absent themselves from the House. I object." This objection prevented passage of the resolution.

That Mr. Dickinson was irritated by this misinterpretation of his motives is shown by the difference in his manner the next time he offered the same resolution, on Tuesday, July 11 (*1*, 1670). This time he had inserted a phrase to the effect that the committee should visit the armories "after the close of the present session of Congress." The resolution was objected to, but without comment. After some discussion of parliamentary technicalities Mr. Dickinson asked:

. . . Is there any time when any one member here who chooses to object and put a veto on the proceedings of this body, cannot prevent us, from the beginning to the end of the session, from offering resolutions, as is the case now, unless members are willing to go into a general raffle—ignoring their own self-respect—for the purpose of introducing resolutions upon Mondays?

The Speaker ruled that "the gentleman from Massachusetts has not, at this time, a right to introduce the resolution proposed by him, under the rules of the House, without the general consent of the body."

To this Mr. Dickinson objected. But when the question was taken, the decision of the Chair was agreed to be the judgment of the House.

And so the select committee was not authorized to visit the armories. Instead, Joseph Foster of Springfield and a few witnesses from Harper's Ferry were brought to Washington. Their testimony before the committee was almost all violently antimilitary.

One further point. It had been maintained by the civilian members of the Springfield Commission, and by others, that a civilian would be more likely than a military man to be well trained in practical mechanics. To this argument a letter from Secretary Davis to the congressional committee replied that a civilian, no matter how skilled a mechanic or ingenious an inventor, would probably lack professional knowledge in regard to military weapons. It is not the business of the superintendent to be a mechanic, for he has his master armorer and his foremen there for the very purpose of working out and checking mechanical details. An officer is also better qualified to devise and conduct experiments to keep the quality of the arms up to and ahead of other countries.

Secretary Davis said that since both modes of superintendency had been tried, the committee need not proceed lacking definite knowledge and understanding of either. In his words:

Having never believed that to devote one's life to the military service of his country was incompatible with the highest respect for the laws and institutions of that country, I have not considered a soldier less entitled to confidence and trust because of his profession; and as the law of the country . . . makes it the duty of the Colonel of Ordnance to attend to the manufacture of arms, and all kinds of ammunition and ordnance stores, and places the national armories under the direction of the Ordnance department, their superintendence would seem properly to devolve upon the officers of that corps. (*6*, 140.)

The Secretary explained what had been in 1841 the chief reason for the change: it was considered desirable, since excellence of arms was so important to the safety of the country, to exclude the national armories from the influence of party politics.

On May 18, 1854, the armory committee passed a resolution introduced by Mr. Faulkner of Harper's Ferry to close the hearings and make a report to the House. Dawson, Keitt and Dickinson voted against it. In the minutes it is recorded that the reason why Mr. Dickinson voted in the negative was that there was insufficient testimony for him to be able to make up his mind, and that he wished to have more witnesses examined, specifying John Chase, the manufacturer, and Joseph Weatherhead and David Legro, workers in the Springfield armory. The committee refused to keep the hearings open for this purpose, but the members agreed that the testimony of these three men, as given the previous autumn in Springfield, should be included in the printed committee documents. Accordingly, Stanton asked to have the testimony and documents referring to the national armories ordered to be printed. It was so ordered.[6]

On June 13 Stanton presented the majority report of the select committee (*1*, 1382). It included "A bill to restore the civil superintendence at the national armories," and took its place in the regular order of business before the House.[7] Mr. Stanton introduced the bill in routine fashion. If this fact is kept in mind later events which set the stage for Edward Dickinson's speech will be more clearly understood.

On June 21, eight days after the bill representing the majority opinion had been introduced, Lawrence Keitt submitted the minority report of the committee which was referred to the Committee of the Whole and ordered to be printed. The report is a delight to read both for accuracy in the use of the English language and for skill in pricking and collapsing bombast, particularly that of the four civilian members of the Springfield Commission. "It is true," the report says, "that there is not, and never has been, any such thing as a military or a civil system, and that the superintendence by a military man is no more a military system than would the superintendence by a religious man be a religious system" (*7*, 15-16).

Richard Stanton had introduced the bill providing for the restoration of civil superintendence at the armories on June 13. Just one month later, on July 13 (*1*, 1713), when the regular Bill for Army Appropriations came up for consideration by the House, being in the Committee of the Whole, Stanton proposed the following amendment:

Provided, That so much of the laws heretofore passed which authorized the appointment of military officers to superintend the operations at the national armories be, and the same is hereby, repealed; and from and after the passage of this act it shall be the duty of the President of the United States, by and with the advice of the Senate, to appoint a competent and well qualified civilian, as superintendent at each of said armories.

6. This material is contained in *House Miscellaneous Document* No. 76, 33 Cong. 1 Sess., 82-114.

7. Both majority and minority reports are included in *House Reports*, No. 191, 33 Cong. 1 Sess.

Mr. Stanton spoke for an hour in support of his amendment (*1, App.,* 1050-1054). He said that the armory committee had recommended the change; that the military men were wasteful and extravagant particularly in the matter of the superintendent's quarters at Springfield, which would certainly cost not less than $50,000, twice the amount that had been appropriated. Stanton also took occasion to read some of the testimony of the witnesses brought from Harper's Ferry about the extravagance there, and the oppressive and degrading regulations affecting the mechanics, and the way in which suggestions for improvements were followed by a loss of pay, and various other complaints of that nature. It was an interesting speech, and must have been particularly so to those representatives who had not previously heard much about the armory question. But the subject had been brought up by Mr. Stanton in such an unexpected way that the minority of the armory committee were stunned.

Edward Dickinson was granted the floor for one hour in which to reply. As this was his only long speech in either session of the Congress it is given in full.[8]

Mr. Chairman: I was never more surprised in my life than to find myself thrust into a debate under the circumstances in which we find ourselves this morning. In reference to the manner in which this debate comes up, I have to say that this is not the time and place to discuss this question.

I propose to occupy a portion of the time allowed me, in making some remarks on this point—the unfairness of discussing this important question in this indirect manner.

It was stated yesterday, by one of the select committee, of which I am a member, that that committee, appointed by the House, had been in session about four months, and that for more than three months of that time the question of the change in the superintendency of the national armories was the only subject which occupied their attention, although the subjects referred to that committee embraced reforms in many departments of the public service. It is legitimate, I believe, for that committee to consider and investigate the manner in which the affairs of the Government, in all those departments, are carried on. It is due to the committee who have been called upon to discharge the duties connected with the resolution introduced just now by the chairman of the committee, under peculiar circumstances, and after the committee had devoted more than three months to this matter—meeting from two to five days in the week—and after the presentation of the report of the majority, and of the report of the minority—which, I suppose, have not been read by half a dozen members of the House—that the matter should be fully discussed by this body as a distinct measure. As far as I am aware, one of these reports—that of the minority—was only published yesterday; and, for my part, I have not been able to read them through since they were published.

Mr. STANTON. Will the gentleman from Massachusetts permit me to make a single remark on this point? I will not interrupt him any more.

Mr. DICKINSON. Certainly.

Mr. STANTON. The testimony taken before the committee was published on the 18th of May, more than two months ago. The majority report was published on the 13th of June, a month ago to-day. The minority report was published more than two weeks ago. If members of the House have not taken the trouble to

8. Edward Dickinson's speech on July 13, 1854, is here quoted from *The Congressional Globe,* 33 Cong. 1 Sess., *App.* 1061-64. It was also printed, with minor differences, in *The Hampshire and Franklin Express,* August 4, 1854.

keep up with the report[s], and to read and consider them, surely that is not my fault. I had nothing more to do in the matter but to introduce the subject at the proper time.

Mr. DICKINSON. I am not finding fault with the gentleman from Kentucky at all. I was merely arguing that the House could not be in possession of the facts stated in these reports, they having been published so short a time. The minority report has only been published, or, at least, has not been obtainable, till yesterday. I know that members of the committee sent for it yesterday without being able to get it. The chairman of the committee, who has seemed to have a complete monomania on the question whether the public money shall be expended for the prosecution of public works under the management of military men, as he calls them, or of civilians, has made a long speech on this point; but I shall try to show him, before I sit down, that this distinction between civil and military is more shadow than substance, more imaginary than real. Under the influence of this engrossing sentiment, this matter has been brought before the House on every occasion where an amendment of the kind could be introduced, to test the sense of this House on the point as to whether expenditures should be made under men who never held a military commission, or under those who now hold one. Why, I suppose that every man on this select committee has a commission; I believe they are all colonels but myself, and I am nothing but a major. [See page 489.] I was afraid to go a grade higher, lest I should get too strong a thirst for military glory. I believe, as I have said, that all the members of this select committee, except myself, are colonels, and yet a majority are opposed to military rule. I think that if the history of these armories should be traced **from their establishment to the present time,** it will be found that there has not been a single civil superintendent, as it is called, in charge of them, who did not hold a colonel's, or at least a major's commission.

It was not my desire to serve on that committee. I was a member of it against my will. I would have made almost any sacrifice rather than to have been placed upon it. But I would not incur the censure, after having been appointed, of shrinking from the performance of the duty imposed upon me. I had no preconceived opinions on this subject to maintain, or prejudices to gratify. I engaged in the investigation with an honest desire to learn the truth, and a determination to follow wherever that might lead.

I say it is discourteous to this committee to undertake in this indirect way to settle the matter here under this amendment, when it has been so long under investigation before the select committee, and when the report of the minority was published but yesterday, and has not been seen by a large proportion of the members, and when there are other bills on the Calendar to be disposed of.

This proposition, sir, is to change the superintendency of the Government establishments from military to civil. It has been a matter of agitation, as the chairman of the committee [Mr. STANTON of Kentucky] says, for the last fifteen years. Previous to the change, from civil to military superintendence, made by Congress some twelve years since, there was a committee appointed to examine into the matter, and their report was in favor of placing these establishments under the Ordnance Department. Congress placed them there, and they have ever since been kept there. This proposition is to repeal that law, and place them under their former superintendence, and allow the President of the United States to select from all classes of the people of the United States, except the officers of the Army or Ordnance Board, men whom he supposes qualified to be placed at their head.

The amount of property at each of these armories cannot be less than three millions of dollars. And if the charges which have been alluded to, and which have been made against these military superintendents, of extravagance, despotism, tyranny, and other improper conduct, are one tenth of them true, the men deserve to be executed. They are here on trial before the Government and the country; and I say that to undertake, in this indirect way, without notice to anybody, without even all the members of the select committee being here, and having a chance to be heard; to undertake in this way to settle such a proposition as is here involved, is in itself a direct act of discourtesy, in my judgment, to the committee.

But if I allude to the course of the committee itself—which I am very sorry to do—the reference would not be any more complimentary. A commission, consisting of four civilians and two military men, appointed by the President of the United States to inquire into the affairs of those armories, made an examination, or what they called an examination, of the matter. They staid at Springfield and about there for three months, during all which time, according to the testimony of one of their number, the board did not call on Colonel Ripley, the superintendent or commandant, for a statement relative to the management and condition of that armory, but resorted to the expedient of giving notice through the newspapers that they would hear such persons as saw fit to present themselves, and proceeded to hear every grievance that anybody chose to make; they heard testimony from any and every quarter whatever, except from the persons in charge of the establishment, and their books, the sources of the most reliable information. And I undertake to say in my place, as a member of the select committee, as a member of this House, and as a Representative of the Springfield district, that there never was a commission authorized by anybody on earth, for the discharge of important duties, which failed so completely in the performance of the duties prescribed, as this. We have their report, and what does it contain? We have a large body of evidence here, of some hundred or two of newspaper pages, transmitted to this House by the President of the United States, which was sent to him to be examined and read. He sent it to us, with the reports of the commissioners, and other papers, when the order was introduced to refer the whole matter to a select committee, and I have not been able to induce the majority of the members of that committee to have this evidence taken before the commissioners, read in the sessions. We are to take their reports as our guide, and the majority of the committee are satisfied with the result to which they have come. I am not satisfied with it. If I were sitting upon a jury, I would not take the opinion of anybody else as to the result of the evidence. I would have the testimony before me, and judge for myself as to what it proved. Sir, as a member of the select committee, I asked that the evidence should be read before the committee. They told me that I might read it myself, if I wished. My reply was that, in my opinion, the evidence should be read before the whole committee, and that I would be satisfied with nothing short of that. It has not been read. But, in the place of it, we have the report of the commissioners sent to the President some time in the month of November or December, and received by us some time in the month of February. Our committee have taken this report, and have adopted the conclusions of the majority of that board, without ever having read the evidence upon which it was founded, so far as I know, with, perhaps, the exception of one or two members. If the evidence contained in the reports is sufficient to satisfy the House that great abuses and great wrongs exist in the management of these armories, they can adopt their recommendations. They do not contain enough to satisfy me, consisting, as they do, more of the opinions of the members than of the facts on which such opinions are founded.

Let me state one other thing. While our committee were examining witnesses it was proposed by the minority of the committee to send to Springfield for witnesses, but their request was not granted, and the investigation was closed by order of the majority, without having heard these witnesses.

Mr. VANSANT. I desire to ask the gentleman from Massachusetts a question. Did not the minority of the committee have full liberty at all times to send for any persons, as witnesses, they might name? Were not they notified, from day to day, to bring forward the names of the witnesses they might wish to examine, that the chairman of the committee might summon them? Did not they delay to present the name of any one for months, during which time the witnesses which had been summoned, were examined, and the testimony closed?

Mr. DICKINSON. I will answer the gentleman's question cheerfully.

Mr. STANTON. I wish to ask the gentleman if the majority of the committee did not give notice to the minority of the committee to furnish the names of such witnesses as they desired to examine, and when they delayed to furnish them, did not the majority propose, for their benefit, that the testimony of such persons as they desired be taken from the rest, and published in the report?

Mr. DICKINSON. I will answer the questions asked by both my colleagues upon the committee with pleasure. The circumstances to which the gentleman from Maryland alludes were these: It is true as he states, that the majority did give notice to the minority that they would summon such witnesses as we would name. But we were not then acquainted with the names of the persons for whom we wished to send, and we could not, therefore, furnish them at once. But it is also true, that we did afterwards furnish them, and that the majority then refused to send for them, and the hearing was closed without their evidence.

Now, in reference to the question put by the gentleman from Kentucky [Mr. STANTON], as to whether the majority did not propose to take the testimony of some three or four witnesses taken before the commissioners, I will say that they did so propose, but the minority thought if they could not have the witnesses before them to examine it would not be satisfactory, but the best that could be done was to have the testimony of a few of the witnesses, as given before the commissioners at Springfield, embodied in the report of our committee. The committee did thus condescend to let the evidence of some three or four of these witnesses come in, evidence taken on examination, not before the committee, but before the commissioners, and not on all the exact points of our inquiry. It is in the committee's majority report.[9] That is my answer to the gentleman.

I do not intend to reply to the gentleman's points now. I can do it fully, I think; but, if I am not competent, I know that my associates on the committee are, and I hope they may be heard. If the committee now desire, in this random discussion, got up out of order, and as I think discourteously to the committee and unwisely for the country, to take action on a matter as important as any which can come before us at this session, I wish to be heard, and I want to hear what other gentlemen have to say. But I desire of all things—it is what I as well as others expected, I believe—that the matter should be allowed to come up in its regular course, and as business by itself. That would be right. It is a matter of no importance whether the appropriation for the armories, to be expended a year hence, is determined now or at the next session. But I have no desire to postpone the discussion, or to delay the action of this body. I am perfectly ready, whenever it can be done legitimately, to have a fair and full discussion, to take my part in it, and to do what I can to elucidate truth and spread the whole case before this body.

Another reason. It cannot have been unobserved by a large part of this committee, that I have twice within the last two weeks asked leave of the House to introduce a resolution from the majority of this very select committee; one of the gentlemen, who voted for the majority report, going with the minority—a resolution to permit the select committee to visit these armories before this subject was discussed and decided. I stated on a former occasion that within a few weeks I went to the Springfield armory, and spent two half days there for the purpose of investigation. I learned more facts there within that brief time than I had during the entire three months of the committee's examination; and I was perfectly satisfied that the select committee was acting in the dark; that it had not the light which the country and this body had a right to expect on the

9. *House Misc. Doc.* No. 76, 33 Cong. 1 Sess., and *House Report* No. 191, same Congress.

subject. I remember that for a long time before these reports were made, I again and again suggested a visit of the committee to the armories, but the proposition was not acceded to.

After I had returned from Springfield, having made such investigation as the time spent enabled me to make of the state of things there, I then proposed formally to the committee, that they should visit the armories at Springfield and Harper's Ferry, for the purpose of satisfying themselves with regard to the truth of the charges that had been made against the then superintendents. I endeavored, upon two different occasions, to introduce a resolution in this House, making provision for such investigation on the part of the committee, but leave was not granted me. We are now called upon to decide this matter, without having had an opportunity afforded us of giving such an examination to this subject as its importance demands at our hands. The board of commissioners who were appointed to visit the armories, remained three months at Springfield, and they then adjourned to meet at Harper's Ferry, but the Secretary of War, or some one who had the authority so to do, notified them that their services were no longer desired, and that they need not proceed to Harper's Ferry, and to this day neither of these commissioners appointed by the President of the United States, have ever been there. We have had here from Harper's Ferry witness after witness—men who have been connected with that armory, but are not now, and who, individually, have the strongest prejudice against it, and, of course, testify under that strong bias.

We have, then, this state of facts, and we are now asked to vote upon this matter without having had the opportunity of a full investigation of the question. I am not satisfied with it. If the committee are ready to adopt the resolution I offered that the select committee may be authorized to visit these armories, after the adjournment of Congress, for the purpose of making inquiries into the state of things there, I am willing to waive the privilege of making any further remarks at this time. I hope the Committee of the Whole will be willing to postpone the discussion of this matter, and let it come up in its legitimate place and form, and that the chairman of the select committee will be willing to withdraw his amendment. If he refuses to do this, I must go on without any connected preparation whatever, and must follow the argument of the chairman of the committee, as well as I can, with what light I have upon this subject; and I will try to be as brief as possible.

Mr. STANTON, of Kentucky. Will the gentleman from Massachusetts allow me to say, if there was any other possible chance to get this proposition up, I would withdraw the amendment I have offered, in order to gratify the gentleman; but I am perfectly conscious that there is no other opportunity, and that there will be none during this session of Congress; and I must, therefore, decline to withdraw it.

Mr. DICKINSON. I am then obliged to ask the indulgence of the committee for the little time I have remaining. The subject is certainly one that requires an extended and thorough investigation at our hands. We cannot begin to do justice to the matter without having the evidence on both sides of the question. And I say here, in the outset, that, without this evidence, all action of Congress will be regarded as having been done in the dark. There will be a necessity for a reinvestigation of the matter if we undertake to decide it now, whatever the decision may be. If the friends of military superintendency are defeated, or if the friends of civil superintendency are defeated, the defeated party will be satisfied that there has not been that fair investigation of the matter, nor that full eliciting of facts which it should have received by the House, prior to any final action upon it.

The chairman of the committee, in the outset of his remarks, gave a history of the legislation on this subject. He has informed the committee that from the establishment of the armories, in 1794, down to 1841, they had been under the management of civil superintendents, as contradistinguished from the officers appointed by the War Department or Ordnance Office. An investigation was had at that time by a board of competent mechanics of the highest character, as to the propriety of continuing the civil superintendency, or of placing the armories under the control of the Ordnance Board; and, after the fullest investigation, it was decided to place them under the Ordnance Board. They have been so placed, and have ever since continued under that control by order of Congress. Efforts have been made—as the gentleman says—every year, from that time to the present, to induce the Secretaries of War to change the system. It has been constantly urged upon them that the ordnance officers should cease to have the control of these armories, and that the superintendents of them should be appointed by the President of the United States from the people at large, without reference to the Ordnance Board. Each Secretary of War, from 1841 down to the present time, has replied to these solicitations, and refused to comply with them. Each of the Secretaries has been convinced that the present system was the best, the most efficient, the most economical, the safest, and the best calculated to promote the interests of the Government. The gentleman from Kentucky has stated to the House the comparative cost of the muskets under the one system and under the other. If any members of the House will read the reports of this select committee, if they will read the tables prepared by the chairman of the committee, and examine the computations that he has made of the expenses and of the cost of muskets, and then take the reports of the ordnance officers containing the items of the expenses and cost of muskets, they will see at a glance how the matter stands. The ordnance officers give you a report reliable and trustworthy showing that the muskets have been made constantly at a less expense since the change has been effected than before.

The committee will see that the gentleman draws together the expenses of the land, the expenses of buildings, and various other things, and prepares them for his own use in his own way, and in a way which I cannot comprehend. I assure you there is a delusion about them. I have examined them with some care, and I am satisfied that they will lead the committee into error, if they follow his tables. Still I will do the gentleman the justice to say, that he is perfectly honest and sincere in his efforts; but his great enthusiasm, his mania, as I have called it before, to substantiate these charges, has led him astray. And while he is in error himself, he will lead the committee, if they follow him, after an *ignis fatuus*, as they will sooner or later find out.

There is but one way by which we can arrive at a correct result in relation to this matter, and that is by examining the history of these establishments, from their foundation down to the present time. By doing so, you will find, by the records in the Departments, the cost, and what entered into the cost, of each musket manufactured. There can be no mistake about that. The result will be, that since the Ordnance Department has had the control of those establishments, the cost has been one dollar or more less per musket, than before that time.

Mr. STANTON (interrupting). I would state to the gentleman that every figure of my report has been derived from the Ordnance Department itself. I have not changed one single figure in the whole tables. The difference between us is this: I have calculated the cost of the muskets from the aggregate of expenses, and they have calculated the cost from what they say enters into the cost of the musket, excluding improvements in machinery, the cost of lands, and building houses, &c.

Mr. DICKINSON. If the gentleman relies upon the Ordnance Department for his figures, for the report made by the committee, it will appear exactly as I say. If, as he states, he derives every one of his figures from the Ordnance Department, I should like to know how he comes to a result so different from that arrived at by the office itself?

Again, the gentleman says no reliance can be placed upon the accounts kept at the armories. If the gentleman will go to the Springfield armory, if he will look at the different sets of books kept there, showing every dollar which comes into the hands of the paymaster; if he will follow me through the establishment, and trace the course of the money from the time it gets upon their books; if he will follow every piece of iron or wood, from the time when it is purchased to the time when it comes out a complete and perfect arm; if he will then say these accounts are not to be relied upon, I will not hesitate to say to him, that he cannot go into any department of this Government, into any bank or insurance office of the United States, and find a system of accounts more perfect than that which will be found there, and that he can find nothing reliable anywhere. I was perfectly astonished to see the number of checks and balances which are employed. The accounts, as made out by the officers, must be examined, before they leave the armory, by the paymaster and some of the clerks, and by the superintendent. They are then sent to the Ordnance Office at Washington; then to the Secretary of War, and again examined; then to an Auditor in the Treasury Department; and if so much as one cent fails to be accounted for, they are sent back to the armory to be corrected.

Mr. STANTON. I presume the accounts are kept in the same manner at Springfield and Harper's Ferry—at least they ought to be. Now, sir, I have before me a report from the armory at Harper's Ferry, giving the items of cost for building the commandant's quarters, in which is laid down the sources from which the information is derived, from which I was certainly not able to draw as favorable a conclusion in reference to the manner in which their accounts were kept, as the gentleman from Massachusetts does.

Mr. DICKINSON. Was that report before our committee?

Mr. STANTON. Certainly it was; and was published in the report of the majority. I will read it.

Mr. DICKINSON. I cannot yield for that purpose now, if it is to come out of my time—read it after I sit down.

Mr. STANTON. Just a moment. It says—

Mr. DICKINSON. Well, sir, I do not know anything about Harper's Ferry. The commissioners appointed by the President have not been there; the select committee have not been there, and I do not know anything about the management of that establishment. But I do know in reference to the armory in my own district, and it is of that I speak. From what I have heard of Harper's Ferry I have not formed so high an opinion of the manner in which the armory there is conducted as of that at Springfield.

Sir, I do not wonder that the gentleman from Kentucky did not like to be questioned by Mr. KEITT, a member of the select committee, in relation to the commission which was sent here from England to examine our national armories. I presume that gentleman does not know what admiration they expressed in relation to them, and that in their opinion arms could be manufactured at our armories for half the price they cost in England, and vastly superior in quality.

But again, the gentleman says that no regard is paid to estimates; no regard is paid to appropriations. Since reference was made to the appropriation of $12,000 for the construction of commandant's quarters at Springfield, my attention has been called to the facts, and I find that although the proposition was made and carried in the House, to refuse the appropriation, yet an amendment was made in the Senate granting the appropriation, which was afterwards concurred in by the House, and became a law. The gentleman from Kentucky was not aware of this latter fact, I am sure, or he would not have made the statement that Congress had refused to make the appropriation. But, sir, as to the way in which these estimates are made. The superintendent first makes them, and they are submitted to an inspector, who visits the armories once or twice a year, to examine into the condition of the establishments, and learn their wants, examining the buildings, the machinery, and everything connected with the establishment; revises the estimates submitted by the superintendent, and usually cuts them down; for it is seldom that as much is granted as is asked for. The estimates then go before the chief of the Ordnance Corps, where they are again revised. They are presented by the Ordnance Bureau to the Secretary of War, where they undergo another examination, and such items as he approves are embraced in the estimates submitted to Congress by the War Department. These estimates are referred to the Committee of Ways and Means, scrutinized by that committee, and brought before the House. All the estimates sent from the armories must go through all these examinations before they come before the House and the Senate. And when the appropriations are made by Congress, the chief of the Ordnance Corps notifies the respective superintendents what amount is appropriated for different objects, and they proceed to expend the money in accordance with that notice; and I feel authorized to say that no money has been expended for the erection of "quarters" for the superintendent, either at Springfield or at Harper's Ferry, until after the giving and receiving of such notice. Whatever extravagance there has been in the amount expended for "quarters" is chargeable to Congress, who voted the money.

Now, Mr. Chairman, I desire in a word to explain the difference between the military and civil systems. One of the leading men in my district, and who understands all about this matter, hearing that some armory men had left because they were dissatisfied, asked one of them what the difference really was? The man replied: "Why, sir, to tell the truth, it amounts to just this: Under the civil system the men do just as they have a mind to, and under the military system they are obliged to do as they ought to." Such is the description of the difference, and the only intelligible one which I have yet heard. The regulations for the government of the armories are the same under each kind of superintendency. Under the existing system the regulations are more regarded, and more strictly enforced, than under the former superintendency; and the most favorable results are obtained for the Government for the amount of money expended, consistently with justice to the workmen employed. More depends upon the character of the superintendent himself as a *man*, than upon the particular system under which he administers the affairs of the establishment. Under the present, no partisanship enters into the appointment or removal of any of the officers or men; if changed, these Government manufactories will become the constant theater of strife for political power and patronage.

Now, as to quarters, and the extravagance of the military men. It has been stated by the gentleman from Kentucky, over and over again, that the quarters at Springfield cost more than $50,000. The gentleman is mistaken. When at Springfield, to my great surprise the committee may be assured, after the gentleman's reiterated statements, I found from the books kept, and which show each day's, half day's, and quarter day's work, and the amount paid for every material, from the laying of the corner-stone, from the beginning to the completion of the structure, that the whole cost was $21,534.56. There was afterwards gas introduced, house painted, fences erected, water carried to the house, &c., which swelled the amount up to $23,773.87. When the gentleman was upon the floor I called on him to state specifically his understanding in reference to the cost of this building. He stated that it cost $50,000. It is true that the head of the Ordnance Department said there was nothing in his office showing the cost of the commandant's quarters at Springfield, but he also said that he would send to the armory for the account, and furnish it to the committee. He did so, and the statement is now in the chairman's hands. I saw the books at the armory, and, so far as I can recollect, the figures in the statement from the Ordnance Department are precisely those in that book. Now, if the gentleman undertakes to say that the building cost $50,000, I should like to have him state his authority for the assertion.

Mr. STANTON. Here it is.

Mr. DICKINSON. I want to know whether his statement is to be taken in preference to those of the Secretary of War, the statement of the Ordnance

Department, the books kept for the very purpose of showing the cost, and everybody else? I cannot admit the correctness of his statement, to the impeachment of all the other evidence before us, and I am sure it will be so regarded by this committee. The gentleman then says that the cost of the building and the grounds, the purchase of which was made necessary by the present location of the building, cannot be less than $50,000. If the gentleman will go there with me, I will show him grounds which were not made necessary by that building. It is a fine house, and I do not wonder that some of the commissioners want to be appointed superintendent. I think I should like to be superintendent; and, if the system is changed, perhaps I shall be an applicant for the office. The house is a fine one, and is no doubt worth all it cost, and will last for generations to come. It has been built and paid for, and will be kept in repair by the Government, and the great question now is, *Who shall occupy it?*

This house stands in one corner of a large tract of land, the furthest removed of any building from the highway. Next to it, and on the site formerly occupied by the old quarters, stands the arsenal. It is a beautiful building, an honor to the Government, to the State, and an honor to the men who built it. The Government ought to feel proud of it. No extravagance was involved in its completion, erected, as it is, for the purpose of storing the great amount of arms of which the Government is the owner. Next, we have several houses for the different clerks and officers of the establishment. In the rear of all these buildings is a large open grass lot, undivided by any fence. It is just as proper to charge the expense of the ground in the rear of these buildings, to which the gentleman from Kentucky [Mr. STANTON] alluded, to any one of the houses occupied by the clerks, or other officers of the establishment, as it would be to the commandant's quarters. The superintendent has converted this land, by his own agricultural skill, from a mere sand bank into a most fertile field. I have not time to say more about the extravagant expenditures charged against the superintendency here than that I deem them to be, to a very great extent, mere assertions, without reasonable foundation, or sustained by the evidence before the House. If gentlemen of the committee will take the pains to inform themselves upon the subject, they will find that many of these charges of extravagance against the management there are unfounded in point of fact.

The charge is frequently made, also, of tyranny and oppression exercised by the officers there towards the workmen in their employment. We hear very often of the military despotism and espionage practiced there in the removal of men without just cause of offense. As I shall not have another opportunity, I think it my duty to remark, briefly, upon some of these matters. Upon my visit to Springfield, I went into several of the workshops, where the manufacturing is carried on. I did not visit those carried on by water-power. I understand them to be in a state of comparative decay, for the reason that steam power having been introduced into the other shops, it was not deemed worth while to keep these in repair, and spend money upon them as they are, as it was expected every year that there would be an application to Congress to make an appropriation for the erection of buildings near the shops, where the machinery is now operated by steam power to do the work now done at the water-shops. I believe the officers at Springfield, the inspectors, the Ordnance Board, and the commissioners, who were there last year, all agree in [the] opinion that it would be judicious to make the proposed change. All the buildings would then be within a convenient distance, the machinery could all be carried by one steam engine, and the whole business be much more conveniently done. So much for that. Now as to the tyranny—the despotism—that has been spoken of. I went into the shops of the Springfield armory. I did not go there on the invitation of the superintendent, nor by his advice, nor under his guidance. I had even told him that I did not want him to accompany me. I went there to learn for myself, to understand how affairs stood there, for my own enlightenment as a member of the special committee of this House, so as to be able to report what the truth was in regard to this whole matter. I saw the foremen of these shops, and many of the men that worked in them. I saw the machinery for the manufacture of guns; and I was completely astonished at the perfection of that machinery. Not that it was of an extravagant description; not that it was so highly finished, as the gentleman says, as to have been very expensive, in comparison with the machinery in other manufacturing establishments. No such thing; it was the completeness, cleanness, and good order of the machinery, that I admired. I found some of the wheel or gear coverings of some parts of the machinery made of brass, instead of being made of iron or steel. And on inquiry, I was told by the men that brass was cheaper for the purpose than any other material. The steam engine was a very beautiful affair. There was some brass upon that, and some brass balls on the railing about it, but this was not for the sake of ornament merely, but to protect it from injury. It was the most beautiful piece of machinery that I ever saw. And it was capable of carrying not only all the machinery in those shops, but also that in operation at the water shops, if placed in buildings where the power could be applied. If not sufficient for the whole, it could be exchanged for one that would carry all the machinery. I inquired of the foremen as to the character of the work; and I learned from them that within the last ten years, the character of the arms manufactured there had been much improved. I learned, too, from inquiries among them that the workmen were contented and satisfied, and the evidence before the special committee was, that the workmen and mechanics in the best private manufactories in the neighborhood, earning the highest rate of wages, would willingly leave these establishments to work at the national armory. They stay there year after year, for the space of ten or twenty years, and have not the least desire to leave. The foreman informed me that if any man wished to leave, he had only to come, at any hour of the day, and say that he wished to leave, and that he could go to the paymaster's office and draw his pay. As to the thrift of the men now compared to what it was formerly, I saw and heard enough to convince me of the good effect of the present system upon them. I was pointed to a long row of neat and tasteful white houses, covering a whole street, which were occupied principally, and many of them owned, by the armorers, purchased out of their savings. Their children are being properly educated, and they and their children go regularly to church. They are not obliged to go, as the gentleman says, nor to attend that particular church to which the superintendent belongs. They go to whatever place of worship they choose, and when they choose. Their children are neat and well dressed. Many of them are, in a pecuniary point of view, quite independent men. They stay there voluntarily, and are not removed, as charged by the gentleman—and this I could show, if I had the opportunity of offering the evidence to the committee. Men are not removed because they are not in favor of this system; and when removals have been made, it has not been the work of the superintendent alone. For instance, within the last year there have been a large number of removals, but they have taken place because the appropriation for each of these armories has been reduced from $180,000 to $125,000. This reduction has been made because the Government now has some five or six hundred thousand stand of arms on hand, independent of all they own in the several States.

When a removal is made from that establishment, the question is not asked whether the individual is in favor of this kind of superintendency or that, but each of the foremen is called upon to say how many men he has under him, how many he can dispense with, and do the work of his shop. They are asked who are their poorest workmen, and whom they can best spare, for if the number is reduced they dispose of men whose services they can best spare, without reference to whether the man believes in a military or a civil superintendency.

And now let me say a word in reference to one of the commissioners who figures largely in this report, and who came before the committee, not only as a witness, but as one employed by somebody to get evidence against the present system. I refer to ex-Governor Steel[e], of New Hampshire. That gentleman, I am told—and there are lots of witnesses to prove it—went on to the establishment at Springfield, as one of the commissioners appointed by the President. He staid there, took a note book, and went to each of the shops to see and converse with the employees in that establishment, privately, and asked their individual opinions about the matter of the superintendency; and he reports that a large majority were in favor of a change. How did he arrive at that result? He told those men—and I have abundant proof of it—that there would be a change; that the military superintendent would be removed, and they had better be on the right side; that if there was to be a change, and they were in favor of a military superintendency, they would be removed. But if they were in favor of a civil superintendency, and they should be removed now, that he knew the President of the United States, and that he would give them assurances in his name that they would be reinstated within thirty days.[10] That they need not have any fears on that account.

That is the man who comes here and talks about the tyranny and despotism of those military establishments, and about removals from office for opinion's sake.

Now, I am told that those men will come forward and say that, up to the time when the commission came there, they were perfectly satisfied, and perfectly contented, and that they knew nothing about this military tyranny and despotism of which we have heard so much. They were prosperous, happy, and contented. Now, it ill becomes ex-Governor Steel[e], of New Hampshire, to talk about despotism of opinion, when he assured those men, in the name of the President of the United States, that they should be retained there, notwithstanding their opinions, and that their opinions upon that point should not be disclosed, and then, without notifying the commission of what he had been about, comes forward and offers these facts, in order to help his own case along.

That is a specimen of one of the commission authorized to ascertain the facts to be used to enlighten the President of the United States, in reference to a change in the superintendency. That is a specimen of a civil superintendent undertaking to say to those men, if they are deposed from their present places because they are in favor of a civil superintendency, he will restore them.

[Here the hammer fell.]

On July 17, four days after Edward Dickinson delivered this speech, he again tried to introduce a resolution providing for a visit to the armories by the committee, and once more it was objected to and blocked. In Northampton, Mr. Dickinson's shire town, the *Hampshire Gazette* (July 18, 1854) reported the second failure in these words: ". . . Mr. Dickinson, of this state, made an ineffectual effort to introduce a resolution authorizing the select committee to whom was referred the subject of the superintendence of the armories, to visit Springfield and Harper's Ferry during the recess, to make examinations, etc. . . ."

On the same day Mr. Stanton's amendment was discussed on the floor of the House. He again spoke in favor of civilian superintendence; Lawrence Keitt argued for continuation of the military; Nathaniel Banks of Massachusetts supported the civilians; while Charles Skelton of New Jersey, objecting to both forms of superintendency, suggested that the national armories be discontinued and that the arms be made under contract in private plants.

10. President Pierce, being from New Hampshire, made plausible this claim by ex-Governor Steele.

On the eighteenth, Dickinson proposed adding to Stanton's amendment a clause which would transfer management and control of the armories from the Ordnance Department to the President, to be his sole responsibility. For it was manifestly unfair, said Mr. Dickinson, for the President to have the power to appoint the superintendent, and for the Ordnance Board to have to take the responsibility for how the armories were administered. He continued (*1*, 1785 ff.):

I should be glad, Mr. Chairman, if I could be allowed, under the rules, to reply to one or two suggestions which have fallen from gentlemen during the discussion on this matter. I desire to make some corrections. Gentlemen have stated what they believe to be facts, but which are not facts, and there is danger of the committee [i.e., the House] acting under misapprehension.

This request not being objected to, Mr. Dickinson took up the points one by one, disproving each in turn. He began:

When gentlemen stand up in their places and assure us from their own knowledge that there are no regulations accessible to the men, or that there has been a change of regulations since the military superintendency was established, I desire to inform the House what the facts of the case really are (*1*, 1785).

He said that, contrary to evidence in the case, it had also been charged that pieceworkers' pay had been docked without notice, on the ground that the tariff had been reduced. And it had been stressed by advocates of civilian administration that before 1841 good reports had been turned in by Army inspectors of the arms. But the gentlemen did not mention the fact that equally good reports had been submitted since 1841 by the same inspectors. And furthermore, that the arms had improved in quality since that date, not only private manufacturers, but the Ordnance Board, the Secretary of War, and the leading mechanics at the armories all agreed.

Mr. Dickinson then indulged in his only flight of oratory:

It is said, too, that the military system discourages enterprise, paralyzes inventive genius, is an insult to the mechanics of the country, and weakens their attachment to our republican institutions. Sir, the mechanics of this country are above the need of any eulogium from me—their reputation for skill is world-wide; and if I believed the charge to be true, I should be found among the foremost in my efforts to put an end to a system which produces such results. Not believing the charge to be true, the obvious answer to it is, that while our mechanics, as a body, are superior to those of any other country in intelligence, skill, and mental power, and while the instances are numerous of those who have made the most brilliant discoveries, and signalized themselves by the highest scientific and literary attainments, and been conscious that no circumstances could control or diminish the power of the "Divinity that stirs within them"—while we are proud, as American citizens, of the honor they have earned for us as a nation, and while they are acquiring wealth and power by the force of their own talents, they need not the feeble aid which we can render them in placing them in responsible positions—they need not our praise to make them conscious of their own deserts. They are entitled to receive, and will ever receive from every intelligent man, the respect due to them for their mental and moral qualities, and for their manly virtues; and will ever look above all distinctions of class or caste, and render to every man according to his desert, and cordially adopt the noble sentiment of the poet:

"Honor and shame from no condition rise;
Act well your part, there all the honor lies" (*1*, 1786).

In spite of these somewhat condescending remarks Mr. Dickinson was quick to recognize outstanding ability. When a mechanic had in truth "signalized" himself by his scientific attainments Mr. Dickinson tried to aid him in every possible way, as in the case of Cyrus Buckland, for whose ability he was later to obtain proper recognition.

Mr. Dickinson's amendment to the amendment was defeated. He had apparently introduced it not with the hope of getting it passed but as a pretext to discuss it, hoping thereby not only to clear the air of one or two misapprehensions but also to put himself on the record as appreciating mechanics' deserts. The debate went on for several days.

On July 31 in an attempt to uncover the devious tactics of some of his associates Mr. Dickinson said that certain facts had come to his knowledge which he felt it his duty to bring to the notice of the House (*1*, 2024). He offered a resolution directing the Secretary of War to communicate any information he might have regarding application for office in the armories by members of the Springfield Commission, the witnesses who testified before the select committee of the House, the members of that committee themselves, or an application sponsored by any of these persons. This resolution was adopted. It was fairly common knowledge that ex-Governor Steele, for one, wanted the superintendency of Harper's Ferry. Secretary Davis' report, confirming Mr. Dickinson's allegations, was dated August 3, 1854, the very day on which the Army Appropriations Act, including the Stanton amendment replacing military men with civilians as superintendents at the national armories, was passed by Congress.[11] It was signed by President Pierce on August 5 after Mr. Dickinson had left Washington. The Secretary's report verified the rumor of Steele's own ambition for the superintendency of Harper's Ferry; Charles Faulkner of the select committee had in fact recommended Steele for the position. Steele in his turn, together with the other two civilian commissioners, had recommended Commissioner Henry Smith for the superintendency at Springfield. Nor were these the only ones.

As a result of Mr. Dickinson's resolution, however, political patronage was eliminated—the two superintendents, appointed to Springfield and Harper's Ferry respectively, were James S. Whitney of Massachusetts, and Henry W. Clowe of Virginia, neither of whom had taken any part in the fight to restore civilians.[12]

Colonel Ripley's letter dated U.S. Armory, Springfield, August 16, 1854, relinquishing his command, is in the National Archives (Records of the War Department, Office of the Chief of Ordnance, Springfield Armory).

11. *House Executive Document* No. 128, 33 Cong. 1 Sess.
12. See U. S. Senate, *Executive Journal*, IX, 393-394, for their confirmation on December 19, 1854.

Activities of "the Select Committee of the House on the Superintendency of Public Works," again appear in the record of the second session of the Thirty-third Congress. The subject of military superintendency of civil works was brought up on February 20, 1855 (2, 847 ff.), this time with reference to the building of the wings of the Capitol. Richard Stanton's brother Frederick, representative from Tennessee, tried to amend a proposal from the Committee on Public Buildings, submitted by Mr. Keitt, so that a civilian architect should be in charge. Richard Stanton took up the argument, asserting that a military man could not, no matter what his experience, direct work on a public building.

Mr. Dickinson asked under whose direction it was proposed to place the construction of this building. Richard Stanton replied that it was to be under the direction of the President and executed by such a civil architect as he might appoint.

"I should like to make another inquiry," said Mr. Dickinson. "I ask the gentleman from Kentucky whether there is any objection to the manner in which the work of the Capitol extension is carried on?"

Stanton did not propose to answer this question, as it would, he said, take more time to explain than he thought proper.

Representative Thomas B. Florence of Pennsylvania inquired whether this discussion was not out of order and the chair replied that it was not; whereupon Mr. Dickinson continued, "I should like to make still a third inquiry. I ask whether the propriety of the manner in which the work of the Capitol extension is progressing has not been referred to a special committee of this House, which committee have taken no steps to enlighten the House as to the charges made against those having the work in charge? And whether that committee are making any progress in their investigations, or whether they have become satisfied that there is no foundation whatever for the charge of mal-administration?"

Stanton answered that his committee had looked into the armories during the previous session. They were now examining other questions, and had elicited some important facts, which, he said with sarcasm, "the gentleman can examine when he chooses to call at the committee room."

Burton Craige of North Carolina rose at this point to say that he was a member of the Committee on Public Buildings and Grounds, to which a portion of the subject had been referred. His committee was unanimous in finding no mismanagement whatever by the military.

Stanton turned to face this new attack, attempting to prove that the law clearly implied that civil officers should be in charge of the extension. Craige replied that he and Stanton differed in their construction of the law. Furthermore, Craige added, his committee were in unanimous agreement that the President usurped no power, while Stanton's committee were equally divided.

"No, sir," put in Lawrence Keitt, a member of both committees, "you are mistaken. A large majority of [Stanton's] committee are in favor of the present mode."

This conversation concluded, Mr. Dickinson resumed speaking, as quoted in *The Globe* (2, 849):

Mr. DICKINSON. I believe that the discussion which this subject has given rise to in the House, has done some good, even if it should proceed no further. We have heard, during this Congress, frequent complaints made in regard to officers in charge of public works. We have had repeated attacks made upon officers who had charge of the construction of the wings of the Capitol. As early as the fore-part of the last session, a committee was appointed, of which the gentleman from Kentucky [Mr. STANTON] was made chairman, and of which I was a member, to consider the charges which have been constantly brought before this House with regard to these officers who had charge of this work, the national armories, and various other civil works. And at one time during the last session, so loud was the clamor in this Hall, in regard to the malconstruction of the wings of the Capitol, and in regard to the impossibility of Congress being ever able to do business in them, that the committee was called together, at my own suggestion, on purpose to see whether the work should be permitted to proceed; or whether the committee should not bring before the House a proposition to order the work to be suspended until some change should be made. That committee convened and summoned the architect before them; and the result of their examination was—and I think the committee were unanimous about it, for I never heard anything more from the chairman—that the work was progressing in the most skillful, the most scientific, and the best possible manner.

Mr. STANTON. Will the gentleman allow me to correct him? The architect was, on a single morning, brought into the committee room, and informally, without being under oath—but his word was just as good to me as his oath—he was examined touching the question of ventilation, and touching nothing else. . . .

Mr. DICKINSON. The gentleman says that the architect employed by Congress was not *under oath*. Why did not the gentleman place him under oath? I undertake to say that all of the committee, with the exception of himself, were perfectly satisfied with the statement of the architect. If the gentleman wanted to elicit more information, why did he not ask the architect to come again? and if he were not satisfied with his answers, why did he not examine him *under oath?*

Mr. STANTON. I will answer the gentleman from Massachusetts. He knows as well as I do, that we had just concluded our labors on a single branch of the investigation. The session of Congress was just about to expire; and the committee had no time to enter into the investigation as to the management. We had not time to do so. The whole time of our session was occupied in other portions of the investigation. That is the reason why I did not call upon the architect to answer as to the manner of the management.

At the present session of Congress, when the committee met, I proposed to enter vigorously upon that examination, but the committee seemed disposed not to sustain me, and, therefore, I dropped it. I did not want to stand singly and alone on the question, when it was obvious to me that the rest of the committee were indisposed to enter into it. But I was willing to take off my coat and go to work, so as to show to the country that the more economical plan of management was not to place the management under military control, not to place it in the hands of an engineer officer, who was never brought up to such a business, and who would take the plans of others and sign his name to them, and claim the credit of them.

Mr. DICKINSON. I think, Mr. Chairman, the committee had abundant time before the close of the last session of Congress, to make as full an examination of this matter as could be of any practical benefit. We had time to make any other inquiry which the chairman of that committee might choose to make of the architect or otherwise. And if the work on these Capitol wings, to be erected at the expense of some hundreds of thousands of dollars, was to be continued during the recess of Congress, and if the chairman of that committee considered that, when completed, they were to be unfit for the purposes for which they were intended, I am astonished that he should undertake to state to this House, in the presence of all the other members of that committee, that we had not time to enlighten them in regard to this great matter, and to protect the country from an expenditure which was to be worse than useless, and that he should not have insisted upon the further and prompt action of the committee in the exigency. I do not so recollect the facts as stated by him; and in regard to the gentleman's taking off his coat at the commencement of this session, I can say that we were as ready as he was to examine engineers, and architects, and everybody who knew anything about the matter. But we did not see the necessity of further investigation; and that is why he says the majority of the committee were not disposed to go into it. It was not for the reason which the gentleman assigns, but because the majority of the committee had become satisfied that these charges were a farce, that they were without foundation, and that the subject had become a perfect monomania with him. . . .

I am prepared to say that there is not a gentleman anywhere, who has any knowledge of the engineer and architect and their plans, who is not perfectly satisfied with their integrity, their eminent capacity, and the perfect sympathy which exists between these two officers, and the perfect coöperation which these gentlemen show in all these public works. If the amendment be adopted to construct a Post Office or Treasury Building, without the amendment to the amendment offered by the gentleman from Tennessee ([the other] Mr. STANTON), this same engineer and architect may go hand in hand in the same manner to construct them, and the country will have great reason to feel proud of such eminent professional skill, and abundantly satisfied with the result of their joint labors and responsibilities. . . .

I do not desire to discuss this question any further than to state to the House that this House, and the country, have been most unmitigatedly imposed upon by the charges that have been made here against the military superintendency of the public works, without any ground to sustain them; and I think it is high time for members to understand what they are legislating about. I say this with all respect for the intelligence of the body. We have spent the greater part of one session already in investigating one branch of this matter, and heard continually the charges of fraud which have been committed by officers having in charge the public works.

MR. STANTON, of Kentucky (interposing). The gentleman from Massachusetts, as well as other gentlemen here, know that I never made any such charges of fraud.

MR. DICKINSON. I do not mean to make any charges against the gentleman from Kentucky, or any other member upon this floor; but the resolutions upon record bear me out in saying—or else they mean nothing—that charges of fraud were made against these officers. There were resolutions of inquiry offered by the gentleman himself, as to the mode of expending money in constructing public works by Army officers, and the expediency of providing by law that no military man should have the charge of their construction; and no gentleman has occupied the time of the House so much as he in trying to convince the country that great frauds have been committed by officers connected with the Army while engaged in this service. If the country does not understand that these charges have been made, and that resolutions of inquiry were offered in this House to draw out facts to sustain these charges, then all I have to say is, that I have entirely misunderstood its proceedings; that I have misunderstood the proceedings of the select committee upon this subject, of which I am a member, that sat here for nearly six months of the last session; and that I have misunderstood the whole object of these inquiries.

I think, then, that it is high time that the House was enlightened upon this subject; and I undertake to say, with the most perfect confidence, that if the question of changing the superintendency of the national armories, which was practically done at the last session, were to be reconsidered to-day, I have great confidence that I should be able to convince the House, notwithstanding there was a majority of nearly a hundred votes in favor of the change from military officers to civilians, that it would be better for the country to restore the management of the armories to military officers. There is no justice, every time we made an appropriation for a Government building, in saying, when the President of the United States is authorized to take charge of the work and select the men under whose superintendence it shall be built, that he shall be restricted and precluded from making a selection of Army officers for that purpose, if he desires to do so, and thinks the public interest demands it. It is very unjust to single out Army officers as incompetent, from education, to take charge of these works, when it is well known to everybody that the officers who are educated at the military schools of the country are approved practical engineers; and while the demand for engineers is so great, not only for the service of the Government, but for private enterprises, shall the President of the United States be prohibited from employing an officer to superintend any public work because he has been educated at a military school? I think we have been legislating upon this subject with very narrow views. . . . I make these remarks because it does seem to me that it is quite time to make some demonstration against the daily introduction of this political humbug, and repudiate this demagogical idea that is urged so unceasingly, that these gentlemen are unfit for the duty of superintending these works. I have no desire to discuss the matter further at this time. I hope that the amendment will not prevail.

The question was then taken, and the amendment was disagreed to.

For once Mr. Dickinson's words were heeded. Meticulous, thorough and fearless, determined to defend those who were maligned or unjustly criticized, nowhere in the record of his remarks on the floor of the House does Edward Dickinson's candor stand out more clearly than here. It is perhaps not too much to suppose that this earnest and sober presentation of the case, while too late to save the armories, did serve to consolidate opinion and so, to defeat Stanton's latest amendment. In any case, the question of military versus civil works did not come up again during the Thirty-third Congress.[13]

The most important measure passed by the Thirty-third Congress was the Kansas-Nebraska Act. This law, extending in effect the area of the slave states, had been introduced in the House on January 31, 1854, and had been referred to the Committee of the Whole to be debated and voted upon in turn.

A corresponding bill had been pushed through the Senate on March 4, 1854, chiefly by the efforts of Senator Douglas.[14] The Senate debate had roused

13. On August 6, 1861, Congress restored military control of the armories, which have been in charge of ordnance ever since. On April 18, 1861, the Harper's Ferry armory was destroyed and was never rebuilt. The Springfield armory, although not essentially different in function from the six United States arsenals, still bears the traditional name. For nearly ninety years it has been the only "armory" in the country. See *A Collection of Ordnance Reports* (Washington, 1890), III, 572.

14. The Senate met to pass the Nebraska Bill on March 3, 1854. They talked all night. The bill was passed early in the morning of March 4 after continuous session; so, although the vote was not taken until March 4, *The Congressional Globe* gives the date as March 3. See also Rhodes, *op. cit.*, I, 470-475.

public feeling in the North to fever pitch. When the Senate bill reached the House on March 21 (*1, 701*), it was introduced by William A. Richardson of Illinois, Douglas' lieutenant in the House, who moved to refer it to the Committee on Territories, hoping to report a bill from there which would have to be acted upon promptly. Instead, it was again referred to the Committee of the Whole, where it took its place fiftieth in line in the order of business. Its opponents thought it had been killed; but it came up again much sooner than anticipated. For, in spite of Whig opposition, Mr. Richardson again succeeded in introducing the Nebraska Bill on the floor of the House on the eighth of May (*1. 1130 ff.*).

Meanwhile, an old and bitter controversy between Massachusetts and South Carolina had been revived, one in which Mr. Dickinson became involved. It had to do with the treatment of free Negro citizens of Massachusetts employed on cargo vessels touching at southern ports. In November, 1844, Massachusetts had sent the Honorable Samuel Hoar[15] on a mission to South Carolina in order to test in the courts the constitutionality of a South Carolina law providing that such Negroes should be held under arrest while their ships were in port. Here is what was said about the incident in Congress ten years later.

On April 27, 1854, William Smith of Virginia speaking in favor of the Nebraska Bill referred to the abolitionists as follows (*1, App., 554*): "Yes, sir, they were scattering all over the country incendiary publications, agitating the subject of slavery, and in every way and form, disturbing the repose and peace of the country. Nor was that all. A great State even sent her missionaries into southern States, for the purpose of raising questions as to the constitutionality of their police laws. She issued manifestoes to all the States of the Union arraigning the States of South Carolina and Louisiana in consequence of their course in reference to those agents."

It was several days before a member from Massachusetts got a chance to present the northern point of view. Samuel H. Walley of Massachusetts, in the course of a speech on May 9, said (*1, App., 635-636*):

The same gentleman [Mr. SMITH] has not spared the Commonwealth which I have the honor in part to represent upon this floor, but has seen fit to rebuke her for the course which she pursued in relation to the mission of Hon. Samuel Hoar to South Carolina.

Sir, I would reply to that gentleman in the words of Daniel Webster:

"There is a more tangible and irritating cause of grievance at the North. Free blacks are constantly employed in the vessels of the North, generally as cooks or stewards. When the vessel arrives at a southern port, these free colored men are taken on shore by the police or municipal authority, imprisoned, and kept in prison till the vessel is again ready to sail. This is not only irritating, but exceedingly unjustifiable and oppressive. Mr. Hoar's mission some time ago to South Carolina was a well-intended effort to remove this cause of complaint. The North thinks such imprisonments illegal and unconstitutional; and as the cases occur constantly and frequently, they regard it as a great grievance."

This, sir, is the whole case, and Massachusetts sought, in a quiet and friendly

15. Distinguished jurist, father of Judge Ebenezer Rockwood Hoar and Senator George Frisbie Hoar.

manner, to test the question in the proper courts. For this she is now reproved by the gentleman from Virginia. Sir, Massachusetts does not plead to the indictment. She does not recognize the right, to say nothing of the courtesy, of a gentleman from Virginia, to arraign her at this or any other bar. . . .

On the day following, May 10, Mr. Dickinson's friend Thomas D. Eliot, of Massachusetts, made an impassioned speech against the measure from which a few paragraphs are quoted (*1, App.,* 574-576):

The friends or the supporters of those last acts [of 1850] may well exclaim, "Away with compromises. We have tried them, and our fathers have tried them in vain. We have bound ourselves, and have submitted to be bound, by acts of legislation we have disapproved, because we loved the Constitution and the peace and progress of the Union. Our fathers compromised when they consented to give back the fugitive. But it was contended that unless they yielded then and in that, no Constitution could be formed, and no Union made; and so the southern interest prevailed. And then, again, Missouri asked to come among us, and our fathers yielded, and again compromised, and again brought the convictions of duty and laid them down before the altar of the Union. And that sacrifice, which presupposed and rested on a faith great as Abraham's, gave to the South a slave State in the hand for wild freedom in the bush. And last of all, when it was said that the master was not secure in his rights, we ourselves yielded. The South asked, and the North gave; and another compromise was made. But it was said that that was to be the last. The new born principle of non-intervention was to be applied to lands recently acquired. The master was to have his hand made stronger, and the North was to have peace; and the covenant was struck, and the bargain was made, and the seal was set, and upon the whole 'FINALITY' was inscribed."

"But now again the cry of 'Give, give,' comes to us! The bush where freedom was to live has been cut down, and the cabin of the sovereign squatter rests there; and we are asked to yield again, and let the laws of slavery prevail where freedom had secured a home. And now we say to gentlemen of the South, if this is to be the way in which compromises are kept, we enter into no more of them from this time forth." . . .

The argument of "compromise" and "compact" has been exhausted. The father of compromises, if he were in this Hall, made classic by his lofty form and his persuasive voice, could find no logic that had not been employed by eloquence kindred to his own.

But he would have heard some squatter logic about which he had not read. The people have a right to govern themselves. The squatters are the people. Therefore, the Missouri Compromise should be repealed. There is the syllogism.

"This is a question of self-government, and the people have a right to form their own institutions." That is the proposition.

But does it follow from that that we cannot legislate to inhibit slavery in the Territories? What people have a right to form their own institutions? Can colored people form such institutions as they wish to establish? If these bills shall be so amended that free colored citizens may remove their families and their effects into Nebraska and Kansas, and be considered as good as squatters, one objection to the bills would be obviated. But this House have decided that colored citizens, however free and however educated they may be, cannot "squat." It takes a white man to do that. He may be what is called a "poor white man"; but the color of the skin secures the right. It is not, then, all people that may form their own institutions, but white people only.

Mr. Chairman, the time will come when we shall see the iniquity of such exclusive legislation. There is not another nation upon the face of the earth, that is civilized and not barbarous, that would condemn, and ostracize, and degrade a freeman because God had not made him white. . . .

W. W. Boyce, of South Carolina, took the floor to say (*1*, 1154):

I desire briefly to make an explanation of the facts concerning the visit of Mr. Hoar to the State of South Carolina, to which the gentleman from Massachusetts referred in his speech to-day.[16] In 1822, when a civil insurrection was upon the eve of breaking out in South Carolina, and it was discovered that free negroes were coming from the West India Islands to head that insurrection, it was found necessary, for the public safety, to pass an act that no free negroes should come into that State.

Many years passed along, and the Abolition excitement came up, and Massachusetts, which, I am sorry to say, has always been found at the head of this agitation, sent one of her citizens to have the constitutionality of this law tested. As soon as Mr. Hoar arrived in the State, he was looked upon as a fire-brand, and great public agitation ensued upon his arrival; but there was no mob violence threatened against him. Some of the most respectable citizens of Charleston waited upon him, and urged upon him the necessity of leaving the State. The manner in which the honorable gentleman from Massachusetts referred to this matter would lead one to suppose that some infuriated mob had forced him to leave the State; but the facts of the case present the matter in an entirely different light. He was waited upon by several respectable gentlemen of the place, and requested to leave the city, and he did so.

Mr. Dickinson interrupted: "I should like to ask the gentleman from South Carolina a question."

"I am ready to answer the gentleman's question."

"I should like to ask . . . whether the municipal authorities of Charleston did not notify Mr. Hoar that they could not protect him, and they would not insure his safety if he did not leave? They allowed him to take his own choice, and so he left."

"I do not know that," replied Mr. Boyce. "I know that some gentlemen waited on him at the hotel, and represented to him that he had better leave, as, though the citizens did not intend to injure him, he might be liable to insult and annoyance."

"I have got the facts from the official report," said Mr. Dickinson, "and I have no doubt it is true. I do not wish to have my State improperly represented in this matter."

The Globe interpolates here, "Some little misunderstanding here took place between Mr. Boyce and Mr. Dickinson, as to the language used by the latter gentleman." The actual words are not recorded, but Mr. Dickinson went on to say:

I rose to make an inquiry of the gentleman from South Carolina. I stated the facts from the official report of Mr. Hoar, of Massachusetts, which he made when he returned. He stated that he was informed by the authorities of Charleston that he could not be protected, and was advised by them to leave, because they could not answer for his safety if he remained. The gentleman from

16. This is a confusing point. Thomas D. Eliot had just finished making a speech in opposition to the Nebraska Bill, and *The Globe* identifies him as the "gentleman from Massachusetts" to whom Boyce referred. But as there is no mention of Hoar or his mission in the printed record of Eliot's speech (*1, App.*, 574), it is clear that the reference is to Walley's remarks on May 9, (*1, App.*, 632 ff.)

South Carolina replied to my question, substantially, that he did not understand the facts to be so. Sir, there is not a purer man in the United States than Mr. Hoar. He is a man for whose prudence, and judgment, and candor, every one who knows him has respect. He was sent there for the purpose of testing the validity of the law of South Carolina, which we, in Massachusetts, regarded as unconstitutional. He was known to be a person who would conduct himself with great propriety; and he was only asked to have the proper means taken to test the validity of the law in the United States courts. But he was advised that he could not remain there safely, and that he could not try the case. He came home and made that report. I took that report as an official report after it had been acted upon.

Nothing more was heard of Mr. Hoar's mission. And it was almost the last point made by Edward Dickinson in relation to the Nebraska Bill. The minority opposing it began a filibuster on May 11, the day after this "misunderstanding" with Mr. Boyce, to prolong which they used every rule of the House: they offered motions to adjourn, motions to adjourn to a fixed time; they proposed resolutions, speaking on them under the five-minute rule; then a member would ask to be excused from voting; and on all these motions the yeas and nays were called for. The filibuster lasted all day and all night, and all the next day, which was the Friday (May 12) after the bill had been introduced. Mr. Dickinson made one of these delaying motions, but he did not stay all night—his name is missing from the later lists of voting members. During this fracas the Speaker had all he could do to preserve any semblance of order in the House. Edward Dickinson, trying among others to interfere in every way possible, managed to have a resolution read which would have restored the bills on the calendar of business to the places which they had occupied before Mr. Richardson had moved to lay them aside on May 8. This move would automatically have stopped debate and prevented passage of the bill. But the resolution was violently objected to and when brought to a vote was defeated 121 to 75 (*1*, 1189).

Although Mr. Dickinson's attempt to restore the bills on the calendar does not indicate that he was more of an obstructionist than any other Whigs, when the resolution was read the Speaker rebuked him sharply:

"The Chair was totally mistaken in his understanding of the paper the gentleman from Massachusetts asked to have read. . . . He had no right to make the motion that it be read. The Chair understood him to call for the reading of the resolution offered by the gentleman from Illinois [Mr. Richardson]" (*1*, 1188).

On Monday, May 22, the bill was finally brought to a vote although it took all day and until nearly midnight to do it, for the minority were again using all the delaying tactics they could think of. Mr. Dickinson took only a minor part in it though present throughout the debate. Needless to say, he voted against the bill, which passed by a vote of 113-100 (*1*, 1254).

On May 23, the day after the passage of the Nebraska Bill, at the instance of Israel Washburn, Jr., a Whig from Maine, a meeting of some thirty members of Congress was held in the rooms of Edward Dickinson and Thomas Eliot of Massachusetts. These men met in order to focus their opposition to slavery.

After a good deal of discussion, during which some of them argued that anti-slavery sentiment should be embodied in the old Whig party, it was decided that the most striking act of opposition would be to form an entirely new party. The name Republican was selected as most suitable. This group of Congressmen were, then, the very first Republicans, the nucleus from which the party sprang.[17]

Thomas Eliot, Mr. Dickinson's friend from New Bedford, was active in the preliminary arrangements in Boston followed by the first Massachusetts Republican Convention in Worcester on September 7, 1854, less than six months after the meeting in Washington. Edward Dickinson, on the other hand, one of those who held that the Whig party should itself embody the principles of antislavery, remained a loyal Whig as long as there was such a party, accepting their nomination for representative in 1854 and again in 1855. Although he had been present at the very beginning of the Republican party and might have been justified in feeling a proprietary interest in it as did Mr. Eliot, he felt nothing of the kind. Mr. Dickinson, in common with many other conservative Whigs, regarded the Republicans as upstarts. He considered that a party founded on but one principle, opposition to slavery, was not a sound party. As a matter of fact, the political scene in Massachusetts for two or three years after the passage of the Kansas-Nebraska Act was one of confusion amounting to chaos. Political leaders changed parties with astounding rapidity, or remained silent even in the face of acute need for leadership. Edward Dickinson not only stayed by his party after it had ceased to exist; a Whig he remained to the end of his days.

Aside from incidental participation in details of parliamentary procedure, the name of Edward Dickinson appears in *The Globe* from now on only two or three times.

After the passage of the Nebraska Bill, and toward the end of the first session of the Thirty-third Congress in late July, there was discussion of a request from citizens of Indiana, Illinois, and Iowa for a mail route by rail between certain specified places (*1*, 1822). When the memorial was first presented to the House it was referred by the Speaker to the Committee on the Post Office and Post Roads, the chairman of which was Edson B. Olds of Ohio. The Speaker, Linn Boyd of Kentucky, had not looked at the memorial very carefully; he took it at face value, not realizing that since it concerned grants of public lands for railroads it should have been directed to the Committee on Public Lands. So, when it came up in July, Mr. Olds, having obtained the floor, was defending the position of the Post Office Committee, which refused to pass the memorial to the public lands when Mr. Dickinson interrupted:

17. Henry Wilson, *History of the Rise and Fall of Slave Power*, II, 410-411. See also George S. Merriam, *Life and Times of Samuel Bowles*, I, 117; and Allan Nevins, *Ordeal of the Union* (New York, 1947), II, 322. (A meeting held at Ripon, Wisconsin, on March 20, decided against using the name "Republican" for a new party.)

"Will the gentleman from Ohio permit me to ask him a question?"

"Certainly."

"Is there any post route now over the road referred to in the memorial?"

Mr. Olds said he was glad the question had been asked, for it showed the propriety of the Post Office Committee having charge of the memorial.

"I wish to ask the gentleman a question," said Dickinson. "I want the gentleman to answer the question I put to him, and that is, whether he knows that there is a road now upon this very route? and if there is any road, what kind of a road is it?"

Mr. Olds replied, "That very question shows the propriety of this matter going before the Committee on the Post Office and Post Roads, in order that they may make themselves more familiar with this very question."

"I wish," Mr. Dickinson repeated, "the gentleman would answer my question, and not evade it in this way. I want him to answer my question."

"The gentleman might ask me if there was a route to the moon," said Mr. Olds, "but I could not answer him without going to the Post Office Committee room and consulting the post route book."

"Well," declared Mr. Dickinson, "if the gentleman cannot answer such a question as that, he is not fit to be at the head of the committee, and he ought to resign and allow some one to be appointed in his place, who can answer such a question."

Now Olds, instead of returning insult for insult, said to Dickinson, "If the gentleman will, under the rules of the House, refer to the Committee on the Post Office and Post Roads a memorial, asking for the establishment of a post route from here to the moon, the petition will receive the respectful consideration of that committee, and they will make a report upon it to the House." (Laughter.)

Mr. Dickinson took no further part in the discussion.

During the second session Mr. Dickinson presented two resolutions, neither of which passed. The first came from the Committee on Elections, of which he was a member; a routine proposal, it provided for the usual mileage and per diem to be paid to William Carr Lane, "from the commencement of the last session until the day upon which the contest between himself and the Hon. Jose Manuel Gallegos for a seat in this House, as Delegate from the Territory of New Mexico, was finally decided."

The first time this resolution was offered, on February 23, 1855 (2, 903), it was referred to the Committee of the Whole. Dickinson had misunderstood the agreement of the day, to the effect that there was to be no debate or any bills introduced; so he withdrew the resolution, inquiring of the Chair "whether there is to be any time when a member can offer a resolution or make a motion?" The Chair could not tell him. "I have been trying to offer it for a number of days," protested Dickinson, "but never could get the floor." Next time he offered the resolution (2, 1007), just before adjournment, it was objected to and not voted upon.

The other subject with which Mr. Dickinson had been entrusted, by the Committee on the Library, had to do with printing certain copies of the scientific and narrative reports of the exploring expedition under Captain Charles Wilkes of the United States Navy.[18] During March, 1854, Dickinson had offered a resolution, which was passed, directing the Library Committee to inquire into the expediency of replacing the volumes lost by the burning of the Library in 1850, and of printing other copies if it seemed proper (*1*, 682). The Committee did not report to the House until the following February, almost a year later, when Mr. Dickinson, on his third try, finally managed to have the resolution read (*2*, 949). It provided for ten thousand copies of the work to be printed and bound under the direction of the Library Committee, to be distributed by the members of Congress (one copy or set of volumes to a library in each district) and by the Department of State.

Over an objection by George W. Jones of Tennessee, Dickinson got the rules suspended for consideration of the measure; whereupon Richard Stanton, out of order and with cries of "No!" "No!" echoing through the House, proposed that the resolution be amended so that the volumes would be printed under the direction of the Committee on Printing, and by the public printer of the House. Otherwise, said Stanton, it would cost infinitely more than there was any necessity for. (Cries of "Order!") Dickinson insisted that the resolution be put to the House, but when someone inquired how much the printing of the work, as proposed in the resolution, would cost, Dickinson said:

"I wish the House would hear me one minute in reference to the inquiry of the gentleman from Pennsylvania."

"No remarks are in order," said the Speaker.

"It will cost $160,000," continued Mr. Dickinson, out of order in his turn. "The House, some years ago, authorized the work to be printed, at a cost of about $1,000,000. Only one hundred copies were ordered to be published, which were distributed to the different States of the Union, and to foreign nations."

At this point Mr. Keitt interrupted. "I call the gentleman to order," said he. "The main question has been ordered to be put."

"I must be heard by the House," insisted Mr. Dickinson. "The plates were prepared at all this cost, and only one hundred copies were ordered to be printed. They are not worth a dollar, unless they are applied to this purpose."

Mr. Florence then asked, "Is it contemplated that the public printer shall print this work? I want to ask one question, and I want to hear an answer."

"No debate is in order," said the Speaker.

"I am not debating," retorted Florence, "I merely wish to ask a question."

The Speaker then asked: "Is it the pleasure of the House that the gentleman from Pennsylvania shall ask a question in reference to the resolution under consideration?" (Cries of "No!" "No!")

The vote was then taken, and decided in the negative: yeas 66, nays 101. It is surprising to note that Edward Dickinson voted against this resolution for

18. The Wilkes expedition took place between 1838 and 1842. The report consists of 19 volumes (28 were planned), of which Captain Wilkes wrote the narrative volumes, six in number. The other thirteen were written by various scientists, members of the expedition.

which he had fought so doggedly. Apparently he had presented it on instructions from the Library Committee and defended it accordingly; but when it came to a vote he acted as he thought best.

The last record of Mr. Dickinson's activity in the House of Representatives is in connection with the final passage of the Army Appropriations Bill as approved by the Senate. It was discussed, amendment by amendment, on the first of March, 1855. Charles Faulkner managed to obtain for the new civilian superintendents of the armories the right to live in the quarters which had been built for superintendents, without payment of rent as had been customary. Dickinson maintained that the proposed salary, $2,500, was too low, and he attempted to get it raised, but without success. He also failed to have the superintendent's clerk's salary fixed at $1,200, with quarters, and the other clerks' at $1,000. Both motions were ruled out of order by the chairman (2, 1016).

Mr. Dickinson's final act was a generous one which bore fruit after he had left Congress. He proposed an amendment which would pay Cyrus Buckland of the Springfield armory $15,000 in compensation for inventions which the United States had been using gratis for twenty-five years (2, 1016-1017). Both Richard Stanton and William Richardson also tried, unsuccessfully, to secure passage of this amendment. Such payment was long overdue. From the time Buckland first entered the armory until 1857, a span of nearly thirty years, he had never taken out a patent on any of his inventions, believing that since invention was his job the government had a right to profit from any machine he devised. But in 1857, two years after Edward Dickinson had tried unsuccessfully to obtain for him any compensation from Congress, Buckland found himself in failing health; so when he was called upon to invent a special rifling machine he notified the Secretary of War that he intended to take out a patent on it. The Government paid him $10,000 for the rights to this invention. Payment did not reach him until 1858, after he had retired.

Mr. Dickinson's interest in Cyrus Buckland illustrates once again his fascinated preoccupation with the creative spirit as expressed in the construction of machines and railroads. It is fitting that this appeal for Buckland should have been Edward Dickinson's last act in Congress. And it is gratifying to reflect that not only Richardson, champion of the Kansas-Nebraska Bill, to which Dickinson had been so bitterly opposed, but Richard Stanton himself, Dickinson's opponent of long standing, in this instance supported his efforts.

SUPPLEMENT

One of the statesmen admired by Edward Dickinson, even though a former member of the opposition, was the Honorable Salmon Portland Chase. In spite of the fact that in 1848 Mr. Chase had been one of the founders of the Free Soil party, the Whigs were inclined to gloss over that indiscretion because of his vigorous stand against slavery. As a United States Senator he opposed the Compromise of 1850 and, in 1854, stood firm against passage of the Kansas-Nebraska Bill.

For bringing to my attention the three following Dickinson letters in the Library of Congress (Division of Manuscripts, "Salmon P. Chase Papers," vols.

27, 36 and 93) I am indebted to Jay Leyda. The first, written at the time of Mr. Chase's election as governor of Ohio in 1855; the second, in 1860, before he was elected to the Senate on the Republican ticket (two days after taking his seat he resigned to become Lincoln's Secretary of the Treasury); the third, after his appointment as Chief Justice of the United States on December 6, 1864. These letters give a hint of Mr. Dickinson's political philosophy, thus helping us to understand why even though, in the words of James Bryce (*The American Commonwealth*, I, 3), the Republican in the North and West is the "party in whose ranks respectable, steady, pious, well-conducted men are to be looked for," Mr. Dickinson never joined it.

Two letters to Mr. Dickinson written in 1854 and 1855 by the Secretary of War, Jefferson Davis, in reply to requests which were not granted, are with the Records of the War Office, National Archives, Military Book No. 35, page 169, and Book No. 36, page 431.

M. T. B.

Amherst July 23. 1855.

My dear Sir,

The Republican Convention of Ohio have nominated you for Govr of that State. They have done well. I admire their good judgment, as it respects themselves—and they pay you but a just compliment for your devotion to the principles of true Republicanism.

I can not forego the privilege of saying that I am most highly gratified with your nomination—and have full faith in your election, by an overwhelming majority—I hope so, not more on your own account, than to rebuke the meanness, and the badness of electing an unprincipled demagogue as your successor, in the Senate of the U. S. and to show to the rest of the Country, that Ohio has yet a reserve force of much character and honest political principle, sufficient to reward fidelity in the public confidence & to stigmatise servility to *mere party,* by repudiating it, & discarding its tools.

There will yet be a day for honest men to hold up their heads—it dawns, even now.

My best wishes will attend you—and your State will be honored by honoring you. I should rejoice to stump my State, if it could help you, and it was a case requiring it.

But you are safe—So is the State, and we have enough to do here to root out, reform, & bring to daylight the wickedest, & most hypocritical political rascalities that any set of men were ever guilty of,—since the days of Judas Iscariot.

Under the guise of extending time of naturalisation, & having *"Americans rule America"*, the "K. N." have made their secret cabals, a mere conspiracy to secure office—without merit—& for no reason—except to use the machinery to boost them, where no intelligent open acting public would ever dream of hoisting them.

Their day is drawing to a close—and such a night as will close over the party, is nowhere foretold, or even remotely foreshadowed!!!—With the most cordial esteem & regard, and a strong desire to see you, I remain your sincere friend,

Edward Dickinson

Mr Chase

Amherst, Mass, Jany 23, 1860

My dear Sir

I thank you for your repeated remembrances of me, in sending your messages, as Govr of Ohio.

I hope to see the Legislature elect you again to the Senate of the U. S. to succeed your successor [George E. Pugh], for whom I entertain to-day, the same measure of contempt, which I felt when I saw him in the Crow-bar case before the U. S. Supreme Court, after his election, and before he took his seat. I hope Ohio will soon be purged of the contempt she has suffered by giving a seat in the National Legislature to such a person.

I should be very happy to see you when you come to N. England. I had hoped, the last two summers, to have seen you at my house—and hope still, that I may have that pleasure.

I send you a copy of the proceedings of the *Union Meeting* in Boston—erasing the concluding portion of Gen¹ Cushing's speech, which is, at the least, in bad taste.

I do not sympathise with the Republican party in Mass^tts—although I am a Republican, upon the true principle of republicanism—the present dominant party in this State being composed of Know Nothings, and ultra abolitionists and some whigs, & more democrats—

The real, true anti-slavery party, is the Whig party—30, or 40,000 of whom have not voted, for years past; because they would not vote for Know Nothingism, by name or by the *name* of Republicanism. The Union Meeting, includes the great Mass of the old Whig & Conservative party, which contains the talent, character & property, of Mass^tts, to a greater degree than all other parties together—and this element will claim to be considered, hereafter, in our State Elections, and will be heard on the subject of the Presidential Election.

We have been dragged through the depths of radicalism, for the last six years, and the bone & sinew of Mass^tts, will be, in fact, are aroused and indignant at the oppression which has been exercised towards the most deserving portion of our citizens, and, in my opinion, there is strength enough here, to place ourselves in a position to deserve more respect than we have had, since the overthrow of every thing good, by the K. N. party.

I was pleased with your course towards Virginia in the Harper's Ferry affair, and should not have much fear of your want of Conservatism—I think you are about as good an *"Union Man"*, as I am, and hope you will soon be in a position to give the Country the benefit of your experience & your integrity. Your views upon the Tariff as lately expressed, will be found acceptable to N. England.

With the highest esteem & personal regard,
I am very truly yours

Edward Dickinson

Mr Chase.

Amherst, Mass, Decr 8. 1864

Hon. S. P. Chase
My dear Sir,

Will you allow me to congratulate you upon your appointment to the highest judicial position in the United States—and to express the satisfaction it gives me, in common with the great majority of the most intelligent, educated, & high minded Lawyers & Judges in New England, to see you placed at the Head of the Court of last resort, in this country—and at a time when not only judicial, but Statesmanlike qualities & qualifications of the highest character, are and will be imperatively demanded, in settling the great questions growing out of the war—as well as those resulting from Peace, when it comes; (as come it must, sooner, or later) You have the confidence of the country, in advance— and all the friends of law & order and Constitutional liberty, will hail your elevation to the Presidency of this august tribunal, as the harbinger of the perpetuity of our Republican Government. With the Court, as now constituted, we can all breathe freely, & rest securely.

Pardon my intrusion—and place it to the credit of my warm personal regard, since my acquaintance with you, at Washington, ten years ago.

With the highest esteem & regard,

I am very resp^y yours

Edward Dickinson

REFERENCES

Government Publications
1. *The Congressional Globe,* 33 Cong., 1 Sess.
2. *The Congressional Globe,* 33 Cong., 2 Sess.
3. *The Congressional Globe,* 32 Cong., 2 Sess.
4. *House Document* No. 207, 27 Cong., 2 Sess.
5. *Senate Document* No. 344, 29 Cong., 1 Sess.
6. *House Miscellaneous Document* No. 76, 33 Cong., 1 Sess.
7. *House Report* No. 191, 33 Cong., 1 Sess.
8. *Journal of the House of Representatives,* 33 Cong., 1 Sess., 2 Sess.

Miscellaneous
The Hampshire and Franklin Express (Amherst), 1854 and 1855.
The Hampshire Gazette (Northampton), 1854.
The History of the Town of Amherst, Massachusetts, 1731-1896, compiled and published by Carpenter & Morehouse (Amherst, 1896).
The Massachusetts Register: a State Record for the year 1852 . . . (Boston, 1852), 321-323.
Mason A. Green, *Springfield, 1636-1886,* etc. (Springfield, 1888).
James Ford Rhodes, *History of the United States from the Compromise of 1850 to the End of the Roosevelt Administration* (New York, 1928), I.
Henry Wilson, *The History of the Rise and Fall of the Slave Power in America* (Boston, 1874), II.

V. NOTE ON EDITING EMILY DICKINSON'S POEMS

In the spring of 1944, as *Bolts of Melody* was about to go to press, one poem still disturbed me. Though written in Emily Dickinson's latest script, the sententious lines were not like her terse quatrains of the 1880's. The stanza as she copied it reads:

> Though love repine and reason chafe
> There comes a voice without reply,
> 'Tis man's perdition to be safe
> When for the truth he ought to die.

I asked Mark Van Doren about it. He said it was by Emerson, a poem called "Sacrifice." This had been caught in time to prevent its appearance in the book. But what if among Emily's penciled notes there were other poems not her own?

The incident intensified a fear which had dogged me from the moment when, after my mother's death, I first began to edit the poems, a task to which she had devoted several years nearly half a century before. In 1932 I was in the midst of unraveling the story of the first editing, a long, difficult undertaking to be sure, but one for which my own professional training, linguistic and scientific, had to a certain extent prepared me. A volume of new poems, however, was another matter. But as I thought it over, what seemed no less important than proficiency in prosody and poetics was the fact that from infancy I had breathed the Dickinson atmosphere. Nor was English poetry new to me. Even as a baby my grandfather, holding me in his arms as he paced the floor, had lulled me to sleep with ballads of Scott and Tennyson. Later, as a schoolgirl in Boston, and throughout my years of graduate study in the University Museum at Harvard, I lived in the home of Professor George Herbert Palmer. In the library of his house in the Yard, taking from the shelves his precious first editions, while the fire blazed on the hearth through long winter evenings, he used to read aloud to me great poetry, from Shakespeare to Masefield. Especially and most frequently he read the poems of George Herbert, whose namesake he was, and of whose works he brought out (1905) the definitive edition in six volumes. Had Professor Palmer lived, the manuscript of *Bolts of Melody* would have been without blemish.

Late in 1944, galleys of the book were sent to a few reviewers. From Professor Whicher of Amherst College I received a letter dated 24 January 1945. He had noted that two lines,

> "If my bark sink
> 'Tis to another sea,"

were identical with the last line of a poem by W. E. Channing.

On January 27 I replied as follows:

Dear Mr. Whicher:
I am much indebted to you for drawing my attention to the last line of Channing's "A Poet's Hope." It is just the sort of thing I have been on the

lookout for ever since I found among the scraps, in Emily's latest handwriting, a quatrain which didn't sound like her. It proved to be by Emerson!

You have given me the opportunity to re-read Channing's poem in the copy of Emerson's *Parnassus* which he dedicated to Sophia Thoreau and which she gave to my grandmother. I had not looked at it for years.

The page proofs of *Bolts of Melody* have not come yet, so if you discover any more quotations, or lapses of mine, will you please be so kind as to let me know?

Gratefully yours,
Millicent Bingham

It was not too late to insert a footnote to the poem on page 223.

No other instances of this sort were drawn to my attention by anyone and on April 4, 1945, *Bolts of Melody* was published.

A month passed without incident. On the thirteenth of May the Reverend Henry Scott Miller, Saint James's Church, Skaneateles, New York, wrote me a letter containing this paragraph:

Did you know that the poem numbered 232 in "Bolts of Melody" is not by Emily, but is two stanzas from George Herbert's "Matins"? She must have copied it and in some way it got into her manuscripts.

"While we were fearing it, it came"!

Something must be done and at once. I telephoned to Arthur Rushmore, head of the manufacturing department of Harper & Brothers. Incredible as it seemed to me, I thought his voice sounded actually amused. But he said he would attend to the matter. Two or three days later he wrote:

. . . I wouldn't give it a thought. We can take it out of the next printing and that will be that. The 3rd Ed. should be pure as snow.

The mistake was still unpublicized when, a month later, on June 16, this paragraph appeared in *The New Yorker*:

One of the poems in the new Emily Dickinson volume not only contains as clumsy a line as ever was penned but was not even written by Emily. It is the one beginning "My God, what is a heart?" The author is George Herbert, he of the seventeenth century. The clumsy line is "That thou shouldst it so eye and woo." (My God, what is a mouthful?) Emily presumably liked this poem, jotted it down, and tucked it away in the famous camphor-wood chest, where it lay until Mrs. Bingham pulled it out with a glad cry and presented it to Harper & Brothers. We have no comment to make on this funny coincidence, except to point out to poets that it is dangerous to jot down any thought but your own, and sometimes inadvisable even to do that.

To the editor I wrote forthwith:

Dear Sir:

In your issue of June 16th you comment (with becoming restraint for which I thank you) on those two stanzas by George Herbert beginning "My God, what is a heart," which mistakenly were included in *Bolts of Melody*, by Emily Dickinson.

By way of explanation, not excuse, may I say that when I came across those lines, in Emily's latest handwriting, they seemed so familiar that I hunted through all her poems, published and unpublished, expecting to find them somewhere. But I never once thought of George Herbert. I am the more humiliated inasmuch as I was brought up on George Herbert by no less a person than his namesake and final editor, the late George Herbert Palmer. In apologizing to

Professor Palmer's memory I should like to add one word that is not without interest. Emily did not copy the complete poem, only the two stanzas, which she lifted out of their pious context.

If the book contains another such blunder I hope it may be exposed by *The New Yorker*.

Very truly yours,
Millicent Todd Bingham

On July 10 another letter came from the Reverend Mr. Miller:

I am writing to call your attention to the fragment numbered 627, which is practically identical with the opening couplet of Swinburne's "Tristram of Lyonnesse." As this poem was published in 1882, according to the Encyclopaedia Britannica, it is possible that Emily Dickinson had read it shortly before her death, and as in the case of the Herbert stanzas, had copied the two opening lines which she liked. The fragment is also given in page 5 of "Bolts of Melody." Certainly there is not the slightest suggestion of plagiarism in either case: such a thing is unthinkable of Emily Dickinson.

The first two lines of the Prelude of "Tristram of Lyonnesse" read:

> Love, that is first and last of all things made,
> The light that has the living world for shade.

And Emily's lines:

> Love first and last of all things made
> Of which our living world is but the shade.

Up to the present time no more such coincidences have been brought to my attention.

INDEX

Set in Linotype Baskerville
Format by Marguerite Swanton
Manufactured by The Haddon Craftsmen, Inc.
Published by HARPER & BROTHERS, *New York*

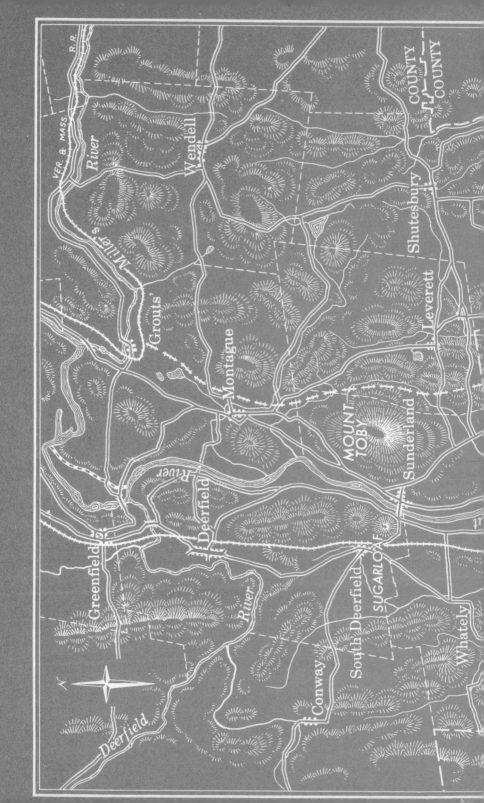